This book is to be returned on or before
the last date stamped below. 2764

LIBREX

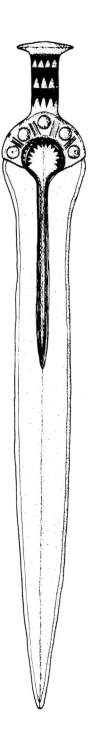

Prehistoric

Europe

TIMOTHY CHAMPION   CLIVE GAMBLE   STEPHEN SHENNAN

University of Southampton,
Southampton, UK

ALASDAIR WHITTLE

University College Cardiff,
Cardiff, UK

ACADEMIC PRESS
Harcourt Brace Jovanovich, Publishers
London   San Diego   New York   Boston
Sydney   Tokyo   Toronto

ACADEMIC PRESS LIMITED
24/28 Oval Road
London NW1 7DX

United States Edition published by
ACADEMIC PRESS INC.
San Diego, CA 92101

This book is printed on acid-free paper

British Library Cataloguing in Publication Data

Prehistoric Europe.
1. Man, Prehistoric—Europe
I. Champion, T. C.
936   GN803

ISBN 0-12-167550-5

ISBN 0-12-167552-1 Pbk

Photoset by Dobbie Typesetting Service, Plymouth, Devon
Printed in Great Britain by Thomson Litho Ltd, East Kilbride, Scotland

Preface

This book owes its existence to a need felt, we believe, by many people who are trying to teach European prehistory, for an elementary textbook suitable for students taking their first course in the subject with little or no previous experience in archaeology. Several years of struggling with the literature in its present form finally convinced us that there was no alternative but to write it for ourselves. The primary evidence, where published at all, is notoriously scattered through a bewildering range of books, pamphlets and journals, written in almost every European language and in any case frequently unobtainable except in a few specialist libraries. For some areas and periods secondary works, sometimes excellent, exist, but their coverage is far from complete and they are mostly at too advanced a level for first-year students. Some general books exist, but none covers the chronological and geographical range that we thought desirable, with a proper concentration on the themes characteristic of modern archaeology at a level suitable for our intended readership.

It was clear from the outset that the book should have as long a chronological range as possible. The earliest evidence for man in Europe forms an obvious starting point, but the finishing point is more problematical. The unfortunate distinction between classical and prehistoric archaeology, with the late Bronze Age and early Iron Age of Italy and Greece sitting uncomfortably on the fence, has obscured the essentially similar nature of developments in Mediterranean and temperate Europe, and we have therefore adopted the somewhat unusual path of including some periods that many would not regard as prehistoric. On the other hand, from a northern European point of view, prehistory would not end until well into the second half of the first millennium AD, and we have therefore, by ending our coverage at the beginning of that millennium, omitted some periods that could be thought prehistoric. There is perhaps no solution to this problem that would satisfy everyone.

It was also clear that within the scope of this book it would not be possible to expound and illustrate the full complexities of the established regional culture sequences of prehistoric Europe. It has not been our intention to do that, nor would we regard it as an essential or even desirable aim in such a book. We have no doubt, nevertheless, that we will still incur the criticism of some of our colleagues for paying too little attention to the material of Prehistoric Europe. Our answer is that it has not been possible since the days of Gordon Childe to do so on a European scale, that we have not been tempted to rewrite *The Dawn of European Civilisation*, and that such studies are often better pursued at a more advanced stage and through books dealing with particular periods and areas. We hope through the text, illustrations and chronological charts to be able to show the general nature of the existing evidence on which our arguments rest, and to provide a sufficient basis of information for students to be able to use the more detailed books satisfactorily.

We have chosen instead to organize our treatment of European prehistory around the discussion of certain themes, especially those which have been most prominent in recent research. This means, in particular, a study of settlement, subsistence, technology, exchange and social organization. In order to focus on these ideas, it has been more convenient to abandon the traditional Three Age System of Stone Age, Bronze Age and Iron Age for the main division of the book into chapters, though the terms remain invaluable for other purposes. We have not attempted to impose any sort of undue uniformity on our treatment of the various themes in the different periods. The very varied nature of the evidence and of research makes this impossible. Thus within each chapter we have not tried to give complete geographical coverage, because in many areas the evidence does not exist or has not been adequately exploited. Similarly, there are differences between the various chapters in the importance attached to each theme. In the earliest periods studies of subsistence and technology predominate, and the evolution of human society has not always formed a major focus of research. At the other extreme, studies of subsistence in the first millennium, though becoming more common, are not as numerous and have not had the impact that they have in earlier post-glacial times, and studies of social organization have been correspondingly more important. Within the general approach adopted for the book as a whole, we have therefore allowed the particular circumstances of the current nature of research to determine the priority of different themes.

The sheer quantity of information on prehistoric Europe is now so great that it is almost impossible for a single person to have an equal command of it all; hence the collaboration of four authors. The initial idea and subsequent organization and editing were the responsibility of one person (TCC) and individual chapters were written by single authors. Drafts were circulated for comment by other authors and we hope we have in this way achieved a certain uniformity, coherence and continuity, and that, despite the inevitable differences in style, the joints are not too disturbing to the reader. It is part of the concept of this book that it should be presented as a whole, as the collaborative work of the authors rather than as an edited collection of papers.

We would like to thank Academic Press for their help and patience in completing a somewhat complex operation, Martin Oake and Michael Jones for producing many of the drawings, and a variety of people, especially Susan Stephenson, Anke Elborn and Sabina Thompson, whose typing skills made order out of chaos. We hope that they think it has all been worthwhile.

Figure 6.9 is reproduced by the courtesy of the Committee for Aerial Photography, University of Cambridge; Figs 9.7 and 10.5 by courtesy of the Trustees of the British Museum; Fig 10.4 by the courtesy of the Ashmolean Museum, Oxford (photograph by Major Allen); the photograph of Stonehenge on p.173 by courtesy of Meridian Airmaps Ltd; Fig. 6.23a is from an original by Roger Gorringe.

March 1984   TCC

Contents

Preface   v

1   The Study of European Prehistory   1

2   Earliest Humans in Europe   17

3   Subsistence and Society in Palaeolithic Europe   59

4   Post-glacial Developments: Hunters, Gatherers and Beyond   89

5   Early Farming Societies: Seventh to Fourth Millennia BC   113

6   Settlement, Expansion and Socio-economic Change:
     3200–2300 BC   153

7   Prestige, Power and Hierarchies: 2300–1400 BC   197

8   The Rise of the State in Mediterranean Europe   239

9   Competition and Hierarchy in Temperate Europe   269

10   Town and the State in Temperate Europe   297

References   327

Index   351

Fig. 1.1   Europe, showing modern political boundaries.

1

The Study of European Prehistory

The foundations of serious prehistoric research were laid in the early nineteenth century, with the establishment of the antiquity of man and the development of the Three Age System for ordering the archaeological record. The quantity of material increased rapidly in the nineteenth century, and local sequences were worked out. This enabled a synthesis of European prehistory to be written by Childe, though the interpretation of the past was heavily influenced by ideas of diffusion from the east. Radiocarbon dating provided an independent means of establishing a prehistoric chronology, and this revolutionized the pattern of Europe's past.

Recent studies have concentrated on prehistoric society and the inferences that can be drawn about it from the archaeological record. A wide variety of new approaches have been pursued, and new types of data collected to answer new questions.

THE DEVELOPMENT OF EUROPEAN PREHISTORY

The serious study of European archaeology did not really begin before the eighteenth century. It was then that the physical remains of the classical civilizations of the Mediterranean were rediscovered, and this new awareness had a profound effect on the intellectual and aesthetic development of Europe. At the same time the remains of Europe's non-classical past were beginning to be appreciated, but no framework of knowledge existed into which they could be fitted. In the succeeding decades European economy and society were transformed by revolutions in agriculture and industry, which had an equal effect on the landscape. Improvement schemes such as the drainage of lakes, the construction of towns, canals, roads and railways, and greatly increased mining and quarrying produced a rapidly growing quantity of archaeological finds, and the pace of research and observation has been maintained since then. At first, recording and publication of these discoveries were in the hands of interested amateurs, for professional archaeologists were almost non-existent before the end of the nineteenth century. Even today, the provision for archaeological work of this sort varies considerably from area to area, and it is therefore inevitable that our knowledge of some parts of European prehistory is somewhat patchy.

In the early days, the only version of the past against which these discoveries could be interpreted was that given by the writings of Greek and Latin authors. These were naturally most complete for the Greek and Roman world itself, and the study of the ancient history of these civilizations was already well advanced. Classical archaeology therefore developed as a means of illustrating and amplifying ancient history, rather than as a primary source of information for it. This trend has in general continued, and classical archaeology has tended to concentrate on such topics as the history of art and architecture, on the assumption (not always consciously made) that questions of economy and society can be adequately answered on the basis of the historical evidence alone. In recent years, it is true, there has been a tendency for classical archaeology to consider a wider range of questions, but there still remains a considerable gulf between the approaches of classical and non-classical archaeology.

With only the most sketchy and unreliable evidence from the classical authors, the study of pre-classical and 'barbarian' societies could not progress very far without certain fundamental advances made in the first half of the nineteenth century (Daniel, 1975). The first was the realization of the true antiquity of the earth and of man. This was largely brought about by the pioneer of geology, Charles Lyell, and by Charles Darwin. It thus became clear that the period recorded in biblical and classical history was only a small fraction of the total existence of the earth and of man's presence on it.

The second advance was the development of the Three Age System by the Danish archaeologists, C. J. Thomsen and J. J. A. Worssae. This suggested that man had passed through three technological phases in which stone, bronze and iron were successively used for the production of tools and weapons. It was rapidly confirmed by observation of archaeological finds in the field, and thus became the first method for ordering discoveries chronologically. Much of the research effort in prehistoric archaeology in the late nineteenth and early twentieth century was expended on cataloguing the accumulating mass of material and organizing it into local chronological sequences.

These concerns have continued to the present day to dominate one school of prehistoric research, particularly common in the Germanic tradition, which concentrates on the study of artifacts, particularly pottery and metalwork. The economy has received little attention, while statements about the nature of society have tended to be based on intuitive impressions and dubious historical analogies. This school has had two complementary aims: the presentation of an ever more detailed picture of spatial variation in pottery and metal types on the one hand, and the documentation in increasingly fine detail of the chronological sequence of these types on the other. In the German school the presentation of this material culture sequence and its regional dimension has tended to be regarded as an end in itself, under the title *Kulturgeschichte* (culture history), and the explanation of the changes observed in those sequences has also been assumed to lie within the cultural sphere, in the 'influence' of one local tradition on another.

Throughout the late nineteenth and early twentieth

century the amount of prehistoric material of all kinds accumulated steadily, and rudimentary local sequences were gradually evolved, based mainly on stratigraphy and typology, though with no firm absolute chronology. The next major advance was the correlation of these many local studies into a pan-European framework, and the synthesis of all this information to form a coherent account of prehistoric Europe. This was very largely the achievement of the remarkable Australian prehistorian, Gordon Childe, who laid the groundwork for future studies in such books as *The Dawn of European Civilization* (1925) and *The Danube in Prehistory* (1929).

The principal concept used in the formulation of such explanations was that of a culture, taken over from German anthropology. Childe defined a culture as a constantly recurring assemblage of types such as houses, pottery and burial rites, and regarded it as the physical manifestation of a particular social or ethnic group. When a trait characteristic of one such culture was found in association with those of another, it was explained as the result of the inter-action of the two peoples, though the nature of the 'influence' exerted was frequently unspecified. In the more extreme case of the replacement in a particular region of one culture by another, it was taken as a sign of the replacement of one people by another through migration and conquest. In this way it was hoped that a sort of history could be written about the relations between prehistoric peoples approximating to the political and military history of more recent centuries. The recognition of such cultures became a principal aim of prehistory, and where suitable recurring assemblages could not be seen, cultures were frequently defined on the basis of no more than pottery types. The nature of the fundamental relationship between the material culture studied by the archaeologist and the social groups inferred by him was not seriously considered, although it can now be seen to be much less simple than was supposed, and questions of how past societies and economies could be reconstructed from present archaeological evidence were largely ignored.

In their place, it became important to ask where a feature observed in a particular culture had come from. A concern with tracing connections of this sort between cultures largely precluded the possibility of the independent invention of such features, and indeed one of the main themes of the interpretation of European prehistory was the diffusion or spread of ideas and inventions from one area to another. In the early part of the century there was some discussion as to whether the origin of this diffusion should be located in Europe itself, with Germany favoured in particular, or more traditionally in the Near East. The latter view prevailed, and all or most of the major innovations of prehistory, such as farming, stone architecture and bronze and iron metallurgy, were attributed to diffusion from a single centre of invention in the Near East.

The pursuit of such links between Europe and the Near East was essential since there was no method of dating prehistoric finds from Europe except by correlation, however tenuous, with the historically dated chronologies of the Near East. The dependence of archaeology on these connections for the establishment of a prehistoric European chronology tended to be confused with the dependence of prehistoric Europe on the East for all its advances. The next advance of critical importance was, therefore, the development of a means of dating European prehistory independent of alleged cultural connections. With the discovery of the possibilities of radiocarbon dating from the late 1940s onwards, this became a reality. Renfrew (1973) has described the shock to archaeological thinking that the new dating method administered, which became even greater when it was later realized that the radiocarbon dates, early though they were, had to be calibrated against tree-ring dates to give a better approximation to calendar dates (see box). In this process the dates became earlier still, and the need for rethinking the traditional prehistory of Europe therefore even greater. It was shown that many of the links on which the old chronology was based are no longer tenable, and that some events which had previously been thought contemporary were in fact separated by many centuries. Above all, it has greatly lengthened the time-span of European prehistory; the neolithic period in particular can now be seen to have lasted millennia rather than just centuries.

Recent Developments

Since the Second World War there has been a steady quickening of the pace of archaeological research. This has been caused partly by an increase in the number of people and institutions involved in archaeology and a consequent increase in resources, and partly by a renewed phase of destruction of archaeological sites through building projects and agricultural activity. The advent of new scientific methods for dating and analysis, and the growth in archaeology of a much wider range of research interests have also been responsible in part for this resurgence. New approaches to the past are gradually being explored, and they form the basis on which this book has been written, but they are meeting considerable problems in the legacy left by the typological tradition. The typological studies it has produced are not for the most part especially helpful and their orientation has meant that much of the data that would currently be of interest was not collected in the course of earlier investigations. Settlement archaeology in particular, though pursued in some regions, has in others tended to be neglected, as has the collection of quantitative data of virtually every kind. This state of affairs has led to two responses: on one hand, the undertaking of new fieldwork programmes designed to answer new questions; on the other, the use of often considerable ingenuity in trying to apply old data collected for other purposes to new problems. In some cases, progress has already been remarkable, but in other periods and other regions, work has barely begun.

One particular theme has been the reconstruction of prehistoric subsistence economies. This is by no means new, for an interest in the economy has regularly marked the work of some prehistorians, notably Grahame Clark's *Prehistoric Europe: the economic basis* (1952), but its importance has increased greatly in recent years. New techniques have been devised for the recovery of plant and animal remains from archaeological sites, and, with their use becoming more frequent, the amount of basic data is rapidly growing. There has also been a great increase in research on the prehistoric environment, especially the earth's vegetation and man's effect on it, studied through the analysis of pollen deposits; in areas without known archaeological sites, the evidence for man's agriculture is frequently only the pollen record of forest clearance and the growth of grasses or cereals. With this evidence as a starting point, attempts can be made to reconstruct the actual system of farming or hunting and gathering

CALIBRATION OF RADIOCARBON DATES

Cross-checks between dendrochronology and radiocarbon dating revealed a recurrent discrepancy between calendar and radiocarbon years such that from c. 250 BC backwards, radiocarbon dates are too young. This error is systematic, however; when compared to the absolute chronology based on counts of the yearly rings of the long-lived bristlecone pine, the error gets progressively bigger, until c. 5300 BC. The error is about 350 years at 2000 BC, and 800 years at 5000 BC. The radiocarbon chronology is therefore ''calibrated'' to correspond to calendar years. There is disagreement as to how exactly this should be done statistically; the graph here follows R. M. Clark (1975), but completion of the curve requires further dendrochronology. Present indications from other sources are that the error continues. ^{14}C dates by Tauber (1970) on peat samples correlated pollen-analytically with varve or glacial meltwater lake sediments in Scandinavia, themselves supposedly capable of yielding absolute dates — c. 8300 BC for the beginning of the final ice retreat — suggested that the error had diminished by then. But Stuiver's ^{14}C dates (1970), directly on lake sediments from the period of glacial retreat, though from North America, could suggest an error at 8000 BC similar to that at 5000 BC. The early post-glacial period is not therefore foreshortened, but the extrapolation made here should be regarded as a working estimate only.

in use at any point in time. Particular attention has been paid to the careful scheduling necessary on the part of hunter-gathering communities for successful use of the local resources, which may include a wide variety of foods, but which may also be highly seasonal in their availability and of fluctuating occurrence from year to year. The complex variations that can exist in the relationship between man and animals, between the extremes of hunting and domestication, have also merited considerable notice. Yet another major theme has been the origin and spread of agriculture, though the later development of agricultural economies has received rather less attention.

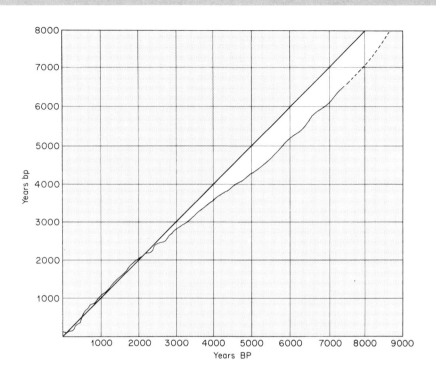

Optimal calibration curve for conversion of conventional radiocarbon dates (bp) to calendar dates (BP) (after R. M. Clark, 1975, with hypothetical extension into the immediate post-glacial period).

In the course of these investigations, it has become increasingly clear that the subsistence economy cannot be understood in isolation from the society which practised it, for the two are inseparable. Economy is clearly an important influence on social organization; among hunter-gatherers, for instance, the exploitation of the available resources and the necessity for mobility set limits to population density, group size and settlement pattern. For farmers, however, the domestication of a new crop could provide valuable new resources, and the need to organize maximum labour for the short seasons of sowing and harvesting was one of the keys to the arrangement of the whole annual timetable. Equally,

social considerations could affect the pattern of subsistence production; it has been argued, for example, that the transition from food-gathering to food-producing was a response to a demand for greater production to promote social status, and the emergence at the end of the prehistoric period of towns with a mostly non-agricultural function certainly necessitated reorganization of the agricultural economy to provide food for them. The social organization of subsistence has, therefore, been a topic of growing importance; the ability to store food at times of surplus to meet future shortages, and the development of systems to exchange food to even out variations in production, were obviously of great importance and have been particularly studied, as has the role of elites in managing and regulating the food supply.

Another theme has been the growth of settlement studies. One element conspicuously missing from much of earlier archaeology was a concern with the size and density of the population, but now in several areas large-scale landscape studies, either by survey on the ground or by aerial photography, are making possible an estimate of prehistoric population figures. These surveys can also document the entire pattern of human use of a region and its resources, and the range of types of settlement occupied. There has been particular interest in the locations chosen for occupation sites, since the resources available in their immediate neighbourhood can give an indication of the economic basis of the site; in the range of sites used by a single community; and in the emergence of a site hierarchy, that is a pattern of sites in which some are of greater importance than others, and might have acted as centres of power or authority in more complex societies.

New approaches have also been developed to the study of material culture, in addition to the ordering of artifacts into chronological sequences. The evidence recovered by archaeologists can be examined as the product of many different processes, including particularly the natural effects of the environment in which it is deposited, such as the decay of most organic materials, and also the modes of past behaviour which led to its original formation (Fig.1.2). The structures and artifacts of a settlement site, for example, and the patterns in which they are found can be used as the key to reconstructing the patterns of behaviour of its occupants. This has been an important factor in the recent study of settlement sites, with particular emphasis on exploring all, or at least the majority, of the site to recover these patterns, to allow understanding of the function of the site as well as its chronology.

New scientific techniques of analysis have also been perfected for the study of certain categories of material, especially pottery, stone and metal, which enable specific groups to be distinguished from each other on the basis of different chemical or petrological composition; these differences can represent sources of production, and in some cases the precise point of origin can be identified. In this way production centres can be studied, and also the systems of exchange which distributed the products from them. Results have been particularly good from the analyses of stone tools, especially of obsidian, and our understanding of prehistoric pottery production has been revolutionized. Whereas previously most pottery was thought to have been a domestic product, it is now known that specialist producers existed from very early times, and that their products could travel very long distances. Studies of such trade have therefore played a large part in recent research, and led to a better understanding of the part played by trade in early societies.

Perhaps the most important area of advance has been the study of prehistoric social organization, and in particular of changes in social organization through time. Much use has been made of classifications of social organization borrowed from modern anthropology, especially that of Elman Service (1962) who proposed a series of four progressively more complex forms of organization, termed respectively band, tribe, chiefdom and state. Although there has been a temptation for effort to be wasted in arguing whether a particular society belongs to one category or another, rather than in explaining the structure of its organization, the scheme has proved useful, if very much oversimplified. European prehistory offers a great variety of types of social organization, especially of the more complex sort, which cannot readily be described in the simple categories of chiefdom and state. It has proved useful, nevertheless, in focusing attention on the very different types of organization that existed in prehistory and on the need to appreciate the level of social organization attained in any region or society before the rest of its archaeology can be properly understood.

Insight into social organization has been gained principally through the study of cemeteries and settlements. In the cemeteries, the grave goods deposited with the body frequently symbolize the person's former role in society; part of that role may have been defined on the basis of distinctions in age or sex, but in non-egalitarian societies part may have been derived from a position of superior power or status, whether that was inherited at birth or achieved in some way during life. Thus the analysis of variations in mortuary practices can offer a valuable key to at least one aspect of the organization of a society.

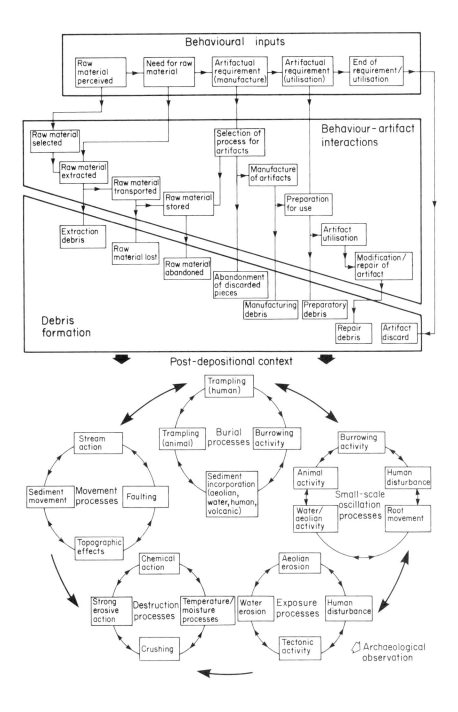

Fig. 1.2 Flow chart to show the manufacture, usage, deposition, survival and recovery of artifacts (after Foley).

Further evidence can be sought in the pattern of settlement, especially in the emergence of marked differentiation between the houses of a single site or between sites within the total settlement system. Individual houses or sites of this sort, distinguished by distinctive architecture or fortification or by artifacts indicating unusual wealth or functions, can express the nature of the social system as much as variations in the wealth of burial deposits. One topic of particular interest has been the general characteristic of complex societies, especially early states, to symbolize their identity by the construction of monumental public buildings, such as palaces, temples, shrines or elaborate funerary monuments.

The effect of a social hierarchy in stimulating change has also been studied. The need for distinctive or exotic objects or materials for display purposes was an important factor in the development of trade and technology. Exchange could provide materials not available locally, such as shells, tools of superior stone or very fine drinking vessels, which thus acquired a prestige value. Technological innovation could give local materials a similar value, if access to the material or the skill to transform it was limited; the first experiments with gold and copper metallurgy and the subsequent development of the bronze industry owed much to the need of rapidly diversifying societies to display their differences.

Attempts have also been made to improve our understanding of one of the most interesting questions, the explanation of why these changes in social organization occurred. Among the factors whose possible significance has been assessed are changes in subsistence economy, themselves caused by environmental change, whether of human or natural origin, and the opportunity offered by the production of a surplus through the introduction of a new subsistence resource. The need to manage increasingly complex agricultural systems, and to regulate production and distribution in order to even out spatial and temporal surpluses and deficits has also been considered, as has the stimulus provided by access to new trade links, which could offer the opportunity for acquiring power and the encouragement to reorganize society and economy in a new orientation towards trade. Further factors which have been discussed are population growth, though it is seldom possible to discern independent archaeological evidence to document such growth, nor to suggest reasons why the population should have been allowed to grow, and, finally, the need for greater political centralization to cope with the expansion of neighbouring polities. There has also been a growing realization of the complexity of even prehistoric societies, and the consequent need for explanations that are not necessarily simple; the interrelationships between the different elements of culture, such as subsistence, exchange, settlement, population, technology and social organization, are so varied that a small change in one can produce changes in some or all of the others, and can indeed be multiplied to produce much greater consequences through these links. It is in the realization of the complexity of social change and in the examination of some possible causes of it that the greatest advance has been made in recent years, but it is there nevertheless that the greatest progress remains to be made.

Many of these lines of enquiry had, of course, been latent in prehistoric research for many years, only awaiting the availability of adequate resources, techniques or methodology. Such interests, however, have played a large part in the so-called 'New Archaeology', a reorientation of approach within the Anglo-American archaeological tradition particularly linked with the names of Lewis Binford and David Clarke. This approach argued for the necessity of a 'systemic' framework for understanding prehistory which views culture as a system which comprises interrelated subsystems such as population, subsistence, exchange and technology, and regarded the interactions between subsystems as critical for explaining the past. This approach also emphasized the vital importance of the links between material culture and the society that produced it, and believed that all areas of prehistoric culture could potentially be explored through the archaeological record, given the right methods. Great weight was therefore given to methodology, in the pursuit of the general principles that would help to explain the whole pattern of man's past. Though fired with a concern for understanding human societies and drawing inspiration from anthropology, much of the work done in this tradition was still orientated towards artifact types and cultures. It was, none the less, basically optimistic about the power of archaeology to understand the past.

Some of that early optimism has been disappointed in practice, and a variety of criticisms and reactions have emerged. The extreme functionalism of the approach adopted to the connection between society and material culture has been criticised, as have a number of generalizations, which stressed similarity rather than variety of behaviour. There has also been a greater contribution from social anthropology, in particular to study the uses of material culture, and such topics as ideology, symbolism and group identity. This has also stimulated the growth of ethnoarchaeology, the study of the material culture and physical record of modern primitive societies.

The current state of European prehistory is therefore characterized by a wide variety of approaches and interests. These range from the traditional artifactual and typological studies, through specific studies of economy, settlement, exchange and social organization, to a concern with the fundamental principles on which societies were based. These varied activities in fact reflect an equally varied conception of the aims and possibilities of prehistoric research.

EUROPE: THE PHYSICAL BACKGROUND

The evolution of the physical form of the land of Europe, and its climate and environment up to the end of the last ice age are some of the themes of the next chapter. Subsequent changes in the environment, both in climate and in vegetation, and man's impact on it, will be examined in the following chapters. It seems appropriate, nevertheless, to give a brief account of the physical background to human settlement and the varied environments offered for it in post-glacial times.

The skeleton of Europe is formed by a series of major mountain ranges which, with one exception, are found in the southern part of the continent, in a zone running broadly east–west (Fig.1.3). The highest are the Alps, which stretch from southern France through Switzerland and northern Italy to eastern Austria; at their highest they reach over 4500 metres, but, though in places they are more than 240 kilometres wide, they are crossed by numerous passes and are far from being an impenetrable barrier. To the west, the line is continued to the Atlantic coast by the Pyrenees on the borders of France and Spain and the Cantabrian Mountains of

northern Spain. To the east, the mountain chain divides into several parts: the northern line, the Carpathians, runs south-eastwards and then westwards in a ring which, though rising to over 2500 metres in places, is narrow and has plenty of passes; to the south of it there are parallel ranges in Bulgaria, the Balkan Range and the Rhodope Mountains; the main southern continuation is the Dinaric Alps, which form the backbone of Yugoslavia and continue on into the mountain ranges of Greece. Another offshoot of the Alps is the Appenine Mountains which run the length of Italy. The one exception to the southern grouping of the major European mountains is the Kjolen Range of Scandinavia.

A second major topographical category is formed by regions of hills and low mountains. A broad band of such landscape spreads through central Europe to the north of the main mountain ranges, from central France to Czechoslovakia; it comprises a large number of small hilly regions, such as the Massif Central of France, the Ardennes of Belgium, the Harz and Erzgebirge Mountains of central Germany, and the Bohemian Forest of Czechoslovakia. There are also other upland areas, such as the Highland zone of Britain, including Wales and Scotland as well as part of western and northern England.

The third terrain category includes the plains and lowlands, which are found predominantly in the north. From the Atlantic coast of western France, through south-eastern England and southern Scandinavia, northern Germany and Poland to Russia runs a continuous belt of lowland plains. It is not uniform, but various distinct regions can be recognized such as the Paris Basin, the Low Country, and the North European Plain; in Russia, the vast East European Plain stretches from the Caspian Sea in the south to the Barents Sea in the north. Much of this zone is highly fertile, though the North European Plain was greatly affected by the glaciers of the last ice age, resulting in poor drainage, lakes and broad tracts of infertile heathlands. There are also smaller blocks of lowland in the hill and mountain zones of central and southern Europe, as well as the many small valleys and coastal plains to be found even in the most mountainous regions. Some of the more important of these lowlands include the Po valley in northern Italy between the Alps and the Appenines, the Alpine Foreland comprising the Swiss and Bavarian plateaux, the Bohemian Basin around Prague, the Hungarian

Fig. 1.3 (above)   Europe, showing major terrain regions (after Jordan, 1973).

Fig. 1.4 (opposite)   Europe, showing modern climate zones (after Jordan, 1973).

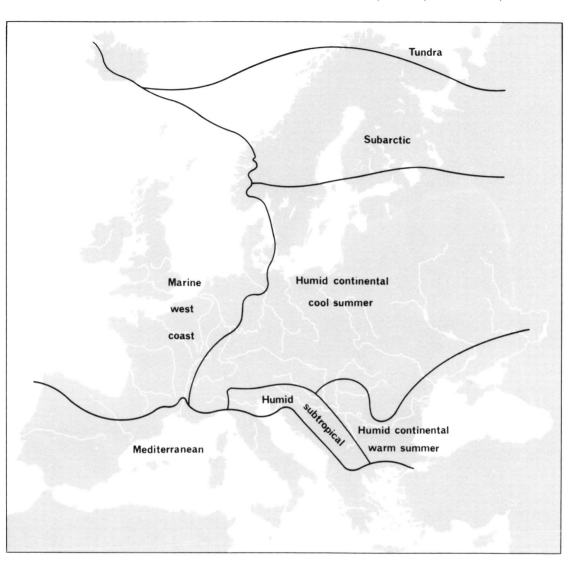

Plain and the Wallachian Plain on the middle and lower Danube respectively, and the Carpathian Basin enclosed in the Carpathian Mountains.

The main mountain ranges form the watersheds of Europe, and most of the rivers flow northwards across the lowlands, like the Loire, Seine, Rhine, Elbe, Oder and Vistula. Only the Rhône flows southwards into the Mediterranean, and with its tributaries it formed a main line of communication between central Europe and the south. The only line of easy communication in an east–west direction through the hill and mountain country of central Europe was offered by the valley of the Danube, rising in south-western Germany and flowing through the Hungarian and Wallachian Plains to the Black Sea.

Europe's position places it firmly within the world's northern temperate zone, but there are great differences in climate along both the north–south and east–west axes (Fig.1.4). The northern and

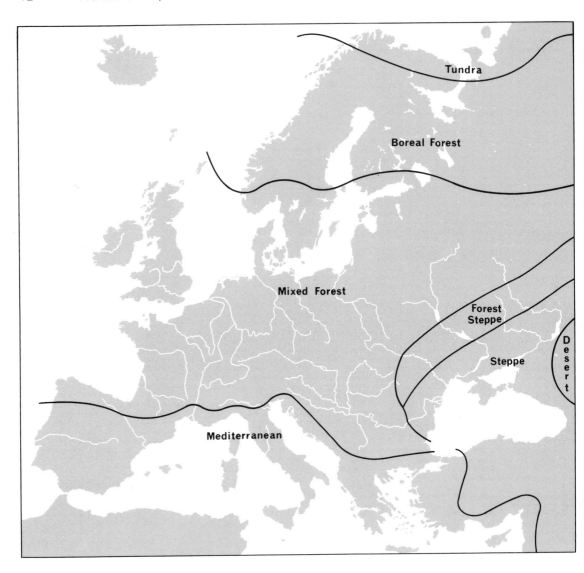

southern extremities of Europe are more than 3500 kilometres apart, while on the west it is exposed to the moderating influences of the Atlantic and on the east it is attached to the great land mass of Asia. These factors and the major topographical features of Europe have resulted in a variety of climatic zones, and although there has been considerable climatic change through the period since the last ice age, these zones have remained distinct. Four main zones can be distinguished. The marine climate of the west coast is characterized by the effect of the Atlantic, ensuring cool summers and mild winters, and adequate rainfall. The Mediterranean climate of southern Europe has hot, very dry summers, mild winters and rain predominantly in the winter. The majority of central and eastern Europe is a zone of

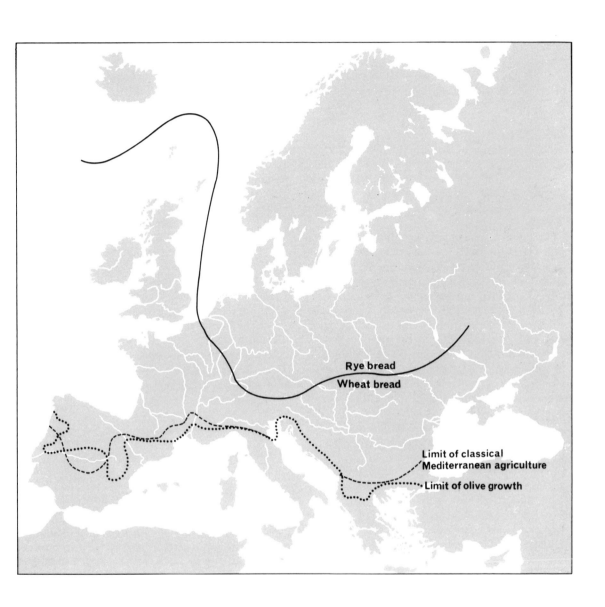

Rye bread

Wheat bread

Limit of classical
Mediterranean agriculture

Limit of olive growth

Fig. 1.5 (opposite)   Europe, showing major zones of modern natural environment (after Hoffman, 1977).

Fig. 1.6 (above)   Europe, showing traditional patterns of agriculture (after Jordan, 1973).

humid continental climate, influenced by the Asian land mass, with rainfall and summers not unlike those of the western coastal area, but with very cold winters which become increasingly bitter towards the east. To the north of this zone is one of subarctic conditions, with short, cool summers and long, very cold winters. Other smaller zones could also be distinguished: parts of the highest mountain areas in the Alps and Scandinavia have almost tundra-like conditions, while in south-eastern Europe the summers become progressively hotter until they approach subtropical or even semi-desert steppe climates.

Climate and topography have been two of the most important factors in controlling the types of vegetation in different parts of Europe, and the types of agricultural regime practised by man. Natural vegetation zones correspond broadly to those of climate (Fig.1.5): in the far north is the tundra region, supporting at the most low bushes and dwarf trees, and to the south of it, in the subarctic climatic zone, is a region of coniferous forest. The modern natural vegetation of western temperate Europe is a deciduous forest, while in the area to the east, in central and eastern Europe, a mixed forest of deciduous and coniferous varieties prevails. The Mediterranean region is characterized by trees able to withstand the prolonged summer droughts, such as the olive, cork oak, chestnut and cypress. In eastern Europe, the increasing aridity and extremes of climate have produced a series of zones, from forest-steppe through steppe to semi-desert, in which open grassland progressively predominates. It must be emphasized that these zones are based on natural vegetation and ignore man's influence, which has in some places modified them enormously, especially by clearance for agriculture and the creation through over-farming of open heath and moor; and also that the nature and composition of the natural vegetation has changed considerably in post-glacial times with variations in the climate. The broad pattern of vegetation has, nevertheless, been constrained by the same geographical features throughout this period, and the relative distinctions between the zones have remained largely constant.

The same constraints have affected the patterns of traditional agriculture practised by man in this period (Fig.1.6). Although in recent centuries farming has been transformed in many areas by increased specialization and new technology, the patterns of pre-industrial, traditional agriculture can still be made out. In the Mediterranean, the climate dictated the use of cereals that could be grown in the mild, damp winters and be harvested in the spring, other species such as the vine and the olive that could survive the dry summers, and flocks of sheep, goats and pigs that did not require well-watered grassland. To the north, the cooler, damper climate led to a very different pattern, in which crops were grown during the summer and harvested in late summer or autumn and cattle were more important. To the north again, in the subarctic zone, agriculture has been possible only in the periods of milder climate, and the northern limits of crop-growing are now further south than they were in the second millennium BC.

Europe's location, therefore, has provided a great variety of topographical, climatic and environmental conditions within a comparatively small area; the use man made of these opportunities and conditions from region to region is described in the remainder of the book.

SUGGESTIONS FOR FURTHER READING

The development of archaeology, especially European prehistory, is described in a number of works by Glyn Daniel, particularly *150 Years of Archaeology*. There is as yet no good account of the developments of the last twenty years, but the sort of ideas that have prompted these changes can be seen, for example, in L. R. Binford, *An Archaeological Perspective*, D. L. Clarke, *Analytical Archaeology*, and A. C. Renfrew, *Before Civilization*, which were all, in their different ways, influential works.

The most important of the classic accounts of European prehistory are, in chronological order, Gordon Childe, *The Dawn of European Civilization*, C. F. C. Hawkes, *The Prehistoric Foundations of Europe*, J. G. D. Clarke, *Prehistoric Europe: the Economic Basis* and Stuart Piggott, *Ancient Europe*. An account which concentrates on some of the more important research of recent years is given by Patricia Phillips, *The Prehistory of Europe*.

Good descriptions of the geography of Europe can be found in G. W. Hoffman (ed), *A Geography of Europe* and T. G. Jordan, *The European Culture Area*.

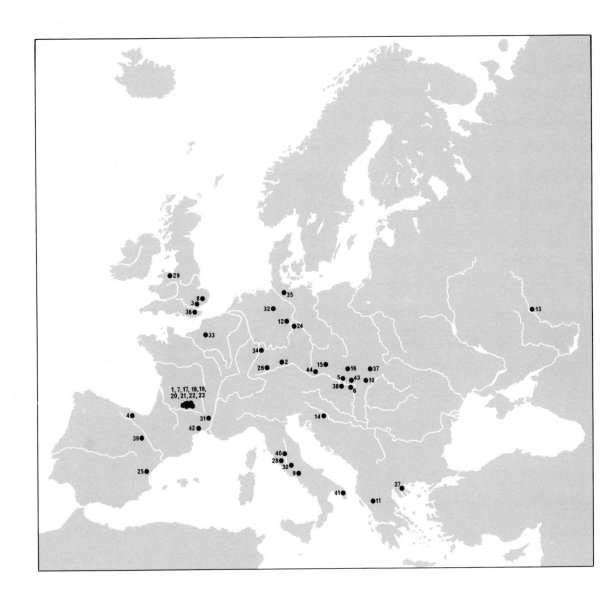

Fig. 2.1   Principal sites mentioned in Chapter 2. 1 Abri Pataud. 2 Bockstein. 3 Clacton. 4 Cueva Morín. 5 Dolní Věstonice and Pavlov. 6 Érd. 7 Fontéchevade. 8 Hoxne. 9 Isernia. 10 Istállóskö. 11 Kokkinopolis. 12 Königsaue. 13 Kostienki. 14 Krapina. 15 Krems Hundssteig. 16 Kůlna. 17 La Chapelle-aux-Saints. 18 La Ferrassie. 19 La Madeleine. 20 La Micoque. 21 La Quina. 22 Laugerie Haute. 23 Le Moustier. 24 Markleeberg. 25 Parpalló. 26 Petersfels. 27 Petralona. 28 Polesini. 29 Pontnewydd. 30 Saccopastore. 31 Salpêtrière. 32 Salzgitter-Lebenstedt. 33 St. Acheul. 34 Steinheim. 35 Stellmoor. 36 Swanscombe. 37 Szeleta. 38 Tata. 39 Torralba, Ambrona. 40 Torre in Pietra. 41 Uluzzo. 42 Vallonet. 43 Vértesszöllös. 44 Willendorf II.

2

Earliest Humans in Europe

This chapter provides a brief description of the origins and aims of palaeolithic (old Stone Age) studies. A chronological and climatic framework for studying early hominids in Europe is now based upon the continuous record of pleistocene events that is recorded in the deep sea ocean cores. These form a yardstick for studying changes in recent earth history. Local regional sequences within Europe are illustrated by using information from the discontinuous land-based record.

The fossil evidence for early hominids in Europe is reviewed, together with the question of when they arrived in the continent. Some of the interpretations that have been put forward to account for differences between neanderthal and modern populations are used to show the problems of studying fossil material.

Our understanding of the material culture of palaeolithic groups is dominated by the study of chipped stone artifacts. This involves studies that experimentally manufacture flint implements, flakes and blades as well as the typological analysis of stone tool assemblages. These investigations are now enhanced by recent breakthroughs in the microscopic investigation of stone tool edges and the interpretation of patterns of stone tool use as determined by experiment.

Finally, the changes in chipped stone assemblages are presented in three major chronological divisions that see a variety of regional traditions.

INTRODUCTION

The aims of palaeolithic (old Stone Age) research are to document the earliest societies in Europe and answer that basic archaeological question, 'why do human cultures change?'. The first aim has led to refinements in the methods and techniques of analysis. The excavation of palaeolithic sites now involves micro-stratigraphic observations of both vertical sequences and horizontal occupation. The chipped stone assemblages that are recovered from these precisely defined and measured contexts are now described in a quantitative manner so that comparisons can be made between collections. The sediments from which they are excavated are analysed for a variety of environmental information about the climatic conditions that existed at the time of deposition. These observations can then be compared with other lines of environmental reconstruction such as the information now available from deep sea and polar ice cap cores and the analysis of pollen grains preserved in lake muds. The advent of absolute methods of time reckoning by measuring the decay of isotopes in volcanic rocks and organic material is beginning to provide a framework for establishing rates of change in human cultures.

The second objective has made use of these improved methods in order to understand the processes of physical, material and social evolution as applied to the genus *Homo*. While the reconstruction of palaeolithic society at any one point in time is an important aim, we also want to understand *why* such long-term adaptations underwent change. The main interest of palaeolithic studies lies in tracing the relationship between biological and social evolution through the scarce remains of the human fossil record and the abundant remains of the tools and equipment that have survived.

ORIGINS OF PALAEOLITHIC STUDIES

The first task of palaeolithic studies was to prove that distinctively chipped stones were indeed human artifacts and to relate them to an early phase of the prehistoric record. The arguments put forward by Prestwich and Evans in 1859 marked a turning point in the general acceptance of a remote prehistory for man. Their case rested on the association of such implements with the bones of extinct animals and their demonstration appeared in the same year as Darwin published *The Origin of Species*. This book was followed in 1865 by Lubbock's classification of prehistoric implements into a number of stages, the earliest of which he termed 'palaeolithic'. By the early years of this century, there existed a considerable body of palaeolithic material, much of which had been recovered from the caves of southern France and the river gravels of the Somme in northern France, and the Thames in southern England. The material was grouped into three palaeolithic stages, lower, middle and upper, based on the shape of the implements. A chronology was provided by observing their position in stratigraphic sequences. These typological studies, where classification is based on the observation of repeated shapes, have more recently been supplemented by technological studies of the different methods used to make stone tools.

Other lines of evidence have also been used to support this tripartite division of the palaeolithic period. The finds of fossil man indicate that the lower palaeolithic was associated with small-brained hominids of the genus *Homo*, the middle palaeolithic with neanderthals, *Homo sapiens neanderthalensis*, and the upper palaeolithic with *Homo sapiens sapiens*, or anatomically modern man. In the upper palaeolithic, tools of bone, ivory and antler first appeared and a number of them were decorated with carved animals and schematic ornamentation. By 1895 the painted caves which had been discovered, such as Altamira in northern Spain, were also accepted as being upper palaeolithic in date. The appearance of an 'aesthetic sensibility' combined with a greater technological competence agreed well with the appearance of modern man in the fossil record.

The association of different hominid types with different categories of stone tools has led to a central concept in palaeolithic studies. This states that changes in material culture during the palaeolithic can be explained by the associated fossil evidence. It was assumed that increasing intelligence was the factor that led to advances, such as technological expertise and the broadening of human culture to include art, language and religion. Cultural evolution, according to this point of view, is dependent upon biological evolution and in particular upon the development of the brain.

As another way of accounting for the major divisions of the palaeolithic, archaeologists introduced the concept of social traditions. Thus, within the upper palaeolithic, it is common to find that the archaeological classifications applied to collections of stone tools are also used as social labels with the effect that we refer to, for example, the Aurignacian culture, the Gravettian people or the Magdalenians.

Different assemblages, e.g. aurignacian, solutrean or magdalenian, were held to represent different human groups who were in a state of competition as Burkitt, writing in 1933, suggested in this dramatic sketch:

The Solutreans broke into Western Europe as a horde of invaders. Armed with the laurel and willow leaf lance points . . . they seem to have completely dominated the scene and yet to have been always aliens . . . while here and there the old Aurignacians must have been driven out or exterminated, elsewhere they probably managed to survive.

This way of interpreting the palaeolithic owed much to Gordon Childe's use of the term *culture* whereby a prehistoric human group, or people, was identified archaeologically by the distinctive tools they made. The patterns that archaeologists detect through either typological or technological studies of these tools are then a result of these binding traditions whereby human groups used their material culture to demonstrate their social differences.

These two concepts — increasing intelligence and social traditions — do not, however, provide an adequate explanation of either changes or differences amongst palaeolithic data. Increasing intelligence may explain why the path of evolution was such a slow one, but still leaves us with the question of why and how changes in intelligence took place. Nor does the idea of social traditions stand up to the evidence that is readily available from contemporary cultural traditions. While it is possible to draw dividing lines based upon differences in material culture between modern societies, it is also possible to see many items or traits that pass over such classificatory lines, thus blurring the categories we are seeking to impose and indeed questioning their validity. An ethnographic study (Thomson, 1939) of an Australian Aboriginal

group showed that at different times of the year the same group made and utilized a completely different set of artifacts. An archaeologist digging up the remains of this group would, if he followed the social tradition argument, conclude that he was dealing with two distinct peoples or cultures. In reality, the patterns that he was seeing were due to changes in technology as the seasonal availability of resources dictated what equipment would be needed.

An alternative concept for understanding the palaeolithic states that what we are studying is adaptive behaviour. Material culture is the means by which people adapt to their environment — the latter includes both the physical environment, from which food and other resources are obtained, and the social environment, which ensures biological reproduction (White, 1959). At a very basic level, it is possible to speak of human societies, at whatever level of brain development or cultural complexity, as aiming to fulfil two goals: the maintenance of the present population and its continued existence into another generation. Failure in either of these goals results in extinction. In this sense we can see that lower palaeolithic societies were as successful in attaining these goals as those in the upper palaeolithic. While the material culture of the lower palaeolithic may seem simple to us, it was none the less both sufficient and efficient in ensuring a successful long-term adaptation to the conditions of the time. Were these conditions to change, either through factors external to human society such as climatic change or internal factors such as population growth, then adjustments would be necessary. These might involve changes in the seasonal location of settlement, a change to hunting different animals, developments in the means of passing on information, or changes to the existing technology in order to cope with the new circumstances. The explanation of change would not, therefore, be dependent upon a single factor such as intelligence but rather the result of the interplay between many variables, among which environment, subsistence, population pressure on resources, biological development and social organization would all be relevant.

Palaeolithic research has shown that it is possible to identify repeated patterns in the data. The direction of present research is towards reconstructing the past in terms of the behaviour that gave rise to such patterns and the variation that exists between the patterns. It is also concerned with providing explanations of the organizing principles that produced such repeated and predictable human behaviour. As Kent Flannery has described it, we are not only looking for the Indian behind the artifact but also for the system behind the Indian.

FRAMEWORKS

The chronological framework for palaeolithic studies has traditionally been based on geology (Zeuner, 1959; Butzer, 1971; Flint, 1971). The position of moraines left behind by the ice sheets indicates the extent and number of glacial advances, while periglacial phenomena, including the deposition of wind blown particles, or loess, point to climatic conditions beyond the margins of the ice sheets. Changes in river profiles, which resulted in the

creation of step-like terraces, indicate fluctuations in sea level as the oceans shrank in size during the glacial advances and expanded during intervening periods of warmer climate. This effect can also be traced in fossil shorelines that were cut by the sea when it stood at much higher levels during those same interglacial periods. The analysis of pollen grains laid down in old lake muds allows the vegetation of the palaeo-landscape to be reconstructed and, by comparing changes in the presence and abundance of tree pollen species, it is possible to assign any associated implements to either a particular glacial or interglacial stage (Frenzel, 1973).

These techniques have provided a great wealth of environmental data both for the reconstruction of palaeo-landscapes and as a means for assigning relative ages to sites (Butzer, 1971). They have, however, the drawback of providing a *discontinuous*

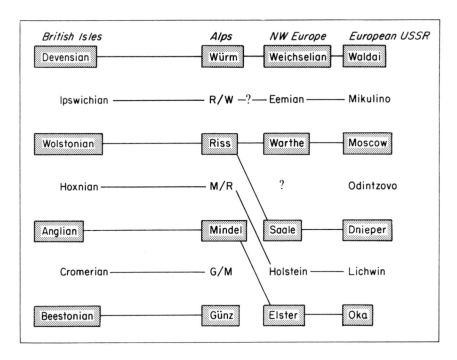

Fig. 2.2 *Regional pleistocene sequences from Europe north of the Alps. These include the classical Alpine scheme that was first proposed by Penck and Brückner in 1909. Some of the conventional correlations are shown between glacial stages (shaded) and interglacial episodes. Notice the difficulty of correlating northwest Europe with the Alps. Correlation charts of this form which are based upon discontinuous records of the pleistocene are now being replaced by continuous records backed up with absolute dates. These show that the classical pleistocene framework of four glacial stages is no longer tenable (based on West, 1977).*

record of pleistocene events. Comparisons between regions have sometimes proved difficult. An example of this is provided by the moraines of north Europe and the Alpine Foreland. In the former area, three major ice advances have been identified (Weichsel, Saale and Elster), while to the south, four glacial episodes are present (Würm, Riss, Mindel, Günz). This has led to considerable confusion over the relative age of some sites and to which glacial period they belong (Fig.2.2).

The discontinuous nature of these terrestrial sequences has been further highlighted by the evidence from deep sea cores that do provide a *continuous* record (Bowen, 1978; Kukla, 1975, 1977). Sediments on the ocean floor are made up of the skeletons of small marine foraminifera which are laid down at a constant rate. Changes in global climate not only affect which types of species are present in such sediments, but also alter the isotopic composition of the surface water. One effect of the continental glaciations in Europe was to enrich the oceans in terms of a particular oxygen isotope, ^{18}O. The amount of ^{18}O can be measured in the skeletons of the foraminifera and, when compared with the stable ^{16}O isotope that is also present, a ratio can be determined. Fluctuations in this ratio are then plotted against depth in the core and a curve produced of changing ocean volumes. This occurred as a result of a fall in world temperature and the growth of continental ice sheets.

In one of these cores, number V28-238 from the Pacific (Shackleton and Opdyke, 1973), it was also possible to identify, at a depth of 1200 cm, a change in the polarity of the earth's magnetic field, from reversed to normal (Fig.2.3). This event, which has also been noted on land and dated by absolute methods to 700 000 BP, provides a clear stratigraphic marker that allows this and other cores to be tied into terrestrial events. In core V28-238, it is also possible, assuming a constant rate of sediment accumulation, to date the fluctuations in the ^{18}O curve that are present. No less than nineteen major stages have been identified, of which eight are full glacial episodes, between the top of the core and the magnetic event at 700 000. In terms of pleistocene stratigraphy, this event at 700 000 is now taken as the baseline between the lower and middle pleistocene. This latter period of time covers the majority of palaeolithic settlement in Europe. Any correlation between this continuous

record and the discontinuous evidence from continental areas has to be supported by absolute dates. For example the Hoxnian interglacial of eastern England might be thought to correspond with stage 7, but this simple procedure of counting from the top and fitting named land events to isotope stage numbers is not permissible. It is still not clear to what extent an interglacial defined palynologically corresponds to an interglacial defined isotopically. However, the study of several old lake deposits in eastern England, including the site of Hoxne itself where palaeolithic artifacts have been recovered, has shown four major vegetational stages during this interglacial (West, 1977). In the early part of the sequence, birch and pine dominated and were replaced by a more temperate vegetation consisting of oak, hornbeam, elm and lime. In the final stage, there was a return to colder conditions with pine and birch reappearing before the onset of Wolstonian glacial conditions. Between stages II and III at some of these localities, there is evidence for rapid deforestation which, it has been claimed, may be due to burning of the forests by man in order to facilitate the capture of game (Turner, 1970). At this time, the local fauna of southern England included giant beaver, large fallow deer, elephant, hippopotamus and rhinoceros. Mean summer temperatures during the Hoxnian interglacial were of the order of 20°C.

The upper pleistocene (stages 2–5 in the cores) is the best understood part of the entire sequence. The deep sea core record is supplemented by a core drilled through the Greenland ice cap at Camp Century (Fig.2.4). Annual layers of ice can also be measured for their ^{18}O content and provide a further check to the information recovered from the ocean floor. The interglacial stage 5 in the deep sea cores has been divided into five sub-stages (Shackleton, 1969), two of which were very short-lived but extremely cold. The cores have been tied in with dated raised beaches in Barbados (Mesolella *et al.*, 1969) to give accurate estimations of the duration of these events. Full interglacial conditions were relatively short-lived between 128 000 and 110 000 years (sub-stage 5e) and the descent to glacial conditions was under way between 80 000 and 70 000 years ago. Within this final glaciation, there are several subdivisions. The early last glacial was a time of moist, cold conditions interspersed with temporary ameliorations known as interstadials (Amersfoort, Brørup, Odderade,

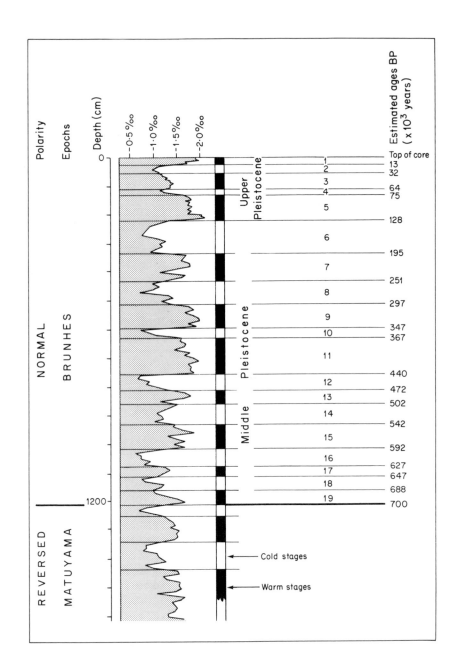

Fig. 2.3 *The climatic record for pleistocene events from deep sea core V28-238 taken in the Pacific Ocean. The core shows the variation in the amount of* ^{18}O *plotted against depth in centimetres. At 1200 cm the sediments show a change in magnetic polarity which can be dated by absolute methods to 700 000 years. The other ages are estimates based upon their depth within the core. Compare the number of warm and cold phases with those recognized from terrestrial studies in Europe (Fig. 2.2) (after Shackleton and Opdyke, 1973).*

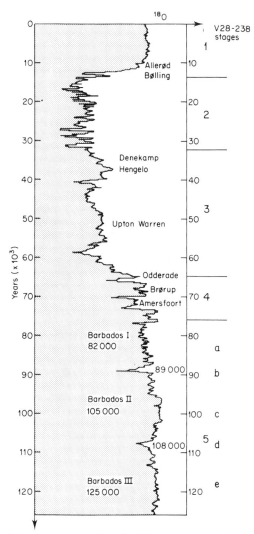

Fig. 2.4   Changes in values for ¹⁸O from Camp Century, Greenland. The isotope record over the last 120 000 years monitors changes in ice volume and shows that after 70 000 the amount of ice increased, which points to colder climatic conditions. The highest values are recorded between 28 000 and 16 000 BP. The threefold division of the isotope record between 125 000 and 78 000 is now supported by a comparable curve derived from pollen studies in north-eastern France (Woillard, 1978) and conforms to the deep sea isotope record where it has been suggested that true interglacial conditions were shortlived between c. 128 000 and 115 000 BP. Possible correlations with interstadial events recognized from terrestrial deposits in northern Europe are also shown (after Dansgaard et al., 1971).

Moershoofd). These have been identified in pollen spectra from peat bogs in Holland (van der Hammen *et al.*, 1971) and a suggested temperature curve plotted (Fig.2.5). Between 39 000 and 29 000 BP was a period of considerable amelioration, the central Würm interstadials of Hengelo and Denekamp. These interstadials have been traced in central and eastern Europe through the formation of soil horizons in loess deposits. They are within the range of radiocarbon dating.

After Denekamp at 29 000 BP, there was a rapid worsening of climate as the dry cold conditions of the full last glacial commenced. It was during this period that the ice sheets began to advance across northern England, the north European plain and out from the Alps. The maximum extent was reached between 20 000 and 18 000 BP (Peterson *et al.*, 1979), after which they began to retreat. The succeeding late glacial is subdivided on the evidence from radiocarbon dated pollen profiles into a series of short interstadials and colder periods before the climate improves in the post-glacial.

GEOGRAPHICAL FACTORS

The combined investigations of pollen analysis, pleistocene stratigraphy, and the existence of an absolute chronology have enabled general reconstructions of the European landscape to be made for various points of the last glacial. Europe never reached the extreme tundra conditions that are now associated with the arctic regions of the world. Because of the latitude at which the unglaciated part of the continent lay, it would always have received more direct solar energy than the arctic regions of today. At any one time, there would have been a complex mosaic of vegetation influenced by local conditions of topography, soil formation, and the degree of continentality. The productivity of the environment during glacial times is well demonstrated by the diversity of the animals that existed and which included such large herbivores as the woolly rhinoceros, mammoth, bison and horse, as well as the reindeer and red deer, and large carnivores, such as bear, lion, hyena and wolf (Soergel, 1943; Toepfer, 1963; Kurtén, 1968; Kahlke, 1975).

The effect of these pleistocene events was not uniform across the continent of Europe. There

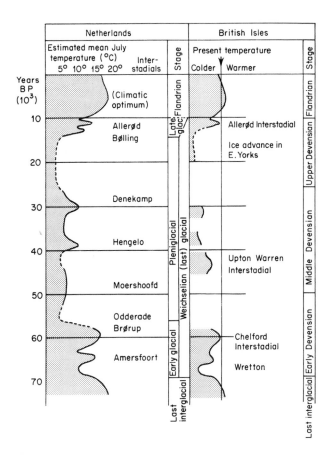

Fig. 2.5   A comparison between the climatic sequence during the last glaciation in the Netherlands and British Isles. The Netherlands curve is based on ¹⁴C dated pollen profiles. The British curve is constructed from several lines of evidence that include glacial deposits, beetle evidence and palynological data (after West, 1977).

would have been certain areas, such as Spain and southern Italy, where the direct effects of glaciations in the north would have been modified by their geographical position. The area of central Europe, Germany and Austria would, however, have had intensified effects, since this area formed an ice-free corridor between the Scandinavian and Alpine ice sheet (Fig.2.6) (Poser, 1948; Kaiser, 1960). Further east, it is clear from the increasing quantities of loess deposits that the degree of continentality in the prevailing climate must have played a part. The amount of these wind-blown deposits indicates extensive areas with poor vegetational cover that allowed such erosion to take place.

THE FOSSIL EVIDENCE

Middle Pleistocene 700 000–130 000 BP

The fossil material from the middle pleistocene of Europe (isotope stages 6 to 19) is meagre when compared with the wealth of discoveries from the East African Rift valley. The available evidence points to East Africa as the area where early hominids developed. Finds from Hadar in Ethiopia, Lake Turkana in Kenya, Olduvai Gorge and Laetoli in Tanzania and a number of limestone quarries in South Africa have produced a complex picture of early hominids grouped under the genus names

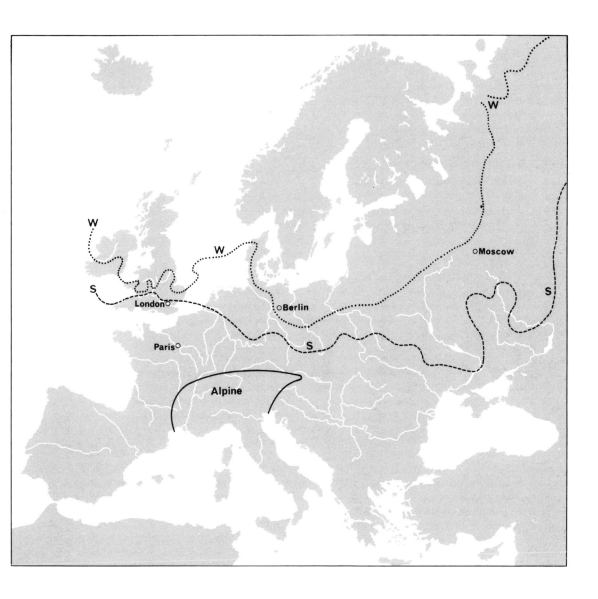

Fig. 2.6 A simplified map of ice sheet advance in northern Europe. The map shows the maximum extent of pleistocene ice sheet advance that occurred during the Saale/Dniepr (S) stage. The most recent Devensian/Weichsel/Waldai (W) stage is also shown.

FINDSPOTS IN PALAEOLITHIC EUROPE

The varied geography of Europe and its pleistocene history have produced differences in the location and recovery of palaeolithic information. In general terms we can divide the continent into three zones.

(a) The northern plains. The area of southern England and Northern France has produced the majority of European lower palaeolithic information from gravel pits in the terraces of the Thames, (Wymer, 1968), Somme and Seine (Breuil and Kosłowski, 1932). The artifacts are often sorted and rolled by stream action. Raised shorelines along the coasts of southern England and Northern France also contain lower palaeolithic material. In northern Germany (Taute, 1968), Poland (Schild, 1975) and Russia (Klein 1969, 1973) many middle and upper palaeolithic sites have been found in loess deposits and have come to light when the loess has been dug for brick making or through agricultural activity and natural erosion.

(b) The central uplands. This is the area of cave exploration, especially in the limestone areas of Europe. Caves have their own microclimates and a considerable amount of climatic information can be gained by studying the shape and size of the weathered fragments, from the roof and walls, that form the deposit in which large collections of middle and upper palaeolithic artifacts have been found (Laville *et al.*, 1980; Farrand, 1975; Schmid, 1967). Open sites are also known along the major river valleys and are often buried in loess (Kukla, 1977; Freund, 1952).

(c) The Mediterranean littoral where sea-cut caves and raised shorelines contain traces of palaeolithic occupation (H. de Lumley, 1969). The Mediterranean is a tectonically unstable area so that the height above present sea-level of these fossil shorelines is not a good guide to their relative position in pleistocene chronology. The lower palaeolithic is more abundantly represented in this area than in the caves of the central uplands.

Homo and *Australopithecus*. The variety of fossil hominids between 4 and 1·3 million years ago is most striking. We know from the footprints preserved in a lava flow at Laetoli that there was an upright walking hominid at 3·8 million years and the earliest tools so far known come from the Omo river region and are dated to 2·5 million years. By 1·3 million years a large brained hominid, *Homo erectus*, had evolved and is found in deposits with a robust Australopithecine. Equivalent finds of *Homo erectus* have been made in China and Java and it appears that this species was widespread throughout parts of the Old World by 1 million years ago.

The fossil evidence for early hominids in Europe is not only sparse, it is also fragmentary (Fig.2.7) (Day, 1977; Oakley *et al.*, 1971). The Steinheim, Arago (M. de Lumley, 1973, 1976) and Petralona specimens are represented by the facial areas of the skull and to differing degrees by the brain case itself. Fontéchevade, Vértesszöllös, Swanscombe (Ovey, 1964) and Bilzingsleben (Vlček, 1978) are incomplete skull bones, while the finds from Atapuerca (Aguirre and de Lumley, 1977), Mauer and Montmaurin are

lower jaws. This has made the taxonomic grouping of these specimens extremely difficult and highly contentious. Scientists cannot determine whether the earliest European specimens should be assigned to *Homo erectus* or *Homo sapiens*.

The skull bones show a flattening of the brain case in contrast to the high domed skull of modern humans. The volume that was enclosed can only be calculated with any degree of accuracy for three specimens and shows a smaller brain than that possessed by modern humans. It is not certain whether this can be interpreted as a difference in intelligence and mental ability. The facial area shows heavy brow ridges and a sloping face. The teeth are generally larger than those in modern humans and the mandibles particularly massive.

The Petralona skull has now been dated to between 160 000 and 240 000 years old (Hennig *et al.*, 1981) while there is a ^{230}Th/^{234}U date for the skull horizon at Swanscombe of 326 000 BP, $+99 000 - 54 000$ (Szabo and Collins, 1975). The finds of skull fragments from the East German site of Bilzingsleben (Mania *et al.*, 1980) are incorporated in travertine deposits,

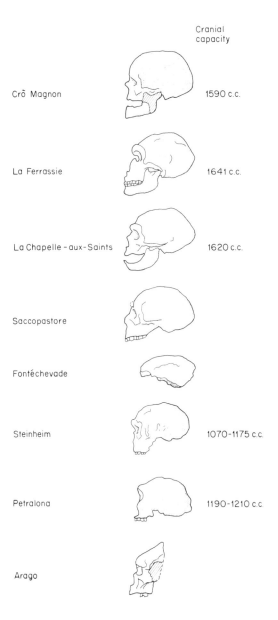

Cranial
capacity

Crô Magnon   1590 c.c.

La Ferrassie   1641 c.c.

La Chapelle - aux - Saints   1620 c.c.

Saccopastore

Fontéchevade

Steinheim   1070-1175 c.c.

Petralona   1190-1210 c.c.

Arago

Fig. 2.7 The outlines of some of the most complete crania from the European fossil record. Note in particular the presence of a chin in Crô Magnon, the shape of the forehead, high domed cranial vault and contours at the base of the skull. The cranial capacity of these skulls as measured by cubic centimetres is also given for some of the specimens in order to convey an impression of comparative size. The skulls have all been orientated in the same profile for the purposes of visual comparison.

which are formed under warm climatic conditions. At the latest this would put the site in stage 7 (Harmon *et al.*, 1980) with every likelihood that this material is from an earlier interglacial stage. Vlček (1978) has claimed that all these fossils date to the Holsteinian interglacial. According to his interpretation of the cranial evidence, two populations existed in Europe at this time. In the east the finds from Petralona, Bilzingsleben and Vértesszöllös are representative of *Homo erectus* while in the west of the continent the material from Steinheim and Swanscombe (Fig.2.8) is, he believes, part of the *Homo sapiens* lineage. This interpretation raises considerable problems of tying in terrestrial chronologies with the continuous chronology of pleistocene events provided by the deep sea cores. Moreover, many other specialists would dispute the attribution of the eastern material to a separate species (Stringer, 1974) and have instead placed all the fossil material within a grade of *Homo sapiens* (Table 2.1).

More recently the molar of a young adult has been excavated from the cave of Pontnewydd in north Wales (Green *et al.*, 1981; Green, 1981). Absolute dates point to an age of around 200 000 years for this specimen. In appearance the tooth is most closely paralleled with the so-called early Neanderthalers from the Yugoslavian site of Krapina which have often been dated to the last interglacial (Brace, 1979). An important series of fossil finds from La Chaise cave in France and which M. de Lumley (1975, 1976) places between *Homo erectus* and *Homo sapiens neanderthalensis* have a Uranium series date of 146 000 ± 16 000 BP.

The few absolute dates for these fossils all indicate that man was present in Europe after 350 000 BP. A longer chronology for the colonization of the continent has been put forward by H. de Lumley (1976) on the basis of his excavations along the coasts of southern France (1969). The cave of Vallonnet near Nice was cut by a very high sea level and contained a few technologically simple artifacts (Fig.2.17). Deposits within the cave were analysed for their magnetic information and found to be of normal polarity. This would imply either a date during the Brunhes epoch of normal polarity that began at 700 000 BP or one of the shorter normal polarity events that occurred during the Matuyama epoch of reversed polarity. H. de Lumley (1976) favours the Jaramillo event for the age of Vallonnet which would

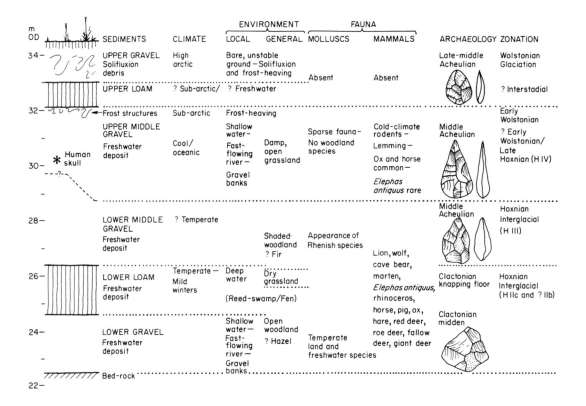

m OD	SEDIMENTS	CLIMATE	ENVIRONMENT		FAUNA		ARCHAEOLOGY	ZONATION
			LOCAL	GENERAL	MOLLUSCS	MAMMALS		
34—	UPPER GRAVEL Solifluxion debris	High arctic	Bare, unstable ground — Solifluxion and frost-heaving		Absent	Absent	Late-middle Acheulian	Wolstonian Glaciation
	UPPER LOAM	? Sub-arctic/	? Freshwater					? Interstadial
32—	Frost structures	Sub-arctic	Frost-heaving					Early Wolstonian
	UPPER MIDDLE GRAVEL Freshwater deposit	Cool/ oceanic	Shallow water — Fast-flowing river — Gravel banks	Damp, open grassland	Sparse fauna — No woodland species	Cold-climate rodents — Lemming — Ox and horse common — *Elephas antiquus* rare	Middle Acheulian	? Early Wolstonian/ Late Hoxnian (H IV)
30—	✱ Human skull							
28—	LOWER MIDDLE GRAVEL Freshwater deposit	? Temperate	Shaded-woodland ? Fir	Appearance of Rhenish species		Lion, wolf, cave bear, marten, *Elephas antiquus,* rhinoceros, horse, pig, ox, hare, red deer, roe deer, fallow deer, giant deer	Middle Acheulian	Hoxnian Interglacial (H III)
26—	LOWER LOAM Freshwater deposit	Temperate — Mild winters	Deep water (Reed-swamp/Fen)	Dry grassland			Clactonian knapping floor	Hoxnian Interglacial (H IIc and ? IIb)
24—	LOWER GRAVEL Freshwater deposit		Shallow water — Fast-flowing river — Gravel banks	Open woodland ? Hazel	Temperate land and freshwater species		Clactonian midden	
22—	Bed-rock							

Fig. 2.8   *The lower palaeolithic site of Swanscombe located in the Boyn Hill terrace of the Thames. Several investigations at this site have now made it possible to place the human skull and the clactonian and acheulian artifact assemblages within their environmental setting.* Elephas antiquus *is an extinct straight tusked elephant that is commonly found in interglacial deposits (after Evans, 1975).*

put the site at between 0·9 and 0·95 million years old.

A new site has come to light at Isernia in central Italy (Sevink *et al.*, 1981) which has the advantage that its early age is confirmed by both palaeo-magnetic and absolute dates. A diverse large mammal fauna together with chipped limestone pebbles has been found in ancient marsh deposits that are stratified below a tufa that has been dated to 0·73 million years. Palaeo-magnetic studies also show the expected reversal in the polarity of sediments below this chronological marker. This combination of a securely dated fauna and artifact collection extending over an area estimated at 20 000 m² makes this a most important site for understanding the middle pleistocene occupation of Europe.

Another site at Anagni (Biddittu *et al.*, 1979) in central Italy has also produced some stone tools dated to between 360 000 and 450 000 years old. Much earlier dates still have been put forward for tools at Chillac in France where Guth (1974) places them below an absolute date of 1·6 million years. None of these four sites has so far produced any fossil human material.

Upper Pleistocene 130 000 — 10 000 BP

The fossil record from the upper pleistocene, isotope stages 2–5, is much richer in material. All the fossils from this period are regarded by all authorities as

Table 2.1   A possible grade structure for the European fossil specimens of Homo sapiens. *The italicized fossils are the suggested type of fossils for that grade; the placing of those fossils shown on the right is less certain. The system is based upon similarities, or morphoclines, in cranial shape. The scheme implies no chronological positioning and avoids drawing arrows between specimens to indicate evolutionary relationships. This is a reflection of the uncertainty of the age of many of the specimens and the realization that unilineal models of human evolution, which have often been favoured in the past, are no longer applicable to the complexities of the palaeontological record. The purpose of this grading system is to establish categories that can then be used to investigate the range of variability among fossil populations as a step in unravelling the evolutionary process (after Stringer et al., 1979).*

Grade 3	*Sub group*		
	(a) *La Ferrassie* 1, La Chapelle-aux-Saints		
	(b) *Crô Magnon* 1		
		Grade 2 or 3	Krapina
Grade 2	(a)? *Saccopastore* 1, La Chaise, Ehringsdorf, Fontéchevade		
		Grade 1 or 2	Steinheim, Swanscombe, Montmaurin, Arago, Atapuerca
Grade 1	(a)? *Petralona*, Vértesszöllös, Mauer, Bilzingsleben		

Homo sapiens and only differentiated at the sub-specific level into either neanderthal or modern man. The type fossil for neanderthal man was discovered in the French cave of La Chapelle-aux-Saints in 1908 and was described and classified by Boule (1908; Day, 1977; Reader, 1981). The skull had strongly developed brow ridges and cheek bones and a sloping face when compared with modern man. The top of the skull was slightly flattened and there was a noticeable bun at its base. Boule's reconstruction of the limbs produced a stooped, shambling creature. The skeleton was re-examined in 1957 (Cave and Straus, 1957) and found to be that of an old man suffering from arthritis. The posture of neanderthal man was therefore no different from that of modern man and it has been claimed that given the right clothes it is unlikely that he would excite much interest if seen walking down the street. The size of neanderthal brain cases is generally larger than modern man and the differences in the face may be the result of eating habits. This interpretation has been put forward by Brace (1979) who has been a supporter of the view that neanderthals should be regarded as a direct ancestor of modern populations (1964; Brose and Wolpoff, 1971). His argument is based on the reduction in tooth size among fossil populations. A series of neanderthalers from the Yugoslavian site of Krapina, dated to the last inter-glacial, have large front teeth. By contrast the neanderthalers and *Homo sapiens sapiens* fossils from the last glaciation all show a marked reduction in incisor size and this trend continues into present day populations. The inferred function of the large incisors is to grip objects, principally food, that was then manipulated by the hands. Brace suggests that the reduction in tooth size that began with the early modern humans is related not only to developments in manipulative technology but also to techniques of food preparation that made chewing easier, thus making the large size of teeth a redundant feature. The remains of hearths from the upper palaeolithic could represent earth oven cookery where heated stones, pot-boilers, were used to soften the food. This 'culinary revolution', as Brace refers to it, provides an example of how biological change might be dependent upon cultural evolution.

A second view maintains that the differences in cranial features are too marked between the fossil populations of neanderthals and *Homo sapiens sapiens* to place the former as an ancestor of the latter (Howells, 1974; Stringer, 1974). Howells, for example (1975), has provided a detailed series of measurements on the jaws of neanderthals and modern populations. These reveal that it is not just a matter of the size of the teeth but rather their positioning within the mandible that is important in assessing relationships between fossils. The last molar, M3, sits well forward in the jaw of the classic neanderthalers such as the specimens from La Ferrassie, La Quina (France), Krapina (Yugoslavia), Shanidar (Iraq) and the Mt. Carmel specimens from Israel. However, in modern populations this tooth is located further back in the jaw and is hidden by the mandibular ramus. This relative positioning is also to be found in the mandibles from the early fossils such as Mauer (Germany) and Arago (France). This suggests a closer relationship between some of the early European fossils and the anatomically modern populations that first appear at 35 000 BP in the rock shelters of western Europe. The find from the Crô Magnon shelter at Les Eyzies (France) is often used to describe the modern populations that were present at this time.

The detailed analysis of cranial and facial structure between neanderthal and Crô Magnon fossil populations has been undertaken by Stringer (1974) using a large number of measurable attributes and comparing them by means of multivariate statistical tests. This analysis further reveals the statistical separation of the early last glacial, classic neanderthal fossils from either earlier or later material.

The neanderthalers therefore pose a number of questions; where did they come from and where did they go to? The question of their demise during the middle of the last glaciation has excited much debate and comment (Trinkaus and Howells, 1979; ApSimon, 1980; Stringer, 1982). One reason for this is, as we shall see in more detail below, the very marked change in the archaeological record at 35 000 BP as represented by the transition from the middle to the upper palaeolithic (White, 1982). This link between fossil types and contrasted cultural assemblages has led to a variety of explanations. These range from the extermination of neanderthalers and their culture by invading Crô Magnon populations to the very rapid genetic assimilation of neanderthalers and their characteristic features, as well as their cultural adaptations, by interbreeding with those

same immigrant populations. Finally, as we have seen, a third explanation argues for a seamless biological and cultural evolution from one to the other.

One aspect of the debate is, however, becoming clearer. We should not link the change in fossils with contemporaneous changes in archaeological material and then make the inference that developments in culture were dependent upon advances in intelligence. A recent find at St. Césaire in western France (Lévêque and Vandermeersch, 1980) shows clearly, for the first time under controlled conditions of recovery, a neanderthal skeleton associated with a flint assemblage that is characteristic of the earliest upper palaeolithic in the area. This find suggests that neanderthalers were not limited by intelligence in passing to the upper palaeolithic. We simply do not know how to interpret differences in cranial shape in terms of differing levels of intelligence. It has been claimed (Lieberman and Crelin, 1971; Lieberman, 1976) that differences in the reconstructed voice boxes of neanderthals combined with the weak development of those areas of their brains connected with speech control would have placed them at a disadvantage in rapid verbal communication using a phonetic system. While their study shows that the mechanisms connected with speech had to undergo evolution, it still does not demonstrate that these early populations lacked the ability to communicate or to organize behaviour in the complex ways suggested by the material record of the upper palaeolithic, with for example the appearance of art and other forms of symboling. Instead we must conclude that the neanderthalers did not require the opportunities for information processing and exchange that these mediums provide since they were not a necessary part of their successful long term adaptations. We shall return to this question in the next chapter. The question of where the neanderthalers went is one of evolutionary theory predicting either a very rapid or a very long period of time to account for the appearance of such morphologically different populations. The opposed views of 'punctuated equilibrium' (Gould and Eldredge, 1977), where speciation occurs in rapid bursts after long periods of no change in geographically marginal populations with small breeding sizes, and 'phyletic gradualism', where evolution follows lineages in a slow cumulative manner (Cronin *et al.*, 1981), currently form a major debate in evolutionary biology (Dunnell, 1980).

THE ANALYSIS AND INTERPRETATION OF CHIPPED STONE

In 1872 de Mortillet proposed that the classification of the palaeolithic should be based on the evidence of chipped stone artifacts. This replaced a system of stages based upon the predominant kind of fauna from caves: these were the 'ages' of the cave bear, mammoth and finally the reindeer. The names of type sites were used to distinguish distinctive *assemblages* of chipped stone, and where these were found to occur many times in a particular region and at a particular time they came to be spoken of as *industries* and *traditions* (Table 2.2).

The division of the European palaeolithic into lower, middle and upper stages was based on these industrial differences. They were regarded as significant stages in the evolution of man and his culture. The evidence that we now have for the great antiquity of tool making from east Africa, and the techniques of analysis that have been developed to investigate differences in chipped stone assemblages have removed some of this significance. When placed in the world picture of human evolution, it now appears that the only clear developmental break in the European palaeolithic occurs at around 35 000 BP with the appearance of the upper palaeolithic stone

and bone technology. Prior to this date there is evidence of both continuity and great variation in assemblages and industries at all times since the earliest colonization of the continent. This makes it difficult to talk of time-related trends in the development of the earlier lithic technology of Europe. We have had to abandon schemes which, for example, claimed that over time handaxes passed from coarsely flaked to finely finished forms (Breuil, 1939). The reality is much more complex than this, as shown by the much better understanding that we now have concerning the manufacture and use of stone tools.

TECHNOLOGY PRIOR TO 35 000 BP

The technology of this early period can be reconstructed from the fashioned implements and the waste material that was a by-product of their manufacture; this work has been supplemented by experimental stone knapping. In Europe the most common raw material is flint, a fine grained siliceous rock with a predictable pattern of fracture and a sharp cutting edge (Oakley, 1949; Bordaz, 1970; Brézillon, 1971). It occurs as both beach and river pebbles and in underground veins that outcrop on

---

Table 2.2   Three important palaeolithic terms and their definitions (Laville et al., 1980, pp.13–14).

Assemblage.	*A collection of artifacts from a specific segment of an archaeological site* This is an unstandardized term. Assemblage may be used to refer to material dug from an open site such as the Clacton channel or the Clacton golf course site (Singer *et al.*, 1973), while at the same time used to describe material coming from within or outside a cave, or referring to the collections recovered during the course of an excavation such as Peyrony's collection from La Ferrassie (1934). The term may refer to working floors, stratigraphical units, material associated with features such as huts and hearths and any other division which an archaeologist may think relevant. As a result, care needs to be taken in deciding which assemblages can be compared.
Industry.	*A distinctive complex or configuration of artifact types and type frequencies that recurs among two or more assemblages.* Examples of this would be divisions of the Acheulian into an upper and lower industry or the Perigordian into six main industries (de Sonneville-Bordes, 1960).
Tradition.	*A group of industries whose artifactual similarities are sufficient to suggest that they belong to some broader culture-historical block of technological ideas and practices.* The terms used to describe these traditions are often derived from different bases. The acheulean (St. Acheul), clactonian (Clacton) and mousterian (Le Moustier) are all named after an artifact collection from a type site. On the other hand Perigordian is named after sites from the Périgord region of modern France. The Federmesser (arched bladelet) tradition found on the North European plain in the late glacial is named after a distinctive artifact type (Schwabedissen, 1954; Schild, 1976)

the surface in the chalk areas of Europe. Less fine grained rocks such as chert and even coarser quartzites were used when flint was not readily available. The industries from this period are characterized by multi-purpose tools that vary greatly in both shape and size.

The largest tools by weight and size are chopping tools, handaxes and cleavers. The former are made by a few blows to a rock nodule that produces an irregular but serviceable cutting edge. Greater expertise is needed in making a handaxe. A recent experiment started with a flint nodule weighing almost three kilogrammes and from this a handaxe weighing 230 grammes was flaked. Fifty-one by-product flakes were produced and a further 4618 small chips also resulted from the experiment (Newcomer, 1971). Further experiments showed a possible three-stage process to handaxe manufacture (Fig.2.9). A large hammerstone was used to *rough out* the handaxe from the nodule and this resulted in some 10 large thick flakes with massive striking platforms and the cortex or skin of the nodule on their upper surface.

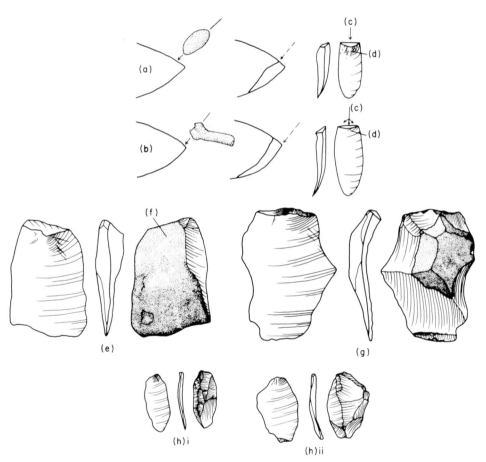

Fig. 2.9 *Making a handaxe. The two types of flake produced by using either a hard or soft hammer are shown (a and b). This is clearly shown in the shape of the striking platforms (c) and the degree to which the bulb of percussion is prominent (d). The rough out flakes (e) carry a large amount of cortex (f). The shaping flakes carry less cortex and often have paper thin edges (g) while the final finishing flakes are small and carry hardly any traces of their striking platforms (h). A finished handaxe is shown in Fig 2.20 (after Newcomer, 1971).*

This was followed by a *thinning and shaping* stage where a soft hammer of either antler or wood was used. The surfaces of these thinning flakes bear the traces of previous flake removal scars on their upper surfaces. Their striking platforms are thin or shattered and the edges of these thin flakes are irregular. About 20 of these flakes were needed in the experiment before passing to the final *finishing* stage. A smaller soft hammer was used to correct the final outline and the 20 flakes removed were small and thin with flatter bulbs of percussion and less irregular outlines. Therefore between 45 and 55 flake removals produced a handaxe from a nodule. The time taken would be between 5 and 10 minutes. At the end of the process there emerged a pear-shaped tool with a thick butt and two straight edges converging to a point. It bears evidence for working on both sides hence its description as a bifacial implement.

Handaxes were also made on large flakes. While a suitable flake may be produced by chance, it is more likely that considerable care will be expended on producing a blank of the desired dimensions before passing to the shaping and finishing stages. The production of large standardized flakes from nodules is often known as the levallois technique of stone working, from a gravel pit in the Seine valley, France, where this technique was first recognized by archaeologists. This method of flake preparation trims the nodule to leave the outline of the flake on one surface (Fig.2.10). The platform of the flake is then often prepared, by striking off small facets, while it is still on the core and then the flake is struck off. Typically a levallois flake is long, broad and has roughly parallel sides. The remnant core, once the flake has been detached, is often described as a tortoise core. Triangular levallois flakes which could have served as projectile points are also common. The essence of the levallois technique is that the size and shape of the flake is predetermined before it is removed from the nodule (Bordes, 1980).

The levallois technique generally produces five or six typical levallois flakes from a nodule. The disc core is the end result of a more continuous process of flake removal, and although the degree of predetermining the flake size is not so marked, a considerable number of flake blanks can be produced since the object is to strike flakes off at angles which will allow further flaking to proceed.

The majority of flakes produced by these two techniques were not subsequently modified, although their sharp cutting edges may have been used for some immediate task in hand. This is also true for the anvil technique of flint working where flakes are removed by the simple procedure of cracking one rock against another. This results in thick, large flakes of highly irregular outline and with massive striking platforms.

The production of a flake tool often involves further flaking known as secondary working. The aim is to correct the outline and by small flake removals to either strengthen, sharpen, or blunt the natural stone edge. Retouch of this nature is commonly found along only one part of the flake's circumference and on one face. Complete bifacial working of these smaller tools is not common.

These retouched implements have been classified

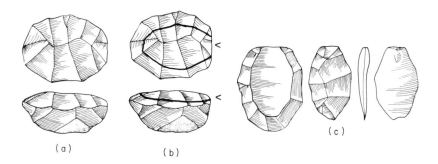

(a)

(b)

(c)

Fig. 2.10   The stages involved in making a levallois flake.

according to the functions that archaeologists think they might have had. The handaxes and choppers are thought to be heavy duty cutting and pounding tools. The smaller flake tools are classified according to their shape into scrapers, points, knives and borers. The repeated shapes have been grouped according to a typological scheme in order to provide a basis for making comparisons between assemblages and industries. The most widely adopted typological analysis is that developed by Bordes which employs a type list of sixty-three recognizable artifacts and a further twenty-one handaxe forms (Fig.2.11). The main list of sixty-three types can be divided into four main groups (Fig.2.12). Group I (numbers 1–4) are levallois flakes which are generally not retouched but because of the effort that went into their manufacture are considered as tools. Group II (numbers 6–29) consists of mousterian tools of which numbers 6 and 7 are points and numbers 9 to 29 various types of side scrapers. Group III is called by Bordes the upper palaeolithic typology and consists of knives, borers, and scrapers, burins and truncated blades and flakes (numbers 30–37, 40). Group IV has a single type, number 43, which are denticulated or notched pieces of irregular outline but clearly retouched as tools. Bordes's typology provides a method for classifying a chipped stone assemblage and, by means of a cumulative percentage graph, a way of comparing one assemblage with another.

Two counts are made of the assemblage. The *real count* includes all sixty-three types while the *essential count* leaves out the unretouched pieces in the list (numbers 1–3 and 46–50).

The analysis also compares aspects of the technology by means of indices. The levallois index provides a percentage figure for levallois flakes, points and blades, whether they are retouched or not, as a total of all pieces. The faceting index gives a percentage of the number of pieces with faceted butts which is a common characteristic of prepared flake removal by the levallois technique.

Bordes's scheme does not take into account the size and weight of the tools. It is based only upon the repeated shapes. It has been applied to lower and middle palaeolithic industries in France and many other parts of Europe and provides a most useful systematic method of identifying patterns in chipped stone assemblages. We will return later to the interpretation of these patterns.

These typological analyses demonstrate that assemblages differ in terms of their composition of type artifacts and the technology involved in producing them. But assemblages also differ in terms of the numbers of pieces available for typological study, which may vary from less than a hundred pieces in an assemblage to many thousand. The same tool type may also vary enormously in respect to its dimensions, as the study of a large number of English handaxes has shown (Roe, 1964, 1968, 1981). This variation may be due to many factors and one that is currently under investigation concerns the possible function of these implements. For a long time it was thought that we would never be able to determine the uses to which palaeolithic tools were put but this gloomy forecast is now changing. When either unmodified flakes or retouched implements are used for cutting, scraping, boring and pounding organic materials, this leaves traces of utilization on the edge of the implement. The examination of these edges under high powered microscopes has revealed a set of distinctive polishes on the flint tool (Keeley, 1980; Anderson, 1980; Hayden, 1979). Experiments using flint tools for tasks such as skinning animals or shaving wood and bone have provided a comparable set of distinctive polishes that allow the interpretation of the palaeolithic microwear polishes to proceed. Keeley (1980) has identified six polishes which result from working wood, bone, antler, hide, meat and non-woody materials. The first step in the analysis is to identify which areas of the tools and flakes carry traces of utilization and then examine them for their polishes. The study of 408 artifacts from the lower acheulean industry at Hoxne, England, demonstrated that some 9% of the unretouched flakes bore utilization traces. The retouched implements showed that utilization was not directly equivalent to the length of the retouched edge (Fig.2.13). In most cases only a small part of the retouched edge had in fact been used. Some of the side scrapers did carry the hide-working polish, thus supporting the intuitive assessment of archaeologists that this was indeed one function of such tools. The other polishes present in this assemblage showed that the palaeolithic occupants at Hoxne used tools for butchering, woodworking, hide-working, and for boring wood and bone. Two of the handaxes carried the meat polish. A similar analysis by Keeley (1980) on a chopping tool from the site of Clacton, England, indicated that this

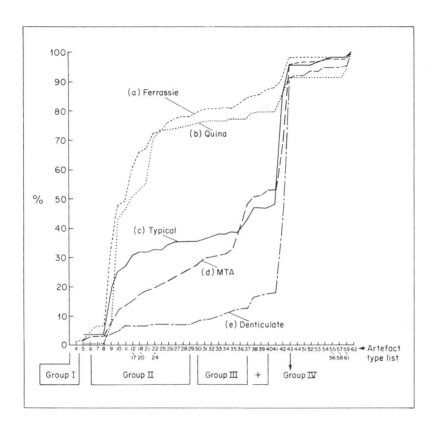

Fig. 2.11 These five cumulative graphs display the differences between mousterian assemblages from France. The different shape to each curve reflects the varying proportions of individual artifact types in each assemblage. These are listed on the horizontal axis and some examples are shown in Fig. 2.12.

The five variants described by Bordes in his typological study are as follows:

Group   (a) Ferrassie mousterian with high proportions of side scrapers (e.g. 17) and a marked use of the levallois
Charentian   technique
             (b) Quina mousterian with a great many transverse scrapers (23) and only a slight levallois index.
(c) Typical mousterian with variable amounts of points (6) and side scrapers.
(d) Mousterian of Acheulean Tradition (MTA). This group is divided into MTA A where handaxes (Fig. 2.20) are common, and MTA B where they are rare and instead a common form is the naturally backed knife. (38).
(e) Denticulate mousterian where assemblages are dominated by denticulate and notched tools (43).
All of these different groups and sub-groups were found by Bordes in a single stratigraphic sequence at the site of Combe Grenal (Fig. 2.22) (after Bordes, 1972a).

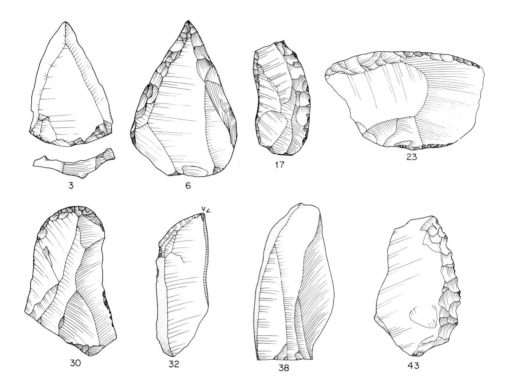

Fig. 2.12   Examples of flake and blade tools from Bordes' typological list of the lower and middle palaeolithic. The numbers refer to this type list (Fig. 2.11).

3   Levallois point: note the prepared striking platform.

6   Mousterian point: obtained by retouching a levallois point.

17   Double side scraper where one retouched edge is concave and the other convex.

23   Convex transverse side scraper.

30   Typical end scraper.

32   Typical burin: the arrows point to the position and number of facets.

38   Naturally backed knife: the cortex surface forms a natural dull edge: characteristically this edge is curved.

43   Denticulate, with contiguous notches down one edge (after Bordes, 1961a).

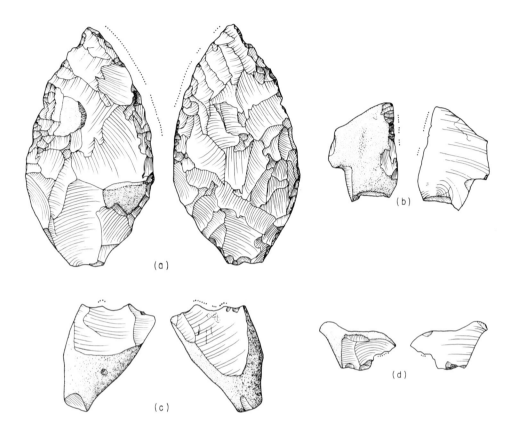

Fig. 2.13 *Microwear studies on lower palaeolithic artifacts. Two artifacts examined by Keeley for traces of use on their edges are illustrated from the site of Hoxne. The handaxe (a) shows just how small an area of this large retouched tool was used. At the point of maximum breadth there are traces of battering while a meat polish can be clearly identified on the upper edges. The location of the polish suggests that it was used in a cutting motion. A few centimetres away from this piece lay a small backed side scraper (b) made on a primary roughing out flake. A fresh hide polish can be identified along a portion of the retouched edge. Keeley suggests that these two implements formed part of the same toolkit.*

At Clacton where the implements are rarely secondarily retouched it also proved possible to identify a number of polishes. The chopper-core (c) bore traces of wood polish and some edge damage scars suggest that it was used for chopping or adzing. The side struck flake retouched with the distinctive Clacton notch (d) carries a small trace of meat polish. Keeley interprets this as an ad hoc meat knife (after Keeley, 1980).

large tool had been used for boring holes in wood.

Microwear studies have only just begun and these first conclusions from a small sample of artifacts and an even smaller sample of assemblages should not be taken as an indication that we have finally sorted out the functional rationale behind the shape of palaeolithic implements. However, such studies do point to the important conclusion that the absence of retouch cannot be taken as a sure indication that the piece was not used as a tool. Furthermore, it seems possible to suggest that a greater use of perishable organic materials such as wood did form part of the palaeolithic tool kit. The tip of a thrusting spear made of yew from the site of Clacton is a rare survival from the era represented by isotope stage 7 of what must have been an important component of palaeolithic technology during interglacial periods (Fig.2.14).

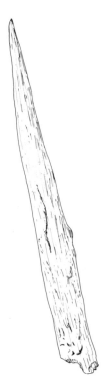

Fig. 2.14 The tip of a thrusting spear made of yew. This wooden fragment is almost 40 cm long and came from the Clacton channel that has yielded many stone artifacts and animal bone remains (after Oakley et al., 1977).

TECHNOLOGY IN THE PERIOD 35 000 TO 10 000 BP

The change during this period is threefold. The heavy duty tools such as handaxes and choppers disappear completely. A new form of nodule preparation appears and involves the production of long, thin, parallel-sided blades. Finally, artifacts made of bone, antler and ivory are found for the first time.

Blades are known from the earlier period but they are often massive in comparison with those from the upper palaeolithic and they are not struck from blade cores. It is clear from the examination of such cores (Fig.2.15) that a more economical use of raw material was being made since many times as much useful working edge can be produced than was possible earlier. Blanks were struck from the core by either direct percussion with a hammer or by indirect percussion whereby a bone punch was placed on the core platform, which in turn was hit with a hammer.

The use of blades as opposed to flakes fostered a reduction in tool size. It is also possible to see a gradual reduction in the size of the blade blanks during this period and a movement toward smaller unretouched tools as with the scalene triangles in the magdalenian of the late glacial.

A type list for the upper palaeolithic also shows that there was an increase in the number of tool classes. In France the list extends to ninety-two implements of which different types of projectile points, knives, end scrapers, borers and chisel-ended tools known as burins form the main part (de Sonneville-Bordes and Perrot, 1954–6; de Sonneville-Bordes, 1960). Geographical variation is most marked, with regionally distinct tool types such as the Kostienki knives from Russia, Poland, Czechoslovakia and Austria or the solutrean leaf-shaped points from France and Spain (Schild, 1975; Kozłowski and Kozłowski, 1979; P. Smith, 1966). These latter artifacts display a novel form of retouch by pressure flaking, where the implement is thinned by squeezing off flakes on either one or both surfaces. It is possible that such skilful flint working was facilitated by preheating the flint before it was worked. This alters the structure of the stone and makes it easier to execute such finely controlled flaking. Other forms of secondary retouch include sharpening retouch, where flat flakes are skimmed off the edge of the implement, and blunting

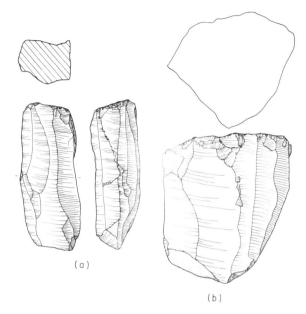

Fig. 2.15 Two common types of upper palaeolithic blade cores: (a) prismatic (b) single platform blade core.

(a)

(b)

retouch where the sharp flint edge is reduced to a blunt right angle. This form of retouch is also known as backing.

The reduction in tool size probably corresponds to developments in hafting technology. While stone projectile points are known from the earlier period, the upper palaeolithic is remarkable for the range and diversity of such tools. They would have been hafted either singly or in combination at the end of throwing spears. Their size is such that many could have formed the tips and barbs for arrows. The site of Parpalló in eastern Spain has produced the earliest evidence for barbed and tanged arrowheads at 18 000 BP (Davidson, 1974) and by inference the bow must have been available by this time.

Hafting developments can also be seen among the bone points. These are often small with split or bevelled bases to make hafting easier. A recent study (Newcomer, 1974) of bone and antler points and awls has shown that in one eastern Mediterranean site a clear preference was given to making awls from bone and points from antler. This was most probably due to the relative strengths of these two materials. Antler can be easily worked with stone tools after it has been soaked in water and its size allows longer points to be made than is possible with bone. Antler

was also used to make small barbed harpoons in the late glacial period. These took the forms of detachable heads that could be fitted to a spear shaft. This meant that the hunter needed to carry only a single throwing haft and a number of such heads when out in search of game. If the animal escaped with the head embedded in it then a new projectile could be fitted and the hunt resumed.

Spear throwers made of bone and antler are also found (Fig.2.16) and point to further developments in throwing technology.

One implication of these developments is that considerably more planning was being put into hunting. This resulted in more effort being expended on the manufacture of implements which were designed for a variety of particular planned tasks. The additional effort was repaid by the time saved in hunting and the more secure results this produced for subsistence strategy.

Bone and antler were also turned into needles and ornaments and were sometimes elaborately carved, as at the cave site of Isturitz in the French Pyrenees where many antler rods, decorated with deeply incised spirals and loop engravings, were found (Saint Perier, 1930, 1936, 1950). Other objects appear to have had a utilitarian role, such as pierced

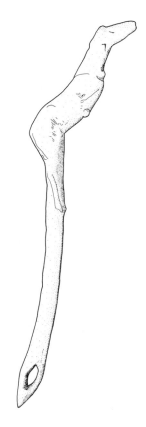

Fig. 2.16   Antler spear thrower decorated in the form of a leaping horse. Magdalenian from Bruniquel, France. Max. length 28 cm.

animal skin in order to make it soft and pliable. Both types were generally hand held. His studies also revised opinions about the use of burins. A burin is formed by vertical flaking on a blade so that a thin facet is removed. In many cases several intersecting facets are removed and typologists have used this to classify a number of different burin types. Semenov showed, however, that not all such distinctive facets necessarily indicate that the tool was used as a burin. Single facet burins did reveal microscopic striations indicating that they had been used to work bone. However, on other tools the facets bore no trace of such striations and the use-wear was instead located on the back of the blade. In this case the purpose of the burin spall removal seems to have been an easy way of blunting the end of the tool so that it could be held in the hand and the back of the blade used as a whittling knife on either bone or wood. Other burins which formed a distinct 'beak' were used, he believes, in the true sense of the term burin: that is as an engraving tool for drawing designs on bone.

A final example from Semenov's work concerns the shouldered points from Kostienki mentioned above. Microscopic study revealed use-wear in the form of polish along both sides of the point and around the shoulder. The degree of polishing argues for a prolonged use of the implement and Semenov's suggested interpretation of its method of use indicates that it should be classified as a knife rather than a point. This interpretation underlines the caution that is necessary in using the intuitive functional terms applied by archaeologists as a guide to the actual function of stone tools.

segments of reindeer antler that may have served as shaft straighteners and knife-like implements (Efimenko, 1958).

Upper palaeolithic tools have also been subjected to use-wear analysis by the pioneer in this field, the Russian archaeologist Semenov (1964). The material came from open camp sites located in European Russia. Semenov did not identify distinct polishes but argued that end scrapers with a wide, sharply retouched edge would be used for removing flesh, fat and muscle fibre from the skin. Blunt-ended end scrapers would have been used for rubbing the

VARIABILITY IN MATERIAL CULTURE PRIOR TO 80 000 BP

Chronology

The early stone industries of Europe can be placed in three periods. The first includes pre-stage 7 industries, the second those from interglacial deposits of stage 7 age, and the last those from glacial stage 6. Assemblages that can confidently be dated to the last interglacial complex, stage 5, are very few in number (Gamble, 1983a).

Assemblages and Industries

Occupation that can be reliably dated to before stage 7 is scarce. The high level sea cave of Vallonnet contained only a small stone assemblage of five chopping tools made on pebbles and four struck flakes (Fig.2.17). The site of Vértesszöllös in northern Hungary, with a minimum age of 350 000 on the basis of absolute dates, yielded a collection of 2800 artifacts of which 700 were tools and the rest stone flakes (Kretzoi and Vértes, 1965). The most characteristic tools were chopping tools made on pebbles and varying in length between 3–4 cm and in width between 1·5–3 cm. These small tools appear to be little standardized in terms of morphology but show a very consistent method of manufacture. Over 2000 fragments of burnt bone were also recovered although there is no evidence for fire in the form of either hearths or charcoal. Other comparable assemblages, although smaller in the number of tools they contain, are also known from east Europe as at Stranská Skála and Přezletice in Czechoslovakia, where representative tools of a simple chopper core industry have been found.

This pattern is continued in the stage 7 interglacial. The unstandardized assemblages with few retouched tools and the presence of chopping tools have been grouped into the clactonian industry named after the type site found in an old stream channel at Clacton, England, and dated by absolute methods to 245 000 BP (Szabo and Collins, 1975). The size of these chopping

tools and flakes is large. While it is difficult to see a standardized set of shapes among the stone artifacts it is clear that the anvil technique of stone working was consistently used. The flakes have massive striking platforms and are generally thick with irregular outlines. The chopping tool element comes in all shapes and sizes. A recent excavation at the site (Singer et al., 1973) showed that most of these tools weighed less than 300 g although some weighing over a kilogram were found. Clactonian assemblages have been found in the two lowest layers at the Thames gravel pit site of Swanscombe (Wymer, 1968). They have also been found in the river terraces of northern France and comparable assemblages have also come from the plains of East Germany (Toepfer, 1976).

The acheulean during this same period is known primarily from the river terraces of southern England, northern France and the Paris basin. The assemblages are highly varied in terms of the shapes and sizes of the handaxes that are present (Fig.2.18) and the numbers and frequencies of the flake tools. A large collection of crudely made handaxes comes from Abbeville on the Somme (Breuil and Kozłowski, 1932). The handaxes have irregular edges and display a generally poor degree of final finishing. These have to be contrasted with more refined handaxe forms from findspots in the same area and from English sites such as the upper levels at Swanscombe which overlie the earlier clactonian industries (Ovey, 1964). At the site of Hoxne there are two assemblages in the stratigraphic sequence (West and McBurney, 1955). The lower series produced a number of finely flaked pointed handaxes while the upper level does not show this same high degree of finished flint working on the bifacial implements (Roe, 1981).

A further form of assemblage variation comes from the East German site of Ehringsdorf (Behm-Blanke, 1960) which has been dated to c.200 000 BP. The assemblage has a number of well retouched flake tools forming points and sidescrapers. Handaxes are not present. In the following glacial stage, there are no clactonian assemblages which can with confidence be dated to this period. However, we find variation in the abundance of handaxes within assemblages and in the shapes that these take. It is during this stage that we find the first clear evidence of the use of the levallois technique, although the presence of this technological feature is once again highly variable.

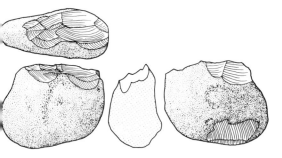

Fig. 2.17   Four views of a simple pebble chopping tool from the site of Vallonnet (after H. de Lumley, 1976).

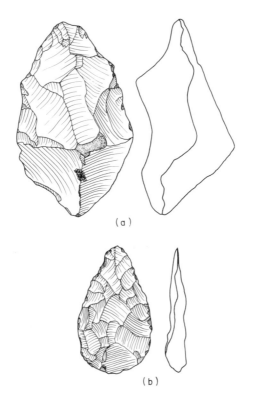

Fig. 2.18 *Lower palaeolithic handaxes from northwest Europe. These two examples from Northern France show some of the variation in size, degree of finishing and shape of the cutting edge that can be found among this class of bifacial tools: (a) Abbeville; (b) Commont's workshop.*

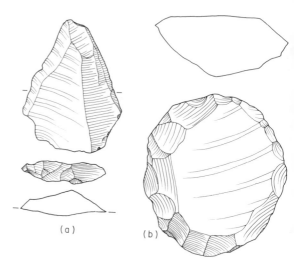

Fig. 2.19 *Triangular levallois flake (a) and tortoise core (b) from Reutersruh in Germany. The raw material is quartzite (after Luttropp and Bosinski, 1971).*

The open site of Markleeberg in East Germany (Grahmann, 1955) has very few handaxes but a number of flake tools, side scrapers and points, made on levallois flakes and flake-blades. Handaxes are still common in northern France and in sites such as La Cotte de St. Brelade (McBurney and Callow, 1971) which is a coastal cave in the English Channel Islands. Large workshop sites where raw material was flaked into artifacts are also known. Bakers Hole on the Thames (Roe, 1981) and Reutersruh in West Germany (Luttropp and Bosinski, 1971) both have many tortoise cores and levallois flakes, although a different raw material was being used. At Bakers Hole a local abundance of flint was exploited while at the site at Reutersruh (Fig.2.19), where chipped stone

covers several acres, the raw material was quartzite. Another Somme site near Amiens, called Commont's workshop after the excavator, shows similar activities but without the use of the levallois technique. Nearby at the Rue de Cagny (Bourdier, 1976) in another gravel pit and at a similar geological age the levallois technique is clearly present.

In southern Europe the acheulean is found throughout Spain, as at the excavated sites of Torralba and Ambrona (Howell, 1966; Freeman, 1975) and in numerous gravel pit exposures along the Manzanares and Jarama rivers near Madrid (Santonja *et al.*, 1980). Acheulean sites are also well known from Italy where one of the best investigated is at Torre in Pietra near Rome (Piperno and Biddittu, 1978). The finished artifacts number just over 300 and were recovered in association with animal bones from an area of 200 m². The sedimentological studies reveal that the material is bedded in fluviatile deposits and there are indications that the handaxes and flakes have been moved both vertically and horizontally from their original resting place. This is possibly an instance where the bones and stones have been collected together by stream action and consequently we should be careful about interpreting the association of these two lines of evidence as an accurate record of human behaviour.

The interglacial complex, stage 5, that followed the penultimate glaciation is very poor in sites. It has been claimed that in some parts of Europe the subsequent erosion of interglacial deposits may account for this (Laville *et al.*, 1980). Fontéchevade in southern France, Krapina in Yugoslavia, and Tata in Hungary where small pebbles formed the major raw material (Vértes, 1964), have produced predominantly flake tool assemblages which may date to some part of the stage 5 complex.

Geographical Variation

A number of geographical patterns can be seen for these early industries. The acheulean and clactonian are entirely lacking in the western part of the USSR (Klein, 1966) although recent finds of pebble tools and flakes in the Tashkent region (Ranov and Davis, 1979), at the loess section at Karatau I, have been dated by thermoluminescence readings on the loess to 200 000 BP. This suggests that some environmental constraints in the northern regions acted against the expansion of palaeolithic populations onto the northern Russian plains.

A second geographical pattern can be seen in the distribution of the distinctive acheulean artifact, the handaxe. It was pointed out by McBurney (1950) that lower palaeolithic handaxes were rarely found in northern Europe east of the Rhine (Collins, 1969). Instead the assemblages either consist of flake tools, as at Markleeberg and Ehringsdorf, or combine a core/chopping tool component as at Vértesszöllös, Tata, Stranská Skála and Přezletice (Valoch, 1968). The site of Bilzingsleben with some 60 000 chipped stone artifacts contains both bifacially worked flakes, some pointed pieces that are reminiscent of handaxes as well as very many small flakes, some of which are worked into scrapers, borers and denticulates (Mania, 1975). In the west of the continent, flake-based assemblages, as at High Lodge in England, are found in the same geographical areas as the classic acheulean handaxes and the chopping tool/core industries that are best known from Clacton. Amongst the acheulean assemblages the distinctive cleavers, which were often made on large flakes and have a transverse cutting edge, are more commonly found in Spain (Jelinek, 1977) than elsewhere.

VARIABILITY IN MATERIAL CULTURE 80 000 TO 35 000 BP

Chronology

The industries and assemblages of this period are commonly referred to as middle palaeolithic. The period marks the return of glacial conditions in Europe although it is not until later that the ice sheets once again covered northern Europe. The period was interspersed with temperate interstadials of which Amersfoort and Brørup are the most important. Frozen ground existed in many parts of northern and central Europe and the climatic information from cave sediments indicates moist humid conditions within a prevailing cold climate. In France this early glacial stage has been divided into two parts known respectively as Würm I and II. In the caves from the Périgord region of southern France these major divisions have been further divided on the basis of sediment studies into a further nine and eight stages respectively (Laville *et al.*, 1980). In central Europe the loess sections show the development of soil horizons that indicate the more temperate conditions of the interstadials. These have been used as chronological markers.

Assemblages and Industries

The variation in assemblages that we saw for the earlier period continues during the early last glacial. Handaxes of various types are found, although in general they tend to be smaller in size than those from the earlier acheulean and less numerous in the assemblages. Samples no longer come in the main from the river systems of northern Europe but instead from the caves and rock shelters of central and southern Europe.

Two cave sites in France, Le Moustier (Peyrony, 1930) and La Micoque (Peyrony, 1938), have given their names to widespread middle palaeolithic industries. The mousterian has been defined as a flake industry where the assemblages grouped within it show variable proportions of points, side scrapers, handaxes and denticulate tools (Bordes, 1968). The use of the levallois technique also varies in importance. The term micoquian encompasses a diverse set of assemblages that are generally small in the number of retouched pieces (Bosinski, 1967; Gábori, 1976; Bordes and Bourgon, 1951). The most distinctive tool type is a thin, sharply pointed handaxe (Fig.2.20). These take a variety of shapes and several have been interpreted as large bifacially worked knives. The rest of these small assemblages consist mainly of side scrapers and points made on flakes.

The micoquian has been identified from the caves of central Europe, as at Balve, the Bockstein and the Klaussenische in Germany (Bosinski, 1967; Schwabedissen, 1970). It is also known from open sites, as at Königsaue in East Germany (Mania and Toepfer, 1973). This site was located by the banks of a lake which has provided important climatic and stratigraphic information. The two assemblages, which number only 90 and 116 retouched tools, have been dated by means of ^{14}C and climatic data to the early last glacial Brørup interstadial. Micoquian assemblages are also known from the Black Sea littoral in eastern Europe as at Ilskaïa and along the Donets river at Krasny-Iar (Gábori, 1976).

On the plains area to the north of the central German highlands are found handaxe assemblages which have been described as upper acheulean. Amongst these the open site of Salzgitter-Lebenstedt (Tode, 1953) produced a fauna dominated by reindeer and mammoth and a collection of some 200 retouched implements. The site has been dated by ^{14}C to > 55 000 BP. The handaxes are thick and heavy in contrast to the more finely worked, smaller micoquian examples.

There are also many assemblages in central and eastern Europe which lack both handaxes and other large bifacial tools. The Hungarian open site of Érd (Gábori-Csánk, 1968) contains a series of small assemblages which are dominated by side scrapers made on small quartzite pebbles. At the Dniestr river sites of Molodova I and V (Chernysh, 1961; Goretsky and Ivanova, 1982: Klein, 1973) scrapers made on flakes are also the most common tool type along with points, denticulates, naturally backed knives and burins. These sites, stratified in thick loess deposits, both have two middle palaeolithic levels which are overlain by a series of upper palaeolithic occupations.

The caves of central and eastern Europe have also produced a varied array of middle palaeolithic assemblages. At the cave of Kůlna in the Moravian karst of Czechoslovakia (Valoch, 1980) over 16m thickness of deposits have produced a number of flake assemblages including a micoquian level. In the entrance to the cave the excavator recovered a flake assemblage that contained some very distinctive bifacially worked leaf shaped points. This tool type (Fig.2.21), while varying considerably in shape and size, has been found elsewhere in Europe in clear middle palaeolithic contexts. These include the eroded open sites in north western Greece at Kokkinopilos and Morfi (Dakaris *et al.*, 1964; Higgs and Vita-Finzi, 1966) and in open sites along the Váh river in Czechoslovakia (Barta, 1967). The *Blattspitzen* (leaf points) are also known from the Ilsenhöhle near Ranis in East Germany (Hulle, 1977)

Fig. 2.20 Middle palaeolithic handaxes from the last glaciation: (a) triangular MTA handaxe from France; (b) a micoquian handaxe from the Bockstein cave in southern Germany: these tools are more commonly referred to as Bockstein knives or scrapers; (c) a small pointed handaxe from La Micoque in southern France.

(a)   (b)   (c)

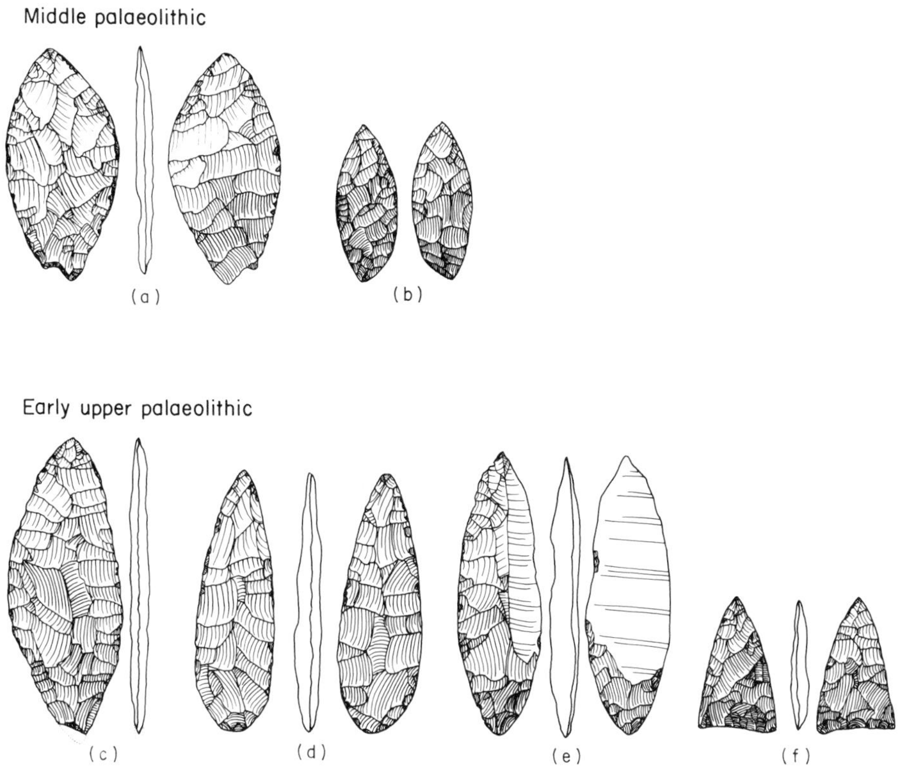

Middle palaeolithic

(a)   (b)

Early upper palaeolithic

(c)   (d)   (e)   (f)

Fig. 2.21   Bifacially worked leaf points from the middle and early upper palaeolithic: (a) Weinberg caves at Mauern, southern Germany: note the hafting notch; (b) open site of Kokkinopilos, northern Greece; (c) open site at Ipswich, England; (d) Szeleta cave in Hungary; (e) Jerzmanovice point from southern Poland only shows partial bifacial retouch on the underside of the blade; (f) hollow based point from the lowest level at the open site of Kostienki I on the Don river in Russia.

and from a few caves in southern Germany, notably the Weinberg caves at Mauern (von Koenigswald *et al.*, 1974), Ofnet (Freund, 1952; 1963) and Urspring (Hahn *et al.*, 1973). At Mauern these distinctive leaf points, many of which bear a hafting notch at their base, date to the Hengelo interstadial at *c.* 38 000BP.

Geographical Variation

One very clear development during this period is the extension of human settlement onto the Russian plains and around the rivers of the Donets and the Dniestr. Gábori (1976) has provided a detailed analysis of assemblage variation in the material from central and eastern Europe. In many cases the assemblages are small and do not come from multi-level sites. Variation in the techniques of flake preparation and the use of a number of different raw materials also add to the problems of drawing up crisply defined industrial groupings.

A very different picture comes from south-west France, Italy and Spain. In France there are many multi-level sites and in many cases each stratigraphic unit contains a large quantity of retouched implements that can be used to conduct a Bordian analysis. While it is an extreme example the site of Combe Grenal (Bordes, 1972a) produced a total of 55 separate mousterian levels the majority of which had enough artifacts to conduct a typological analysis.

This combination of a compact geographical area, detailed stratigraphies which contain rich assemblages and a long history of palaeolithic research have all combined to make the Périgord and surrounding districts of southern France the classic area for mousterian studies (Bordes, 1961b). It was for these rich data that Bordes devised his typological system based on a 63 tool type list. By means of this and his observations on technological aspects of the assemblages he distinguished five major variants that were found repeatedly in the caves and open sites of the area (Fig.2.11).

The most important element in distinguishing these variants are the side scrapers. Rolland (1981) has shown in a quantitative analysis of 120 assemblages, the majority of which come from France, that the Charentian scraper group consistently has higher proportions of retouched implements than the other variants. A further plot of the 120 assemblages shows a clear relationship between high implement frequencies and the proportion of side scrapers in the assemblages. This relationship cannot be seen for the miscellaneous tools as represented by denticulated and notched pieces. In other words, side scrapers are the major cause of assemblage variability.

The Mousterian Debate

The identification through typological analysis of these five variants has produced an important discussion on the interpretation of differences in archaeological assemblages. Bordes has argued that the differences are the result of cultural traditions and that they may be taken to represent an ethnic entity, a people (Bordes and de Sonneville-Bordes, 1970). In their view, the five variants are the cultural remains of five tribes which led separate existences during the early Würm in the Périgord region. A cave containing a level of denticulate mousterian followed by a level with the Quina variant was therefore occupied on two occasions by different populations.

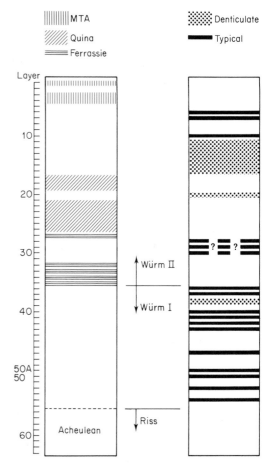

Fig. 2.22 Vertical distribution of different types of Mousterian industries throughout the Combe-Grenal succession (after Mellars, 1969).

These traditions persisted for many millennia and underwent little cultural admixture.

Mellars (1969, 1970) has pointed out that the stratigraphical position of the variants produces two clear patterns. The Quina variant is always found above the Ferrassie variant and MTA A below MTA B. Moreover the MTA assemblages are always at the top of the stratigraphic sequences and are not overlain by any other variant. Typical and denticulate variants show no precise stratigraphic position. This relationship can be seen in a single column at Combe Grenal (Fig.2.22). Mellars argued that there is a time-related trend, an evolutionary pattern, to the variants. This has been answered by Bordes with detailed stratigraphic arguments and cave sediment studies. According to the chrono-stratigraphic phases proposed by Laville *et al.* (1980), many of the variants can be regarded as contemporary or in different chronological positions to those suggested by single stratigraphic profiles. This system of intricate relative dating therefore apparently contradicts Mellars's argument of chronological development within the mousterian. The validity of the chrono-stratigraphic scheme based on sediment studies must however await the establishment of an absolute chronology which will perhaps be possible by sample enrichment techniques in ^{14}C dating of these early periods.

The third argument in the debate, proposed by the Binfords (1966, 1969), suggests that the variation is to be understood in terms of function. They recognized two main types of hunter-gatherer settlement, base and work camps, which were occupied by different numbers of people, at different seasons and for different lengths of time. The tasks that were carried out there would be expected to differ and these can be divided into extractive tasks (work camps), where food, plants and raw materials were procured, and maintenance activities (base camps) where food was prepared, distributed and eaten and where raw materials were turned into tools. These major activities, they argued, would be carried out in different locations. They then took Bordes's type list and assigned functions to the tools that related to these activities. Then by means of a factor analysis they measured the degree of correlation amongst all the tool types from seventeen assemblages. This produced five clusters of associated artifact types (Table 2.3) and allowed the Binfords to classify the assemblages according to their functional attributes and moreover to suggest an interpretation of the types of settlement systems from which they were derived.

These original arguments have subsequently been modified and extended, as we shall see later when discussing the upper palaeolithic. Detailed work on the settlement systems and activities of contemporary hunters (Binford, 1978, 1980, 1982; Silberbauer, 1972; Winterhalder and Smith, 1981) has shown both Bordes's and the Binfords' initial cases to be oversimplified. However, this does not diminish the importance of the debate in addressing the question:

Table 2.3 Summary of the Binfords' study of assemblages variability in the mousterian. The five factors represent five groups of statistically interdependent artifacts among mousterian assemblages and it is suggested that these differences can best be understood by considering the assemblages as tool kits which performed different tasks.

Factor	Artifact types from Bordes list	Suggested activity	Type of activity	Analogy to Bordes variants
I	Borers, scrapers, burins	Manufacture of tools from non-flint materials	Base camp maintenance tasks	Typical mousterian
II	Points and scrapers	Hunting and butchery	Work camp extractive tasks	Ferrassie
III	Flakes and knives	Cutting and incising (food processing)	Base camp maintenance tasks	MTA
IV	Utilized flakes, denticulates	Shredding and cutting (of plant materials?)	Work camp extractive tasks	Denticulate
V	Point, blade, scrapers and typical burin	Killing and butchering	Work camp extractive tasks	Ferrassie

why do cultural assemblages vary in space and time? One approach adopts a commonsense view that different peoples have different artifacts and this is why the archaeological record is so varied. The alternative approach admits that the answer is much more complex since we simply do not know all the causes of variation which result in the distinctive patterns in our data. This view maintains that, instead of assuming we know why assemblages vary, we should instead explore the ways in which assemblages are created as a result of variable human behaviour, as for example in the separation of activities at different camp sites.

VARIABILITY IN MATERIAL CULTURE FROM 35 000 TO 10 000 BP

Chronology

The term upper palaeolithic embraces a very wide range of different regional traditions and sequences of lithic assemblages. This can be simplified into two major divisions, early and late upper palaeolithic (Campbell, 1977).

The upper palaeolithic of Europe falls within the time range that can be dated by existing methods of radiocarbon measurement. Blade-based technologies first appear before the Denekamp interstadial that commenced some 32 000 years ago. In the caves of southern France this episode is represented by the Würm II/III erosion horizon, while in the loess areas of central and eastern Europe the climate improved sufficiently to allow the development of a soil horizon.

The early upper palaeolithic is also found in the following glacial stadial that began at 29 000 BP and marked a rapid decline in climate. At 18 000 BP the ice sheets had expanded to their maximum extent (CLIMAP, 1976, Peterson *et al.*, 1979). This was followed by an improvement in the climate and the ice sheets began to shrink in size, a process that was completed by 8 000 BP. The late upper palaeolithic is associated with the period between 20 000 and 10 000 BP during which two important but short interstadials took place. The first at 12 400–12 000 BP is known as the Bølling and the second at 11 800–11 000 BP is termed the Allerød (Coope, 1977).

EARLY UPPER PALAEOLITHIC 35 000 TO 20 000 BP

Assemblages and Industries (Fig.2.23)

The earliest upper palaeolithic assemblages in at least some areas of Europe appear to develop from the mousterian (Bordes, 1968, 1972b). In central and east Europe there are several sites with small collections of artifacts that show a mixture of upper palaeolithic technology and middle palaeolithic typology. In central Czechoslovakia and north-eastern Hungary these small assemblages have been grouped under the name szeletian after assemblages in the Szeleta cave in Hungary. Leaf-shaped points and end scrapers made on blades occur with mousterian side scrapers made on flakes and the continued use of the levallois technique. Bone projectile points appear for the first time. The earliest of these assemblages are dated to between the Hengelo and Denekamp interstadials. Leaf points of different form (Fig.2.21) also occur outside this area at an early date and in an upper palaeolithic context at Jerzmanovice in Poland (38 000 BP) and Kents Cavern in England (Kozłowski and Kozłowski, 1979; Campbell, 1977). None of these assemblages is comparable to the mousterian foliate assemblages of southern Germany that have already been mentioned, although they are not far removed in time from each other.

The few bone points found with szeletian assemblages provide a link with the aurignacian assemblages of the area (Albrecht *et al.*, 1972; Hahn, 1977). These are clearly upper palaeolithic industries employing the full use of blade technology. The number of artifacts in these assemblages is small. At the Hungarian cave site of Istállóskö (Vértes, 1955) the bone points were more frequent than the chipped stone artifacts. This occurred in the lower of two aurignacian assemblages and amongst the stone artifacts was a szeletian leaf point.

In Italy and southern France the earliest upper palaeolithic shows a similar mixture of middle palaeolithic typology with upper palaeolithic technology. In France there are assemblages with

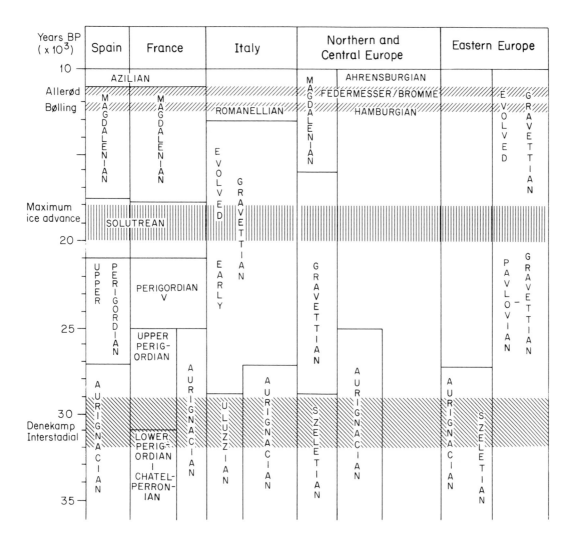

Fig. 2.23   Outline of upper palaeolithic industries in Europe. Major interstadials and the maximum ice advance are marked.

distinctive curved, blunted backed knives made on blades which overlie mousterian assemblages. These châtelperronian knives have given their name to a more widely recognized industry. At the site of Arcy-sur-Cure (Leroi-Gourhan and Leroi-Gourhan, 1964) some 50% of the tools could be classified as middle palaeolithic although the three châtelperronian levels also produced carved ornaments and bone objects

(Movius, 1969). The uppermost of these three levels has a ^{14}C date of 33 000 BP. The presence of naturally backed knives in the MTA B of southern France has led to suggestions that the châtelperronian was a development from an earlier mousterian industry. In the Dordogne area such assemblages are referred to as the first two stages of the perigordian tradition which we will examine later.

At Lecce in southern Italy comparable châtelperronian points have been found in uluzzian assemblages named after a cave at Uluzzo (Barker, 1981). There is again the mixture of upper and middle palaeolithic features and a ^{14}C date of >31 000 BP.

Thus, in southern, western and central Europe there is evidence between 35 000 and 31 000 BP of assemblages that show a mixture of middle and upper palaeolithic features. Moreover, there is evidence that such assemblages were contemporary with the first widespread, full upper palaeolithic industry, the aurignacian. At two sites in France, Piage and Roc de Combe, the châtelperronian is found stratified between aurignacian assemblages. At the Dordogne site of the Abri Pataud the earliest aurignacian levels have been dated to 34 000 BP (Fig.2.24). This site serves as a classic dated sequence for the early upper palaeolithic in the Périgord region (Delibrias and Evin, 1978).

The aurignacian is the first widespread upper palaeolithic tradition (Sonneville-Bordes, 1960; Hahn, 1972, 1977). It is thought to have been introduced to the continent rather than to have developed from local traditions. The use of blades struck from blade cores is the dominant lithic manufacturing technique. Secondary retouch is variable but often involves shallow, flat retouch which results in the sharpening of edges (Fig.2.25, e). The scrapers are often very distinctive, made on thick flakes (Fig.2.25, g and h). Dufour bladelets (Fig.2.25, i) are also commonly found at some sites and consist of semi-abrupt retouch that alternates down either one or both edges. These are particularly common at the Austrian loess site of Krems-Hundssteig (Hahn, 1977). The bone and antler tools also display some stratigraphic ordering as at the rock shelter of La Ferrassie excavated by Peyrony (1934). The early aurignacian contains split-based bone points which are replaced by solid-based and then later with bevelled bases. In central and eastern Europe this development is not so clear-cut. The split-based bone points only occur in caves such as at Istállóskö (Albrecht *et al.*, 1972) and the Vogelherd (Riek, 1934) and are often found together with solid points which are also found in many open sites.

The second widespread early upper palaeolithic tradition is the gravettian (Otte, 1981). Blunted back points are the most distinctive element that serves to distinguish it from the aurignacian. It first appears some 27 000 years ago. In France these gravettian assemblages are referred to as later stages of the perigordian which began with the châtelperronian. The link is provided by the use of steep, blunting retouch. This was Peyrony's (1933) scheme and the interpretation for the stratigraphic hiatus between the lower and upper perigordian, when the aurignacian intervened, is that the perigordians moved into more peripheral locations and only re-occupied the Dordogne area at a later stage. In sites along the Rhône Valley we find levels of aurignacian overlain by upper perigordian/gravettian and then followed by a further level of aurignacian. The cave of Salpêtrière (Escalon de Fonton, 1966) provides a good example of this stratigraphic relationship. In southern Germany the early gravettian is at least contemporary with a later aurignacian (Hahn, 1977), although sites with assemblages that can be attributed to either tradition are very scarce. In eastern Europe this interstratification and contemporaneity does not exist. The gravettian sites in this area have a rich abundance of artifacts as at Pavlov, Dolní Věstonice (Klima, 1957) and Předmost in Czechoslovakia and Molodova V and the Kostienki sites in European Russia (Chernysh 1961; Klein 1969, 1973). Perigordian/gravettian assemblages are found in south-east Europe and in Italy and Spain where the Cueva Morín (González-Echegaray and Freeman, 1973) provides an important stratigraphic sequence with five separate aurignacian and two upper perigordian assemblages.

The upper perigordian assemblages of south-west France are distinguished by several distinctive type fossils (de Sonneville-Bordes, 1973). In stage Va of the French sequence are found distinctive Font Robert points with long tangs (Fig.2.25, k). In perigordian Vb truncated pieces (Fig.2.25, o) with retouch on the truncation appear to have been hafted in a row to give a sharp cutting edge. Stage Vc is distinguished by the abundance of burins which have been truncated and retouched to produce a number of burin facets. These are known as Noailles burins (Fig.2.25, p). At the Abri Facteur in the Dordogne this assemblage has been dated to 23 000 BP (Delport, 1968).

The distinctive Kostienki knives from sites in European Russia also date to this period in central and eastern Europe. They are found at the Crakow-Spadzista street site in Poland (Kozłowski,

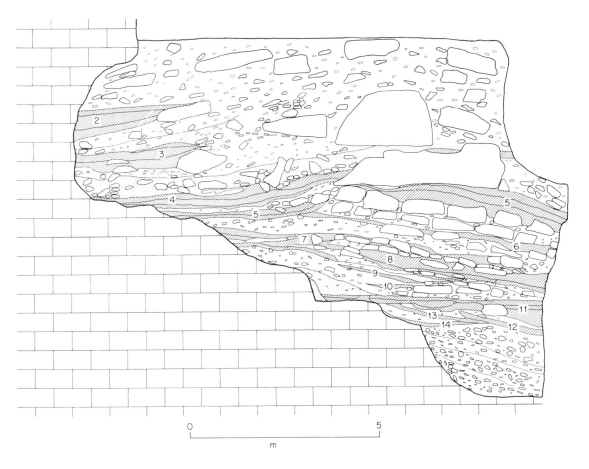

Fig. 2.24 A section through the deposits at the Abri Pataud. The numbers refer to the stratigraphical levels that were recognized by the excavators and which contain artifacts and hearths (after Movius, 1977). The sequence is as follows:

	level 2	Proto-magdalenian		21 940 BP ± 250
	3	Perigordian VI		23 010 BP ± 170
	4	Perigordian Vc		27 060 BP ± 370
	5	Perigordian IV	front c.	29 000 BP
			rear	27 900 BP ± 260
	6	Evolved aurignacian	c.	32 000 BP
	7	Intermediate aurignacian		32 8000 BP ± 500
8, 9, 10		Intermediate aurignacian		no date
	11	Early aurignacian		32 600 BP ± 800
	12	Basal aurignacian		33 260 BP ± 500
	13	Basal aurignacian		no date
	14	Basal aurignacian		34 000 BP ± 675

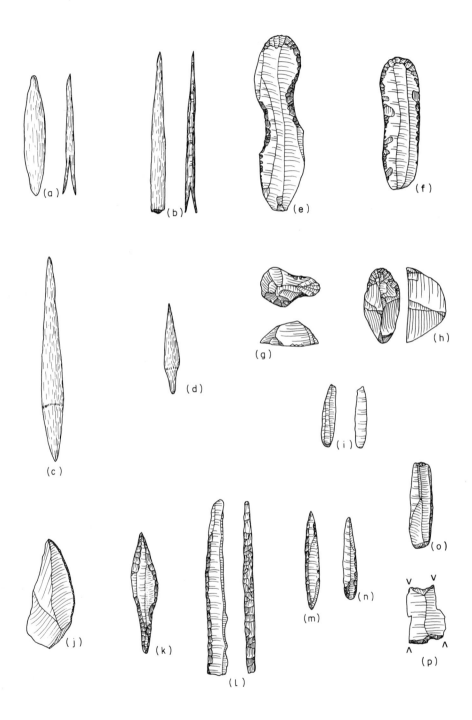

(a)

(b)

(e)

(f)

(c)

(d)

(g)

(h)

(i)

(o)

(j)

(k)

(m)

(n)

(L)

(p)

1974), and in level 9 of the multilevel loess site which contains both aurignacian and gravettian assemblages at Willendorf II in Austria (Felgenhauer, 1956/9).

Geographical Variation

The aurignacian is found throughout most of Europe although few assemblages have been attributed to this industry in either Russia or Italy. It is not found on the north European plain (Bánesz, 1976) but clusters in the central highlands and around the river valleys of central and eastern Europe. Aurignacian and szeletian assemblages have been found in close geographical proximity in the Bükk mountains of Hungary. In Czechoslovakia, however, the distributions of such assemblages are mutually exclusive with the szeletian concentrated along the Váh river and the aurignacian in Moravia and eastern Slovakia. Aurignacian assemblages are present in Belgium (Otte, 1979) but lacking in England, where Campbell (1977) has grouped a small series of occurrences, which includes material with leaf points, into a general category of early upper palaeolithic.

The gravettian is particularly common in Italy (Leonardi and Broglio, 1962; Laplace, 1966) and on the Russian plains (Koz∤owski and Koz∤owski, 1979). It is however also lacking on the north European plain. These assemblages were being created at the same time as the ice sheets were expanding out from the Alps and Scandinavia.

UPPER PALAEOLITHIC TOOL-KITS AND TECHNOCOMPLEXES

The contemporaneity of perigordian and aurignacian assemblages in south-west France has been used by Bordes (1973) as further proof that the underlying causes for variation in stone assemblages relate to ethnic traditions. The Dordogne region appears as a favoured area for settlement which, he felt, was competed for by different and unrelated groups. In reply, Binford (1973, 1977) has put forward an argument that views the variation as the result of different ways of organizing technology. The essence of his argument is that technologies differ with respect to the amount of forward planning and manufacturing effort that goes into them. Where both of these factors are high then we expect the following:

(1) that tools will be made at some location away from where they will be used in the future;
(2) the effort that went into making such tools means that they will be looked after, *curated*, and brought back from the locations where they were used for further use elsewhere. They may even be repaired and recycled.

If these circumstances prevailed then we would expect little direct association between the tools recovered from a site and the activities which their shapes and frequencies might suggest were carried out there. We would only expect such a direct association when the tools were made, used and thrown away all at one location. Such an expedient method of organizing technology might apply either to certain tool types or to whole assemblages. A change in the way technology was organized, from *expedient* to *curated* behaviour, may well explain the changes in assemblage composition both within and between stages in the palaeolithic. The development in many upper palaeolithic assemblages of well made projectile points in stone and bone and the use of a hafting technology may well be indicative of such a behavioural change. It may be that the differences between châtelperronian and aurignacian assemblages are not related to who made them but rather to

Fig. 2.25 Aurignacian and perigordian/gravettian implements: (a, b) aurignacian split-based and (c, d) solid-based bone/antler points; (e–f) end scrapers on blades; (g) nosed scraper; (h) steep scraper on a thick flake; (i) Dufour bladelet; (j) châtelperronian knife/point, a distinctive type fossil of the lower perigordian; (k) Font Robert tanged point; (l) backed blade; (m, n) micro-gravette points with blunting retouch on one edge; (o) retouched truncation; (p) noailles burin.

different ground rules that governed the way these tool-kits were organized.

This model suggests that we need different ways of measuring the differences between artifact assemblages than is provided by conventional typological means. Rather than comparing the number of backed blades and the shape of the burins, we instead require measures of the degree of effort that went into stone tool manufacture. Some indication can be provided by experimental studies and as we shall see in the next chapter by the study of raw material procurement. The numbers of broken tools compared to complete tools and the degree to which unmodified flakes were used would also provide measures about the organization of lithic technologies in the past.

The term technocomplex (Clarke, 1968) was originally proposed to act as an umbrella concept for the investigation of assemblages and industries that showed some degree of similarity, and which probably arose as a common technological response to environmental conditions. This has been used to describe these early (Hahn, 1977; Otte, 1981) and late upper palaeolithic (Schild, 1976) industries. The term is useful since it makes us consider the common functional purposes of technology. As a result much greater variation in assemblage composition and the occurrence of distinctive tool types is allowed in the way palaeolithic materials are compared and classified. However, it must be remembered that these terms and concepts are just stepping stones to understanding, and naming a group of industries as a *technocomplex* does not explain why they differ one from another.

THE LATE UPPER PALAEOLITHIC — 20 000 TO 10 000 BP

Chronology

The last glacial climatic minimum serves as the base line for the beginning of the early upper palaeolithic. At this time the ice sheets reached their maximum extent and the oceans shrank thereby providing additional broad coastal plains between France and England. This glacial minimum provides us with a very good opportunity to observe palaeolithic adaptation against the extremes of climate and resources (de Sonneville-Bordes, 1979). The closer resolution of the temperate oscillations in the late glacial (Coope *et al.*, 1977) also gives us the possibility of contrasting short-lived climatic events with the cultural remains of the archaeological record.

Assemblages and Industries

This period marks the development of clearly defined regional assemblages within western Europe. These can often be characterized by specific artifact types. This is clearly shown in the appearance between 21 000 and 18 000 BP of distinctive assemblages in France and Spain known collectively as the solutrean (Fig.2.26). The Dordogne site of Laugerie Haute (Smith, P. 1966) provides a detailed stratigraphic history of these assemblages which employed the use of pressure flaking to make large leaf points. These take a variety of forms, unifacial and bifacially worked, and the solutrean has been divided into a

Fig. 2.26 Solutrean, magdalenian and tanged point implements: (a, b) pressure flaked solutrean leaf points: (a) point of face plane or unifacial form, (b) laurel leaf; (c) shouldered point; (d) barbed and tanged arrow head from Parpalló, Spain; (e) awl/borer; (f, g) magdalenian double and single row antler harpoons; (h) denticulated backed element; (i) burin; (j) shouldered point; (k) azilian antler harpoons; (l, m) antler harpoon found with tanged point assemblages on the north European plain; (n) ahrensburgian tanged point; (o) bromme tanged point; (p) hamburgian shouldered point; (q) Federmesser backed segment.

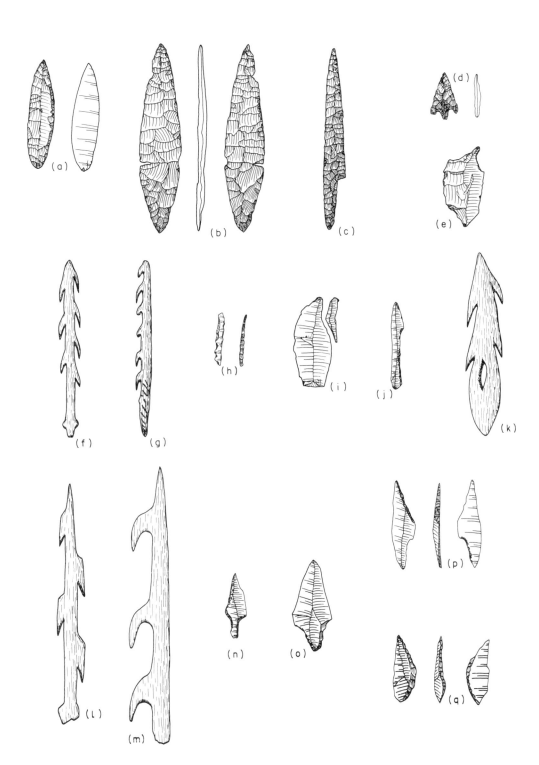

number of stages on the basis of these types. In a late phase shouldered projectile points are found and at Parpalló in eastern Spain (Pericot, 1942) the late solutrean, now dated to 18 000 BP, also contained barbed and tanged arrowheads. The solutrean is not found outside western Europe; one reason may be that it developed at a time just prior to and during the maximum extension of the continental ice sheets. It is probable that in central Europe groups abandoned the area during this period of climatic severity. In eastern Europe the assemblages show a continued use of gravettian blunting techniques in the manufacture of backed points and knives. Within western Europe there was a contraction of settlement into the most favoured areas. The artifact assemblages that follow the maximum advance of the ice caps can be grouped into three major geographical technocomplexes (Koz̷owski and Koz̷owski, 1979).

In France, Belgium, Spain and the upland areas of central Europe through to Czechoslovakia are found magdalenian assemblages with antler harpoons and an abundance of burins (Fig.2.26). Small serrated backed blades are also common, and we find awls, end scrapers and raclettes, which are blade scrapers with light retouch around their edges. Bone and antler artifacts are particularly common and many of them are decorated. The magdalenian is named after the rock shelter of La Madeleine on the Vézère river in the Dordogne. This remarkable site has been excavated on many occasions and yielded many thousands of stone and bone tools as well as engraved bones. The antler harpoons at the site have both single and double rows of barbs. The antler tools include the so called bâtons which are a segment of reindeer antler with a hole drilled through, as well as elaborately carved spear throwers. It has been suggested that these served as a shaft straightener for arrows. Recent excavations by Bouvier (1977) have shown how the small size of some of the stone tools requires careful recovery. Small backed bladelets formed a dominant part of the various assemblages in the site and these are so small that some 8000 can be fitted into a litre bottle. At the magdalenian site of Petersfels in southern Germany a recent excavation by Albrecht (1979) of the spoil tips from the earlier digs of Peters (1930) showed that some 95% of all the smaller tools had been missed. The 6500 tools that were recovered by Peters must therefore be regarded as a gross under-representation of the actual number

of tools present. At La Madeleine the recent excavations have revealed 18 archaeological levels (Bouvier, 1977) in contrast to the three described by Peyrony for the same profile (Capitan and Peyrony, 1928). Of these 18 levels, level 7 is dated to 12 640 ± 260 and level 14 to 13 440 ± 300 b.p.

In Italy and eastern Europe, however, the assemblages lack this distinctive bone work, and are not called magdalenian. There is a development toward smaller implements, still retouched with steep blunting. Small blade segments and micro-gravette points are characteristic tools. These are regarded as part of a gravettian technocomplex and so provide a continuation in tradition with the early upper palaeolithic (Laplace, 1966; Bartolomei *et al.*, 1979). The size of these sites is again impressive as at the cave of Polesini (Radmilli, 1974), where 392 000 chipped stone specimens were recovered and of these 7% were retouched tools. More than one half of the implement category consisted of small backed bladelets. Small blunted backed bladelets and rods are also a common feature in the large lithic collection from Kastritsa cave (Bailey *et al.*, 1983) in northwest Greece.

This period also sees the repopulation of the north European plain, which was last used as a regular focus for occupation during the early part of the last glacial period (Taute, 1968). Antler harpoons are common in assemblages from this area but the most distinctive tool is the *Stielspitze*, or tanged point. At the site of Stellmoor near Hamburg two main occupation levels were excavated. In the lower, dated to stage Ia of the late glacial, the Oldest Dryas, shouldered projectile points were common. In the upper level, dated to another cold period, III, the Younger Dryas, tanged points were found. The earlier assemblage is representative of the hamburgian industry while the upper is termed ahrensburgian (Fig.2.26). The divisions into younger and oldest Dryas have been established through pollen studies. The presence of *Dryas octopetala* in pollen profiles indicates a period of cold climate and reduced summer temperatures.

The three cold climate dryas zones, Ia, Ic and III are separated by periods of greater warmth; the Bølling and Allerød oscillations. During the Allerød we find assemblages that lack the shouldered and tanged points but which possess curved blunted backed points and knives. These Federmesser groups (Schwabedissen, 1954; Schild, 1976) are contemporary with magdalenian assemblages in the highlands to the south, as at Gönnersdorf near Köln (Bosinski, 1979).

These late glacial assemblages show large regional groupings. After zone III the climate improved markedly and with it the vegetation and animal resources available to hunting groups also changed. Large projectile points were replaced by smaller forms, as with azilian assemblages in France (de Sonneville-Bordes, 1973), and industries using microlithic flint segments became common. This marks the transition from the palaeolithic to mesolithic. In many areas this transition is not clear cut and we find classifications such as epi-palaeolithic and epigravettian. This is especially true for southern Europe. While it is an arbitrary boundary in terms of both human adaptations and technology, the date of 10 000 BP and the beginning of the post-glacial period mark an end to palaeolithic Europe.

Geographical Variation

The most striking feature is the repopulation of the north European plain as the ice sheets retreated. The dearth of sites in this large area during the early upper palaeolithic is replaced by many hundreds of flint scatters (Taute, 1968). At this same time human populations were moving up to the latitude of the arctic circle in Russia (Klein, 1973; McBurney, 1976), while in eastern Siberia populations had reached the Bering land bridge and moved into north America. While the date of human entry into this continent is still fiercely debated it is likely, on the basis of present ^{14}C evidence, to have taken place at the same time as the late upper palaeolithic of the western end of Eurasia.

SUGGESTIONS FOR FURTHER READING

The revolution in quaternary stratigraphy, which is still not fully felt in palaeolithic studies, is clearly presented by D. Q. Bowen, *Quaternary Geology* and should be preferred to other schemes which still use the four glacials/interglacials of the Alpine sequence. The human fossils are well described and illustrated by M. H. Day, *Guide to Fossil Man*, who sorts out the confusing array of names which have been assigned to certain fossils. Cave excavation and typological analysis is dealt with by F. Bordes, *A Tale of Two Caves*, who reports on his own excavations at Combe Grenal and Pech de l'Azé. General works on the European palaeolithic, which are well illustrated and describe in considerable detail the sites and sequences, include F. Bordes, *The Old Stone Age* and J. M. Coles and E. S. Higgs, *The Archaeology of Early Man*. D. K. Bhattacharya, *Palaeolithic Europe* is good on individual site descriptions and *The Palaeolithic Age* by J. J. Wymer is especially strong on the palaeolithic sequences of Europe. Finally, the most accessible corpus of illustrations and site accounts is provided by H. Müller-Karpe's monumental *Handbuch der Vorgeschichte*, vol. I.

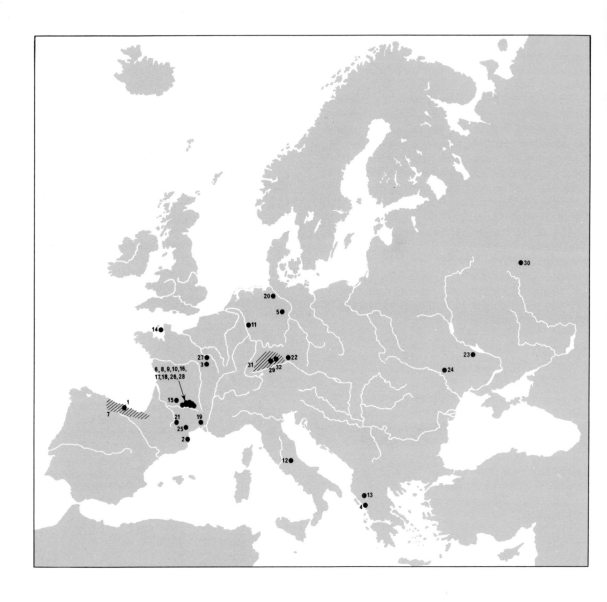

Fig. 3.1   Principal sites mentioned in Chapter 3. 1 Altamira. 2 Arago. 3 Arcy-sur-Cure. 4 Asprochaliko. 5 Bilzingsleben. 6 Bruniquel. 7 Cantabrian Mountains. 8 Cap Blanc. 9 Combe Grenal. 10 Crô Magnon. 11 Gönnersdorf. 12 Grotta Paglicci. 13 Kastritsa. 14 La Cotte. 15 La Marche. 16 Lascaux. 17 Laugerie-Basse. 18 Laussel. 19 Lazaret. 20 Lehringen. 21 Mas d'Azil. 22 Mauern. 23 Mezhirich. 24 Molodova. 25 Niaux. 26 Pech Merle. 27 Pincevent. 28 Rouffignac. 29 Stadel. 30 Sunghir. 31 Swabian Uplands. 32 Vogelherd.

3

Subsistence and Society
in Palaeolithic Europe

The two themes of this chapter, subsistence and society, are used to investigate patterns in palaeolithic data. With subsistence this involves looking at the decisions which determine the location of camp sites in relation to resources, as well as the problems associated with interpreting animal bone samples from palaeolithic sites. The importance of hunter-gatherer mobility and their use of space is stressed in the analytical framework for investigating settlement systems and adaptations at a variety of spatial scales.

The subsistence economies are discussed as variations in food management strategies rather than as economic types involving selection upon particular animals. Ethnoarchaeological studies have shown how important it is to consider variations in these strategies for the creation of distinctive archaeological residues. The analysis of patterns in excavated sites is discussed together with specific instances of hunting behaviour.

Other aspects of the palaeolithic record such as burials, raw material transfers and art, are discussed from the point of view of increasing social complexity and changes in social organization. The contrast between middle and upper palaeolithic materials at 35 000 BP is examined, and the implications for changes in systems of information exchange that used material culture as a medium for communication are examined. This involves the use of a model of palaeolithic social systems which stresses the importance of alliances for populations coping with a high-risk glacial habitat.

The summary of palaeolithic Europe presented in the last chapter has dealt with the data along two dimensions: time and space. Typological and technological changes in material culture have been linked to a time scale that incorporates climatic reconstructions and to regional variation within the European continent. In broad outline we have seen *what* changes, and *when* it changed. There has however been comparatively little mention of *why* change took place and this chapter will add to the framework by discussing the data in terms of human behaviour and cultural adaptation.

There are many aspects of human activity that need to be considered when an understanding of changes and variation in culture is being sought. This chapter will select certain aspects, and in the first place those concerned with exploiting the environment and getting food. This does not mean that these are the only aspects that need considering, but rather that an investigation of food-getting strategies has proved immensely valuable in analysing the patterns in large amounts of palaeolithic data. The second aspect that will be discussed in this chapter concerns the evidence for social evolution during the palaeolithic period in Europe. While the environment determined what resources were available for exploitation and posed problems for long-term group survival, the form of social system laid down how the habitat was to be used. It is to this aspect that we must look for differences in the degree of exploitation and the changing use of the environment over periods of time.

SUBSISTENCE ECONOMY

The old established view of hunter-gatherers, both modern and palaeolithic, has been that they lead a catch-as-catch-can existence, taking from the land the resources that are most readily available and moving on to new supplies when those at a particular location can no longer support them.

This view is now considered misleading since it implies random, unstructured behaviour that would leave nothing for the archaeologist to discover in the form of repeated patterns. If this were the case then our task would be simply that of identifying and listing the animals and plants that turn up on palaeolithic sites. Once this had been done one would have made an analysis of prehistoric subsistence activities.

We should, however, be less concerned with listing what palaeolithic man ate and more interested in the choices that were available and the factors that influenced the decisions that went into planning a subsistence strategy (see box). For instance, we are now beginning to understand the true significance of hunter-gatherer mobility, which exists as one of their major tactical devices, operating within their overall food-getting strategy (Lee and De Vore, 1968; Bicchieri, 1972; Smiley *et al.*, 1979-1980). This strategy can be said to have a goal which is to *minimize risk*. When resources such as rainfall or the

---

MAKING DECISIONS IN A

The many subsistence decisions that hunter-gatherers make have been modelled by Jochim (1976). Their strategic goals are:

(1) To attain a secure level of food.
(2) To keep energy expenditure to within acceptable limits.

Their tactics for achieving these goals consist of three interlinked components.

The *resource use schedule* dominates the decision-making process, as shown by the larger arrows. Deciding on this blueprint involves an assessment of the available resources in terms of the following attributes: weight, density, aggregation size, mobility, fat content, non-food yields.

Jochim has used this attribute analysis to predict the pattern of resource use for the south-west German mesolithic where during the post-glacial climatic conditions favoured the exploitation of both plants and animals.

The *location of sites* is one means by which the cost of exploiting resources can be reduced. In general we would expect to find that sites are located closer to resources which are less mobile, which have a higher density and which are less clustered. Where to place a site is often a decision involving multiple choices. Other factors may be important here such

migratory patterns of large herbivores are unpredictable, then the ability of hunter-gatherers to secure food is at risk. Personal and group mobility is one means by which information about the position and abundance of resources is acquired and helps to minimize this risk. It is also a way of achieving the optimal strategy for the exploitation of the environment by making adjustments to the distribution of people across it.

Some environments in which we find hunters and gatherers contain a higher degree of risk than others. In particular those habitats where animals form the bulk of the diet, the arctic regions of the globe, are high-risk since the mobility of the resources makes it difficult to predict herd movements, and the herds themselves are also prone to natural cycles of population rise and crash. Time and energy have to be spent in search and pursuit before the prey can be secured. Effort expended in this manner represents a *cost* since the calories that were used up have to be replaced. Risk and cost have to be judged together in any subsistence decision. They provide two of the principles which govern the activities of hunters and gatherers and which contribute to the creation of patterns in the archaeological record.

The problem for the archaeologist lies in transferring these principles to a study of palaeolithic data. One way this can be done is by using a spatial framework for the investigation of subsistence decisions and the various costs that were involved.

HUNTER–GATHERER SUBSISTENCE ECONOMY

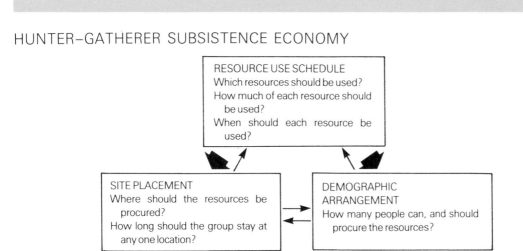

Reconstructed schedule for the use of resources in mesolithic southern Germany (after Jochim, 1976).

as proximity to firewood and water. It is also the case that the aspect of a possible site, particularly caves and rock shelters, will be important in determining the internal temperature of the shelter and hence making it more or less attractive for occupation. Visibility over the surrounding terrain for watching game may also recommend some localities in preference to others. The *size of the population unit* and the duration of settlement may also depend upon other factors such as social interaction: for example, participation in group ceremonies and the acquisition of marriage partners. This may result in larger groups staying together for longer periods of time than would be predicted by the cost models of exploitation since the members would be prepared to accept a higher series of exploitation costs.

This would take the following form:

Scale	Analytical concept	
Site	Exploitation territory	Features influencing choice of location and the relation of the site to the environment
Local region	Site extended territory, seasonal territories	Adaptation to an area local settlement system adjusting personnel to resources
Region	Annual territory, home range	Total area patrolled by a group
Inter-regional	Lifetime territory Alliance networks	Area from which marriage partners are obtained and contacts maintained with other groups

Site Analysis

An analytical device which has made use of the principle of cost is *site catchment analysis* which was first proposed by Vita-Finzi and Higgs (1970). It was developed in order to investigate the locations of palaeolithic sites in relation to resources. The model is based on the ethnographic observation that a foraging radius of two hours walking time, about 10 km, represents a critical cost threshold. Beyond such distances returns diminish rapidly so that it becomes uneconomic, as measured by calories expended for calories returned, to continue exploitation beyond this point. Vita-Finzi and Higgs referred to this as the *site exploitation territory*, and an example using a smaller radius of 5 km for an important series of middle and upper palaeolithic caves at Mt. Carmel, is shown in Fig.3.2. The site exploitation territory forms the area around the site that was regularly exploited by groups based at that site. The model also employs the concept of a home base settlement system since the two hour threshold has significance only if the hunting or foraging parties intend to return to the main camp in the same day. The model therefore states that *distance* is an important factor in understanding prehistoric site locations since we can use this as a measure of exploitation costs. When these rise the result is that either another resource is exploited, or the size and

composition of the group is altered, or the group moves to another location. In this manner costs are lowered to within acceptable limits.

The home base was defined archaeologically by Vita-Finzi and Higgs as a densely occupied location. Examples would be the Mt. Carmel caves (Garrod and Bate, 1937) and the lower and middle palaeolithic site of Combe Grenal (Bordes and Prat, 1965) in the Dordogne region of southern France. Changes at this latter site in the relative importance through time of reindeer, red deer, bovids and horse bones are thought to reflect a combination of climatic factors (Fig.3.3), which led to different proportions of these animals being taken from the area around the site.

Changes in the various species represented in the animal bone assemblages from caves and open sites often contrast with evidence of occupational continuity. A study of palaeolithic occupation in the south German Swabian uplands provides such an example (Gamble, 1978, 1979; Hahn, 1979,1981). The available resources consisted of mixed herds of large herbivores and the excavated faunal assemblages indicate that a large number of different species were exploited (Table 3.1). The Swabian uplands form a roughly rectangular block of limestone that can be divided into an area of high, broken relief in the north and a flat plateau in the south. This southern area has a width of some 20 km, a diverse series of soils, and permanent water sources in the small,

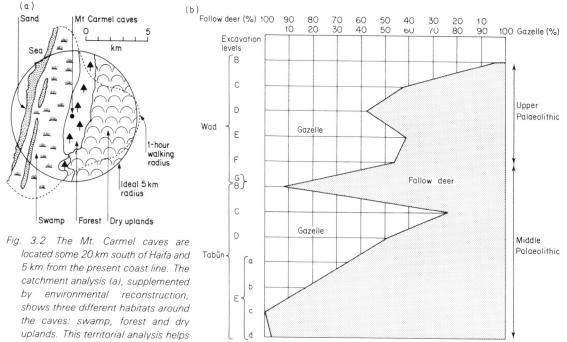

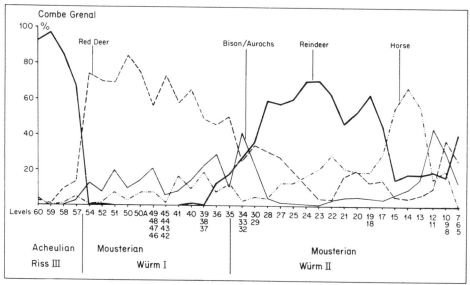

Fig. 3.2 The Mt. Carmel caves are located some 20 km south of Haifa and 5 km from the present coast line. The catchment analysis (a), supplemented by environmental reconstruction, shows three different habitats around the caves: swamp, forest and dry uplands. This territorial analysis helps account for the changing proportions of the two main animal species found in two of the caves. Note how fallow deer increases under increasingly moist conditions which favour forest growth (after Higgs, 1976; Garrod and Bate, 1937).

Fig. 3.3 The animal bones from Combe Grenal in southern France: the graphs plot the changing proportions of the four main animal species identified. The archaeological levels spanned part of the penultimate and last glacial periods (Riss III, Würm I and II in the French sequence) and contained abundant artifact assemblages. The changing proportions of animal species are interpreted as the effects of climate upon the availability of prey for human hunters (after Bordes and Prat, 1965).

Table 3.1   The proportional representation of the main animal species from faunal collections associated with palaeolithic assemblages from southern Germany (after Gamble, 1978). The percentage indicates the frequency with which a particular species has been identified from the total number of archaeological levels dated respectively to each of the three time periods.

	Middle palaeolithic (micoquian/ mousterian) c. 75 000– 35 000 BP	Early upper palaeolithic (aurignacian/ gravettian) c. 35 000– 20 000 BP	Late upper palaeolithic (magdalenian) c. 16 000– 10 000 BP
Mammoth	63%	90%	19%
Woolly rhino	79	55	19
Bison/aurochs	59	50	38
Horse	93	100	83
Red deer	61	35	46
Reindeer	71	100	81
Ibex	24	70	27
Chamois	6	25	4
Cave and brown bear	77	95	44
Lion	47	45	4
Hyena	67	30	10
Wolf	67	70	27
Red fox	47	75	27
Arctic fox	35	60	34
Number of archaeological levels	49	20	47

steep-sided valleys that dissect it. We should expect this area to have provided the best grazing land within the limestone uplands. Palaeolithic settlement would therefore have been located in the centre of this southern region in order to establish a least cost solution to the problem of exploiting the herds. From such a location a local group would have been optimally positioned, according to the 10 km radius model, to exploit the diversity of the faunal community that surrounds them. The distribution of sites (Fig.3.4) shows that this was indeed the locational strategy employed. At the centre of this flat grazing area a small cluster of sites was located within each of the three occupied valleys. It is clear that occupation returned to these central locations throughout the middle and upper palaeolithic even though there are notable changes (see for example mammoth, rhino, bison and ibex in Table 3.1) in the species composition of the animal bones associated with the lithic assemblages of these periods.

The faunas from these German caves also contain many bones of carnivores, of which cave bear, hyena, wolf and lion form the most significant component (Musil, 1980-1). The cave bear used these sites as winter hibernation dens, and natural mortalities have added their remains to the archaeological record. Hyenas and wolves also used these caves as den sites and both these carnivores are known to bring bones of other animals back to their den areas. These particular cave sites with their faunal assemblages are therefore a combination of both palaeontological and archaeological evidence.

By contrast, a series of sites in southern Europe, from Cantabrian Spain (Altuna, 1979; Freeman, 1973; Straus, 1977, 1982), have produced comparatively few carnivore remains indicating that these cave and rock shelter sites were rarely used as dens. This should result in the animal bone faunas being more directly representative of human rather than animal activity. It has been noted by Freeman

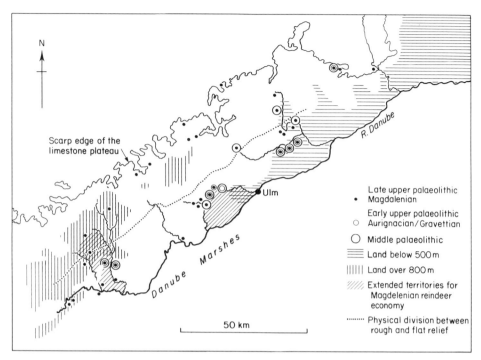

Fig. 3.4 Palaeolithic occupation in the limestone Swabian Alb of southern Germany. The majority of sites shown are cave and rock shelter locations (after Gamble, 1978).

(1973) that different parts of this area were settled during different phases of the palaeolithic. During the mousterian and early upper palaeolithic this upland area displays a pattern of regularly occupied base camps that were centrally located with respect to the range of exploited resources. These included red deer, roe deer, ibex, chamois and horse. By contrast the magdalenian pattern of site location dispersed the population. The faunal counts associated with magdalenian assemblages point to a greater reliance upon hunting red deer and this dispersion of personnel into a larger number of smaller groups was accompanied by a broadening of the resource base to include shell fish and small game. Painted caves, such as Altamira, which appear at this same late upper palaeolithic period, may have served as foci for the seasonal meeting of a larger group (Conkey, 1980) since the resources now available did not permit the same degree of residential permanence in base camps that was possible in the earlier periods.

Local Settlement System

The study of the location of palaeolithic sites in relation to resources can also be used to link sites together into a local settlement system. In an example from the magdalenian of the Swabian uplands of southern Germany, Sturdy has suggested that the pattern of a number of dispersed sites, each with a small artifact assemblage and a fauna dominated by reindeer bones, formed part of a settlement strategy where population was purposefully positioned at the *edges* of blocks of grazing land. These are clearly defined naturally by obstacles such as the steep sided valleys and the marsh. Sturdy interpreted these sites as watching stations where the members of the group were positioned so as to block the movement of the herds of reindeer from these upland areas. The sites were therefore located to a territory of very irregular shape which Sturdy called a *site extended territory* since it clearly did not conform to the ideal shape of the site exploitation territory. He interpreted this settlement pattern as a reflection of close control of the animal herds. The human groups were staying in close contact with their critical resources — the reindeer — during the summer months without disturbing them. In the example used here, the area enclosed by the Blau and Ach rivers and the Danube is some 185 km², which at a stocking density of 4·75 reindeer per km² would have supported 880 animals. This number of reindeer would have been of sufficient size to sustain two nuclear families, ten people, culling the herd at a level which would not affect its long-term survival chances.

Regional Settlement Systems

These examples of seasonal settlement patterns have to be fitted into a much larger system of exploitation in what Vita-Finzi and Higgs (1970) termed an *annual territory*. This formed the total area exploited by a human group throughout the year. It has however, proved difficult to define, archaeologically, the dimensions of these annual territories. An example of what an annual territory might look like was proposed by the same authors for north-west Greece, Epirus. Here two caves, Kastritsa and Asprochaliko, contained late upper palaeolithic assemblages of comparable date. The reconstructed snow cover at the height of the last glaciation (Fig.3.5) strongly suggested that Kastritsa was a focus for summer exploitation of red deer, while Asprochaliko, located near the edge of a large coastal plain, provided a winter base (Legge, 1972). They suggested that as the herds of red deer and steppe ass moved up the valley from their winter to summer grazing lands, the human groups would have also followed their principal quarry (Bailey *et al.*, 1983).

This model of extreme mobility brought about by a need to follow the herds has also been used to reconstruct annual territories for the reindeer hunters of south-west France (Bahn, 1977) and southern Germany (Sturdy, 1975). In these cases distances of 300 and 600 km have been suggested as the annual movements of palaeolithic groups that were almost entirely dependent upon this one animal species for their livelihood.

The implications of these reconstructions of subsistence behaviour are considerable. We would need, for example, to reconsider the significance of variation in cultural sequences, since the same group would have been responsible for the manufacture of artifacts that were separated by large geographical distances. In the German case Sturdy argued that the southern groups moved 600 km when following the herds to the winter grounds on the north European plain around Hamburg. This could have involved a change in material culture from magdalenian to tanged point assemblages as the groups moved from south to north during the year. It is not, however, clear why such changes in technology should be related to seasonal or functional factors. It is also difficult to find evidence among ethnographically known hunters for such a system of long distance herd-following. This appears to be a strategy adopted by groups who have domesticated their animals rather than by hunters, who generally adopt an *intercept* strategy. The latter involves killing the deer as they pass through an area on their way from winter to summer grazing grounds. For the rest of the year other resources are exploited; and most importantly the group makes use of the stores of meat that were cached from the brief periods of migration hunting (Smith, 1978; Binford, 1978a; Ingold, 1980). It is therefore common to find several groups using the migrating herds at different points on their yearly cycle of movement, rather than to find a single group closely following the herds throughout the entire year (Burch, 1972).

Storage is an important adaptation since it introduces a considerable degree of flexibility of choice into the planning of a subsistence strategy. It conditions the duration of occupation and the amount of group aggregation. It can also affect the degree of group mobility, thus making the definition of annual territories a difficult task for the archaeologist. Food storage represents a necessary solution to the problems of resource availability and predictability for any group that is primarily dependent upon animals for food. The way that we shall identify a storage strategy in the palaeolithic is by the study of animal bones. In particular the existence of stores of meat will affect the types of bones that come into domestic contexts and which eventually find their way into the archaeological record as rubbish.

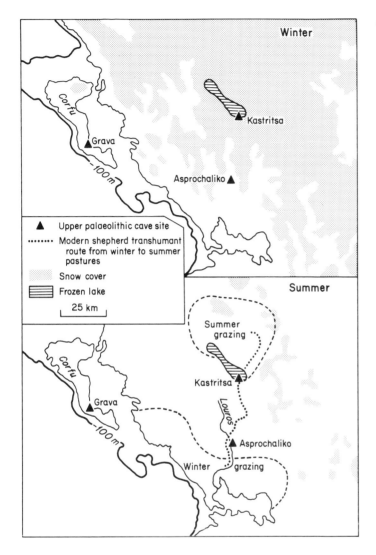

Winter

Corfu

▲Grava

Kastritsa▲

Asprochaliko▲

▲ Upper palaeolithic cave site
······ Modern shepherd transhumant
        route from winter to summer
        pastures
▨▨ Snow cover
▤▤ Frozen lake
|—— 25 km ——|

Summer

Corfu

▲Grava

Summer
grazing

Kastritsa▲

Louros

Asprochaliko▲

Winter grazing

*Fig. 3.5   Summer and winter snow cover and
sea level in Epirus, Greece, 20 000 years
ago, reconstructed from physiographic and
climatic sources (after Vita-Finzi, 1978).*

Another adaptation which also modifies the extreme mobility argument is the use of time saving facilities, for example traps that, once set, will save the hunter valuable time that can be used in the search and pursuit of other game. Such facilities may range in size and complexity from simple deadfall traps for catching small animals to large collective drives where herds of animals can be stampeded, penned and slaughtered (Oswalt 1976; Torrence, 1983).

THE SETTLEMENT SYSTEM
AND FOOD RESIDUES

The original site catchment model of Vita-Finzi and Higgs recognized only two types of settlement, the home base and the transit camp. A more detailed scheme has been put forward by Binford, who describes two different settlement systems (1980, 1982). These reflect the different decisions that face hunter/collector and gatherer/forager strategies (Table 3.2).

Table 3.2   Differences between extreme collector and forager settlement systems (after Binford, 1980). These different systems for getting food result in different types of site for each settlement system. Both systems have residential bases *from which foraging and hunting parties set out and where manufacturing, food preparation and other domestic tasks take place. Within the daily foraging radius around these camps are found* locations *where plants are gathered or animals killed. Three further site types are only encountered in a collector system.* Field camps *are overnight stops for work parties operating at some distance from the residential base. They may be used for some time while the work party carries out its planned task.* Stations *most commonly take the form of observation points for watching game and gathering other information about the environment and its resources. Finally* caches *are formed on many occasions, when animals have been killed, in order to keep off scavengers. The food is brought back to the residential camp when it is needed.*

Foragers/gatherers (e.g. !Kung San of the Kalahari desert: Lee and De Vore, 1976)	Collectors/hunters (e.g. Nunamiut Eskimo of northern Alaska: Binford, 1978; Campbell, 1968)
Bulk of the diet is provided by plant foods which are gathered daily	Bulk of the diet is animal protein and at some seasons of the year this food comes from stores
The foragers set out from, and return to a home base camp every day	Work parties leave the home base to collect specific resources and may not return every day to the main camp.
The consumers move to the available plant resources which means that the base camp is moved many times during the year	After the animals have been intercepted and killed, a cache is made and the food moved to the consumers where and when it is needed. Although very mobile, there are not the same large number of base camp moves during the year.

The collector strategy, where animals are the main staple of the diet, can be described as a logistical strategy. This means that a great deal of time and energy goes into *planning ahead*. Parties set out from a home base with specific objectives in mind, for example to hunt an animal species in a location where it is known to occur, or to make use of seasonally abundant resources such as fish. The planning is very clearly seen in the preparation of hunting gear that is selected for the job in hand and which is designed to provide the best possible chances of success. Careful preparation and planning ahead is a critical part of surviving in harsh environments where the penalties for any mistake are swift and drastic.

Once resources have been intercepted, the collectors' response is often to make a cache of the food. It can then be taken back to the base camp as required. In this way stored food resources are moved to consumers.

What is in these stores will obviously affect both the composition and formation of the archaeological record. For example, the age of hunted prey and the anatomical parts of the animal carcass will vary

between stores depending upon the time of the year when the animal was killed and the techniques of butchery used in partitioning the animal. As a result, there will be little direct relation between the location where hunting took place and the location where the meat is finally eaten and the bones thrown away to form part of the archaeological record.

The existence of such *food management strategies* will strongly influence archaeological interpretation about the season at which cave and open sites were used if the evidence for determining seasonal use is based on animal bones. A study by Bouchud (1966) on the mandibles of reindeer excavated from middle and upper palaeolithic sites in south-west France led him to conclude that these caves and rock shelters were occupied all the year round by human groups. The state of tooth eruption, and the degree of attrition on their grinding surfaces pointed to a continuous sequence from very young to very old reindeer in these faunal assemblages. The lack of any clear peaks in the data, that might indicate a preferred season of occupation, led Bouchud to argue for the unbroken use of these sites by groups that hunted reindeer in the vicinity. If, however, these groups were using stores of reindeer meat then it would be possible to offer an alternative reconstruction. A small hunting party, for example, would use the caves on an infrequent basis bringing with them small parcels of meat from store. Depending upon which store they were using they might bring parts which contained evidence for reindeer killed in spring when in fact they were visiting the site in summer or fall. Repeated visits of this kind over many hundreds of years, during which time different stores would be used, could produce a faunal assemblage with no clear indications of the season when it was visited!

The animal bones are, in the first instance, informing us about which stores were being used, rather than, as is usually assumed, which time of the year a group was camped in a rock shelter. The study of seasonality in a collector settlement system will need a clear understanding of the conditions under which stores of meat are created and the way in which they are used throughout the rest of the year. Moreover, the bone residues in a site belonging to a collector settlement system have first to be analysed in terms of food management strategies before we can proceed to wider interpretations of hunting activity (re-examine, for example, the assumptions made in the studies of the Mt. Carmel and Combe Grenal faunal assemblages (Figs 3.2 and 3.3)).

By contrast with the hunter-collector strategy, the gatherer/forager settlement system generally sees a much closer link between the creation of the archaeological record and the activities which might be directly inferred from the artifacts and food residues. Their strategy is the simple one of finding food within a foraging radius from the residential camp. This is of course the basis of the site catchment model that has been discussed above (Lee, 1968; Silberbauer, 1972; Yellen, 1977). When plants form the bulk of the diet it is easier to predict where they will be located and so the amount of time spent in searching for resources will be much less than is the case with collectors. Once the exploitation costs rise, the answer is to move camp to a new location where the time and distance spent in searching for food are reduced. In this strategy consumers are moved to resources. Food is gathered near the base camp and brought back to it where it is prepared and cooked.

The debris within a residential camp will generally indicate directly the season of the year when the group was there and the foraging activities that went on around the camp. In other words, the relation between the settlement and the environment is recorded in the material left behind to form the archaeological record.

The examples used earlier in this chapter all came from the last glaciation. This fact suggests that both settlement systems and food management strategies in palaeolithic Europe would have been toward the collector end of the spectrum. It should, however, be emphasized that the presence of a storage strategy, although suspected, has not yet been demonstrated for this period.

If we turn to the earlier palaeolithic it is more difficult to determine the type of subsistence strategy that was practised. Much of the data comes from marsh (Torralba), lake (Bilzingsleben, Hoxne) and above all stream (Swanscombe) deposits. The associations of large mammals such as straight tusked elephant and rhino with stone tools has led to reconstructions of big-game hunters driving the megafauna into the water where they can be killed (Freeman, 1975; Steiner and Wagenbreth, 1971). On occasion artifacts have been found, such as the 2·5m long wooden spear with fire hardened point, at Lehringen, north Germany (Oakley et al., 1977) which provide unambiguous evidence for the killing of an elephant. However, the depositional context of these finds must not be forgotten and, as we have already seen at Torre in Pietra (Piperno and Biddittu, 1978), river sorting can produce comparable results to big-game hunting by gathering material together. Moreover there are many riverine localities in Europe (Toepfer, 1957; Vereschagin, 1974) where the remains of elephants and mammoths have accumulated and yet *no* artifacts have been found. This does not rule out the likelihood that several of the large mammal carcasses were indeed utilized. Recent work on early hominid sites in East Africa (Bunn, 1981; Potts and Shipman, 1981) has revealed clear traces of marks left by stone tools and carnivore teeth on the bones of animals. At Bilzingsleben (Mania and Dietzel, 1980) similar observations have been made on the bones of rhinoceros.

These observations tell us that meat and marrow were being obtained and eaten. The use wear on lower palaeolithic artifacts from Hoxne and Clacton (Keeley, 1980) also points to the same conclusion. This does not answer the question of how the meat was obtained either through hunting or scavenging and as yet does not provide a firm platform for testing models about cooperation in group hunting (Howell, 1971) or food sharing (Isaac, 1978) of this valuable resource. As we learn more about the subsistence strategies of the earliest colonizers of Europe, it is most probable that, instead of reconstructing dramatic changes in terms of developments in big-game hunting, we shall instead see variation in the spectrum of food management strategies that were constrained by the importance of animal protein to any mobile, non-food producing population inhabiting the northern latitudes of the world. In other words, there is little reason why the earliest colonizers should have had food management strategies that differed much, in terms of the animals taken, from those last glacial groups for which we have a less distorted archaeological record.

THE ORGANIZATION OF SITES

It should by now be apparent how the type of sub-sistence strategy will affect the patterns that we see in the archaeological record. We can begin to see how different settlement *systems* are characterized by particular *types* of settlement (Table 3.2).

The purpose of models such as those presented above is to help our understanding of the past by coming to terms with the principles of human behaviour that lie behind the creation of the archae-ological record. In the narrative above, the importance of subsistence has been stressed. Many of the observations, such as that having to do with storage, have been derived from work among contemporary hunter-gatherers. While such studies may help the development of general models, such as the settlement system model, we as archaeologists are still left with the problem of selecting the appropriate site types when we deal with archaeological materials. Ethnoarchaeologists can also assist here by observing the creation of modern camp sites where patterns in the material deposited or abandoned can be directly related to such everyday activities as eating, sleeping, cooking food, mending tools and other tasks (Yellen, 1977; Hayden, 1979b; Binford, 1978b; Gould, 1971).

In fact, it would be more accurate to say that the investigation of the palaeolithic is the study of the residues left behind by these commonplace activities rather than any observation of some grand theme such as hunting.

Ethnoarchaeological studies of camp sites do not, of course, have to contend with the long-term natural processes of erosion, sorting and the transportation of materials. These factors make the archaeologist's task particularly difficult, especially in a palimpsest of human occupations, as is the case with many rock shelter deposits.

However, it is possible to find recently abandoned rock shelter sites where these natural processes have not occurred and which give a good impression of the initial phases of the creation of an archaeological deposit. One example (Fig.3.6) comes from south-west Africa where Clark and Walton (1962) mapped the undisturbed surface of a rock shelter in the Erongo mountains. The rock shelter has good views of the surrounding countryside, and was probably used by male hunting parties as an overnight field camp during the late Stone Age of the region. The materials were undisturbed in the positions where the last hunters to use the shelter had abandoned and discarded them. Notice the regular spacing of the hearths and sleeping hollows along the back wall of the shelter, a pattern which is determined by the size of the human body and the useful heat retention qualities of the shelter wall. The hearths provide a focus around which activities took place, such as repairing hunting equipment. In amongst the sleeping hollows the archaeologists found a wooden arrow shaft and a throwing club which had been stored for use on a future occasion by the last hunters to use the cave. Sixty-one stone artifacts came from the surface immediately surrounding the bedding places, indicating that hunters had sat on their beds to make and repair their gear. Cooking and eating areas were most probably in other parts of the cave.

A comparable arrangement of hearths within a rock shelter can be seen from the excavations at the Abri Pataud (one of the classic rock shelter sites above the modern village of Les Eyzies in France). In level 3 at this site were found a row of five hearths, their centres spaced some 2 m apart and running parallel to the shelter wall (Fig.3.7). The excavator, Movius (1966), interpreted this arrangement as the

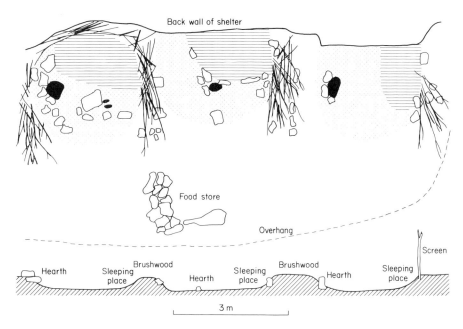

Fig. 3.6   Plan and section of North West Settlement, Big Elephant Cave, Erongo Mountains, South West Africa (after Clark and Walton, 1962).

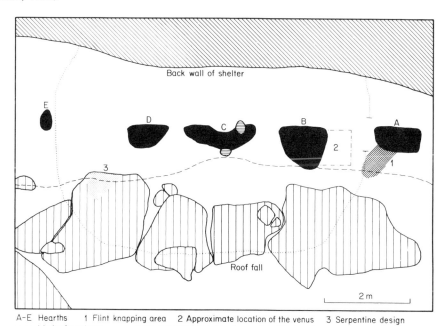

A–E Hearths   1 Flint knapping area   2 Approximate location of the venus   3 Serpentine design
---- Limit of overhang   ········ Area, according to excavator, enclosed by long house

Fig. 3.7   Plan of level 3 in the Abri Pataud rock shelter (after Movius, 1977).

remains of a long-house with central hearths that was positioned between the back wall of the shelter and the collapsed roof blocks. The spaces between the hearths would, however, have been sufficient for sleeping areas, as shown in the example from the Big Elephant cave, and rather than long-houses, we are most probably seeing the remains left behind by a small hunting party operating away from their base camp. The substantial size of the hearths indicates that this shelter was re-used in this manner on many occasions.

The hearths contained quantities of ash and heat-cracked pebbles that had presumably been placed in the fire to retain heat. Engraved stone slabs, one of which is a bas-relief female carving in the 'venus figurine' tradition, were found around the hearths,

as well as an assemblage of some 1900 flint artifacts. The level is classified as a phase of the upper perigordian dated by ^{14}C to $23\,010 \pm 170$ b.p.

The arrangements of hearths in palaeolithic sites have often been interpreted as evidence for huts since it is thought that only an intentional construction could produce such clear patterning as we have seen, for example, at the Abri Pataud. This is also the situation at the Lazaret cave where H. de Lumley (1969b), in a detailed study, reconstructed a large tent from the distributions of bones and stone tools around two hearth complexes. However, the spacing of hearths and *people* so as to exploit the benefits of the sun and fire-warmed shelter wall can also produce patterning without there ever having been a roofed or tented structure.

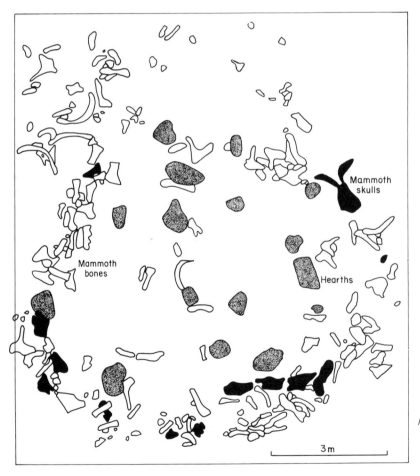

Fig. 3.8 Plan of hearths, flints and animal bones in level 4 of Molodova I (after Klein 1969a).

This may also have been the case in many open sites. At the open site of Molodova I, level 4, (Goretsky and Ivanova, 1982; Klein, 1969), an oval arrangement of mammoth skulls and long bones was found enclosing an area of 8m × 6m (Fig.3.8). Within this oval area were fifteen hearths and a dense scatter of mousterian flint cores and tools. These residues are interpreted as representing the remains of a hut where the large heavy mammoth bones served as weights to hold down skin coverings. However, as can be seen in Fig.3.8, several of the hearths are in fact located within the walls of the structure. It is possible that the mammoth bones served as small windbreaks where hunters sheltered while watching for game. The repeated use of this location under different conditions of wind direction and varying numbers of hunters could explain the repositioning of hearths within the basic structure.

This same factor may account for the positioning of hearths at the magdalenian open site of Pincevent in France (Leroi-Gourhan and Brezillon, 1966). This site has three substantial hearths placed 3m apart. Associated with each hearth are clearly defined arcs of stone and bone debris. The two hearths with large quantities of chipped stone around them both have a single stone seat placed respectively on the west and east side. The arcs of debris have been interpreted as the remains of small circular tents but equally plausible is the interpretation of two working hearths which were used in the open air. The choice of which hearth, and its seat, was used depended on the wind direction that day and the fact that smoke gets in your eyes.

The size and complexity of the internal features at Molodova contrast with the late upper palaeolithic Russian site of Mezhirich (Pidoplichko, 1969). Here some 385 mammoth bones were found above a shallow depression containing two small hearths and a scatter of flint and bone artifacts. The mammoth long bones and jaws had been stacked to form a wall that enclosed a circular space of about 5m². The 'hut' at Molodova would, if it ever existed, have enclosed 48m². The excavators at Mezhirich found 35 mammoth tusks lying on top of the mammoth bone pile and these were interpreted as the curved supports for a roof which might then have been covered by skins. Two large hearths lay just outside the structure. No doubt the structure at Mezhirich

was used on a number of occasions, as with the finds at Molodova. The full investigation of the activities at these sites and a complete reconstruction of the significance of these concentrations of bones would depend upon a more detailed examination of the spatial patterning of the various materials in the sites.

Recent advances in such analytical techniques are shown in Fig.3.9 where a detailed analysis of the distribution of flint artifacts has allowed the reconstruction of two specific flint knapping events.

HUNTING EPISODES

The majority of palaeolithic cave and open sites consist of many superimposed activities which make reconstruction of the sort outlined above a difficult task. The presence of bones of cave bears and the unmistakable evidence of bones gnawed by hyena and wolf points to the role of other agencies than man in the creation of archaeological deposits. As a result most sites are palimpsests of natural and human origin. The two examples in this section come from complex sites and represent only a small part of the archaeological deposits. They show that even within cave sites, where re-use by man and carnivores has made interpretation difficult, it is possible in some instances to isolate specific activities.

The site of La Cotte, in the English Channel Islands, contains, within a long stratigraphic sequence dating mostly to the penultimate glaciation, two piles of mammoth and woolly rhino bones (Scott, 1980). In layer 3 the bone pile consists of nine skulls and two lower jaws of mammoth and comparatively few limb bones. However, the latter are common in the other bone heap in layer 6, where skulls of mammoth are rare. Skulls and limb bones of the woolly rhinoceros also occur in both piles. No other animal species were found in these bone heaps which had been piled up against the rock wall of this coastal cave. Stone artifacts which were abundant elsewhere in the site were also absent in the vicinity of the bones. Scott has interpreted these concentrations as the end result of two different hunting episodes. The pile in layer 3 resulted from the middle palaeolithic hunters stampeding the mammoths and rhinos over the headland of which the cave of La Cotte forms a part. The ageing evidence, obtained from a study of the teeth and bones, shows that a small herd

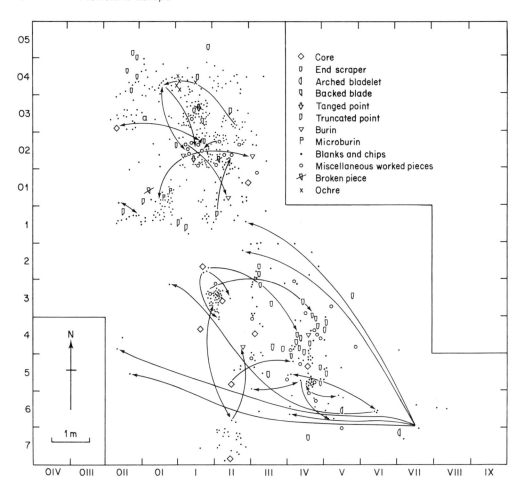

Fig. 3.9   Plan of chipped stone artifacts in level III of the late palaeolithic site at Calowanie, Poland. Arrows link pieces which could be fitted together: in the top scatter arrow (a) connects an endscraper with the core from which it was struck. The separate articulation nets, as they are called, point to the number of separate manufacturing events and the location of the stone knappers. Notice the lack of truncated points in the lower net, though they are common in the upper one (after Schild, 1976).

of adult mammoth females and their young were driven in this hunting episode. The close proximity of this event to the cave helps explain why the heads, which have comparatively little food value, should be found at all. In layer 6 these are much rarer, which suggests that primary butchery of the carcasses took place elsewhere and that only selected portions were brought back and stacked in the shelter of the cliff. This example shows how important factors of

distance and the size of the animal carcass can be in determining what, and how much, will be transported from a kill site to some other location.

The second example also concerns mammoth bones. In an upper palaeolithic level in the Weinberghöhlen at Mauern in southern Germany (Bohmers, 1951; von Koenigswald *et al.*, 1974) the excavators found wedged between two rocks a mammoth skull together with six segments of

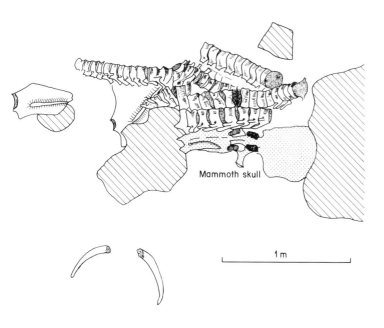

Mammoth skull

1 m

Fig. 3.10 Cache of mammoth bones from the Weinberg caves, Mauern in southern Germany. This layer also produced a gravettian chipped stone assemblage. One of the vertebral columns carries the unmistakeable traces of hyena gnawing (after von Koenigswald et al., 1974).

backbone from the same species (Fig.3.10). These backbones had been butchered into 60 cm long segments for ease of transportation from the kill site back to this cave, where presumably a cache was made. The backbone contains a good amount of meat and the decision to transport these segments probably depended upon both the amount of time needed to strip the meat from them and dry it, and the number of people who were available to carry out such a task.

CHANGES IN PALAEOLITHIC SOCIETY

This emphasis on subsistence has shown differences within rather than between time periods. There are many unresolved questions about the form the food management strategies took at particular times and places. Did they include storage? Was hunting rather than scavenging or trapping the means by which meat was obtained? Moreover, to what extent are the samples of bones the result of human or carnivore accumulation?

It is for these reasons that the food management strategy model has been used. We simply do not understand our faunal samples well enough to use

them to talk of economic stages with specialist reindeer or mammoth hunters; or of generalist hunters, who took a wider range of prey, replacing the big game hunters who apparently killed enough animals on a single occasion to keep a small town in steaks for several months.

There are, however, a number of other aspects in the palaeolithic record which do show clear changes through time and which are commonly linked to developments in social complexity. Many of these help to mark the boundary at 35 000 BP, that is between the middle and upper palaeolithic (Mellars, 1973). As a result, the distinctions between these archaeological periods are often explained by developments in social organization.

Burials

Burials are occasionally found in amongst the deposits of cave and open sites. These have to be distinguished (S. Binford, 1968a; Harrold, 1980; Rowlett and Schneider, 1974) from the natural incorporation of human remains within carnivore deposits, as with the skull from Arago (M. de Lumley, 1976). The appearance of intentional burials at the beginning of the last glaciation is one reason why we have both more, and completely preserved, crania and limb bones for neanderthal and modern man.

The earliest burials are associated with neanderthals and have so far all come from caves and rock shelters. They form two main geographical clusters in south-west France and the caves of Israel, as at Mt. Carmel (Garrod and Bate, 1937). Some thirty-six individuals from sixteen sites are presently known, although several of these are disputed by some authorities as not being true burials. Only single burials are known. The graves are shallow scoops in the cave floor into which the body was laid. Most frequently this was placed in a flexed position with the head resting on one arm. All age and sex classes have been found in the burials. These range from the funeral pit of a young infant excavated by Bordes (1972a) at Combe Grenal, where the bones had not survived, to the recovery of the old man of La Chapelle-aux-Saints who had hardly any teeth and a bad case of arthritis. Grave goods (Table 3.3) have been claimed for several of these burials but since most consist of animal bones and flint tools this evidence must be considered as ambiguous.

The upper palaeolithic sample is much larger, some ninety-six skeletons from forty-one sites (Harrold, 1980). Burials are known both from cave and open sites. Multiple burials are a common feature and the presence of ornaments provides clear evidence for grave goods being intentionally placed with the corpse.

This is well shown at the Russian site of Sunghir (Bader, 1978), dated to 23 000 BP, where amongst a series of graves was found the burial of two young boys (McBurney, 1976). The bodies were fully extended and lay in the grave with their heads touching. By their sides were large spears of straightened mammoth ivory, and pendants, flint tools and animal figurines were lying on their bodies. At the same site an adult male inhumation was covered in many thousand of small pierced ivory beads, the arrangement of which across the body suggesting that they were sewn onto clothing. Around the upper arms were large ivory bracelets. Finds of comparable age were made some years ago in the Grimaldi cave complex on the Italian Riviera and more recently in an accurately recorded context at the Grotta Paglicci (Fig.3.11) (Mezzena and Palma di Cesnola, 1972).

Display and Design

These burials provide a vivid glimpse of the use that upper palaeolithic populations made of material culture for the purpose of display. Dress and ornament are common ways by which social position and status are signalled to other people and it is common to recover beads and pendants from upper palaeolithic occupations throughout Europe. A variety of raw materials were used including drilled fox canines, sections of mammoth ivory and shells. The size and shape varies from the elaborate fish-tailed pendant in châtelperronian levels at Arcy-sur-Cure (Leroi-Gourhan and Leroi-Gourhan, 1964) to the simple ivory bead necklace found with gravettian implements from the Brillenhöhle (Riek, 1973) in

Table 3.3   The occurrence of the main categories of grave goods in middle and upper palaeolithic burials for which adequate information is available. Only reliable information has been included (Harrold, 1980). It appears from these burial data that the upper palaeolithic reflects a greater number of social distinctions than is the case for the middle palaeolithic material.

	Middle palaeolithic	Upper palaeolithic
Total of reliably documented burials	33	67
Tools	7	36
Animal bones	7	24
Manuports	8	5
Shells	0	18
Red ochre	0	35
Art/decorative objects	0	33

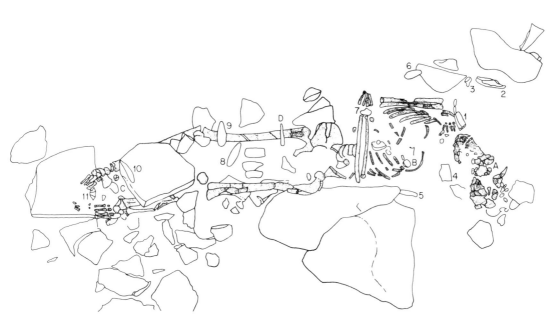

Fig. 3.11 Burial in the Grotta Paglicci, Italy. The burial, dated to between 23 000 and 24 700 BP, is of a 12–13-year old youth. The numbers (1–11) mark flint tools thought to be grave goods. Around the skull (A) were some 30 pierced deer canines that may have been sewn on to a cap. Other grave goods include a poorly preserved shell bracelet (B), a slab of haematite (C) and a bone awl (D). The skeleton indicates a stature in life of between 157 and 165·5 cm (after Mezzena and Palma di Cesnola, 1972).

southern Germany. These beads are often incised with repeated patterns (Hahn, 1972b). Ivory bracelets are known from the gravettian site of Pavlov in Czechoslovakia (Klima, 1957) and circular ivory disc pendants engraved with animals have been found at Laugerie-Basse, Mas d'Azil and Bruniquel in France (Leroi-Gourhan, 1968 p.403).

Small figurines have been recovered from the Russian site of Kostienki I level 1 (Efimenko. 1958; Abramova, 1967) where there are many carved heads of animals as well as several female figurines. These date to c.23 000 BP. A much earlier group of animal figurines was discovered in the aurignacian levels of the Vogelherd in southern Germany (Riek, 1934; Wagner, 1981) and included a small ivory horse, mammoth and other animals. At the nearby cave of the Stadel and also associated with aurignacian stone tools is a small anthropomorphic statuette (Fig.3.12) carved from a juvenile mammoth tusk.

The earliest designs from south-west France are

Fig. 3.12 Anthropomorphic figurine from the Stadel cave in southern Germany. It is fragmentary and has been carved from a small mammoth tusk; it comes from a layer containing aurignacian artifacts, dated to 31 750 BP (after Hahn, 1977).

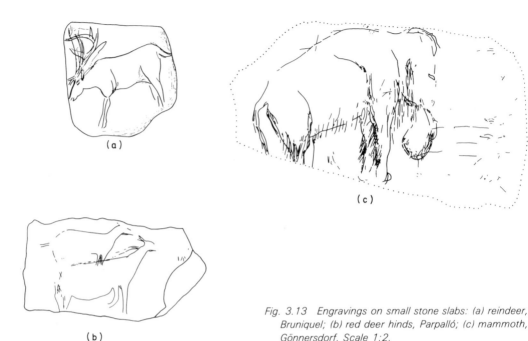

Fig. 3.13 Engravings on small stone slabs: (a) reindeer, Bruniquel; (b) red deer hinds, Parpalló; (c) mammoth, Gönnersdorf. Scale 1:2.

engraved signs of undeciphered meaning on limestone slabs (Collins and Onians, 1978). These come from the aurignacian levels at La Ferrassie and a few other sites in the Les Eyzies areas (Delluc and Delluc, 1978).

In the late upper palaeolithic there are several sites which contain a great wealth of engraved stone plaques (Fig.3.13). These include the 1500 slabs from La Marche (Pales, 1976) on some of which are engraved representations of human heads (Fig.3.14). At Gönnersdorf in west Germany the engraved slabs littered the floor of a dwelling structure. At both sites, which date to the late magdalenian, the engravings are a mass of superimposed sketches of animal figures, scratched lines, and at Gönnersdorf, outline human profiles (Fig.3.15), which are thought to be female representations. The engravings lack the finished completeness of the art from the painted caves.

Another aspect of visual display is to be found in the sculpted friezes of animals. At the Abri Cap Blanc (Lalanne and Breuil, 1911), this forms a great frieze of horses sculpted on the back wall of the rock shelter and dated to the late upper palaeolithic. The rock

shelter at Laussel (Lalanne and Bouyssonie, 1941–6), also near Les Eyzies, produced a number of limestone blocks which had bas-relief engravings, in an upper perigordian level, of female figures and other anthropomorphic representations.

The decorated mammoth skull from the dwelling at Mezhirich (Pidoplichko, 1969) points to another domestic context of display in upper palaeolithic society.

It is impossible to see chronological developments in art styles amongst these data. In broad outline the earliest display and design consists of animal figurines, pendants, ornaments and a few engraved blocks. Between 25 000 and 20 000 years ago we find a great concentration of such display items in the burials, as at Sunghir, and in domestic contexts as at Dolní Věstonice and Pavlov (Klíma, 1957), and Kostienki (Efimenko, 1958; Klein, 1969b). In the late upper palaeolithic we find those sites with many thousand engraved stone slabs, some of which can be deciphered as animal and human sketches. Moreover at this time there is an increase, as at La Madeleine (Capitan and Peyrony, 1928), in the decoration of

Fig. 3.14   Three engraved human faces from La Marche. Over 1500 engraved stone plaques have been recovered from this magdalenian site in western France; many are engraved with superimposed images of human figures and profiles. These three examples are drawn to the same scale and orientation for comparison (after Pales, 1976, and Hadingham, 1979).

hunting equipment, for example spear throwers, and the appearance of pierced antler staffs engraved with animal designs (Fig.3.16).

Marshack (1972) has made a careful study of much of this portable art and has suggested that some of the pieces depict, through the portrayal of plants, animals and fish, the various seasons. He has also claimed that a microscopic study of some of the enigmatically scratched bone plaques reveals an intentionality to these scorings and markings that points to systems of notation and time reckoning. Developments of this nature would clearly be advantageous to groups coping with harsh glacial environments since it provided a means of estimating the available resources and passing the information on to other hunters.

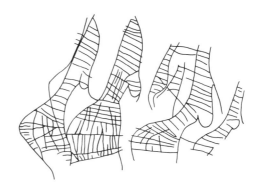

Fig. 3.15   Small stone slab from Gönnersdorf, engraved with what are interpreted as female figures in profile. Similar engravings and statuettes have been found in sites in western, central and eastern Europe (after Bosinski and Fischer, 1974). Scale 2:3.

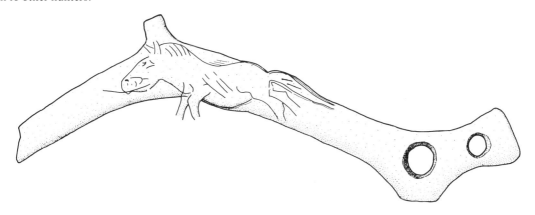

Fig. 3.16   Pierced antler rod or bâton, engraved with a figure of a horse, from La Madeleine.

Cave Art

The main period of cave painting was during the late upper palaeolithic and is contemporary with magdalenian lithic assemblages.

The painted caves of Europe are found, with one exception in the Urals, in Spain and France. There are a great many caves in varying stages of preservation, and with different quantities and styles of painting. Mineral pigments were used as colouring materials and these generally occur naturally in the caves. Engraving on the walls was also very common, as at Les Combarelles and Lascaux (Breuil, 1952; Leroi-Gourhan and Allain, 1979). Clay modelling is known at Le Tuc d'Audoubert where two recumbent bison have been found in the far reaches of a cave that is very difficult of access. Tracings in the soft clay are also a frequent feature as with the drawing of a bison at Niaux, and mammoth at Rouffignac (A. Leroi-Gourhan, 1968).

Styles in painting (Table 3.4) are also variable, ranging from the simple black outlines of horses, bison and mammoths at Pech Merle to the polychrome horses from Lascaux and the bison at Altamira (Breuil, 1952). Finally a very naturalistic style is thought to represent a late phase in the 'Salon Noir' at Niaux where realistic drawings of horses and bison can be found.

The cave art consists predominantly of paintings and engravings of animals of which the most common are shown in Fig.3.17. Scenes, as we understand them in art, are rare although this does not mean that composition was unknown. Leroi-Gourhan (1968, 1982) has argued that palaeolithic artists followed an intentional layout when painting their caves, which is reflected in the positions of the paintings and the association of certain subjects together. He stresses the importance of the signs that are also found in these caves: dots, rectangles, hands and wound signs. These, according to Leroi-Gourhan, delimit particular areas in what he calls these palaeolithic sanctuaries (see box describing Pech Merle). His interpretation as to why this layout should exist is that the art expressed for palaeolithic man ideas concerning the natural and supernatural organization of the living world. The male–female principle, which he believes was translated into animal images, here represents the obvious and potent principle of organization that deals with fecundity.

The content of the art, its message, is still debated (Ucko and Rosenfeld, 1967; Leroi-Gourhan, 1982; Pfeiffer, 1982). The contexts in which it occurs suggest some of the functions for the actors involved. It is possible that one purpose of the cave art hidden in underground chambers, difficult of access, was to provide a 'theatre' for a framework of belief that was enacted out through ritual. The great caves of Niaux and Pech Merle have yielded evidence in the clay floors of footprints. These are frequently of children

Table 3.4   The four major style periods recognized by Leroi-Gourhan for palaeolithic cave art and decorated objects. The dates are very approximate.

10 000 BP	*Style IV*	
	Les Combarelles	Le Tuc d'Audoubert
	Font de Gaume	Les Trois Freres
	Rouffignac	Altamira
	Niaux	Cap Blanc
15 000 BP	*Style III*	
	Lascaux	Cougnac
	Pech Merle	
19 000 BP	*Style II*	
	Pair non Pair	Laussel
25 000 BP	*Style I*	
	No cave paintings, only engraved slabs;	
	La Ferrassie	
32 000 BP		

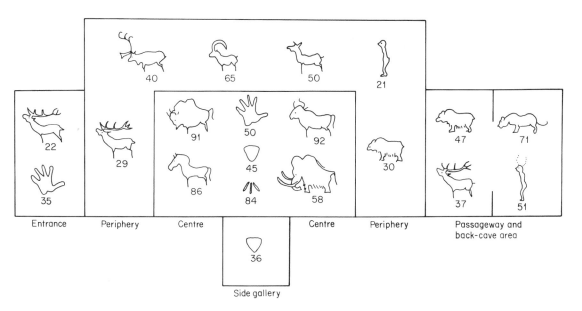

| 40 | 65 | 50 | 21 |

22	29	91 50 92	30	47 71
35		86 45 58		37 51
		84		

| Entrance | Periphery | Centre | | Centre | Periphery | Passageway and back-cave area |

36

Side gallery

Fig. 3.17   Occurrence of animal figures and other motifs in five specific areas of decorated caves. The numbers refer to the percentage frequency of individual motifs in each area. These figures (after Leroi-Gourhan, 1968) lend support to the idea of intentional planning of cave sanctuaries.

and it is probable that one reason for the location of the art in these secret places was to act as a suitable hidden setting for rites of initiation into the full status of hunters. Paintings and sculpted friezes also occur in the daylight areas of caves and rock shelters and most probably provided a backdrop to common ritual and ceremonies associated with visiting and group aggregation (Conkey, 1980). These sites provided a means of integrating widely dispersed populations by giving them a common focus, a permanent symbol in the landscape.

Social Networks

Display and design are ways that information is transmitted through the medium of material culture. It is there to be seen and the messages, while not directly intelligible to us, are part of a visual communication code (Wobst, 1977; Sackett, 1977, 1982). On occasion the similarity in stylistic rules governing the manufacture and design of particular objects allows us to trace very extensive information networks.

In the early upper palaeolithic, associated with upper perigordian assemblages in France, and with gravettian in other parts of Europe, have been found a series of distinctive female figurines. These are small in size, ranging from 4 to 22 cm in height, and all of them show the same exaggerated proportions of the body, and schematic treatment of the head. In southern France these same features have been found on bas-relief engravings, as at the Abri Laussel (Fig. 3.19) and the Abri Pataud. The examples from the rest of Europe are carved on stone, mammoth ivory and at Dolní Věstonice made out of baked clay mixed with pulverized bone. They are found from the Pyrenees to the Don river in Russia and they also occur in Italy. They can be dated to between 25 000 and 23 000 BP. The similarity in design points to a common set of stylistic rules and conventions in a shared system of communication. This visual similarity expresses, in one small way, how dispersed human populations over such large distances were integrated into a coherent social network. This integration was of great importance for the gathering and dissemination of information, about environmental exploitation and the distribution of personnel.

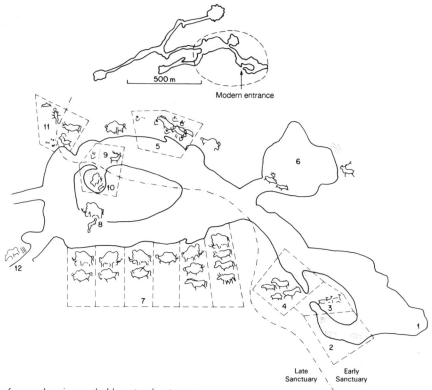

THE PAINTED CAVE OF PECH MERLE NEAR CABRERETS, LOT, FRANCE

Plan of cave showing probable natural entrance.

Detailed plan of cave: 1, possible site of entrance at the time of the earliest decorations; 2, 3, 4, Le Combel chamber with figures in the earliest style; 5, main decorated chamber of the early sanctuary with a frieze of horses surrounded by hand signs; 6, ossuary; 7, large black fresco often referred to as the chapel of the mammoths; 8, area with scraped ceiling; 9, figures just outside the chamber; 10, chamber with the woman/bison panel; 11, side chamber with the wounded man and brace sign; 12, narrow gallery with engraving of a bear and other signs.

Side chamber (11): the wounded man sign with what are called brace signs and which have been interpreted by Leroi-Grouhan as female symbols. As with many of his interpretations, it is impossible to assess objectively such descriptions.

Material culture is part of the information system that is put to social uses. Interactions, which involve the exchange of information in the contexts of ritual, trade, marriage and communication, use not only figurines, cave art, dress, and distinctively shaped weapons and tools (Clark, 1975, pp.66–85; Close, 1978), but also raw materials. An example of social networks traced by these means comes from a study

The cave was first discovered in 1922 and subsequently some more chambers were found in 1949. The underground passages extend for about 2 km and of this about 150 m contains paintings. The original entrance is thought to have been in the back of the Le Combel chamber; the modern entrance is entirely artificial.

The paintings in the cave indicate the wide range of subjects and styles that are common to palaeolithic art. They also serve as a good example of Leroi-Gourhan's thesis that the grouping of particular subjects follows a logical and repeated pattern.

He recognizes two successive sanctuaries in Pech Merle. The earlier is characterized by quadrangular signs and it is indicated on the plan. It includes the panel of horses that is placed in early style III and includes two side panels; one with a red hand in one chamber and the other panel with a paired ibex and ox. The quadrangular signs made up of red dots in the recesses of Le Combel are, according to Leroi-Gourhan, the place where the representations begin, the point of departure for understanding the layout of the earlier sanctuary.

The later sanctuary, still in style III, consists of one very large panel of black outline figures of mammoth, bison, ox, and horse. From left to right he identifies the following pairings: ox/horse/mammoth, then bison/horse/mammoth and finally bison/mammoth pairings. This, Leroi-Gourhan considers, shows very clearly the male/female symbol pairing. The scraped ceiling is also in this later sanctuary, and consists of a space of some 40m², in which the soft clay in the ceiling was scraped with a stick. A great mass of superimposed representations can be broken down to reveal a mammoth and some female figures drawn schematically in profile.

Finally, in the same side chamber as the ox and ibex we find the brace sign, interpreted as a female symbol, and the wounded man. This combination of signs is repeated at the cave of Cougnac that lies some 30 km north-west of Pech Merle. Footprints in the clay floor have also been found at Pech Merle.

source. Schild (1976) has compared the distances away from source (Fig. 3.18) for the Allerød interstadial and the succeeding cold late Dryas phase. He found that in the warmer period the sites with the most tools of this flint are those that lie within 100 km of the source. Sites further away than this only have a very few pieces of this same flint. The late Dryas phase presents a different picture. The Holy Cross flint often exceeds 90% of all the flint found in sites that lie within 200 km of the source. Moreover, the flint has been found up to 400 km distant.

This study points to the effects that changes in climate and resources can have upon the distribution of palaeolithic materials. It is not certain by what means the flint was distributed over these distances — whether it was collected by groups visiting the area or by exchange between neighbouring bands.

The raw material sources from this same area of Poland were also used in the early upper palaeolithic. The chocolate-coloured flint is found in Czechoslovakian and Hungarian assemblages of the szeletian, aurignacian and gravettian. The volcanic glass, obsidian, is also found at some distance from its source at Tokaj in Hungary and is found in Austrian and Czechoslovakian sites with aurignacian and gravettian assemblages.

Small, portable art objects have also been found over large distances. They provide evidence for the existence of these social networks which were important to maintaining population in the harsh glacial environments of northern Europe.

Fossil shells and marine molluscs also point to contacts that extended over considerable distances. At the Kostienki sites on the Don river in Russia shells were found from the Black Sea, which lies some 450 km to the south (Klein, 1969b). The magdalenian sites of the Les Eyzies area in southern France contain fossil shells which come from geological deposits 300 km to the north and marine mollusca that originated from the Atlantic (Bahn, 1977). Two fossil shells from the coast of East Anglia in England have been found in the Spy cave in Belgium at a date of 22 000 BP (Campbell, 1977). Many of these shells were used as ornaments or sewn onto clothing as decoration. These items point to the many links that existed in later palaeolithic Europe and which assisted in the successful adaptation of small, scattered populations to a harsh northern continent.

of a distinctive raw material from the Holy Cross mountains in Poland during the late glacial. This chocolate-coloured flint has been found in sites that lie many hundreds of kilometres away from the

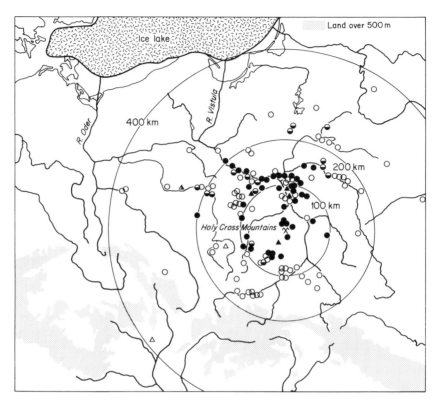

Fig. 3.18   Distribution of tools made of chocolate-coloured flint from the Holy Cross mountains of central Poland (after Schild, 1976). This was more extensive during the late Dryas cold phase, when tools typical of the tanged point assemblages of the European plain were used, than in the Allerød interstadial, when the plain was forested and Federmesser assemblages were common. Circles: tanged point assemblages; triangles: Federmesser assemblages; open symbols: sites where some tools were present; half-filled symbols: sites with many tools; filled symbols: sites where such tools outnumber others.

Social Evolution

The appearance of these elements — burials, display, painted caves, raw material transfers — after 35 000 BP all strongly suggest some major changes in palaeolithic adaptations. Other changes in the upper palaeolithic package have been listed by Mellars (1973) and discussed by White (1982). These include, for southwest France, an increase both in the number and size, as measured by area covered, of upper palaeolithic sites when compared with those from the middle palaeolithic. From this it has been inferred that there was a population increase in this region during the upper palaeolithic. This view is supported by Klein

(1973, pp.121–6) in his review of upper and middle palaeolithic material from the Ukraine. He also notes that in this area the settlement evidence indicates that upper palaeolithic populations were less nomadic than those of the middle palaeolithic.

However, elsewhere in Europe, this increase in the number of sites in the early upper palaeolithic is not apparent (Hahn, 1977; Gamble, 1983b; Otte, 1981). This is particularly so for the early upper palaeolithic in central and eastern Europe which would have been faced with very severe glacial conditions from 30 000 to 20 000 BP as the ice sheets advanced. The most striking feature, however, is that there should be occupation at all in these areas during such extreme conditions. The settlement evidence from the middle palaeolithic (Gamble 1983b) points to the abandon-

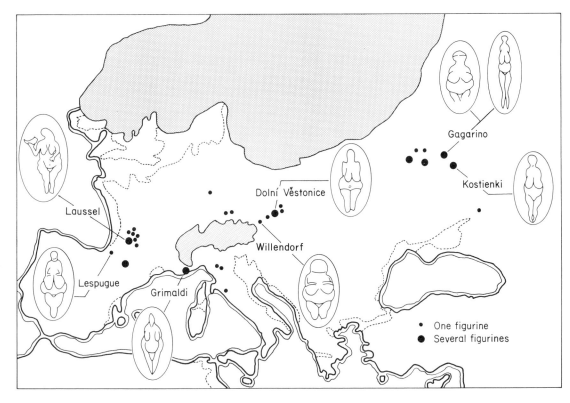

Fig. 3.19   Distribution of 'venus' figurines and bas-relief carvings.

ment of these same regions by neanderthal groups when conditions deteriorated in the early last glacial. In other words, the upper palaeolithic populations of central and eastern Europe had solved some of the problems connected with exploiting ecologically specialized environments caught in the grip of the last ice age.

What can account for this? In the last chapter we saw that it is no longer possible to explain away the differences by claiming that Crô Magnon populations were in some way more intelligent than neanderthalers and thus had better adaptations. Neither is it possible to say that someone came up with the idea of blade and bone technology or even sewn clothing and this lucky break made everything else possible. While developments in technology were no doubt required, this would have depended on the appropriate stimulus from other areas of the cultural system. Technology by itself could not lead the way.

Klein (1973) has pointed out that any explanation of the transition is unlikely to rest with a single cause. Instead he argues for a complex feedback between biological, environmental and cultural factors—in other words, factors that are both internal and external to palaeolithic adaptations. The former would include population growth and the development of new social institutions while the latter takes into account the changing climate and resources that might place stress upon the cultural system and so precipitate change. This has been examined for the transition in the Levant by S. Binford (1968b). The animal bone assemblages from sites in this region suggest a move from generalized hunting of a wide array of animals to the selective concentration upon fewer species between the middle and upper palaeolithic. This she believes would lead to pressure on human groups to form larger aggregations in order to utilize the large amounts of meat obtained as a result of intercept hunting during the migration of herds of wild cattle and fallow deer. These bigger populations would need new ways of integrating personnel and establishing corporate identity, which is reflected in the display items left in the graves. Harrold (1980) agrees that the upper palaeolithic burials indicate a greater number of social distinctions and these reflect the more complex mechanisms of social integration that were now required. In Binford's terms the changes in ecology applied selective pressure to many parts of the cultural system. As a result of these environmental changes, social organization underwent a dramatic transformation. The small-sized societies of the middle palaeolithic were thus replaced by larger systems which saw the widespread exchange of marriage partners as one element in establishing ties among a larger regional human population.

This view suggests that we look at palaeolithic society as a web of alliances (Bender, 1978, 1981; Gamble, 1982) which defined many different types of social relationships and which in turn specified how the environment was to be exploited and how groups were to be integrated into social units of different size.

One purpose of these widespread alliance networks would be to provide a safety net for dispersed populations living at low densities in such high-risk environments as those which characterized Europe after 30 000 BP (Gamble, 1983b). The ties established through kinship, the exchange of marriage partners, trade and many other means gave any individual or local group a form of insurance policy so that if and when resources failed in their area they had access to alternative hunting grounds and the resources they contained (Burch and Correll, 1972). These links would have been an essential component for any cultural adaptation faced with the climatic conditions and changes in resources in glacial Europe. They would have been as necessary for a successful long term adaptation as skin clothing and other technological items that kept out the cold.

We cannot, of course, dig up a palaeolithic society or network of alliances since these are merely conceptual devices which help us in exploring the problem of change. What we can recover are some measures, provided by material culture, of how these networks varied through time.

These safety nets could only be maintained with some extra cost to the means by which information about personnel, groups and resources was exchanged and processed. One consequence of a larger society would be defining the social ties and relationships between an increased number of people so that, instead of meetings and visits breaking down into conflict, they actually resulted in resources being made available and the insurance policy being cashed. With more people to account for, there was clearly a need to develop systems of information exchange which were rapid, easy to interpret and which could integrate scattered regional populations whose members met infrequently.

The solution appears to have been to utilize the information content that is inherent in all material culture and which is expressed symbolically in the shapes and forms of all objects (Conkey, 1978; Wobst, 1977; Sackett, 1982). For example, by adhering to a set of stylistic rules for the design of the Venus figurines, these objects then possessed the ability to signal information that could be used in this process of integrating population at a very extensive spatial scale. We do not understand the precise content of the visual message contained in these little figurines but we can see why at this time of climatic severity these similar-looking objects appear over such large areas of the continent (Fig. 3.19). Dress, ornament, painted huts and stone tools all served as mediums for visual display which assisted in the all-important flow of information about who people were, how to behave towards them and, as a by-product of such meetings, to discover information about the disposition of mobile animals and other critical resources. The key to success on the steppe-tundras of Europe was to gather information in order to be able to plan ahead and devise the best schedule to position personnel to resources. The alliance networks provided the framework along which this information travelled and the explosion in the obvious use of this potential of material culture during the upper palaeolithic is understandably dramatic.

We should, however, be quite clear about one point. It was not developments in the way information could be exchanged that made it possible to inhabit the high risk environments of the last glaciation. These developments were required by changes in the way social relationships, the pattern of alliances, were constituted. It was this framework which specified how dispersed populations were to be integrated and how the social system could function.

By implication the system of alliances that characterized neanderthal society did not specify such relationships under this sort of extreme environmental circumstances. As a result, the selective pressures of the environment led to the abandonment of areas when climate deteriorated and their recolonization only when conditions improved.

Under different environmental and social conditions there may be a need to restrict access to resources contained within the territory of a single group. The fixed locations of cave art and the variety of local painting styles associated with them point to the possible role of these developments as symbolic markers within a very complex social mosaic during the late upper palaeolithic. Jochim (1983) has suggested that the concentration of late glacial cave art in south-west France and Cantabria may reflect a set of advantageous environmental conditions which only occurred at that time. This made it possible for groups in these areas to intensify their exploitation strategies by utilizing the abundant salmon fish runs as well as migrating herds of reindeer and red deer. The tighter packing of population to resources would require the stricter definition of territories and the resources they contained. Cave art sites formed the focus for this emerging group identity and territorial commitment. As Conkey (1978) has pointed out, these upper palaeolithic populations appear to be coping with adaptational stress, both social and environmental, by participating in certain classes of symbolic behaviour. This is the inference placed upon the appearance of art, ornament and other features of the upper palaeolithic package which were governed by rules embodied in stylistic outcomes.

The difference between the middle and upper palaeolithic can therefore be viewed as necessary developments in material culture related to a fundamental restructuring in the pattern of alliances. These networks specified how ecologically specialized environments were to be exploited. The material culture which we recover is a symbol of the variety of tactics (unique to man) which are utilized in the process of cultural adaptation. Why the pattern of alliances changed to one of dominance over the environment is open to question (Ingold, 1981). Increasing competition for resources which define social position such as prestige goods or social knowledge (Bender, 1978), and population growth

leading to adaptational stress as more people have to be accounted for (Conkey, 1978; Jochim, 1983), are possible causes for this major shift. What is clear is that the results of these shifts led to an increase in the spatial and demographic size of population units which regularly interacted. This also involved the expansion of population above the Arctic circle and into the environments of eastern Siberia and so into the New World. The change to symbolically organized behaviour brought changes in the status and roles of individuals between groups and societies. When these developments in society were finally faced with the dramatic upturn in climatic conditions at 10 000 BP, the entire global system of hunters and gatherers was poised for some further fundamental changes in the forms of society and the means of obtaining a livelihood from the environment.

SUGGESTIONS FOR FURTHER READING

A model for investigating aspects of subsistence behaviour among hunters and gatherers and backed up by a case study is provided by M. A. Jochim, *Hunter Gatherer Settlement and Subsistence.* Palaeolithic site location and the reconstruction of last glacial environments forms a significant part of C. Vita-Finzi, *Archaeological Sites in their Setting.* Ethnoarchaeological approaches to the study of hunters and gatherers and the relevance of such observations to palaeolithic studies are presented in contrasting styles by R. A. Gould, *Living Archaeology* and L. R. Binford, *Bones: Ancient Men and Modern Myths.* An informative survey of modern hunters from a number of contrasted environments and social settings is M. G. Bicchieri, *Hunters and Gatherers Today.*

The literature on palaeolithic art is very extensive. For a critical account of the main theories, see P. J. Ucko and A. Rosenfeld, *Palaeolithic Cave Art*; and a more recent general treatment by E. Hadingham, *Secrets of the Ice Age.* Case studies which deal with palaeolithic adaptations at a regional scale can be found in E. S. Higgs (ed.), *Palaeoeconomy*, in R. G. Klein's synthesis, *Ice Age Hunters of the Ukraine*, and G. N. Bailey (ed.), *Hunter-gatherer Economy in Prehistoric Europe*, where questions of culture change are also discussed.

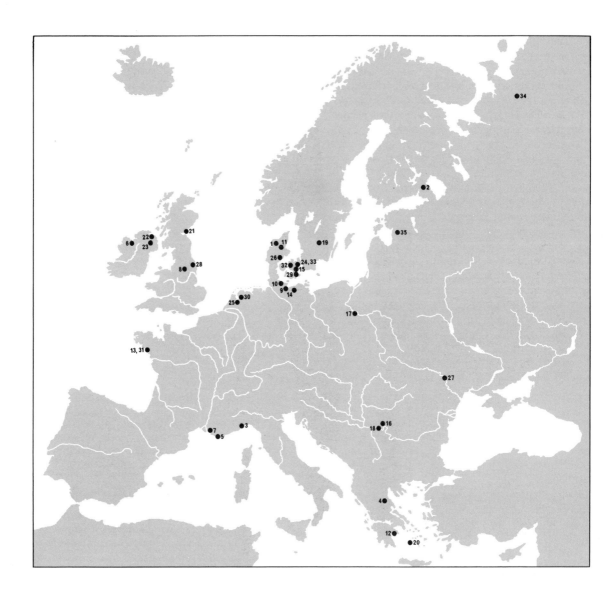

Fig. 4.1   Principal sites mentioned in Chapter 4. 1 Aggersund. 2 Antrea. 3 Arene Candide. 4 Argissa. 5 Cap Ragnon. 6 Carrowmore. 7 Châteauneuf-les-Martigues. 8 Deepcar. 9 Duvensee. 10 Ellerbek. 11 Ertebølle. 12 Franchthi cave. 13 Hoëdic. 14 Hohen Viecheln. 15 Holmegaard. 16 Icoana. 17 Janislawice. 18 Lepenski Vir. 19 Loshult. 20 Melos. 21 Morton. 22 Mount Sandel. 23 Newferry. 24 Ølby Lyng. 25 Pesse. 26 Ringkloster. 27 Soroki. 28 Star Carr. 29 Svaerdborg. 30 Swifterbant. 31 Téviec. 32 Ulkestrup. 33 Vedbaek. 34 Wis. 35 Zvejnieki.

4

Post-glacial Developments: Hunters, Gatherers and Beyond

The ninth millennium BC saw the culmination of profound environmental changes which altered the conditions in which well-established communities of late-glacial hunters had flourished and their way of life ended. Economic and social adaptations to altered landscapes, higher temperatures, spreading forest and differently composed fauna were numerous and profound. A wide range of resources — large forest ungulates, plant food, birds, fish, sea mammals, and shellfish — was exploited and control over them may even merit the label of food production. Settlement was largely mobile but permanent bases may have developed, and though often small, communities need not necessarily be viewed as simple or autonomous; the development of cemeteries and long-range exchange of artifacts may point to complex social relations. Though replaced by a cereal-based economy probably of non-European origin from the seventh to fifth millennia BC — of an immense importance which later chapters demonstrate — this way of life was no mere interlude since it may have foreshadowed later developments, created some of the conditions in which they were acceptable and helped to control the rate at which they were accepted. The contrast between the two ways of life may be one of degree rather than of kind, and this chapter avoids a rigid chronological treatment in discussing the extent of indigenous European post-glacial adaptations.

THE SETTING

The end of the glacial period is conventionally dated by the beginning of the final retreat of the main Scandinavian ice sheet. According to sediment or varve chronology, this was *c.* 8300 BC. This point is often used as a convenient marker of environmental and indeed other sorts of change. In discussing these, however, one must bear clearly in mind that environmental change, involving temperature rise, ice retreat, vegetational and faunal change and so on, had in fact begun several millennia previously. In Denmark for example forest cover, forest fauna and forest hunters flourished in warmer phases of the final glacial period. The ninth millennium BC must therefore be seen as the point after which environmental fluctuations on the previous scale ceased, not the beginning of entirely novel conditions. The dominant factor in post-glacial environmental change (Fig.4.2) was a rise in temperature, rapid in northern though less marked in southern Europe. In one study on Gotland in the Baltic (Mörner and Wallin, 1977), it was found that summer temperature, after fluctuating in the final millennia of the late-glacial period, rose rapidly from the ninth millennium BC to reach present-day levels by the eighth and its peak (1·5°–2·0°C higher than today) by the fifth. A major result was the final and rapid melting of ice sheets in northern Europe. As they retreated, human settlement expanded into such newly available areas as northern Ireland, Scotland, the Baltic area and Scandinavia; in the latter case, this was partly to maintain the previous way of life based on reindeer following, but elsewhere to take advantage of new land. A rise in sea level due to the melting of the ice led to extensive land loss, as in the North Sea basin which had gained roughly its present coastline by the seventh millennium. The complementary effect of a rise in the level of land now relieved of the weight of ice can be seen in the complicated history of the Baltic, which changed from open water to land-locked lake around 7500 BC after land rise and then back to open water by 5000 BC as sea-level continued to rise. Vegetation spread as temperature (and humidity) rose, and forest replaced open or sparsely wooded tundra in northern Europe, and scrub or open woodland in southern Europe, at varying rates (Watts, 1980). Forest composition changed in a succession in northern and central

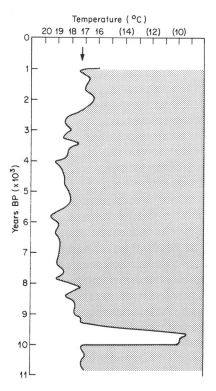

Fig. 4.2   A curve for mean summer temperature through the late-glacial and post-glacial period, established from oxygen isotope analysis of lake sediments on Gotland in the Baltic (after Mörner and Wallin, 1977).

Europe from birch, through pine and hazel, to climax 'mixed oak' by the sixth millennium. In more southerly Europe there was a change to a dominant oak component by roughly the same time, with the possible exception of the more open steppe environment of the southern USSR. The labels of these stages in north-west Europe (Table 4.1) have been applied elsewhere, though the changes were neither synchronous nor uniform. The glacial megafauna disappeared, reindeer herds moved north to follow cold conditions, and the fauna of forested Europe was dominated by aurochs or native cattle, red deer, roe deer and pigs. In the north, elk persisted for a while, and in the south ibex, and perhaps sheep

Table 4.1 *Late pleistocene and holocene climatic and vegetational periods and sea-level stages of the Baltic Sea in northern Europe (after Milisauskas, 1978).*

Name of period	Dates (BC)	Dominant vegetation	Climate	Sea level stages of the Baltic Sea	
Subatlantic	After 300	Beech	Maritime		
Subboreal	3000–300	Oak, beech	More continental	Present Baltic Sea	2000 BC
Atlantic	6200–3000	Oak, elm	Warmer and maritime	Litorina Sea	5500 BC
Boreal	7500–6200	Hazel, pine, oak	Warmer and continental	Ancylus Lake	
Preboreal	8300–7500	Birch, pine	Warm continental		7800 BC
				Yoldia Sea	8300 BC
Younger Dryas	8900–8300	Forest tundra	Arctic		
Allerød	9800–8900	Birch, pine	Temperate continental	Baltic Ice Lake	
Older Dryas	10 100–9800	Tundra	Arctic		
Bølling	10 800–10 100	Birch parkland	Subarctic		
Oldest Dryas	Before 10 800	Tundra	Arctic		

and goats, though their indigenous status is doubted.

These different aspects of the ecosystem, which changed throughout the period, should always be viewed together. For example, vegetation growth in lakes and ponds formed in morainic landscapes caused peat growth which led to their transformation first to fens then to drier land; these changes for increased, then reduced, animal and plant life for human exploitation (e.g. Welinder, 1978). Such changes may have been more obvious in northern Europe but should be considered everywhere. Attention has sometimes been paid to the effects on human adaptation of the initial changes towards a forested environment, presenting it as a disadvantageous situation, but the advantages of new staples such as plants with edible seeds or roots and nut and fruit bearing trees should not be minimized. On the other hand the long term trend to thicker forest cover, which reduced the variety and density of both plant and animal food resources, may have been more serious, and required more radical adaptations. This chapter follows indigenous adaptations into this situation, as far as the seventh millennium in southern Europe and the fifth in the north.

CHRONOLOGY AND CULTURAL SEQUENCES

Artifacts of flint and to a lesser extent of other stone are the dominant surviving items on most sites of this period, depressingly so in comparison with those favoured sites, especially in north-west Europe, where bone, antler, wooden and other organic artifacts are also preserved (e.g. Star Carr, Clark, 1954; Hohen Viecheln, Schuldt, 1961). Such abundant material has been and remains difficult to order chronologically (Fig.4.3), while the basic need for such a sequence is more important than ever as research moves on to wider interests. Long vertical stratigraphies are everywhere rare; Newferry in northern Ireland (Woodman, 1977) is not in an area which helps with the construction of wide regional artifactual sequences, though the Mediterranean with several sequences such as at Arene Candide in northern Italy (Cardini, 1946) is better served. Environmental information derived from lake sediments, shorelines or pollen analysis which can help to date a site relatively or absolutely is most abundant in northern Europe (but regional vegetational sequences may not be synchronous), but

Phase Date bc 9000	Oldest 8000	Old 7000	Middle 5900 6700	Late 4500 5300
Region BC				
Southern Belgium	Ahrensburgian	Limburgian	Limburgian	Limburgian
Northern France	Les Blanchères Pretardenoisian	Tardenoisian Kerjouanno	Tardenoisian Grotte de l'Ouest	Northern Tardenoisian Southern Tardenoisian Belloy Retzian
South-western France	Laborian	Sauveterrian	Sauveterrian	Sauveterrian
Languedoc		Grottes des Causses	Grottes des Causses Montclusian	Grottes des Causses Late Montclusian
Provence	Valorguian	Montadian	Montadian	Castelnovian
North-western Switzerland		Birsmattian	Birsmattian	Birsmattian

Fig. 4.3   *Part of Rozoy's four-stage arrangement of local cultural development in France and neighbouring areas from the ninth to fifth millennium. The names generally mark key sites and important microlith styles. There is no generally agreed scheme of this kind for Europe as a whole.*

even the sequence of so well endowed an area as Denmark was incomplete until after the last war, though it is now secure. Extrapolation from better dated areas or sites may ignore regional variation in the rate of adoption of style changes or be simply irrelevant, a particular problem for eastern Europe where there was greater continuity with late-glacial traditions than elsewhere. Radiocarbon dating clearly offers the greatest hope for reliable chronologies across Europe, but has so far been applied most in north-west Europe where other aids are available — and hardly at all in eastern Europe, where they are not (e.g. Tringham, 1973, p. 556).

Amongst flint assemblages, projectile points or insets are the most diagnostic items, and there were several fashions which are of use in dating. Other tools, as well as the techniques to produce them, also deserve consideration (Fig.4.4). There was in most areas a progressive modification of late-glacial traditions; eastern Europe stands out as an exception because of the duration of its 'epigravettian'

assemblages. The labels 'mesolithic' and 'epipalaeolithic' have thus been variously used for such differing cases (with the additional connotation of accompanying extreme environmental change for 'the mesolithic'). The production of small flint blades and of flint axes, adzes and picks was of wide importance, while ground stone axes were used in parts of northern and western Europe. Projectile points become initially smaller (microliths) than their late-glacial ancestors, as in the north European Maglemose complex, or the Azilian industry of south France and Spain though once again the reduction in size can be traced back to the late-glacial period. A further widespread fashion in western Europe in the eighth millennium was the addition of smaller, more geometric, 'Sauveterrian' microliths — probably both points and insets; these were followed in the seventh millennium by 'trapeze-shaped' 'Tardenoisian' microliths produced on regular narrow blades — in reality chisel-ended and piercing points and sharp cutting insets.

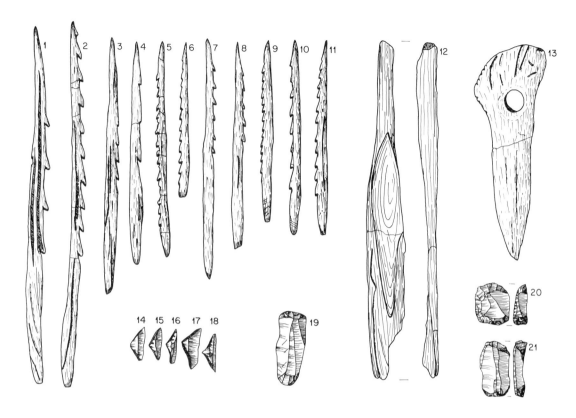

Fig. 4.4 A selection of material culture from Star Carr, Yorkshire, England: barbed antler points (1–11), wooden implement, possibly paddle (12), antler mattock (13), flint microliths for arrow tips or barbs (14–18), flint scrapers (19–21) (after Clark 1954). Scale 1–11, 13 at 1:4, 12 at 1:6, 14–21 at 2:5.

Regional exceptions abound: Britain was outside the fashion for 'blade and trapeze' industries, Denmark largely outside the 'Sauveterrian' orbit. Wide-ranging schemes such as those of Kozłowski (1973) may tend to overemphasize superficial inter-regional similarities, but detailed variation is more interesting from the point of view of social territories, discussed below. Since most sites are represented by surface or unexcavated material, it is to be hoped that detailed typological studies (e.g. Rozoy, 1978) are combined with radiocarbon dating to produce further refinements in regional sequences. Such a need is compatible with another, to use flint assemblages for the functional and social analysis of all sites in an area. Nor should an understandable

obsession with projectile points, such as those preserved mounted in wooden shafts at various sites (e.g. Loshult, Sweden, Peterssen, 1951) and embedded in an aurochs' skeleton at Vig in Denmark (Hartz and Winge, 1906), encourage the assumption that hunting was the only way man came into contact with animals.

SUBSISTENCE

While there are clear indications in the late-glacial period that man was well adapted for more than mere survival in a range of conditions, the post-glacial period provides the first well-preserved examples in wood and other perishable organic materials of the skills available for active exploitation of and movement across the landscape. This is demonstrated by dug-out canoes (Pesse, Holland, van Zeist, 1957), sea-going skin-boats which may be indirectly inferred from the early colonization of northern Ireland, the Scottish Islands, or Melos in the Aegean, skis (Wis, USSR, Burow, 1973), self bows (Wis; Holmegaard, Denmark, Broholm 1931; available probably since the Ahrensburgian group of the late-glacial), seine-nets (Antrea, USSR, Clark, 1975) and birch bark containers (Star Carr, England, Clark, 1954). No less skill should be assumed for subsistence itself.

A varied post-glacial fauna was available for exploitation, as indicated above, and it is striking that a variety of species is typical of the faunal remains on most sites. Red deer and pig are found on sites across Europe but rarely does one species dominate. In the north, elk (until the onset of deciduous forest) and aurochs are frequent additions, in the south sheep and goat, and ibex and others occur in more mountainous southern regions.

Table 4.2 *Recorded population densities of various species in different habitats (after Bay-Petersen).*

Region	Hectares per animal
Red Deer	
Northwest Scotland	16
Dune Plantations, Denmark	20–25
Voronezh Reserve, USSR	36
Caucasus Reserve, USSR	100
Sikhote-Alin Reserve, USSR	140
Roe Deer	
Belovezhsk Nature Reserve	55–1000
Tuwinisch Nature Reserve, USSR	20–40
Pig	
Kazakhstan (maximum), USSR	16–20
Mongolia (maximum), USSR	25–33
Caucasus Reserve, USSR	125–250
Elk	
Ontario — early regrowth of woodland	62
plus 16–30 years	125
plus 30–45 years	250
European Russia — mixed forest	1000–1200
coniferous forest	1400

When specialization is indicated, it was not the largest species that were usually involved. Two excavated Danish sites are therefore unusual; pig and roe deer were found to dominate at the Maglemosian site of Svaerdborg I (Friis Johansen, 1919), and pig at the Ertebølle site of Ringkloster (74%, Andersen, 1975). The latter may have been a specialized winter extraction camp. Ireland, with its impoverished post-glacial fauna lacking aurochs, elk and roe deer, and with perhaps few red deer, is an interesting exception to prove the rule, while the dominance of elk in east Baltic sites (Clark, 1975) may again reflect a restricted local fauna. Such variety represented security. Each species must have differed in its social behaviour (red deer and aurochs were probably more 'social' and grouped in bigger herds than elk, pig or roe), its habitat, mobility and density (which is difficult to calculate for the ecological conditions of the time), as well as its meat yield (Tables 4.2, 4.3; Fig.4.5). The last factor is more important than the number of individuals represented on a site; at Star Carr, England (Clark, 1954) for example, fewer elk or aurochs were found than red deer (and the site has often been interpreted in terms primarily of deer exploitation), but they may have contributed almost as much meat. The substantial size of the early post-glacial fauna is notable; a red deer stag at 165 kg clean carcase weight could have fed a family of five for over thirty days. Subsidiary products should not be ignored, such as skins, bone and antler for tools, and even teeth for pendants, or in the case of beaver for scraping tools (e.g. Hohen Viecheln, western Germany, Schuldt, 1961). Ringkloster on Jutland shows specialized exploitation of marten, presumably for furs (Anderson, 1975).

It is likely that hunting was a widespread means of cropping these resources, as projectiles in animal skeletons (as at Vig, mentioned above) or healed wounds (Noe Nygaard, 1974) suggest. The possible extinction of the aurochs on Zealand by the beginning of the Atlantic period (Degerbøl and Fredskild, 1970) is another indication of hunting, though perhaps in connection with habitat change unfavourable to the species. The seasonal pattern of occupation inferred from the settlement of most regions (Fig.4.6), though perhaps less accentuated in the Mediterranean, may also support the hunting hypothesis. Examples of seasonally occupied sites abound in the literature, though the evidence is rarely direct and often negative

Table 4.3 Relative frequencies of different ungulate species in Danish Mesolithic sites, calculated as percentages of the total ungulate fauna (after Bay-Petersen). The figures are based on either the minimum numbers of individuals (A) or total numbers of specimens (B) identified. Owing to certain ambiguities in the literature, all of the figures should be regarded as approximate.

	Red Deer	Roe Deer	Pig	Aurochs	Elk	Sample size
Boreal						
Svaerdborg	12·0	31·0	38·0	7·0	12·0	100(A)
	12·6	23·1	34·1	8·6	21·6	880(B)
Holmegaard	30·8	24·6	33·8	4·6	6·2	65(A)
Atlantic						
Dyrholmen	34·3	25·4	32·8	6·0	1·5	67(A)
	35·2	14·8	38·8	8·5	2·7	1442(B)
Ertebølle	17·1	43·4	35·5	1·3	2·6	76(A)
Norslund	25·9	13·1	32·6	27·6	0·8	659(B)
Ringkloster	15·8	2·2	74·0	7·3	0·6	1445(B)
Ølby Lyng	58·0	29·6	12·3	—	—	1114(B)

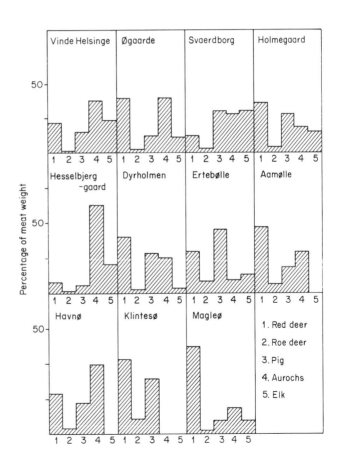

Fig. 4.5 The contribution of different ungulates to the meat diet at Danish Mesolithic sites, assuming male red deer = 220 kg, roe deer = 19, pig = 166, aurochs = 800, elk = 500 (after Bay-Petersen, 1978).

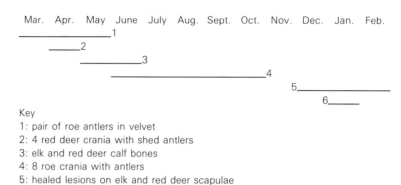

Fig. 4.6   Summary diagram of evidence for seasonal activity at Star Carr (after Pitts, 1979).

or inferential (and is often based on out-dated techniques of recovery in excavation). It has been suggested that Star Carr was a winter site on the basis of unshed red deer and elk antlers, but unshed roe deer antler, which, unlike the others, is carried for more of the summer, indicates a more varied occupation. The unpublished site of Holmegaard V on Zealand, which is on the edge of a marsh, is seen as a winter site by comparison with its neighbours further into the marsh, which are interpreted as summer sites. Site V is bigger than its neighbours, and lacks the pike bones and barbed points found on them. Upland sites provide firmer examples of non-winter occupation, as on the Pennines of England, and small sites everywhere seen as 'extraction camps' (discussed below) suggest transient occupation. Such movement would be ecologically sound, in order to exploit the seasonally most abundant resources — not always animals of course — and to follow some species such as red deer which in modern conditions tend to move their territory according to the season. But such movement would imply a lack of control over the animals' own movement, necessitating cropping by hunting. Large-scale game drives may have been as or more important than individual stalks; widespread flint scatters on the hills of central England have been seen as the remains of just such communal activity (R. Jacobi, 1978). But practice must have varied to suit local topography and vegetation, and to minimize game disturbance in these conditions. The presence of domesticated dog has been claimed on early post-glacial sites such as

Star Carr, on the basis of morphological changes in the jaw. Dogs would have aided hunting of all kinds, though similar use in earlier periods is hardly disproved by these criteria. (Dogs, or wolves, were probably also exploited for their fur, and their meat, since their bones appear to be treated or preserved no differently to those of other species.)

It is unlikely, however, that hunting was a random or wholly opportunistic process. Danish sites provide perhaps the best series of faunal remains from a restricted area in Europe, and show concentration on older rather than younger animals (Bay-Petersen, 1978; Fig.4.7). A similar pattern and an emphasis on males can be seen in individual sites elsewhere, again such as Star Carr. Some problems should be pointed out, such as the fact that even the Danish samples are rather small. There is little control now over the recovery techniques employed, and it has been shown how small bones escape excavation surprisingly easily (Payne, 1972). Nor is there control over the processes by which bones were deposited on a site and remained there (Binford and Bertram, 1977). Binford has distinguished between food management and herd management, the former producing similar faunal patterns to the latter. Experimental random hunting is also said to produce structured faunal samples (Wilkinson, 1976). But at face value the Danish sites do support a commonly held hypothesis, that hunting was a carefully controlled activity, designed to extract particularly the excess part of a herd not required for breeding, and probably with the minimum of disturbance.

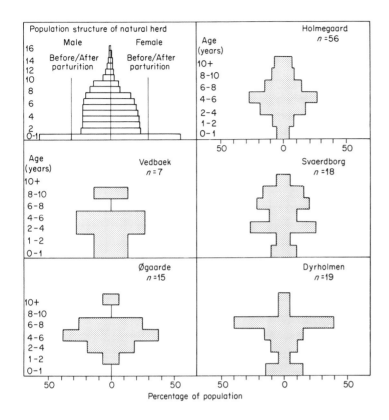

Fig. 4.7 Age distribution of (a) red deer herd in nature (b) red deer represented on Danish mesolithic sites by lower jawbones (after Bay-Petersen, 1978).

Other man-animal relationships may however be envisaged (see box on p.98), involving greater control or closer contact. The probable use of ivy as a fodder plant on sites in southern England is suggestive (Dimbleby and Simmons, 1974), though it could also have been used as a lure. Deliberate clearances seen in pollen diagrams in various parts of England (Simmons, 1975) would have had the effect of creating enriched, resprouting vegetation (Mellars, 1976a), attractive to all species, especially deer. Such a policy would be compatible with structured hunting, but also with greater control of herd movement, blurring the distinction between 'hunting' and other forms of exploitation. Particularly as forests developed towards their vegetational climax state, such a policy could have created mutual interdependence between man and animal. Closer control even than this, involving periodic corralling or herd separation for culling purposes, can hardly be disproved, and can be compared with some modern ranching practices for free-range cattle or sheep. Such practices are hardly likely to have been uniform. The English evidence includes also the case of the southern Pennines where the upland vegetation may have been deliberately suppressed on a greater scale than envisaged in the lowlands (Jacobi et al., 1976). Unfortunately, animal bone is rarely preserved on English sites. The abundant pollen analyses of Denmark have not apparently shown the same kind of clearances, though the optimal size might well escape detection. The valley and loess soils of eastern Europe may have had little early post-glacial settlement (Tringham, 1973), suggesting perhaps an inability to cope with climax vegetation.

Control of animal breeding is also hard to disprove, since morphological criteria can be ambiguous or negative (Higgs and Jarman, 1972). The steady diminution in size of red deer in Italy since the late-glacial (Barker, 1976) suggests that the controlling factor was climate. On the basis of

MAN–ANIMAL RELATIONSHIPS

A great range of man–animal relationships can be envisaged in the post-glacial period. Game drives and selective breeding are extremes of forms of exploitation; others may lie in between such as loose herding or free-range ranching. It is in the case of most sites no easier to substantiate the hunting hypothesis directly than to deny the herding or breeding hypothesis, and the interpretation of faunal remains has been governed in large part by assumptions. Morphological criteria of 'domestication' are weak (Higgs and Jarman, 1972), and useless for grading degrees of control. The age and sex composition of cropped herds may produce greater insights though they too are subject to ambiguity. Few faunal assemblages have been excavated by proper recovery techniques and on- and off-site distortions are rarely allowed for. How is research then to proceed in this vital area? As many criteria as possible need to be tested against each other, on properly excavated samples. As well as this, areas rather than individual sites deserve greater consideration, to pick out overall trends. As much supporting evidence should be included as possible concerning other resources. Sophisticated plant use for example may have bypassed or delayed any necessity for close animal control, or vice versa. And if hypotheses have run ahead of data such a situation is healthy enough, if the need for problem-oriented research in favourable areas is adequately recognized.

morphological criteria, claims for selective breeding of pigs have been made at Soroki on the river Dniester and other sites in the Crimea and of sheep or goats at La Adam in coastal Romania and other sites in the region; both remain uncertain and disputed (Tringham, 1971). The increase in numbers of sheep and goats claimed at Châteauneuf-les-Martigues in the south of France from the seventh millennium onwards (Escalon de Fonton, 1967) could indicate a shift towards greater reliance on species which were, it is certain, later closely controlled; doubts remain about the chronology and indigenous status of the animals.

The situation is therefore uncertain. Hypotheses of close control cannot be rejected, and are increasingly attractive as the period continues. It can also be argued that selective hunting was sufficiently advantageous for other practices to be unnecessary, in that they would merely have increased the amount of human labour required. Knowledge of other resources and factors is also required, and details of these will be given before the potentially revealing transition to a cereal-based economy is discussed.

Ethnographic studies of modern 'hunter-gatherers' have shown that there is a positive correlation between increase in latitude and dependence on meat. It would be surprising if early post-glacial communities did not exploit the increasingly abundant plant resources of their environment, from the seed-bearing grasses of southern Europe to the root plants, fruits and nuts of temperate Europe. The direct evidence, however, is sparse. Hazel nuts are common, sometimes in pits or even layers. Water chestnuts were found on several north European sites, and yellow water lily at the Holmegaard sites. The residues of several edible species were recovered at Star Carr, including the latter and bog-bean, fat-hen and nettle. Raspberry was recorded at Newferry. There is no direct proof that such plants were deliberately collected and eaten. In southern Europe, the almonds, pistachio nuts, pears and vetch from the Franchthi Cave in the Argolid, Greece (Jacobsen, 1973), and the cereal or large grass pollen grains in coprolites from Icoana at the Danube gorges in Romania in the seventh millennium (Carciumaru, 1973) are indications of wider possibilities. Material equipment for plant preparation is everywhere rare. The potential is, nevertheless, far greater than the record suggests, and Clarke (1976) listed the numerous edible plant species available. Recovery techniques have not yet matched the problem, particularly for root plants. The technology of deliberate control is not complicated, from coppicing or clearance to encourage hazel, to transplanting root- and seed-bearing plants. The prominence of hazel in Boreal phases of pollen diagrams from Britain might be a clue to such control. Clarke has envisaged several varieties of horticulture and arboriculture in early post-glacial Europe, and the seasonal availability of the resources is no barrier to these possibilities, since many are storable. The succession to climax forest may have tended to diminish plant resources, providing strong motives for greater human intervention, and the almost universal adoption of cereals by the fifth millennium BC may have been a transformation of native experimentation or practice—a solution of indigenous problems—as much as the imposition of an exotic or wholly foreign subsistence economy.

Fish remains have not been systematically recovered but a wide range are represented in the record. Pike is a large lake fish present at such Danish sites as Holmegaard or Svaerdborg but absent from Star Carr, in which region the date of its immigration is uncertain. Salmon is a notable river fish in northern Europe, and occupation deposits beside the river Bann at Newferry presumably reflect a very long exploitation of it. Species of carp were important at the 'late' site of Lepenski Vir in the Danube gorges (Srejovic, 1972). Fish may have been a more important resource on the coast and several sites have a wide range of species—cod, haddock, turbot, sturgeon and salmonid at Morton, Scotland (Coles, 1971); tunny, grouper, wrasse, sargus, seabream, and others, at Cap Ragnon, southern France (Phillips, 1975), and small and large fish at the Franchthi Cave, Greece (Jacobsen, 1973). The largest fish were probably caught out at sea in deep water. Other sites have fewer fish and more of other marine resources such as both grey and Greenland seals, as at Ølby Lyng, Zealand (Petersen, 1970). It was suggested that fish found at Ølby Lyng had been dried since skull fragments did not match vertebrae in the correct proportions. Whale bone was also found at the inland site at Ringkloster, in Jutland, perhaps for winter occupation, as it is 15 km from the coast where the site of Flynderhage (perhaps for autumn occupation) was concerned with fishing and sealing, as well as large land animals. Porpoises and whales are, however, only occasional finds.

Sea level changes have destroyed many earlier post-glacial coastal sites. In the north, however, sealing was practised by the Ahrensburgian group, and there are also early post-glacial coastal sites (Clark, 1975). By the sixth and fifth millennia,

however, there may have been greater use of coastal resources. Ølby Lyng and Flynderhage are late sites of this sort. Another example of this possibility are the so-called coastal shell middens. They are found in such areas as Denmark, western Scotland, Brittany, or the Tagus estuary and have generally been seen as a sign of pressure on food resources. Preliminary indications from investigations at several middens on the small west Scottish island of Oronsay may bear this out, since four sites each represent a different season of the year (on the basis of fish ear-bone growth) and hence allow the possibility of year-round occupation of a small, rather exposed island (Mellars, 1978). This is not what a model of sophisticated seasonal resource use would suggest (e.g. Jochim, 1976).

Bird bones on many sites show another resource which was not neglected. Concentration on migratory swans at the winter coastal site of Aggersund in northern Jutland (Andersen, 1979), to the exclusion of other winter fowl, shows interesting specialization.

As with the diversity of faunal remains, so the overall diversity of resources exploited is striking, again designed presumably to obtain security of food supply. The balance between the various sources of food is unclear, and food remains at any one site cannot be expected to yield simple answers. Careful predictions have been made by setting probable resources against human requirements month by month through the year for part of the Upper Danube basin, within a framework of repeatable and safe levels of exploitation of each resource (Jochim, 1976). Such models may tend to be self-fulfilling but point the way to the enormous value which detailed ecological studies could have. They also raise the question again of how sophisticated early post-glacial subsistence was. It has been shown that a wide variety of resources was exploited, and animal exploitation even if limited to 'hunting' is likely to have been at the least selective and structured. The various resources each had periods of maximum abundance, and any purely predatory system of exploitation would try to crop each at this point. Given the nature of the animal and plant world, this would tend to involve human movement by the season to the point of greatest abundance of food, on a larger scale in areas of sharper relief, on a lesser scale with less relief or topographical diversity. Examples of transient or seasonally occupied sites in the archaeological record support this likelihood. By such carefully timed exploitation at chosen levels of repeatable cropping, communities could have been maintained in equilibrium in their environments, at densities of up to one person per 10 sq km (e.g. Jochim, 1976). Human population could have been stabilized at a safe level well below the maximum 'carrying capacity' of the given environment. According to this model, sophistication lies in the careful adaptation of human numbers and exploitation by a rather simple technology to available resources. The knowledge that such a system has, in recent situations, rather low labour inputs has been an added theoretical attraction.

Such a model is however essentially static, perhaps assuming equilibrium in the natural and human world, besides implying a rather passive human response to predetermined ecological conditions; the choice of the level of exploitation of each resource is also problematical, especially with fish and plants. It may therefore be preferable to suggest a more dynamic model which could begin to account for regional variability and for long-term change, while still recognizing the value of the alternative model. According to this, the preferred model here, the changing post-glacial environment is of considerable importance and provides an element of inbuilt instability. The loss of the North Sea basin, perhaps previously a vast resource of plants, fish and fowl, the silting up of lakes and ponds, the crowding out of nut-bearing hazels from climax forests, the susceptibility of species with probable low density, such as the aurochs, to over-hunting in finite areas are all examples of the potential consequences of this environmental change, which could have required positive human readaptations. Even without this long-term environmental instability, it is uncertain whether population *was* at this period stabilized below carrying capacity, particularly in the early post-glacial period as animal and plant resources increased in abundance, and even a very low rate of population increase would be serious in time (Meiklejohn, 1978).

Human choice cannot be discounted either. Intenser levels of exploitation may have been achieved, or aimed at, to satisfy group or individual needs for status through the abundant provision of food (Bender, 1978), or to allow a more sedentary existence. In such a model therefore there would

have been a need through time to readapt to changing conditions, to use all available resources and to maintain or increase returns by achieving greater control over them. Sophistication in subsistence would then lie not in the equilibrium achieved but in the varieties of control established over plant and animal resources, hardly necessary in a state of balance but vital in a changing situation. The final post-glacial adaptation, the adoption of a cereal- and animal-based economy, though by general agreement originally derived from outside Europe, could then be seen in European terms as in many ways a logical solution to indigenous problems. The division of Europe from other areas is anyway arbitrary and similar processes can be envisaged in the Near East. But the fact that the ultimately successful form of food production was adopted from outside does not detract from the possibility that native forms of food production were in the process of being developed. If no clear choice is possible yet between the competing possibilities, at least an exciting stage of research lies ahead. In the interim, the process of transition to a cereal-based economy may briefly be surveyed for the clues it may provide from region to region to the previous state of subsistence. Any such attempt may be subject to serious alteration as the quality of recovery improves in the future.

New resources were introduced or spread along three main axes into Europe according to available data—from Greece and the Balkans to the northwest, westwards through the Mediterranean, and eastwards of the Carpathians on to the steppes beyond. Part of the process is likely to have been the result of colonization by intrusive groups or communities, and is discussed further in the next chapter (see Fig.5.7). Part, however, seems to have been the result of further adaptation by indigenous communities, and the rate at which it happened may therefore give some additional indications of the state of native economies. The establishment of mixed farming economies along most of the first axis, in Greece and the Balkans from the earlier seventh millennium and in central-western Europe by the late sixth is generally attributed to colonization. The apparent avoidance of alluvial and loess soils by native communities in the Balkans (Tringham, 1973) may reflect an inability to cope with climax forest; and at the Franchthi Cave the introduction of sheep, goats and cultivated cereals (emmer wheat and barley) and a shift from other previously used animals and large fish is apparently rapid, in the seventh millennium (Jacobsen, 1973; Payne, 1975). This shift, however, is not synchronous with the appearance of pottery here (similar to the 'aceramic Neolithic' sites of Thessaly like Argissa). Agnosticism about the extent of direct colonization (Dennell, 1978) is worth serious attention; wild barley and oats were recovered from the Franchthi cave from the eleventh millennium BC onwards and might be taken to reflect local experimentation in plant use. The very varied economy of the Körös culture in the Danube alluvial basin could be another clue to the possibility of native evolution; cereals in particular were adopted at a stage when the temperature was becoming increasingly favourable, and when the vegetational succession was reducing the edible plant and animal biomass. Further north in north-west Europe the situation is also unclear, but native adoption of new resources is probable in the Ertebølle–Ellerbek culture in the fifth millennium, and possible in other areas like Britain around the fringes of presumed primary colonization on the loess. Investigations at Swifterbant, Holland (van der Waals and Waterbolk, 1976) show native communities adding cereals to the seasonal exploitation of estuaries and the inner coastal zone. Cereal cultivation was extended to its limits in the Baltic area, but rather slowly and not as a major resource; Broadbent (1979) has observed in north-east Sweden that it was the success of sealing and fishing that made agriculture a viable additional minor resource.

In the west Mediterranean, direct agricultural colonization may be restricted to southern Italy from the earlier or mid-seventh millennium. Elsewhere the picture may be of gradual change by native communities. Pottery was early and widely adopted, though lithic traditions continued. Sheep and goat may have been introduced into the area only at this date (e.g. Lewthwaite, 1981), though this is disputed, and widely distributed by exchange, without substantial human population movement. Cereals were apparently not widely used till the later sixth or early fifth millennia BC, long after pottery and sheep and goats. The situation in inland northern Italy, where investigation has been good (Phillips, 1975) shows a range of practices and resources; deer remained important for a long time (Jarman, 1971). This may therefore reflect the relative stability of native economies, either less affected by sea level rise

or vegetation change than elsewhere or sufficiently well readapted on lines discussed above, and potentially able to draw on seed-bearing grasses as well as a diverse fauna, including even rabbit, fish, shells and the rest. By the argument presented earlier, shell middens in the Tagus estuary may reflect pressures, but unfortunately much of Iberia is poorly investigated. The better sequences from south French caves and other sites (Phillips, 1975) do support the process of slow transition, but recovery of plant remains seems to have been erratic.

To the east colonization is generally seen to have extended little past the Carpathians initially, from the later sixth millennium. Further east till the late fifth or early fourth millennium the Bug-Dniester culture seems to have possessed a stable economy, based either on the broad range of resources available or on the greater control of resources such as pig which claims for selective breeding suggest.

This analysis has raised serious problems with the data but at the very least the varying rate of adoption of new staples indicates that in many areas their success may have depended as much on local developments as on their own inherent superiority.

SETTLEMENT

The pattern and units of settlement from region to region have generally been seen as dependent on the major economic strategy practised within it, and a general model of mobility has dominated, now refined by the detailed studies by Jochim and others of the changing seasonal density, yield and accessibility of various resources. At a crude level of analysis, sites are certainly widespread in Europe as a whole, from coast to above 1000m in Switzerland. Gaps in this kind of distribution, as in eastern Europe or on the larger blocks of chalk downland in southern England, are relatively rare and can be explained within the ecological model. More detailed study is of course required, and even the best wide surveys, as in England (Wymer, 1977), raise uncomfortably the question of what is meant by a 'site', without extensive excavation. This factor greatly reduces the area with any reasonable number of well-investigated settlements. But detailed studies in areas such as Britain, the Low Countries,

Table 4.4 Approximate dimensions of some British Mesolithic sites, based on the observed distribution of stone implements and flaking debris (after Mellars, 1976b).

| | Dimensions | | Estimated | |
	Length	Breadth	total area	Structural features
Type I Settlements				
Dunford 'A'	2·4m	2·4m	4·5m²	?Roughly paved area
Broomhead '5'	4·5m	4·0m	14·9m²	Linear setting of five stake holes
Thorpe Common	5·6m	1·8m	8·4m²	Rock-shelter with limestone wall
Oakhanger VIII	4·2m	2·1m	8·8m²	
Type II Settlements				
Deepcar	7·5m	7·5m(?)	44·0m²	Sub-circular stone structure
Iping Common	7·5m(?)	7·5m(?)	44·0m²	Roughly circular area of stained sand
Oakhanger V	12·0m	11·0m	100·0m²	
Thatcham I	13·5m	12·0m	116·0m²	
Star Carr	16·5m	14·5m	184·0m²	Birchwood platform
Type III Settlements				
Morton	15·0m	>10·0m	>150·0m²	Multiple stake-hole arrangements
Selmeston	>100·0m	?	>2000m²	Multiple 'pit-dwellings'
Farnham	?	?	?20 000m²	Multiple 'pit-dwellings'

Table 4.5 Two types of British Mesolithic artifact assemblages (after Mellars, 1976b).

Site	Estimated area of site in square metres	Micro-liths %	Scrapers %	Burins %	Saws %	Axes/ adzes %	Cores %	Micro-burins %	Total essential tools
Type A assemblages									
Upland									
Broomhead 5	14·9	90·0	10·0	—	—	—	31·2	21·6	41
Dunford A	4·5	93·2	—	6·8	—	—	15·9	31·8	44
Lowland									
Thorpe Common	8·4	94·0	—	6·0	—	—	23·9	11·1	67
Iping Common	?44·0	90·8	8·4	0·8	—	—	46·2	24·1	119
Type B assemblages									
Upland									
Deepcar	44	59·6	32·5	7·0	0·9	—	14·9	150·0	114
Lowland									
Star Carr	195	27·0	35·4	36·3	0·4	0·8	31·8	10·9	920
Thatcham	116	57·0	25·8	11·4	3·8	2·0	53·0	25·3	500
Oakhanger V	100	46·1	37·9	0·04	16·0	0·04	25·4	27·0	2779
Morton	150	26·8	61·3	11·9	—	?	33·2	21·7	845
Farnham	?20 000	75·5	19·8	2·8	0·1	1·6	124·3	64·7	913
Selmeston	>2000	71·0	21·8	1·1	6·0	x	90·1	20·8	183

Denmark and parts of France, Italy and central Europe do support the kind of settlement model outlined. Indications of seasonal occupation are characteristic of well-investigated sites, though the problems of interpretation were noted above and the absolute rarity of proof of long-term or all-year occupation even on later sites (see p.131) should be stressed. This information can be joined with factors of location and environmental situation, variation in site size, and in on-site activities as reflected in flint assemblages and other artifacts, further to support the model. The balance of analysis tends to follow the conditions of preservation. The emphasis in Denmark, for example (Petersen, 1973), has been on location, with a range of coastal, lake or swamp and inland sites known, and on direct seasonal indicators

in the well preserved sites of such notable areas as Zealand, with Holmegaard and others to the fore. This may be partly contrasted with the much more detailed studies of site size and artifact composition in areas with poorer organic preservation such as England (Mellars, 1976b) or the Netherlands (Newell, 1973; Price, 1978), though location is not here ignored. Mellars found a range of site sizes, the smallest with the least number of artifacts and the fewest number of different types, usually projectile points, the largest with a converse situation; small sites were more typical of upland locations (Tables 4.4 and 4.5). A similar situation is evident in the Netherlands, though without differentiation according to relief (Fig.4.8).

A rough typology of settlements may be built up,

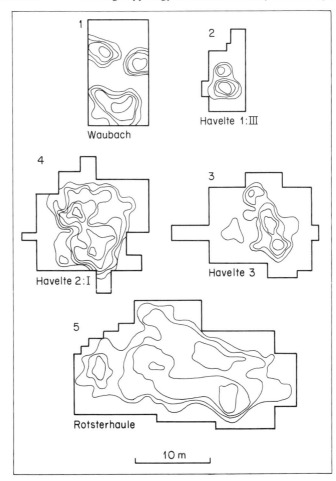

Fig. 4.8 Settlement types in the Dutch mesolithic. Artifact concentrations are represented by contours of the artifact density, at contour intervals of 10, 20, 40, 80, 160 and 320 artifacts per sq. m. (after Price, 1978).

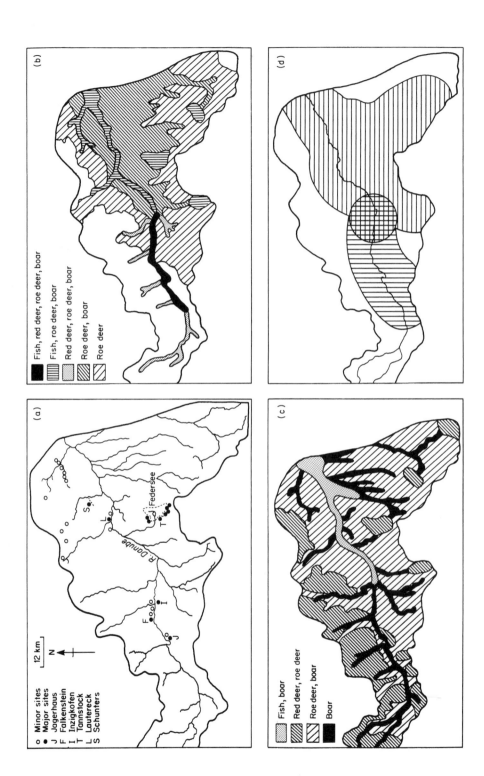

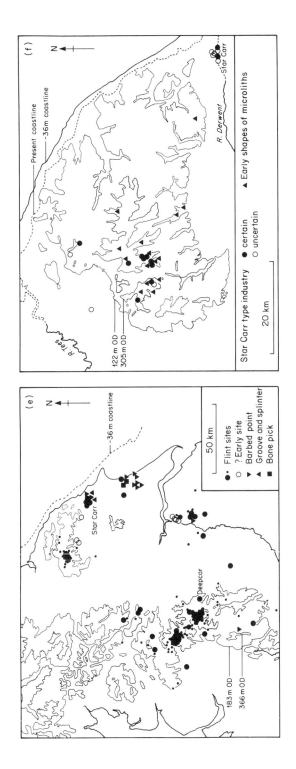

Fig. 4.9 Territory around Mesolithic sites. (a) Mesolithic sites in Jochim's study area. (b) Predicted primary resource distributions, January — March. (c) The same June — August. (d) Comparison of winter (vertical hatching) and summer (horizontal hatching) zones (after Jochim, 1976). (e) Distribution of early mesolithic sites in northern England. (f) Distribution of early mesolithic sites of the northern York Moors and environs (after Jacobi, 1978).

Star Carr type industry   ● certain   ▲ Early shapes of microliths
                           ○ uncertain

20 km

Present coastline
—36 m coastline
R. Derwent
Star Carr
122 m OD
305 m OD
R. Tees
N

Flint sites ●
? Early site ○
Barbed point ▼
Groove and splinter ▲
Bone pick ■

50 km

—36 m coastline
Star Carr
Deepcar
183 m OD
366 m OD
N

from smaller more transient 'hunting' or 'extraction' camps, to longer-stay larger 'bases' in areas of resources favourable to greater agglomerations of population. A regional example is the upper Danube basin, where an area of 6700 sq km was supposed to have supported a population of probably well under 700 or 800 people, moving according to resource availability, in smaller units in the winter, spring and autumn, but with greater nucleation possible in the summer for up to seventy-five to 100 people (Jochim, 1976) (Fig.4.9). Variation is likely from region to region, as suggested in Chapter 2. Individual sites may be hard to classify. Star Carr has been seen firstly as a winter lowland base camp, supporting perhaps four to five families exploiting deer and other animals and restocking supplies of harpoons and points (Clark, 1972), contrasting with summer upland hunting sites on the nearby north York Moors (R. Jacobi, 1978); secondly as a specialized site for hide tanning with summer as well as winter occupation (Pitts, 1979); and thirdly as a hunting stand used over long periods in different seasons (Andresen *et al.*, 1981).

The rather small size of most sites seems to give further support to the mobility model, and the largest sites are rare in well-studied areas such as Britain, Denmark and the Netherlands. The character of preserved structures also tends to support this, since traces of windbreaks, huts (sometimes in the form of elongated pits) and floors are few on most sites (e.g. Deepcar in the English Pennines, Radley and Mellars, 1964) and perhaps better known on 'base' camps, such as the series of carefully laid floors of brushwood and bark at sites like Star Carr, Holmegaard, Duvensee or Ulkestrup (Clark, 1975, p. 104). But even here there is ambiguity of evidence, since even the longer-stay bases with good organic preservation have not yielded much in the way of structures. Leather tents could have provided quite adequate, permanent shelter, and caves in southern Europe would suffice by themselves. Occasionally favourable circumstances suggest alternatives, as in the post- or stake-supported hut at Mount Sandel beside the river Bann in northern Ireland (Woodman, 1978) or the trapezoidal hut platforms with plastered floors, internal hearths and other fittings in successive levels at Lepenski Vir in

Yugoslavia (Srejovic, 1972). (Of sixth/fifth millennium date, this fishing village is of controversial status and some would postpone discussion of it till the next chapter.) Flimsiness of superstructure should probably therefore be discounted from discussion of the status of settlements (Fig.4.10).

The 'ecological functionalism' of the general model of mobile settlement should be recognized, however, and every allowance made for regional variation from the idealized picture. Even within the model, the scale of mobility may be greatly overdone, since on Zealand there are summer sites at Holmegaard as well as the larger single winter site; to the north in the Aamosen area there is also a range of sites, though further winter sites have not been suggested. On a local level, the Star Carr analysis suggested that an area of only 10-kilometre radius could support four families in winter, and resources would be more abundant in summer. Some areas may have had the greatest population concentration in summer, others however in winter bases, and there is a potential confusion of short-range movement within a favoured home range with larger scale seasonal mobility. Summer movement to uplands is certainly on a dramatic scale but — compare later transhumance — may not always have been a major or dominant part of economic strategy for all the population. Less mobility than the ecological model allows may have been possible from region to region and is certainly a trend to be looked for through time. Shell middens and other coastal sites could be seen in this light (contrast the 'stress' model discussed above), with all available resources being called upon to support permanent settlement. Greater control of resources than the ecological model allows would also support it, and the possibility of essentially *social* desires for sedentism might be supported by the analogy of the Natufian and other cultures in the Near East, where settled life preceded developed food production based on cereals and the rest. Social factors may have affected settlement in another way, periodic 'fusion' or agglomeration of population being replaced by 'fission' or dispersal in communities with loose internal social structure (Flannery, 1972). Whether this in its turn is an ecological safety device is unclear.

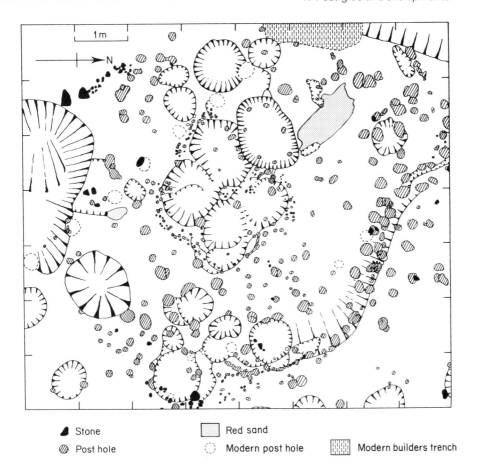

Stone

Post hole

Red sand

Modern post hole

Modern builders trench

Fig. 4.10   Plan of Mesolithic hut at Mount Sandel (upper site) (after Woodman, 1978).

SOCIETY

The assumption has been dominant that there was little differentiation within or between communities at this time and social organization like settlement has generally been seen as a variable dependent on economy. Within this viewpoint good reasons could be advanced for this—the conditions of the food quest with many resources on the hoof, high human mobility and low population density; the lack of storable wealth or fixed food sources; the lack of craft specialization and the wide sharing of

technological skills and the lack of fixed territories would all tend to deny the establishment of permanent differentiation. This view is both suggested and confirmed by relevant ethnographic studies which document details of food sharing for example, or the low labour input required for subsistence even in marginal areas, and the importance of kin groups. In evolutionary schemes (e.g. Service, 1962) the 'band' has been seen as an appropriate label for this level of organization, contrasted later with first tribes, then chiefdoms and ultimately states. The role of individual families and wider alliances has been outlined above in Chapter 3. A model of egalitarian society has therefore been widely applied, and allowance has been made only for division of labour and perhaps status between the sexes. Further attention to social organization has been largely devoted to population movement within the appropriate ecological-economic framework via the ethnographic as well as the archaeological record (e.g. Lee and Devore, 1968; Wobst, 1974; Jochim, 1976). Such studies have been illuminating in their own right. Population densities at or below one person per 10 sq km for example or seasonal nucleations of a maximum of around 100 emerge from many ethnographic studies.

Whether such studies can directly help the study of the early post-glacial period is another matter. Once challenged (e.g. Bender, 1978) the egalitarian model like so many other assumptions about this period looks less secure, and a flexible attitude to the variety of social organization possible is more appropriate. As stressed already in this account, long-term environmental changes could have created stress or an uneven distribution of resources from region to region; greater control of resources is compatible with some evidence. In this kind of setting the reasons for suggesting an undifferentiated society may be harder to sustain.

Substantiating this alternative in the archaeological record is difficult, and it may be irrelevant to look for exactly the same kind of material indicators of individual wealth or status as are so evident by the third or second millennia. Group differentiation may be an initially more appropriate concept, and burials, exchanges of artifacts and 'social territories' may all be used to examine it. The burial record of the period is sparse, with many gaps—none is known in Britain for example—and relatively few cases known overall. The recent discovery at Vedbaek, Zealand of a cemetery of a least seventeen graves with 22 people (Albrethsen and Petersen, 1976) (Fig.4.11) beside a settlement known for over 50 years raises questions of the survival of the evidence. Most other known examples of collective burial in the period are within settlement areas or deposits—as at Arene Candide, north Italy (Cardini, 1946), Hoëdic and Téviec, Brittany (Rozoy,1978), the Tagus estuary, Portugal

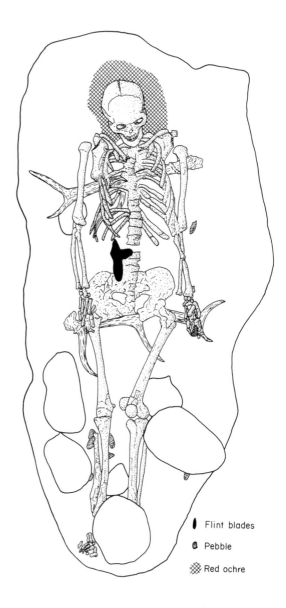

Flint blades

Pebble

Red ochre

Fig. 4.11 Adult man's burial at Vedbaek: grave no. 10 (after Albrethsen and Brinch Petersen, 1976).

(Roche, 1972) or at Lepenski Vir and its neighbours (Srejovic, 1972) as well as the very late or transitional examples at Swifterbant, Netherlands (Meiklejohn and Constandse-Westermann, 1979)—though the cemetery at Zvejnieki, Latvia (Zagorskis, 1973), also beside a settlement, shows that the Vedbaek case in not isolated. The mere existence of these burials may denote a greater concern with group identity and possibly with territory than in the late-glacial period, understandably if mobility were reduced and resources increasingly under pressure; most known cemeteries are also late. Men, women and children are found in these burials (infant mortality is, no doubt, as later, underrepresented). Most burials are in simple pits but are often marked by ochre, antlers or large stones, and most bodies have artifacts accompanying them. In as far as skeletons may be accurately aged and sexed—a difficult problem at Vedbaek for example—men tend to be distinguished from women, and older men may receive slightly more special treatment. The generalization is difficult; women and infant children receive special treatment, too, perhaps casualties of childbirth. Both cases may suggest greater than average status, perhaps in the case of older men achieved during life, and in the case of young women belonging to their family or kin group. The very fact of formal burial at all may denote status; apparently cannibalized bones in the settlement refuse at Vedbaek, and also at Dyrholm (Mathiassen et al., 1942), do not need to have belonged to unfortunate enemies from other communities. Isolated burials are known too within sites, most notably in Denmark as at Vedbaek Boldbaner, and at Janislawice, Poland (Chmielewska, 1954), with an extensive grave inventory; their significance is as yet unclear.

Another possibility which has begun to emerge is that late mesolithic communities in Atlantic Europe may have been responsible for the construction of the first megalithic barrows and cairns (e.g. O'Kelly, 1981). These monuments are described and illustrated in the next chapter, to whose period they are conventionally assigned, since they date on the whole from the mid-fifth millennium BC. The possibility remains however that their emergence is due to native traditions of burial and to accelerated social change, marking perhaps an increased sense of territory and some degree of social differentiation. A recent example comes from the group at Carrowmore, Co. Sligo (Burenhult, 1981) where the simple cairn and chamber with collective burials of no. 4 have a series of such early radiocarbon dates. The example, like others, however, is controversial, since the earliest dates are strictly from contexts predating construction.

Long range movements of artifacts or raw materials of restricted source are known in the period, as in the case of slate tools in the east Baltic (Clark, 1975), sandstone pebbles in southern England from the south-west (Rankine, 1949) or obsidian tools on the Hungarian plain from the Bükk and Matra mountains (Tringham, 1971, p. 46). Some movement may be due to direct human movement, but some at least is the likely result of various sorts of exchanges (cf. Sahlins, 1972). If so, a greater concern with group or individual identity is again suggested than in the more meagre record of the late-glacial period.

Finally the abundant flint and stone artifacts may be used not just for the vital establishment of sequence but for the differentiation of separate 'social territories' (Clark, 1975; Clarke, 1968). Many techniques were held in common over wide areas, as seen in projectile and other types, and social mechanisms clearly existed for the rapid dissemination at times of advantageous innovations. Such areas of contact have been dubbed 'technocomplexes'. Within these, particular styles may be related to the existence of separate human groups, probably based on kinship, responsible for their creation and maintenance (Fig.4.12). Such 'social territories' have definable if overlapping territorial expression (e.g. Clark, 1975, map 6; Kozłowski 1973, Fig.9) (Fig.4.13). Their existence is often overlooked in the welter of typological detail or long-range comparison. Communal identity is perhaps less consciously reflected in these areas, but the possible definition of territory is of great interest. A further hypothesis worth examination is that their size decreases through the post-glacial period (e.g. the Horsham group in southern England, Clark and Rankine, 1939, Teverener, Hülstener, Nollheider groups between the rivers Rhine and Weser, Arora, 1973). What these possibilities imply for social organization within

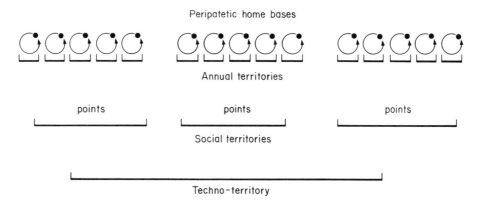

Fig. 4.12   *A possible hierarchy of human territories in the early post-glacial period (after Clark, 1975).*

communities at 'social territory' level or the more local level is unclear, but this very uncertainty confirms the need for a flexible approach. The maintenance of group identity, particularly in times of stress, may have required or fostered internal differentiation.

SUGGESTIONS FOR FURTHER READING

The literature on chronology and cultural sequences is vast. S. Kozłowski (ed.), *The Mesolithic in Europe* and B. Gramsch (ed.), *Mesolithikum in Europa* are important collections of surveys. J. Rozoy, *Les Derniers Chasseurs: L'Epipaléolithique en France* illustrates several eponymous sites and the variability of sequences from area to area.

R. Lee and I. Devore (eds), *Man the Hunter* provides the first of several ethnographic reference points for the conventional model of hunter-gatherer subsistence and dependent settlement and society, of which M. Jochim, *Hunter-gatherer subsistence: a*

Predictive Model and P. Mellars (ed.), *The Early Post-glacial Settlement of Northern Europe*, are important developments. Often quoted sites can be found in J. G. D. Clark, *Star Carr: a Case Study in Bioarchaeology* and *The Earlier Stone Age in Scandinavia*. Mediterranean examples are to be found in Rozoy (cited above), P. Phillips, *Early Farmers of West Mediterranean Europe*, G. Barker, *Landscape and Society: Prehistoric Central Italy*, and interim reports on the Franchthi cave published in *Hesperia* and *Nature*.

The importance of the social context is explored by B. Bender in *World Archaeology* **10**, 1978 and T. Ingold, *Hunters, Pastoralists and Ranchers: a Study in Reindeer Economies*. Control of resources is discussed in E. Higgs (ed.), *Papers in Economic Prehistory* and *Palaeoeconomy*, by P. Mellars in *Proceedings of the Prehistoric Society* **42**, 1976, and D. Clarke in G. Sieveking *et al.* (eds), *Problems in Economic and Social Archaeology*. Other sources are quoted in the text, where references to burial practice, exchange and social groupings are also individually cited, since there are as yet no comprehensive accounts which emphasize these aspects.

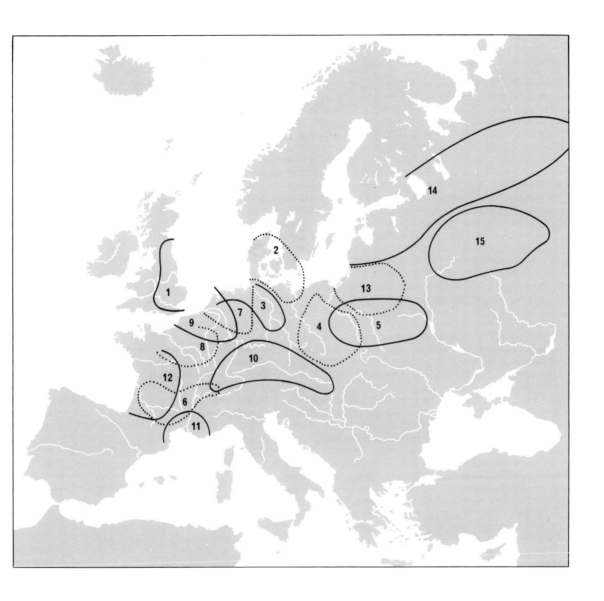

Fig. 4.13   Possible social territories at the end of the Boreal period (after Kozłowski, 1973). 1 Broxbourne. 2 Maglemose. 3 Duvensee. 4 Komornica. 5 Janislawice. 6 Sauveterre. 7 Boberg. 8 Tardenois. 9 Rhein. 10 Beuron. 11 Châteauneuf. 12 Cuzoul. 13 Neman. 14 Kunda.

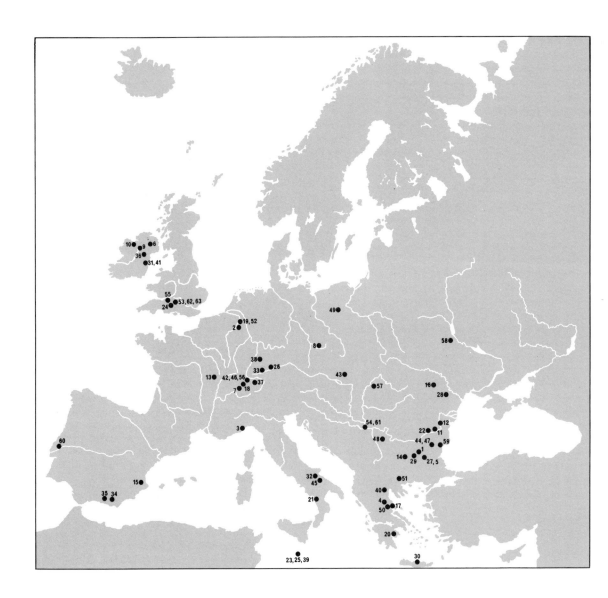

Fig. 5.1 Principal sites mentioned in Chapter 5. 1 Aibunar. 2 Aldenhoven. 3 Arene Candide. 4 Argissa. 5 Azmak. 6 Ballynagilly. 7 Burgäschisee. 8 Bylany. 9 Carrowkeel. 10 Carrowmore. 11 Cāscioarele. 12 Cernavoda. 13 Chassey. 14 Chevdar. 15 Coveta de'l Or. 16 Cucuteni. 17 Dhimini. 18 Egolzwil. 19 Elsloo. 20 Franchthi Cave. 21 Grotta Della Madonna. 22 Gumelnitsa. 23 Hal Saflieni. 24 Hambledon Hill. 25 Haġar Qim. 26 Hienheim. 27 Karanovo. 28 Karbuna. 29 Kazanluk. 30 Knossos. 31 Knowth. 32 La Quercia. 33 Lautereck. 34 Los Millares. 35 Los Murcielagos. 36 Loughcrew. 37 Meilen-Rohrenhaab. 38 Michelsberg. 39 Mnajdra. 40 Nea Nikomedeia. 41 Newgrange. 42 Niederwil. 43 Nitra. 44 Ovcharovo. 45 Passo Di Corvo. 46 Pfyn. 47 Polyanitsa. 48 Rudna Glava. 49 Sarnowo. 50 Sesklo. 51 Sitagroi. 52 Sittard. 53 South Street. 54 Starčevo. 55 Sweet Track. 56 Thayngen-Weier. 57 Tiszapolgár. 58 Tripolye. 59 Varna. 60 Vila Nova De São Pedro. 61 Vinča. 62 West Kennet. 63 Windmill Hill.

5

Early Farming Societies:
the Seventh to Fourth Millennia BC

The economic adaptations of the early post-glacial period were replaced from the seventh to fifth millennia BC by an economy based on cereal cultivation and the husbandry of a restricted range of closely controlled species. Over much of Europe wheat and barley, sheep and goats were new resources, though cattle and pig were previously available. The exotic origin of such staples is not so much of interest as the yields and diversity which all in combination offered. These favoured more permanent settlement and a securer, more productive source of food. As a basis for intrusive colonization and as a solution to indigenous problems or an improvement on native experimentation, they were rapidly spread across Europe, and once established fostered an irreversible and complex process of further economic change, population growth and social development. In its own way predatory, the economic system was in the long term unstable, leading to environmental side-effects and further agricultural change. Population growth, if both cause and effect of agricultural innovation, was another major factor favouring long-term change. Social complexity, which may have contributed to the emergence of food production, favoured economic specialization and greater productivity, with further effects on environment and agricultural innovation. These themes continue in the rest of prehistoric development; this chapter surveys the first major phase of agricultural settlement in Europe, down to the later fourth millennium BC.

THE SETTING

Physical, climatic and vegetational changes continued. Sea level rise in northern Europe reached its peak in the seventh to fifth millennia BC, subsequently to be offset by continued isostatic recovery. Major adjustments—such as the opening of the Baltic (the Litorina Sea phase)—had been effected by the time of the establishment of agriculture, but local effects were still important, such as land recovery in the inner Baltic or land subsidence in the southern North Sea Basin (Louwe Kooijmans, 1974). The Boreal phase is generally considered to have been drier at least in northern Europe, on the basis of bog and lake shrinkage, and the Atlantic to have been both wetter and warmer, with temperatures at an 'optimum'. It is disputed whether the sub-Boreal period (fourth to first millennium BC) was any drier or much colder; frost-sensitive species such as elm, holly or ivy do not show a clear response to any such changes in the earlier fourth millennium. There may however have been increasing aridity in southern Europe after a maximum of humidity in the earlier

fifth, producing summer drought in low-lying areas by the fourth, on the basis of both pollen analysis and isotope analysis of sea shells. The generalizations are difficult, and regional and local variation is likely to have been substantial. The process of the change to climax forest cover was finished by the sixth or fifth millennium in northern Europe, by the seventh in southern. As far as the regional possibilities for pollen analysis allow one to say, forest cover was the predominant natural vegetation, though it may already have been permanently reduced by deliberate clearances. A great range of soils existed by the seventh to fifth millennia, whether in origin products of weathering, erosion, alluviation, periglacial wind-laying (such as the great drifts of loess to the south of late-glacial ice limits with sands closer to the ice limits) or of glaciation itself. These soils were probably at the peak of their potential fertility, though in some areas soil structure may already have been affected by this date—in northern Europe, for example, by the wet Atlantic climate or by deliberate human clearance. Increasingly, therefore, man has to be seen as a vital part of the ecosystem.

Karanovo level	Culture	Contemporary sites in S.E. Europe
VII	Cernavoda-Ezero (Dipsis)	Baden-Pecél, Hissar II, Bubanj Hum Ib, Troy I-II, Early Helladic I-II (Eutresis)
VI	Gumelnitsa-Kodjadermen	Gumelnitsa, Salcutsa, Vinča C-D, Bodrogkeresztúr, Tiszapolgar, Cucuteni A, Tripolje B, Dikilitash, Photolivos III, Bubanj Hum Ia, Dhimini, Saliagos, Aegean Later Neolithic, Early Emborio
V	Maritsa	
IV	Kalojanovetz	E. Boian
III	Vesselinovo	Vinča A-B,, Paradimi I, Sesklo
II, I	Karanovo	Starčevo, Cris, Pre-Sesklo, Early Elateia

Fig. 5.2   The cultural sequence at Karanovo, Bulgaria and simplified regional equivalents in the Balkans (after Renfrew, 1969).

CHRONOLOGY, CULTURAL SEQUENCES AND THE EVIDENCE

While organic materials are rarely preserved, notably in the settlements of the Alpine foreland and in the trackways of the Somerset Levels in England, a greater range of materials survives on sites of this period than previously, with the new additions being pottery and other clay objects and towards the end metal in some areas. Pottery was subject in many areas to continual changes in manufacture, form and decoration. Such abundance of material amenable to typological arrangement is combined with long

stratigraphical sequences in many areas—the product of more stable settlement. The best sequences come from the direct superimposition of layers in the tell settlements of the Balkans and Aegean, with such key sites as Vinča (Vasić, 1932), Karanovo (Mikov, 1959; Georgiev, 1961), Sitagroi (Renfrew, 1971) or Knossos (Evans, 1971) outstanding (Figs 5.2–5.4). Even at sites like these, however, the usually limited scale of excavation has made evaluation of stratigraphic problems, especially discontinuities, risky. Farther north and west sequences are shorter; the rock shelter deposits at Lautereck, west Germany (Taute, 1967), are

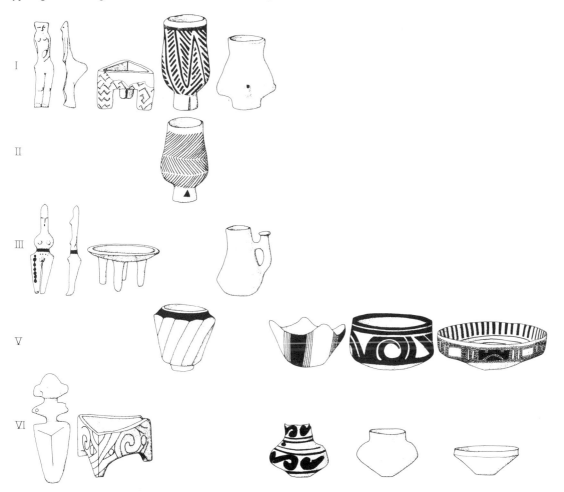

Fig. 5.3 A selection of clay objects from the sequence at Karanovo (after Georgiev, 1961).

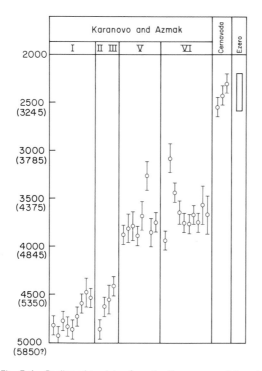

Fig. 5.4   *Radiocarbon dates from the Karanovo and Azmak tells in Bulgaria (after Renfrew, 1971).*

unusually long, covering the Late Mesolithic to the Bronze Age (e.g. Lüning, 1969; Meier-Arendt, 1974). Less direct and less reliable sequences are sometimes available in ditch fills, as in the enclosure at Windmill Hill, in southern England (I. Smith, 1965). Some compensation is available in the horizontal stratigraphy of extensive settlements of timber-framed houses on the loess in the sixth and fifth millennium BC. Long cave and rock-shelter sequences are available in the Mediterranean, as at Arene Candide (Brea, 1946/56), or at the Grotta del Santuario della Madonna, Praia a Mare in Calabria, southern Italy (Trump, 1966a); Iberia, however, is for the most part poorly investigated. Regional sequences have thus been tolerably well worked out in many areas, subject to the difficulties noted. The addition of radiocarbon dating has helped to iron out such problems, and by giving an absolute framework has put regional sequences in their proper relationship. The classic example is the final placing of the Vinča culture long before that of Troy I. No complacency is

called for; the application of radiocarbon dating has been uneven, and usually most consistent in areas where sequences were already best known. Problems for the long-term study of change are still posed in some areas by this failing and detail everywhere remains to be improved.

No survey such as this could hope to do more than indicate some of the major regional cultural groupings (Fig.5.5). Innovations such as the use of polished or ground stone (see the previous chapter) or metallurgy were not regionally synchronous, and terms like 'the Neolithic' and 'Chalcolithic' or 'Eneolithic' are probably best dropped. More importantly, matérial equipment cannot be used directly to sustain assumptions about economic adaptation. The presence of pottery has often been seen as virtually synonymous with the practice of full 'mixed farming'. Its presence may indeed suggest greater permanence of settlement, as in the Ertebølle (Troels-Smith, 1967) or Bug-Dniester cultures (Tringham, 1971) discussed in the last chapter, but its introduction may precede, lag behind or be independent of economic innovation.

The very varied nature of the evidence for this period across Europe deserves emphasis. Survival of different categories of evidence follows the physical conditions of different regions. The abundance of peat deposits for pollen analysis in much of northwest Europe is offset by the paucity of alkaline or neutral soils to preserve bone. Molluscan analysis on calcareous soils lacks the refinement of pollen analysis. The situation is largely reversed in eastern Europe, while the loess of west and central Europe is both now decalcified—destroying bone—and generally devoid of peat or other suitable material. Palynological work such as near the later sixth and earlier fifth millennium settlement at Hienheim in the Bavarian Danube valley (Bakels, 1978) is therefore rare. Pollen analysis is also scattered in Mediterranean Europe. Inherent problems such as these are compounded by prehistorians' failure until recently (or perhaps even up to the present) to recover systematically the full range of economic and social evidence which does survive. New techniques of recovery provide many grounds for optimism for the future, though the limitations of the evidence may still make the study of nutrition, for example, over and above the study of diet, difficult or

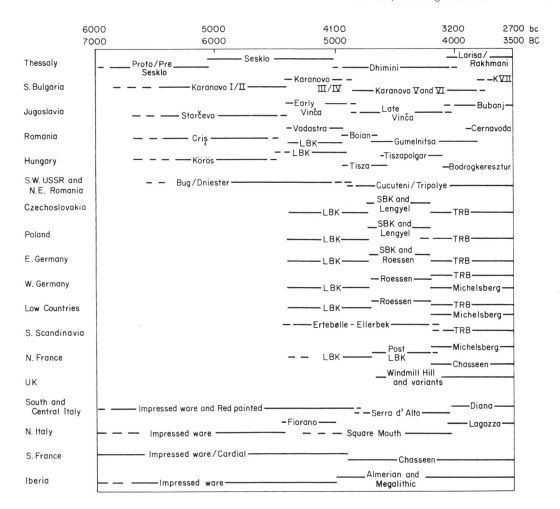

Fig. 5.5 *Highly simplified cultural chart for the Neolithic and Chalcolithic periods. This is intended as a preliminary guide only, as it cannot give enough allowance to regional variation, overlap or indeed controversy. LBK = Linearbandkeramik, SBK = Stichbandkeramik, TRB = Trichterbecherkultur (sources: various).*

impossible (Dennell, 1979). Older data of all kinds are less reliable, though individual pieces may be of excellent quality. In the thematic account of early farming economy and society which follows, therefore, no one region can provide good evidence for all relevant aspects, and themes must be illustrated by examples from a wide geographical and chronological range. Regional and chronological variation, however, was substantial and important,

and major developments will be noted within the thematic framework as appropriate.

SUBSISTENCE: NEW RESOURCES AND THEIR ESTABLISHMENT

The resources which came increasingly to dominate subsistence economies, starting from the earlier seventh millennium BC in south-east Europe, were cereals, legumes, sheep, goats, cattle and pig, although others such as deer and indigenous plants remained in use, and fish and other marine resources were also exploited where available. Many people have seen such an economic shift as 'allowing' subsequent social developments, others prefer the converse relation and agnostics or realists would see both processes as inextricably combined. Whatever the case, there is no doubt that such an economic shift was of fundamental importance. As in the previous chapter, the major resources deserve consideration for their individual food yields and their combined diversity. Such an approach to some extent by-passes assumptions about how exactly each was used or controlled. The problem of reliable criteria of domestication is eased by the fact that cereals and ovicaprids were not indigenous to much of Europe. Their spread implies that they were closely controlled, and by extension therefore so also were cattle and pigs. But doubts as to the range of control of animals must remain, and the greater confidence that is possible for this period must not set up assumptions about lack of control in an earlier phase.

Wheat and barley, the dominant cereals, offer highly productive land-use. Comparison of yields in reasonable conditions of soil fertility and climate in medieval, classical and recent times suggests a minimum figure of four-fold returns, or of some 400 kg per hectare (e.g. Dennell, 1978); a person might be supported by some 250 kg in a year, the bulk of the residue being required for seed, but with a possibility of surplus in a good year. Other advantages include adaptability to a range of soils and climatic regimes — wheat is best suited to heavier and wetter soils in warmer conditions, and barley and rye are more tolerant of lighter, drier and more acid soils and are cultivable up to relatively high altitudes. They can also be sown either in autumn as in their natural state or in spring (Harlan, 1972). Conscious or unconscious selection seems to have led to the emergence as crops in their own right of species such as oats and possibly rye which were probably initially weeds (Hillman, 1978). This further increased the diversity available to the cultivator. Cereals can be stored, though this was not perhaps an innovation in food sources. The technology for their cultivation can be simple, and its continuation over many years

in the same place is possible as long as soil conditions can withstand the predation of the natural ecosystem that a harvest represents. At the outset of their use in Europe highly fertile and well-watered soils were available, and their state could additionally be maintained by growing nitrogen-fixing legumes — peas, lentils and vetches — and by manure from animals, or restored by a period of lying fallow. It is hard to quantify the advantage that cereals would have offered over indigenous plants, many of which were still collected, but these generalizations, based partly on modern cereals, help to explain their increasing dominance in food remains and settlement strategy (Fig.5.6 and Tables 5.1, 5.2).

Whether the range of animals that were now favoured offered greater individual meat yields is uncertain; sheep and goats are after all smaller than deer, and cattle and pig continued to decrease in size. Gross meat yield from a herd over a period of time, however, could have been increased by the possibilities of greater control; this would have involved perhaps less mobility for husbandman and herd or probably greater selectivity and efficiency in

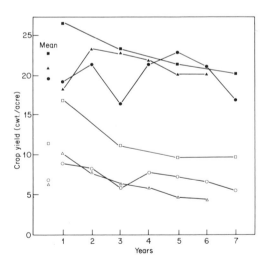

Fig. 5.6   Crop yields under differing conditions of cultivation at the experimental station at Rothampsted, southern England (after Dennell, 1978).

Table 5.1   Principal plants represented on early neolithic sites in South-east Europe (after Dennell, 1978).

Plant	Settlement												
	5	6	7	8	9	10	11	12	13	14	15	16	17
Einkorn	x		x	x	x	x	x	x	x	x	x	x	x
Emmer	x	x		x	x	x	x	x	x	x	x	x	
Bread-wheat					x				x	x	x		
Barley	x	x		x	x	x			x	x	x		
Vetch	x				x				x	x	x		
Lentil	x			x	x	x	x	x	x	x	x		x
Pea	x	x			x				x	x	x		
Flax									x	x			
Cornelian cherry					x				x	x	x		
Apple									x	x	x		
Blackberry									x	x			
Walnut										x			

Greece: 5: Ghediki (aceramic) 6–5000 bc (Renfrew, J. M., 1973). 6: Sesklo (aceramic) 6–5000 bc (Renfrew, J. M., 1973). 7: Achilleion (aceramic) 6–6000 bc (Renfrew, J. M., 1973). 8: Argissa (aceramic) 6–5000 bc (Hopf, 1962). 9: Nea Nikomedeia c. 5500 bc (van Zeist and Bottema, 1971).
Crete: 10: Knossos (aceramic) c. 6000 bc (Evans, 1968).
Bulgaria: 11: Azmak, E. N. c. 5000 bc (Renfrew, J. M., 1969). 12: Karanovo, E. N. c. 5000 bc (Renfrew, J. M., 1969). 13: Chevdar c. 5000 bc. 14: Kazanluk, E. N. c. 5000 bc.
Yugoslavia: 15: Anza I. c. 5000 bc (Gimbutas, 1974). 16: Vřsnik c. 5000 bc (Garašanin, M. and D., 1961). 17: Selevac late Vinča (Hopf, 1974).

Table 5.2   Composition of foods per 100g of edible portion for various plants and animals consumed by early villagers (after Redman, 1979).

Food	Food energy (kcal)	Protein	Fat/Oil	Carbohydrate
Cereals				
Bread wheat	331	14·8	1·7	67·1
Emmer wheat	333	12·5	2·4	68·3
Six-row barley	337	10·0	1·6	70·2
Legumes				
Peas (dried)	339	22·3	1·1	56·3
Lentils (dried)	345	24·9	1·2	57·2
Vetch	343	27·6	1·7	55·2
Tree nuts				
Almonds (dried)	605	16·8	54·9	21·5*
Pistachios (dried)	598	18·9	54·0	19·7*
Acorns	268	3·0	2·6	57·8*
Fruits				
Figs (dried)	303	4·0	1·2	62·6
Dates (dried)	318	2·2	0·6	73·0
Grapes (raisins)	289	2·5	0·2	76·5
Olive (ripe)	207	1·8	21·0	1·1

*Includes fibre content.

cropping the herd. Secondary products would have included milk, hides and short wool (but see below) as well as bone and horn. The different species seem to have had different habitat requirements; ovicaprids preferred or tolerated drier and more open conditions, cattle needed water close at hand, and pigs preferred woodland pannage. All three could be exploited within range of a settlement given suitable environmental diversity and the local environment might determine their balance; cattle seem to have been more successful further into temperate Europe for example. Local conditions might also entail considerable mobility on a seasonal basis. The ability, particularly of ovicaprids, to maintain clearances could have been initially another advantage, and close control would have allowed concentrated use of manure. Gelded cattle offered possibilities for traction.

Animal domestication has often been defined in terms of deliberate genetic difference via selective breeding leading to changes in behaviour and morphology. Problems with morphological criteria have already been discussed, and they remain even at this stage. Breeding itself may not have been closely controlled at all times in each of the species other than by gelding the undesirable males. A range of types of herd control could be envisaged, from stalling and curtailed feeding to free-ranging movement in which husbandmen were virtually followers of more amenable herds for much of the year. Breeding seems not to have led to such rapid variation as in cereals; the major development was that of the full use of secondary products like milk and wool, but that was not until the third millennium onwards and is discussed in the next chapter. Again the advantages of the shift in exploitation are hard to quantify, though they are clearly perceptible in outline.

Together both cereals and animals surely presented a high-yielding, diverse and above all secure blend of resources. Their relative contributions must have varied from region to region, but overall it seems that cereals were the dominant partner of a successful marriage and represent the ultimate post-glacial triumph of the plant. They are lower in the food chain and can yield more food per unit of area. More settlements seem to be sited with the needs of cultivation in mind, and animal exploitation may

already have been well advanced at an earlier stage. The side-effects of the system — the probable need for increased labour input, and the environmental disequilibrium entailed in the predation of over-harvesting and over-grazing — will be discussed later.

The transition to this economic shift has partly been outlined already (pp. 100–101) and it remains only to emphasize the apparent role played by direct colonization in many areas (Fig. 5.7) notably on the south-east/north-west axis as well as in the central Mediterranean and to the immediate east of the Carpathians. Colonization is difficult to prove directly, though in Greece and the southern Balkans, for example, similarities in painted pottery, clay figurines and stamp-seals and other material equipment to that in the adjacent Near East are cited as supporting evidence for the hypothesis. Even with colonization there may regularly have been an indigenous contribution of population and skills; cattle for example seem to have been domesticated (at least on morphological criteria) earlier in Greece (Protsch and Berger, 1973; Evans, 1971) than in the Near East, where in the seventh millennium cattle were still a subject of awe in the cults of Çatal Huyük on the Konya plain of Turkey (Mellaart, 1967). The spread of the new economic adaptation was varied both in pace and character, and the averaging of its rate (e.g. Ammerman and Cavalli-Sforza, 1971) may do its complexity little justice.

There is no room for discussion of the Near East except to emphasize that the emergence of new resources and novel methods of exploiting these resources in the period 9000–7000 BC (e.g. Bender, 1975), can be seen from the European perspective not just as a foreign, isolated process but as a parallel one of adaptation to changing conditions. The fact that part, at least, of the most advantageous long-term post-glacial adaptation originated in the Near East is by no means the limit of its interest. It is equally profitable to consider such processes as the gradual shift to a broad spectrum of resources in the late glacial period, experimentation with single species of animal like gazelle, and the geographical restriction of large grasses in the steppe conditions of this period (Binford, 1968; Bottema, 1978). Also of interest is the establishment of more sedentary settlements *before* the emergence of domesticated animals and cereals both of which had undergone morphological

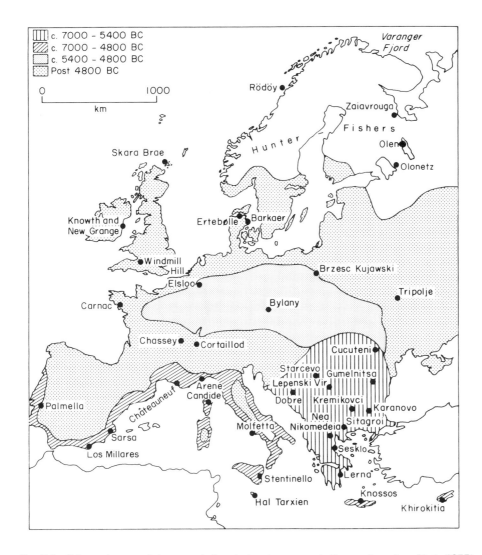

Fig. 5.7 Schematic map of the spread of agricultural economy in Europe (based on Clark, 1977).

change (as at Mureybit or Tell Abu Hureyra; Moore, 1975), and the early creation of substantial settlements like Jericho.

EARLY FARMING PRACTICE

If the long-term aim of research is for more studies of subsistence at a local, detailed level and the demonstration of the view that economy and society are indivisible, a general model of early farming practice can usefully be built in the meantime on the basis of widely-drawn examples, taking as much account of temporal and regional variation as the quality of the evidence allows. On the assumption that it had the most effect on the location of settlements, cereal cultivation will be treated first.

In virtually all areas of primary agricultural settlement it can be seen, by mapping sites against soil types and topography, that the most favourable soils and locations were chosen (see box). Later, as population grew, a process of infilling began with the expansion of farming settlements on to less highly favourable soils and locations. Three examples illustrate the first point. In the southern Balkans, as in the Maritsa valley of Bulgaria, substantial and long-lived settlements (forming 'tells' or settlement mounds), such as Karanovo, were sited on light and workable fertile valley soils, and favourable areas like this could support several such sites spaced at regular intervals. Even here there were variations in the distribution of usable soil types, and the height of tells as a rough index of the length of their occupation has been positively correlated with the amount of high quality arable land within a radius of 2 km around them (Dennell and Webley, 1975). There is a problem in this sort of case of determining the extent of usable land; heavy soils were discounted for arable given their poor drainage and the available technology. In southern Italy large settlements on the Tavoliere plain of Apulia were regularly sited on a particular light fertile soil type (Jarman and Webley, 1975) and in central and western Europe

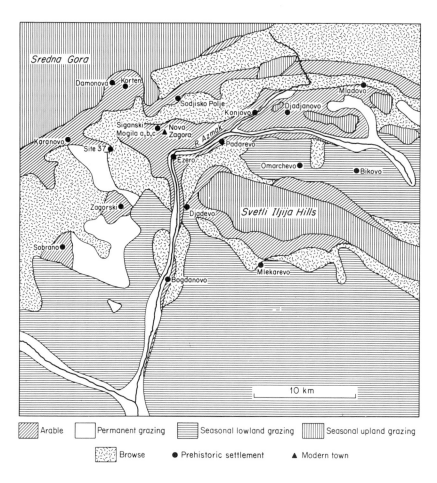

Fig. 5.8   *Neolithic and Chalcolithic sites in the Nova Zagora region Bulgaria, in their reconstructed environmental setting (after Dennell, 1978).*

primary agricultural settlements (of the so-called *Linienbandkeramik* or Linear Pottery culture), again often substantial, were regularly sited on deposits of loess, a well drained and easily tillable soil.

In all three examples, soil types are varied in distribution, and many settlements are sited so as to have other soil types within reach. The frequent siting on the edge of loess deposits reflects also location near streams or rivers, an important factor in the maintenance of fertility (Figs 5.8-5.10). Such a strong pattern in temperate Europe of primary settlement oriented on the river network and flood-plain edge shows clear developments at a later stage.

Detailed studies in southern Poland (e.g. Kruk, 1980) and elsewhere show a shift through time off the loess and up and out of valleys on to drier 'interfluves'. The same sort of process can be seen in the colonization of the Alpine foreland, as in Switzerland, where primary settlement occurred in the Rhine valley from the sixth millennium, extending gradually to the glacial lakes and then the morainic landscape of the foreland itself by the late fifth and early fourth. In some areas of less differentiated soil quality such a pattern is harder to discern, as in Britain or parts of southern Scandinavia, and soil choice may have been more eclectic; the process only becomes clearly

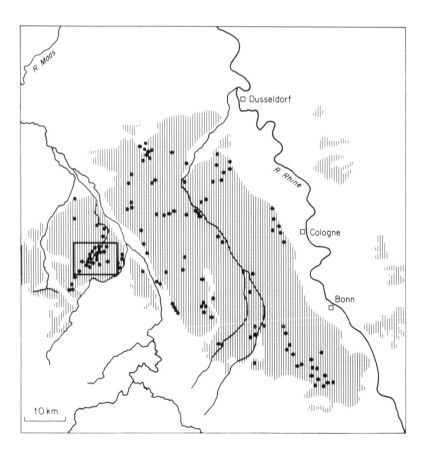

Fig. 5.9   *Linear Pottery sites between the Rhine and Maas rivers in northwest Germany. Vertical hatching shows loess soils and the inset the Aldenhoven plateau (after Kuper et al, 1975).*

visible with the intaking of marginal sandy soils in the third millennium, discussed in the next chapter.

Forest cover would regularly have had to be removed, or, in the case of old clearances from the previous phase, secondary scrub or even established grassland. Forest removal was probably strenuous but not essentially difficult. Large trees of climax forest could have been felled by axe, by fire-setting or by ringing, and the probably meagre understorey cut and burnt; cultivation could have started around dead trees and roots. Ringing is suggested by the use of older wood later than younger wood in the superimposed levels of the bog settlement of Niederwil in northern Switzerland (Mook *et al.*, 1972). Burning of waste can be seen in charcoal fragments beneath the Sarnowo barrow in Poland, from the phase of secondary colonization in the late fifth and early fourth millennium (Dąbrowski, 1971). This process is variously seen in pollen diagrams of north-west Europe, sometimes rapid, sometimes gradual, and may have led to clearances of many square kilometres

(e.g. Sims, 1973). It is paralleled there, in the area of secondary colonization, by a vast increase in the production of stone and flint axes, themselves often of substantial size. Primary clearances on the loess or in the Balkans may, however, have been smaller in extent, or possibly in alluvial situations involved less tree removal, reflecting again the favourable nature of primary settlement. Axes and adzes in eastern Europe are noticeably smaller than in the north-west (e.g. Tringham, 1971, Fig.11), and the 'shoe-last' adzes associated with primary settlement on the loess may be essentially splitting tools not felling axes. There is also clear evidence for the careful management of woodland itself as a resource, as in the coppicing of hazel around the Somerset Levels, England, for wattle production (Rackham, 1977).

Soil preparation on ground previously under forest cover, relatively free of weed and grass, or in continuous cultivation would have been easily achieved by digging sticks or hoes. Such a technology probably goes back to the previous phase and some

SETTLEMENTS AND RESOURCES

Much attention has rightly been focused in recent years on the quality of land around agricultural settlements. The primary focus of the farmer's life is likely to have been within an hour of his settlement; wheeled transport was an innovation of the third millennium. Detailed study of soil and other resource distribution within such an area — 'site catchment analysis' — offers many insights into subsistence strategy, as in the relation of tell duration to surrounding soil quality. On its own, however, it best achieves the aim of raising further questions rather than answering them. Apart from problems of reconstructing contemporary soil types and environment and quantifying their value, such analysis may avoid the issue of the status of different settlements; it tends to treat each as a self-contained unit. Such an economic unit may have been widespread. It has immediate implications for society, if that is indivisible from economy. Cereal cultivation provides food for the farmer, and perhaps his animals, but it also characteristically offers the possibility of large storable surpluses, regularly or irregularly.

Animals provide meat and other products for the husbandman; they are also a controllable mobile resource, capable of being given to or exchanged with others. The export of grain may be hard to detect, though irregularities in faunal remains — underrepresentation of certain age brackets or species, for example in Swiss Alpine foreland sites (Sakellaridis, 1979) — may suggest such movement. The development of ditched enclosures from the mid-fifth millennium in central and western Europe, present also in southern Italy from the seventh, could also reflect it. In some areas therefore it may be appropriate to envisage a hierarchy of settlement units (the existence of other sites around surviving tells has hardly been looked for, though a range of settlement sizes exists within the loess of west and central Europe) or at least considerable interaction amongst neighbours. Later agricultural intensification and specialization do not preclude an early start to the process, and at no stage can the study of economy be divorced from that of society.

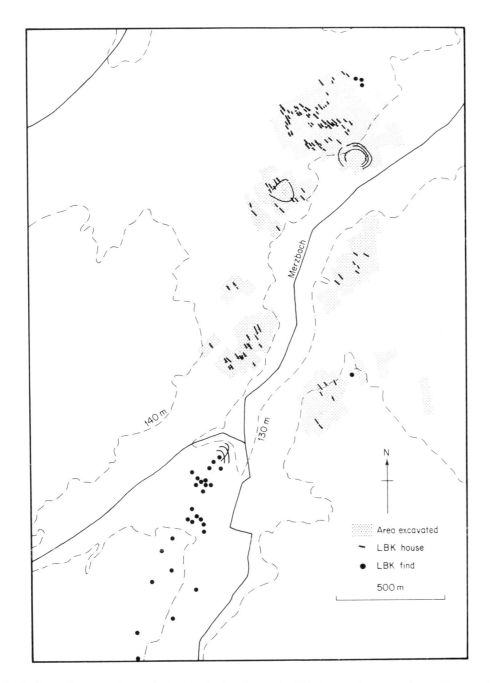

Fig. 5.10 Linear Pottery settlement in the Merzbach valley on the Aldenhoven plateau, northwest Germany (after Kuper et al, 1974).

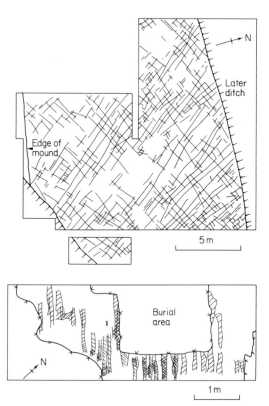

Fig. 5.11   Ard-marks under barrows. Top: South Street, Wiltshire, England. Below: Sarnowo 8, Kujavia, Poland (after Fowler and Evans, 1967; Dąbrowski, 1971).

perhaps ploughing in eastern Europe from the fifth millennium onwards has been inferred from wear on limb bones (Mateescu, 1975; Todorova, 1978). There were castrated cattle in central Europe from the sixth millennium, and ploughs are first documented in the Near East before 3000 BC. There is thus a range of possibilities: such a tool may have been present in Europe from the beginning, or it may be a later response to changed conditions, either of European or external inspiration. Whatever the case, it would also have been vital for the intaking of temperate grassland created through forest clearance.

Crops could be chosen to suit soil type and location (p.118). It is probable that from an early stage considerable discretion was exercised by the farmer, since finds of cereals are known in settlements dominated by or composed exclusively of one species, as of emmer, bread wheat and six-row barley in contexts at Chevdar, Azmak and Karanovo in Bulgaria from the seventh to fifth millennia (Dennell, 1974). Crop purity unlike crop differentiation may have increased little with time. Weeds are well represented, and monoculture seems not to have been practised; diversity provided not only a range of products but greater security. Better data on these aspects are a prime requirement of future research. Whether crops were sown in autumn or spring is unclear and a complicated issue; regional practice may have varied, with autumn sowing common in southern Europe. It is, however, worth challenging the common view that autumn sowing was introduced in northern Europe only in the late second or first millennium. The species in question, emmer (of which spelt is only a natural variant), was available in northern continental Europe from the sixth millennium, and the versatility of crops as a package would have provided the early farmer with further means of hedging his bets, since their sowing season could be varied. Further recovery of weeds and study of their flowering seasons is required.

It has been a common model that cultivation on one spot was at first of short duration with long fallow periods in between, and that those gradually shortened as cultivation periods lengthened, with increasing labour input required (e.g. Boserup, 1965). The model has also been supported by ethnographic data (e.g. Coles, 1976) and by famous experiments such as those of Iversen in Denmark,

so-called stone axes or adzes may now have helped such tasks. The development of the plough may have been related to the secondary phase of agricultural colonization on to poorer, often drier soils in north and north-west Europe where longer fallow periods were required, though the evidence is complex and ambiguous. The existence of a variety of ploughs, light and heavy, is seen in marks scored in the subsoil and preserved under barrows dating from the earlier fourth millennium, from southern England to Poland, on a variety of soils, chalk and sandy (Fig.5.11). Possible wooden examples are preserved beside the Sweet Track, England (Coles *et al.*, 1973) and at Seeberg Burgäschisee-Süd in Switzerland (Müller-Beck, 1965) at a similar horizon. Similar conditions of preservation do not exist in central and eastern Europe, though the use of cattle for traction and

suggesting the need of soil for ash enrichment and its inability to give good returns for more than two or three seasons. The whole question is more complicated. Some undistinguished soils may support continuous cultivation with steady if low yields for years (Dennell, 1978, Tables 17 and 31) and highly fertile, well-watered post-glacial soils may reasonably be supposed to have done better; ethnographic data generally relate to mineral-poor tropical or northern soils. Careful manuring would have helped yields, though there is little direct evidence of its practice; high bracken pollen counts under the South Street barrow, southern England in the fourth millennium (Dimbleby and Evans, 1974) might reflect mucked-out bedding. The use of nitrogen-fixing pulses and vetches, which are widely found, though probably under-represented, would also help, together with short periods of grass fallow. It may even be possible to detect such a practice at Bulgarian tells in the relative composition of samples of plant remains, particularly in the high representation of legumes (Dennell, 1978), though further research is required. Certainly such tells were large and long-lived, and there was too little land in their vicinity for large tracts of forest fallow. Where forest history can be more directly studied, in the pollen diagrams of north-west Europe, clearances were both long-lived — up to 400 years in northern Irish examples (Pilcher et al., 1971) (Fig.5.12) — and perhaps extensive — one calculation has an upper limit of 80 km^2 over a similar timespan (Sims, 1973). Primary settlement in favourable locations, therefore, could have been supported by continuous or near continuous cultivation, perhaps in some cases on quite limited plots. In the areas of secondary settlement more varied practice can be envisaged. The plough would have helped to cope with long periods of grassland fallow if these were required, but pollen data suggest more or less continuous use of these more extensive clearances. The evidence is, however, compatible with shifting foci within a larger cleared area, and poorer soil types may have required this too. Even this is far from the common model of 'slash and burn' shifting cultivation for early farmers, and the general use of forest fallow is unproven.

The existence of permanent fields is therefore likely to have been widespread, but conditions for their preservation are more restricted and a detailed insight into land-use is denied, a particularly frustrating loss in the case of tell settlements. There is evidence from the fourth millennium in southern England in the form of soil build-up with criss-cross ploughing under the South Street barrow (Ashbee et al., 1979) and of extensive ditches around Hambledon Hill (Mercer, 1980) that hints at our loss elsewhere, and palisades and fences are well represented in contemporary settlements in Switzerland and earlier in west and central Europe on the loess. It is also of the greatest interest that the best early example of permanent land division, in western Ireland, is in the third millennium, is extensive and probably involves both arable land and pasture (Caulfield, 1978). Its complexity may reflect agricultural intensification by this date, but the practice of enclosure was probably an early feature.

Harvesting is reflected in a variety of sickles and sickle flints, but hand plucking is likely as well. High-magnification study of silica gloss on flints (e.g. Keeley, 1980) is required, as well as further study of weed remains, since some crops or the lower stubble may have been harvested as fodder for animals. After harvest, grain must have been treated in a variety of ways; stages in the process of clearing a crop of weeds and chaff, with different products at each stage, from animal feed to human food to seed crop, have been studied in the Bulgarian tells of Kazanluk and Chevdar (Dennell, 1978) and this approach deserves wider imitation. Notable finds from Swiss settlements with good organic preservation include separate jars on hut floors of wheat, peas and wild plants, as at Egolzwil 2 (Sakellaridis, 1979). Such preservation is rare, but systematic recovery techniques must be used elsewhere. Pits beside houses were widely used in the more open settlements of west and central Europe for storage, and their contents offer similar analytical possibilities (e.g. Bakels, 1978, Fig.10).

Animal husbandry was a versatile and valuable partner of cereal cultivation. By-products like manure could help arable, and surplus crop could in turn feed animals. Animals could be moved to or allowed to reach by themselves the best grazing available, without being limited by the cereal-oriented location of settlements. Whatever the argument at an earlier phase, there is little doubt that by now

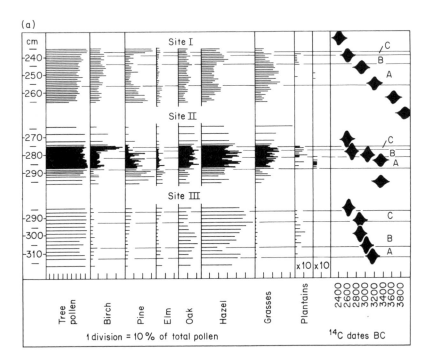

(a)

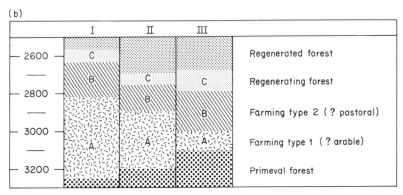

Fig. 5.12   (a) Simplified radiocarbon dated pollen diagrams from Ballynagilly (1) Beaghmore (2) and Ballyscullion (3) in northern Ireland, and (b) summary interpretation. Dates are in radiocarbon chronology (after Pilcher et al., 1971).

considerable skills in animal management were available. Sheep and goats were introduced far beyond their natural habitat, even if this did extend across southern Europe in the early post-glacial Europe. The large native cattle were extensively used,

and their great size seems not to have been an obstacle in handling them. The process of local domestication of cattle has been studied in central Europe, using morphological criteria (specifically size variation) to contrast native, imported and interbred populations (Bökönyi, 1974) and this was no doubt repeated widely elsewhere. The ability was important in other ways; it is unclear whether it would have been possible to maintain herds in isolation from other stock in the wild, and it must therefore have been necessary to control a variety of animals in any one area. Size reduction is, however, an ambiguous criterion, as noted above, and is not necessarily just the result of deliberate selection for docility or ease of handling, particularly if herds could not be isolated securely. The presence of castrated cattle is shown by detailed measurements of legbone proportions in central Europe from the sixth millennium (Müller, 1964) and in Britain from the early fourth (Harcourt, 1974). Oxen would have provided traction not only for ploughs but also for timber in clearance and for use in house construction, and later for the stone used in barrows.

In forested environments stocking rates have been estimated to be rather low (see Table 4.2), and it is unclear how much better results could be achieved with cattle and pig than other combinations of large ungulates such as deer, aurochs or elk; the likely contribution of animals to the economy as a whole may have been relatively small in such situations. As with other ungulates, densities would have been increased with more open vegetation such as browse on the edge of forests or in regenerating clearances, valley bottom grassland or man-made grassland. In favourable circumstances here stocking rates could have been much improved (Fleming, 1972). Animals were therefore not only a vital part of the clearance process, preventing regeneration, but would themselves have directly benefited from it, and some clearances of woodland may have been as much for pasture as for cultivation. It is, however, difficult to discriminate between these possibilities. The ratio of 'arable' to 'pasture' weeds may be calculated from pollen diagrams (Turner, 1965) but this makes little allowance for the previous distribution of each species or detailed local ecology, and the presence or absence of cereal pollen itself may not be reliable because of its poor dispersal. Study of soil profiles in conjunction with molluscan analysis suggests that few clearances in southern England of the fourth millenium were not accompanied by some kind of soil disturbance (Evans, 1972). It may have been more normal for pasture to succeed cultivation

wherever this was possible, a pattern also suggested in north Irish pollen diagrams (Pilcher et al., 1971). In the long run, therefore, animals may have made a more significant contribution to the economy as the amount of open country increased, with settlement expansion and more extensive clearance and cultivation. Such a suggestion is compatible with the long-term trend towards greater specialization in animal management, discussed in the next chapter.

Variation on this pattern would be possible by animal mobility, on a seasonal basis, to get the best grazing in valley bottoms, in marshes and fens, and on more open uplands. Upland sites in caves and other locations are known in many areas beyond the main foci of lowland settlement, as in eastern Europe (Tringham, 1971), or southern and central Italy (Jarman and Webley, 1975; Barker, 1975), and these may best be explained by such exploitation. In Britain, early and continued concern with the Somerset Levels may reflect an interest in their rich spring and summer grazing resources, apart from the many uplands available.

It can be seen from faunal remains that it was everywhere possible to overwinter herds, even in northern or north-west Europe, given the warmer climate of the Atlantic period. Winters may have provided some problems from frost and snow in inland, northern continental areas; the orientation of early timber long houses in central Europe has been linked to the direction of severe winds (Soudsky, 1969). Phosphate analysis is needed to establish if animals were regularly kept within them. Such problems would have been most acute perhaps in the Alpine foreland, significantly higher than surrounding settled areas. Stalling of animals within settlements is demonstrated on its lower edge by preserved sheep or goat droppings at Thayngen-Weier (Guyan, 1967), and further suggested by the store of elm branches, other leaf fodder and a high ivy pollen count. That this was at least partly winter stalling is suggested by the discovery of housefly puparia, seen also at Egolzwil 4 on the higher foreland itself (Vogt, 1969). This need for stalling may have limited animal populations in such areas and many cattle were killed before their first winter in such sites (Sakellaridis, 1979). On the other hand, the particular model of early animal management, in which animals were more or less permanently stalled or restricted and fed on elm and other forest browse (Troels-Smith, 1960), does not seem plausible since such a practice would limit animal numbers and increase labour input.

Paradoxically, comparatively little detailed attention has been paid to variations in animal products. If meat were a main aim, one would expect high numbers of juveniles since it is more economic to cull at this stage. Unfortunately, many areas of Europe do not provide the large animal bone samples required for such patterns to be reliably established and inferior recovery techniques have been widely employed; many faunal reports are summarized in terms of species proportions and little else, and ignore age, sex and meat weights. High proportions of juveniles are a regular feature, however, suggesting a widespread concentration on meat. Detailed analysis at Sitagroi and Knossos showed a progressive increase in the numbers of young animals (Renfrew, 1972). At Chevdar and Kazanluk the majority of ovicaprids seem to have been slaughtered after their third year, though far more pigs were killed before this: cattle evidence is sparse (Dennell, 1978) (Tables 5.3, 5.4). It is probably too early for wider generalization but milk and wool, though valuable, may most likely have been of less significance at the outset, on the grounds not only of the breeding required to improve yields of these

products but also of the human need to adapt to milk itself (Sherratt, 1980). There may, however, have been limited use of dairy cows in this phase, seen in the bones of old cows, as in Swiss settlements (Sakellaridis, 1979) or in southern England at Hambledon Hill in the fourth millennium (Mercer, 1980). The gradual increase of cattle at Sitagroi and Knossos has also been related to the gradual development of dairying. Linen, not woollen, textiles are found in Swiss settlements of the fourth millennium. Such specializations seem to be a later development.

One aspect of animal exploitation has not been neglected. While the balance of species represented usually reflects local ecological suitability (discussed above), there are cases where this may not apply — as in the Starčevo-Körös settlements in low-lying parts of the Danube basin in the seventh millennium, where sheep and goat seem ill-adapted to wet conditions (Bökönyi, 1974). Diachronic variations in Switzerland have also been attributed to 'cultural choice' (Higham, 1967), perhaps less reliably, but the notion does highlight the extent of control and choice available now in animal exploitation, even if in the long run ecological constraints tended to prevail. Another possibility here, however, is that the wrong factors are under consideration; it has been

Table 5.3   Principal animals represented on early neolithic sites in south-east Europe (after Dennell).

Site	Sheep	Goat	Sheep/ Goat	Cattle	Pig	Deer red	roe	Dog	Cat
Argissa	x	x		x	x	x	x		
Nea Nikomedia	x	x		x	x	?		?	
Knossos (aceramic)	x	x		x	x			x	
Chevdar	x	x		x	x	x	x	x	x
Kazanluk	x	x		x	x	x	x	x	x
Anza			x	x	x	x	x	x	
Lepenski Vir			x	x	x	x	x	x	

Table 5.4   Estimated sources and intake of meat at Chevdar, Bulgaria (in kg per annum) (after Dennell).

	Sheep	Pig	Cattle	Red deer	Roe deer	Total
Number	30	19	8·6	2·1	6·3	66
Weight per animal	36	40	250	200	25	
Total weight	1080	760	2150	420	157·5	4568

suggested, for instance, that sheep and goats were valued primarily as producers of manure (Lewthwaite, 1981).

In neither sphere of the economy were earlier exploited resources ignored. The continuing use of deer and pig for example has been demonstrated (Jarman, 1971, 1972) and it has been stressed that a great range of practices must be substituted for a simple domesticated/wild dichotomy, not necessarily following clear species divisions. Plants other than cereals were widely used, as shown by the Bulgarian and Swiss data amongst others. As well as being important subsidiary food sources, continuing experimentation in both spheres led to important developments such as the domestication of the horse and of various Mediterranean fruits by the third millennium, the consequences of which are discussed in later chapters. Here it can be noted that in Greece, for example, olives, pears, figs and grapes are represented by occasional finds before this date, and that at Sitagroi gradual changes in the size and morphology of grape pips can be followed through several phases till a culmination of the process by phase IV, just before 3000 BC (Renfrew, 1972).

EARLY FARMING SETTLEMENT

This general model of early farming practice and development can be given greater regional and chronological depth by a consideration of the settlement that it supported from area to area over time. At face value this evidence at present allows greater appreciation of variation than the patchy economic data, but its interpretation, in turn, raises difficult problems and cannot be used simply as a substitute for economic data. As in the previous phase, it has been common to see settlement as dependent upon economy, with now greater permanence or at least stability of settlement possible through improved economic adaptations. That the common basic units of settlement over Europe included not only homesteads (say up to ten people) but also hamlets (ten to fifty) and villages (fifty to 250 plus) and that each unit can be seen in favourable conditions of excavation to include post-framed houses, seems to bear this generalization out.

(Amongst the great variety of architectural forms and details we may note the painted interior walls of Karanovo, the wooden floors of Swiss houses, and the internal ovens and other fittings and furniture seen in east European houses and house-models.) It is sometimes possible directly to justify the hypothesis of permanence by year-round seasonal indicators, notably in Switzerland (e.g. at the Burgäschisee and Wauwilermoos sites of the Alpine foreland, and Meilen-Rohrenhaab on the Zürichsee (Sakellaridis, 1979)). One notes, however, similar evidence in the Bug-Dniester culture (see above). A further general relation between the quality of resources and the scale of settlement is also widely assumed. How far the extensive variation now to be described can be explained wholly in such terms is another question.

A phase of primary agricultural settlement from the seventh millennium to the sixth or early fifth has already been outlined, and four examples have been selected to illustrate some of its characteristics. In parts of Greece and of the southern Balkans many long-lived settlements, probably of village size, have been recognized, such as Karanovo or Argissa and their neighbours in the Maritsa valley and Thessalian plain respectively. Continuity of occupation more or less in one spot and the use of mud brick or daub produced mounds or tells over time. Size of settlement is obviously hard to establish in a tell without extensive excavation at every level, but the first phase at Karanovo is already estimated to have contained up to sixty closely set small houses (Mikov, 1959), arranged in rows with little space between them and with average dimensions of 6 × 6 m appropriate for use by individual families. That other estimates both reduce (e.g. Milisauskas, 1978) and expand (e.g. Todorova, 1978) this figure reinforces its uncertainty. The density of such settlements can be impressive within one area, with the close spacing of apparently contemporary sites, as in the two examples above (Fig.5.6), both on fertile soils. Even such constricted territories would include at 2 km radii (or c. 12·5 km^2) some 1250 hectares, capable of substantial yields (p.118) and even with allowance for fallow and local pasture perhaps with room to spare, but this depends on the size of population at each settlement. This may reflect the very favourable conditions of much early settlement and the possibility in it of high yield and a good margin of safety. Two other unanswered questions are also relevant, however. One concerns the observable continuity of occupation at tell sites. In some sequences there are stratigraphic breaks of a major kind, as in the sterile layer between levels II and III at Karanovo, for example, and there may also be minor stratigraphical discontinuities at most other sites. It is hard, however, to assess the significance of these without fuller excavation since they could as well suggest localized shifts in village focus as discontinuity of occupation with its implications of economic stress and over-exploitation. At the same time even stratigraphic superimposition does not prove direct continuity. It is also uncertain whether the tells themselves reflect the full settlement pattern of their area, since their prominence has distracted attention from other possible sites, which would have suffered from continued land-use in their fertile territories. Shorter-lived settlements have been found, as the low tell of Nea Nikomedeia in Macedonia, perhaps of village size (Rodden, 1965), and the Franchthi cave continued to be occupied. Homesteads and hamlets have not been regularly recognized, but their absence might be illusory.

More varied settlement has been found to the north with shallower though still substantial occupation levels, more obvious stratigraphic signs of discontinuity and rarer tells. Settlement was concentrated again in fertile alluvial or terrace locations. In the Carpathian basin proper many sites of the Starčevo-Körös-Criş complex were sited close to water in the lowest parts of valleys or even on levees and sand-ridges in seasonally inundated parts of the flood plain. Settlement layers were substantial and recent survey suggests homesteads strung out in some density along river margins. Animal exploitation was varied, with both sheep and goat and cattle being regional preferences. Cereal cultivation has been documented; and other animals, fish and shells were also exploited. It may, however, be easy to underestimate the scale of settlement in such a region. There is some evidence for year-round settlement (Tringham, 1971, p. 92) and Körös settlements in parts of Hungary for example appear to have been dense, even though individual units may not have been large or particularly long-lived.

Farther north again on the loess deposits of central and western Europe from the later sixth millennium, both settlement units and settlement patterns may be contrasted with those of the southern Balkans, but to a lesser extent with the Carpathian basin. Villages, hamlets and homesteads, all with the typical post-built long-house — which may have held large or extended families, stalled cattle and upper-storey lofts and granaries — can all be recognized in the dispersed settlement pattern which is most usually concentrated on rivers and streams, where the combination of loess soil and valley-bottom or valley-side location provided highly favourable conditions. Villages such as Elsloo and Sittard in the Netherlands or Bylany in Czechoslovakia have tended to dominate discussion, but the exceptional rescue work on the Aldenhoven plateau (low rolling loess country dissected by streams which feed the minor tributaries of the Maas and Rhine) suggests that in that area at least individual homesteads were the dominant unit. The density of these homesteads, which can only be seen with massive stripping in front of open-cast mining, was high, with spacing at a few hundred metres or less along streams, and occasional loose concentrations (e.g. Kuper *et al.*, 1977; Farruggia *et al.*, 1973) (Fig.5.13). At most sites there was much replacement of individual timber buildings but essential permanence of occupation is likely so that continuity of occupation of favourable locations was possible for up to half a millennium. The Aldenhoven results are exciting for hinting that dense overall occupation is compatible with individually small, dispersed units. Villages may lie in areas with less locational constraints, or reflect the influence on regional variation of other factors including social organization. Certainly, in the area of Sittard and Elsloo other sites such as Stein and Geleen (Waterbolk, 1958/9), perhaps of hamlet size, suggest variation on the Aldenhoven situation, but the scale of investigation has not been nearly so extensive.

In the Mediterranean the evidence for settlement patterns rather than units is discontinuous and fragmentary. In southern Italy on the Tavoliere large ditches enclosed nucleations of huts, which were within ditched compounds. Sites like Passo di Corvo or La Quercia seem of village size, others are smaller. Surveys (e.g. Jarman and Webley, 1975) have established the spacing of such units, though there is still much to learn about their relative frequency. The area seems to contrast with others

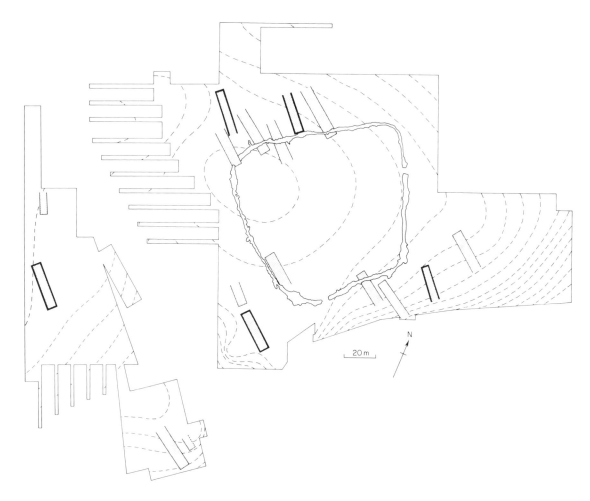

Fig. 5.13   Schematic site plan of the Linear Pottery settlement at Langweiler 9 on the Aldenhoven plateau, northwest Germany. Heavily outlined houses were thought to be in use in the first phase of occupation (after Kuper et al., 1977).

such as central and northern Italy and southern France (Barker, 1975; Phillips, 1975), where individual sites rather than patterns have mainly been recorded, in a range of situations from the coast to inland valleys or upland caves, though again with a discernible preference for light fertile soils. An intensive survey (e.g. Barker, 1977) may rapidly produce more coherent results, and such a survey is badly needed in Iberia to link isolated cave sites like Coveta de l'Or in Valencia or Los Murcielagos in Cordoba (Phillips, 1975) to other sites whatever their economic and cultural status.

In the fifth and fourth millennia there were two major developments, the consolidation and intensification of settlement within many areas and the related expansion of settlement into secondary areas around their periphery. In eastern Europe this is to be seen first in the continued occupation of many tells previously established, such as in the Maritsa valley. There is some evidence, though its incomplete nature is difficult to interpret reliably, for an increase in the size of such settlement units, as seen in the larger houses at Karanovo VI, now in some cases at least double their earlier length. There are hints too of ditches around them. In northern Greece the sites of Sesklo and Dhimini may mark the same kind of process with the addition of strong fortification walls to settlement areas. They may also mark another widespread trend of these millennia, that of the emergence of more specialized sites, in this case of nucleated citadels on low hilltops (Theocharis, 1973).

Settlement appears also to have become more established to the north. Tells of this date are found in the lower Danube basin and in the southern Carpathian basin, and such continuity of occupation is now reflected classically in the sequence from Vinča near Belgrade. Settlement was also extended into uplands surrounding the river valleys, as in the area of Šabac to the south of the River Sava (Sherratt, 1976, Fig.12). In the Carpathian basin itself settlements fluctuated in size and spacing; after large Tisza phase sites, in the Tiszapolgár phase many settlements were again small and short-lived. Despite the difficult alluvial environment, a specialized cattle-breeding economy seems to have developed which possibly served wide areas around it. Amongst more recently investigated tells in the general lower Danube area Polyanitsa, near Trgovishte in north-east Bulgaria, dates from the fifth millennium, and throughout its eight well-excavated levels shows a nucleated settlement of closely-set houses within a square palisaded perimeter, which became steadily more crowded (Todorova, 1978) (Fig.5.14). A similar sort of development is seen in Tripolye settlements to the east of the Carpathians. In the Black Sea area notable cemeteries such as Cernavoda or Varna may reflect the same stability of settlement; though their settlements are poorly known, water-side settlements are recorded at Varna (Todorova and Toncheva, 1975).

External expansion is reflected in the progressively wider adoption of a cereal- and animal-based economy on the steppes, as far as the River Bug and then beyond to the river Dnieper. This had a greater range of site locations and types, representing probably both colonization from the previous zone of settlement east of the Carpathians and further change by the previously well-adapted native

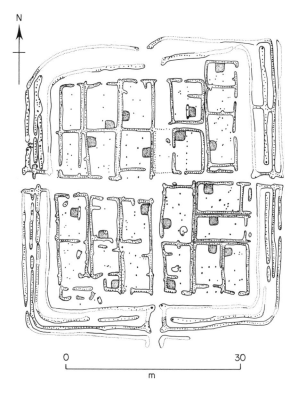

Fig. 5.14   *Level 1 of the small tell at Polyanitsa, north-east Bulgaria (after Todorova, 1978).*

population. Cucuteni on the Prut and Tripolye on the Dnieper typify a large number of sites probably of village size, often with houses radially arranged on promontories and partially enclosed by ditches. A clear analysis of the whole settlement pattern is lacking, despite such indications of increase in site numbers, size and hierarchy, and of settlements placed to exploit a wide range of territory from valley to interfluve.

In central and western Europe the major theme in these millennia is the infilling of the area of primary settlement, with sites spread now over a wider range of the landscape; sites now occur further off the loess, higher on to the interfluves and uplands and even in some parts lower on the flood plain, and with a greater range perhaps in site sizes and statuses. The classic study which outlines such a settlement history is that of Kruk (1980) in southern Poland (Fig.5.15)

(a)

(b)

Permanent settlement

Temporary settlement

Single finds

Corded ware flat graves

- - ➤ TRB settlement concentration

(c)

Fig. 5.15   Settlement types and distribution in southern Poland (a) LBK culture, Dłubnia Valley near Dziekanowice; (b) Lengyel culture, Dłubnia valley at the Baranowka confluence; (c) TRB and Corded Ware cultures, upper Szreniawa river basin near Szczepanowice (after Kruk, 1980).

and the same sort of pattern can be seen in many areas (e.g. Whittle, 1977). In more detail the process was both complicated and regionalized, and requires much further research for full elucidation. In some areas, there seems to have been little direct continuity of occupation from the primary phase, and a shift in the focus of settlement may reflect its gradual expansion. On the Aldenhoven plateau far fewer Roessen settlements of the mid/later fifth millennium are known and such discontinuity is typical. The recently excavated site of Inden-Lamersdorf (Kuper and Piepers, 1966) still has a valley location but seems to represent a much more nucleated unit, larger than a homestead and enclosed with a palisade. Another site at Aldenhoven may be similar (Jürgens, 1979). In the Chassey-Michelsberg-TRB horizon of the fourth millennium, more sites are known again, with ditched enclosures prominent both in valleys and on the edge of interfluves, as at Urmitz in the Rhine valley. The Sarnowo ard-marks come from an area of secondary colonization on the sandy interfluve of the River Vistula. Pollen beneath the barrow indicated cereal cultivation. Locally, however, development may be obscure; on the Aldenhoven plateau there is little indication of Michelsberg settlement.

Beyond the loess there was again secondary colonization and acculturation. The study of vegetational history through pollen analysis, and to a lesser extent molluscan analysis, has yielded information, but an integrated view of settlement and economy has been difficult. The most striking factor is the apparently wide-ranging nature of settlement with an eclectic choice of soils and locations. In Denmark perhaps only the poorer soils of western and central Jutland were avoided; in Ireland the early site of Ballynagilly, Co. Tyrone, lies within the upland area (ApSimon, 1976). Agricultural settlement was rapidly extended to its limits, in the northern isles of Scotland, and in Scandinavia and the Baltic coast where the transition to fishing, sealing, trapping and such economies around 60°N can profitably be studied, with cereal agriculture a slow addition.

The region where the relation of settlement to economy can at present best be studied is the Alpine foreland of north-western Switzerland. Colonization south of the Rhine began in the late fifth millennium

and the following developments were therefore relatively rapid compared with those of the areas of primary settlement. From the Bodensee to Lac Leman there were three main zones of settlement — in the hinterland of the Rhine and along its tributary the river Aare and its environs; on the major glacial lakes; and on the morainic landscape of the Alpine foreland proper, which is broken by frequent small lakes and marshes. It is very striking that all three were so rapidly taken up, with no perceptible difference between them just as in other parts of north-west Europe. Sites in the Aare valley itself are poorly preserved and badly investigated, but elsewhere where preservation is good a contrast in terms of site size can be seen between sites in the immediate hinterland of the upper Rhine such as Niederwil, Pfyn and Thayngen-Weier in the Thurgau, and those on the foreland itself, such as the various sites of the Burgäschisee or of Egolzwil in the Wauwilermoos in the Ober Aargau (Fig.5.16). The sites on the large glacial lakes, such as Zürich-Kleiner Hafner on the Zürichsee or those on Lac Neuchâtel are probably also larger, but have rarely been excavated completely. The contrast may be seen between the nucleated rows of terraced houses set within a strong palisade at Niederwil (Waterbolk and van Zeist, 1978) and the short rows of houses at Seeberg Burgäschisee-Süd (Bandi, 1967) or Egolzwil 5 (Wyss, 1967). These differences can be related to the more favourable climate and larger areas of better soils around the bigger sites (Sakellaridis, 1979). There may also be a comparable contrast in terms of individual site durations but the problem is complex. Many glacial lake sites give long stratigraphies, seen also at Niederwil, whose buildings were many times renewed as they sank into damp ground. Dendrochronological analysis suggests durations of thirty to seventy years for both Thurgau and foreland sites (e.g. Brunnacker et al., 1967), though only twelve to fifteen years at Egolzwil 5 (Wyss, 1976), and similar durations for Zürichsee sites. There is, however, the additional problem of extrapolating from these figures, which relate to the felling of wood, to the actual duration of a particular settlement, and the span of occupation at Burgäschisee-Süd, Niederwil and Thayngen-Weier indicated by radiocarbon dates — though a less precise method — was longer (Mook et al., 1972). In the Thurgau, Burgäschisee and Wauwilermoos cases, small areas have yielded several sites which suggest overall continuity of occupation despite the abandonment of individual sites (whatever their duration). Pollen analysis does not indicate extensive clearance and it is hard to explain individual abandonments in terms of over-use of resources since their small areas were still exploited. There is therefore scope for considering such sites in relation to those of the more fertile zones and not just as independent units. Animal economies were certainly mobile, as the probably seasonal sites on the Thunersee for example indicate, and varied, as frequent remains of deer and in a few cases fur-bearing animals as well as cattle, ovicaprid and pig indicate. Low numbers of bones at sites like Burgäschisee-Süd, and very varied species proportions on the foreland generally would be compatible with the export of animals, probably on the hoof. The find at Burgäschisee-Süd of a string of copper beads which had been in use for some time (Ottaway and Strahm, 1975) raises intriguing possibilities in this direction.

In the western Mediterranean after the slow beginnings emphasized above, there was further consolidation and growth of agricultural settlement through the fifth and fourth millennia. This can most vividly be seen in the colonization of Malta in the early fifth, probably the last small island to be occupied, and can most thoroughly be illustrated by the results of research in southern France. Here too the increase in site size, type and numbers is striking, as well as the extension of settlement into most available locations including upland plateaus (Phillips, 1975). Only in the narrow valleys of inland Provence or the southern Massif Central were deer and other such resources of much concern, in areas where cultivation and stock keeping would be restricted. Similar processes must have been at work in Iberia, though they are again poorly documented (Savory, 1968). The appearance of a series of large nucleated and sometimes fortified settlements in southern Iberia demands them, but can hardly be traced in the available evidence. Their chronology is also unsound; while they continued into the third millennium their beginnings may lie well before 3000 BC and both this and the following chapter therefore mention this same phenomenon (Chapman, in press). The site at Vila Nova de São

Pedro in the Ribatejo was preceded by an unenclosed settlement with evidence of mixed farming and craft specialization in the form of a domed potter's kiln. Los Millares in Almeria is the largest of a group of some twenty similar sites, termed Millaran. Each of the two has a hilltop location with a nucleated settlement area, potentially far above village size, bounded by massively strong stone walls. That at Los Millares is furnished with stone bastions, and supported by outlying stone towers or forts. A simple artificial watercourse apparently led into the settlement area, and a rich cemetery lay outside. Such sites have been investigated since the last century, but without sufficient thoroughness, and cannot be related to a contemporary settlement pattern. Below Los Millares on its promontory above the Andarax valley leading to the coastal plain there lies a virtual archaeological desert, though the site's complexity demands a supporting hierarchy of settlement. This southern European development may reflect in part the pressures of an increasingly arid environment, and Malta too will be later discussed in these terms. In southern Italy, however, there was apparent continuity of settlement through the fourth millennium even though few sites can be assigned a close date.

EARLY FARMING ECONOMY AND SETTLEMENT: VARIATIONS, INNOVATIONS AND EFFECTS

Regional and chronological variation, growth and change almost everywhere are the three most striking factors of these four millennia across Europe, and it is important to seek further understanding of them. The common view of settlement as a variable dependent on economy has been stated. At a crude level we could now, for instance, contrast settlement forms at an early stage in southern Europe (Balkan tells, Apulian enclosures) with those in northern Europe (homesteads and villages on the loess) and relate such differences to the quality of resources in each region; the Alpine foreland provided another general example on these lines. However, there are other factors to take into account, which are significant for the long-term changes also discussed in later

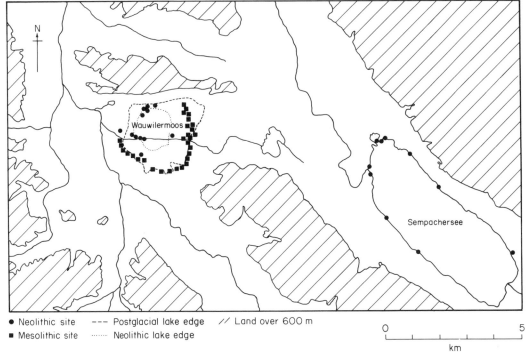

Neolithic site   --- Postglacial lake edge   // Land over 600 m
Mesolithic site   ······ Neolithic lake edge

0   5
km

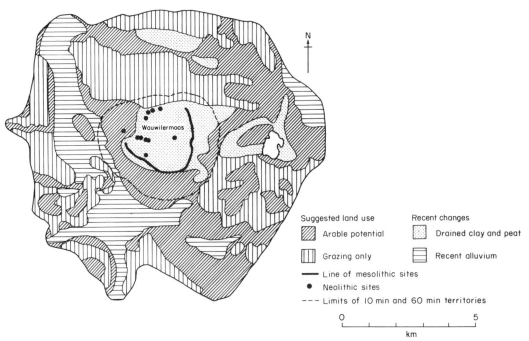

Suggested land use   Recent changes

Arable potential   Drained clay and peat

Grazing only   Recent alluvium

Line of mesolithic sites

Neolithic sites

--- Limits of 10 min and 60 min territories

0   5
km

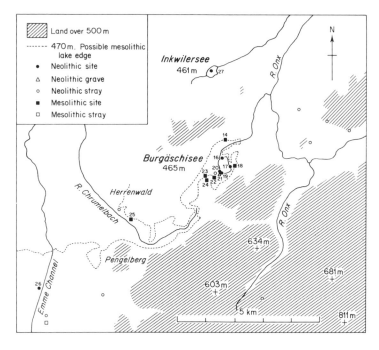

Fig. 5.16 (above and opposite)   Territory around settlements on the Alpine foreland of Switzerland (after Sakellaridis, 1979).

chapters. Apart from the many empirical problems—such as continuity at tells, or their overall settlement pattern—there is a danger in mistaking form for content. For example, dispersed homesteads or hamlets on the loess might support as much population as the more obvious tell villages. Such an admission would restate the importance of social factors alongside that of inherent resources or agricultural skills. Early farming economy and settlement can be seen as interwoven strands in a highly adaptable, manipulative system, but the development of such a system was shaped by social organization. In some cases the agricultural base allowed the emergence of complex society despite moderate resources and an increasingly difficult environment, as in southern Iberia by the end of the fourth millennium. Southern Greece provides another such example by the third millennium. In such cases the social consequences of increased labour input in agricultural intensification or of increased specialization may have been profound.

The extension of agricultural settlement can be documented in nearly all areas of Europe. This seems to have been accompanied by a gradual intensification of the agricultural economy seen, for example, in the development of the plough and perhaps the shortening of fallow periods, but the possibility of intensive but restricted cultivation at an early stage precludes a simple model of development. Intensification is also reflected in specialization and diversification, which can be seen widely in cereal crops and animals, and fruits in southern Europe, and these provided in their turn further adaptability. A concomitant of these developments virtually everywhere was population growth. It is important not to overplay this factor since its beginnings may have preceded the full development of food production, and as noted before even a low rate of increase can have important long-term consequences. Where populations can be studied on a long-term basis in one area, such as the east Mediterranean, there are no obvious immediate changes in life expectancy or health (Angel, 1972). At the same time the rate of increase was surely quickened, and also subject to bouts of rapid acceleration in favourable circumstances, particularly with the opening of new areas. It is important not to be side-tracked into a sterile debate whether population pressure caused agricultural innovation (e.g. Boserup, 1965) or vice versa, since the production of both chickens and eggs is a continuous process. It is important to recognize population growth as one dynamic source of change amongst others, and one which once accelerated entailed irreversible consequences.

The replacement of the first post-glacial adaptations in Europe was initiated soon after 7000 BC and completed virtually everywhere by about 4000 BC, but the second set of adaptations were not in the long term stable, and already about 3000 BC further major changes begin to be detectable. Amongst other interlocking factors under discussion the predatory nature of agriculture itself, over a long time span, is worth a final consideration. The removal of vegetation cover and the suppression of its regeneration by grazing animals may lead to leaching of soils through an excess of water and lack of mineral recycling, or even to waterlogging and peat growth. The British Isles provide upland examples (e.g. Evans *et al.*, 1975). The process may also lead to soil erosion and redeposition, as suggested in the Maritsa valley by the third millennium (Dennell and Wembley, 1975). Cultivation itself may in unfavourable circumstances or on unresilient soils lead to loss of structure or truncation, as on sandy soils in the Netherlands where heath followed arable land by about 3000 BC (Waterbolk, 1956) or on the chalk soils of southern England which had in places been severely reduced by a similar date (e.g. Kerney *et al.*, 1964). To these general effects can be added regional environmental changes, as towards aridity in southern Europe, or towards greater salinity in the Carpathian basin. Changes therefore which begin to emerge around 3000 BC can be related at least in part to such conditions. These were not synchronous, and others are discussed in the next chapter. In southern Europe, many tells were abandoned or show signs of discontinuity; even if this uncertain period has been overemphasized it certainly marks a striking transition. In Apulia settlements on the plains were apparently abandoned around this date, or at least were replaced by a much more varied settlement pattern. In

southern Iberia, further nucleation was in store. In northern Europe, the pattern of development is also uneven, but we may point to many transitions by 3200–3000 BC, as in the end of the Chassey-Michelsberg-TRB horizon of settlement, or in the British Isles where the replacement of cultivated areas by grassland or secondary forest is a common phenomenon. Though such widespread changes need not be linked from region to region, their existence indicates common problems faced by early farming communities, and the need to readapt to these was another factor which led to the rate of change in prehistoric development being crucially altered by about 3000 BC.

EARLY FARMING SOCIETY

Before considering some of the outstanding social developments that had occurred by the end of the period under discussion here, and how best to explain them, it is appropriate to look at some of the basic features of early farming communities, without ignoring regional variation or seeking to derive a unitary model of society.

Virtually wherever they have been discovered, house types, despite variation in size and construction, suggest that the basic social unit occupying them was the family. Floor area of say 50 m² or less would imply a small or nuclear family but very little detailed evidence is available to compare variation in internal arrangements or the density of artifact deposition. It is then unclear whether the larger long-houses of the loess, for example, imply an extended family, or a nuclear family plus animals. The former would be appropriate for the more dispersed settlement pattern discussed above, but the house type is common to homestead and village. Unfortunately their floors are generally destroyed, though one late (Lengyel) example at Postoloprty in Bohemia had four internal hearth-pits (Soudsky, 1969).

Nucleated and dispersed settlements may have been held together by different social relations, but it is noticeable that in both generalized types there is little further variation in the size of the dwelling units in use in any one pattern. Karanovo (Fig.5.17), loess long-houses (Fig.5.18), Swiss settlements or the

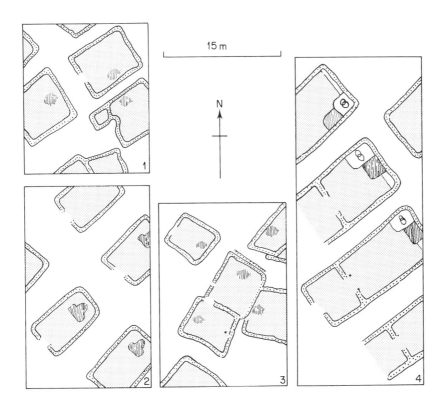

15 m

N

1

2

3

4

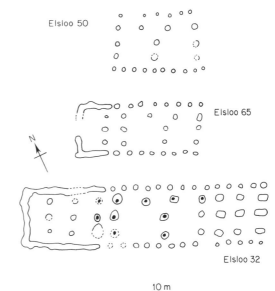

Elsloo 50

Elsloo 65

N

Elsloo 32

10 m

Fig. 5.17 (above) Wattled and mud-walled houses in the stratified layers of Karanovo tell, Bulgaria; 1: phase 1, 2: phase 2; 3: phase 5; 4: phase 6 (after Piggott, 1965).

Fig. 5.18 (right) Plans of large, medium and small long houses from Elsloo, Limburg, Netherlands, of Linear Pottery culture (after Modderman, 1970).

villages of the steppes may all be used again to illustrate this. On this basis — and admitting that artifactual variation has hardly been considered — a model of internally undifferentiated or more or less egalitarian communities has generally been proposed. There is one recurrent exception to this uniformity in the existence of single larger buildings within nucleations, as in the occasional vast long-houses of the loess (Soudsky, 1969). These are generally accommodated within the model as village halls or club-houses, rather than as the dwelling of some more favoured family. Though the evidence is rarely available for this hypothesis to be tested, its plausibility is confirmed by the early site of Nea Nikomedeia in Macedonia where square and rectangular houses not over 8 m wide were grouped around a central square building some 12 by 12 m, with three internal divisions rather than the two of its neighbours, and several clay figurines reinforcing its probably different function (Rodden, 1965) (see box).

As with hunter-gatherer societies, the family was part of a far wider set of relationships, not only in the immediate setting of homestead, hamlet or village (see above, p.131), but also in ties of kinship and alliances beyond the point of its residence. As to how these relationships were articulated or linked together in early agricultural communities, there is a general opinion that there was considerable communal inter-dependence and little individual differentiation. The explanation of this supposed state of affairs is usually sought in the material conditions of agricultural production. There was equal access to resources such as land, crops and animals, these resources were sufficiently productive to satisfy each family's requirements but were not used to create large surpluses, and the social cohesion necessary for cooperative undertakings like housebuilding, clearance and other agricultural tasks, while favouring nucleation of settlement and risk-spreading alliances, did not lead to further social differentiation. The economy reflects, indeed is, the society.

In many respects lack of internal differentiation and an overall concern with communal identity seem to be widely reflected in other such obvious features of the archaeological record as burial and exchange systems, and may also be reflected in cultural groupings. Burial practice varied widely: in eastern Europe individual burials within settlements are known, with only occasional separate cemeteries from the fifth millennium on; separate cemeteries occur occasionally on the loess in central Europe, and more frequently in western Europe; and more varied practices are known from areas beyond, including the construction of earthen, timber and

EVIDENCE FOR RELIGIOUS BELIEFS

The beliefs of past societies are an integral aspect which the archaeologist cannot afford to ignore, however difficult their reconstruction may seem. Burials, for example, have for some years now been interpreted as a more or less accurate mirror of life, on the assumption that a person's living status will be accurately reflected in his or her treatment at death. Ethnographic comparisons show how other factors may intrude. Belief in the impurity of death may affect the extent of ritual treatment at death as much as the deceased's social status; burial can also be an opportunity for various sorts of idealizations, inversions or distortions of social relations in life. Other insights into these important systems of belief may be offered to archaeologists by objects such as the numerous figurines of eastern Europe. Found widely on settlements and sometimes in graves they represent animal, male and, most frequently, female beings, probably deities. Associated evidence from buildings and architectural models suggests that such cults were an important feature of daily life, with both a domestic aspect within the house and a communal aspect in shrines and temples. Models like the one from a Gumelnitsa context at the Danube site of Căscioarele suggest that temples may have been two-storeyed and impressively large. Faced with this sort of evidence, archaeologists make neat divisions between economy, society, belief and other aspects of life at their own peril. Where the evidence is less obvious, it may be easier to ignore, but the need to investigate belief remains the same.

stone monuments ('barrows' and 'megalithic tombs') to hold burials whose numbers again vary widely from area to area—to say nothing of the Mediterranean or the Steppes.

Despite the variety, we may risk the generalization that in earlier stages burials generally do not reflect great social differentiation either in the treatment of the grave or in accompanying goods. Cemeteries from the loess such as Nitra in Czechoslovakia (Fig.5.19) are one example though one may note the attention given again to older men (see above p.109). Many barrows may reflect the same situation, with all ages and both sexes represented in them and little differentiation in goods. This is a particularly Atlantic or western European phenomenon from the fifth millennium on, which is found from Iberia to Scandinavia and is in the north-west concentrated particularly off the loess; a unitary view of it, however, would be disputed, since amongst other factors selection itself for barrow deposition may reflect social differentiation, particularly when a small number of people have been recovered from long-lived monuments, such as West Kennet in

southern England (Piggott, 1962) (Fig.5.20). It is still possible to argue that this is a side-issue to the questions of communal identity which such monuments and cemeteries raise. The former have been seen as attention-seeking devices, imposing architecture with the social purpose of providing a focus for surrounding communities (e.g. Fleming, 1973) and cemeteries may also fulfil something of the same role. Given their distribution, there is a temptation to link both to the generally dispersed pattern and units of settlement around them and to suggest that communities in such an arrangement needed cohesion of this kind to a greater extent than those in larger villages, as in eastern Europe. Cemeteries there appear from the fifth millennium on, mainly from the lowest Danube/Black Sea coast area and the Hungarian plain, where the same settlement dispersal may apply, but other factors such as an increase in population and reduction of territory may also be relevant. The continuity with previous practice will be noted particularly in Atlantic Europe (p.109).

Exchange systems can be widely documented in

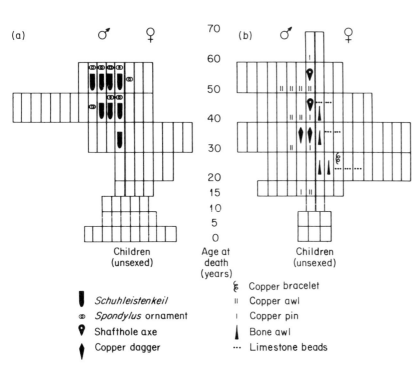

(a)   ♂   ♀   70   (b)   ♂   ♀

Children   Age at   Children
(unsexed)   death   (unsexed)
                (years)

& Copper bracelet
▌ Schuhleistenkeil   ‖ Copper awl
⊕ Spondylus ornament   ▏ Copper pin
♀ Shafthole axe   ▲ Bone awl
♦ Copper dagger   ⋯ Limestone beads

Fig. 5.19 The association of selected grave goods by age and sex in the cemeteries of (a) Nitra, Czechoslovakia (Linear Pottery culture) and (b) Tiszapolgár-Basatanya, Hungary (phase 2: Bodrogkeresztúr culture) (after Sherratt 1976). Each square represents one burial (not all grave-goods shown).

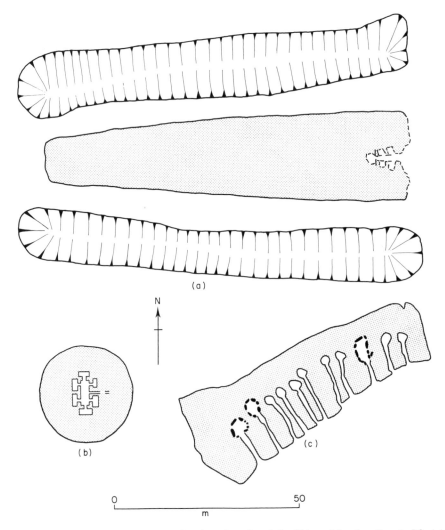

Fig. 5.20 *Ground plans of northwest European chambered tombs of the fifth and fourth millennia BC; (a) West Kennet, Wiltshire, England; (b) Quanterness, Orkney, Scotland; (c) Barnenez, Brittany, France. (after Piggott, 1962; Henshall, 1965; Giot).*

several media, and though not of a uniform character may reflect a general concern with maintaining communal relations. Perhaps the clearest example of the long-range distribution of material of a restricted source for non-utilitarian purposes lies in the use of the East Mediterranean shell *Spondylus gaederopus* (Shackleton and Renfrew, 1970), which is widely found, usually formed into bracelets, discs or beads, on the south-east/north-west axis of Europe as far west as the Paris Basin from the late sixth millennium onwards, though not from the primary phase of agricultural settlement in eastern Europe; on the loess it is associated with the initial settlement. How this distribution was organized, however, is unclear.

A Black Sea source is disputed by preliminary analyses on samples ranging from that coast to inland Yugoslavia, though there is a possible workshop at Constanţa, Romania (Galbenu, 1963) and a quantitative analysis of the spatial distribution of worked and unworked shells is badly needed. The observation that finds are common in Bulgaria and Romania, though of Aegean origin, may support the hypothesis of a 'prestige chain exchange' (Shackleton and Renfrew, 1970).

Other materials have been more closely studied in these spatial terms, though several kinds of movement may be simultaneously involved. Obsidian was distributed as raw material and blades from centres on Melos, in central Europe (p.109) and from four central Mediterranean islands—Sardinia,

Lipari, Pantelleria and the Pontine group near Naples. Flint and stone were widely distributed, mainly in the form of axes or adzes, but with other artifacts represented in flint. Bulgarian flint products are widely found in eastern Europe, Polish in northern Europe and Danish in Scandinavia (Sherratt, 1976, Fig.2). Breton stone axes were distributed to much of France (Le Roux and Cordier, 1974), and stone axes from highland sources in Britain to all of the country (Clough and Cummins, 1979). The movement of a jadeite axe, probably from continental Europe, is seen arrested beside the early fourth millennium Sweet Track in the Somerset Levels, together with a chipped flint axe in mint condition (Coles *et al.*, 1974). Copper products (Fig.5.21) are found beyond the early centres of

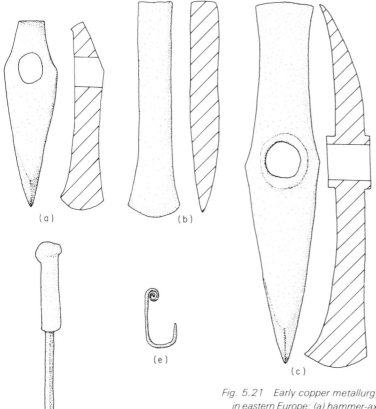

Fig. 5.21   Early copper metallurgy of the later fifth and fourth millennia BC in eastern Europe; (a) hammer-axe, Slivnitsa, W. Bulgaria. (b) chisel, Russe, N. Bulgaria. (c) axe-adze, Timisoara, S. W. Romania. (d) awl in antler handle, Azmak, S. Bulgaria. (e) fish-hook, Azmak (after Tringham, 1971). Scale: (a) c. 1:4; (b–e) c. 1:3.25.

EARLY COPPER METALLURGY

Though of crucial importance in the long run for its technological implications, metallurgy is of greatest interest in its early stages for its social context. Copper metallurgy was developed in the Balkans in the fifth millennium, and in Iberia by the fourth at the latest, both areas probably being independent of each other and of the Near East as well, though this also saw fifth millennium development. A gradual development from the use of native copper to the smelting and hammering and then the casting of copper ores took place from *c.* 4500 BC in eastern Europe. Kiln technology was developed further than achieved by potters, taking temperatures to over 1000°C. By 3000 BC or soon after more difficult sulphide ores were beginning to be worked as well as oxide and carbonate ores, and some closed two-piece moulds began to accompany open moulds. The emphasis of production was on personal ornaments; axes and adzes, of doubtful functional value compared to stone forms and in some case obvious copies of contemporary non-functional stone battle-axes; daggers (mainly in the Carpathian Basin); and on minor functional items, such as awls or hooks. The main emphasis was therefore on social purposes. Many finds are amongst settlement debris, although copper objects and occasionally gold are notable where cemeteries occur. These desirable products were widely dispersed beyond the areas of production in the Carpathians, like the 443 objects found, along with others of different materials, in a 34 cm high pot at Karbuna between the Prut and Dniester. Despite or perhaps because of the social use of many products, the scale of production was impressive, seen best not in the products themselves but in the extent of shafts at known mine sites such as Aibunar, Bulgaria (near the tell of Karanovo) or Rudna Glava, Yugoslavia. A similar diversity of products is shown in the Millaran culture in Iberia, including here also daggers, halberds and knives, as well as simple tools. The addition of this new medium with its varied and changing forms to other kinds of social interaction was both an expression of and stimulus to social change in wide areas.

production in eastern Europe which started in the fifth millennium, as in the Karbuna hoard east of the Carpathians or Danish hoards such as Bygholm, around or soon after 4000 BC (see box). Many products expecially axes must have been acquired and used for timber working and other such tasks—the Sweet Track planks bear their marks—and such acquisition may have been direct from the source. But analysis of spatial patterns of distribution, especially in the best documented areas such as Britain or the central Mediterranean, indicates a general tendency for many products to decline steadily in numbers with distance from source, suggesting that directed movement or trade was not a regular phenomenon and that a major mechanism of movement was exchange. Exceptions such as Cornish (Group 1) axes in Britain may be a third millennium development (Clough and Cummins, 1979). Such patterns of 'fall-off' are not uniform and a variety of processes may be at work; random exchanges over short distances should be contrasted with the rarer and more constrained movement of prestige items (e.g. Renfrew,

1977). Different processes may, however, produce similar spatial patterns. It seems highly probable therefore that a dual use was made of tools like the stone axe and the exchange aspect is of the greatest social interest. It documents a widespread, almost universal, need for regulated interaction or communication between groups, in part perhaps to link widely separated communities but probably in greater measure to help order relations at local or regional level. Sahlins has labelled this 'balanced reciprocity' (1972). The role of individuals within this increased activity is ambiguous. In some cases we are dealing with artifacts both themselves generally little differentiated in quality and produced in vast quantities, and it may be more useful to think again in terms of communal activity. With other objects which were rarer or costlier to produce, or had greater ascribed value, such as *Spondylus* artifacts, stone battle-axes or copper objects, we must think in terms of prestige networks between those able to command such goods.

There is scope for much further research into cultural groupings in relation to this social behaviour. Though individually they have been the subject of innumerable weighty monographs and theses, there has been little use of Clarke's concept (1968) of them as communication systems, for example, or concern with their scale and sharpness of mutual definition, over a broad area and a period of time. Interestingly, as in the previous period, the long-term trend seems to have been towards a reduction in the scale of such groupings at the level of social territory as previously discussed, rather than of technocomplex. For example, in central Europe the Linear Pottery culture of the late sixth and earlier fifth millennium shows wide uniformity which disintegrates towards the end of its tradition and subsequently. There may be a relation with population density; wider communication systems might have served dispersed kin groups, while smaller ones reflect less separation, as well as an increased concern with territory. A similar reduction right through the neolithic period in the size of pottery style distributions in the south of France has been noted by Hodder (1979), and explained as showing greater concern for social conformity and identity in reaction to increasing stress and conflict. It is important not to rely solely on pottery styles or any one cultural trait since the degree of overlap is also at issue, and since petrographic studies have suggested that a certain pottery type found in south-west England in the fourth millennium was produced, probably locally, from a clay of restricted distribution in Cornwall (Peacock, 1969). Potting itself may therefore be at least in part a specialized rather than purely communal activity and the same may hold for other crafts. However, it is tempting to view the development of burial practices, exchange systems and cultural groupings together as reflecting the same processes of social change, from a primary concern with communal identity often over wide areas and with little internal differentiation, to progressive signs of a reduction in the scale of groupings, with perhaps less reciprocity and greater internal ranking.

One characterization of early agricultural communities as dispersed unranked units or 'segmentary societies' (Renfrew, 1979) finds much agreement elsewhere. But one must also note the actual variations, as seen with megaliths and

exchange systems above and recognize the inherent possibilities for further development, which must preclude universal characterizations. It was suggested in Chapter 4 that one motive for a shift to agricultural production in the first place may have come from social conditions of emulation or status-seeking through the provision of food. While there may have been land in plenty for all, fields and pasture may have been more easily held as personal property than hunting grounds, especially with some permanence of cultivation. Cereal products could be stored. Production itself could be intensified, both of animals and cereals, and used to buttress social differentiation; anthropologists have observed how leaders mobilize production rather than vice versa. More people born would represent not necessarily a threat to the food supply but in favourable conditions a welcome addition to the family's productivity and social standing. The sociologist Mauss noted that "to give is to show one's superiority . . . to accept without returning or repaying more is to face subordination". From these generalizations stem many possibilities for variation in the organization of early agricultural communities, and for subsequent developments. The following examples illustrate something of subsequent changes up to 3000 BC.

The striking change in the layout of settlements seen at Dhimini and Sesklo in Thessaly, northern Greece, from the later fifth millennium on has already been described. The architectural layout of the new site at Dhimini may be stressed, with encircling walls between some of which are megaron houses and a great central court entered opposite a large megaron house. The remodelled acropolis at Sesklo shares these features. Unlike Sesklo, settlement has not yet been found outside the acropolis at Dhimini. These changes may demonstrate a change in the character of some sites and the development of a settlement hierarchy, in turn suggesting social differentiation. Dhimini was able to attract copper and gold artifacts though there was no local production. The high quality of the elaborate decorated pottery also suggests craft specialization, but it is interesting that the zone of distribution of Dhimini pottery is confined to eastern Thessaly; elsewhere other styles were in competition. Defensive walls and ditches have been noted at one or two other sites, and Sitagroi to the north had copper and gold from its later fifth millennium level (III).

Similar processes of social change can be discerned in eastern Europe from the fifth millennium BC. The increase in number of tells and their extension to new areas, already referred to, testify to favourable conditions for permanent settlement. Disappointingly, few tells have been completely excavated or published, and little change in layout is evident at this stage, except in the north-eastern Bulgarian sites such as Polyanitsa (p.134). Some buildings were now very large, up to 19 m long in Azmak tell in the Maritsa basin (Georgiev, 1965) but it is not clear how great the normal range of variation in house size was. Palisade and bank defences have been recorded at Polyanitsa and other sites in north-east Bulgaria, and also at sites in north-west Bulgaria such as Gradeshnitsa and Zaminets (Nikolov, 1978). Attention can usefully be directed to other features such as craft specialization, including pottery and metallurgy, and evidence for an increasing emphasis on ritual. The most spectacular recent example of high-quality craft products found together in abundance is the late Chalcolithic cemetery at Varna on the Black Sea (Ivanov, 1978), still under excavation but with at least 200 graves. Here the material includes fine graphite-painted pottery, stone and cast copper tools, and abundant gold objects, in the form of beads, flat ornamental pieces, coverings of other materials, and tubes and three-dimensional artifacts such as rings, ornamental quoits and token axe-heads. The gold itself was probably of Caucasian origin. Ritual elaboration can be seen in the generally increased number of figurines and associated objects, in the greater number of categories of figurines, and also in the more numerous evidence for buildings within settlements, which even if not differentiated in size can be distinguished as shrines or something similar on the basis of their contents. Amongst many examples (e.g. Gimbutas, 1974), the recent one of Ovcharovo, a site in north-east Bulgaria rather like Polyanitsa, is interesting (Todorova, 1974), with house model and 27 other miniature cult objects including figurines, furniture and pots. In the Vinča culture several sites stand out as centres of regional ritual importance (J. Chapman, 1981) and in eastern Europe as a whole there may have been a trend to the emergence of regional centres which in various ways controlled the networks of exchange and even ritual.

Cemeteries adjacent to several tells in north-east and northern Bulgaria (e.g. Todorova, 1978) may have served to reinforce the social importance of selected sites. Though the Varna settlements are not yet well investigated it may then be no accident that so many spectacular and exotic objects were concentrated in so large a cemetery. Returning to the subsistence sphere, one may note that the largest and most long-lived sites had generally the best land around them (e.g. Dennell and Webley, 1975), not necessarily simply to provide enough food for their inhabitants but also crucially providing the capacity for surplus production. The available archaeological vocabulary is not adequate to describe the social situation. There was a great range of site sizes and types; craft specialization and exchange were highly developed; ritual was important. Internal differentiation within sites is not obvious, nor generally within cemeteries. Differences within society may have been masked, and the special role of ritual may have been to paper over increasing social cracks. Eastern European communities did change radically at the end of this period (see Chapter 6), and many of the changes may be due to just such internal factors. The changes were neither uniform nor simultaneous; the rather earlier end to the Vinča culture in the early fourth millennium BC (J. Chapman, 1981) reinforces the likelihood of internal social turmoil.

Moving to the other end of the Mediterranean one is struck by the social change suggested by the development of Millaran sites already partly described, probably, but not certainly, by the later fourth millennium. Nucleation, defence, and craft specialization are again notable features. Developed exchange networks must also have been in operation, and amongst the profusion of elaborate ornaments and prestige items found chiefly in the cemeteries of 'passage grave' tombs, as directly outside Los Millares itself, there are objects made of north African ivory and ostrich shell. The tombs themselves were carefully built, some with corbelled vaults, and many were plastered and painted within. Within the Los Millares cemetery, the largest tombs with the biggest range of exotic goods seem to act as foci for the rest (R. Chapman, 1981a). Such nucleated cemeteries seem therefore to reflect established social ranking as much as communal identity, and their wide distribution (e.g. Savory, 1968, Fig.44) as well as the fortified sites suggest a general process of social differentiation in southern Iberia by this time.

Such change can be studied above all in terms of the complex interaction of local conditions and factors, and long-range influence or colonization of Iberia from the eastern Mediterranean is now generally rejected. Purely local conditions can be seen most clearly perhaps in the case of islands, which can profitably be examined throughout Europe from the Orkneys and Shetlands to the Cyclades. One example, the Maltese islands, will serve to make the point. Colonized in the early fifth millennium, they saw from c. 4000 BC to c. 2500 BC (Trump, 1966b) the steady development of a remarkable series of so-called temples—stone buildings based on a clover-leaf plan but often extended, with facades sometimes as high as two storeys, internal courts perhaps partly roofed, and clear indications of ritual and ceremonial use. The buildings tend to be distributed in pairs or clusters at reasonable distances from their neighbours, such as Mnajdra and Hagar Qim on Malta itself. In the absence of a range of other evidence it is unclear whether these imply social differentiation. The underground version of one near the Tarxien temple, the Hal Saflieni hypogeum cut in limestone, contained the remains of several thousand people, implying unrestricted access, but its construction like that of the larger 'temples' may have required centralized organization.

Evidence from temperate Europe by the fourth millennium does not suggest on the whole such developed social change, though the variety of settlement forms, exchanges and burial practices does not support any uniform model of social organization. One example must serve to illustrate the possibility of the emergence of marked social differentiation by the end of this period. Amongst other communal monuments in Ireland the circular passage graves are notable for their tendency to be grouped closely together, as in the four great cemeteries of the Boyne, Loughcrew, Carrowkeel and Carrowmore. Their date range is unclear, though some at least were built almost as early as other types. In the Boyne cemetery two of the largest monuments, Knowth (Eogan, 1969) and Newgrange (O'Kelly, 1982), may have been built in the later fourth millennium, though some of the satellites closely grouped around Knowth were earlier (Eogan, 1974). The mounds of both are impressively large, up

to 80 m in maximum diameter and c. 15 m high, constructed of vast quantities of stripped turf, soil, clay and river stones. The external architecture was elaborate with a vast facade at Newgrange (O'Kelly, 1979) and a ring of decorated kerb-stones at both. The internal structures of long passage leading to central chamber (one at Newgrange, two at Knowth) were also finely built and decorated. The central chambers and their recesses held numerous cremations with a specialized selection of ornaments and pottery out of a much wider range of contemporary artifacts, and decorated stone basins (Fig.5.22). Such monuments may have served the same general social purpose as other more dispersed types in Ireland and elsewhere. Their nucleation, size, deliberately eye-catching and imposing architecture and specialized grave goods are distinctive, however, and could suggest that a greater degree of centralization and organization lay behind their construction. However, in the absence of supporting economic and settlement data, it is difficult to reject an alternative social context of gradual construction over a long period by communities contributing to centralized foci as—speculatively—a means of reducing or sublimating communal competition for resources. After all, the four main sites lie on a rough transect of about 150 km at more or less regular intervals. In this model one may envisage communities using both local and regional monuments, at different levels. The wider relations of the passage graves have been long debated, and an international aspect could reflect not so much the movement of architects or people as a further means of sublimating local stresses, whether or not widely spread beliefs or cults are involved.

More differentiated societies have been dubbed 'chiefdoms' (see box on p.170), a label which, if of strictly limited value as a 'catch-all' characterization, usefully directs attention to a wide range of social factors which are not so evident amongst the earliest farming communities. At the end of this part of the book we have returned to the question posed in the opening chapters: why do societies change? We can elaborate this question: why are there different sorts of change in different parts of Europe, and why does Europe as a whole have a less intense development than the Near East? This account has stressed in a general way the importance of the interaction between a wide number

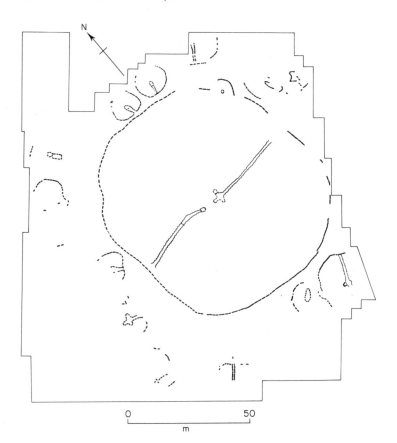

N

0   50

m

Fig. 5.22 Schematic plan of the central passage grave monument and satellite mounds at Knowth, Boyne valley, Ireland (after Eogan, 1974).

of factors, but further analysis is required. Most explanations at present reject the notion that societies change simply because of successive stages being reached in human evolution; this is non-analytical. They also reject the notion of success or prosperity in favour of seeing stress or imbalance of various kinds as the key condition for promoting change. Within this framework opinions vary enormously. Various materialist interpretations stress the importance of environmental and economic factors. In this way in Mediterranean Europe we could examine the aridity of the climate, the instability of resources such as soil or vegetation, the adaptability of the agricultural system and the potential of population to increase. These could be seen to produce competitive social relations within and between communities, in an accelerating conflict over scarce resources. Other interpretations emphasize the primacy of social relations over material conditions which at best can only constrain, not determine, the nature of society. Attention could be given to the inherently competitive nature of social relations. In Mediterranean Europe this could be seen to influence or direct the extension of settlement and the intensification of agriculture, creating surplus needed for the production of wealth and exchange items and at the same time exaggerating the consequences of arid climate or population increase. Differences in temperate Europe could be seen as related to its wider resource base within this social context. Others again advocate that not all of a society's activities need be intimately linked at all times in a coherent adaptive way. If each activity is not to be seen automatically as a 'function' of another or others, its explanation may have to be sought in its own terms, rather than by reference to the familiar link with others. The elaboration of burial monuments and settlement forms in Mediterranean Europe, for example, may have been the result of particular social conditions without close reference to the basic conditions of climate, environment or agricultural production. If this claim is made it becomes far harder of course to predict the nature of the social conditions involved, though again stress, imbalance and competition are useful general concepts. That argument rages on all these issues shows that though the complex nature of many changes has begun to become clear, the detailed tasks of suitable data collection and satisfactory explanation have hardly begun.

SUGGESTIONS FOR FURTHER READING

The literature on chronology and cultural sequences is vast. Particularly useful regional surveys are R. Tringham, *Hunters, Farmers and Fishers of Eastern Europe* and D. Theocharis (ed.), *Neolithic Greece*; J. Guilaine, *Premiers Bergers et Paysans de l'Occident Méditerranéen* and P. Phillips, *Early Farmers of West Mediterranean Europe*. The literature for central and western Europe is more fragmented; examples are cited in the text.

Useful discussions of agricultural practice are in R. Dennell, *Early Farming in Bulgaria: 6th to 3rd Millennia BC* and by various authors in E. Higgs (ed.) *Papers in Economic Prehistory* and *Palaeoeconomy*, and in R. Mercer (ed.) *Farming Practice in British Prehistory*; but there are now many others. Detailed pollen investigations can be seen in I. Simmons and M. Tooley (eds), *The Environment in British Prehistory*. Agricultural settlement can also be followed in these same references apart from others detailed in the text. J. Kruk, *The Neolithic Settlement of Southern Poland*, is an important indication of the results to be gained by detailed survey. The social context of agricultural practice and settlement can be considered through — amongst others — M. Sahlins, *Stone Age Economics* and *Culture and Practical Reason*; some relevant interpretations are in A. Sheridan and G. Bailey (eds), *Economic Archaeology: Towards an Integrated Approach*, and I. Hodder (ed.), *Pattern of the Past*.

Burial and ritual can be followed in regional studies, such as H. Todorova, *The Eneolithic in Bulgaria* and J. Chapman, *The Vinča Culture of Eastern Europe*, or T. Powell (ed.), *Megalithic Enquiries in the West of Britain*. Problems in the interpretation of burial are discussed in I. Hodder, *Symbols in Action*. Exchange is widely documented. One case study is T. Clough and W. Cummins (eds), *Stone Axe Studies*. Metallurgy can be considered through the works of Tringham, Chapman and Phillips cited above and Renfrew's paper in *Proceedings of the Prehistoric Society* **35**, 1969.

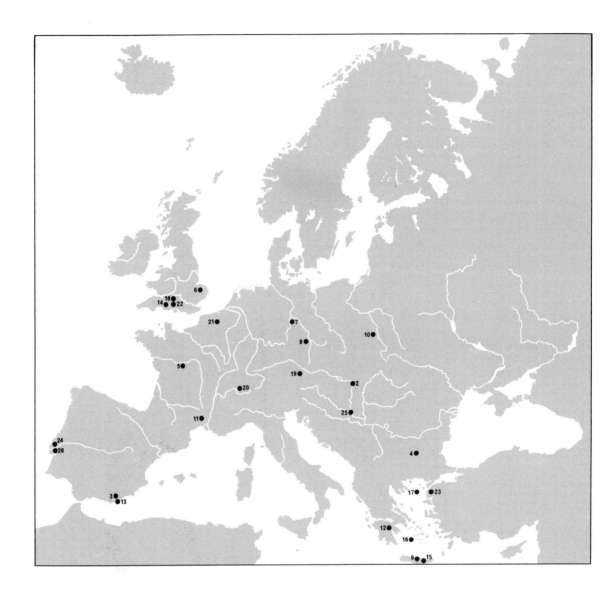

Fig. 6.1   Principal sites mentioned in Chapter 6. 1 Avebury and Silbury Hill. 2 Budakalasz. 3 Cerro de la Virgen. 4 Ezero.
5 Grand Pressigny. 6 Grimes Graves. 7 Halle-Dölauer Heide. 8 Homolka. 9 Knossos. 10 Krzemionki. 11 Lébous. 12 Lerna.
13 Los Millares. 14 Mount Pleasant. 15 Myrtos. 16 Phylakopi. 17 Poliochni. 18 Roundway. 19 Salzburg. 20 Sion-Petit
Chasseur. 21 Spiennes. 22 Stonehenge and Durrington Walls. 23 Troy. 24 Vila Nova de São Pedro. 25 Vučedol. 26 Zambujal.

6

Settlement Expansion and Socio-economic Change 3200-2300 BC

This is a period of major change in the European prehistoric sequence. Beginning in the later fourth millennium many parts of Europe underwent a process of agricultural intensification. In temperate Europe this involved the integration of plough agriculture and wheeled transport involving animal traction with the keeping of animals for milk and wool production, to form an expansive mixed farming system. In the Mediterranean, especially the Aegean, the incorporation of the olive and the vine into the existing agricultural pattern resulted in increased productivity and settlement expansion; in some areas irrigation was practised. Throughout Europe the settlement expansion which occurred resulted in a move into zones which were agriculturally less stable. The response to this situation was varied. In the Aegean and parts of Iberia there was a distinct trend towards more hierarchical forms of society. In temperate Europe dispersed forms of settlement appeared over wide areas, linked by the presence of a small number of distinctive artifact forms, and social patterns became established which were relatively egalitarian for the most part, but formed the basis for the developments of the succeeding Bronze Age.

INTRODUCTION

The preceding chapter has provided an account of the introduction of agricultural economies into Europe and of the major developments which stemmed from it. It is doubtful if any of the subsequent changes which occurred in European prehistory is as immediately striking as this one. Perhaps symptomatic of this is the fact that until recently the subsequent changes in the prehistoric record have been described and accounted for in terms of a constant succession of changing peoples and their ideas. Little thought has been given to any social or economic dimension the changes might have and as a result the nature of the developments which led from the establishment of an agricultural economy to the appearance of state forms of organization in various parts of Europe during the Bronze Age and Iron Age is poorly understood. Similarly, while the sequences of changing archaeological material have now been quite well documented, in some areas at least, the varying dimensions of change have never been properly examined.

This chapter attempts to examine some of the main dimensions of change in the period *c.* 3200–2300 BC. The treatment is broadly regional in that temperate and Mediterranean Europe are considered separately, and within the latter broad zone the Aegean area is further singled out. In each case a brief outline of the cultural sequence is followed by a discussion of socio-economic change during the period.

The main thesis of this chapter is that beginning in the later fourth millennium BC large parts of Europe underwent major changes in settlement and subsistence economy which marked a very significant break from the earlier neolithic. These developments were themselves associated with social changes and it is the socio-economic patterns which came into being at this time which in fact form the basis for the subsequent Bronze Age. The major break does not lie where it has always been placed by the technological subdivisions of the Three Age System, but well over a millennium earlier.

TEMPERATE EUROPE

Regional Sequences

In south-east Europe from the east Balkans to the western edge of the Carpathian Basin the changes which occurred in the cultural sequence around 3200 BC are certainly among the more significant. The long-established cultures of the earlier Copper Age disappeared and were replaced by new ones showing a continuity into the succeeding Bronze Age. Changes occurred not simply in pottery styles but in metallurgy, settlement pattern and subsistence around this time (see *inter alia* Georgiev, 1961; Kalicz, 1963; Tringham, 1971; Müller-Karpe, 1974; Dennell, 1978).

A chronological chart indicating the regional cultural variations for the period from *c.*3200 to 2300 BC is given in Fig.6.2. Despite the great variety of different cultural names there is in fact a marked similarity in the ceramic inventory over the whole area from the middle Danube eastwards, including the Aegean and western Anatolia; an impression of the pottery is given in Fig.6.3. The similarity has two main elements: a generally dark grey burnished surface on the finer wares, which in many areas follows on a period of elaborately painted fine wares; and the appearance in the ceramic inventory of a range of cups and jugs, which had previously been either rare or non-existent. This basic ceramic assemblage with its different functional elements continued in use for a period of the order of 1500 years in the south-east European area.

North and west of the Carpathian Basin the period around 3200 BC does not represent the significant break in the cultural sequence which it does further east. What we see at this time is a more diverse regional picture of essential continuity from the previous period (see Fig.6.2). The north-western parts of central Europe and the north European plain from eastern Poland across to the Low Countries are characterized by the later phases of the various regional versions of the TRB culture group (see, for example, Bakker, 1979; Wislanski, 1970; Behrens, 1973). The upper Danube and the middle and upper Rhine areas have their own local cultural groupings, while France (Guilaine, 1976) is largely unified by the material culture similarity of the late Chassey culture

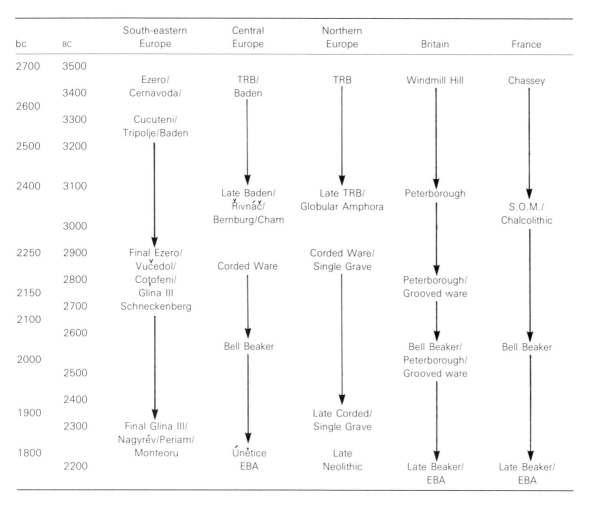

bc	BC	South-eastern Europe	Central Europe	Northern Europe	Britain	France
2700	3500					
	3400	Ezero/ Cernavoda/	TRB/ Baden	TRB	Windmill Hill	Chassey
2600						
	3300	Cucuteni/ Tripolje/Baden				
2500	3200					
2400	3100		Late Baden/ Řivnáč/ Bernburg/Cham	Late TRB/ Globular Amphora	Peterborough	S.O.M./ Chalcolithic
	3000					
2250	2900	Final Ezero/ Vučedol/	Corded Ware	Corded Ware/ Single Grave		
	2800	Cotofeni/			Peterborough/ Grooved ware	
2150		Glina III				
2100	2700	Schneckenberg				
	2600		Bell Beaker		Bell Beaker/ Peterborough/ Grooved ware	Bell Beaker
2000						
	2500					
1900	2400			Late Corded/ Single Grave		
	2300	Final Glina III/ Nagyrév/Periam/				
1800		Monteoru	Únětice	Late	Late Beaker/	Late Beaker/
	2200		EBA	Neolithic	EBA	EBA

Fig. 6.2   A regional chronological chart for temperate Europe.

(see Fig.6.4 for examples of some of these assemblages).

Although gradual cultural changes went on in the immediately succeeding period, it is the interval from c. 2850 to 2350 BC which sees major changes in the cultural sequence of temperate Europe north and west of the Carpathian Basin. Around 2850 BC the various regional cultures of central, northern and north-west Europe were replaced by the widespread Corded Ware assemblage (Fig.6.5) (named after the characteristic cord-impressed decoration on many of the pots) whose appearance in many areas seems to have coincided with a marked change in settlement form, as well as in settlement pattern (see, for example, Behrens and Schlette, 1969; Behrens, 1981). In northern Europe relatively little changed versions of this assemblage continued into the local early Bronze Age, but in central, north-west and the southern edges of northern Europe there was another fairly marked change in the material culture sequence around 2500 BC, with the appearance of an assemblage, whose most characteristic type is a vessel known as a Bell Beaker (Harrison, 1980) (see Fig.6.6). Varieties of this assemblage are also widely found in

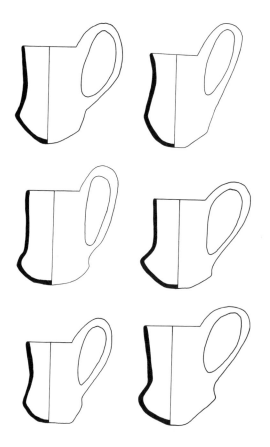

Fig. 6.3   Examples of Baden culture pottery (after Kalicz, 1963).

ment of an acceptable alternative framework for European prehistory. Many dimensions of change are not immediately tangible to the archaeologist but play a key role in understanding the past. It will be apparent that many of the arguments presented below concerning these remain at a very speculative level.

Socio-economic Processes

It has already been suggested that within the period considered in this chapter temperate Europe underwent, at different times in different places, some significant socio-economic changes, albeit nothing on the scale of the beginnings of agriculture two and a half millennia earlier. These changes occurred in a variety of spheres, including subsistence and settlement, social organization and ideology, and the technology of metallurgy. An attempt will be made at the end of this chapter to suggest the interrelations between these changes and how they might account for some of the changes observed in the cultural patterning of the archaeo-logical record, but it will first be necessary to give a separate treatment to the individual dimensions themselves.

Changing agricultural strategies. At the beginning of the period with which this chapter is concerned the socio-economic organization of prehistoric Europe still showed a great deal of uniformity. During the course of the third millennium, however, developments took place which led to an increasing divergence between different regions, perhaps most notably between the Aegean and the rest of Europe, but also more generally between the Mediterranean zone and temperate Europe to the north. Of particular importance in this trend was a growing differentiation in subsistence, as early horticultural systems (Sherratt, 1980) gave way to systems more closely adapted to specific regions and making use of a number of important agricultural developments. In temperate Europe the critical factors included the use of the plough and the cart, with associated animal traction, the development of wool in sheep, and the milking of domestic animals. The evidence for these subsistence changes and their significance

Britain and France, which had been largely unaffected by the Corded Ware distribution, as well as in the western Mediterranean. In all the areas where the Bell Beaker assemblage occurs it forms the prelude to the local early Bronze Age and in north-west Europe it is in Bell Beaker contexts that metalwork first appears in any quantity; this question will be discussed further below.

With this outline in mind it is possible to go on to an examination of the social, economic and ideological dimensions of the changes which took place, but it should be stated at the outset that although the inadequacies of the traditional 'normative' model for explaining change in the archaeological record have been exposed, work has barely begun on the develop-

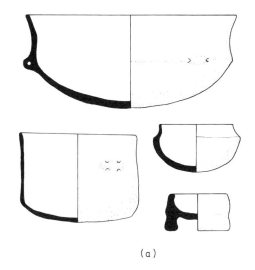

(a)

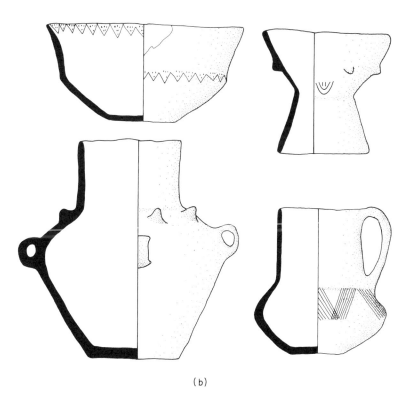

(b)

Fig. 6.4 (a) Later fourth
millennium Chassey
pottery from northern
France (after Bailloud,
1976).
(b) Later fourth millen-
nium pottery from
northern Europe: the
Salzmünde group, central
Germany (after Preuss,
1966).

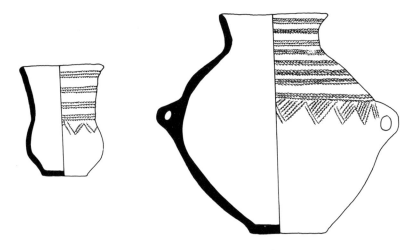

Fig. 6.5   Corded Ware pottery from central Europe; a beaker and an amphora from central Germany (after Matthias, 1974).

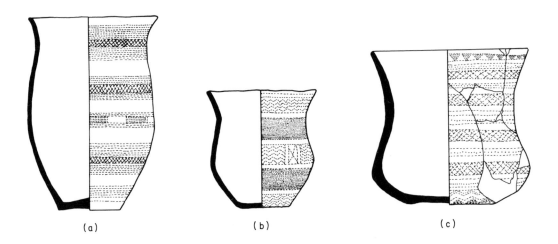

(a)   (b)   (c)

Fig. 6.6   Examples of Bell Beaker pottery from different parts of Europe (a) southern England (after Clarke, 1970) (b) central Germany (after Behrens, 1973) (c) central Spain (after Harrison, 1977).

has recently been reviewed by Sherratt (1981).

The earliest evidence for carts in Europe comes at the end of the fourth millennium with such finds as the well-known cup in the form of a wagon from the Baden culture site of Budakalasz in Hungary, while solid wooden disc-wheels found in water-logged contexts in north-west Europe have been dated to c. 2850–2400 BC, the time of the local Corded Ware phase (Fig.6.7) (van der Waals, 1964). The evidence for ploughing, on the other hand, comes not from the objects themselves but from the discovery of plough marks preserved under burial mounds, from Britain in the west to Poland in the east and dated to the later fourth millennium BC. Ox traction generally is suggested by a number of double ox burials which appear at this time in central Europe.

The evidence for the use of milk and specifically its introduction as an innovation at this time is more tenuous, but one source is the functional analysis of pottery. It was noted above that around 3200 BC there was a major change in the pottery assemblages of south-east and central Europe, with a new emphasis on cup and jug forms. In the Aegean this phenomenon has been attributed to the appearance of wine, but as Sherratt (1981) notes the change affects a much wider area than this could satisfactorily explain. It is certainly tempting to suggest that the widespread distribution of these new forms clearly designed for the drinking and pouring of liquids is in fact related to the first large-scale use of milk. The association of this assemblage with the spread of such an innovation certainly provides a more plausible explanation for it than the massive invasions of Europe from Anatolia which used to be invoked (e.g. Kalicz, 1963).

Finally, the evidence for the use of wool remains to be considered. Early domestic sheep did not bear wool and the earliest textiles of prehistoric Europe were made of flax. How swiftly and generally the changeover took place is unknown but in the lakeside

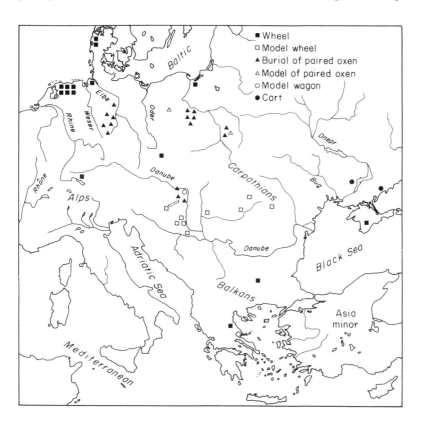

Fig. 6.7 The distribution of evidence for wagons/animal traction in third millennium BC Europe (after Piggott, 1975b).

villages of the Swiss uplands, with their good organic preservation, a change from linen to wool can be seen at the end of the third millennium. In some areas far greater quantities of spindle whorls are found at this time than in previous periods, for example at Homolka in western Czechoslovakia (Ehrich and Pleslová, 1968).

The dates of first appearance of some of these subsistence innovations are still not entirely clear and it may be that some of them go back to a period earlier than that discussed here (see the previous chapter), while wool may be relatively late. Nevertheless, there are strong indications that it was in the course of the late fourth and third millennia that they came together to form a related complex which led to a radically changed agricultural strategy. Application of the plough would have led to greater productivity in the immediate task of land cultivation, but at the same time a larger cleared area would have been necessary as grazing for the larger number of animals which now had to be maintained for traction and which were also worth keeping for milking. More extensive clearances would also have made the landscape more suitable for sheep rearing and associated wool production, while manure would have helped to maintain the fertility of permanent fields; finally, larger numbers of domestic animals would have discouraged forest regeneration. Thus more intensive cereal agriculture and increased stock raising would have been closely associated in an expansive agricultural system.

But the evidence just described of agricultural innovations is not the only indication of changes in subsistence and settlement in the period from c. 3200–2300 BC. At rather differing times within it, major changes occurred in the settlement pattern of many regions of Europe north of the Mediterranean. Site locations preferred in earlier periods were no longer used and in many places there was an expansion of the settled area.

In southern Bulgaria many of the tell settlements were abandoned at the end of the fourth millennium and never reoccupied (Dennell, 1978). In the Hungarian plain there is a striking contrast between the numerous dispersed settlements of the Tiszapolgár culture at the beginning of the fourth millennium, and the very small number of Baden culture sites, in new locations, at the end of the millennium. It is noteworthy that in Hungary, as elsewhere, the shift

was long-lived, since the founding occupation of many of the second millennium bronze age tell sites dates back to the period c. 3000–2700 BC.

Perhaps the best documented case of settlement change at this time is that in southern Poland (Kruk, 1980), where survey work has been able to produce a very clear picture of the development of settlement (Fig.5.15). In the TRB phase in the late fourth millennium there was a major change in land-use, with a move away from small-scale settlement areas in the valley bottoms. In addition to areas along the main rivers, the population exploited the surroundings of small valleys that penetrated the large watersheds, and the majority of sites, including all large settlements, lie on the plateau area between the rivers, especially its marginal zone. In the succeeding Corded Ware phase, in the first half of the third millennium, there was a further change. The TRB settlements were abandoned, and indeed virtually all traces of settlements disappear: only burials, often under mounds, are known from this phase, although their distribution is almost identical to that of the TRB settlement sites.

A similar sequence is known from other parts of central and northern Europe (Fig.6.8): the area of settlement expands in the later fourth millennium, to be followed by a further change in settlement pattern in the Corded Ware phase, c. 2900–2500 BC, when the little evidence available suggests that settlement was highly dispersed, and the area occupied appears in many cases to be extended still further than before. Further west too such phenomena are apparent. In France it has been noted (Bailloud, 1976) that the distribution of settlement in the period beginning c. 3200 BC, characterized by the Seine-Oise-Marne culture, was much less selective than in previous periods and a great variety of different types of terrain were occupied, while in the Netherlands there are indications of a more open landscape developing in the Corded Ware phase, beginning c. 2900 BC. Britain too shows a similar pattern, although here the period of extensive clearance in the mid-third millennium follows on a phase of forest regeneration which had succeeded the initial colonizing period in many places (Whittle, 1978; Bradley, 1978b). Some of the British evidence indicates extensive grassland at this time; for example, evidence from buried soils beneath mid-third millennium ceremonial monuments such as Durrington Walls in the southern

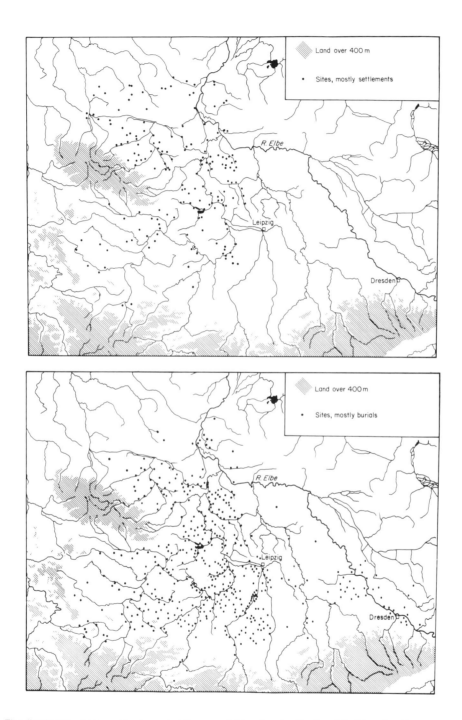

Fig. 6.8   The distribution of occupation in central Germany (a) late fourth millenium BC, (b) earlier third millenium BC (Corded Ware). Scale: c. 1:2,500,000.

chalk area suggests a period of about 500 years during which an environment of grassland existed, maintained, it is assumed, by grazing animals (Evans, 1975).

It is difficult to avoid relating these changes in settlement and its distribution to the subsistence developments described above; the expansive characteristics of a system based on these have already been described. Specifically local factors should not be neglected, of course; in the Hungarian plain, for example, where the animal component of the economy seems to have become more important, it is likely that one of the major factors which resulted in a change in agricultural strategy was the increasing salination of the soil, which meant that earlier arable farming strategies were no longer viable. In general, however, what we are seeing is a change from continuous localized use of the same small areas of land to a geographically more extensive approach in which the animal component increased in importance together with the use of plough agriculture. The fact that the expansion was onto soils which could not sustain continued cropping meant that increasing areas were cleared, leaving land fallow which could in turn be used to feed more animals. At the same time, in central Europe there developed a more differentiated settlement pattern than earlier, including both nucleated settlements, sometimes quite large, and hamlets (e.g. Kruk, 1980). As we have noted, however, in the course of the continuing clearance and expansion of the Corded Ware phase, the settlement pattern became much more dispersed and settlement units smaller, so that a pattern of small hamlets, often of quite ephemeral construction, became generally prevalent and continued until the beginning of the local early Bronze Age *c.* 2200 BC (see, for example, Schlette, 1969). In Britain the settlement pattern always seems to have been a small-scale dispersed one so there was no major change here, while in south-east Europe the pattern seems to have become more nucleated: in Bulgaria, for example, although many tells were abandoned, a small number continued in occupation during the third millennium and some, such as Ezero, were fortified (Dennell, 1978).

In the past the change to a dispersed settlement pattern in central and northern Europe and the appearance of Corded Ware pottery over wide areas around the same time used to be ascribed to the invasion of nomadic pastoralists from the south Russian steppes (Gimbutas, 1965). It can now be seen that although there may have been an element of truth in the idea, inasmuch as it recognized the increasing importance of domestic animals, in fact the changes are much more likely to have been the result of local settlement and subsistence developments involving expansion and the adoption of new agricultural strategies; the detailed archaeological arguments are discussed by Häusler (1981).

Production, exchange and interaction. The previous section has been largely concerned with subsistence at the level of the individual community. It is now necessary to turn to the topic of the relations existing between these communities. As we have suggested already, studies of this topic have generally concerned themselves with documenting the extensive areas of material culture similarity which are so characteristic of the earlier third millennium in temperate Europe, and explaining them in terms of influences and migrations of one kind and another. Before discussing such thorny questions it is necessary to devote some attention first to the general issues involved and then to the evidence for exchange of materials of known source.

In considering the scope of inter-community relations it is important not to neglect the possible role of subsistence commodities. In the context of prehistoric temperate Europe in the earlier third millennium the bulk transport of subsistence commodities over any distance must be regarded as unlikely because of transport difficulties; although by this time a wide variety of different environments was in use, their complementarity could not be exploited in this way. On the other hand, individual communities must have been vulnerable to the risk of agricultural failure throughout prehistory and needed some kind of safety-net in an emergency. Movements of animals would have been one possibility in such a situation and movement of people to resources would have been another. Either way, it is likely that such arrangements depended on the local kinship network, and this links in to another important aspect of exchange, that of people in marriage. In order for a population to survive there must always be a sufficiently large pool of available marriage partners to overcome the random fluctuations in the number of individuals of opposite sexes in the relevant age groups at any given time. If communities are small, there is a constant need for exogamy, marrying out from the community, to maintain such a pool. This may have been particularly necessary for the very small communities which the archaeological evidence indicates in the Corded Ware and Bell Beaker phases of central, northern and western Europe from *c.* 2900 to 2300 BC. It is likely that the kin relations created by exogamy formed the medium for the equally essential mutual subsistence support at times of localized disaster, the two elements forming a cohesive system of inter-community relations at the local scale which was especially important at this time, not just because of the small size of the communities concerned, but also because the agricultural expansion onto less durable soils mentioned above had increased the potential for failure.

The way in which such relations might have been organized will be considered in the next section; here it is important to remember that even though they may be archaeologically relatively intangible, ethnography suggests that they must have formed the matrix in which the exchange of other materials was embedded.

The clearest archaeological evidence for exchange comes, of course, from those materials sufficiently durable to survive in quantity up to the present. The exploitation and exchange of hard stones for the manufacture of axes and other utilitarian tools has been described in the previous chapter, but there are indications that it became particularly intense in the later part of the fourth and the earlier part of the third millennium. It is at this time that some of the major flint mines in prehistoric Europe were in operation, such as Grimes Graves in England (Mercer, 1981a), Grand Pressigny in France, and Krzemionki in Poland (Tabaczynski, 1972). Although locally available surface flint was satisfactory for most purposes, the manufacture of large objects required flawless flint which was only obtainable by mining. This was carried out on a large and complex scale, involving the digging of numerous shafts and interconnecting galleries (Fig.6.9). The material obtained was highly prized and consequently travelled long distances from its sources (Fig.6.10).

It is likely that one of the main reasons for the increased scale of flint exploitation at this time was

the greatly increased extent of forest clearance involved in the expansion of settlement already discussed, for axes were generally the major product of the mines. But this was not universally the case. In the early part of the third millennium very large flint blades began to be produced, particularly in the more northern and western parts of Europe, most probably in response to the appearance of copper daggers further south-east. It is striking that the flint from Grand Pressigny, of a rich honey colour not dissimilar from that of copper, was particularly used for this purpose. The complementary relationship between the use of copper and flint for large blades continued through to the end of the third millennium BC, when the production of flint alternatives to metal reached its climax in southern Scandinavia, a region remote from any metal sources (Lomborg, 1973).

The distribution of items of flint and other hard stones is relatively easy to trace because it is straightforward in many cases to assign them to particular sources. Other materials do not allow one to be so specific, although it is still possible to say something: thus, shells of Mediterranean origin are found in Baden culture graves in the Carpathian Basin (Banner, 1956), while amber, which had been widely used in its Baltic area of origin as early as the mesolithic, began to percolate southwards (see box on p.219). It is likely that fine pottery would also have been exchanged, but here the characterization work remains to be done, while evidence is completely lacking for the exchange of textiles, a likely concomitant of the larger scale of textile production which seems to be associated with the beginning of the exploitation of sheep for wool; this probably became much more important in the period dealt with in the succeeding chapter.

Of all these different types of materials and artifacts which were the object of exchange, it seems that only a relatively small proportion were immediately utilitarian. The rest were of social rather than practical significance. It is likely that metal too falls into the non-utilitarian category at this stage of the development of its extraction and use.

It has been seen in the previous chapter that in the later fifth and earlier fourth millennia an extensive copper metallurgy flourished in south-east Europe and the Carpathian Basin, based on the use of local sources of easily worked oxide and carbonate ores from mines such as Rudna Glava in northern

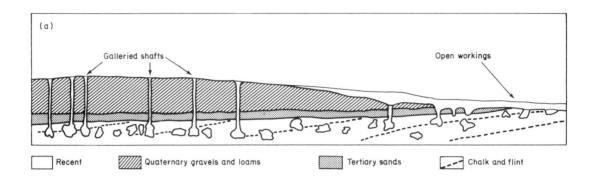

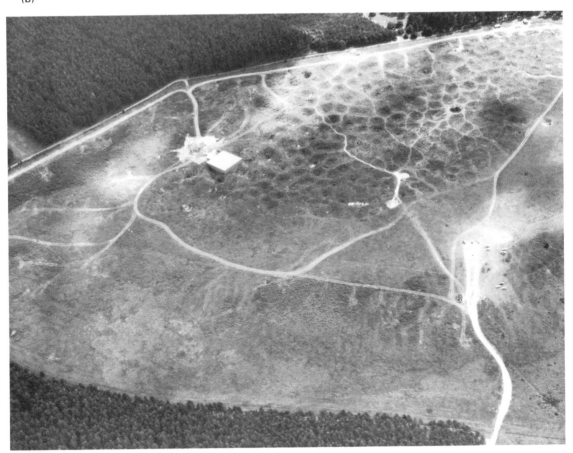

Fig. 6.9   (a) A section through the flint mines at Spiennes, Belgium (after Clark, 1954). (b) An aerial view of the flint mine complex at Grimes Graves, Norfolk, England; the depressions indicate the tops of the former mine shafts. (Reproduced with the kind permission of Cambridge University Collection: copyright reserved.)

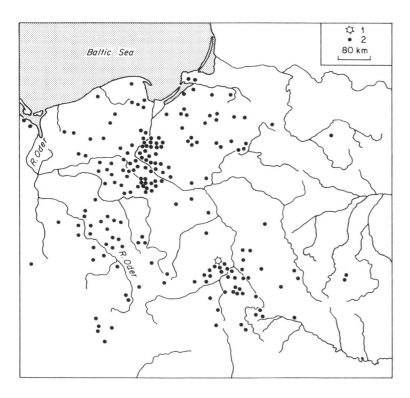

Fig. 6.10 The distribution of banded flint axes from the Krzemionki mines, Poland (after Tabaczynski, 1972). 1, Source; 2, finds.

Yugoslavia and Aibunar in Bulgaria. A number of different types of items were produced, in particular a wide variety of shaft-hole axes, sometimes found in graves and hoards but largely as isolated finds. Metal finds belonging to the period around the end of the fourth millennium, however, are much less common, and the inference is generally made that this results from a scarcity of available metal at the time (Sherratt, 1976). Whether or not this was the case, it is certainly a time of major change in the metal industries. It may be that the more easily worked copper ores were now largely exhausted; at all events, some of the rare copper finds of this period, found in Baden culture contexts (see, for example, Müller-Karpe, 1974), have proved on analysis to be made from the sulphide ores which formed the basis of the European Bronze Age industry (Novotna, 1973). Sulphide ores are more complex to work since they require an initial roasting process before they can be smelted. They are, however, more widely available, being found extensively in central and western Europe (Fig.6.11).

As I have already indicated, the number of finds is not large but it is sufficient to show that in the early third millennium BC metallurgy continued in the Carpathian Basin and south-east Europe and began over a wide area to the north and west (Ottaway, 1973). In the former area the small number of finds from the first half of the third millennium is made up of small hoards, occasional grave finds and one or two moulds for the manufacture of metal objects, and includes such types as sheet metal ornaments, daggers and axes (Fig.6.12). By this time the Caucasian metallurgical tradition had come into being at the eastern end of the Black Sea (see, for example, Häusler, 1976) and it seems fairly clear that some of the forms which first appear in central and south-east Europe at this time, such as the single-edged shaft-hole axe, are of Caucasian origin; however, evidence of more extensive Caucasian and steppe connections is, it should be added, extremely restricted in its distribution (Ecsedy, 1979; Häusler, 1981).

North and west of the Carpathian Basin metal

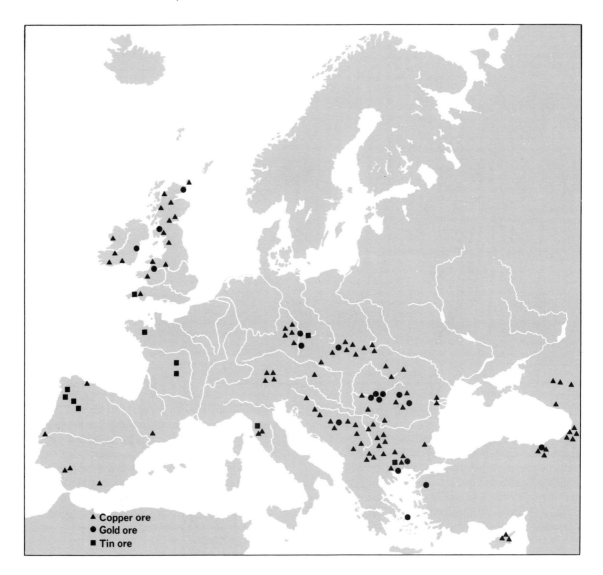

Fig. 6.11   Copper, tin and gold sources in Europe (after Coles and Harding, 1979).

items had been in circulation in small numbers for much of the fourth millennium, even occurring as far north-west as Denmark (Randsborg, 1980), but it seems that prior to the end of the fourth millennium either the metal or the objects themselves originated in the south-east. After this time local sources in Germany, Austria and western Czechoslovakia

began to be exploited (cf. Ottaway, 1973). In the first half of the third millennium the most commonly found items are small sheet copper ornaments from graves, but copper versions of the characteristic Corded Ware stone battle-axes were also produced and distributed in west-central Europe at this time (Fig.6.13) (Kibbert, 1980). A mould for one of these

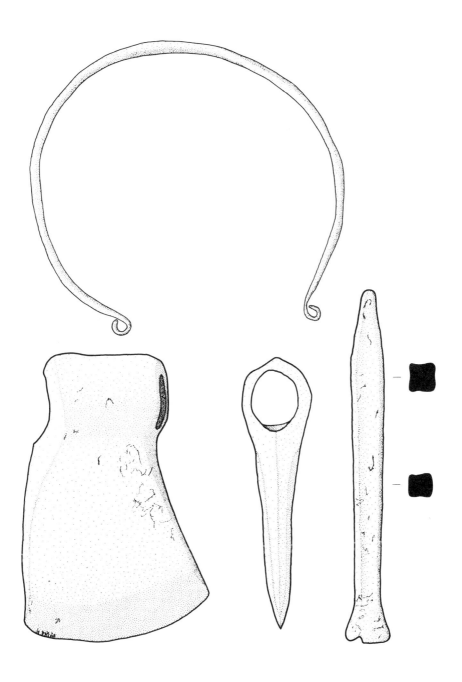

Fig. 6.12 Examples of metal types from late fourth/early third millennium BC central Europe (after Müller-Karpe, 1974).
  Scale: c. 1:1.4.

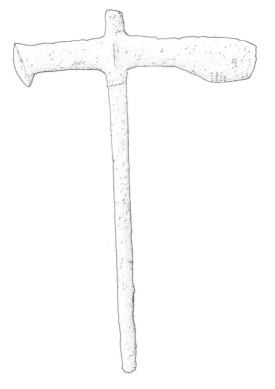

Fig. 6.13   A metal battle-axe from central Europe; both the axe-head and the shaft are made of copper (after Kibbert, 1980). Scale: c. 1:4.2.

from a site near Salzburg, Austria (Müller-Karpe, 1974) suggests that the ore sources of this area, so important later in the Bronze Age, were already being exploited. The Bell Beaker phase, however, *c.* 2500–2200 BC, sees a marked increase in the quantity of metal in the archaeological record of temperate Europe west of the Carpathian Basin. Copper daggers were regularly deposited in graves, as well as various copper and silver ornaments (Fig.6.14). It was not until this time that local copper metallurgy was introduced to northern France, coastal north-west Europe and the British Isles, a development associated with the appearance of Bell Beaker assemblages in these areas. As we will see in the next chapter, the bronze industries of the western part of temperate Europe follow on directly from these Beaker traditions.

This discussion of the Bell Beakers brings us back again to the general question of inter-regional inter-action and material culture similarity in the third millennium BC. As we have already seen, this period is characterized by a number of widespread cultural phenomena, the Baden, Corded Ware and Bell Beaker culture groups in traditional terminology. Although strong arguments have been presented recently against regarding them as indicative of invading groups of people from different sources, the problem of explaining the phenomena remains. They certainly do not relate to the patterns of contact indicated by the exchange of objects of known source. Many of these cross-cut the cultural patterns, such as the distribution of flint from Grand Pressigny mentioned above, while many of the areas of cultural similarity include the distribution zones of a variety of raw materials and exchanged objects.

It is clear that if progress is to be made it is essential to specify very closely the nature of the similarities. It has already been suggested that the Baden distribution may be explicable at least in part as the introduction of a new range of vessels associated with new functions. The Bell Beaker distribution, which stretches from Ireland to Hungary and Norway to North Africa, in fact proves to be a very variable phenomenon (Lanting and van der Waals, 1976; Harrison, 1980). Only in north-west Europe does there seem to be an extensive Bell Beaker material assemblage, although even here much of the settlement material belongs to the later phases of local sequences and not to the beginning (Whittle, 1981). Elsewhere the Bell Beaker 'culture' is limited to the occurrence of finely decorated Bell Beaker vessels, together with a small range of metal and other decorative items, generally in burials, in the context of local assemblages. On the evidence of the grave associations in many parts of Europe, it seems likely that it is part of a new form of the expression of male status (Shennan, 1976, 1977a), but in western Europe it may conceivably mark a more radical break and the introduction of a more inegalitarian ideology than had previously existed in this area (S. J. Shennan, 1982b; cf. Whittle, 1981; but see also Burgess, 1980). The widespread Corded Ware assemblage, with its burial associations of cord-decorated beaker and battle-axe, which precedes the Bell Beaker in much of central and

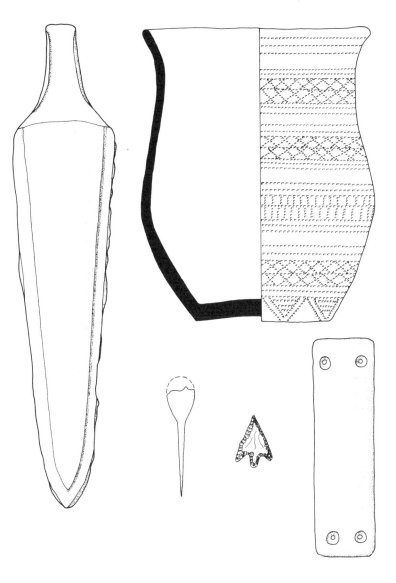

Fig. 6.14 A Bell Beaker assemblage with metalwork, from Roundway, Wiltshire, England (after Clarke, 1970).

north-west Europe, seems to be a similar status-related phenomenon.

Social organization. In many respects the discussion of the previous themes depends on various implicit assumptions about the nature of society in the different regions of Europe during the period under consideration. It is now necessary to examine this topic explicitly.

The main emphasis in the studies of social organization in the third millennium BC which have been carried out in recent years has been on the growth of socio-economic inequality. Inferences concerning this subject have been made on the basis of a variety of different lines of evidence, including the existence or otherwise of a settlement hierarchy, the presence or absence of large-scale ceremonial monuments, and the nature of differentiation among burials. These studies have tended to be dominated by the stages of Service's (1962) and Fried's (1967) evolutionary typologies of society and in the period under consideration here, specifically with the development of chiefdoms (see box). As we will see, for many parts of Europe evidence of a variety of different kinds suggests the existence of hierarchical societies which are not states (chiefdoms in Service's terminology) at least from the late fourth millennium until well into the iron age, so it might appear at first sight that we are dealing with an unchanging situation. In fact, it is highly unlikely that this is the

case, since it is increasingly clear that hierarchies may be of a variety of different types which it is not satisfactory simply to place at different points on a single unilinear scale.

In the British Isles the building of ceremonial monuments goes back to the beginning of the neolithic, but during the course of the fourth millennium it increased markedly in scale. The great tomb complexes of Ireland such as New Grange and Knowth, mentioned in the previous chapter, date to around 3500 BC, while in widely separated parts of Britain, from the Orkneys in the north to Wessex in

TYPOLOGIES OF SOCIETY

Probably the most important framework for the archaeological study of social change in the last two decades has been provided by the neo-evolutionary typologies of society developed by the American anthropologists Elman Service (1962) and Morton Fried (1967), who proposed that it was possible to categorize societies according to their position on a scale of social complexity.

Service's categories were band, tribe, chiefdom and state, based on the nature and scale of social integration. Band societies consist of local groups relatively tenuously linked to one another at a larger scale and generally associated with economies based on hunting and gathering. Tribal organization, on the other hand, is associated with agricultural economies and characterized by a variety of means of linking the members of different local social groups, so that tribes have considerably more cohesiveness than bands. Nevertheless, in both tribes and bands social relations are conducted on a basis of reciprocity and do not involve any centralized institutions. It is these which define the chiefdom on Service's scheme: the presence of a central figure, the chief, who coordinates social activity and has special privileges. In chiefdoms the characteristic mode of exchange is not reciprocity but redistribution: tribute goes from the population to the chief, who then redistributes at least some of it on such occasions as feasts. Finally, at the highest level of organizational complexity, comes the state. This too is centralized but is marked by a much greater degree of institutional differentiation at the centre than are chiefdoms, and the state apparatus has a monopoly on the socially

sanctioned use of force. It is characteristic of states that they integrate much larger numbers of people than the other forms of organization and that kinship ceases to be the basic idiom of social relations, which instead come to depend much more on a codified framework of legal rights and obligations.

Fried's scheme is similar to Service's but is based on the nature of social differentiation rather than the means of social integration. Thus his categories are egalitarian society, rank society, stratified society, and the state. Although these follow the same broad trend as Service does, because of their different basis they do not coincide with his categories exactly but rather overlap with them.

Both these schemes are empirical generalizations derived from the study of societies existing in the present or the very recent past. Their application to archaeology has been criticized on the grounds that knowledge of the defining characteristics of the different stages is simply inaccessible to inference from archaeological data. However, such a viewpoint is likely to be hostile to any attempt to study past societies by means of archaeological evidence and is not shared by the authors of this book. More serious is the criticism that it masks a great deal of significant social variation to think in terms of these simple unidimensional typologies, and that the empirical generalization of social types is less profitable than the development of general explanatory principles to account for social variation. Nevertheless, they have played an extremely important role in directing the attention of archaeologists towards significant questions of social change.

the south, new monuments on a larger scale began to be constructed around 3000 BC (see box on Henges).

It is arguable whether the major monuments had a settlement function, so that they can be regarded as the upper level of a settlement hierarchy, but such hierarchies have been postulated for parts of central and south-eastern Europe at the end of the fourth and the beginning of the third millennium BC. The upper level sites or centres in a settlement hierarchy usually have a number of features which distinguish them from other settlements. They are often larger and have additional functions of an economic, social or religious kind, generally associated with functionally differentiated individuals. As we will see in the next chapter, in the early states of the late Bronze Age Aegean the special character of these centres, with their storage facilities and evidence for administrative and craft activities, is clearly apparent; but are the supposed centres of the third and fourth millennium BC Europe of the same character?

Undoubtedly, the most frequently presented argument for the existence of a settlement hierarchy in the period around the end of the fourth millennium is the existence of fortified settlements. These are found widely in south-east, central and western Europe at this time, from Bulgaria to Germany and Poland (Milisauskas, 1978), as well as in France and Britain (Mercer, 1980; Passard, 1980). Very often the sites themselves are naturally defensible hilltop or spur situations, while the defences consist of palisades and/or ditches; Halle-Dölauer Heide in East Germany is an example (Behrens and Schröter, 1980). All this is suggestive of endemic local raiding, but of how much more is less clear. In some of the better researched areas of Europe, such as Bohemia, it is clear that they are not the only settlement type and that they were permanently occupied. It has also been suggested that there is a tendency for indications of craft activities and items obtained through long-distance exchange to occur more frequently at such sites (Pavelčik, 1973), but the evidence for this is rather more dubious. What is certainly true is that many of the defended sites, for example Homolka in Bohemia (Ehrich and Pleslova, 1968), are extremely small and could not have contained large populations (Fig.6.15). They may be indicative of some degree of institutionalized hierarchy but in many cases at least can hardly represent more than the household of a figure such as

a lineage head with a very localized degree of power.

It remains to consider the other main avenue which has been used to make inferences about social organization, the evidence of burials, in relation to this period. Over the greater part of western, north-western and west-central Europe various forms of collective burial generally prevailed at the beginning of the third millennium, as they had for a considerable time. At this point there was a major change in those parts of these areas where the Corded Ware assemblage appeared since this was associated with the introduction of an individual inhumation burial rite. Further west, however, this change did not generally occur until the Bell Beaker phase, or immediately after, at the end of the third millennium, and in some parts of France collective burial continued until well into the second.

It should not be thought that collective burial means undifferentiated burial (cf. Shanks and Tilley, 1982). It is increasingly clear that collective burial practices were extremely complex and it has long been suggested that not all the population could have been buried in the British collective tombs. Nevertheless, prior to the Corded Ware phase, and to the Bell Beaker phase further west, individual inhumation burial was relatively rare and there does not seem to have been a consistent use of grave goods to mark inter-individual distinctions, although Denmark may be an exception to this generalization (Randsborg, 1975).

The change in settlement pattern associated with the appearance of the Corded Ware has already been noted and one aspect of it in central Europe is the disappearance of any sites which might be regarded as central places. Corded Ware settlements seem to be very small in scale and undifferentiated, a situation largely paralleled by the burials, although there is an indication of differentiation in terms of grave goods among both adult males and adult females as well as between age and sex groups (Neustupný, 1973). In Britain and France the building of monuments of various kinds continued at this time. These areas lie to the west of the Corded Ware distribution and did not undergo the changes which correlate with its appearance. Here it seems to be the appearance of the Bell Beaker burials which represents the introduction of inter-individual differentiation in terms of the differential consumption of goods at burial, although there are indications that it may

HENGES

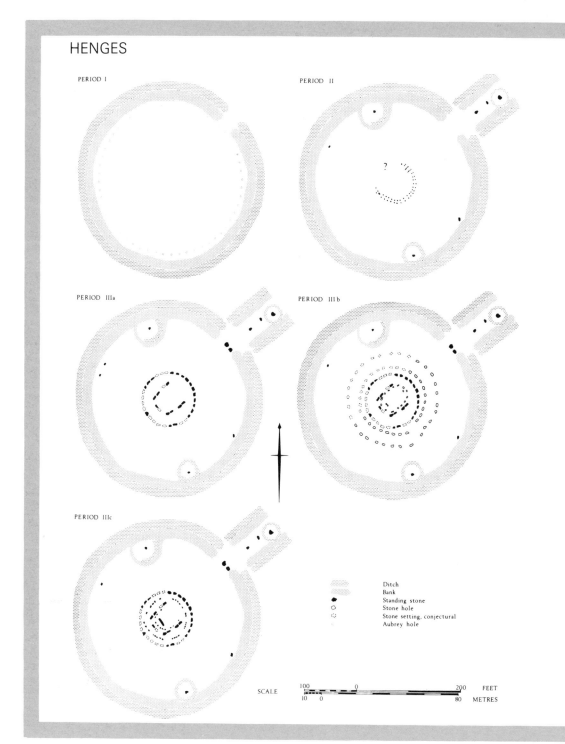

PERIOD I

PERIOD II

PERIOD IIIa

PERIOD IIIb

PERIOD IIIc

Ditch
Bank
Standing stone
Stone hole
Stone setting, conjectural
Aubrey hole

SCALE

| 100 | 0 | 200 | FEET |
| 10 | 0 | 80 | METRES |

The third millennium BC ceremonial enclosures of southern England are some of the most remarkable monuments from this period in the whole of Europe. By analogy with the most famous of all these sites, Stonehenge (Atkinson, 1956), they have been called 'henge monuments'.

Enclosures are a feature of the earlier neolithic throughout much of north-west Europe (see the previous chapter), but the major henge monuments of southern England, such as Avebury (I. Smith, 1965), Durrington Walls (Wainwright and Longworth, 1971) and Mount Pleasant (Wainwright, 1979), were enterprises on a vastly greater scale. They were bounded by a very large ditch and bank, with the ditch generally on the inside rather than the outside. Within the enclosures stone circles and/or wooden circular structures have been found. The great mound of Silbury Hill, near the Avebury henge, was a work of similar scale.

Renfrew (1973) used calculations of the man-hours

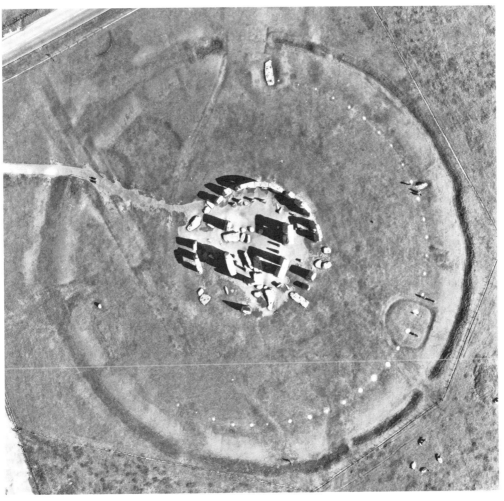

1. (a) The successive structural phases of Stonehenge (after Royal Commission on Historical Monuments, 1979). (b) An aerial view of Stonehenge.

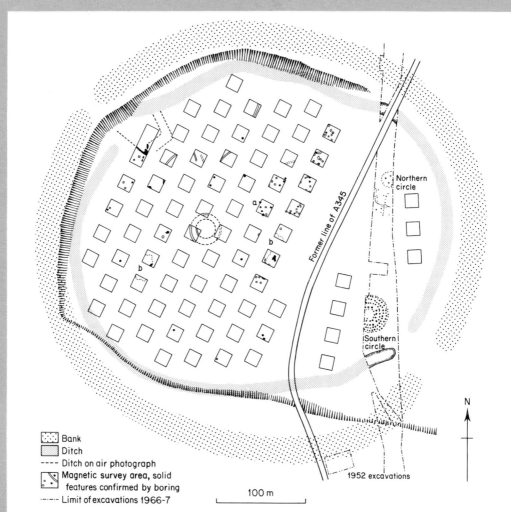

Bank

Ditch

---- Ditch on air photograph

Magnetic survey area, solid
features confirmed by boring

—--— Limit of excavations 1966-7

100 m

Northern circle

Former line of A345

Southern circle

1952 excavations

N

2. Plan of the Durrington Walls henge monument (after Royal Commission on Historical Monuments, 1979).

of labour involved in the construction of the monuments of the British neolithic to argue that those of the earlier neolithic were relatively modest undertakings which could have been accomplished by small-scale egalitarian groups, but that the monuments of the late neolithic, and the final phase of Stonehenge in the early Bronze Age, when the trilithons were erected, were several orders of magnitude greater in scale and must have involved some kind of centralized planning and control as well as a call on the manpower resources of a relatively wide area.

More recently, Startin and Bradley (1981) have made further calculations and arrived at lower total man-hour figures than those Renfrew used, although the significant difference in scale between earlier and later monuments remains. However, the nature of the power which was exercised, the nature of the social institutions which existed, or of the forms of rank and status associated with this centralization, if that is indeed what the major henge monuments represent, are topics of key importance on which work has hardly begun (cf. Whittle, 1981).

start rather earlier (Bradley, 1982). Subsequently there was a drastic decline in the scale of monument building since the new form of social system operated in a very different fashion from the one which preceded it. Society became re-oriented around the control and consumption of prestige goods, as we will see below (Renfrew, 1974; S. J. Shennan, 1982b).

In the more eastern parts of Europe, including the Carpathian Basin, the situation with regard to burial was very different. Collective burial was never prevalent and there is no very marked break in the form of burial practice to be seen between the late fourth and the late third millennium BC. This area had long been characterized by a great deal of variation in burial practices, including cemeteries of earth-pit graves in which individuals were differentiated by means of grave goods, as well as disposal in pits within the settlement. Such practices continued into the third millennium, and indeed into the second, but were increasingly accompanied by cremation, in a pattern which is differentiated both at the intra-cemetery level and at the regional scale (see Kalicz, 1968; Bona, 1975).

The tendency towards a mutual exclusion of settlement and burial evidence seen in the more western parts of Europe, so that where settlements are archaeologically detectable burials tend not to be, and vice versa, is much less marked in eastern Europe; for example, the fortified hilltop sites discussed above are occasionally accompanied by relatively richly equipped individual burials; the site of Vučedol in Yugoslavia is an example (Müller-Karpe, 1974). The evidence from both burials and settlements, including the occurrence of a limited number of metal items, such as tanged copper daggers, suggests the existence of at least some degree of social ranking to which the control and consumption of prestige items was relevant.

Conclusion

This chapter covers the period to near the end of the third millennium. The lower boundary to the period was fixed in terms of the Bell Beaker phase which, as we have seen, was of considerable significance in much of western, north-western and central Europe. From the Carpathian Basin eastwards, however, the break at *c.* 2200 BC is of little significance. Here the

major break in the sequence occurred around 3000 BC and after that time developments followed in the same pattern until a further marked change is visible in the region's archaeological record early in the second millennium; this will be considered in the next chapter.

Before going on to consider developments in the Mediterranean area in the third millennium it is necessary to indicate some of the interrelationships between the different changes and trends which have been outlined. The most sustained recent attmept to do this has been made by Gilman (1981), who has argued that the subsistence innovations discussed above, which were widely introduced and adopted in the course of the fourth millennium, resulted in a 'capital investment' in the agricultural land of the community which meant that the option of community fission was no longer available in the face of attempts by individuals to exploit their fellow community members. As a result of this, in the course of time stratified societies became established based on the differential ownership of the means of production.

Coherent though it is, there are problems with this argument when it is brought up against the archaeological evidence. One to which attention may be drawn is the long time gap between the adoption of the innovations in the course of the fourth millennium and the appearance of what are believed to be stratified societies at the beginning of the second (see next chapter). This is less important, however, than the evidence which we have already noted that the third millennium was a time when the area of cultivation expanded in many parts of Europe, counter to the specifications of Gilman's model; furthermore, the light plough which would have been used was not a major piece of capital equipment. It was, in fact, one of the most important factors enabling the expansion of settlement which has been described. This in turn must have depended ultimately on increased population density leading to the fissioning of settlements and the consequent need for further colonization.

A suggestion that has been made in relation to the Netherlands, which may be relevant for much of northern and north-western Europe, is that by the time of the Corded Ware period it may no longer have been possible for daughter settlements to be established close to their parent; relatively long-

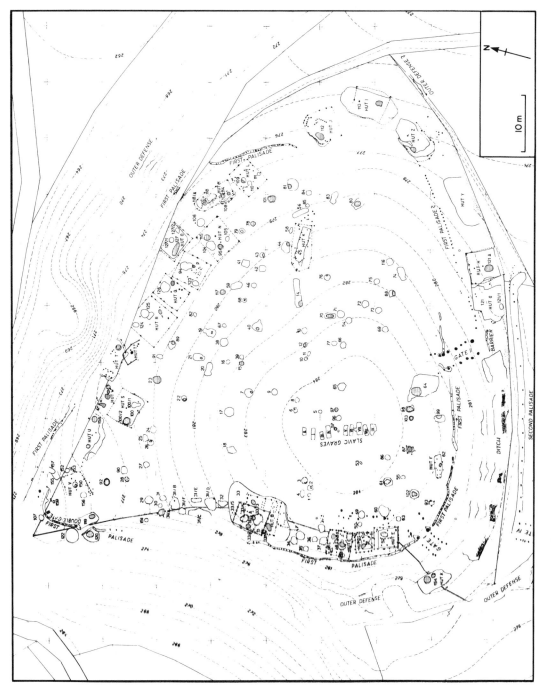

Fig. 6.15 Plan of the late fourth millennium BC hilltop enclosure of Homolka, western Czechoslovakia (after Ehrich and Pleslová, 1968).

distance 'leap-frogging' migration may have become necessary, resulting in an unprecedented break-up of previously close networks of communities related by kinship. One aspect of this process may have been the creation of an ideological framework which facilitated the incorporation of outsiders, and the large-scale homogeneities in material culture which we have already seen may be part of this. A feature of particular interest in this development, characterizing much of Europe north and west of the Carpathian Basin, where the Corded Ware and Bell Beaker distributions were prevalent, is the disappearance of fortified settlements already noted. In the small dispersed settlements of the late neolithic and beginning of the Bronze Age in this broad zone there are no indications of defences, nor the selection of defensible settlement locations. These locations show a regular pattern of abandonment at the beginning of the third millennium BC with reoccupation a millennium later in the later early Bronze Age; Homolka is again an example (Ehrich and Pleslova, 1968). It would seem then that the expansion process which is apparent in many areas was a peaceful one involving the integration of many small domestic units in the way already described above, an integration all the more necessary in view of the increasing instability of the environments being occupied.

At this point it is worth considering again the large-scale appearance at this time of the practice of single burial with grave goods. Whether one considers Corded Ware or Bell Beakers there is much emphasis on male prestige goods, such as stone battle-axes and copper daggers, the warlike aspect of which contrasts markedly with the disappearance of evidence for fortification and defence; it may well be that their significance was symbolic only. As we have seen, the cemeteries and graves of this period, unlike the preceding one, provide evidence for the representation of inter-individual distinctions by means of grave goods, and associated indications of some degree of ranking (Shennan, 1977b). Given the small size of the settlements and the lack of evidence for regional centralization, these distinctions cannot have been great but it does suggest some interesting possibilities. The breakdown of rigid localized kinship networks, stemming from the postulated necessity for long distance migration, may well have led to an increased emphasis on the explicit exhibition

of status by means of material symbols. Furthermore, the process of integrating disparate communities would have had built into it an initial asymmetry, that between newcomers and existing inhabitants. This asymmetry may well have provided a ranking principle which operated in the course of the incorporation of newcomers into local kinship networks. That the large-scale homogeneities in material culture seen at this time may have been associated with the incorporation of outsiders has already been noted, but if symbolic incorporation was important, it is worth asking what aspects of material culture were used in this way. Many were not, as the pronounced local differentiation of much Corded Ware and Bell Beaker pottery makes clear; those that were so used were those associated with the key area of personal status.

In Britain the situation was very different, as we have seen, with the continued expansion of regionally organized monument building well into the third millennium; here, as elsewhere in western Europe, the appearance of Bell Beakers most probably ushered in the forms of ritual and social organization which were to characterize the Bronze Age and which replaced the monument-based hierarchies of the third millennium. In the Carpathian Basin and southeast Europe, however, there was no such change as that associated with the Corded Ware and Bell Beakers. In the same period cultural traditions became increasingly regional and localized, fortified sites continued to exist, while individual inhumation cemeteries and burials were far less prevalent (Kalicz, 1968; Bona, 1975). Whether or not it is because the very different, generally more abrupt, topography and soil distribution of the south-east European area did not have the potential for gradual expansion which existed in the more variegated and gentle landscape of the north and west, it seems likely that competition, in the form of endemic raiding, continued between small-scale hierarchical groups.

MEDITERRANEAN EUROPE

The ecological differences between Mediterranean and temperate Europe have been outlined earlier in this book. As we have seen, the adaptations to them of agriculturally-based societies differed from an early date. However, in the course of the period from the late fourth to the late third millennium BC these differences increased and a major division also arose between the Aegean area, developing towards the first European civilization, and the Mediterranean area to the west. It is most straightforward to follow this division and to begin with an examination of the Aegean.

The Aegean

A chronological table showing the cultural sequence for the various parts of the Aegean is shown in Fig.6.16. Like most such sequences it is heavily dependent on changes in pottery styles, seen in stratigraphic sequences at certain key sites, such as Troy in north-west Anatolia or Phylakopi on Melos

in the Cyclades. In fact, the pottery styles of much of the Aegean at the beginning of the early Bronze Age have a great deal in common with the Baden styles of south-east Europe and the Carpathian Basin discussed above; the same dark grey burnished appearance and a similar emphasis on vessels for containing and serving liquids, which Renfrew (1972) has related to the innovation of wine drinking in the Aegean (Fig.6.17), but which, as we have seen already, Sherratt (1981) links to the increasing importance of milk; it may more generally reflect an increased *social* importance of drinking.

Substantively far more significant than changes in pottery, however, if perhaps initially less obvious archaeologically, were some of the other developments of the third millennium, since it is increasingly clear that it was at this time that much of the basis of the second millennium Aegean civilizations was

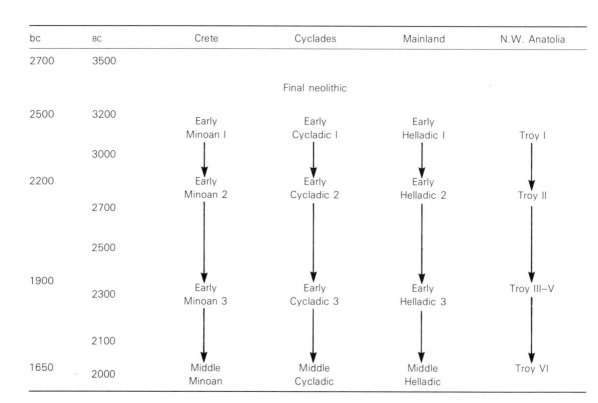

bc	BC	Crete	Cyclades	Mainland	N.W. Anatolia
2700	3500				
			Final neolithic		
2500	3200	Early Minoan I	Early Cycladic I	Early Helladic I	Troy I
	3000				
2200		Early Minoan 2	Early Cycladic 2	Early Helladic 2	Troy II
	2700				
	2500				
1900	2300	Early Minoan 3	Early Cycladic 3	Early Helladic 3	Troy III–V
	2100				
1650	2000	Middle Minoan	Middle Cycladic	Middle Helladic	Troy VI

Fig. 6.16 A regional chronological chart for the Aegean area.

established. During the neolithic it was the plains of Thessaly and Macedonia in the north of Greece which seem to have been the most prosperous and developed. Southern Greece with its more arid climate and smaller pockets of viable agricultural land was less densely settled, while the islands of the Aegean, the Cyclades in particular, show little sign of permanent settlement until the end of the neolithic (Renfrew, 1972; Halstead, 1981a).

In the early Bronze Age this pattern changed markedly. As Renfrew (1972) has shown, whereas in the northern part of Greece populations remained relatively static, in the south there are indications of marked population increase and the Cyclades are characterized by extensive settlement (Fig.6.18). It is likely that the domestication and adoption of the olive and the vine played an important role in this process; their use is documented by the finding of grape pips and olive stones in archaeological contexts. The olive in particular would have made areas more productive since it would not have competed with cereals for either land or labour while it provides a very high calorific yield. Recently, Halstead (1981a) has emphasized that the increased exploitation of sheep may also have played a role in

this expansion, and has suggested that wool was beginning to become important at this time, possibly as a result of the diffusion of a more woolly type of sheep; the potential role of sheep as manure producers improving soil fertility also should not be neglected.

The settlement pattern associated with the expansion was a dispersed one: settlements were generally very small, of farmstead or hamlet size in contrast to the larger village size settlements in the north. In this way they were matching themselves to the small pockets of arable soil available to support the mixed farming base on which they depended. Unfortunately, in the interpretation of the settlements of the Aegean Bronze Age there has been

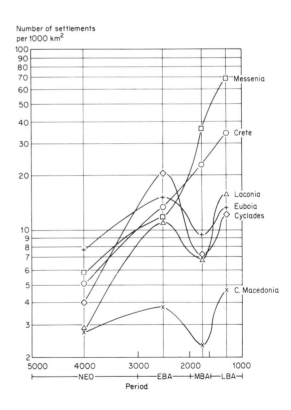

Fig. 6.18 Patterns of differential regional growth in settlement numbers in the prehistoric Aegean (after Renfrew, 1972).

Fig. 6.17 Drinking and pouring vessels from the Aegean early Bronze Age (after Renfrew, 1972).

a tendency to see all of them too much as prototypes of the palaces of the second millennium when, in fact, they are no more than small-scale agricultural settlements, as, for example, the site of Myrtos in Crete (Warren, 1972; Whitelaw, 1983). Even so, it is undeniable that not all the sites which have been examined were agricultural hamlets. Some were almost certainly regional central places, a step higher in the settlement hierarchy. It is clear, for example, that Knossos on Crete was already an order of magnitude larger than other Cretan settlements by the end of the neolithic (Whitelaw, in press), while at third millennium BC Lerna, in the Peloponnese, a large building called by the excavators the 'House of Tiles', is in some respects similar to the later palaces and contained numbers of clay seal impressions (Fig.6.19) (Caskey, 1954, 1955; Heath, 1958). Lerna, like a number of other third millennium sites, was fortified (Fig.6.20), a further indication of a special status for certain sites, and also of the existence of warfare. Fortifications continued to be elaborated into the second millennium on the islands and the Greek mainland but, strikingly, do not occur on Crete. Nevertheless, it remains important not to exaggerate the size of the majority of these sites. Many of them are extremely small, no larger than their temperate European equivalents of the same period, but tend to be regarded as more significant than these merely because for local geological and vegetational reasons they were constructed in stone rather than timber, and because of the tendency already mentioned to project features of the second millennium back into the third. However, the suggestion of some regional centralization in the

settlement patterns of the third millennium is also accompanied by evidence from a number of places of considerable differentiation between burials in terms of their contents, and also of increasingly elaborate specialist craft activity, most notably in the developing field of metallurgy (Renfrew, 1972; Branigan, 1968).

Rich early Bronze Age burials are known from throughout the Aegean; they occur in the Cyclades, Crete, and to a lesser extent in mainland Greece, and show that quantities of valuable materials were being taken permanently out of social circulation. Perhaps most striking of all, however, are the remarkable hoards from third millennium BC Troy II, a site whose special status is also indicated by its fortifications and its internal buildings (Fig.6.20) (Blegen, 1963). It is difficult to avoid the conclusion that in many parts of the Aegean at this time regionally centralized forms of organization were prevalent, with a corresponding social hierarchy. In Service's (1962) terms we are already dealing with complex chiefdoms. The elites in these societies had at their command the services of what must have been full-time specialist craftsmen to achieve the high standard of workmanship which is the most striking feature of many of the items from graves and hoards.

The growth of specialist craftsmanship developed hand-in-hand with the hierarchies it served, but was particularly intimately linked with the growth of metallurgy, which provided a potential unavailable in other materials. Copper metallurgy had been known in the Aegean for a long time prior to the early Bronze Age but it was undoubtedly in this period, and particularly in its second phase, that its scale

Fig. 6.19 Seal impressions from early Bronze Age Lerna (after Renfrew, 1972). Scale: c. 1.4:1.

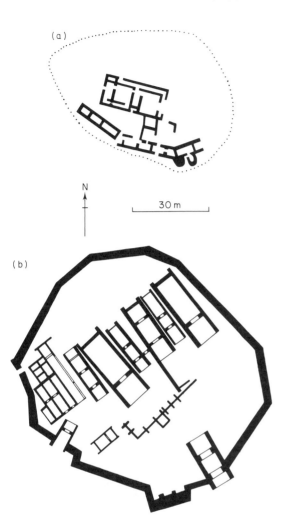

Fig. 6.20 Plans of Aegean fortified sites of the third millennium BC (a) Lerna III (b) Troy II (after Renfrew, 1972).

increased considerably (Renfrew, 1972). Moreover, it is at this time too that the alloying of copper with tin to produce tin–bronze first occurs; earlier objects were of copper only, as they were in temperate Europe until rather later. Where tin was unavailable arsenic was used to produce the same effect of increased hardness and improved workability; its use seems to have been particularly prevalent in the Cyclades and Crete. It is hard to assess the importance of the different categories of use to which

metal was put since there is no reason to believe that the archaeological record provides us with a representative picture: as elsewhere in Europe weapons and ornaments are present in far larger quantities than tools, which nevertheless exist in considerable variety. However, the level of craftsmanship involved in the production of some of the jewellery and weapons suggests that the social aspect of metallurgy was of considerable significance (Fig.6.21); the innovation of the dagger is strikingly evident, but whether it really revolutionized warfare, as has been suggested, or was simply of symbolic significance is more arguable.

Conclusions. It remains to consider the explanations which have been offered for the social and economic developments of the Aegean early Bronze Age described above, and it may be worth going into these in some detail as an example of the way in which a particular set of developments generates competing hypotheses.

In the past they would have been ascribed to the influence of diffusion from the Near East and it has been suggested recently that arguments about the importance of outside influence for developments within a given area cannot be decided on the basis of archaeological evidence for external contacts. Nevertheless, such evidence, or the lack of it, must be taken into account, while models which suppose non-visible influence must be very clearly specified so as to be testable in other ways. In the case of the Aegean early Bronze Age the lack of evidence for external contacts is striking, with the partial exception of Crete, where a number of imports from Egypt and the Near East are known, but even here the indications are slight. Trade and contact within the Aegean were undoubtedly important (Renfrew, 1969), and it is to processes going on within this area that the developments of the Aegean early Bronze Age are best ascribed, although it may yet turn out that external trade with Anatolia was a relevant factor.

At the end of the first major treatment of these processes Renfrew (1972, pp. 480–85) outlined two rather different models to account for the changes observed. The first, his *subsistence/redistribution model*, depended on the domestication of the vine and especially the olive. The fact that both cereals and

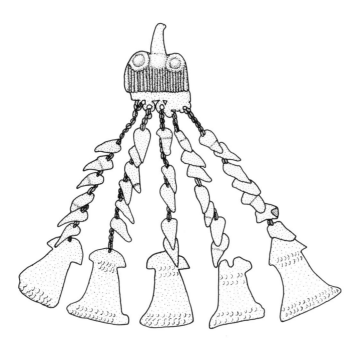

Fig. 6.21   An example of Aegean early Bronze Age ornamental metalwork: an earring from Poliochni on the island of Lemnos (after Müller-Karpe, 1974.

olives could be grown, in different areas, from a single village led to internal redistribution of these products, in the hands of what came to be chiefs. Specialized services came to be concentrated round the resources controlled by the redistributive agent, and the larger population which followed on the adoption of the new food crops was increasingly able to support such services on a full-time basis.

In the second, the *craft specialization/wealth model*, a different set of factors is selected, based on the importance of bronze, whether tin or arsenic based, in producing weapons which could give their possessors an advantage in combat, as well as status items, for which metal ornaments too were relevant. A demand for these developed which led to increased specialization and an enhanced status for the village chief controlling their production, who would himself have been the main consumer of the products. In turn, the result was an increase in competition and ultimately hostility and warfare, for the control of these new goods.

There are problems with both these arguments although they undoubtedly include some of the key factors. Gilman (1981) puts the building blocks together in a different way. For him the importance

of the olive and the vine is not the basis they provide for redistribution by a benevolent managerial elite, but the opportunities they give for exploitation. Olive trees in particular represent a long-term capital investment in agriculture. This means that communities dependent on them for subsistence are tied to them. People are not able to move away if any member of their own community starts breaking the social rules and trying to establish a dominant position, while they also become more open to 'protection-racket' politics at the hands of other communities and dominant members of their own. The argument certainly seems to have more in its favour when applied to the olive trees of the Aegean than to the plough agriculture of temperate Europe, although it remains the subject of considerable dispute and is in competition with a fourth alternative which again makes use of a very similar set of variables.

This is the 'social storage' model (Halstead, 1981a; O'Shea, 1981; Halstead and O'Shea 1982). One of the key problems faced by early agricultural communities was that of the fluctuation in harvest yields from year to year, as we have noted above, but Halstead's argument is that the marked changes in settlement pattern which characterized the Aegean in the fourth and third millennia, particularly the great expansion of settlement in the islands and small pockets of arable land in the southern mainland, posed this general problem in a rather specific way which led to a particular solution. One way of coping with harvest fluctuations is exchange, so that communities which are in surplus one year will share with their more unfortunate neighbours in the expectation of similar treatment if they should be in the same circumstances; the debt thus created may be seen as a form of indirect storage for the creditor. In fact, food in such contexts is often exchanged against material prestige items, which in emergencies provide a kind of currency which can be used so that food exchanges are not restricted to specific pairs of communities. The argument is that such complex networks are predisposed to simplification through centralization, perhaps by means of a redistribution agency of the type which figures in Renfrew's models. One important parameter of such systems is their scale. They can only work in contexts where agricultural disaster is sufficiently localized for the transport of foodstuffs to be possible with the available technology. This is much more feasible in the southern Aegean than in the agricultural plains of northern Greece since in the former there is greater local diversity of topography and micro-climatic conditions, while much of the available agricultural land is close to the sea and consequently better bulk transport facilities. The potential of animals in such a 'social storage' system is obvious and Halstead's suggestion of the importance of sheep, which could be used for wool and manure when they were not required as an emergency food supply, is very plausible in the light of the role of sheep in the second millennium palace economies which will be examined in the next chapter.

The model as presented tends to emphasize the redistributive managerial role of centralized elites in such a system, but it is also possible to look at it from a point of view which is closer to Gilman's. In the unstable environments of the southern Aegean some locations are more favourable than others and communities in those locations would have been continually in the position of creditor, so that ultimately they would have controlled not just the more reliable food sources but also the majority of the prestige items. This could have been the basis for

two further developments: a gradual influx of population to the key location, which would have put new pressures on the internal organization of that community, and the reduction to a position of dependence of less well-situated groups. Such a process may well be relevant to the growth of Knossos mentioned above.

These different models show some of the ways in which the kaleidoscope may be turned in attempting to account for the developments of the Aegean early Bronze Age, and give some idea of the way archaeologists go about trying to explain their observations. The subsequent growth towards the palace economies of the second millennium will be considered in the next chapter, but there seems little to disagree with in Renfrew's (1972) argument that by the end of the early Bronze Age the pattern had already been set.

The Central and Western Mediterranean

Although the area from Italy to Portugal tends to be viewed from a distance as a unity in terms of its ecological conditions, which are subsumed under the general heading of 'Mediterranean', on closer inspection it proves remarkable for its diversity, which is mirrored in many aspects of the development of the third millennium. This is particularly the case with the cultural sequences of the period, which show a regional variation which defies easy summary until the middle of the period when the appearance of the Bell Beaker assemblage, in different versions in different places, imposes a cultural unity in certain limited respects on the peninsulas and islands of the western Mediterranean (Harrison, 1980). An indication of some of the regional sequences is given in Fig.6.22, but it is interesting to note that whereas in temperate Europe some of the changes in the ceramic sequence seem to correlate with major transformations of the socio-economic system, in the western Mediterranean this seems to be less markedly the case; indeed, some regions at least show considerable general stability during the period.

The area is in a worse position than temperate Europe in that the pace of prehistoric research in the

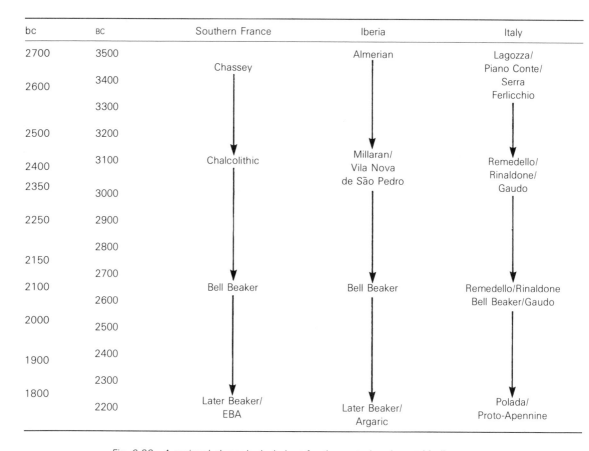

bc	BC	Southern France	Iberia	Italy
2700	3500		Almerian	Lagozza/ Piano Conte/
2600	3400	Chassey		Serra Ferlicchio
	3300			
2500	3200			
2400	3100	Chalcolithic	Millaran/ Vila Nova	Remedello/ Rinaldone/
2350	3000		de São Pedro	Gaudo
2250	2900			
	2800			
2150	2700			
2100	2600	Bell Beaker	Bell Beaker	Remedello/Rinaldone Bell Beaker/Gaudo
2000	2500			
1900	2400			
	2300			
1800	2200	Later Beaker/ EBA	Later Beaker/ Argaric	Polada/ Proto-Apennine

Fig. 6.22   A regional chronological chart for the central and west Mediterranean.

last 100 years has been far slower; on the whole it has been the striking remains of the classical world which have attracted the interest of Mediterranean archaeologists, much less of a distraction north of the Alps and southern France. This situation has begun to change significantly only relatively recently and the area still suffers from the problem discussed at the beginning of this chapter, the fact that research has been largely carried out within a culture historical diffusionist framework. Fortunately, work is now emerging which will in the future enable the construction of a more satisfactory picture.

Subsistence. We have already seen that in many parts of Europe the end of the fourth and the early part of

the third millennia were times of considerable change in settlement and subsistence. There are indications that this was also the case in south-east Spain, one of the key areas of the west Mediterranean during this period because of the precocious developments of the Millaran culture which will be considered below.

Lowland Almeria and Murcia, where these developments took place, is the driest area of Europe, with a rainfall which is unpredictable and torrential when it occurs. It has been argued (Mathers, 1984) that the lack of known early agricultural sites in this area is a genuine one, and that the appearance of agricultural sites there at the end of the fourth millennium BC represents the expansion into the area of populations which could cope with the difficulties it presents. The reasons for the expansion remain unclear, as indeed they do for the similar expansions elsewhere in Europe at this time, but the fact that it occurred raises the question of the means which were used to survive in these conditions and indeed to flourish, as some communities evidently did. Gilman (1976, 1981) has suggested that as in the Aegean the domestication of the vine and the olive may have been important; finds of seeds and stones of both are known from early third millennium Copper Age contexts in Iberia. Another feature which has been proposed as important is water-control. The evidence for irrigation remains slight, although a supposed irrigation ditch has been found at the site of Cerro de la Virgen in south-eastern Spain (Schüle and Pellicer, 1966) while it has also been suggested that the location of Copper Age and Bronze Age sites at the confluences of seasonal streams is a result of the potential of such locations for flood-water farming (Chapman, 1978; Gilman, 1981); there is, however, no reason why this could not have been practised at a very early date (Sherratt, 1980). In fact, it may have been not so much innovations in agricultural practice which were important for coping with the extreme environments of south-east Spain, but organizational developments and changes in society; these will be discussed further below.

This picture of agricultural expansion contrasts markedly with that recently outlined by Barker (1981) for central Italy, where the emphasis during the same period is on stability. Agricultural economies had become established prior to the late fourth millennium, and Barker suggests that transhumance had already become an element in the subsistence economy, since not only are there low-lying sites on good soils with archaeological indications of mixed agricultural economies, but there also exist sites high in the Apennine hills which could not have been occupied all the year round and which must have been summer herding stations. The basis for this movement lies in the summer desiccation of lowland grazing which means that only small numbers of stock can be kept there all the year round, whereas far larger quantities may be maintained by taking advantage of the seasonal complementarity of grazing in the lowlands and the hills.

Since the work of Higgs and his colleagues (Higgs, 1972) first directed attention to the prehistoric sub-sistence economies of the Mediterranean, transhumance has played a considerable role in accounts of the operation of those economies, by analogy with the practices of mediaeval and early modern times. More recently, however, a number of authors (e.g. Lewthwaite, 1981) have attacked this view, arguing that the importance of transhumance in the historically known cases is the result of specific conditions which would not have obtained in the prehistoric period. On this argument, the importance of the pastoral sector of the subsistence economy in the prehistoric west Mediterranean has been over-emphasized. It has been suggested indeed (Lewthwaite, 1981) that until the Roman and medieval periods the importance of animals, particularly sheep, may well have been the production of manure to improve arable yields, rather than dairying or wool production. Such a view does not necessarily conflict with the role assigned by Halstead (1981a) to sheep exploitation in his discussion of 'social storage' in the Aegean, outlined above. He saw sheep as essentially a mobile food reserve which could be consumed in case of emergency, but from which by-products could be taken in the meantime; it is certain that in the Aegean wool was important to the palace economies of the second millennium BC.

Apart from the specific question of transhumance there has been more generally a tendency to see pastoral economies as dominant in the prehistoric western Mediterranean, largely on the basis of inferring that the current degraded ecological conditions also existed in the past. The classic example of this view is the old interpretation of the late neolithic inhabitants of the limestone plateaux of southern France as 'Les pasteurs des plateaux'. In fact, this was not a degraded area but one character-ized by a fertile brown forest soil suitable for mixed farming based on cereals supported by livestock, and indeed superior to the clay soils of the lowlands and depressions between the plateaux (Delano Smith, 1972). Both the limestone plateaux and the coastal lagoons immediately to their south were certainly settled by the mid-fourth millennium because numbers of sites are known from both areas with Chassey occupation (Delano Smith, 1979). Neverthe-less, there does seem to have been an expansion of settlement into the interior of the plateaux in the post-Chassey phase at the end of the fourth millennium, an expansion which may, like that in south-east Spain, be associated with social developments.

Social Organization. Like many parts of temperate Europe at the beginning of the third millennium, much of the western Mediterranean is marked by evidence of social change. Unlike most of them, however, the developments in the western Mediterranean seem clearly to have been leading in the same direction as those going on in the Aegean at the same time, towards the beginnings of regionally centralized organization in the context of a settlement pattern consisting largely although not entirely of dispersed hamlets.

Again some of the clearest evidence for these trends comes from Iberia, in the occurrence of what appear to be fortified centres and in increasing indications in the burial evidence of developing social inequality. Chapman (1981a) has argued for the existence of social ranking on the basis of an analysis

of the cemetery of megalithic tombs associated with the fortified late fourth/early third millennium site of Los Millares (Fig.6.23). Examination of the tomb inventories indicated differences between them in the quantity and types of grave goods deposited, while the richer ones were located closer to the settlement. The grave goods included items of copper, ivory and ostrich egg shell, materials which must have been obtained by exchange (see below), and it has been argued that the quality of workmanship demonstrated by many of the objects is indicative of craft specialization. It has also been noted more generally that a relationship exists between the size and degree of elaboration of the megalithic tombs in Iberia and the quantity and variety of grave goods: they are smaller and less elaborate in areas with fewer prestige items in the tombs (Mathers, 1984). On the basis of all this evidence it appears that while social differentiation was considerably developed in lowland Almeria, in most of the rest of Iberia, particularly the north, it

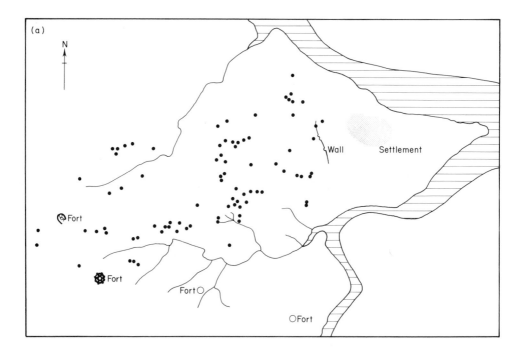

Fig. 6.23   (a) Plan of the site of Los Millares, south-east Spain (after Harding, 1978). (b) Los Millares tomb 40. This contained the remains of at least 100 individuals; the grave goods included more than 120 ceramic vessels and 170 other items. Those illustrated are a decorated piece of ivory, an ivory comb, two stone axes, a stone bead and a copper axe (after Müller-Karpe, 1974). Scale: c. 1:1.6.

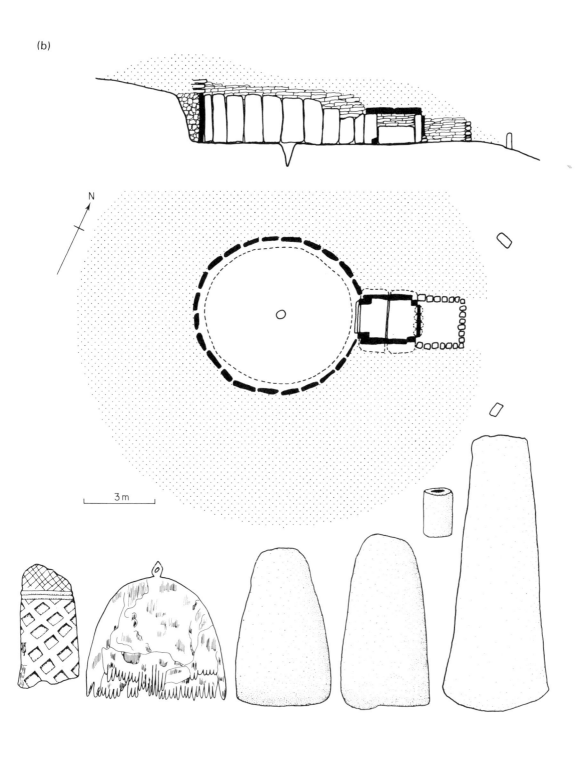

(b)

N

3 m

was far less marked. The main exception to this generalization is the area around the Tagus estuary in Portugal, where exactly the same phenomena occur in the Vila Nova de São Pedro culture at the beginning of the third millennium as in the Millaran culture of Almeria. Fortified settlements are known (Fig.6.24), such as Zambujal (Sangmeister and Schubart, 1972) and Vila Nova de São Pedro itself

(Savory, 1968), as well as small hamlets, and there are the same elaborate collective tombs with rich grave goods including copper, ivory and ostrich egg shell, as well as numbers of objects whose functions are unknown but which most probably served as status symbols (Fig.6.25) (Harrison, 1980).

Although the chronology is not as secure as it might be, it seems that prior to the end of the fourth

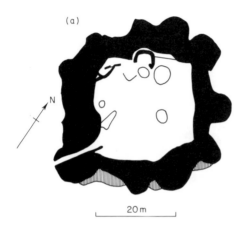

(a)

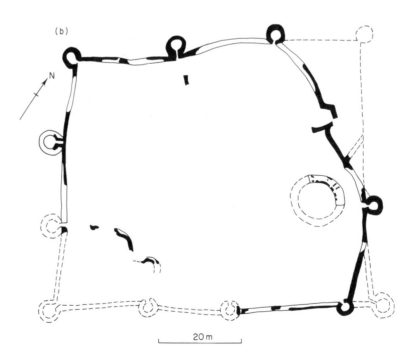

(b)

Fig. 6.24   Plans of late fourth/early third millennium BC fortifications in the west Mediterranean. (a) Vila Nova de São Pedro, Portugal. (b) Lébous, southern France.

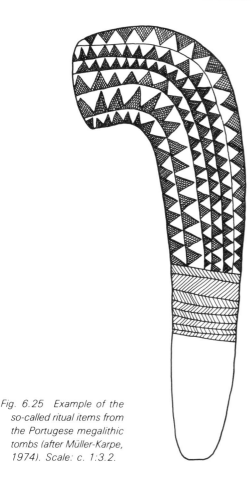

Fig. 6.25 Example of the so-called ritual items from the Portugese megalithic tombs (after Müller-Karpe, 1974). Scale: c. 1:3.2.

Indications of regional centralization are by no means as clear in peninsular Italy in the earlier third millennium BC. Barker argues, however, that the burial evidence is suggestive of some degree of social differentiation, on a scale which varies from region to region, as one might expect. Differentiation between burials in terms of their grave goods is most marked in the Gaudo group in the south, where metal objects again play a role, as they do throughout the western Mediterranean at this time. The Rinaldone graves of central Italy, while less differentiated than the Gaudo group, also frequently contain metal objects, but this can be ascribed to the fact that many of them are close to the metal sources of Tuscany and it was not necessary to exert demand from a distance as it was in the case of groups further away from the sources. It is noteworthy that very few copper daggers and axes crossed the Apennines (Fig.6.26): on the Adriatic side of central Italy social statuses apparently did not need to be represented at burial by means of exotic items obtained from a distance; flint daggers were sufficient.

Interaction, exchange and production. It is now necessary to examine the question of exchange more closely as it has a considerable bearing on the developments in social organization discussed in the previous section.

Perhaps the most detailed work which has been carried out is that on the characterization of obsidian and its distribution patterns (Hallam et al., 1976), which is interesting from a number of points of view, not least for the indications it gives of the patterning of interaction in the western Mediterranean and of the separation of Iberia from contacts which included Italy, southern France and the largest west Mediterranean islands (Fig.6.27). Significant too is the fact that the superior quality of Lipari obsidian for the production of large blades is mirrored in its wider distribution. More generally, obsidian bears witness to a process well-known in ethnographic contexts, in which materials which are used for utilitarian purposes close to their source acquire a greater and often non-functional value with distance. Barker (1981) has noted that the obsidian blades found on neolithic settlements in central Italy are invariably both wafer-thin and undamaged, suggesting that they were never actually used; furthermore, water-sieving of deposits on these sites

millennium no such evidence for social differentiation and hierarchical organization is apparent in either Portugal or south-east Spain so that we are seeing in these two areas, largely to the exclusion of the rest of Iberia, developments which can really only be paralleled in the contemporary Aegean. In southern France some similar sites are now emerging, of which the best known is Lébous in the Hérault (Arnal, 1973). Lébous (Fig.6.24) starts at the end of the fourth millennium with material of the Copper Age Fontbouisse culture and continues into the early Bronze Age. It is likely that this site too represents some kind of regional centre in its contrast with the surrounding hamlets, but the striking wealth and differentiation of the Iberian megalithic tombs is not matched by those of the Hérault.

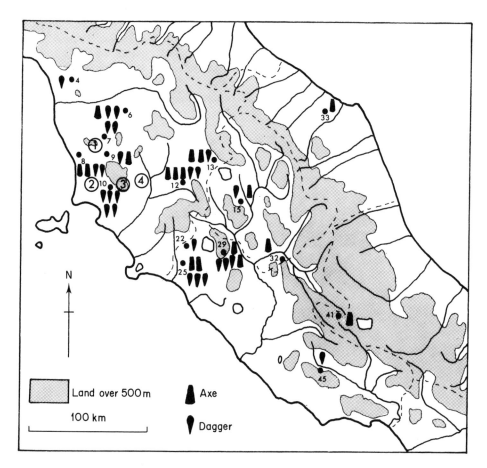

Fig. 6.26 The distribution of copper artifacts in eneolithic burials in central Italy (after Barker, 1981).

has produced obsidian core remnants less than a centimetre in size, worked to the limit of possibility.

There is no suggestion, however, that obsidian moved by any other than a system of sea-transport and hand-to-hand exchange (Renfrew, 1972). This is not the case with some of the other materials exchanged in the earlier third millennium whose provenance is known, specifically the ivory and ostrich egg shell found in the Copper Age contexts of southern Iberia. These are indicative of directional trade (Renfrew, 1972). Their source is north Africa but they do not show a general decrease of quantity with distance from the source; on the contrary, quantities are concentrated some distance away from

the source, in this case in the Millaran and Vila Nova de São Pedro burials of south-east Spain and Portugal. Such a pattern, when it occurs, is indicative if not of a greater demand in those areas, of a greater ability to realize it, and is generally associated with societies of some degree of complexity. Such arguments, of course, fit in very well with the evidence discussed in the previous section that these two areas were indeed exceptional in the degree of social hierarchy and centralization which had developed. Harrison and Gilman (1977) have made an interesting analysis of the exchange of these materials in which they note the concentration of north African materials in southern Iberia and the

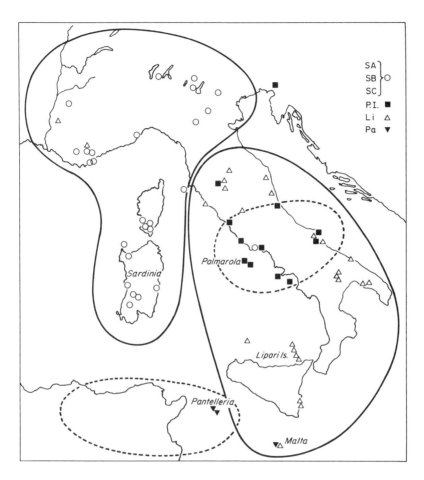

Fig. 6.27 Obsidian sources and the distribution of their products in the west Mediterranean (after Hallam et al., 1976).

contrast it makes with the much smaller number of Iberian items in adjacent north Africa. Their suggestion is that the exchange was an 'exploitative' one, in which ivory and ostrich egg shell, important prestige commodities in Iberia, were obtained for almost nothing from north African hunter-gatherer groups unaware of their 'value'. They also suggest that through time the situation changed and some members of these latter groups were able to achieve a superordinate status by virtue of their involvement in the exchange.

Of all the materials which were being used to represent prestige in the context of growing social differentiation in certain areas, metal was the most prevalent, overwhelmingly copper but occasionally silver and gold. In comparison with earlier periods the occurrence of metal in archaeological contexts in the west Mediterranean is considerably greater in the period from the end of the fourth to the middle of the third millennium BC, which is often referred to as the Chalcolithic or Copper Age.

Copper ores are widely distributed around the

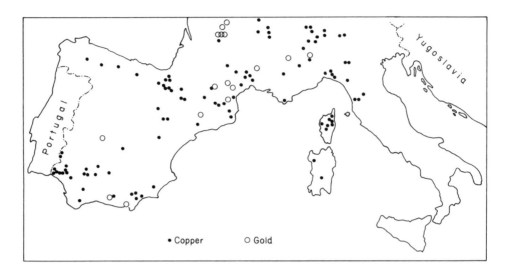

Fig. 6.28   The distribution of copper and gold sources in the western Mediterranean (after Delano Smith, 1979).

western Mediterranean (Fig.6.28) and a number of areas have evidence of early third millennium metallurgy. Nevertheless, there are again contrasts between southern Iberia and elsewhere. In southern France finds of metal objects are very much restricted to the area of the Grands Causses where the metal sources are, and they include axes and knife blades as well as copper beads (Clottes and Costantini, 1976); away from this region it is generally only the small beads which occur, and these very rarely. This pattern only changes in the Bell Beaker phase in the mid-third millennium, when finds become much more widespread and include such objects as daggers as well as ornaments. As we have seen already, central Italy shows a similar picture, with those graves of the early third millennium Rinaldone group containing metal heavily concentrated around the local copper source, although here there is no increase in finds in the middle of the millennium. In Iberia on the other hand copper had to travel some distance to the rich graves of Almeria and the Tagus estuary, another feature which fits in with the greater social complexity of these areas suggested above.

In all these regions it was copper rather than tin–bronze which was used, but there is certainly evidence for technological sophistication in that some items have a high arsenic content derived either from deliberate alloying or from the selection of ore with a high arsenic content; as noted above, arsenic has the same effect as tin in improving hardness and workability. As in the Aegean and temperate Europe, points and daggers of various kinds were one of the main items produced, or at least deposited, a practice which continued in the Bell Beaker phase of the middle to later third millennium. The significance of the dagger, which must be a social one, is further indicated by the high-quality flint daggers which were produced and deposited in burials at this time. In the western Mediterranean as in temperate Europe, where the same phenomenon occurs but on the whole rather later, it seems likely that these were a response to the introduction of the copper dagger to their respective regions. The end of the fourth and the early part of the third millennium is, in fact, the time of the most intensive flint exploitation in the western Mediterranean, as witnessed, for example, at some of the workings in southern France (Courtin, 1976a), and again this parallels developments further north.

After this discussion of exchange and production it remains to consider the more generalized patterns of material culture similarity which are apparent in the western Mediterranean at this time. In the diffusionist framework which characterized European archaeology into the 1960s these were avidly sought in order to establish connections between this area and the Aegean and the Near East. Most notably it was argued that the developments which we have seen in southern Iberia were the achievement of colonists from the Aegean (see Blance, 1971), an argument based on the assumption that local societies could not possibly have produced the tombs and fortifications and their contents unaided, and bolstered by adducing general cultural similarities between the two areas. These arguments are now discredited (Renfrew, 1967) and the only widespread material similarity which remains to be considered is that represented by the Bell Beakers and their associated material.

In the western Mediterranean, as elsewhere in Europe, these items appear in a number of different local contexts. In most places two distinct phases are clearly recognizable; the later one predominates in numbers of finds and is characterized by local developments in the pottery styles, as well as by the presence of elements such as the stone wrist-guards, which had their origin in central Europe. Burials of the early phase are most often the latest interments in the local collective tombs but later phase burials are often single grave inhumations. In general it may be said that the early phase beakers are associated with sites, monuments and artifacts which are characteristic of the earlier third millennium Copper Age cultures, while in the later phase we see the beginnings of patterns characteristic of the early Bronze Age (Sangmeister, 1976; Harrison, 1977). In Portugal, for example, Bell Beakers first appear as a new fine pottery style in the final phases of such fortified sites as Zambujal and Vila Nova de São Pedro, and associated with a variety of rich grave goods in the megalithic tombs.

As regards the significance of the Bell Beaker phenomenon, everything points to its being similar to that suggested for temperate Europe. It represents

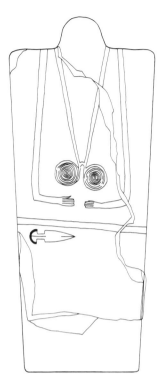

Fig. 6.29 A statue-menhir from the site of Sion-Petit Chasseur, Switzerland (after Wyss, 1969). Scale: c. 1:37.

the introduction of a new set of prestige artifacts to the societies of the area, as well as being associated in some areas with innovations in metallurgical techniques and an expansion of metallurgical activity, or at least of the deposition of metal objects; as we have seen, this occurred in southern France. It is likely, however, that as in parts of temperate Europe the new prestige items were associated with a new ideology of prestige, laying more emphasis on the individual consumption of prestige goods and less on investment in monument building (Gilman, 1976). In the light of this suggestion of ideological change it is also interesting that in southern France, adjacent parts of Switzerland, and Corsica, the statue-menhirs (Fig.6.29) which are a characteristic of the Copper Age cultures of the area in the later fourth and early third millennia are defaced and re-used in other constructions, apparently in the Bell Beaker phase and the succeeding early Bronze Age (Lewthwaite, pers. comm.). At the site of Le Petit Chausseur, Sion, Switzerland, they were re-used in a Bell Beaker burial cist (Gallay, 1976).

Conclusion. Some of the main trends which mark the end of the fourth and the earlier part of the third millennium BC in the west Mediterranean are now becoming increasingly clear as a result of the work of the last two decades, but the reasons for them are much less obvious, not least for the striking contrast with the Aegean, which becomes even more apparent in the second millennium. For central Italy Barker (1981) argues that although both this area and the Aegean were under a pressure for intensification and expansion as a result of population increase, their paths were very different because the Aegean offered very restricted areas of good agricultural land but very good, largely marine communications. Peninsular Italy had much poorer communications but more extensive areas of agricultural land, as well as pasture; thus it was always possible to maintain the less radical option of expansion rather than further intensification and social and cultural transformation. A variation on this theme would emphasize not so much the need for intensification but the problems of agricultural instability faced by the southern Aegean and not by central Italy.

Instability and the problems of coping with an extreme environment are, as we have already seen, the factors advanced by those attempting to account for the development of social hierarchies in south-east Spain (e.g. Gilman 1976); but if such factors can plausibly be seen as relevant to this case, it is more open to doubt that they are applicable to the Tagus estuary of Portugal. Here conditions were by no means as harsh as in south-east Spain; the climate is not arid and the soils are some of the most fertile in Portugal, but all the evidence suggests that a similar hierarchical form of organization had developed. One view relates the developments to the control of the inter-regional exchange which was required to obtain prestige materials and artifacts; inasmuch as

south-east Spain was also involved in such exchange it is not clear why this is not considered a relevant factor there. At least now, however, we have the beginnings of some models to replace the Aegean colonists and other east Mediterranean influences whose inadequacies have been exposed. It remains to develop them further and to start the work necessary to distinguish between them.

SUGGESTIONS FOR FURTHER READING

The period dealt with in this chapter has very little in the way of immediately accessible syntheses for further reading, particularly as far as the detail of the regional sequences is concerned. Exceptions include C. B. Burgess, *The Age of Stonehenge* (Britain), C. Renfrew, *The Emergence of Civilisation* (the Aegean), G. Barker, *Landscape and Society: Prehistoric Central Italy*, and T. Wislanski (ed.), *The Neolithic in Poland*. Of the widely distributed cultural phenomena discussed in this chapter only the Bell Beakers are at all well-served in English, by R. Harrison, *The Beaker Folk*. For German readers, however, Volume III of H. Müller-Karpe's *Handbuch der Vorgeschichte* is an extremely useful and wide-ranging reference for this period.

In recent years a number of studies have begun to deal with social and economic questions concerning this period. Burgess, Renfrew and Barker all attempt to do this for their study areas in the books listed above. The agricultural changes are explored by A. Sherratt in an important paper in I. Hodder *et al.* (eds), *Pattern of the Past*, while J. Kruk, *The Neolithic Settlement of Southern Poland* is an excellent case-study of settlement and agricultural change. Sherratt has also reviewed the evidence for trade and exchange in temperate Europe, in G. Sieveking *et al.* (eds), *Problems in Economic and Social Archaeology*; aspects of west Mediterranean trade are examined by R. Harrison and A. Gilman, in V. Markotic (ed.), *Ancient Europe and the Mediterranean*.

Studies of social change include examples by C. Renfrew in C. B. Moore (ed.), *Reconstructing Complex Societies*, and by A. Gilman in *Current Anthropology* **22**, 1981. K. Kristiansen provides an interesting regional investigation of northern Europe in Renfrew, Rowlands and Segraves (eds), *Theory and Explanation in Archaeology*.

A number of the papers in C. Renfrew and S. Shennan (eds), *Ranking, Resource and Exchange: Aspects of the Archaeology of Early European Society* provide case-studies concerning a variety of different aspects of this period.

Fig. 7.1   Principal sites mentioned in Chapter 7. 1 Akrotiri. 2 Agia Triadha. 3 Brančֲ. 4 Budapest. 5 Bush Barrow. 6 Camp de Laure. 7 Cerro de la Virgen. 8 Dover. 9 El Argar. 10 Grotte du Hasard. 11 Helmsdorf. 12 Homolka. 13 Knossos. 14 Lébous. 15 Łeki Małe. 16 Leubingen. 17 Luni. 18 Malé Kosihý. 19 Mallia. 20 Monte Bego. 21 Mount Pleasant. 22 Mycenae. 23 Narce. 24 Newgrange. 25 Nitriansky Hrádok. 26 Odemira. 27 Peristeria. 28 Phaistos. 29 Phylakopi. 30 Pylos. 31 Pyrgos. 32 Salcombe. 33 Spišský Štvrtok. 34 Toszeg. 35 Tufariello. 36 Únětice. 37 Val Camonica. 38 Veselé. 39 Zakro.

7

Prestige, Power and Hierarchies
2300–1400 BC

The developments of this period represent the continuation of the patterns and trends established in the preceding millennium. In temperate Europe hierarchies emerged in both settlement and society in many areas. This process seems to have been associated with the growth of the copper and bronze industry during this period, and the possibilities that control of the new resources offered as a basis for power. Most of the Mediterranean shows a considerable degree of stability in this period, only undergoing dramatic change in the first millennium BC, but in the Aegean the beginning of the second millennium saw the appearance of the first Cretan palaces and half a millennium later the first palaces appeared on the Greek mainland. These represent complex bureaucratically-based organizations, the first states to appear in Europe. These palace-based societies came to a sudden end at the close of the thirteenth century BC. In temperate Europe the changes which occurred in the latter half of the second millennium are not as striking as those seen in the Aegean; nevertheless, they represent a major break with the patterns discussed in this chapter.

In the previous chapter developments were traced from late in the fourth to late in the third millennium BC, a time coinciding with the end of the main period of widespread Bell Beaker contacts over much of Europe west of the Carpathian Basin, and with the end of the early Bronze Age in the Aegean. In these two areas the period around 2300 BC marks a significant break in the sequence, while in eastern, south-eastern and much of northern Europe the division is more artificial, splitting up local sequences which do not show any major change at this time. In the present chapter the aim is to follow developments to the middle of the second millennium BC, rather later in the Aegean, when further significant changes occur over a wide area. In the Aegean the Bronze Age civilizations come to an end, while over much of the rest of Europe the archaeological record is characterized by the appearance of the so-called Urnfield cultures, and it is now increasingly clear that major social and economic changes were also under way. In the conventional terminology applied over most of Europe this chapter therefore includes both the early and middle Bronze Age, although there is now an increasing tendency to bracket these two together as the 'earlier' Bronze Age, in contrast to the Urnfield and associated cultures of the 'later' Bronze Age (Coles and Harding, 1979), in recognition of the cultural, social and economic threads which link the first two periods together.

Whereas the phase divisions of the European neolithic are largely based on changes in pottery styles, in the Bronze Age the emphasis tends to switch to bronze typology. As in the neolithic, the chronologies are relative ones. Sequences have been established in the archaeological material of individual regions and these have been related to one another by the establishment of typological connections. The results are generally extremely confusing to anyone approaching the material for the first time and are the subject of interminable debate among specialists. In contrast, relatively little effort so far has been devoted to the task of establishing a sound absolute chronology based on radiocarbon dating, even in areas such as Britain where the method is accepted, and this fact needs to be borne in mind in the following account. This will be divided regionally on the same basis as the previous chapter and after a brief outline of the regional sequences the same group of general themes will be pursued, again on the

grounds that these represent key dimensions of prehistoric change, and that the interrelations between them are central to explaining the developments which occurred.

TEMPERATE EUROPE (Fig.7.2)

In central Europe west of the Carpathian Basin the Bell Beaker phase was relatively short-lived. Bell Beaker pottery fell out of use, while the local forms of cup and bowl which had been associated with them continued with relatively minor typological variations until the end of the early Bronze Age (*c.* 1800 BC), to form a zone of material culture similarity in this area generally known as the Únětice culture (see Gimbutas, 1965). Although the whole of the period from the disappearance of Bell Beakers *c.*2300 BC until *c.* 1800 BC has come to be referred to as the early Bronze Age, this is really something of a misnomer (cf. Müller-Karpe, 1974). In most parts of the area few metal objects occur at all in the archaeological record until *c.* 2000 BC and they are all made of copper, not tin–bronze. The development of tin–bronze metallurgy was associated with the appearance of a large number of new types of ornaments and weapons. Both have provided important bases for the chronological sequence. Around 1800 BC a number of types which had first developed further east, mainly in the Carpathian Basin, began to appear in central Europe, including elaborate shaft-hole axes and the first blade weapons sufficiently long to be called swords rather than daggers; metallurgically these changes define the beginnings of the middle Bronze Age.

The middle Bronze Age in central Europe is also often referred to as the Tumulus culture, on account of the frequent occurrence of burials of the period under round mounds of earth and stone, which are less common over early Bronze Age burials. Many of these mounds are situated in areas which have not been subject to arable cultivation since that time, so that the mounds have survived, in contrast to the zones of early Bronze Age distribution, which have been in fairly continuous cultivation; accordingly, this particular distinction between early and middle Bronze Age may be more a result of the vicissitudes of destruction and preservation than of a genuine difference between them.

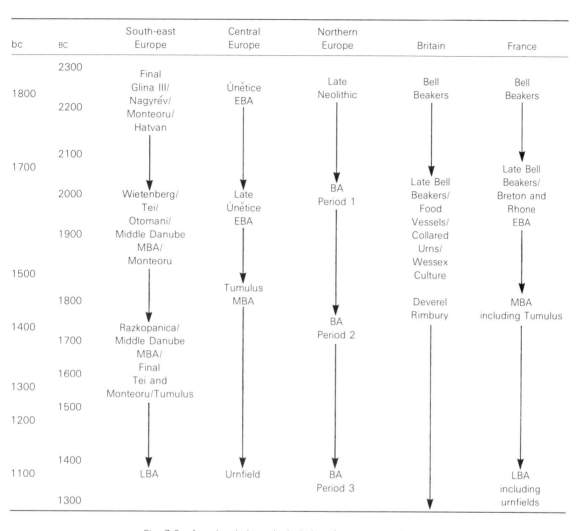

Fig. 7.2 A regional chronological chart for temperate Europe.

Further west, the clear chronological schemes which it is possible to define for the pottery and metalwork of central Europe are much more blurred: types continue in use much longer and many of the central European innovations simply do not occur. This is particularly clear in the case of the pottery, for in many areas, including Britain and the Netherlands for example, Bell Beakers continue in use down to c. 1800 BC, undergoing a considerable local typological evolution (Clarke, 1970; van der Waals and Glasbergen, 1955). In Britain the situation

seems to be particularly complex because chronologically parallel with the Beakers runs a remarkable variety of other ceramic forms, particularly numerous types of urn, which have strongly overlapping spatial distributions; after c. 1800 BC the Beakers disappear while the other ceramic traditions continue and develop (see Burgess, 1980), but they are all essentially local.

In metalwork, similarities between western and central Europe are greater. As in that area, the regions which possess a metal industry are initially

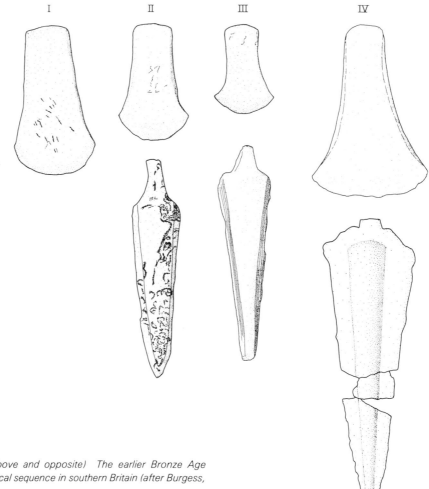

I   II   III   IV

Fig. 7.3 (above and opposite)   The earlier Bronze Age
   metallurgical sequence in southern Britain (after Burgess,
   1980).

rather limited but activity expands in the course of time. By and large the metal ornaments are of fairly local types but at least some of the central European innovations in tools and weapons did reach the west, for example changes in dagger form and the gradual lengthening of the blade (see Gerloff, 1975). The more spectacular types, however, such as metal-hilted daggers and later decorated metal-hilted swords did not find their way to the west; further-more, some types continued in use long after they had gone out of fashion further east; see Fig.7.3 for an outline of the metallurgical sequence in Britain (discussed in Burgess, 1980).

This is in marked contrast to southern Scandinavia, which maintained extremely close contact with the centres of metallurgical innovation in central and eastern Europe (Hachmann, 1957). Southern Scandinavia is of especial interest in the Bronze Age because it had no local metal supplies of its own; everything had to be imported. While many parts of Europe to the south were in their early Bronze Age, with metal items being produced and subsequently deposited in the archaeological record, southern Scandinavia was still in its late neolithic (Lomborg, 1973). This period is sometimes known as the Dagger Age because of the enormous production at this time

V   VI   VII   VIII

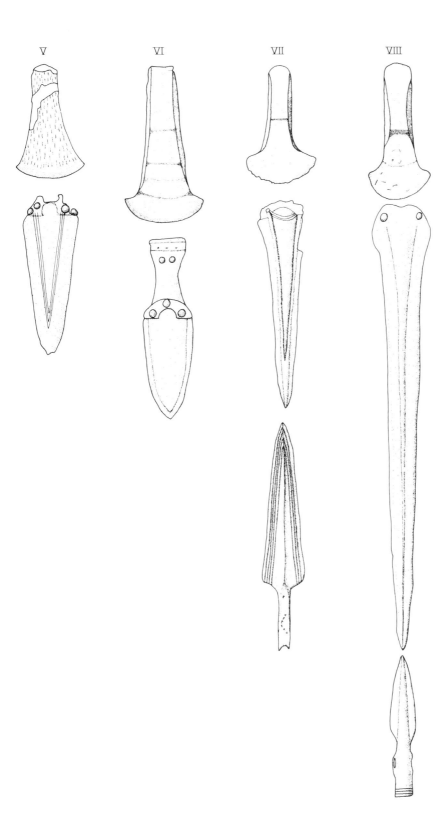

of fine flint daggers; these clearly represent a response to the metal daggers then being manufactured, which they imitate in many detailed respects (Fig. 7.4).

The periods of the southern Scandinavian Bronze Age itself were first defined late in the nineteenth century and are simply known as MI to MVI, the M standing for Montelius, the archaeologist who defined them. Although metal items begin to appear in period I, contemporary with the end of the early Bronze Age in central Europe, only in period II does a large-scale industry develop in southern Scandinavia, producing some very elaborate ornaments and weapons (Fig. 7.5) and parallelling the Tumulus Bronze Age to the south (Hachmann, 1957). Period III is already contemporary with the beginning of the later Bronze Age in central Europe but there are no very marked changes at this time in southern Scandinavia, which indeed shows a remarkable

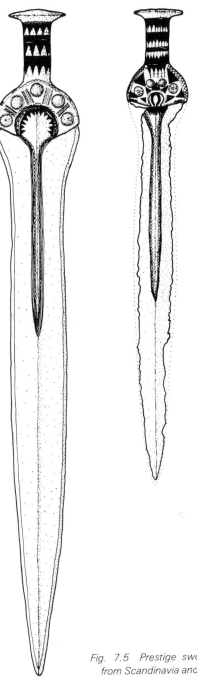

Fig. 7.5 Prestige swords from Scandinavia and the Carpathian Basin (after Hachmann, 1957).

Fig. 7.4 A Scandinavian late neolithic flint dagger (after Lomborg, 1973).

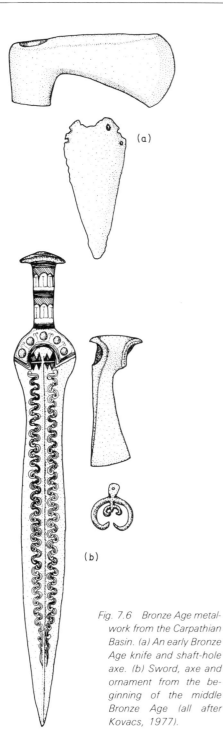

(a)

(b)

Fig. 7.6 Bronze Age metalwork from the Carpathian
Basin. (a) An early Bronze
Age knife and shaft-hole
axe. (b) Sword, axe and
ornament from the be-
ginning of the middle
Bronze Age (all after
Kovacs, 1977).

degree of continuity throughout its Bronze Age
sequence. Other parts of the northern European
plain show similar trends but the material is much
less rich.

Finally, it remains to discuss the sequence in
eastern Europe, from the Carpathian Basin to
Bulgaria (Gimbutas, 1965; Hansel, 1968; Bona, 1975),
and here as elsewhere it is necessary to disregard a
great deal of regional diversity in the material if
general trends are to be defined. As far as the pottery
is concerned, the major common thread which links
the different parts of this large area is provided by
the prevalence of dark-grey burnished cups and
conical bowls which become increasingly baroque
through time in both form and decoration. Urns also
become much more frequent as inurned cremation,
which had existed from the start of this period,
became the generally prevailing burial rite,
considerably before the large-scale appearance of the
custom in west-central Europe c. 1500 BC.

Eastern metalwork also has its own special
character (Fig.7.6) and is best represented in the form
of those caches of metal objects known as hoards.
Although rare in the earliest phases, the Bronze Age
hoards of the Carpathian Basin and adjacent areas to
the east and north are some of the richest in Europe
and a detailed typological sequence for tools,
ornaments and weapons has been derived from them
(see, for example, Mozsolics, 1967, 1973). This
parallels the sequence for west-central Europe, but it
seems clear that whereas up to c. 2000–1900 BC it was
the latter area which was the leader in the establishment of a true tin–bronze industry and metallurgical
innovation in general, after that time this role was
taken over by the Carpathian metalworking tradition.
This question will be considered more fully below.

It was noted above that there is no major break in
the sequences of eastern Europe around 2300 BC, but
in the most south-easterly part, in Bulgaria and
Macedonia, this is not the case. There those multi-
layer tell sites which had continued in occupation
after the end of the neolithic and Copper Age
cultures of the fifth and fourth millennia were
themselves finally abandoned c.2300–2400 BC and
there seems to be a shift to hilltop settlement
locations, a change which has more in common with
developments in the Aegean (see below) than further
north at this time (Dennell, 1978). In and around the

Carpathian Basin, however, occupation continued on many of the same sites from *c.* 3000 BC until *c.* 1700 BC and tell settlements came into existence whose stratigraphic sequences have provided much of the basis for the local chronologies which have been established (Kalicz, 1968); one of the most important in this respect is the site of Toszeg in the Hungarian Plain. Many of these tells were abandoned in their turn *c.* 1800–1700 BC.

Absolute Chronology

So far this discussion has been largely in terms of the sequences of material culture in different areas. These sequences define a relative chronology, important for the classifying of new discoveries; however, the changes they define are themselves in need of explanation, and this is where the importance of absolute chronology lies. Firstly, it is important to be able to define *rates* of change, and secondly it is essential to avoid the circularity which consists of using a similarity in finds between two regions both to argue for the general contemporaneity of the material in the two areas and as evidence for some kind of relationship between them, such as diffusion from one to the other, which actually purports to explain the similarity.

This question is of particular significance in the earlier Bronze Age of temperate Europe because so much emphasis has in the past been placed on the supposed role of the Aegean civilizations in stimulating early Bronze Age development north of the Mediterranean. It is worth looking briefly at why this should have been the case, and the first factor here is the very deep-rooted assumption that any given innovation must have occurred first in the area of higher civilizations and then diffused to prehistoric Europe. On the basis of this assumption the pioneers of European prehistory related regional sequences to one another and ultimately back to the supposed eastern Mediterranean origin of the material concerned. This process had the additional virtue of providing absolute historical dates for prehistoric Europe unobtainable by other means. Historical dates were available for Egypt, which could be transferred to the Aegean, and then by allowing a time-lag for the diffusion of particular types to places increasingly further away, a date could be established

for the contexts in which those types occurred. Subsequently Childe built on this approach what might be called in today's parlance a 'processual model' for the beginning of European bronze working, which posited that it depended on the demand of the eastern Mediterranean civilizations for metal supplies. The chronology then is particularly important, not simply because prehistorians like to have things in the right chronological relationships, but because the validity of the chronology was a necessary although not a sufficient condition for the validity of the model, which was universally accepted until the 1960s.

When the first radiocarbon dates appeared they seemed to confirm to a remarkable degree the dates for the various Bronze Age phases which had been reached by traditional typological methods. The problems arose with the recalibration of radiocarbon dates, which made many of the traditional chronological equations between the eastern Mediterranean and central and western Europe untenable (see for example Renfrew, 1973b). Not only are these equations particularly important for the period from *c.* 2300 to 1500 BC, but this is the period for which the exact extent and form of the calibration have been most debated, mainly on the grounds of an alleged discrepancy between Egyptian historical dates and the most rigorous calibration which has been proposed, that of Clark´ (1975); only recently has it been demonstrated that no such discrepancy exists.

The implications of this are that in the core area of central Europe the early Bronze Age in the conventional definition lasts from *c.* 2300 to *c.* 1800 BC, and the middle Bronze Age from *c.* 1800 to *c.* 1500 BC. This means that the beginning of a large-scale bronze industry in central Europe took place well before the beginning of the Mycenaean civilization whose influence it was supposed to reflect, while certain specific artifact types supposedly of Mediterranean origin which had been used to establish the typological chronology, were shown to be present much earlier in central and western Europe. Conversely, however, radiocarbon dating was also able to demonstrate the conservatism of some of those areas removed from the centres of metallurgical innovation: thus, a grave in England containing a dagger which was typologically early Bronze Age proved to date to *c.* 1500 BC. Because of this problem it may yet turn out that some of the

Aegean connections postulated in the past can be accommodated, but they must have occurred very late in the earlier Bronze Age development of temperate Europe. Far more radiocarbon dates are needed.

Socio-economic Processes in Temperate Europe c. 2300–1500 BC

In the previous chapter it was argued that a number of different processes operating in different spheres of the socio-economic system resulted in major changes in much of Europe between the late fourth and third millennia BC. A more integrated agricultural strategy had developed which was expansive in nature and which in some areas at least had resulted in an extension of the area of settlement onto soils which were not as productive as those settled initially, and where occupation was therefore potentially more unstable. Two distinct tendencies seem to characterize the resulting settlement systems of eastern and western Europe: in the former a pattern of long-lived settlements, albeit not very large, which were often fortified and/or in defensible positions, and some of which may have been local centres; in western Europe a change from such a pattern, which had existed in the fourth millennium, to one where settlements were extremely small and highly ephemeral, and defensive considerations seem to have been irrelevant. Within the western zone, however, there seems to have been a major distinction between a small number of areas, particularly parts of Britain and Brittany, where large-scale monument building was going on early in the third millennium, indicative of some kind of centralized organization, and the rest of the zone, where there are no indications of monuments or centralization but some limited differentiation between individuals is visible in the burials. Throughout temperate Europe, with the exception of the north around the Baltic, copper metallurgy was established.

It is now necessary to follow through these patterns into the following period. It will become obvious in the succeeding account that the studies on which a discussion of such themes has to be based refer very largely to Europe west of the Carpathian Basin; in eastern and south-eastern Europe north of

the Aegean chronologically oriented typological studies of pottery and bronzes still reign supreme.

Subsistence. Wherever the necessary work has been done in central and western Europe all the indications are that the expansion of the area of cultivation which had begun in the early and middle part of the third millennium continued into the second, taking in increasingly marginal soils. In such areas as southern Britain, Denmark and Czechoslovakia burial mounds dating to the first half of the second millennium occur in areas which were never subsequently subject to cultivation, a fact which has been the key to their survival (Grinsell, 1959; Randsborg, 1974; Čujanová-Jílková, 1970). It was believed by Childe that the presence of so much middle Bronze Age material in areas not suitable for agriculture today indicated an invasion of pastoralists, replacing the existing agricultural population, but there is really no need to accept such a view. All the evidence suggests that especially from c. 1800 BC onwards occupation expanded still further onto soils around the margin of the existing area of settlement which were unable to sustain continued exploitation, and that this inability, perhaps aided by the beginnings of climatic deterioration, resulted in the development of acid heathland soils unsuitable for agriculture. The result of this very widespread process of soil exhaustion, visible from Czechoslovakia to Britain and Denmark, was a major retrenchment of settlement onto high quality arable soils which began at various times between c. 1500 and 1200 BC in the different areas (Bradley, 1981; Kristiansen, 1981). In some of these regions, such as Bohemia and the Upper Rhine valley (Balkwill, 1976), this represented a contraction back to the core areas of settlement in the late neolithic and early Bronze Age; in others, however, such as southern England, new areas of settlement seem to have begun to increase in importance at this time; thus in England the Thames valley begins to increase in prominence, while that of Wessex declines.

A further indication of the increasing importance of controlling and allocating rights to land is the growth of field systems, which seems to begin certainly by c. 1800 BC (Fig.7.7). This did not occur everywhere in the western part of Europe at the same time: in some parts of north-west Europe and southern Scandinavia they do not appear until well

Fig. 7.7   Plan of an earlier Bronze Age field system from southern England (after Bradley and Richards, 1978).

into the first millennium BC, long after the period with which we are concerned here. In Britain, however, field systems appear in Wessex well before 1500 BC, in response, it has been suggested (Bradley, 1978a), to the first retreat from the most marginal soils. There are as yet only a few hints of such phenomena in west-central Europe but one can reasonably postulate that this is the result of lack of discovery rather than absence. Whereas in Britain and other parts of north-west Europe prehistoric field monuments have survived under pasture, in central Europe they have been largely covered in forest, while the artifact oriented tradition has

dominated Bronze Age studies virtually to the exclusion of the field tradition so important further west.

It is important to note that it is the landscape evidence which has provided the basis for tracing what must have been very important developments in subsistence at this time. In places the picture has been supplemented by pollen analysis indicating abandoned fields, but the evidence of animal and plant remains from archaeological sites has made very little contribution up to the present, generally indicating no more than that the major domestic animals were kept and the main cereals cultivated. In some areas rock art has proved a valuable source of evidence (see box). Two aspects of animal husbandry at this time deserve mention; the first concerns the horse.

Although it appears that small populations of wild horses survived in much of Europe throughout the mesolithic and neolithic, all the evidence suggests that it was first domesticated in the south Russian steppes early in the fourth millennium and that its use then spread westwards. Until recently it was thought that this process was a gradual one, but it has now been suggested that certain bone objects dating to the mid-fourth millennium in central and western Europe are parts of horse harness (Lichardus, 1980). By the end of the fourth millennium rare horse bones are found on many archaeological sites in central Europe (Nobis, 1971; Sherratt, 1981), and in the Bell Beaker phase, half a millennium later, they appear in very large quantities on sites near Budapest, Hungary (Bökönyi, 1974) and also occur far to the west, for example at Newgrange in Ireland (van Wijngaarden-Bakker, 1974); in the subsequent early Bronze Age they regularly constitute a small percentage of the bones found in settlements. The bone items referred to above are believed to be the cheek pieces from bits; if this is so, it makes it highly probable that actual riding was an important use for the horse from the start. Other bone artifacts interpreted as cheek pieces occur widely in the Carpathian Basin *c.* 2000–1800 BC (see, for example, Točík, 1981ab). Many of them are quite elaborately decorated (Fig.7.8) and may be an indication that by this time, if not earlier, the importance of the horse was at least as much social as it was economic, and that horses, and the equipment associated with them, were status symbols of the high-ranking sections of society which will be discussed below, a role for which there continues to be evidence throughout later prehistory.

Another area of the animal economy whose importance most probably lies in the sphere of social production and exchange is textile manufacture. It has been suggested in the previous chapter that wool was replacing flax as the raw material for textiles by the later third millennium BC, and that an expansion of textile production was already taking place as more sheep were kept and the landscape became increasingly deforested; rather later, woollen textiles are preserved in the well-known Danish Bronze Age

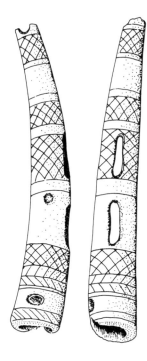

Fig. 7.8   Decorated antler cheek-pieces for horse bits from the Carpathian Basin (after Piggott, 1965).

burials, where some of them are of very high quality (Broholm and Hald, 1935).

The remarkable importance of the control of sheep and textile production which emerges from the Linear B tablets of second millennium Knossos in Crete will be discussed below, and although obviously nothing comparable exists from temperate Europe, there seems good reason to believe that textiles were an important factor in the economy which must be taken into account even if little evidence exists, particularly when considering the balance of exchange between different areas. It has been suggested, for example, that the light sandy soils of Jutland extensively occupied in the earlier Bronze Age were being exploited for pastoral production, including textiles which were exchanged for the metal which had to be imported (Kristiansen, 1978). The fact that in Denmark some of the dead were buried in fine quality textiles, as well as with bronzes which, of course, have a better chance of survival, suggests that textiles, like the bronzes, were items of

ROCK ART

Rock carvings are known from many parts of Europe during the earlier Bronze Age. In many places they simply consist of circle and rings, but a number of widely scattered areas have an enormous wealth of rock art, executed by means of painting as well as engraving, and including figurative representations of people, animals and artifacts. Dating the rock art is by no means easy but it can be done by means of a study of the patterns of superimposition of the carvings and their degree of wear, while the artifacts represented can often be identified as types also known from other archaeological contexts and therefore independently dated.

In southern Europe the two most important areas are Val Camonica in northern Italy and Monte Bego in southern France (Anati, 1961; de Lumley *et al.*, 1976). It seems clear that their art is connected with ritual and religion. There appear to be scenes depicting worship as well as representations of funerals and it has been suggested that some of the elements in such pictures are similar to known features of Celtic religion. At a more mundane level, the art provides information on agriculture, confirming conclusions reached on other grounds. Pictures of oxen, often harnessed to ploughs or carts, are a frequent occurrence.

The other main rock art area is in Scandinavia (e.g. Burenhult, 1973; Hallström, 1960) where there are two different traditions. One of these lies largely in the far north, where the representations consist of wild animals, fish and birds, as well as humans. It is believed to be at least partly Bronze Age in date because of the relationship between the art and the changing coastline of Scandinavia, as it recovered from the weight of the ice sheets on the one hand and was submerged by rising sea levels on the other. The art is taken to be indicative of the hunting and gathering economies and societies which continued in these remote regions. They are Bronze Age in date alone and do not possess any of the characteristic Bronze Age features discussed in this chapter.

The other main tradition lies in the agricultural part of Sweden and Norway, in the south, where, as at Val Camonica, agricultural scenes occur, involving ox ploughs and carts pulled by horses, as well as pictures of men holding battle axes and spears. One special feature of the southern Scandinavian art is the large number of boat representations, showing very varied craft and emphasizing the importance of marine transport to the societies inhabiting this coast with its numerous islands.

prestige. The extent of production is hinted at by the large numbers of spindle whorls and loom weights which occur in many excavated settlements; in particular, it is interesting to note that evidence for textile production occurs in large quantities at fortified sites on the fringes of the Carpathian Basin, such as Malé Kosihý in Slovakia (Točík, 1981a), which there are other grounds for considering to be regional central places (see below).

One of the major problems for Bronze Age studies is the nature of the articulation between subsistence activities and the prestige sphere of the economy, to which some reference has already been made. This relationship will be examined again below but here it is relevant to note that textile production may have been one of the elements of the link, in that control

of people, land and animals could be translated directly into a commodity possessing exchange value within the prestige sphere. For this same reason it may also be relevant to the reasons for the over-exploitation of the land which seems to characterize the middle Bronze Age (1800–1500 BC), and which although not exactly contemporary wherever it occurs seems to reflect a very similar pattern of socio-economic development (see above). One standard response would be to relate the expansion onto marginal land to a continuing population increase which finally exceeded the limits the system could bear, but another is to argue that it was the demands of production for prestige reasons, particularly pastoral production, which led finally to over-exploitation and the subsequent contraction and

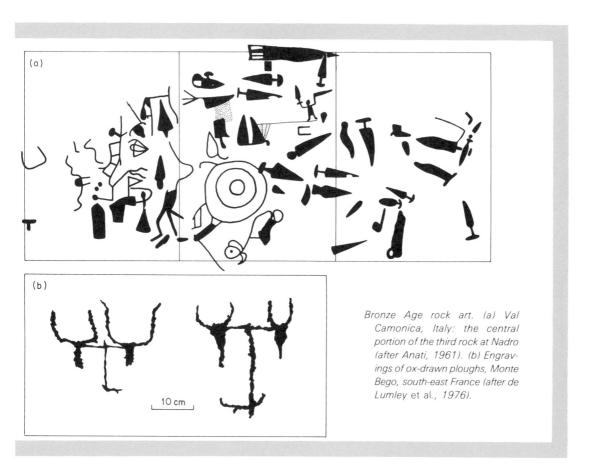

Bronze Age rock art. (a) Val Camonica, Italy: the central portion of the third rock at Nadro (after Anati, 1961). (b) Engravings of ox-drawn ploughs, Monte Bego, south-east France (after de Lumley et al., 1976).

intensification (see, for example, Bradley, 1981). It is clearly important to try and test between these two hypotheses.

The implications of the drastically changed subsistence economies which came into being in many areas around and after 1500 BC will be examined in chapter nine. It is now necessary to review the evidence for the form of social organization in the earlier Bronze Age, on which much of the preceding argument hinges.

Social organization. This is best approached initially by taking a comparative look at those regions in the western half of Europe which always feature in accounts of the early Bronze Age, owing to the relatively attractive nature of their archaeological record.

In the Wessex area of southern England the construction of large-scale ceremonial monuments largely ceased after *c.* 2000 BC. Some sort of activity continued at the existing ones, although altered in character, but only at Stonehenge was a further phase of construction undertaken (Burgess, 1980). Burials in this period continued to include both inhumations and cremations and to vary in their spatial and monumental context, but the most notable new feature was the appearance of a small number of burials richly provided with grave goods (Fig.7.9), the so-called 'Wessex culture' (Piggott, 1938; Burgess, 1980); such burials occur sporadically elsewhere but the concentration and richness of those

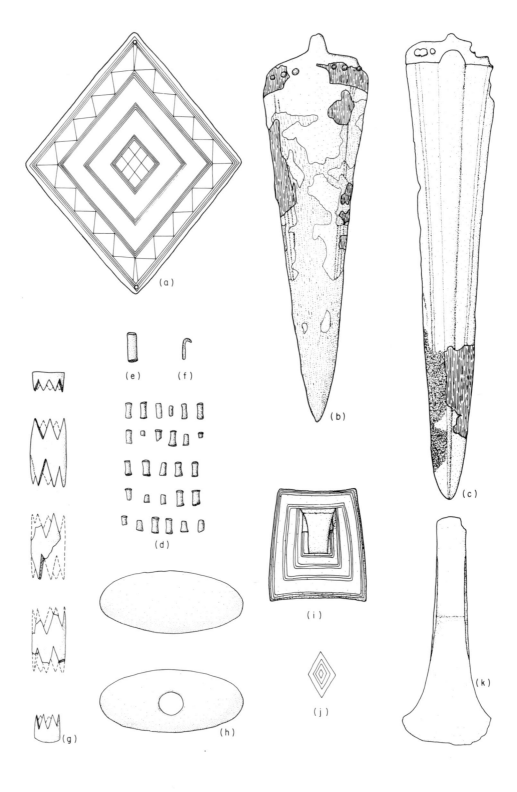

(a)

(b)

(c)

(d)

(e)

(f)

(g)

(h)

(i)

(j)

(k)

in Wessex is unmatched. We have already suggested in the previous chapter that the decline in monumental activity and the growth of individual burial with exotic grave goods was associated with the Bell Beakers and marked a changed form of hierarchy and ultimately a new source of power, associated with the obtaining and consumption of prestige goods. It is this which the rich Wessex burials represent. Renfrew (1973a) characterized the difference between the monument-building phase and the 'Wessex culture' phase as that between 'group-oriented' and 'individualizing' chiefdoms, and while this formulation is not particularly satisfactory the distinction it recognizes seems to be a valid one.

A similar phenomenon may be seen in Brittany, where the elaborate late neolithic megalithic monuments are replaced after a Bell Beaker phase by single-grave burials under round barrows, some of which are accompanied by very rich grave goods, including metalwork (Giot *et al.*, 1979ab). These are dated to *c*. 2300–2000 BC and they are succeeded by a similar but much less rich group of barrow burials, dating to *c*. 2000–1500 BC; this situation also parallels southern Britain, where the rich burials continue until *c*. 1500 BC but the later burials are less rich than the earlier group.

In central Europe the picture with which we are presented at the beginning of the Bronze Age is very different, as we have seen in the previous chapter. Hierarchies seem to have been very little developed although inter-individual differences were being expressed at burial in terms of grave goods. The lack of differentiation changes in the course of the early Bronze Age and around 2100–1800 BC burials with strikingly rich grave goods, including sophisticated craft items and goods obtained by long-distance exchange, appear in central Europe, particularly in the Elbe–Saale area of Germany and in Bohemia;

examples include the burials of Leubingen and Helmsdorf and the cemetery at Únětice (Coles and Harding, 1979, pp. 38-42) (Fig.7.10). In the former area these stand out in a particularly marked fashion because most of the other burials of the period contain very little. In Bohemia and the other regions the richest burials are not so strikingly pre-eminent and the distribution of grave wealth is a much more continuous one (see, for example, Hásek, 1959).

In an early treatment of the social implications of these burials the east German archaeologist K. H. Otto (1955) proposed that four different socio-economic classes could be defined, but the terms and categories of his doctrinaire Marxist analysis seem inappropriate and anachronistic, more relevant to the feudal system of the Middle Ages than to the early Bronze Age. What does seem clear is that hierarchies had now arisen in central Europe which resembled their contemporaries in such regions as Wessex and Brittany in that rituals involving the possession and consumption of prestige goods were very much part of their operation. To summarize, the difference is that whereas in western Europe rich early Bronze Age graves appear as a result of the changed ideology and ritual (and consequently changed nature) of societies whose organization was in some sense already regionally centralized, in central Europe hierarchies actually developed in the course of the early Bronze Age, and the existing burial ritual simply accommodated this by increasing the range of grave goods deposited both quantitatively and qualitatively, so that the same end result was reached as in western Europe.

The factors involved in the development of hierarchical societies in central Europe at this time are by no means clear but the growth of the copper and bronze industry was almost certainly involved. If one examines the spatial distribution of those parts of central Europe which have attracted attention in

Fig. 7.9 A rich Bronze Age burial from southern England: the grave goods from the Bush Barrow. (a) Lozenge-shaped plate of sheet gold with incised ornament. (b) Copper dagger. (c) Bronze dagger. (d) Thirty-three rivets of bronze. (e) Large bronze rivet. (f) Small hook-like bronze object. (g) Three cylindrical bone mounts and two end pieces or ferrules of bone. (h) Polished stone mace-head (i) Belt-hook of hammered gold with incised ornament. (j) Small lozenge-shaped plate of sheet gold with incised ornament. (k) Flanged axe of copper or bronze. (After Annable and Simpson, 1964.) Scale: (a–c), (g–k) c. 1:2.6; (d–f) c. 1:1.6.

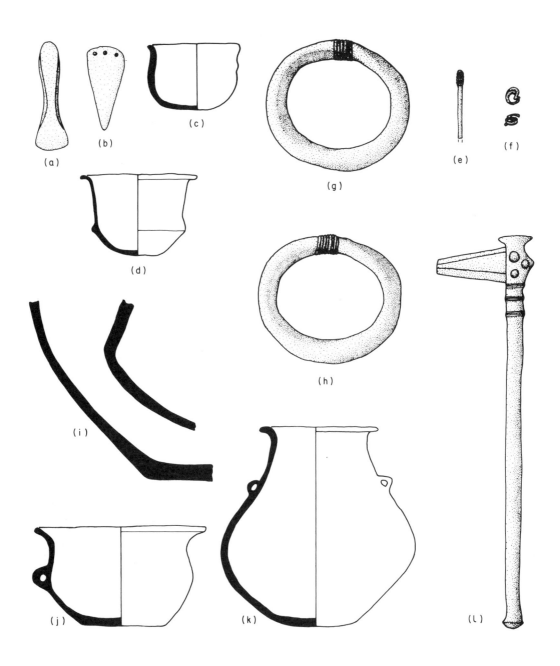

Fig. 7.10   The grave goods from one of the rich early Bronze Age burials in barrow 1, Łeki Małe, western Poland: (a) Flanged axe. (b) Knife blade. (c), (d), (j), (k) Pots. (e) Knot-headed pin. (f) Gold spiral. (g), (h) Bracelets. (i) Profiles of large pots. (l) Metal-shafted halberd. (After Gimbutas, 1965.) Scale: (a, e–h) c. 1:3.5; (b–c) c. 1:3; (d) c. 1:4; (i) c. 1:2; (k–l) c. 1:7.

terms of their evidence for social differentiation, one is inevitably drawn towards those lowland areas of good agricultural soils adjacent to local metal sources. Furthermore, if one compares the dates at which these areas begin to show such evidence with the beginning dates for major bronze age exploitation of the adjacent metal resources a relationship seems to emerge. Thus, at a time when the early Únětice graves of Bohemia and the Elbe–Saale are characterized by largely undifferentiated inventories of ceramic goods, south-west Slovakia and the Danube valley both contain cemeteries which suggest the beginnings of more marked social differentiation (S.E. Shennan, 1975; Vladár, 1973a; Christlein, 1964; Schubert, 1973). South-west Slovakia is close to the Slovakian ore sources, known to be exploited at an early date (Točík and Vladár, 1971), while the Danube valley lies near the Alpine sources, which were also exploited early (Pittioni, 1980). The metal sources of north Bohemia and the Elbe–Saale area, on the other hand, which also included tin, only became important in the later early Bronze Age, with the development of a true tin–bronze industry, and it was only at this time that the rich Únětice graves of the two areas appeared and document the emergence of hierarchies here (Christlein, 1964).

The evidence from south-west Slovakia is particularly good and has recently been the subject of analysis (S. E. Shennan, 1975, 1982). The first part of the early Bronze Age here is known from a number of inhumation cemeteries of varying sizes, in all of which the grave goods accompanying the burials are typologically essentially the same. Furthermore, these items were worn in the same fashion, and the same distinctions between individuals, those related to their age and sex for example, were marked by the same symbolic means. All the communities involved seem to have been very small, in all cases well under 100, but within the cemeteries (for example, Branč) there was clear evidence for internal differentiation, with some individuals having much more elaborate sets of grave goods than others; this was particularly marked within the female burials. The conclusion reached at the end of the analysis was that within each community there was a leading family, and that there was at least a tendency for status and position to be inherited through the male line, while females only obtained the rich and elaborate costumes in which some of them were buried during adolescence or young adulthood, possibly on marriage.

It might be thought that when communities seem to have been so small it is curious that there should have been so much emphasis on the symbolic expression of status, and such strong patterns of differentiation. Here again, however, it is important to bear in mind the alliance links between communities, and especially the question of exogamy: it is highly unlikely that communities of the small size which has been reconstructed would have been reproductively viable for very long. Exchange of marriage partners would have been essential and the symbolic communication of status on a regional scale would have been important for this reason; however, there is no suggestion that any of the cemeteries belonged to a centre which dominated the region (S. E. Shennan, 1982).

The pattern just described characterizes south-west Slovakia from *c.* 2300 to *c.* 2000 BC, but unfortunately there are virtually no known settlements to associate with it. In the final phase of the early Bronze Age in the area (*c.* 2000–1800 BC), however, a major change occurred. It appears that in a relatively short period of time some form of regionally centralized organization became established, since in each of the river valleys of the area one or two fortified sites appeared, together with a large number of other settlements (Fig.7.11); examples of the former include Veselé (Točík, 1964), Malé Kosihý (Točík, 1981a) and Nitriansky Hrádok (Točík, 1981b). In the fortified sites metalwork has been found of a technological sophistication not present earlier, as well as moulds for the manufacture of metal objects and evidence of other forms of craft production, such as bone carving (Fig.7.8); the decorated bone items referred to above which have been interpreted as horse equipment come from sites such as these. Evidence also exists for new long-distance contacts, for example in the appearance of amber, which does not occur in the cemeteries of the first part of the early Bronze Age described above.

This sequence is one which occurs widely in central Europe west of the Carpathian Basin at around the same time, *c.* 2000–1800 BC. Defensible positions are occupied and often fortified; in many cases this

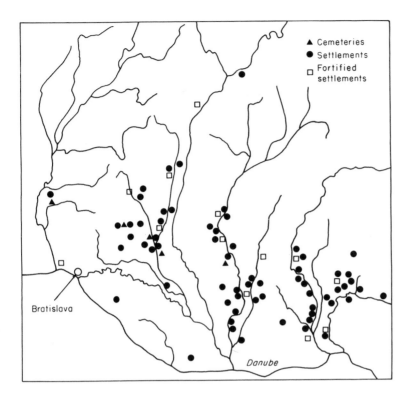

Fig. 7.11 South-west Slovakia in the later early Bronze Age (after Točík, 1964). Scale: c. 1:1,750,000.

represents a re-occupation of sites which had been abandoned 1000 years earlier; for example at Homolka (Ehrich and Pleslová, 1968). The development can be seen as marking a renewed convergence between west-central Europe and the Carpathian Basin and areas to the east, where, as we have seen, a similar pattern of fortified settlements had been in existence since early in the third millennium. A particular feature which some of these settlements of the early second millennium in these different areas have in common is the fortification, or further fortification, of only a part of the settlement, to form what has been called an 'acropolis'; for example at Spišský Štvrtok in eastern Slovakia (Vladár, 1973b). In the past these have generally been interpreted as the strongholds of feudal-type overlords, often supposedly of foreign origin, dominating an indigenous peasant population.

Whether this was the case, or whether it is simply an anachronism based on projecting the socio-economic conditions of very different later periods back into the past, the problem is a particular instance of the more general question currently of considerable interest in Bronze Age studies, concerning the nature of the power base and of socio-economic inequality (Rowlands, 1980). A more general review of this question will follow below; for the moment it is simply necessary to note that by c. 1800 BC over much of temperate Europe from Romania to western Germany a pattern of fortified regional centres was in existence for which the archaeological evidence of 'central-place' functions is considerably better than it is for the fortified sites of the late fourth millennium. At the same time, the burial record of many of these areas is also indicative of considerable social differentiation. If one wants to talk about 'chiefdoms' in the sense of Service (1962; see box on p.170), perhaps these later early Bronze Age societies are particularly good candidates for the term.

The pattern is one which continues throughout the middle Bronze Age, until c. 1500 BC, and as far as the

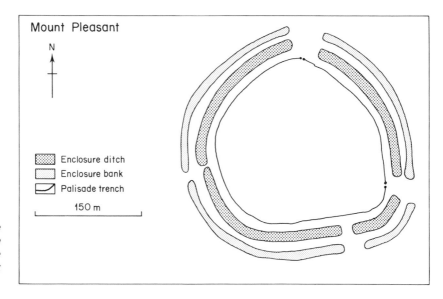

Mount Pleasant

N

Enclosure ditch
Enclosure bank
Palisade trench

150 m

Fig. 7.12 Mt. Pleasant, southern England: the late phase enclosure inside the ditch and bank of the earlier henge monument (after Wainwright, 1979).

differentiated burials are concerned it is one which is parallelled in many parts of western Europe. Far less evidence exists in this area, however, for fortified sites or possible regional centres until the end of this period, although examples are known, such as the late phase of Mount Pleasant in Wessex (Figs 7.12 and 7.13) (Wainwright, 1979). The apparently later development of fortifications must indicate a significant difference between the earlier Bronze Age trajectories of central and western Europe as regards the development of warfare and raiding, but the reasons for this are unknown. Non-fortified centres may have existed which performed similar functions to those of central Europe, but it may be that processes tending towards the extension of regionally centralized organizations did not go on at the same pace in these areas, so that 'central-place' settlements do not occur before the later Bronze Age.

Metallurgy. The development of metallurgy in the earlier Bronze Age has already been considered from the point of view of its use in the building up of regional and inter-regional relative chronologies, and it has been suggested that the control of metal exploitation may have been a key factor in the development of hierarchies in central Europe. It is now necessary to examine the topic in its own right,

on the assumption that whereas in the fourth and earlier third millennia copper was only one of a number of materials widely used and exchanged, by the earlier second millennium bronze had come to far outweigh other materials in its significance.

At the beginning of the early Bronze Age the metallurgical techniques in use were little different from those which had become established in the south-eastern part of Europe more than two millennia earlier. They depended largely on simple forms of casting and extensive subsequent working to transform the object into the artifact desired; metal ornaments were made of hammered metal sheet and/or bent wire (cf. Coles and Harding, 1979, p. 11). The metal itself was copper, some of which has proved on analysis to contain significant amounts of arsenic and impurities indicating the use of sulphide ores, which needed an intervening roasting process before smelting could take place; as we have seen, however, both these innovations had already appeared in central Europe by the end of the fourth millennium.

Industries making use of these techniques and materials were widespread in Europe *c.* 2300 BC, from Ireland to the Black Sea. It was not until the very end of the third millennium that changes began to take place and the centre of innovation seems to

Fig. 7.13 Reconstruction of the east entrance through the Mt. Pleasant palisade (after Wainwright, 1979).

and no doubt in response to these properties, that the two-piece mould came into extensive use, for the solid casting of ornaments and weapons of a previously unknown complexity (Fig.7.14).

These new types, like the techniques which produced them, originated in west-central Europe and were both exchanged and imitated widely. It was not until rather later, probably *c.* 1800 BC, that a large-scale eastern Carpathian industry started, making use of what analysis has shown to be a copper of distinctive composition most probably derived from sources in Transylvania (Mozsolics, 1967). This industry soon developed its own stylistic and technological traditions, for example a greater emphasis on the use of shaft-hole axes as opposed to flat axes than further west, and its products are among the most striking of the European Bronze Age (Fig.7.6). Its technological attainments soon equalled and even exceeded those of the west-central

have been in the area of present-day Czechoslovakia, Austria and Germany. Tin sources are very rare in Europe (see Fig.6.11) and the beginning of copper–tin alloying to produce bronze seems to have depended on the supplies available in the Bohemian Ore Mountains, on the border of western Czechoslovakia and East Germany. Copper also existed in these mountains and other extensive supplies were available not far away in the Harz mountains, the Alps and central Slovakia. Some if not all of these copper sources had already come into use earlier in the course of the third millennium, but if the number and size of archaeologically known metal finds is any guide to the amount of metal being produced and circulated, then this increased drastically just before 2000 BC. The increase no doubt stemmed at least partly from the potential of the new alloy. Tin–bronze is easier to cast than copper alone and the resulting artifacts are harder, a factor of considerable importance for weapons and tools. It was only now,

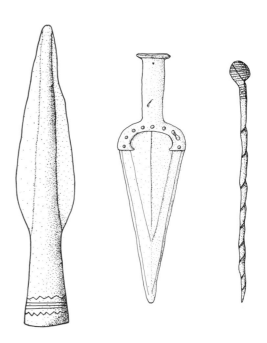

Fig. 7.14 Metalwork of the later early Bronze Age in central Europe (after Hachmann, 1957). Scale: dagger c. 1:4.1; others c. 1:1.95.

European industry and its innovations, including the first short swords, were adopted further west.

The middle Bronze Age is a time of increasing elaboration of ornaments, weapons and also tools. It seems likely that it was during the first half of the second millennium that metal first began to have an impact on practical activities as opposed to social display. Apart from the very large numbers of axes, which may have served as both tools and weapons, specialized woodworking tools are also known and the first bronze sickles appear (cf.Harding, 1976). The use of metal tools for everyday tasks expanded enormously in the later Bronze Age and may have been an important factor in the economic changes which then took place.

The main contexts in which metal items are found are graves and hoards, and it is their distribution in the former which has been one of the main bases for inferring the growth of hierarchical societies discussed in the previous section. The social role of metal production must have been extremely important, in that it was widely used for items of display, both ornaments and weapons, which were regularly removed from circulation when people were buried. As we have already seen, within particular regions and cemeteries this deposition was characterized by considerable differentials between graves with respect to the quantity, quality and types of items deposited.

The burial of hoards of metal items was another means by which they were taken out of circulation. Their significance has long been the subject of argument and was probably as varied as are the hoards themselves. These range from hundreds of axes or neck rings (Fig.7.15) to small groups of high-quality ornaments and weapons, although none of them seem to be scrap metal hoards, which do not appear until the later Bronze Age.

The organization of copper and bronze production and circulation in temperate Europe is a subject about which very little is known except at a basic technological level, although the recent finds off Dover and Salcombe in the English channel of two shipwrecked vessels carrying cargoes of bronze, and dating to the early part of the later Bronze Age, give some insight into the scale of operations which by then had developed (Muckelroy, 1981). Certainly by c. 2000 BC highly specialized bronze craftsmanship existed, most visible in the production of prestige weapons (Figs.7.6 and 7.14). Studies of the distribution of different types suggest that such items as dress pins and working axes were manufactured and distributed locally in particular local styles but high-quality prestige weapons seem to have circulated on a far more international scale and to have followed more uniform styles; Fig.7.5 shows bronze swords from Denmark and Hungary.

The question of the nature of interregional inter-

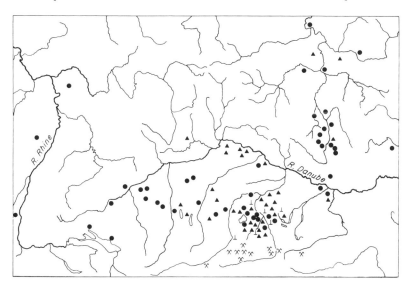

Fig. 7.15 The distribution of early Bronze Age ingot hoards in the upper Danube area; these are believed to represent deposits of the raw products of the east Alpine copper mines. Findspots of ring ingots (dots); rib-ingots (triangles); copper-mining centres (crossed picks); bronze-casting sites (inverted T's). Scale: c. 1:6,000,000 (after Butler, 1978).

action with respect to metal and other materials is an important one. Although there is a not inconsiderable number of copper sources in Europe, they are not evenly distributed. Some regions, the north European plain in particular, are a considerable distance from the sources and would have had to obtain their metal supplies through interregional exchange. In most of these areas local metal industries did not start until after 1800 BC. What is interesting is not only that they were able to obtain metal supplies, but that they too removed metal from circulation in the form of grave and hoard deposits, and used it in the symbolization of the hierarchical social relations which were increasingly developing.

The pattern has been particularly clearly documented in Denmark (Randsborg, 1974; Kristiansen, 1978). It has already been noted that metal does not appear in Denmark in any quantity until *c.* 1700 BC, contemporary with the developed middle Bronze Age further south. From this time on very large quantities of metal were deposited in graves and hoards, and analysis of the burials has indicated a very considerable degree of social differentiation. The quantity of metal desposited has been shown to relate to the agricultural productivity of those areas where the graves and hoards are found so there does seem to be a clear link between control of agricultural resources and trade goods. The removal of metal from circulation by prestige consumption meant that new supplies were constantly needed. This in turn ensured a continuing basis for power in the control of a resource which became more important as time went on and metal became increasingly significant for both tools and weapons. Control, however, was bought at the price of a continuing vulnerability to fluctuations in the supply of metal from the south, as recent work has shown (Kristiansen, 1978).

Where the metal came from must be inferred on typological and *a priori* grounds rather than scientific analysis of the material. Although metal analyses have been able to provide some useful information about the composition of bronzes, they have proved unable to assign specific items to specific sources, as has been done, for example, in the case of obsidian (Coles and Harding, 1979, pp. 12–13). This is a problem which extends to other Bronze Age trade materials. Indeed, when one asks what was being exchanged for the metal supplies which reached areas such as Denmark, few answers are forthcoming. One is the fossil resin amber (see box).

AMBER

Amber is the general name for a variety of different types of fossil resin. Numerous geological sources for these resins are known throughout Europe, but the main sources are in the area around the Baltic sea in northern Europe. One is the west coast of Jutland, where amber is washed up on the beach from submarine deposits after storms; the other is the south-eastern coast of the Baltic sea, in present day Poland, Latvia and Lithuania. Here too large quantities of amber are washed up on the coast but there are also inland deposits which have been mined in recent times. Amber derived from these two main sources has been spread more widely by marine and glacial action.

Amber was used extensively for the manufacture of beads and other ornaments throughout much of prehistory. Initially, in the mesolithic and the earlier part of the neolithic, it was only used in areas close to the Baltic sources, but in the course of the third millennium its distribution expanded to the south and it is found in burials over much of Europe during the Bronze Age. This expansion seems to be closely related to the rise of the social hierarchies discussed in this chapter and their need for symbolic differentiation (S. J. Shennan, 1982a). The amber had to be obtained by long-distance exchange and was clearly a highly valued material, being found in the greatest quantities in graves which are also very rich in other materials, such as the Shaft Graves of Mycenae in Greece (Harding and Hughes-Brock, 1974). Some of the items made from it, such as the two amber cups or the spacer beads with complex perforations from burials in southern England, display a very high degree of craftsmanship.

(a) The location of the main Baltic amber sources (after Coles and Harding, 1979). (b) A necklace of amber beads from a rich early Bronze Age burial in southern England (after Annable and Simpson, 1964). Scale: c. 1:2.25.

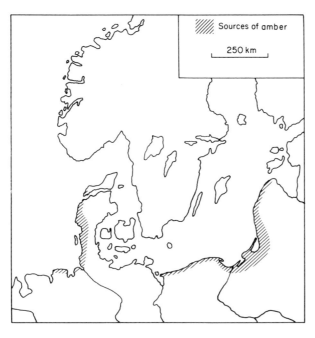

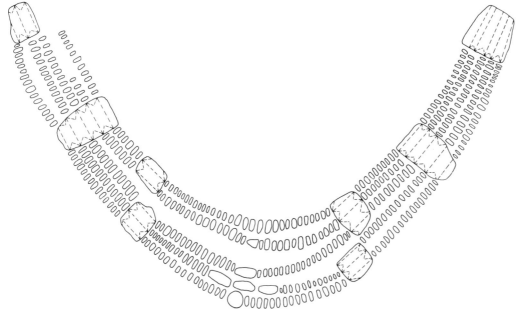

Other commodities are more evasive. Salt was certainly being exploited in some areas at this time: evidence for it exists in the form of the clay containers in which it was transported (Matthias, 1976). As we have seen the large-scale exchange of textiles can only be assumed rather than demonstrated at present.

Conclusion. The preceding pages have outlined the chronology and what seem to be some of the major socio-economic trends of the earlier Bronze Age in temperate Europe. As we have seen, the existence of hierarchically organized societies has long been accepted as a characteristic feature of this period. In general, however, little thought has been given to their nature. One of the very few clearly specified models is that of Gilman (1981) discussed in the previous chapter, who takes the view that power rested directly on the control of land and other productive resources by powerful individuals in a system of stratification, the unequal distribution of the resources necessary to maintain life in Fried's (1967) terms. This had developed by the Bronze Age as the culmination of a process which had begun with the introduction of the plough during the fourth millennium. It was suggested in the previous chapter that the evidence does not fit Gilman's model, nevertheless the importance of the control of land and other productive resources in the earlier Bronze Age remains an open question. Many authorities on the Bronze Age would take the view that with archaeological evidence alone it is simply impossible to distinguish between this suggestion and any of the available alternatives, and that all such matters are in fact inaccessible to us. The position taken here, as throughout this book, is that if we wish to explain the changes seen in the archaeological record of the earlier Bronze Age rather than merely describe the material, then consideration of these questions is unavoidable.

The speculative model sketched here starts from the indications of a concern with prestige artifacts and the representation of individual status seen over much of central and northern Europe at the beginning of the third millennium and described in the previous chapter. In this situation the first archaeologically observable change to occur was the very rapid adoption of the Bell Beaker and associated items as a new set of prestige goods in the middle of the third millennium, likewise described above. The

assumption made here is that the concern with prestige was competitive and that emulation was of considerable importance, so that innovations in prestige artifacts were immediately taken up. Consumption of goods at burial was no doubt the result of a variety of different factors, of which the need for prevention of inflation was no doubt one: the important point about keeping down the number of such goods in circulation was not that the objects themselves would have become devalued if this had not been done, but that this would have happened to the statuses they symbolized.

It was only in the Bell Beaker phase that metal began to become important, as its potential in the prestige system began to be realized, not least its remarkable versatility. It is interesting that metal items are not particularly associated with what on other grounds are considered to be higher-status graves in the Corded Ware period of the early third millennium (Ottaway, 1973). Until metal products began to become important there was relatively little differentiation either within regions or between them in the wider central European area, as there was no basis for it to develop. The demand for metal, however, led to the introduction of an asymmetry into the system, in that those who controlled its distribution, not necessarily the primary producers, now had an advantageous position; this situation eventually resulted in structural changes at the regional and interregional level, starting, as we have seen, with those areas adjacent to the Alpine and Slovakian sources.

The interregional dimension of this process was particularly important. For those involved in local prestige competition in areas distant from the metal sources, to become linked to the interregional prestige exchange system was the key to success. This would no doubt have required the establishment of appropriate alliances, which may itself have involved the competitive mobilization of subsistence resources by local kin groups, in the struggle to become sufficiently influential to join the interregional alliance and exchange system. The power of those at the nodal positions in the system also depended on the continuation and extension of exchange. Without the demand for metal their superior position would have been lost, and conversely, they themselves also needed supplies of exotic materials and objects which required the active seeking out of distant contacts.

Nevertheless, regions differed in the ease and speed with which they were incorporated into the interregional system, depending on the exchange possibilities they offered and the susceptibility of their social systems to penetration by it. In general, the latter was high, since the Bell Beaker phase had already seen the establishment of a considerable degree of ideological uniformity over most of the western half of Europe, but it occurred initially in those areas such as Wessex and Brittany, where, as we have seen, centralized organization and ritual of some kind had developed in association with monument building.

Such an outline is not entirely speculative. Indeed, one could say with little exaggeration that the archaeology of the earlier Bronze Age is the archaeology of its prestige artifacts and the rituals in the course of which they were deposited. Certainly, the archaeological record of the later early Bronze Age and Middle Bronze Age of temperate Europe provides ample evidence for the operation of processes such as those outlined, not just in the rich graves to which emphasis has been given, but in the strong similarities between prestige objects over very large areas, and the widespread use of specific materials obtained by exchange, such as amber, which show that there were extensive contacts between the upper levels of local hierarchies. It was processes of incorporation of the type described which during the middle Bronze Age led not only to the establishment of metal industries in many areas peripheral to the metal sources, but to the development of social systems and consumption patterns at the same time identical to, and ultimately dependent on, the core regions.

The model outlined emphasizes the importance of interregional connections in the earlier Bronze Age and has that in common with Childe's view. We have seen, however, that Childe placed the motor for the changes apparent in the archaeological record of the temperate European earlier Bronze Age in the civilizations of the eastern Mediterranean, and that such a dependency model is no longer tenable. The alternative proposed by Renfrew (e.g. Renfrew, 1973b) of a series of autonomous local processes of change is also unsatisfactory. What we see is a convergence of local trajectories and an interaction between them, based on the influence of a widespread ideology and subsequent elite inter-

actions which followed from it. This pattern prevailed until the middle of the second millennium, when major economic and social changes occurred, establishing the foundations of a new system which lasted until the Iron Age.

MEDITERRANEAN EUROPE

The differences we saw in the previous chapter between the Aegean and the rest of the Mediterranean zone are even more marked when we come to consider the period from the late third to the middle of the second millennium BC. The Aegean sees the rise of the Minoan and Mycenaean civilizations, and their ultimate collapse in the second half of the millennium. In the rest of the Mediterranean there are no such dramatic developments and the period seems in general to be one of stability. However, not the least important of the differences between the two areas lies simply in the amount of archaeological attention each has received. More work has been done on the Aegean in this period than on any other area of Europe, and the chronological sequence has been defined with unequalled precision. The central and western Mediterranean in contrast have been very much neglected, not just by comparison with the Aegean but with the rest of Europe and in many areas even the broad outline of the sequence is only poorly known. In this chapter, therefore, the Aegean and the rest of the Mediterranean zone will again be treated separately.

The Central and Western Mediterranean

While lack of work has been a major reason for our scant knowledge about the Bronze Age sequences in this area, another reason is certainly the stability and isolation which many regions exhibit during the period, and which mean that many patterns continued from the preceding phase. When chronologies depended on establishing sequences of changing material culture, those areas where it changed relatively little inevitably had very coarsely defined chronologies, and this situation has hardly changed with the advent of radiocarbon dating, since it has been so little used in this area. In the central Mediterranean, however, particularly southern Italy and Sicily, some firm dates are provided for the very end of the period of interest, in the form of sherds of Mycenaean pottery in local contexts (Marazzi and Tusa, 1979). An outline chronological sequence is presented in Fig. 7.16.

In northern Italy and adjacent parts of southern France the earlier Bronze Age is characterized by the Polada culture (Barfield, 1971), which in its earliest phase is associated with Bell Beaker material and which extends chronologically well into the middle of the second millennium. Relatively extensive contacts with central Europe mean that it is possible to relate Polada to the well-established sequences we have seen in the previous section of this chapter. In central Italy, however, it has only recently been realized that the material of the so-called Apennine Bronze Age, which it used to be thought represented the early Bronze Age in that area, cannot begin any earlier that

c. 1700 BC, and it is more recently still that material has been found which actually fills the gap in the sequence which the late dating of the Apennine phase produced (Barker, 1981); the key site here has been the settlement of Tufariello (Fig.7.17) (Holloway, 1975).

Further west the gaps in our regional knowledge of the Bronze Age are still greater. In Iberia it is again south-east Spain and southern Portugal which are the best known, as in the preceding period, although in the latter area the centre of gravity has moved south from the area of defended sites around the Tagus estuary discussed in the previous chapter (Schubart, 1975, 1976). In much of inland Iberia next to nothing is known of the Bronze Age sequence, although it is clear that in many areas Beakers continued in use well into the second millennium, as did the use of collective tombs. A continuation of Beaker developments is also seen in parts of southern France (see, for example, Harrison, 1980) and the pattern is the same as in those areas of north-west

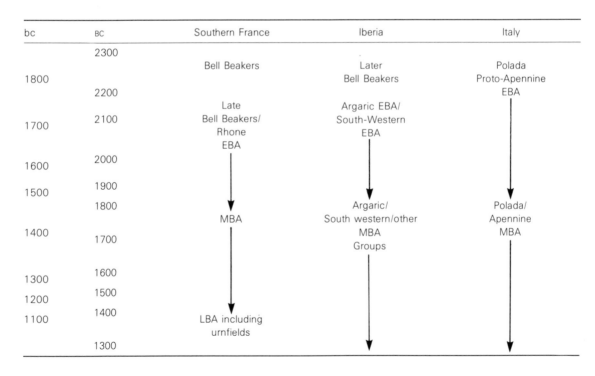

bc	BC	Southern France	Iberia	Italy
	2300			
1800		Bell Beakers	Later Bell Beakers	Polada Proto-Apennine
	2200			EBA
1700	2100	Late Bell Beakers/ Rhone EBA	Argaric EBA/ South-Western EBA	
1600	2000			
1500	1900			
	1800	MBA	Argaric/ South western/other MBA Groups	Polada/ Apennine MBA
1400	1700			
1300	1600			
1200	1500			
1100	1400	LBA including urnfields		
	1300			

Fig. 7.16 A regional chronological chart for central and west Mediterranean Europe.

Europe where it occurs, involving increasingly localized patterns of typological development. Even in those areas where Beaker pottery did not continue in use for a long period other types of Beaker origin continued to circulate, including wrist-guards and buttons of various kinds. Southern France, however, remained reasonably in the mainstream of European developments, the Rhône valley in particular, which was part of a larger cultural zone extending north up the Rhône valley and east into Switzerland, with its own characteristic pottery types and metalwork which was a distinctive local version of that current in central Europe in the earlier Bronze Age (Bill, 1973).

In Iberia the picture is much more one of local isolation in the earlier Bronze Age after the widespread contacts of the Beaker phase, although along the Atlantic coast there are some suggestions of contacts with Ireland and Brittany. However, it is only at the very end of the Bronze Age, early in the first millennium BC, that an international 'Atlantic' Bronze Age comes into being (Rowlands, 1980).

The most spectacular Iberian Bronze Age material is undoubtedly that of the El Argar, or Argaric culture. This is found in south-east Spain in exactly the same area as the rich Millaran copper age material described in the previous chapter. At such stratified sites as Cerro de la Virgen (Schüle and Pellicer, 1966), the cultural sequence can be traced from Copper Age levels, through levels containing some Beaker sherds but otherwise developments of local ceramic types, into levels of the local Argaric Bronze Age. The most obvious contrast between the Copper Age and Bronze Age material is in the sphere of burial. The elaborate collective tombs are replaced by individual burial, very often in large storage jars; at the cemetery of El Argar itself 80% of the 1000 burials were in such jars. Impressive grave goods, however, continued to be deposited, now associated with individual burials and with a much greater emphasis on metal items than in the Copper Age (Gilman, 1976; Coles and Harding, 1979, pp. 221-7).

Most similar to the developments in south-east Spain are those in southern Portugal (Schubart, 1975, 1976), again paralleling the situation we saw in the Copper Age, but they are different in certain important respects. Communal burial gives way to individual burial, here inhumations in stone cists, containing grave goods including metalwork, but the material is not so rich in either quantity or quality as in the south-east (Fig.7.18). The major difference between the two areas, however, lies in the trends they show in the spatial distribution of sites. Whereas

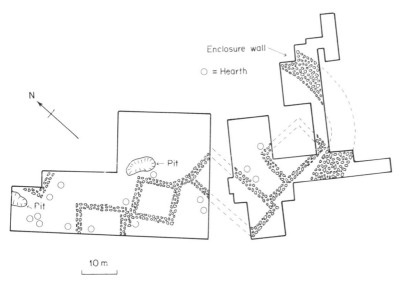

Enclosure wall

O = Hearth

N

← Pit

Pit

10 m

Fig. 7.17 The Protoappennine Bronze Age settlement at Tufariello, Campania, Italy (after Holloway, 1975).

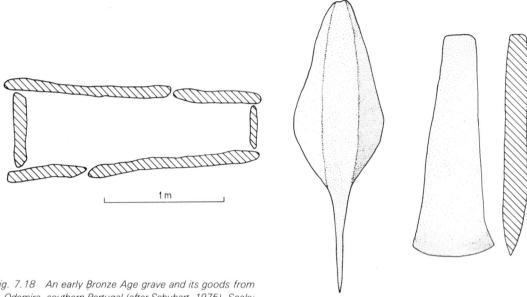

Fig. 7.18 *An early Bronze Age grave and its goods from Odemira, southern Portugal (after Schubart, 1975). Scale: c. 1:1.5 for objects.*

the rich cemeteries of the Argaric Bronze Age are found in the same area as their Copper Age predecessors, in southern Portugal the Bronze Age cemeteries do not show the same distribution. The Copper Age centres and tombs discussed in the previous chapter are centred on the lower Tagus area, whereas the Bronze Age cemeteries are concentrated to the south, in the area of the copper sources, a region in which, in complete contrast to the lower Tagus, Bell Beaker material is virtually non-existent.

As suggested above, the exact dating of these Iberian developments, like those of much of Italy, presents problems. In much of the central and western Mediterranean local developments continued with no major changes until the end of the second millennium and the beginning of the first; later phases of the Portugese south-western Bronze Age and the Argaric continued up to this time in a similar way to the Apennine Bronze Age in Italy. Only in southern France does the sequence of change parallel that in temperate Europe, with the beginning of the Urnfields providing a suitable breaking point.

Social and economic patterns c. *2300–1200 BC.* It has already been noted that even the regional cultural sequences of this area in the earlier Bronze Age are

not well-known and the situation is even worse when we attempt to reconstruct societies and economies. Here it will only be possible to sketch some of the aspects which have attracted attention in different parts of the central and west Mediterranean.

Once again, south-east Spain is an important focus. The strong indications of some form of regionally centralized organization and marked social differentiation which existed in the Copper Age have been seen in the previous chapter. In the Argaric Bronze Age, burials were individual rather than communal and there were very marked disparities in the grave goods which were deposited. Gilman (1976) has suggested that this was the end result of a long process going back to the neolithic, in the course of which incompatibilities had arisen between social organization and ritual. Initially societies were egalitarian and their rituals and ideology were similarly communal and egalitarian. Gradually, society became increasingly differentiated but ritual remained communal even though rich grave goods were deposited. Finally, in the early Bronze Age socio-economic inequalities increased still further and an openly inegalitarian ideology of individual differentiations arose to sanction it. As we have seen, south-east Spain has this pattern of change from communal monument construction to the deposition of individual burials, some with very rich grave goods, in common with Wessex and Brittany. It may be that it was the external contacts associated with Bell Beakers, rather than a further local increase in socio-economic differentiation, which finally led to the changes in burial ritual which characterize the Argaric. In southern Portugal a similar change occurs but here the range of differentiation in the Bronze Age burials is much less marked.

A further factor which these two areas of Iberia have in common with the earlier Bronze Age pattern in temperate Europe concerns the role of metallurgy. Whether or not the basis of power and prestige in the Copper Age depended on control of subsistence resources, as has been suggested, it seems generally agreed that in the Bronze Age metal was critical (cf. Chapman, 1982). This emerges most clearly in Portugal where, as we have seen, the Copper Age centres were around the mouth of the Tagus whereas the Bronze Age ones are clustered in the south, where the rich copper sources lie. Copper sources existed close to the Millaran/Argaric area so such a shift did not occur, but even here there is some indication of a change in settlement pattern, so that where Copper Age settlements tended to be on low hills dominating immediately adjacent rich agricultural areas, newly established Bronze Age sites were further inland, in the foothills of the mountains, often in very steep positions and strongly fortified; defensive considerations seem to have been even more important in the second millennium than they were in the third in this area.

One problem with assessing the importance of metal in sustaining and accounting for the hierarchical forms of organization which undoubtedly existed in the Bronze Age is that so little is known of the possible role of the subsistence economy in this regard; evidence apart from that of site locations is meagre in the extreme. But the indications of the social importance of metallurgy, in the large amounts deposited in burials and the spatial association between metal sources and differentiated societies, certainly suggest that its control was important and provide a close parallel with the temperate European patterns discussed in the preceding section. In this light, the differences between temperate Europe and Iberia are also striking. In Iberia tin–bronze did not come into use until relatively late in the Bronze Age,

even though it is one of the few parts of Europe with its own tin sources. Arsenical copper, which has many of the properties of tin–bronze, continued to be used as it was in the Copper Age, since the local copper ores were generally arsenic-rich. Nor did the products of the industry attain the sophistication of those produced in central and eastern Europe. The other respect in which the Iberian earlier Bronze Age differs from that to the north is its isolation. After the Beaker phase southern Iberia does not share in the exchange and interaction systems of temperate Europe, nor does a comparable expansion of the prestige system and interaction networks occur within Iberia itself, despite the fact that contacts seem to have existed between southern Portugal and south-east Spain (Schubart, 1975).

Parts of southern France seem to have been equally isolated, in that much of the earlier Bronze Age shows little change from the local late neolithic and copper age, but as we have seen, other areas, particularly the Rhône valley, were clearly part of the wider temperate European interaction system. This is apparent not just in the metalwork, which shows similarities with central Europe and includes metal-hilted daggers, but also in the occurrence of amber in southern French sites; particularly large quantities are known from the Grotte du Hasard and it has been shown by analysis to be of Baltic origin (Roudil and Soulier, 1976). As in Iberia, so too in southern France defensive considerations seem to have been important in some places; the site of Lébous in the Causses continued in use and a Bronze Age fortified site, the Camp-du-Laure (Courtin, 1976b), is known from near the mouth of the Rhône. To what extent such sites as these functioned as regional centres, if at all, is unknown, but again there is evidence, particularly from the Rhône group with its metalwork (Bill, 1973), of social differentiation expressed in variations in quantity and quality of grave goods, and this area at least can probably be taken to have had many of the characteristics of the other parts of the temperate Bronze Age system discussed in the previous section of this chapter.

As might be expected, there are considerable variations within the great length of peninsular Italy. In terms of interregional relations, one can roughly divide the north, with its transalpine contacts, from the centre, which was relatively isolated, from the south, which from around the middle of the second millennium has increasing contacts with Mycenaean Greece.

The northern group, the Polada culture (Barfield, 1971; Peroni, 1971), is interesting in that although prestige weapons of central European types occur, as do amber beads, indicating its central European contacts, burials are extremely rare, so that one does not see the socially differentiated patterns of grave good deposition widely prevalent elsewhere, a fact whose implications for the local social system deserve investigation. Settlements of the Polada group are quite well known because many of them are in lakeside situations with good organic preservation, and this has also served to produce extensive subsistence evidence; but a dynamic picture of socio-economic change has yet to emerge.

In this respect most progress has been made by Barker (1981) in his study of central Italy, where there appears to have been a gradual process of agricultural intensification through the second millennium. Subsistence was based on mixed arable agriculture with seasonal transhumance, in some cases to sites at the very top of the Apennine mountains at an altitude of 2000m, but in the later part of the second millennium some of the trans-humant camps seem to have become permanent settlements with their own mixed agricultural sub-sistence economies (Fig.7.19). At the same time there seems to have been a growth of lowland settlement, with an increase in cereal pollen in the pollen diagrams of these areas and suggestions of more intensive animal and crop management at such sites as Luni and Narce (Östenberg, 1967; Potter, 1976). These developments are the background to the dramatic changes in central Italian society in the first millennium BC which are discussed in the next chapter.

It is likewise only late in the second millennium that one sees any great developments in metallurgy and exchange in central Italy. Prior to this time metal items are extremely rare and their metallurgical composition very variable; as in Iberia the use of a consistent tin–bronze does not become established until late. There are also parallels between the two in the restriction of metal items to areas adjacent to the sources; this at least is the case with the copper axes. Rare metal-hilted daggers are distributed more widely across central Italy and are one of the few indications of any kind of status or prestige

differentiation in the population, but again it is to be noted that they occur as isolated finds rather than in burials, which are extremely uncommon.

Altogether, as Barker (1981) has argued, it appears that in the central Italian Bronze Age communities were made up of a few households living at a basically self-sufficient level, with simple technologies and little craft-specialization (Fig.7.17), but with some degree of higher status for their leaders; little evidence exists for any degree of regional centralization.

Southern Italy is different from the areas to the north in that from about 1500 BC there is evidence of contact with Mycenaean Greece, in the form of imported pottery, which by the fourteenth century BC is present in considerable quantities and occurs not only on the Italian mainland but also on Sicily and the Aeolian Islands (Coles and Harding, 1979, pp. 418-20). How much of this interaction involved Mycenaean settlement and how much simply exchange is not clear. Such contacts between more and less advanced societies often lead to considerable changes in the latter; in this case the Mycenaean impact on local societies is unknown and deserves further investigation. It is perhaps significant, however, that when major changes began to occur in the Bronze Age societies of Italy it was in central Italy, and particularly Etruria, not in the area of Mycenaean influence.

Conclusion. Although societies which were hierarchical to some degree seem to have existed throughout most of the central and western Mediterranean, the picture which emerges from the period *c.* 2300–*c.* 1200 BC is generally one of stability and isolation. In Italy this represents a continuation of the pattern of the third millennium seen in the previous chapter. Dramatic developments only began at the very end of the second millennium, culminating in the rise of Rome. In Iberia the stability and isolation could be said to represent a failure to follow the trajectory of the Aegean during this period, since the Aegean at the end of the early Bronze Age and south-east Spain and southern Portugal in the Copper Age, both *c.* 2500–2300 BC, were arguably at a very similar point of socio-economic development. In Iberia changes were to come, albeit not on the scale of those in Italy, when it became part of a larger Mediterranean system with the coming of the Phoenicians (see below, Chapter 8).

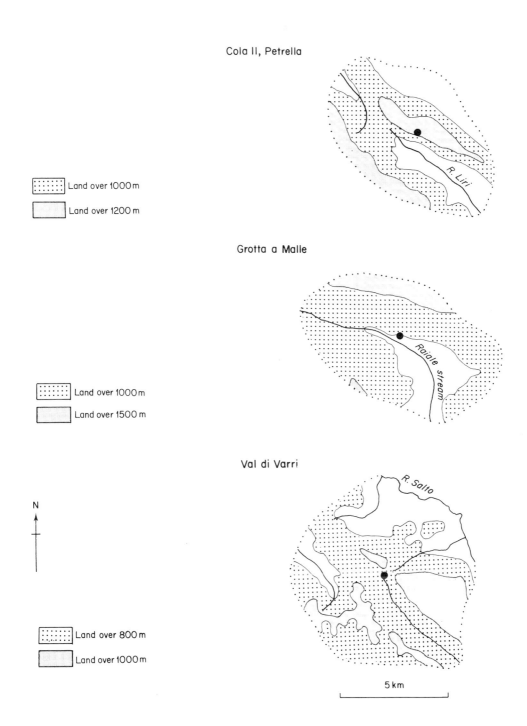

Cola II, Petrella

Land over 1000 m
Land over 1200 m

Grotta a Malle

Land over 1000 m
Land over 1500 m

Val di Varri

N

Land over 800 m
Land over 1000 m

R. Liri

Raiale stream

R. Salto

5 km

Fig. 7.19   The territories within one hour's walking distance of three upland Bronze Age sites in Abruzzo, Italy (after Barker, 1981).

The Aegean

The middle and late Bronze Age sequences of the Aegean are known in a detail unparallelled in prehistoric Europe. The rapid rate of ceramic change and the contacts between the Aegean and the Near East during this period mean that it is possible to define absolutely dated chronological subdivisions much less than 100 years in length in many cases, although one unfortunate side-effect has been the generation of a typological and chronological nomenclature of labyrinthine complexity. Fig.7.20 is a chronological table for mainland Greece and Crete in the period *c.* 2000–1200 BC, indicating the basic outline of the periodization and the main developments which occurred. This will provide a framework for the discussion which follows.

We saw in the previous chapter that the Aegean early Bronze Age marked in many respects a break with earlier patterns. There was a major expansion of settlement in the southern Aegean, most probably associated with the establishment of Mediterranean polyculture—cultivation of the olive and vine as well as cereals and pulses. Although in general the settlement pattern was one of dispersed hamlets, in many

places there is evidence of settlements differentiated from the others in size, the presence of fortifications, or the existence of exceptional buildings. Similarly, differentiation is visible in the burials of many areas, some of which contain elaborate grave goods, often metal weapons and ornaments whose very existence suggests the importance of the symbolization of prestige.

During the early Bronze Age there is relatively little that distinguishes Crete from the rest of the Aegean in social and organizational terms, apart from the lack of defences at major sites. Around 2000 BC, at the beginning of the middle Bronze Age, this situation changes significantly and in Crete the first palaces appear, at Knossos, Phaistos and Mallia (Cadogan, 1976). Although currently available evidence is not decisive, it appears that these were already significantly larger than other contemporary Cretan sites during the early Bronze Age. Some reasons why this might have been the case have been suggested in the previous chapter, but whether or not these are valid, the estimated population sizes of these early Bronze Age communities, which range between *c.* 300 for the smallest and 2000 for the largest, suggest that relatively complex modes of community integration

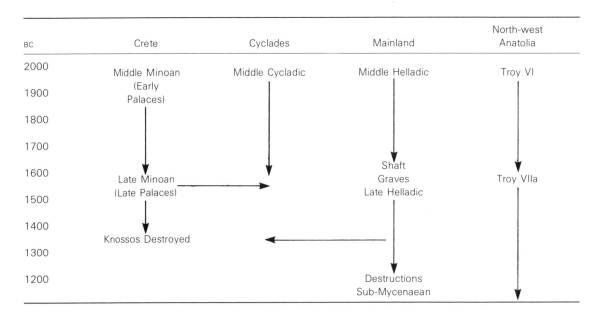

Fig. 7.20   A regional chronological chart for the middle and late Bronze Age Aegean.

would have been necessary, and that some important organizational thresholds had been passed (Whitelaw, 1983). The appearance of palaces at these sites, however, is associated with a further jump in size; the area of occupation at Knossos, for example, expands from less than 5 hectares in the early Bronze Age to about 45 hectares in the middle Bronze Age proto-palatial phase. Whitelaw (1983) has suggested that a new organizational system such as that represented by the palaces may have been necessary before any further growth could take place.

But what do the palaces represent? Physically, they are large integrated complexes of buildings including monumental elements on the one hand and storage facilities on the other (Fig.7.21). Functionally, there

is no reason to doubt the role which has been assigned to them ever since they were first discovered, that they were major regional centres, the seats of local rulers, with a key regional administrative role. That these early palaces were associated with prestigious individuals is suggested, for example, by the treasures from the early palace at Mallia (Fig.7.22) (Renfrew, 1972). The administrative role indicated by the large-scale storage facilities is emphasized by the appearance of the first Cretan script at this time, called 'Hieroglyphic' by Sir Arthur Evans, by analogy with Egypt. Texts in this script have been found at all three of the early palaces, mainly on seals or seal impressions, but occasionally on clay tablets as well. The precise nature of the economy indicated

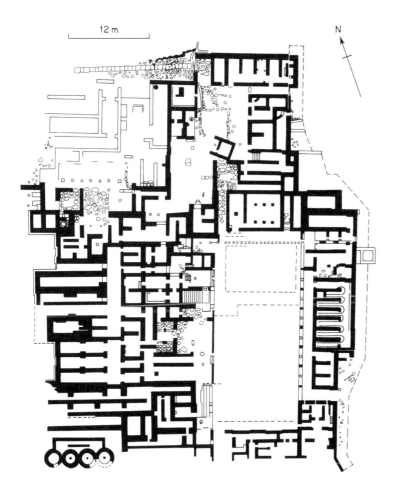

12 m

N

Fig. 7.21 Plan of the middle Bronze Age palace at Mallia, Crete (after Renfrew, 1972).

*Fig. 7.22   The decorated stone mace-head from the middle Minoan palace at Mallia (after Müller-Karpe, 1974). Length =
15 cm.*

by the storage facilities is open to argument: was the
role of the palaces *redistributive*, in the sense that
they provided a means of evening out spatial and
temporal variations in food supply for the
populations of their tributary areas as a whole, or are
we rather seeing evidence of *mobilization*, the
upward movement of resources from the general
population to the elite for the benefit of the latter?
Halstead and O'Shea (1982) in fact suggest that an
initially redistributive role may have changed in the
course of time to one in which the overriding
emphasis was on mobilization for the benefit of the
elite; on the other hand, the fact that the end of the
palace system (see below) apparently resulted in a
catastrophic population decline suggests that there
must have been at least some redistribution which
benefited the general population.

Of most importance, however, are the implications
of the administrative apparatus so abundantly
documented by the archaeological evidence for the
social organization associated with the palaces. In
terms of the standard evolutionary scales for the
development of social complexity none of the
European societies considered so far in this book
could be regarded as anything more complex than a
'chiefdom' in Service's (1962) scheme, but with the
appearance of the Minoan palaces we have to
consider the question of whether or not we are
dealing with the first European states (see box on
p.170). Fried describes the state in the following terms:

A state is not simply a legislature, an executive
body, a judiciary system, an administrative
bureaucracy, or even a government . . . (It) is better
viewed as the complex of institutions by means of
which the power of the society is organised on a basis
superior to kinship (1967, p. 229).

Other authors (Flannery, 1972b; Wright, 1977) lay
the emphasis on the growth of specialization and
centralization in decision-making.

The question of whether the late Bronze Age
societies of the Aegean can be viewed in such terms
has been discussed extensively by Renfrew (1972),
who has coined the term 'early state module' to
describe them. His conclusion is that while they share
many of the characteristics of chiefdoms, the
significance of the palace as an administrative
institution is such that we must see these societies as
minor states, remembering that in fact the Greek
city-states of the classical period were no larger in
size, albeit very different in nature.

The early palaces at Knossos, Mallia and Phaistos
came to an end late in the seventeenth century BC,
possibly as a result of earthquakes, and were swiftly
replaced by new palace buildings of which far more
has survived. At the same time new palaces appeared
at such sites as Agia Triadha and Zakro, as well as
a number of what appear to have been minor centres,
often referred to as villas or country houses
(Cadogan, 1976). If, as seems likely, they represent

an intermediate tier of organization between the major palaces on the one hand and ordinary settlements on the other, they represent in effect an extension of the palace system to cover most of Crete. Certainly they had similarities in both architecture and other aspects of material culture with the palaces, but perhaps most important is the presence of seals and clay tablets bearing inscriptions in Linear A, a new script which appears to have replaced the earlier Hieroglyphic script at around the same time as the end of the earlier palaces. Although, like the Hieroglyphic script, it has not yet been deciphered, it is clear that the inscriptions on the tablets are mostly the documents of a palace-based administrative system, and their presence at these minor centres, such as Pyrgos, strongly suggests that they formed a part of it.

Fragments of Linear A tablets have also been found outside Crete on some of the Aegean islands, such as Thera (Doumas and Puchelt, 1980) and Melos (Renfrew and Wagstaff, 1982), and are one indication of the considerable expansion of overseas Cretan contacts, particularly in the Aegean area, which began at the end of the seventeenth century BC (Davis, 1979). The nature of the relationship between the Cretan polities and the Aegean, especially such sites as Phylakopi on Melos or Akrotiri on Thera, has long been a matter of discussion. During the sixteenth and earlier fifteenth centuries BC these imported Cretan pottery and showed considerable Cretan influence on their own local ceramic styles. It has been suggested that they were colonies controlled from Crete, but the evidence available does not make it possible to be very specific about their political status (Davis, 1979). What is clear is that during the fourteenth century BC Minoan cultural influence and trade contacts in the Aegean, and indeed in the eastern Mediterranean generally, were replaced by Mycenaean links and influence from the Greek mainland (see, e.g. Caskey, 1972; Dickinson, 1977), symptomatic of major political changes which had taken place.

Outside Crete, the earlier part of the middle Bronze Age was not generally a time of growth. Many early Bronze Age sites were abandoned, although it is not altogether clear how much this is due to settlement nucleation as opposed to population decline; Renfrew (1972) has suggested

that piracy first became important in the Aegean at this time and had an effect on local settlement patterns, as it was later to do in the medieval period. At all events, there are no developments nearly comparable to those of Crete until the sixteenth century BC. Then the Shaft Graves of Mycenae and the *tholos* tombs (burial chambers with corbelled roofs and long entrance passages) of Peristeria in Messenia, with their rich grave goods (Fig.7.23), many of them showing Cretan influence in their craftsmanship, indicate the rise of wealthy centres on the Greek mainland (Dickinson, 1977). The explanation usually advanced for Mycenae's growth to wealth and power is that it had a strategic position on trade routes, but there is really very little evidence which can be advanced in support of such a view. As with Crete, we can trace the development but we cannot satisfactorily explain it. Subsequently, during the fifteenth century BC, a number of other places come to share the Mycenaean pattern, including *tholos* tombs, which appear in Mycenae itself in the period after the Shaft Graves (Hooker, 1976).

The contrast with what happened on Crete during this time is striking. About 1450 BC all the palaces and minor centres of Crete, except for Knossos, were destroyed. Knossos itself continued until c. 1370 BC before it too was destroyed by fire, and it is this last period of its existence about which most is known, for the administrative documents which have come down to us were written in the Linear B script, deciphered by Michael Ventris and shown to be a form of Greek (see box). Whether the rulers of Knossos during this period were Mycenaeans who had conquered Crete or not is a controversy which can be left to the specialists. What is apparent is that during this final period Knossos controlled much of the island: the Linear B tablets refer to places all over Crete, except the east, as having to pay tribute of various forms to Knossos (Killen, 1977). The destruction of the other Cretan palaces may well have been carried out as part of a military expansion to achieve this end. The Bronze Age Near East provides numerous examples of the cyclical expansion of local city-states at the expense of their neighbours and their ultimate decline. The reasons for the final demise of Knossos are obscure and have been the subject of much scholarly (and not so scholarly!) debate. The most favoured in recent years has been

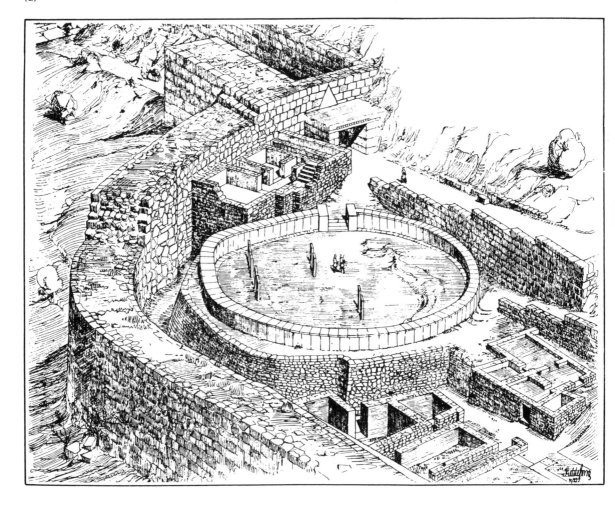

Fig. 7.23   The tombs of Mycenae. (a) Shaft Grave Circle A (after Stubbings, 1972). (b) Grave goods from the Shaft Graves
(after Stubbings, 1972).

THE LINEAR B SCRIPT

The decipherment of the Linear B script is one of the great adventure stories of post-war prehistoric studies in the Aegean (Chadwick, 1958). It had already been established by Sir Arthur Evans, the excavator of the palace at Knossos, that the inscribed clay tablets found there must be lists or accounts. A numerical system was clearly recognizable, as was the fact that some of the signs on the tablets were clearly pictures of the objects they referred to, such as cups, tripods or horses, while others probably represented syllables. Ventris built on the work already done by applying wartime code-breaking methods to the problem and his decipherment of the Linear B script as an early form of Greek was all the more convincing for not being what he or anybody else had expected.

The tablets show the meticulous detail in which the economy was centrally controlled from the palace by its bureaucracy and also give an indication of the form of the hierarchy which controlled it, confirming and amplifying the picture deduced from the archaeological evidence of the palaces themselves, with their state rooms and storage facilities. Of particular interest is the way in which the Knossos tablets demonstrate that by late Bronze Age times textile production had become a large-scale industry (Killen, 1964). It is clear that the palace of Knossos directly controlled enormous flocks of sheep, and that the production of textiles must have been a major activity of the palace economy, a feature which it shares with the palace economies of Mesopotamia, where the clay tablets of the bureaucracy once again provide the evidence.

It is perhaps the tablets more than anything else which confirm the affinities of the Aegean late Bronze Age centres with the Bronze Age states of the Near East, and indicate the qualitative break between them and contemporary societies elsewhere in Europe, which did not have bureaucratic institutions.

(a)

(b)

(c) 'Two tripod-cauldrons of Cretan workmanship, of ai-ke-u type; one tripod-cauldron with a (?) single handle (?) on one foot; one tripod-cauldron of Cretan workmanship, burnt away at the legs, (?) unserviceable; three (?) wine-jars; one larger-sized dipas *with four handles; two larger-sized* dipas *with three handles; one smaller-sized* dipas *with four handles; one smaller-sized* dipas *with three handles; one smaller-sized* dipas *without handle.'*

A Linear B tablet from the palace of Pylos, known as the 'Tripod tablet' because of its subject matter. (a) A drawing of the tablet. (b) The text written out in its constituent groups. (c) A translation. (After Palmer, 1965; Stubbings, 1972.)

Fig. 7.24   Map of the east Mediterranean to show sites with evidence of Mycenaean pottery (after Stubbings, 1972).

that it was in some way connected with the volcanic eruption which largely destroyed the island of Thera, but the investigations which have been carried out tend to refute this hypothesis rather than confirm it. It now seems unlikely that debris from the eruption had a major impact on Crete, while there may be chronological discrepancies between the various events.

After the end of Knossos, and presumably of the palace-based economy associated with it, it is evidence of Mycenaean rather than Minoan trade that one finds in the ports and centres of the east Mediterranean (Fig.7.24), while on mainland Greece itself the later fourteenth and thirteenth centuries BC were a time of major construction at the existing Mycenaean citadels and the establishment of new palaces elsewhere (Hooker, 1976). Of particular interest is the palace at Pylos in Messenia, which was founded at this time and seems to represent the unification of a number of small-scale political units into a larger polity; this has been the subject of intensive investigation concerning both its settlement pattern (McDonald and Rapp, 1972; A. Chadwick, 1978) and its political geography (J. Chadwick, 1977; Cherry, 1977). Like late period Knossos, it has produced an archive of tablets written in the Linear B script, again demonstrating the key role of the palace in every aspect of socio-economic life. The information they record includes the assessment of contributions due to the palace from various localities, details of land tenure, the organization of personnel into work units, and the location of the Pylian army (J. Chadwick, 1976).

The Aegean palace pattern was not of course maintained. Over a period of about 100 years

beginning at the end of the thirteenth century BC the mainland centres were destroyed and there was a breakdown of the cultural uniformity in the pottery which is so striking a feature of the Mycenaean world (Fig.7.25); at the same time, evidence of Mycenaean contact with the eastern Mediterranean also ceases. The reasons for the collapse have been much debated, most of those advanced involving incursions of invaders from one source or another, although some have argued in favour of local insurrections; the matter is discussed by Hooker (1976). The initial cause need not have been cataclysmic in itself. However, once the fragile palace centres and their organizational system were destroyed, serious consequences would certainly have ensued for the populations who depended on them. It would have been necessary for them to revive more localized and

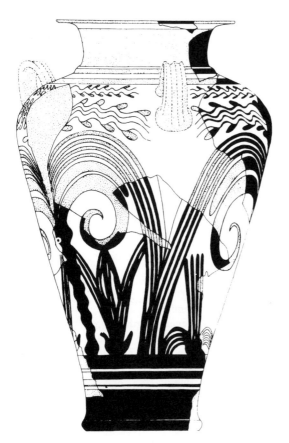

Fig. 7.25   *Mycenaean pottery from Amman and Lachish in the Levant (after Stubbings, 1972).*

autonomous forms of organization in all probability incapable of supporting the population densities which could be maintained by the palace economy, or its functional specialization. The Greek city-states which eventually emerged in the first millennium BC were organized on a very different basis.

SUGGESTIONS FOR FURTHER READING

Unlike the previous period, the earlier Bronze Age is now extremely well-covered as far as detailed synthesis of the material is concerned. *The Bronze Age in Europe* by J. Coles and A. Harding provides a very thorough account which is regionally comprehensive, except for the Aegean. More detailed regional studies of interest include those by Burgess and Barker mentioned at the end of the previous chapter, while M. Gimbutas, *Bronze Age Cultures of Central and Eastern Europe*, remains an important source despite the widespread rejection of many of its interpretations. Detailed coverage of the middle and late Bronze Age in the Aegean may be found in G. Cadogan, *The Palaces of Minoan Crete*, and J. Hooker, *Mycenaean Greece*.

As far as social and economic studies are concerned, A. Sheridan and G. Bailey (eds), *Economic Archaeology*, includes relevant papers by Bradley (Britain and Bohemia), Halstead and O'Shea (the Aegean), and Kristiansen (Scandinavia). The Scandinavian Bronze Age has been a particular focus of such studies. Relevant papers apart from that mentioned include K. Randsborg's study of social stratification in *Praehistorische Zeitschrift* **49**, 1974, and two other studies by Kristiansen, one in K. Kristiansen and C. Paludan-Muller (eds), *New Directions in Scandinavian Archaeology*, the other in C. Renfrew, M. Rowlands and B. Segraves (eds), *Theory and Explanation in Archaeology*.

An important attempt at an overall general synthesis of social change in the European Bronze Age is that referred to at the end of the previous chapter, by A. Gilman in *Current Anthropology* **22**, 1981; at the opposite extreme, Susan Shennan, The social organization at Branc, *Antiquity* **49**, 1975, is a detailed reconstruction of a community, based on a single cemetery. A recent account of society in the Aegean late Bronze Age, based very much on the evidence of the Linear B tablets, is J. Chadwick's *The Mycenaean World*.

A number of the chapters in Renfrew and Shennan (eds), *Ranking, Resource and Exchange* again deal with various aspects of social and economic change in this period.

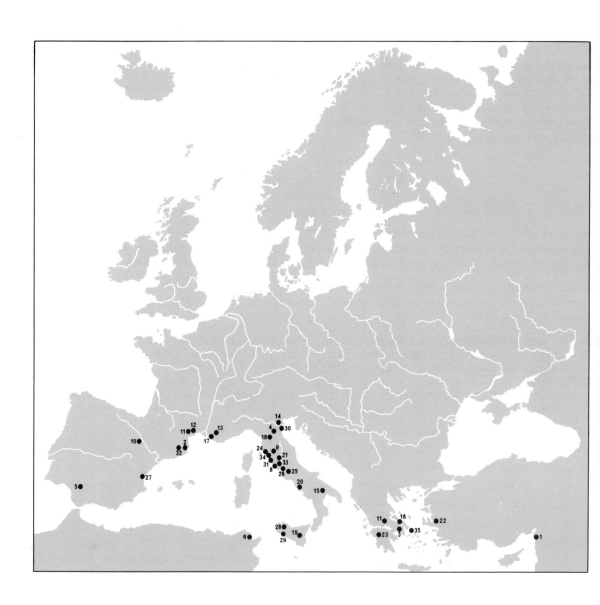

Fig. 8.1 Principal sites mentioned in Chapter 8. 1 Al Mina. 2 Ampurias (Emporion). 3 Athens. 4 Bologna. 5 Carambolo.
6 Carthage. 7 Cayla de Mailhac. 8 Cerveteri. 9 Chiusi. 10 Cortes de Navarra. 11 Delphi. 12 Ensérune. 13 Entremont.
14 Frattesina. 15 Gravina. 16 Lefkandi. 17 Marseilles (Massalia). 18 Marzabotto. 19 Morgantina. 20 Naples. 21 Narce.
22 Old Smyrna. 23 Olympia. 24 Populonia. 25 Praeneste. 26 Rome. 27 Saguntum. 28 Segesta. 29 Selinus. 30 Spina.
31 Tarquinii. 32 Ullastret. 33 Veii. 34 Vetulonia. 35 Zagora.

8

The Rise of the State in Mediterranean Europe

After the collapse of the Mycenaean palace societies in Greece, there are signs of extensive depopulation and a complete lack of centralized political authority. In Italy, southern France and Spain, new burial rites and prestige items were adopted by a hierarchical society closely akin to that in central and western Europe. From the eighth century onwards, however, first Greece and then the other areas of the Mediterranean show a series of dramatic changes. There was a sharp rise in population, a marked intensification in the cultivation of cereals, the vine and the olive, the introduction of new technologies, especially in pottery and metalwork with the widespread adoption of ironworking, and the appearance of towns. These changes were accompanied by new types of political organization, in particular the city-state. The search for raw materials, especially metal ores, and for land to settle excess population led to colonization throughout the Mediterranean by Greeks and Phoenicians, disseminating the new political system which was soon to prevail throughout the whole region. The new political structure led to the adoption of formal laws, of coinage for payments to and by the state, of an alphabetic script and a new level of literacy, and new fighting tactics to use most efficiently the military potential of a citizen army. A fundamental factor in the emergence of the new system was competitive rivalry between individuals and groups, which further led to conflict between the states and the ultimate consolidation of the first European empires.

The distinction between Mediterranean and temperate Europe described in the previous chapter largely disappeared with the collapse of the Mycenaean palace societies, and though Greece retained a distinctive material culture, it was probably not very different in economic and social organization. Italy, southern France and parts of Spain, on the other hand, were clearly linked to central Europe from the end of the second millennium. Yet from the eighth century onwards the Mediterranean lands rapidly diverged from Europe north of the Alps, and the division between the classical and barbarian worlds was drawn. So great was this division that it makes sense to treat the Mediterranean world separately in this chapter, down to the full emergence of the city-state and the beginnings of empire building, and to devote the next two chapters to the further developments in temperate Europe.

Radiocarbon dating has made virtually no impact on this period, and absolute chronology depends on detailed artifactual studies, especially of pottery, ultimately dated by finds from historically known sites or links to the historical chronology of the Near East and Egypt. There are few such links between the twelfth and the eighth centuries, so the chronology of that phase is less certain, but where such finds exist, the frequent changes in style and the detailed decoration employed make the pottery ideal for such study, and a high degree of chronological precision is possible (Fig.8.2).

REGIONAL SEQUENCES IN MEDITERRANEAN EUROPE

The thirteenth century BC saw the climax of the Mycenaean palace societies, and their connections outside Greece at this time form a marked archaeological horizon. The quantity of Mycenaean pottery known from the central Mediterranean is steadily growing (Marazzi and Tusa, 1979) and there are close connections in the bronze industries of Italy and

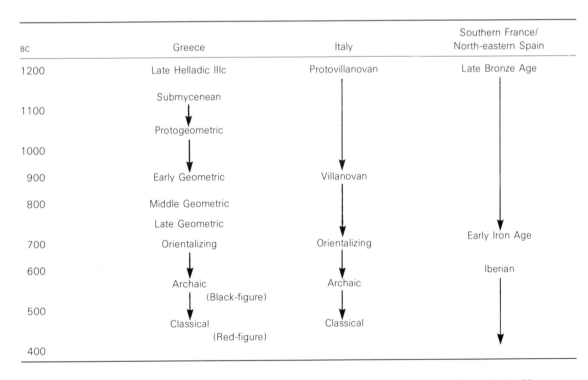

BC	Greece	Italy	Southern France/ North-eastern Spain
1200	Late Helladic IIIc	Protovillanovan	Late Bronze Age
1100	Submycenean ↓ Protogeometric		
1000	↓		
900	Early Geometric	Villanovan	
800	Middle Geometric		
	Late Geometric		
700	Orientalizing	Orientalizing	Early Iron Age
600	↓	↓	Iberian
	Archaic	Archaic	
500	↓ (Black-figure)	↓	
	Classical	Classical	
400	(Red-figure)		↓

Fig. 8.2 Chronological chart for Mediterranean Europe in the late second and early first millennia BC.

Greece (Bietti Sestieri, 1973). There are also strong similarities between Greece and central Europe, especially in weaponry (Müller-Karpe, 1962). These links are valuable for chronological purposes as well as for the evidence of the long-distance connections of the Mycenaean world. With the collapse of that world, these connections were severed and archaeological material in these regions is more diverse.

In Greece the archaeological record is comprised almost entirely of graves and their contents (Snodgrass, 1971). These include pottery and metalwork, especially weapons and personal ornaments. There is a wide variety of local grave rites and pottery styles, and it is the ceramic sequence in the region of Athens that forms the basis for the division of the period into phases on the grounds of the changing decorative styles; these phases are successively Submycenaean, Protogeometric and Geometric, with further subdivisions (Coldstream, 1977) (Fig.8.3). Iron became increasingly common from the eleventh century.

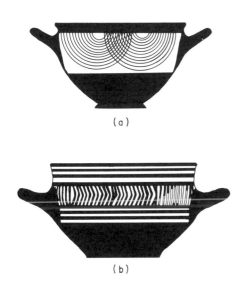

(a)

(b)

Fig. 8.3 Geometric pottery: (a) cup with pendant semi-circles, typical of the products of the Greek island of Euboea, traded widely through the eastern and central Mediterranean, 900–750 BC; (b) Italian imitation of Greek cup with chevron decoration, 800–760 BC, from Veii (after Ridgway).

The western Mediterranean presents a very different sequence. The twelfth century in Italy was a period of major innovation, which saw the extension to Italy of the material culture assemblage of Urnfield Europe, to be described in detail in the next chapter. This Proto-Villanovan culture (Rittatore Vonwiller, 1975; Fugazzola Delpino, 1979) (Fig.8.4) displays the typical cemeteries of single-grave cremations and pins and brooches comparable to those of central Europe; the safety pin type of brooch had been invented around the fifteenth century somewhere in the region of northern Italy or the eastern Alps and its use in a variety of forms became increasingly common from the twelfth century onwards (Alexander and Hopkin, 1982).

The more general use of iron from the ninth century marks the transition to the Iron Age, but this brought little significant change to the cultural tradition, which shows strong continuity from the Proto-Villanovan of the final Bronze Age. A number of regional groups can be distinguished. The Villanovan group (Zuffa, 1976) (Fig.8.5), named after a cemetery excavated at Bologna in the nineteenth century, was located in central Italy, and includes in its later phases the material of the Etruscans; in north-eastern and north-western Italy were respectively the Este and Golasecca groups (Peroni et al., 1975; F. Ridgway, 1979), both of which show considerable continuity throughout the first millennium.

The material culture of Urnfield Central Europe was also adopted in southern France and north-eastern Spain (Maluquer, 1971), possibly well before the beginning of the first millennium (Schauer, 1975b). The sequence is best seen in the settlements and cemeteries of Cayla de Mailhac (Louis et al., 1955/60) and Ensérune (Jannoray, 1955) in France, which successively span the rest of the millennium, though large cemeteries are well known elsewhere in southern France and northern Spain. Pottery and metal styles comparable to those of central Europe were adopted, as well as the cremation burial rite (Fig.8.6).

Elsewhere in Iberia the cultural sequence is much less clear (Savory, 1968, pp.214–38). The centre and west are known primarily for bronzes, which link the region firmly to the later Bronze Age of Atlantic Europe, and subsequently for small defended sites

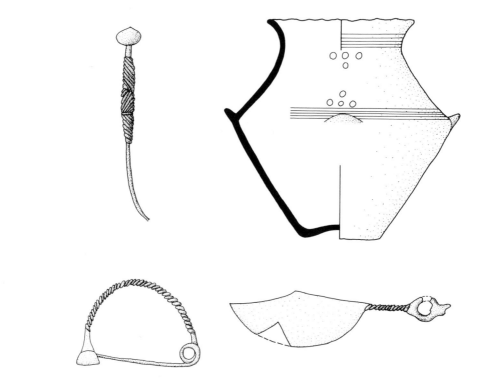

Fig. 8.4

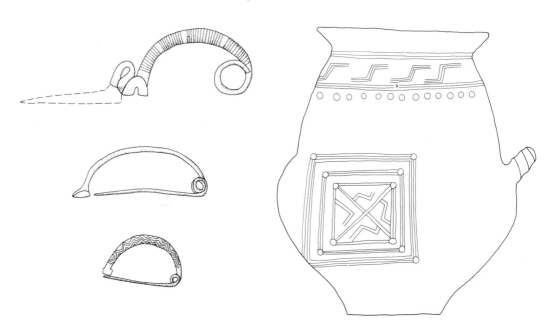

Fig. 8.5

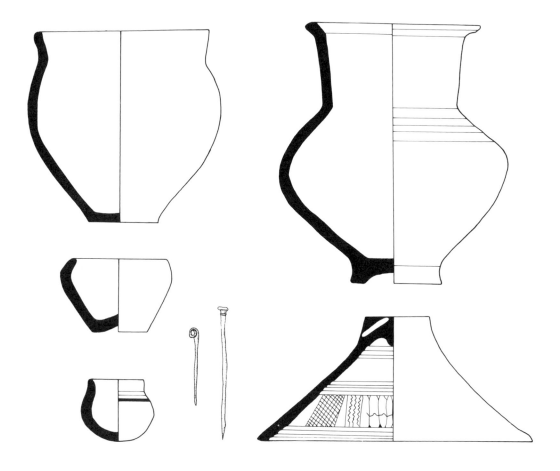

Fig. 8.4 Ceramic and metal types of the Protovillanovan period: biconical urn, pin, brooch and knife (after Müller-Karpe, 1959).

Fig. 8.5 Ceramic and metal types of the Villanovan period: biconical urn and brooches (after Hencken, 1968).

Fig. 8.6 Ceramic and metal types of the final Bronze Age in the south of France, from the cemetery and settlement at Cayla de Mailhac (after Louis et al., 1955).

comparable to those further north. In the south, it seems likely that there was considerable continuity from the local Argaric Bronze Age. Some innovations comparable to those of central Europe occurred, however, as the representation of sheet bronze armour, especially shields, on a series of pictorial grave slabs from the south-west shows (Almagro, 1966) (Fig.8.7).

From the eighth century, the Mediterranean world was transformed, and a cultural complex emerged completely distinct from that of the rest of Europe to the north. This period of more extensive contacts was initiated by the orientalizing phase in the late eighth and seventh centuries in which motifs of Near Eastern origin were copied in Greek, Italian and Iberian pottery and metalwork, and had a profound effect on later artistic developments (e.g. Rathje, 1979) (Fig.8.8). The broadly homogeneous culture which had appeared by the sixth century, and which united most of the Mediterranean coastal regions, included towns with monumental architecture, particularly fortifications and temples, intensive agriculture, coinage, literacy, increased output of specialist craft industries, and a tradition of fine, wheel-thrown pottery, frequently painted. Four main groups can be discerned within this complex as a whole, distinguished as much by their historically known ethnic identity and language as by variations in material culture: the Phoenicians and their colonies (Moscati, 1968), the Greeks and their colonies, the Italians, especially the Etruscans (Pallottino, 1978) and later the Romans, and the Iberians of eastern Spain (Arribas, 1963).

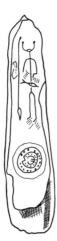

Fig. 8.7 Decorated Iberian stela from Megacela depicting warrior armed with spear, dagger, horned helmet and shield (after Savory, 1968). Height 1·42 m.

SETTLEMENT

After the collapse of the Mycenaean palace civilization in the twelfth century there is little archaeological evidence for the pattern of settlement in Greece (Snodgrass, 1971). Finds are mostly of burials, either singly or in small groups, and their quantity is much less than in earlier and later periods. This suggests not only that there were few, if any, large sites, but also that Greece may have been largely depopulated. This seems to have been true even as late as the ninth century; recent excavations at the important site of Lefkandi (Popham *et al.*, 1979) on the island of Euboia, where it can be reasonably argued that a considerable proportion of the original burials have now been recovered, suggest that, even at its greatest, the population did not exceed a few dozen. All traces of the centralization of the previous centuries had disappeared, and the settlement pattern was one of small villages.

In Italy, the picture is somewhat different. In the south the major sites which had been in contact with the Mycenaean world in the thirteenth and twelfth centuries failed to maintain their position, and there are few signs of any sites with more than ordinary size or status. In central and northern Italy, on the other hand, some such sites are known; the growth of Luni and Narce during the Bronze Age has already been described in the previous chapter, and they continued to be important centres into the first millennium. At Frattesina (Bietti Sestieri, 1975, 1981), a large site which has recently been discovered near the mouth of the Po in northern Italy, there is evidence for considerable craft activity; glass was being worked there, as well as ivory and ostrich eggs imported from the eastern Mediterranean or north Africa. Though little is yet known about the settlement pattern of the Proto-Villanovan period, there were clearly some sites which were centres of population and industry.

In the south of France and Iberia the evidence is less clear. Most attention has been paid to the burial record and few settlements have been adequately explored. In southern Spain some of the sites established in the Argaric phase may have continued into the first millennium, but both there and further north there seems to be no marked hierarchy of sites. In the south of France, too, sites of apparently

Fig. 8.8 Decoration on the Bocchoris vase of faience, made in the east Mediterranean region and found at Tarquinii (after Rathje, 1979).

superior status do not appear to have emerged before the eighth century.

From the eighth century, however, the archaeological record of many areas of Mediterranean Europe is dramatically transformed. The sheer quantity of material increases enormously, and the number of sites and graves known rises very rapidly. Snodgrass (1980a) has argued convincingly from the evidence of the numbers of graves from two comparatively well explored areas of Greece, Attica and the Argolid (Fig.8.9), that this represents a substantial increase in the actual population of

Greece; on the basis of the figures from Athens and Attica, he suggests that in the space of little more than sixty years in the middle of the eighth century the population multiplied approximately sevenfold. The same increase of sites and graves can be seen in much of Italy and southern and eastern Spain, though its precise rate and chronology are less easy to specify. On the basis of site survey evidence from south Etruria, which is less exact than that from cemeteries, Potter (1979) has shown that it probably occurred slightly later than in Greece, perhaps in the seventh century (Fig.8.10). In Spain this phase of

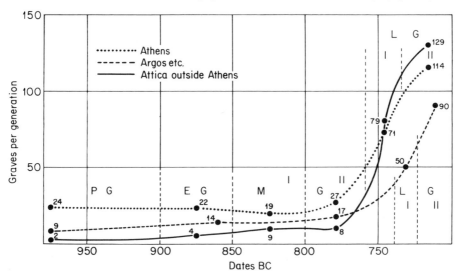

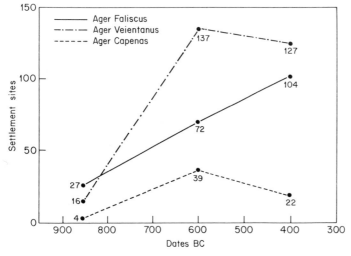

Fig. 8.9   Estimated population growth in Athens, Argos and the Attic countryside, 950–700 BC (after Snodgrass, 1980a).

Fig. 8.10   Estimated population growth in southern Etruria 900–400 BC (based on figures in Potter, 1979).

population growth may have started in the eighth century in the south and the seventh in the east. Not all areas of the Mediterranean world were equally affected, however. Parts of Greece, especially in the north, do not seem to have shared this sudden expansion, and in Italy Barker (1981, p. 214) has shown from survey work in Molise that parts of eastern Italy showed a similar pattern of settlement growth, but not until after the middle of the first millennium. This demographic explosion will be discussed further below, but such a marked and rapid increase in population must have affected the society and economy of the Mediterranean world in a most profound way.

At the same time as the number of sites was increasing, there also appeared new types of sites, in particular towns. The origins of this urban growth are difficult to describe because archaeological exploration has been limited and many of these sites are in any case overlain by classical and even modern successors. Nevertheless, there is enough evidence to show how the settlement pattern throughout Mediterranean Europe was transformed in the period from the eighth to the sixth century. Some of the earliest evidence comes from the eastern Greek area of the coast of Asia Minor and the Aegean islands (Snodgrass, 1980a, pp.31–3). Old Smyrna was a nucleated and fortified site already by the mid-ninth century, closely followed by other settlements such as Zagora on the island of Andros, occupied by about 800 BC (Fig.8.11). Elsewhere on the Greek mainland the development belongs rather to the eighth and

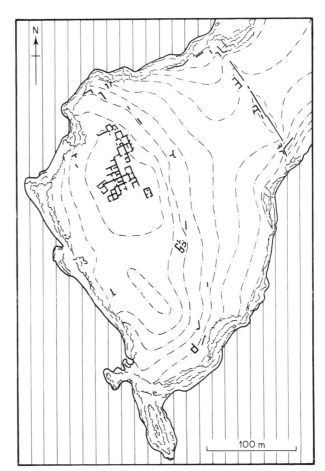

Fig. 8.11 Plan of the eighth century settlement at Zagora on Andros (after Snodgrass, 1980a).

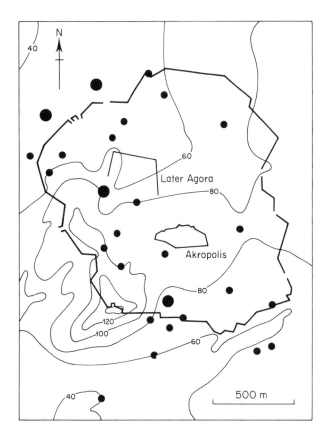

Fig. 8.12   Distribution of ninth and eighth century burials in Athens (after Snodgrass, 1980a).

seventh centuries, as the evidence of settlement nucleation and more particularly of the foundation of associated sanctuaries shows. Even a site as late as eighth century Athens, for example, seems to have been no more than a scatter of small settlements (Fig.8.12) and the major civic monuments were not begun before the sixth century. By the seventh century, however, most of the important sites of the Greek mainland and the Aegean islands had been firmly established, though their resemblance at this stage to the modern concept of a town should not be exaggerated.

The late eighth and seventh centuries were also the period of massive Greek expansion overseas through the foundation of colonies (see box), which introduced towns in the Greek fashion to many areas of the Mediterranean (Boardman, 1980). But this was not the only path to urban growth and in other areas of the central and western Mediterranean native,

non-Greek centres were already well established by the eighth century. In Italy the leading area was Etruria, but remarkably little work has been done on Etruscan towns (Scullard, 1967; Boitani *et al.*, 1975); many, but by no means all, are under modern settlements and excavation has been concentrated on their cemeteries, which therefore have to be used for the chronology of the towns themselves. On this evidence many of the major south Etruscan towns were in existence by the eighth century, such as Tarquinii, (Fig.8.13), Veii (Fig.8.16), Cerveteri and Populonia. Further north some of the Etruscan towns may have developed rather later, but Chiusi was certainly occupied by the seventh century, and Bologna, later to come under Etruscan control, already by the eighth.

Further south similar developments were occurring too. Rome itself (Pallottino, 1979), which was also to come under Etruscan influence in the sixth century,

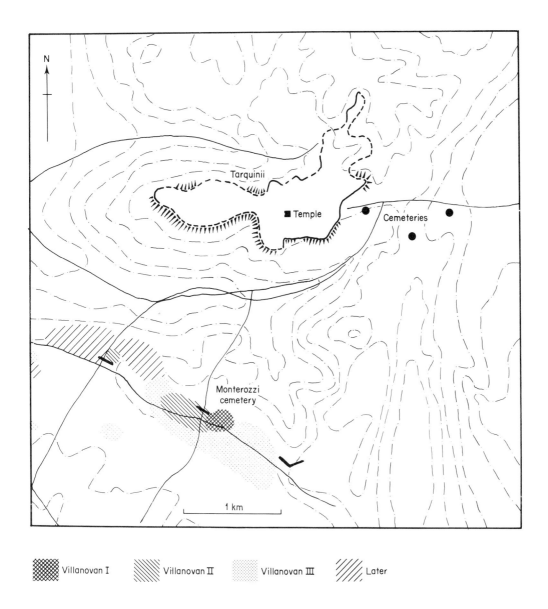

N

Tarquinii

■ Temple

Cemeteries

Monterozzi
cemetery

1 km

Villanovan I   Villanovan II   Villanovan III   Later

Fig. 8.13 Tarquinii, showing defences and development of the Monterozzi cemetery.

GREEK AND PHOENICIAN COLONIZATION

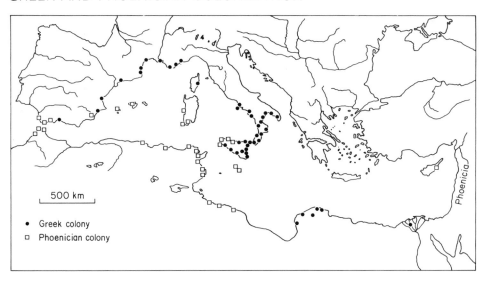

• Greek colony
□ Phoenician colony

Extent of Greek and Phoenician colonization in the Mediterranean.

From the eighth to the sixth century the Greeks (Boardman, 1980) and Phoenicians (Whitaker, 1974) expanded rapidly through most of the Mediterranean basin and the Black Sea region, founding a series of colonies; many of these sites, Naples and Marseilles, for example, are still occupied as important cities today. The areas they colonized were to a large extent mutually exclusive. The Phoenicians settled the north coast of Africa, western Sicily, Sardinia and southern Spain, while the Greeks colonized the Black Sea, the northern Aegean, the Adriatic, southern Italy, Corsica, the south of France and eastern Spain. There were two main reasons for the foundation of these colonies, the settlement of excess population and the acquisition of raw materials and other commodities.

The phase of colonization coincides with the dramatic rise in population documented for Greece, and the ancient historians tell how people were selected, by compulsion if necessary, to take part in the new foundation overseas. On the islands of the Aegean and on the mainland of Greece, where occupation is confined to the coastal plains and the valleys between the mountain ridges, land for agricultural settlement is in short supply, and hence

had an earlier origin. The earliest burials date to the ninth century; the first known settlement sites belong to the eighth century and in the seventh domestic occupation spreads over much of the area of the later city. In the sixth century domestic settlement became more widespread, burials were relocated away from the settled area, and the construction of the first monumental religious buildings and civic works, such as the paving of the Forum, was undertaken.

In southern Italy and Sicily a similar growth can also be detected, though the sites have attracted less attention. The emergence of major sites such as Gravina in Apulia and Segesta and Morgantina in Sicily began as early as the eighth century, and emigration was one solution to the problem of over-population. Some colonies seem to have been exclusively occupied by Greeks or Phoenicians, but in others there is evidence for a considerable native community as well.

The other reason, and perhaps the one that was more important at least in the earlier stages of colonization, was the pursuit of raw materials. Both Greece and Phoenicia were lacking in adequate sources of metals, and other raw materials such as timber and pitch for ship-building. From the end of the seventh century provision of a sufficient supply of corn was also a matter of major concern, especially to Athens. Hence many of the colonies were primarily trading stations, frequently with very mixed populations. The earliest Phoenician colonies were aimed at the mineral wealth of the Tartessian region of southern Spain, and the first Greek colony in the west, at Pithekoussai on Ischia (Ridgway, 1973), also had a major interest in metals. There is extensive evidence for metalworking, and for the importation of iron ore from Elba. Subsequently there was a Greek colony in the Etruscan port of Graviscae, to gain access to the metal ores of Etruria.

Some of these sites seem to be of the type defined by Karl Polanyi as 'ports of trade', that is sites with a purely trading function through which the exchanges between two differently organized societies could be controlled, and located on the boundary between them. Naukratis on the Nile delta is the best example; a Greek colony there coordinated the trade between Greece and Egypt, particularly the import of corn. Al Mina on the north Syrian coast was an important link between Greece and the Near East from the late ninth century onwards. Massalia (Marseilles) and Emporion (Ampurias) in the western Mediterranean and Spina at the head of the Adriatic may also have been of this nature, as trading posts on the borders of the Greek and non-Greek worlds.

known to the early Greek writers as Tartessos are much less well documented than its burials and metalwork, but large and densely occupied sites such as Carambolo (Carriazo, 1973) appear to have been established by the eighth century. In eastern Spain and south-western France hilltop defended sites also became important from the eighth century onwards (Benoit, 1965; Solier, 1976/8). The site of Cayla de Mailhac is known to have been occupied from the mid-eighth century on the evidence of settlement and accompanying cemeteries. At Ensérune (Jannoray, 1955) the original sixth century site was replaced c. 400 BC by an organized settlement with paved roads. Similar sites are also known from Spain, the most extensively excavated of which is Ullastret (Fig.8.14). South-eastern France and north-western Italy, on the other hand, do not appear to have developed major sites of this sort at so early a date, though by the fourth century large hilltop sites such as Entremont (Fig.8.15) were well established (Benoit, 1968).

This urban growth was well under way by the sixth century throughout most areas of the Mediterranean, and though it increased rapidly after the phase of Greek expansion, it was not just a Greek phenomenon. The actual origins of many of the towns are still obscure. Some, especially the new foundations of the colonies, were clearly conceived as towns from the outset (the names of Naples and Carthage are derived from the Greek and Phoenician for 'New Town' respectively), but others grew from the coalescence of a number of small pre-existing settlements. The scattered nature of the occupation of Athens in the eighth century and Rome in the seventh has already been referred to, and similar developments are known to have occurred at Bologna and Veii (Fig.8.16). From a comparatively early date, however, signs of regular planning can be seen, especially in the newly founded colonies; Selinus in Sicily, for example, had a rectangular grid of streets (Fig.8.17). Such planning was not limited to Greek towns, as the reorganization of the Etruscan town of Marzabotto in the early fifth century shows (Mansuelli, 1979) (Fig.8.18). Greek fashions in architecture, especially in temples and fortifications, were also widely adopted throughout the Mediterranean.

The rapid growth of the towns, the expansion of the Greek and Phoenician worlds through colonization

though they existed alongside the Greek colonies and rapidly adopted Greek styles of pottery and architecture, for instance in the Doric temple at Segesta, they are without doubt of entirely native origin.

The eighth and seventh centuries also seem to have been the critical period in the western Mediterranean. In southern Spain the settlement sites of the area

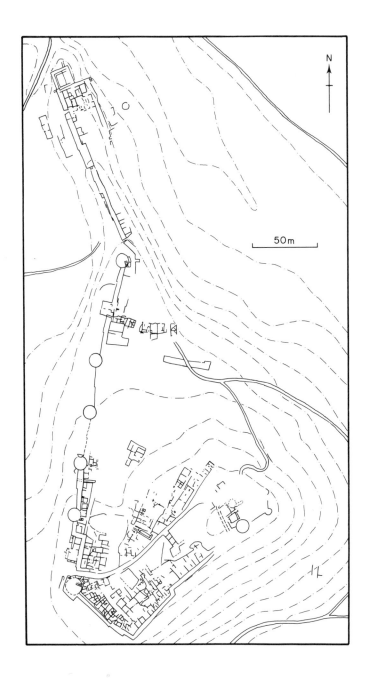

Fig. 8.14 Plan of Ullastret, north-east Spain, showing defences and internal structures.

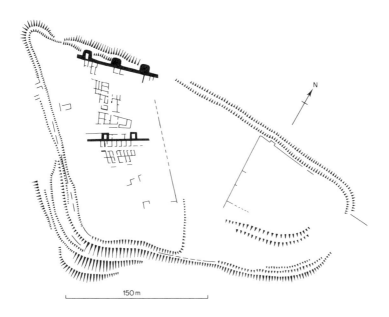

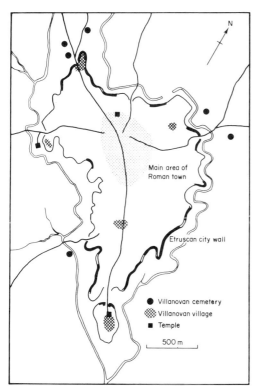

150 m

500 m

Main area of
Roman town

Etruscan city wall

● Villanovan cemetery
▨ Villanovan village
■ Temple

*Fig. 8.15   Plan of Entremont, Provence,
showing defences and the development
of a street plan (after Benoit, 1968).*

*Fig. 8.16   Plan of Veii, showing scattered
Villanovan occupation on the site of the
later Etruscan and Roman town (after
Potter, 1979).*

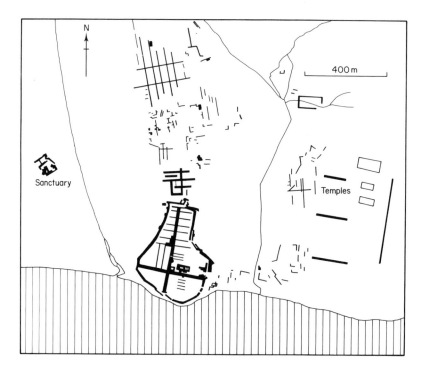

Fig. 8.17 Plan of Selinus, Sicily, showing axial arrangement of streets inside the defences.

and the wide adoption of Greek styles produced a certain degree of homogeneity in the culture of the Mediterranean, and a series of essentially urban societies. The functions of these earliest towns have been little explored, but at least some part of their role can be suggested. Their intimate association with the rise in population is important, and both the coalescence of scattered villages and the foundation of new sites shows the town as one means of accommodating the increasing number of people. Many of the towns show evidence for the practice of non-agricultural craft industries such as pottery and metalwork, and this too must have been important for their inception. The presence of fortification suggests that security was also a major consideration, though many sites may only have acquired defences at a later date. Trade, too, was an important factor, and its role will be discussed more fully below; here it must be noted that many of even the most important sites were not located on the sea or natural harbours,

but some way inland, with associated ports on the coast; again, defence may have been the paramount consideration. The ports of Athens and Rome at Piraeus and Ostia are well known, and the Etruscan towns of Tarquinii and Cerveteri had their ports at Graviscae (Torelli, 1971, 1977) and Pyrgi respectively. Perhaps most important of all was the role of the town as a focus for a new centralized pattern of social, economic, political and religious organization, symbolized by the construction of monumental public buildings. The relationship of the town to the emergence of this new social organization will be examined more fully below.

PRODUCTION AND EXCHANGE

The rise in population and the expansion of settlement was accompanied by great changes in the organization of craft production and the technologies

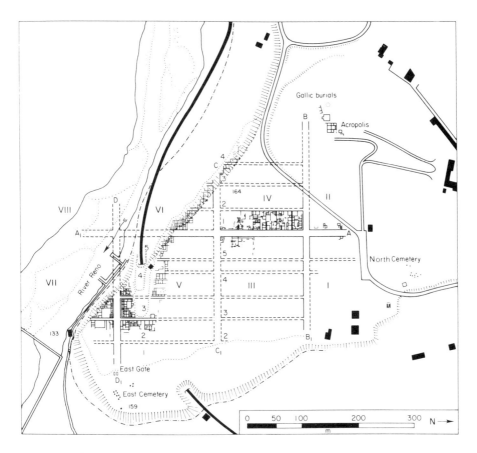

Fig. 8.18 Plan of the Etruscan city of Marzabotto (after Mansuelli).

practised in the Mediterranean region. New and more complex technologies were introduced, and there are clear signs of a greater development of craft specialization and its necessary concomitant, exchange.

The most obvious new industry was ironworking (see box). The increasing mastery of the complex skills needed to work this metal ore, which occurs much more abundantly than copper and tin, enabled a vastly greater quantity and range of items to be produced. Much attention has been paid to the superior weapons possible in iron, but probably of equal importance were the superior specialist tools now available for other industries such as farming, carpentry, masonry and sculpture. The new material therefore played a vital part in allowing the

development of other areas of production, but little is yet known about the detailed organization of iron production at this period.

A similar development occurred in pottery manufacture. The new styles of fine decorated pottery that spread throughout the region from the eighth to the fifth century were the products of a more complex technology using the potter's wheel for shaping the pot and a kiln for firing it. This higher level of organization is known in Greece from the end of the second millennium, and in southern Italy from the ninth century at least; it spread to other areas of Italy, Sicily, Spain and southern France by the sixth. Recent discoveries of kilns and study of the actual material suggests that much of the pottery once thought to have been exported from

EARLY IRONWORKING

The development of the technology of ironworking has frequently been attributed to the Hittites of Asia Minor, who were supposed to have guarded the secrets of the craft most carefully, before the collapse of their empire led to its rapid diffusion in the Near East and Europe. This story, however, is largely based on a misinterpretation of Hittite documents, and a new explanation is needed. In fact, objects of iron are known sporadically in the Near East from c.5000 BC, becoming more common there and in Greece towards the end of the second millennium. From the eleventh century onwards, especially in the Levant, Cyprus and parts of Greece, the number of iron objects increases considerably. The evidence is drawn mainly from graves and sanctuary deposits, and it is difficult to tell whether these are representative of all metal production, but iron does not appear to have been finally adopted as the dominant metal until perhaps the ninth century.

The key factors in producing usable iron objects were the control of carburization, that is the absorption of a small quantity of carbon by the iron to produce steel, and the discovery of quenching, which is the rapid cooling of the hot metal to produce a harder object. Quenching was known from the eleventh century but remained in only occasional use, while controlled carburization was generally achieved by the beginning of the first millennium.

The reasons for the adoption of iron are still hard to discern. The working of iron was known at least in principle for a considerable period before its wide adoption, though difficulties in practice may have been experienced. Snodgrass (1971, 1980b) has argued for Greece that it was the interruption of metal supplies for bronze that forced a resort to iron, although at the time its products were inferior. This may have been temporarily true, but other areas where iron was becoming common did not experience a similar shortage, and Greece itself later maintained a massive bronze industry. This explanation of bronze shortage will not work for the whole of the Near East and Aegean area, and it may be that the shortage was caused by increasing demand for metal objects throughout a wide area, which could only be met with a more plentifully available metal. As skill with iron increased and a regularly successful product could be achieved, so a point was reached where bronze could be quickly supplanted.

In the rest of the Mediterranean the widespread adoption of iron occurred slightly later, in the eighth century in Italy, and the seventh in Spain and France. The original knowledge of iron in these areas cannot be attributed to diffusion from Greece or Phoenicia, since examples are known in all areas in pre-colonial contexts (though the chronology in Spain is not clear). As in Greece and the Near East, the widespread adoption of the new metal and its technology is more important than its first appearance, and is probably best regarded as an integral part of the general intensification of production that was part of the economic and social changes that affected the whole area at this period.

A similar pattern of development is known in temperate Europe, and is described in Chapters 9 and 10.

---

mainland Greece was in fact produced locally. It now seems likely that local pottery industries were rapidly established in many of the Greek colonies and that the new styles and new technology were equally rapidly adopted by non-Greek neighbours, especially in Etruria and Spain. The increased expenditure of labour in preparing and finishing the pots, and the increased investment by the craftsman or an entrepreneur in new facilities such as the wheel and kiln, betoken a greater degree of specialization on the part of the potter and artist. In some cases, especially of figure decoration, the work of an individual craftsman can be recognized.

Other crafts have left less archaeological evidence for their practice, but in some areas the demands of the new social and political order, to be discussed below, significantly stimulated output and specialization. The importance of religion promoted the skills of architecture, engineering, masonry and sculpture for the construction and decoration of temples. New methods of fighting (Snodgrass, 1980a, p.101-7) also led to new areas of production, particularly of bronze armour and in shipbuilding.

Further signs of the intensification and special-ization of production can be seen in the increasing quantity, variety and functional specificity of craft tools, and in the growing number of representations of craftsmen of all sorts on painted pottery. The practice of a craft skill began to form a new basis for achieving status within society.

Increased specialization in craft production, as well as in agriculture (described below), was accompanied by a new organization of distribution and exchange. The clearest signs of this new system are to be found in the plans of the towns, which included open spaces for this purpose. At about the same time in the sixth century the Agora in Athens and the Forum in Rome were being laid out as formal market places. Unlike the redistributive economies of the Bronze Age palace societies, this system was not centrally controlled but was based on the new principle of market exchange, and formed one of the major features which distinguished this pattern of social organization from its predecessors.

The role of these new patterns of exchange should not be exaggerated, however. It is true that they were important within individual communities and that some towns were considerable exporters (Athens, for instance, exported large quantities of olive oil and monopolized the supply of fine pottery), but their economy was not orientated towards exports, and overseas trade was mostly for the purpose of securing necessary raw materials (Austin and Vidal-Naquet, 1977). Much of this trade also took place not within the Greek world, but with neighbouring societies such as the cities of the eastern Mediterranean, Egypt, the Etruscans and the Iberians, or the less developed societies of non-Mediterranean Europe (see the next chapter).

Relations between communities of this sort are probably best not described purely economically in terms of the modern concept of trade, but the material exchanges should rather be seen as one manifestation of the variety of reciprocal relations that existed between societies keen on extending their influence through far-flung connections. The rise of a system of networks exchanging prestige goods has been discussed in the previous chapter, and similar goods continued to be exchanged in the first millen-nium (Cristofani, 1975). Amber from northern Europe is still found in Greece and in Italy, as well as ivory and ostrich eggs from the east Mediterranean or north Africa. With the growing intensity of external contacts in the eighth century the flow of these goods also increased, and the early historians record many cases of such gifts between communities. They clearly continued to be a significant element in the conduct of relationships between individuals and societies, though control of these commodities may no longer have been as important for an individual's status within his society as previously (see below for more detailed discussion).

SUBSISTENCE

Evidence for the pattern of subsistence production in the late second and early first millennia is difficult to find, since it has not formed a regular focus of archaeological attention. Nevertheless, some inferences can be made. In post-Mycenean Greece, pollen analysis suggests that the area given over to arable crop production was greatly reduced; this is perhaps only to be expected if there was a serious drop in population, as argued above. Even so, it is possible that, with large tracts used for pastoral purposes, if at all, there was a greater reliance on animal products for food resources (Snodgrass, 1980a, pp.35–40). By the eighth century, however, this pattern was changing. The earliest Greek literature, which contains reference to this period, clearly shows a society primarily dependent on the intensive production of cereals and pulses, and the urban civilization of the Mediterranean throughout the archaic and classical period relied mainly on crop products rather than livestock for its food require-ments. At the same time, the importance of the olive seems to have increased throughout the early part of the first millennium. There is little evidence for the extent of vine growing and wine production, but the intensive agriculture of cereals, olives and vines was the firm agrarian basis on which classical civilization developed, just as its Mycenaean predecessor had done in the second millennium. The vine and olive again allowed land otherwise agriculturally unpro-ductive to be profitably used, and yielded a product that could be readily exchanged.

A somewhat similar picture emerges from Italy. The vine and the olive had been grown in many areas of the peninsula during the Bronze Age but only on a small scale. Signs of possible intensification of cereal production at Luni and Narce have been referred to in the previous chapter, but in the first millennium the evidence from Narce is quite clear (Potter, 1979, p. 62). The ninth century layers show a great increase in the quantities of cereals, and also in the degree of contamination of the crop with the seeds of weeds of cultivation. This has been plausibly explained as the result of reducing the period of fallow in the cycle of crop growing, in order to increase the total annual yield. The development of Italian vine and olive growing is far from clear, but some evidence suggests that they may have been becoming more common in Etruria and Rome during the seventh century. A clearer pattern can be seen in the Molise region (Barker, 1981, p.214), where the massive expansion of settlement at the end of the prehistoric period onto the valley bottoms and the uplands was accompanied by changes in the system of agricultural production, in particular the adoption of the typical Mediterranean polyculture, with the intensive cultivation of vines, olives and cereals in the lower valleys. In this region the transformation coincided with the historically attested arrival of migrants from more populous areas of Italy, but a similar agricultural system may have been adopted in other areas at the time of rapid population growth. Such agricultural intensification needed an adequate labour supply, either through natural growth or by acquisition of slaves, who grew to be an essential part of the Italian rural economy.

The evidence from Spain and southern France is still more sparse, but the growth of population and urban centres was accompanied by the adoption of Mediterranean polyculture. The vine and the olive are thought to have been introduced by the Greeks at the time of colonization, but they spread through the peninsula and southern France, and by the sixth century a pottery industry had been established to produce amphoras, the large storage vessels in which wine and oil were transported. In classical times Spain was one of the major cereal producing areas of the Empire, and there are some signs of intensive production from early in the first millennium. A series of sites along the lower Ebro, such as Cortes de Navarra (Maluquer, 1954/8), were continuously occupied and regularly rebuilt throughout the later Bronze Age and the early Iron Age, and seem to have been located to exploit the fertile valley for its cereal

growing potential; this area was later famed for its winter wheat production. Southern Spain was the most intensively cultivated area and there a variety of fruits was also grown. The whole of Spain indeed was agriculturally very productive, and it was only later deforestation and over-exploitation that has reduced some areas to heath and steppe.

Another sign of agricultural intensification is the production of specialized tools and other items. Amphoras have already been mentioned, and they were an important part of the output of the pottery industry in many areas of the Mediterranean from the seventh century, producing storage vessels for wine and oil. Agricultural tools are less common, though the vast majority of archaeological finds, such as graves and sanctuaries, would not be expected to produce them. Nevertheless, it seems clear from early literature as well as the archaeological record that from about the seventh century iron tools of many varieties for specific agricultural purposes were becoming increasingly common (Snodgrass, 1980b). These were an important product of the new iron industry and would have been harder, sharper, longer-lasting and therefore much more efficient than their predecessors of bronze, stone or wood.

SOCIAL ORGANIZATION

These changes in settlement, subsistence and production were part of a fundamental transformation of society in most areas of the Mediterranean world in the first half of the first millennium which culminated in the emergence of communities organized as states. The evidence for the growth of this new system is fullest in Greece and Italy and is especially well evidenced in Athens and Rome, where archaeology is supplemented by early historical records (e.g. Humphreys, 1978). Although the exact stages by which individual states emerged may have varied in detail, there was an overall uniformity of social development which can only be understood if studied as a single phenomenon throughout the Mediterranean.

After the collapse of the centralized Mycenaean palace economies there are still indications of social ranking in Greece. Burials continued to be furnished with grave goods, in particular weapons and ornaments, and the variation in wealth of these deposits seems to symbolize differentiation in social status. The first historical records, referring perhaps to the eighth century or slightly earlier, suggest the widespread institution of kingship, though it is far from clear what the basis of such kingdoms was, how large a territory they controlled, how centralized was their authority, or how long they had been in existence. They were certainly of a different order from the rulers of the Mycenaean palaces, and should perhaps be regarded as little more than local chiefs. From the eighth century, however, this picture was changing; kings began to disappear, to be replaced by constitutional aristocracies, and the deposition of grave goods showed a trend away from the traditional symbolization of personal status.

Italy, southern France and Spain followed a rather different course. The adoption of the Proto-Villanovan single burial cremation rite and its associated metal types links many areas of Italy firmly with Urnfield Europe, and these connections are maintained until the seventh century. The further adoption of this complex of burial rite, pottery and metal types in the south of France and eastern Spain united the western Mediterranean basin with temperate Europe to form a single broadly homogeneous zone, in which Greece took no part. It will be suggested in the next chapter that the spread of this new burial rite and its associated material culture and symbolism was connected with the change in the basis of social ranking, from the control of prestige goods to the control and exploitation of subsistence resources as a means to the acquisition of power. The adoption of precisely this set of material culture items in Italy, France and Spain may suggest that the same principle for structuring society was in operation in those areas too; the suggestion is a tentative one, but the evidence cited above for the intensification of crop production might support this argument.

The burial record in all these areas shows a considerable differentiation in grave wealth throughout the period, but it increases dramatically in the eighth and seventh centuries; this process may already have begun before the phase of contact with Greek and Phoenician traders and colonists. One element in the wealth symbolism of the richest graves which is shared with late Urnfield Europe is the weaponry, bronze vessels and armour known from Italian graves (e.g. Hencken, 1968). Iberian carvings are also paralleled in central Europe

(compare Fig.8.19 and Fig.9.15). Another theme, the practice of vehicle burial, is known from Etruscan cemeteries, such as those at Cerveteri, Populonia and Vetulonia (Woytowitsch, 1978), from the south of France at Cayla de Mailhac and from one of the richest burials from southern Spain, at Toya in Andalucia. The wider European context of this tradition is discussed in the next chapter. In both Spain and Italy some of the richest burials were placed in chamber tombs, frequently of some architectural sophistication and sometimes fitted with replicas of domestic furnishings.

Contact with Greeks and Phoenicians brought a new source of wealth and a new way of expressing it. From the late eighth century the variation in grave wealth increases enormously, and imported items from Greece or the Levant are regularly found in the richest graves. The climax of this phase occurred in Italy in the seventh century, when the most lavishly furnished graves were deposited, such as the Regolini-Galassi Tomb at Cerveteri (Pareti, 1947), and the Barberini and Bernardini Tombs at Praeneste (Fig.8.20). Thereafter, although considerable expenditure was incurred in burial rites, for instance, in the remarkable series of painted tombs at Tarquinii, the seventh century extremes were nowhere again matched.

What followed in all these areas was a new form of social organization, the state, which possessed centralized institutions of political and military authority, a monopoly over the exercise of force within the community and a permanent class of specialized rulers and administrators. This new form of organization was to prove extremely successful and rapidly became the dominant one throughout the Mediterranean region, though it should not be thought that it was entirely uniform. There was considerable variation between individual states, and ancient Greek political theorists such as Aristotle distinguished two main types, the ethnos and the polis, which correspond broadly to recognizably different archaeological patterns (Ehrenberg, 1969; Snodgrass, 1980a, pp.31–48).

The *ethnos* comprised a variety of detailed structures, but tended to be a large political unit, either entirely rural or lacking a single dominant urban centre, and frequently with no very powerful central authority. Much of central and northern Greece and southern Italy was organized in this way.

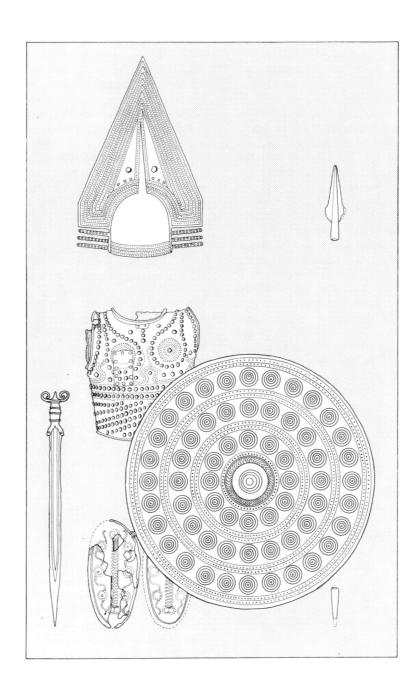

Fig. 8.19   Arms and armour of the Italian early Iron Age (after Schauer, 1975a).

Fig. 8.20   Gilded silver bowl from the Bernardini tomb, Palestrina.

Archaeologically, it can be seen that these areas shared only to a limited extent in the explosion of population, settlement and production from the eighth century onwards and individual status continued to be symbolized in burials. From time to time the *ethnos* could be an effective and powerful force. The Samnites of central Italy, for example, were a group of rural communities each with its own elected leader; they lacked any strong permanent central assembly but at times of crisis met to elect a military leader, and could mobilize a strong and united army. The Macedonians of northern Greece lacked a single major centre, but their rapid military expansion in the fourth century under Philip and Alexander the Great showed the force which a polity of this sort could potentially harness.

It was with the rise of the *polis*, however, that the great changes described earlier in this chapter were particularly connected. The *polis*, or city-state, was essentially an autonomous organization which united a rural hinterland around a single central focus of political and religious control which, as shown above, typically developed into a city. It could vary enormously in size, from very large and populous states such as Sparta or Athens with over 300 000 inhabitants down to the smallest of the Aegean islands, many of which had less than 5000. City-states of this sort were already in existence by the eighth century in the Phoenician towns of the eastern Mediterranean, and this type of organization was very rapidly adopted by many Greek communities during the course of that century (Fig.8.21). Greek and Phoenician colonization propagated the city-state in the central and west Mediterranean, and it was soon taken over by the native peoples as well. The Etruscan towns were organized on similar lines by the sixth century (Pallottino, 1978), as also were the towns of Latium in central Italy. The position is less clear in eastern and southern Spain, though it seems likely that the same principle of political structure was widely adopted there too; certainly a number of cities, such as Saguntum, had constitutions closely akin to those of Greek states (Arribas, 1963).

The general concept of the city-state was therefore rapidly and widely adopted, though with certain local variation, and indeed many of these states show a similar constitutional development. There was a steady trend away from monarchy towards a constitutional oligarchy under firm aristocratic control, and in a few cases, notably at Athens, a further progress towards democracy. The constitutional oligarchies usually took the form of a powerful assembly or senate and elected magistrates who held office, frequently in pairs, for a limited term and according to fixed and known laws. Such constitutions are known, for example, at Athens, Carthage, Rome and among the Etruscan cities.

At the same time there were important changes in

Fig. 8.21 Extent of the polis *(shaded) and the* ethnos *in archaic Greece (after Snodgrass, 1980a).*

the way society was structured within the state. Originally, there had been a comparatively fluid structure, with no permanently defined royal or noble families; social ranking had been based on descent and alliances of friendship and marriages as much as on control of production. The opportunities offered by the intensification of agriculture and production provided a new means of accumulating wealth and hence a new basis for leadership. These realities were recognized, if we can generalize from the history of Athens and Rome, by the recognition of a permanent and stable aristocratic class and by the adoption around the sixth century of a new principle for social ranking based on wealth (assessed in terms of agricultural production), at least as far as concerned the individual's military obligations to the state and his right to hold office in it. A parallel development was the emergence of territorial sub-divisions within the state, for purposes of local administration and military organization.

The new political system also brought a set of other innovations. One of these was the formulation of law codes in place of customary tradition. The new laws regulated the rights and obligations of the citizen, and were frequently inscribed for public display, as at Gortyn in Crete where they still survive. Another innovation of fundamental importance and enormous long-term consequence was the reintro-duction of writing. A version of the Phoenician script, with the addition of symbols for vowels, was adopted by the Greeks around the middle of the eighth century (Jeffery, 1964). It may have had a particular importance in the keeping of administrative, legal and commercial records, but from the very start it proved more flexible than the syllabic system of the Mycenaean palaces, and literacy was by no means confined to such limited purposes, within a short space providing a vital stimulus to artistic and intel-lectual achievements. The Greek alphabet was borrowed by the Etruscans as early as the seventh century and from them in turn by the Romans and other Italian peoples. It also spread to the south of France and to parts of Spain, though other systems of writing were also in use there; in these areas it is mainly monumental inscriptions that survive and the true extent or use of literacy is not known (Arribas, 1963).

Another important innovation was coinage

(Kraay, 1964). The first coins seem to have been invented by the Lydians of Asia Minor, and adopted from them by the Greeks in the early sixth century. In the previous centuries wealth had been stored and assessed in various commodities such as oxen, tripods and iron spits, but the use of small discs of precious metal, although no more than a refinement of these earlier practices, was very much more flexible at a time when transactions involving payments were becoming more common. The earliest coins were all of fairly high value, and not at all comparable to modern currencies for everyday commercial use. The coins were part of the wealth of the state and their appearance represents the growth of a new set of state functions. They would have been used to make payments to the state for taxes, fines or other dues, and in turn would have been dispensed for such things as military service, shipbuilding or construction of monumental buildings. All of these were state concerns and the earliest coinages seldom circulated outside their city of origin. Later, however, some coinages, especially that of Athens, were used in foreign trade and gained a wider acceptance. Many of the Greek and Phoenician colonies minted their own coins from an early date, and by the third century other states in Italy, France and Spain were producing their own local issues. In all these areas the basic function of the coins was the same, to pay for the state's activities.

Apart from military operations, the state engaged in large construction projects such as fortifications, docks, and public buildings. There was also one other area where the state was particularly active, in religion. Each city had its own protective deity and the festivals associated with the cult of these gods were an important part of its life and an expression of the identity of the state. From the very beginning of the city-state the growth of the town was ac-companied by or even preceded by the appearance of sanctuaries, and in particular of temples. The great interest focused on these buildings led to rapid progress in architectural and engineering skills as temples became larger and more impressive (Fig.8.22).

Religion was also the means of uniting states into wider groupings. City-states were essentially autonomous entities and whatever common bonds they had were in a shared language and a shared religion. The states of Greece, for instance, were only

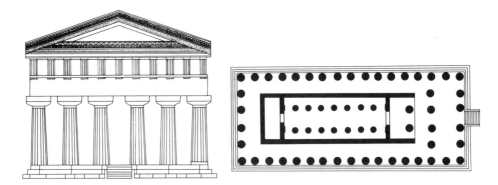

Fig. 8.22   *Greek temple at Syracuse, Sicily; built in the late sixth century, it was probably the first major stone temple in the west.*

rarely capable of any combined political action, but all recognized the importance of sanctuaries such as Olympia and Delphi. These major religious sites grew up at the same time as the towns and temples (Table 8.1) and must have played a part in that process. Similar loose groupings of cities around a religious focus are also known elsewhere. The most important Etruscan cities formed such a confederacy, which met at a shrine at Voltumna, but its political powers were minimal. The cities of Latium, of which Rome was one, likewise made up the Latin League with its meeting place at the shrine of Aricia.

SOCIAL PROCESS AND THE DEVELOPMENT OF THE STATE

It remains now to consider the relationship between the changes described above in settlement, population, subsistence and production and the new model of political organization that emerged. It is true that some of the most important elements of this new order, such as coinage and the alphabet, and probably the very idea of the city-state itself, were borrowed from the Near East by the Greeks and spread by them with the Phoenicians throughout the Mediterranean, and then further borrowed by the native communities of Italy and Spain, but it is not enough simply to account for this phenomenon as an example of diffusion from the east. That would not explain why the new ideas were found useful, and it

has been one of the most important contentions of this chapter that the changes described in the different areas of society and economy were all interlinked to produce the final emergence of the archaic state. It is also important to realize some of those processes, especially in subsistence and settlement, had already begun before any significant contact with the Near East or with the Greeks. Any explanation will have to consider the adoption of these new forms in the light of local social conditions, and of the geographical extent of these developments throughout the Mediterranean basin.

It does not seem likely, either, that there was a single new discovery or invention which provided a unique stimulus to this remarkable phase of growth. The mainstays of the agricultural economy, cereals, the vine and the olive, had all been known and used before, and it was the way they were cultivated, rather than what was cultivated, that changed. Similarly, in productive technology, the widespread adoption of iron was undoubtedly an important factor in supplying superior weapons and tools for other industries and crafts, but it too had been known, though little used, in previous centuries. The development of ironworking is therefore perhaps best regarded as another part of the general phenomenon of growth to be explained, rather than as an explanation for that growth.

One of the most dramatic changes was in population, and it could be suggested that it was this sudden rise in numbers that brought about the

Table 8.1   Changing rates of deposition of various types of bronze object at archaic Greek sanctuaries (after Snodgrass, 1980).

	Eleventh and tenth centuries BC	Ninth century	Eighth century
Bronze figurines at Delphi	0	1	152
Bronze tripods at Mount Ptoön (Boiotia)	0	0	7
Bronze dedications on Delos	0	1	19
Terracotta figurines at Olympia	10	21	837

	Eleventh and tenth centuries BC	Ninth and early eighth	Later eighth and seventh
Bronze fibulae at Philia (Thessaly)	0	2	1783+
Bronze pins at Philia	1	4	37
Bronze fibulae at Perachora	7	1	50+
Bronze pins at Perachora	0	15	81
Bronze fibulae at the Argive Heraion	16	10	88
Bronze pins at the Argive Heraion	3	c.250	c.3070
Bronze fibulae at Lindos (Rhodes)	0	52	1540
Bronze pins at Lindos	0	0	42

reorganization of economy and society. Barker (1981), for instance, has argued that the rising population in Italy eventually created a crisis in the supply of subsistence resources which was solved by the adoption of more intensive agricultural methods, a greater degree of specialization and consequently a new pattern of exchange. Though Barker does not do so, the argument could be extended to account for the new political organization on the grounds of the increasingly complex social and economic relationships and the consequent need for greater managerial control and administration. There is without doubt a very close and important connection between population growth, subsistence intensification and political change, but it is difficult to see population as the sole responsible agent. Such an explanation would not explain why population was growing at all, or why it grew so rapidly in the course of the eighth and seventh centuries, nor would it account for the remarkable homogeneity of these changes throughout the Mediterranean.

Another way of approaching the problem would be to look at the nature of society at the point where the city-state begins to emerge, and at the main functions of the state. The archaeological record suggests a markedly hierarchical society with a basis in agricultural wealth, and this is confirmed by such early historical records as are available, which agree

in describing an aristocratic and oligarchic society whose foundation was in land and its products. Competition for status continued to be one of its principal features, achieved primarily through controlling and increasing agricultural production, though alliances, particularly with friends abroad, continued to be important. The Greek poet, Hesiod, writing about 700 BC, spoke of the 'gift-devouring' aristocrats, and of the advantages of more sons to produce more resources. Competition for status could therefore lead to agricultural intensification and population growth. The earliest historical records suggest a general pattern at the beginnings of state emergence, in which land had become increasingly concentrated in the hands of the aristocratic class, whose status was becoming more stable and permanent, and who firmly controlled rights to office and power in the state.

In these circumstances the institutions of the state may have offered a means of solidifying aristocratic control of the society. Institutional rather than purely personal positions of office would make the survival of the social group less dependent on the abilities of the individual, and the widespread trend from monarchy to aristocratic oligarchy would have guaranteed a share in power to all aristocrats at the expense of the chance to wield absolute power. The change from the demonstration of individual status in graves to the construction of major public and religious monuments was part of the process by which this new social order was legitimated.

The state was, therefore, a means of increasing and perpetuating aristocratic control over society, and was also an efficient means of mobilizing the people. Apart from religion and the construction of public monuments, both of which were important in providing an identity for the city as a whole, the one area where the state was most active was in warfare. Relationships between states were mostly of two sorts, friendly and characterized by the reciprocal exchange of gifts, or unfriendly and warlike, and these were alternative means of achieving status — either through alliances or by conquest. Warfare was for the acquisition of territory to increase the wealth and power of the successful state, and the *polis* was a remarkably successful means of organizing military force. Rights of citizenship incurred obligations of military service, and for the first time the mechanism existed to mobilize a large citizen army. From the late eighth century in Greece a new style of bronze armour with helmet, breastplate and shield became common, and from the seventh century in Greece and Italy new tactics were evolved to use the available manpower most effectively; armoured infantry relying mainly on spear and shield and operating in large disciplined bodies presented a formidable new fighting force (Snodgrass, 1980a, pp.101–07). The new state organization also allowed the construction and manning of specially designed warships, and naval warfare began. The wealth acquired as a result of successful wars was used by the state to pay for the campaigns and to raise public monuments, but there was no outlet for expenditure beyond these items, and surplus wealth was sometimes distributed to the citizens. The welfare of the state was therefore the welfare of the individual citizen.

These considerations may also help to explain the rapid diffusion of the city-state organization. Individual aristocrats are known to have entered into alliances with members of other states, often sealed by marriages, and a network of such links would have provided a means for the dissemination of new ideas for the increase of wealth and the organization of society. The obvious military superiority of the state organization, moreover, would have been a powerful stimulus to imitation, for rival societies could not have hoped to compete on such unequal terms. This competitive rivalry was indeed one of the hallmarks of the early city-states, frequently carried on in open war in which ever larger infantry and naval forces were used, and mercenaries were increasingly employed. The states which prevailed were those with the most efficient military organization, and in due course they began to put together political structures of a higher order. The Athenian empire of the fifth century, which held sway over much of the Aegean was the first, and the rapid Macedonian expansion in the fourth century through Greece and the Near East to India showed something of the potential of the system. The most lasting, however, was that of Rome. Until the end of the fifth century Rome was just one of the many states of Italy and had been largely overshadowed by Etruscan neighbours to the north. In the fourth century, however, she began to dominate first her neighbours in Latium, then the rest of central Italy, until by the end of the third century she was firmly at the head of a confederacy which embraced the whole of the peninsula. This was the secure power base from which the later expansion into empire was to evolve.

SUGGESTIONS FOR FURTHER READING

The archaeology of Mediterranean Europe in the first millennium has been particularly well studied, though much remains unpublished and much is almost hidden in journals and monographs. General treatments of some of the themes discussed in this chapter are not common.

The evidence from Greece is presented in A. M. Snodgrass, *The Dark Age of Greece* and *Archaic Greece*, and in J. Coldstream, *Geometric Greece*. Greek trading and colonizing, as well as something of the barbarian reaction, are described in J. Boardman, *The Greeks Overseas*. For the Phoenicians, see S. Moscati, *The World of the Phoenicians*.

A most important collection of papers on Italy is published in D. and F. S. Ridgway (eds), *Italy before the Romans: the Iron Age, Orientalizing and Etruscan Periods*. G. Barker, *Landscape and Society: Prehistoric Central Italy* is useful, though its coverage only just extends to this period. There are several good introductions to the Etruscans: M. Pallottino,

The Etruscans, L. Banti, *Etruscan Cities and their Culture*, M. Cristofani, *The Etruscans: a New Investigation*. For a study of the social and economic development of a region, see T. Potter, *The Changing Landscape of South Etruria*.

Much of the material from Spain remains unsynthesized. For eastern Spain, A. Arribas, *The Iberians*, is still useful.

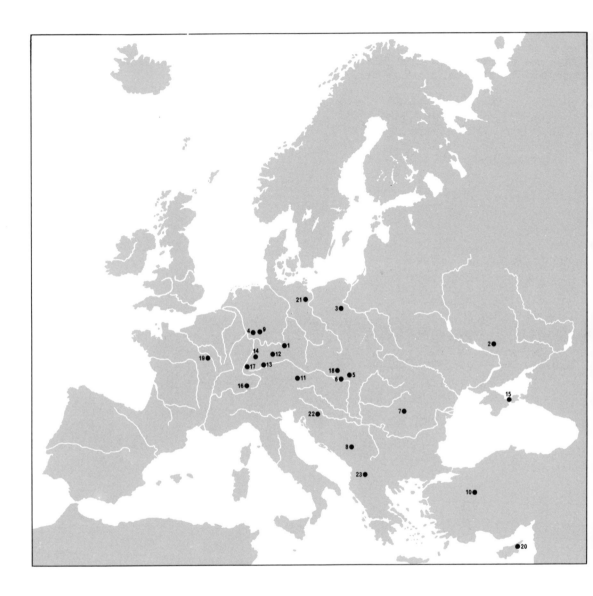

Fig. 9.1 Principal sites mentioned in Chapter 9. 1 Acholshausen. 2 Belsk. 3 Biskupin. 4 Bleibeskopf. 5 Čaka. 6 Chotín. 7 Ferigile. 8 Glasinac. 9 Glauberg. 10 Gordion. 11 Hallstatt. 12 Hart an der Alz. 13 Heuneburg. 14 Hohenasperg. 15 Kul Oba. 16 La Tène. 17 Magdalenenberg. 18 Molpír. 19 Mt. Lassois and Vix. 20 Salamis. 21 Senftenberg. 22 Stična. 23 Trebenište.

9

Competition and Hierarchy
in Temperate Europe

A far-reaching transformation of European society and economy was initiated towards the end of the second millennium. New forms of burial rite, new technologies, new weapons, a new level of intensification of agricultural and industrial production, and proliferation of defended sites mark this new phase. These indicate a new basis for social organization and a new level of differentiation within society. Relationships between the elites were carried on through competition for status, achieved by prowess in arms or generosity in giving. This competition produced a widespread uniformity of culture at the elite level. From the eighth century onwards the transition to iron and the rise of the Mediterranean world to the south produced significant changes in temperate Europe. Exchange networks were reorientated towards the south, and a new level of wealth was achieved by those elites on the fringes of the classical world best able to profit from the new conditions.

The centuries at the end of the second millennium mark a period of great change in temperate Europe. In many areas local sequences of classification and terminology have been worked out which show a significant break in the Bronze Age cultural tradition at this point, and continue with a new phase which embraces both the later Bronze Age and the first stage of the Iron Age. The archaeology of this period is still very largely the archaeology of its prestige items, but the quality and range of the evidence increases steadily, and is sufficent to show that European society underwent a major transformation at this time. The chronology of these changes was not, of course, exactly contemporary in all areas, but within the space of a few centuries most regions of Europe were affected. The date of the start of this new phase has traditionally been established by connections, especially through common weapon types, between central Europe and the Mycenaean world; these have been used to argue that the transition in central Europe was contemporary with some of the final phases of Mycenaean civilization, hence about 1250 BC. Radiocarbon dates are gradually becoming available in greater numbers, however, and these tend to show that, especially in parts of eastern Europe, the onset of the changes may have been rather earlier. There are still too few dates for certainty, and the traditional chronology is used here.

REGIONAL SEQUENCES 1250 – 400 BC

Over much of central and western Europe a considerable degree of cultural uniformity was established during the final centuries of the second millennium (Coles and Harding, 1979, pp.335–532). The most characteristic feature was a new burial rite of urned cremation, and the discovery of many cemeteries of this sort has given the name 'Urnfield' to this cultural tradition and this period. The generally accepted scheme of classification was worked out by the German archaeologist Paul Reinecke, and comprises four phases, Hallstatt A to D, named after a large cemetery in Austria excavated in the nineteenth century. Hallstatt A and B belong to the late Bronze Age Urnfield period, C and D to the ensuing Iron Age (Fig.9.2).

This cultural uniformity existed particularly at the elite level, and is to be found especially in metalwork and fine pottery (Müller-Karpe, 1959; von Brunn, 1968). The pottery vessels selected for use in burials frequently conformed to a standard type, with a tall cylinder-shaped neck (Fig.9.3). There was also considerable homogeneity of bronze types, especially weapons and ornaments, and particularly pins. New techniques for making complex sheet bronze objects were developed, and applied to armour (Schauer, 1975a) and to vessels, especially buckets and cups (Sprockhoff, 1930; Merhart, 1970; Furmánek, 1970). There was also great uniformity in the use of symbols, which clearly had an important but unknown ideological meaning. Sun symbols and birds' heads, among others, are regularly found decorating bronze vessels, armour and other objects (Kossack, 1954).

Within the general pattern of uniformity there was great local variation. A number of local groups within the Urnfield culture can be distinguished, mainly on the basis of styles of pottery and metalwork, but also showing a wide variation in the actual form of burial (e.g. Württemberg, Dehn, 1972; Hesse, F. R. Hermann, 1966; Bohemia, Bouzek *et al.*, 1966). The Lausitz group in southern Poland and eastern Germany is particularly well known for its well-researched cemeteries and its numerous fortified sites (Malinowski, 1961; J. Herrman, 1969; Coles and Harding, 1979, pp.341–52 and 359–62).

The transition to this Urnfield culture may have begun earliest in parts of central Europe, perhaps in Hungary, but within a short space of time the new complex incorporated many areas further west, including much of Italy, as we saw in the previous chapter. By soon after 1000 BC, and possibly even earlier, further areas still had been included, and the Urnfield complex spread as far as Belgium (Desittere, 1968), southern and western France (Chertier, 1976ab; Cordier, 1976; Schauer, 1975b) and north-eastern Spain. This cultural tradition was maintained until towards the end of the eighth century.

Other areas to the north and west of the Urnfield region shared some of its developments, but were not fully incorporated into it, and in particular did not adopt the characteristic burial rite. In northern Europe (Baudou, 1960), Periods III to V of Montelius's system run parallel to the Urnfield phase (Fig.9.2). There was a general trend from inhumation

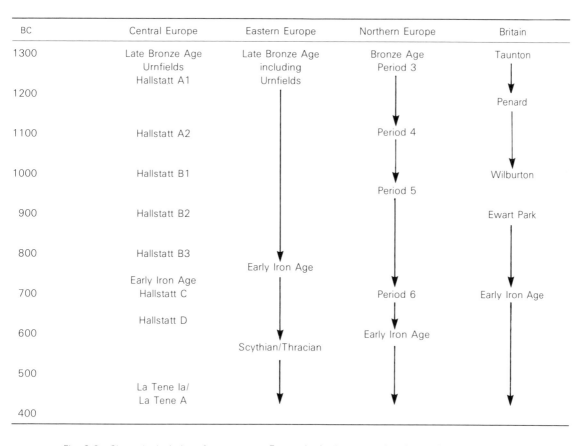

BC	Central Europe	Eastern Europe	Northern Europe	Britain
1300	Late Bronze Age Urnfields Hallstatt A1	Late Bronze Age including Urnfields	Bronze Age Period 3	Taunton
1200				Penard
1100	Hallstatt A2		Period 4	
1000	Hallstatt B1		Period 5	Wilburton
900	Hallstatt B2			Ewart Park
800	Hallstatt B3	Early Iron Age		
700	Early Iron Age Hallstatt C		Period 6	Early Iron Age
600	Hallstatt D	Scythian/Thracian	Early Iron Age	
500	La Tene Ia/ La Tene A			
400				

Fig. 9.2   Chronological chart for temperate Europe in the late second and early first millennia BC.

to cremation burial, but the pottery and metalwork of the region show marked continuity from earlier periods (Coles and Harding, 1969, pp.491–532). Connections with the Urnfield world can be seen in the adoption of related sword types and in the appearance of sheet bronze objects such as armour and large vessels (Baudou, 1960; Thrane, 1975).

In western Europe many areas lack a consistently recoverable burial rite, and the study of their later Bronze Age has revolved particularly around the bronze metalwork (e.g. Butler, 1963; Briard, 1965; O'Connor, 1980). Associated finds, especially in large hoards, have formed the basis for a chronological sequence, established primarily on material from southern England and northern France (Fig.9.2). Local developments include particularly

the adoption of socketed axes to replace the previous solid forms but there are also changes parallel to those of the Urnfield region (Fig.9.4). Weapon types, especially swords, changed in a similar way, and sheet metal objects also appear. Armour in Britain and Ireland was apparently restricted to shields (Coles, 1962; Needham, 1979), though they are very similar to central European types, and throughout western Europe large bronze vessels were generally in the form of cauldrons (Hawkes and Smith, 1957).

To the east of the Urnfield region, a series of local traditions can be distinguished (Coles and Harding, 1979, pp.386–414). The later Bronze Age sequence is still largely unknown in many areas of south-eastern Europe, but in southern Yugoslavia there was a long-lasting tradition of cremation burial under barrows,

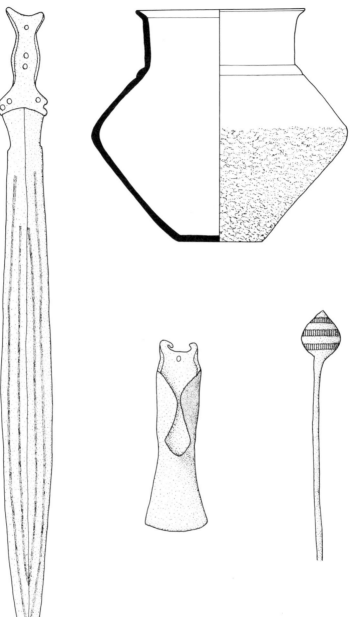

Fig. 9.3 (above)   Ceramic and metalwork types of the Urnfield period: cylinder-neck urn, sword, pin and axe from south-west Germany (after Müller-Karpe, 1959).

Fig. 9.4 (opposite)   Bronze types from the north-west European late Bronze Age: sword, spearhead, winged axe, socketed axe and socketed chisel from south-eastern England (after Burgess).

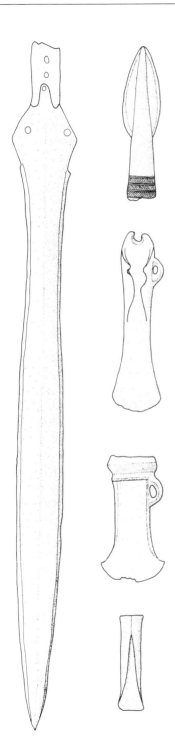

as at Glasinac (Benac and Čović, 1956), and the finds from graves and hoards show a similar trend in bronzeworking to that of central Europe. In Rumania and the southern Ukraine are a series of local variants on the Noua culture (Florescu, 1964), best known for its inhumation cemeteries and many undefended settlement sites. Further east still in southern Russia was the Timber Grave culture (Sulimirski, 1970, p. 256), in which the characteristic burial rite was crouched inhumation in a wooden chamber under a large mound; evidence of horses and horse-harness is particularly common.

About 700 BC the cultural homogeneity of the Urnfield region was disturbed. The widespread adoption of iron at this time (Pleiner, 1980) can be used to define the beginning of an Iron Age, but there were also other changes. The early Iron Age Hallstatt culture, extending with considerable regional variation from France to Czechoslovakia and northern Yugoslavia, adopted an inhumation burial rite, frequently under a barrow (Fig.9.5). The wealthiest burials were now placed in a wooden chamber, often accompanied by a four-wheeled vehicle (Pauli, 1971; Joffroy, 1957; Drack, 1958; Dvorak, 1938; Schiek, 1953) (Fig.9.6); an eastern origin for such rites has often been proposed, since the wooden chambers recall those of the Timber Grave culture and the practice of vehicle burial also has second millennium antecedents in western Asia. This new prestige burial rite, found from the late eighth to the sixth century in Bohemia, southern Germany, Switzerland, Alpine Italy and eastern France, was also practised, as we have already seen in the previous chapter, in Etruscan Italy, southern France and parts of Spain, and even as far away as the royal cemeteries of Salamis in Cyprus and Gordion in Asia Minor.

Many regional variations in burial rite and artifact typology can be identified within the Hallstatt culture (e.g. Kossack, 1959), which shows a broad division into an eastern and a western group. General trends such as the development of an iron technology, burial rites, and the adoption of new ornament types, especially the brooch to replace the pin, were common to both areas. Within the eastern group (Wells, 1981), the site of Hallstatt itself (Kromer, 1959) was an important salt-mining centre; large defended sites with associated groups of burial mounds, such as Stična (Gabrovec et al., 1970; Gabrovec, 1974) are

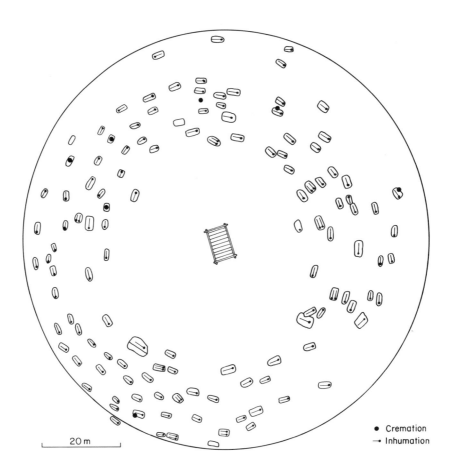

• Cremation
→ Inhumation

Fig. 9.5   The Magdalenenberg barrow, south-west Germany: a large burial mound of the sixth century BC.

also found. In the western group similar associations of defended sites and cemeteries are known, such as the Heuneburg in southern Germany and Mont Lassois in eastern France (see below), though few settlements have been excavated.

From the seventh century onwards imported material from Greece and Italy begins to occur in these areas, especially in the context of the richest sites and burials (Wells, 1980; Schaaf and Taylor, 1975). Much of this material, including fine pottery and bronze vessels, was concerned with the serving and consumption of wine; it will be discussed further below.

In the course of the fifth century there is a transition to the second phase of the Iron Age, named after the Swiss site of La Tène (Schwab, 1974; Navarro, 1972). Most of this phase will be the subject of the following chapter, but its initial stages in Champagne (Bretz-Mahler, 1971), the Rhineland (Haffner, 1976) and parts of central Germany, Czechoslovakia and Austria (Penninger, 1972; Moosleitner *et al.*, 1974; Pauli, 1978) are marked by a series of rich burials which continue some of the traditions of the sixth century (Schaaf, 1969). Many of these burials include vehicles, but now two-wheeled chariots instead of the four-wheeled ones of the earlier period (Harbison, 1969; Joachim, 1969). Imports from the Mediterranean world are now found in these graves,

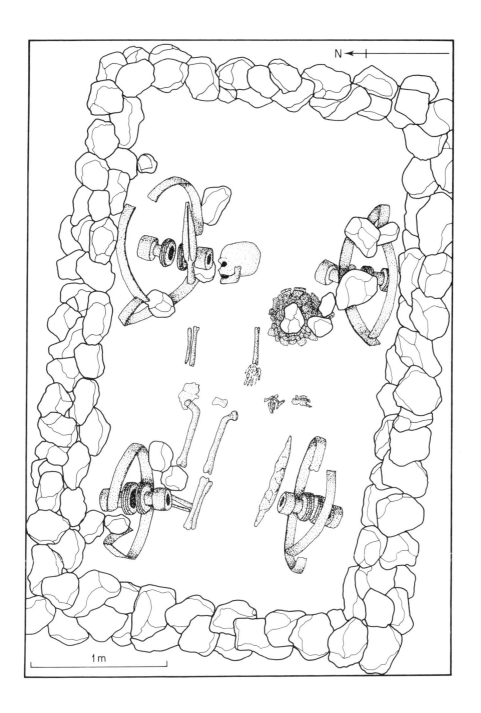

N ← |

1 m

Fig. 9.6 Burial at Offenbach-Rumpenheim, west Germany, containing a four-wheeled vehicle.

as well as rich locally-made items, often decorated in an elaborate ornamental style known as early Celtic (Jacobsthal, 1944; Schwappach, 1973) (Fig.9.7).

On the fringes of the Hallstatt culture other regional traditions can be distinguished. The cemeteries and sites of the Lausitz group of the Urnfield period continue to form a recognizable local phenomenon. The barrow building tradition of southern Yugoslavia also continued (Benac and Čović, 1957), but here too classical imports begin to occur in the richest graves.

In northern and western Europe the connections with events in central Europe were greatly reduced. In the north the local pre-Roman Iron Age shows a pattern of isolated development. In Britain some areas, especially south-eastern England, shared some of the changes in weapon and ornament types in central Europe, but the picture was predominantly one of indigenous development of pottery and metal-work types (Cunliffe, 1978a).

In eastern Europe a new regional complex developed covering the area from Hungary and Slovakia to the Black Sea (Dušek, 1974a). The cemeteries show some regional variation (e.g. Chotín in Slovakia, Dušek, 1966; Ferigile in Rumania, Vulpe, 1976) and employ both inhumation and cremation rites, but are linked by the presence of common weapon types, particularly arrows and daggers, and the frequent occurrence of horse-harness and horse burials (Fig.9.8). These and other features, such as

Fig. 9.7   Bronze flagons from a rich early La Tène grave at Basse-Yutz, France; though ultimately inspired by Mediterranean prototypes, these flagons are in shape and decoration entirely of local manufacture.

bronze mirrors, connect this region with areas further east, and this complex is often attributed to Scythian invaders, though there is no definite evidence for such an ascription (Gazdapuzstai, 1967).

SETTLEMENT AND SUBSISTENCE

The earlier part of the Bronze Age, as described in Chapter 7, had witnessed the steady expansion of agricultural activity onto increasingly marginal soils in the search for greater production. This trend of expansion continued in many areas in the later Bronze Age and the Iron Age, but at the same time some areas were being abandoned and other methods of increasing output were being sought. In many regions the best evidence for agricultural activity is still pollen analysis, but from this period onwards actual settlement sites become more common and the evidence of site distributions and site finds of plant and animal remains provide valuable information.

The evidence for agricultural expansion comes from many different parts of Europe. In Poland there was a marked phase of deforestation, perhaps early in the first millennium, accompanied by increasing quantities of cereals and grasses. In Scandinavia the pollen evidence shows a more dramatic impact on the environment from man's

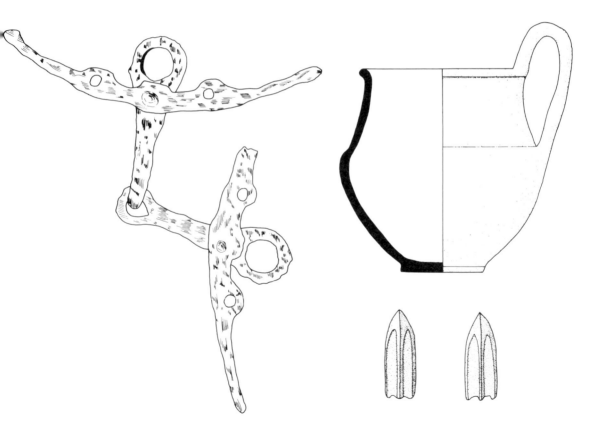

Fig. 9.8   Grave-goods from a so-called 'Thracian' cemetery at Chotín, Slovakia: horse bit, pot and arrowheads (after Dušek, 1966).

agricultural activity than would have been supposed from other archaeological remains (Welinder, 1975). In France deforestation occurred higher up the mountainous regions of the Massif Central and Pyrenees than previously, though human exploitation may only have been seasonal. In Britain too there are signs of decreasing woodland and greatly increased pastoral and arable activity (Turner, 1981). In some regions, the French mountains for example, this expansion may have been into areas previously little, if at all, used for agriculture, but in others it was rather a question of the more intensive use of areas already exploited; more frequent cropping and shorter periods of fallow, together with the keeping of more animals, would have allowed less chance for woodland to regenerate.

The pattern was not one of uniform expansion, however, for many areas were becoming increasingly hostile to human agriculture and some had to be permanently abandoned. The expansion of agriculture in the third and early second millennia had brought into use increasingly marginal soils; some were at high altitudes approaching the limits of profitable agriculture, while others were vulnerable to over-exploitation and exhaustion. Many of the acid and infertile heathlands of Britain and northern Europe are the result of such over-exploitation at this time, and were already being abandoned by the end of the second millennium. Elsewhere the problem was caused by the growth in upland areas of blanket bog, which produced an extensive layer of peat. In parts of western Ireland, for instance, whole prehistoric landscapes, including settlements and field-systems, were covered by a thick layer of peat (Lynch, 1981). Peat growth was caused by water-logging of the soil and led to conditions unsuitable for agriculture. What initiated the development of blanket bog is less clear, however (Evans *et al.*, 1975). The waterlogging may have been due to increasing rainfall, or to impeded drainage caused by previous human ploughing. Whatever the cause, peat growth had begun in some areas perhaps as early as the beginning of the second millennium, but by around 1000 BC was certainly rendering large tracts of upland unable to sustain further agricultural activity. Mountainous regions such as western Ireland and parts of the highland zone of Britain (e.g. Dartmoor, K. Smith *et al.*, 1981; Balaam *et al.*, 1982), which had previously supported extensive pastoral and

some arable farming, had by this time undergone irreversible changes to infertile moorland, and were abandoned.

Other areas also may have been under stress. As mentioned in Chapter 7, some regions which had supported large communities in the third and early second millennia may have suffered declining yields by the end of the millennium as a result of the previous excesses of production. Problems may also have been caused by non-anthropogenic changes in the environment. Changes in the climate at this period have for a long time been thought to have had important consequences for man; though the precise nature and chronology of such changes is still obscure (see box), colder and wetter weather would undoubtedly have put further stress on the established system of agricultural production. By the middle of the first millennium, a further problem may have already begun to affect coastal areas of north-western Europe, for rising sea levels in the North Sea were to pose a constant threat of marine transgression of the land, which became particularly severe during the first millennium AD.

One solution to the problems posed by such a contraction of the area available for agriculture was to be found in the further expansion and more regular cultivation of areas still usable, described at the beginning of this section. Such possibilities were somewhat limited, however, and other methods of increasing output had to be sought. The first millennium saw a variety of such strategies, including new crops, new tools and a more complex and intensive organization of agriculture.

In many areas of central and especially northern Europe rye became increasingly common, and has remained the most important cereal of that region. The reason for its adoption was its ability to withstand very cold and wet conditions in winter, which would have recommended it at a time of deteriorating climate. Elsewhere, wheat and barley remained the dominant cereals, though different varieties were now common; in some areas, especially the west, emmer wheat was largely replaced by spelt wheat, and naked barley gave way to hulled barley (Knörzer, 1976). The advantages of these varieties are not clear, but they may have been hardier or more productive. One very early reference in classical literature spoke of two harvests a year in Britain, and it is possible that this records the practice of sowing in both winter

CLIMATIC DETERIORATION IN THE EARLY FIRST MILLENNIUM

There has been considerable discussion of the role of climatic change in later prehistory (e.g. Turner, 1981), and many of the important developments from the mid-second millennium onwards, especially in the organization of the subsistence economy and settlements, have at some time been attributed more or less directly to a worsening climate. It is, however, far from clear whether the climate changed significantly, or how it affected man.

The clearest evidence for climatic change is to be found in the pattern of peat growth seen in many areas of Europe, especially in the bogs of the north and west. It has been recognized for a long time that in many areas a twofold division of peat bogs and blanket peats can be seen: a lower layer of dark-coloured, highly humified peat, and an upper layer of fresh-looking, light-coloured, weakly humified peat. These were formed under different conditions, respectively drier and wetter. The junction between two such layers, known as a recurrence surface, therefore represents a time of climatic change to wetter conditions, but research has shown that there is no single synchronous surface throughout Europe. On the contrary, many such recurrence surfaces have been noted, with considerable variation in date.

Some studies have suggested that even within the same bog a single recurrence surface may have widely differing dates at different points; such an argument would tend to support the conclusion that local factors were particularly important in determining the precise rate of peat growth and that universal factors such as climate were insignificant. Other workers, on the other hand, have reported exactly the opposite results. There has also been discussion of the effects of human activity, since clearance of forest or continued ploughing, for instance, could alter drainage patterns sufficiently to produce local changes in peat growth.

Despite the disagreement over the relative contribution of anthropogenic and natural factors and of local and universal ones, it seems certain from the peat evidence that climate was changing from perhaps as early as the late second millennium BC. This conclusion may be supported by the evidence of snail assemblages in central Europe, which show a trend from species preferring a warmer, drier climate to those of colder, wetter conditions.

The extent of the change is difficult to estimate. A drop of one centigrade degree in mean winter and summer temperatures has been suggested, which would have been sufficient to affect the length of the growing season and the altitudinal limits of agriculture. Increased rainfall would have affected farming in very different ways, depending on how it was distributed throughout the year. Too little is yet known about the seasonal effects of, or regional and local variation in, any such climatic deterioration, and it is not yet possible to suggest with any confidence precisely how prehistoric society and economy were affected.

and spring, in order to increase output per person; more land could have been cultivated at one time, but hardy varieties would have been needed to survive winter sowing.

New tools were also introduced, as first bronze and then iron became increasingly applied to domestic and agricultural purposes. Bronze sickles are known in very large numbers from the later Bronze Age, and many of the axes, which make up the most numerous type of bronze objects, must have had functions in clearance and cultivation. Tools such as axes and sickles were also among the first to be made plentifully in iron.

Other features of this new intensification include the provision of special facilities for agricultural purposes. The digging of pits and the construction of granaries, which became increasingly common during the first millennium, indicate the need to store grain efficiently, above or below ground. Wells also became more common, and so too did field systems (Bradley 1978a). The latter would have made it easier to control some agricultural activities, such as manuring, but would also have been important in dividing and demarcating land as pressure on agriculture became greater and rights in land became more critical. It is possible too that the growth of the salt industry (see below) should be seen in the same context, providing a means of storing and distributing meat more efficiently.

These developments taking place during the late second and the first half of the first millennium produced a very different and more intensive pattern of agriculture in temperate Europe. There were other effects too. First, as already mentioned, further expansion of agriculture, being limited or impossible, could no longer provide the whole solution to the demand for more resources, and so, perhaps for the first time, control of rights in land became of great importance. Secondly, those soils which had not been exhausted by previous agriculture and which could support the new intensive strategy of farming were particularly valuable. That meant in particular the valleys, which henceforth became the focus for a shift of population, settlement and wealth away from many areas which had in earlier periods prominently figured in the archaeological record (Rowlands, 1980).

This shift is seen in many areas of Europe. In the west, for example, the lower valleys of the major rivers such as the Loire, Seine, Thames and Rhine are distinguished by concentration of finds, especially of bronze, which are clearly superior in quantity and quality to those of intervening areas. In Denmark too, Kristiansen (1978) has noted the correlation of bronzes and the better agricultural soils.

The evidence for actual settlement sites is more extensive in this period than in any previous one, though in few areas have they formed a major theme of research. The numbers of known sites might suggest an increase in population, but though this conclusion is tempting and may well be correct, it cannot yet be supported by evidence of sufficient quality; the increasing recognition and recovery of settlements could be, at least in part, due to the more substantial nature of the features such as pits and house foundations to be found in sites of this period.

In most areas the settlement pattern is composed primarily of small agricultural villages, with a particular preference for sites in valleys, especially beside rivers and lakes. Little is known about internal organization except in exceptional cases such as the Swiss lakeside settlements (F. Keller, 1878; Guyan, 1954; Wyss, 1971). About 100 such lakeside sites are known, especially on Lakes Neuchâtel and Leman, which were occupied throughout the Bronze Age

until the eighth century, when they were abandoned in the face of rising water levels in the lakes. Preservation is unusually good, and there is evidence for the exploitation of a wide range of domesticated and wild plants and for the practice of crafts such as carpentry, metalworking and weaving.

The other important element in the settlement pattern of most areas of Europe is the fortified sites. As described in Chapter 7, defended sites had appeared throughout Europe during the earlier part of the Bronze Age, but from the end of the second millennium they became much more common (e.g. Schindler, 1968; Jockenhövel, 1974). They differed greatly in their size and construction, and it should not be thought that they necessarily performed similar functions in all areas. Although extensive excavation has been rare, it is already apparent that there were considerable regional variations. Some regions, especially northern Europe, show no signs of such fortifications, while in others their distribution is neither uniform nor stable. Nevertheless, in many areas of temperate Europe defended sites were common.

The numbers of such forts are particularly striking in the region of the Lausitz culture in Poland and eastern Germany (J. Herrmann, 1969). They vary considerably in their construction (Fig.9.9), size, density of occupation and location. Some are on hilltops, others by lakes or marshes; some may be sited for strategic defensive purposes, others for exploitation of local resources. Some, such as Biskupin or Senftenberg (Fig.9.10), were without doubt densely occupied, and show evidence for a wide range of industrial and agricultural activity.

In other areas the defended sites were less numerous and perhaps played a different role. In Britain, recent excavations have suggested that one of the major functions of the early forts may have been the storage of grain (Fig.9.11) on the grounds of the large numbers of granaries found (Cunliffe, 1978a, p. 268). In central Europe, some of the sites show particular evidence for the practice of metalwork, in bronze and in iron, frequently on a very large scale, as at Glauberg and Bleibeskopf in Germany (Jockenhövel, 1974b), and Molpír in Czechoslovakia (Dušek, 1974b). The same pattern can be seen in southern Russia, where strongly fortified sites had been occupied by the seventh century; at Belsk, a vast enclosure of over 4000 hectares including three strongholds, there is

Fig. 9.9   Diagrammatic reconstructions of Lausitz fortification types: 1–2, plank and palisade types; 3, box type; 4, grid type; 5, dry stone wall type (after Coblenz).

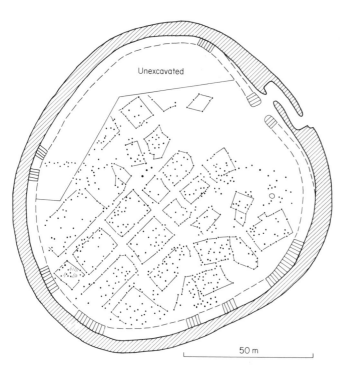

Unexcavated

50 m

Fig. 9.10 Plan of Phase I occupation at the defended site of Senftenberg, East Germany (after Herrmann, 1969).

Fig. 9.11 Four-post structures interpreted as granaries, and circular houses, in the hillfort of Moel y Gaer, North Wales (after Guilbert).

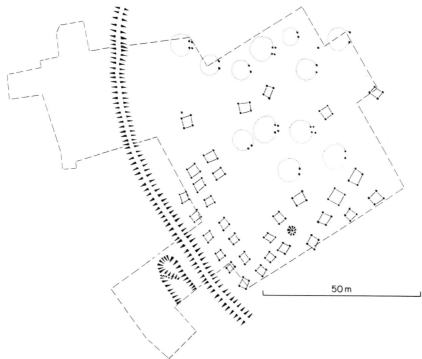

50 m

extensive evidence for iron and bronze production, the bronze being especially used for prestige items such as horse trappings and mirror handles (Sramko, 1974).

Similar connections in the form of status-related items between rich burials and defended sites are known in other areas of Europe, but can be seen most clearly in sites in eastern France, Switzerland and south-western Germany in the sixth and early fifth centuries (Härke, 1979, pp.67–148; Wells, 1980, pp.22–103) (Fig.9.12). These frequently exhibit a pairing between the fortified site and a cluster of rich burials. The Vix burial, for example (Fig.9.13), near the defended site of Mont Lassois, contained a large bronze crater, or wine-mixing jar, and a pottery drinking cup, both imported from Greece, together with the remains of a vehicle and many other wealthy items (Joffroy, 1954, 1960). Among the many rich

graves around the Hohenasperg, two are of particular note. The Grafenbühl (Zürn and Herrmann, 1966) contained a wagon, ornaments of amber, bone and gold, and ivory from the eastern Mediterranean, but had been robbed in antiquity. The recently discovered burial at Eberdingen-Hochdorf, however, was intact (Biel, 1982), and revealed, among other things, gold ornaments made specially for the burial, a large cauldron containing the remains of a drink, drinking horns, a wheeled bronze couch of Italian or Etruscan manufacture, and textiles pinned to the walls of the chamber. The best known and most extensively excavated complex is the Heuneburg and its associated burials (see box), but the whole group of sites, and others elsewhere, for example in the south-eastern Alps (Wells, 1981), clearly demonstrate the connection between the inhabitants of the defended sites and the deceased buried in such style.

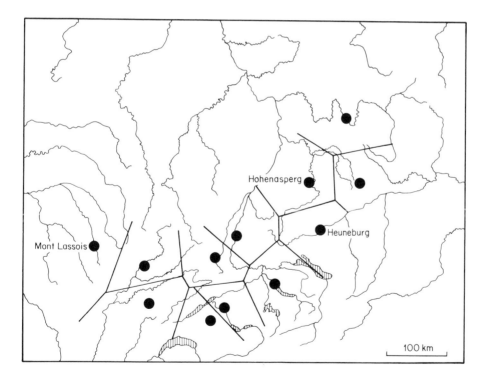

Fig. 9.12   Distribution of important defended sites and rich burials of the sixth century in eastern France, Switzerland and southern Germany (after Härke, 1979).

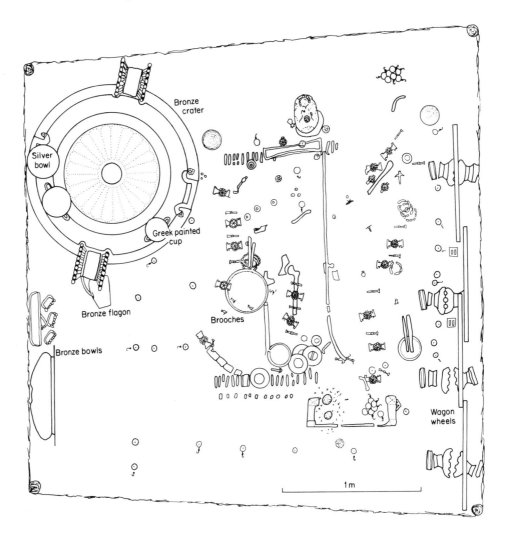

Fig. 9.13   Plan of the late sixth century grave at Vix, eastern France (after Joffroy).

TECHNOLOGY

One of the most remarkable features of this period was technological development, especially in the metal industries. Bronze production was transformed by the perfection of new techniques, the appearance of new products, a great increase in the volume of output and a new level of craft organization. Iron became increasingly common, especially from the tenth century, until it had largely replaced bronze for

many tools and weapons by the seventh. Other industries such as salt became of greater importance, and new materials such as glass and coral were worked.

New techniques for the manufacture and use of bronze were perfected and exploited. One of the most important of these was the use of sheet bronze. Some items of sheet metal, in gold, silver and bronze, are known from the early Bronze Age, but they are mostly small and simple, such as earrings, neck

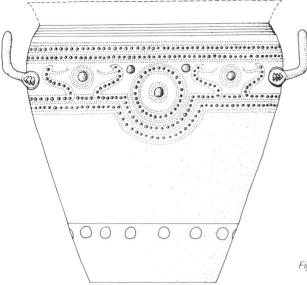

Fig. 9.14 Bronze amphora with bird-head decoration, from Unterglauheim, Germany (after Müller-Karpe, 1959).

ornaments or decorative plaques, and have little in common with the complex products made from the thirteenth century onwards. These were mainly of two sorts, vessels and armour. The vessels (Sprockhoff, 1930; Furmánek, 1970) included cups, buckets and cauldrons (Fig.9.14) while the armour (Schauer, 1975a) comprised helmets, breastplates, shields and greaves (Fig.9.15). All the items in this range posed rather similar technical problems for the smith, including hammering out a large sheet of metal, forming it to a complex three-dimensional shape, rivetting and strengthening. Larger objects such as shields, buckets and cauldrons all had to be given extra rigidity, and this was achieved by beating up ribs and bosses, which served a mechanical as well as a decorative function, and strengthening the rim by rolling it over a stiff wire. There was particular difficulty in fixing handles to the larger vessels, designed to hold considerable quantities of liquid, and one of the best solutions was the casting of a solid bronze handle directly on to the rim of the vessel, a technique shared with those swords where a solid bronze hilt was cast onto a previously made blade.

Other improvements in the techniques of casting were also mastered. Moulds were made of clay, stone

or bronze and increasingly complex shapes were cast in them. Successful casting of longer items became possible, and the first swords thus produced were substantially longer than the daggers and rapiers that had preceded them. Another important technique was hollow casting, achieved with a core of sand or clay in the centre of the mould. This allowed a greater variety of castings to be produced, with more efficient use of available metal and more effective finished products.

These techniques seem to have been first mastered and employed in the production of weapons and other items of high status, and there can be no doubt that it was demand for such objects that stimulated these advances. They did, nonetheless, have a wider significance, for bronze was coming into much more common use for a variety of domestic purposes, with a consequent decline in the reliance on stone tools. Bronze objects from this period are found much more frequently on settlement sites, especially small ornaments and agricultural and craft tools.

Another sign of the changing pattern of the bronze industry is the discovery of increasing numbers of hoards. To describe a find of several or many bronzes as a hoard says more about its discovery than about its original deposition, and hoards are a

THE HEUNEBURG

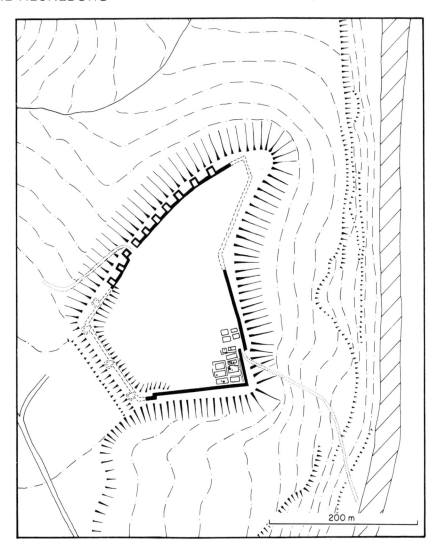

1. Plan of the Heuneburg, showing bastions on the defences and excavated buildings in the south-east corner.

The Heuneburg is the only extensively excavated example of an early Iron Age defended site in central Europe (Kimmig, 1975), but it was also one of the wealthiest sites of the period. It was first defended in the middle of the second millennium BC, or perhaps even earlier, and again in the late first millennium AD, but the climax of its occupation was in the sixth and early fifth centuries BC. The site lies on a triangular promontory overlooking the upper reaches of the Danube in southern Germany. About 3 hectares was enclosed within a defensive circuit that was rebuilt many times. The defences were of the standard local timber-framed type with a stone facing and rubble filling, except for one phase,

Period IV, in which a different technique was used. This consisted of a plan which incorporated bastions on the north-west side, sharp angles and a tangential gateway, and a technique using plastered mud-brick on a limestone base for the walls. Both plan and technique are of Mediterranean inspiration. This circuit was destroyed by fire and rebuilt in traditional local style.

Occupation deposits in the interior are several metres thick in places, and many successive phases and changing plans have been distinguished. Some parts of the interior were quite densely occupied, and a variety of different activities can be documented. As well as dwelling houses and granaries, there were workshops for bronzesmiths; bronze brooches were made on the site, and a mould for a copy of an Italian jug handle has been found. Iron was also worked, as were lignite, antler and coral, imported from the Mediterranean; amber came ultimately from the Baltic. Exploitation of these materials seems to have been primarily to produce ornaments or other prestige items. Among other imports were fine pottery from Athens and amphorae, presumably with their contents of wine, from the south of France.

There are several groups of burial mounds in the vicinity, including the large mound of the Hohmichele (Riek and Hundt, 1962). This lies about two kilometres to the west and is one of the largest burial mounds in Europe, being eighty metres in diameter and fourteen metres high. The original burial in the centre of the mound had been robbed shortly after deposition, but had been a burial in a wooden chamber with a four-wheeled vehicle. The mound also contained a series of secondary burials, one other of which was also a vehicle burial. The grave goods included the harness sets for two horses, a large sheet bronze cauldron, textile furnishings and a bow and quiver full of iron-tipped arrows.

The Heuneburg was clearly the residence of an elite who were able to mobilize local resources to connect themselves to very far-reaching exchange networks. Apart from the imports from France and Greece, silk and the domestic chicken are also known from here, the first occurrence of these Oriental items in temperate Europe. The intensity of the contacts with the Mediterranean world is shown by the adoption in one phase of exotic building styles, probably designed at least in part as an impressive display of power and status.

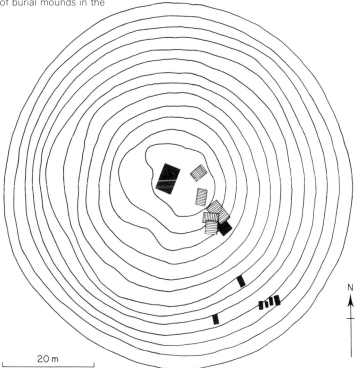

2. The massive burial mound of the Hohmichele; the central burial had been robbed in antiquity (after Riek and Hundt, 1962).

20 m

N

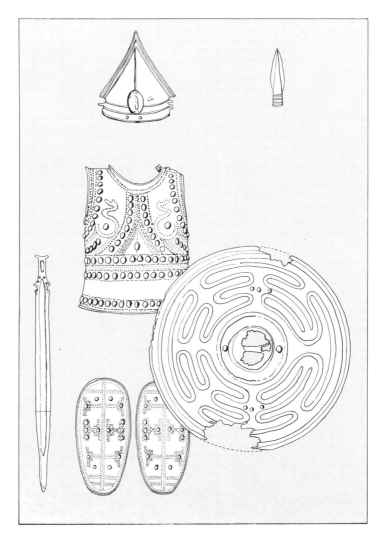

Fig. 9.15   Arms and armour of the late Bronze Age in western Europe, 1000–700 BC (after Schauer, 1975a).

phenomenon as yet not totally understood. It is clear that from the end of the second millennium they became much more common; and that some were personal collections of ornaments or craftsmen's tools, while others may have been of a ritual or votive nature, is a point to be further discussed below. Of the others, some at least represent different stages in the system of bronze production. Hoards of bronze bar ingots indicate that the supply of raw material was becoming more standardized, while finds of

groups of similar objects in a nearly or completely finished state suggest the stock of a smith or trader awaiting distribution (Rowlands, 1976, pp. 163-68). This is itself an important observation, since it shows that the smiths were working to meet anticipated rather than actual demand. Both of these types of hoard are known from about the thirteenth century.

From the tenth century onwards hoards of rather a different type are found. These are composed mainly or totally of scrap—old, worn items, frequently broken into small pieces. They are sometimes associated with clear indications of metal working such as moulds or ingots, and are therefore closely connected with bronze production. They are found widely throughout Europe, but occur particularly in the main centres of the bronze industry, sometimes totalling several thousand objects. These hoards are a clear sign of a growing concern with the supply of metal for bronze casting, and the development of a system of scrap collection and recycling. The recent discovery (Muckelroy, 1981) of two shipwrecks dating from the end of the second millennium off the south coast of England, bringing quantities of bronzes of French types otherwise almost unknown there, further suggests the existence of a complex system of transporting bronze from one area to another for recasting, possibly to even out temporary or chronic shortages.

Another innovation known from the later Bronze Age in Britain and northern France was the addition of about 7-10% lead to produce a copper–tin–lead alloy (Northover, 1982). Though earlier examples are known, this became increasingly common from the tenth century. The lead would have produced a metal that was easier to pour and produced fewer faulty castings, at the cost of a less hard finished product, and so might have been added to increase output, but it is also possible that it was introduced because the copper and tin needed to produce a standard tin bronze were not available in the quantities necessary to meet demand. In either case, it looks as though a major concern of the bronze industry in its later phases was a desire to maintain or increase output to satisfy a growing demand for a much wider range of objects.

The other important area of technical innovation was in ironworking (Tylecote, 1962; Pleiner, 1980). As in the Mediterranean region (see previous chapter), the beginnings of iron in temperate Europe can no longer be assigned to the collapse of the Hittite empire and a consequent diffusion of its knowledge. Recent finds have suggested that iron was in fact known for a considerable period before the start of a real Iron Age. Objects of iron are now known in increasing numbers from the second millennium (Kimmig, 1964, p. 274; László, 1977), and studies of the decoration on bronze implements (Bouzek, 1978) show that iron tools were being used with greater regularity from about 1000 BC. More important

perhaps are signs of actual ironworking from the second half of the second millennium (Brongers and Woltering, 1978, p. 97), to show that not all iron objects need have been imported. It is clear that iron was known and worked, though perhaps on quite a small scale, during the second millennium, and what needs explaining is not so much its first appearance as the processes by which working techniques were improved and it gradually came to replace bronze. Perhaps as early as the tenth century in parts of the south-eastern Europe, and certainly by the seventh century in most of the rest of the continent, iron had come to be used in place of bronze for most weapons and tools.

These early stages do not show a highly developed iron technology; it was rather a case of long, slow development. The earliest objects show few signs of a mastery of the technique of carburization, which was mostly irregular or absent. Only slowly was this skill mastered, but the smiths of temperate Europe never seem to have practised quenching and tempering. They did, however, learn how to harden the edges of tools, and to use carburized and uncarburized metal to best advantage in the same product. Even so, quite late in the Iron Age the fashion for long swords outran the smiths' ability to produce efficient weapons, and they needed straightening after each blow. The first iron objects were also made for the most part in the same form as their bronze predecessors, and it was only later that shapes more suitable to forging in iron were developed.

The superior potential of iron over bronze was, therefore, not the reason for its widespread adoption, for the skills to exploit it did not exist. The relative merits of late Bronze Age bronzes and early Iron Age iron objects are as yet little understood, and it is probably the very much greater abundance of iron ores that is the key to its use. Mention has already been made of the concern during the later Bronze Age to secure an adequate supply of raw material, and the switch to iron may be one further step in the readjustment of the organization of the metal supply industry to meet demand. The problems may have arisen through actual exhaustion of copper and tin ores, or through an increase in the demand for metal products, especially tools, which seems to characterize the later phases of the Bronze Age; possibly both factors may have played a part. However that may have been, the eventual mastery of the potential of iron was one of the most important elements in the growth of a more complex society in later prehistory, but its original adoption on a large scale is best seen in the light of the continuing history of the supply of metal products, and the general intensification of production that occurred from the end of the second millennium.

Another industry that expanded dramatically at this period was salt. The beginnings of salt extraction have already been mentioned in Chapter 7, but from about 1200 BC the scale of production increased enormously (de Brisay and Evans, 1975). The terrestrial deposits of the Halle region of eastern Germany and of Poland were exploited, and extraction from sea-water was increasingly practised on the Atlantic coasts of France and southern England. Some of the richest sites of central Europe owed their wealth to salt. The site of Hallstatt itself in Upper Austria was a salt-mining centre; radiocarbon dates suggest that mining may have started before 1000 BC (Coles and Harding, 1979, p. 380), though the greatest wealth of its cemetery came in the seventh and sixth centuries (Kromer, 1959). The nearby site of Dürrnberg bei Hallein (Maier, 1974) may also have been in use in the late Bronze Age, and replaced Hallstatt as the major centre in the fifth century. Another very rich site of the sixth and fifth centuries, Camp de Château in eastern France, also owes its importance to salt.

Salt was obviously a valuable commodity in later prehistoric times, but its uses are not so clear. By comparison with later periods, it was probably needed primarily for preserving meat and fish, but also possibly for tanning leather. Salting provided a means of storing meat for later use or for exchange, and was therefore particularly critical in a society in which the ability to control and mobilize foodstuffs was important.

Other industries are also known to have expanded in the period from 1200 BC onwards, though some have left little trace. The importance of textiles in the earlier Bronze Age has been described in Chapter 7, and the almost ubiquitous occurrence of loom-weights throughout Europe attests to their continued role in the first millennium. Leather also seems to have become more important, and specialist leather-working tools are found from the late Bronze Age onwards (Roth, 1974).

A wide variety of materials was worked to provide ornaments, frequently associated with people of high rank. Gold ornaments are quite widely distributed, but particular concentrations are found in Hungary (Moszolics, 1973) and in western Ireland in the late Bronze Age (Herity and Eogan, 1977, pp.186–221), and in the rich graves of the sixth century in southern Germany and the fifth century in the Rhineland (Wells, 1980), and south Russia. Amber also continued to be traded from the Baltic and was widely used for personal ornaments (Malinowski, 1971), but new materials were also introduced. Glass begins to occur from the beginning of the Urnfield period (Haevernick, 1975, 1978): compare the contemporary Proto-Villanovan site at Frattesina in northern Italy (see previous chapter), where evidence of actual glass-making has been found. At first, it was used only for beads, but later for a wider variety of objects, especially bracelets; some locally produced glass vessels are also known, particularly from the cemetery at Hallstatt. From the fifth century an opaque red glass, usually but wrongly called enamel, began to be used as a decorative inlay. Other materials were also brought into use; shale and lignite (Rochna, 1962) were worked to make ornaments, and red coral (S. Champion, 1976, 1982) from the Mediterranean was widely distributed into central Europe from the seventh century as a decoration on its own or attached to other ornaments.

Many objects of these types, as well as the vessels and armour of the late Bronze Age, are particularly associated with the rich graves and their accompanying sites (compare the discussion of the Heuneburg above). There was an increasing differentiation and specialization of production among craftsmen, especially smiths, and those who produced the higher status items and ornaments, perhaps working directly for specific patrons, were distinct from those who made more everyday domestic or agricultural products.

SOCIAL ORGANIZATION

In Chapter 7 it was suggested that the social hierarchies of the earlier Bronze Age were based on a principle of competition for status in which an important role was played by control over access to prestige items such as metal. In the later Bronze Age and the earlier Iron Age the evidence for the existence of such hierarchies continues, and in some areas is greatly increased, but the detailed forms which its expression takes are now different and it must be asked whether there are any significant changes in the basis of social organization.

There were in fact two major readjustments in the way in which social status was symbolized, particularly in the burial record. The first was the adoption of the Urnfield cremation rite and its associated set of objects, including swords, armour and bronze vessels. Though there are some variations in the wealth of grave goods throughout the period, there are two phases of more extreme differentiation. The first is at the very beginning of the Urnfield period, perhaps in the thirteenth to eleventh centuries, when particularly rich burials were deposited in a number of areas such as Hungary, Slovakia, Bohemia, Austria and Bavaria (Coles and Harding, 1979, pp.363–66). At Čaka in Slovakia, for example, a large mound contained a series of graves, one of which produced a sheet bronze corslet (Točík and Paulík, 1960; Paulík, 1963). Two of the richest burials in Bavaria were at Hart an der Alz (Müller-Karpe, 1956) and Acholshausen (Pescheck, 1972); in the former the finds included sheet bronze vessels and the remains of a wheeled vehicle, in the latter a sword, vessels and a miniature wheeled bronze vessel for some ritual function, while in both bird symbols of typical Urnfield type were found. In finds such as these the association of the new weaponry, the new technology for vessels and armour and the new symbolism with the new burial rite is clearly confirmed. Subsequently these extremes of wealth are not matched until the graves of the eighth century, when again a greater degree of differentiation, expressed in very similar style, is found.

The second major readjustment came around 700 BC, when these Urnfield forms of rich burial gave way to the practice of inhumation, frequently in a chamber of some form, with a wheeled vehicle. This was the form taken by the rich burials of Bohemia, southern Germany, Switzerland and eastern France during the earlier part of the Iron Age, and the examples from Vix and the Hohmichele have already been mentioned. Further east in Europe, as we have already seen, a different complex emerged, with its own characteristic forms of prestigious funerary rites, including horse burials.

The adoption of these various new styles of burial, and particularly of burial for the elite, has seemed to many prehistorians so important and so widespread a phenomenon, and marked so definite a break from previous practices, that it could only be explained as the result of migration, or in particular of conquest by a new ruling group of external origin. Thus the archaeology of the later second millennium has been seen in terms of Urnfield migrants, spreading out from a notional point of origin perhaps in Hungary, while the inception of the Iron Age has been attributed to invaders from the east, though their precise origin has often escaped recognition. These explanations have faced serious difficulties, not least because the identification of the origin, chronology and causes of the migration has posed often insuperable technical problems. It remains to ask whether a more satisfactory answer could be found, as also in the case of the Bell Beaker phenomenon, in terms of the adoption of new principles for the organization of society, together with the means of displaying new statuses and legitimating them.

The close association of Urnfield arms, technology and symbolism with burial rites and defended sites has already been mentioned, as also has the concentration of settlement and wealth on prime agricultural land. These correlations are therefore of great importance in understanding the Urnfield phenomenon. By the end of the second millennium the opportunities for further agricultural expansion were, as we have already seen, greatly reduced, and land had become a critical resource. If we take as our starting point the competition for status within society and the augmenting of subsistence production as one means of initiating such competition, then in the conditions prevailing at the end of the second millennium one possible strategy would have been the intensification of agricultural activity; some of the ways this was achieved were described in the previous section. Another course would have been the forcible acquisition of additional land, or even actual produce, through raiding. The dwindling supply of available land for expansion had made land a valuable item and created the conditions for more aggressive competition and raiding. The emphasis placed on the sword, spear and armour, the development of new technologies to improve these items and the proliferation of defended sites all point to the increasing importance of armed raiding. Warfare may only have been practised by a limited section of a society, in particular by the elite, but it was assuming a greater role in the relationships between societies (T. Champion, 1982).

It is perhaps significant that some of the functions associated with the earliest defended sites are concerned with the control of subsistence resources. Also of great importance was the control of technology, not only as a means of intensifying production, but also to provide the weapons, armour and other status-related items such as bronze vessels (Rowlands, 1980). New methods of controlling and increasing subsistence resources, new ways of controlling and exploiting metal technology, new responsibilities for the conduct of aggression and defence would all have contributed to forming a new set of principles for the structuring of relationships within society; control over the allocation of rights in land would have been particularly important. It is perhaps in the promotion and justification of such a new structure that the new symbolism of the Urnfield period and the ideology it represents were used; the adoption of a new burial rite throughout society may also have been part of this pattern of change.

Given the existing principle of competition between individuals and interaction between societies, such changes were inherently likely to be adopted rapidly over a large area. Relationships may have been peaceful, for instance through the exchange of gifts, or more warlike, even to the point of actual conflict; either way, the knowledge of new technologies, new fighting methods and new structures of organization would have been quickly disseminated. It is remarkable how rapidly and uniformly throughout Europe changes, particularly in sword styles, occurred at this time; competitive emulation or even the need for survival would have ensured rapid acceptance and local copying.

The same explanation applies to the acceptance of certain Urnfield items, such as weaponry, armour and bronze vessels, outside the area of Urnfield burials, for instance in western and northern Europe. The Urnfield world eventually encompassed most of central Europe from Hungary to eastern France and, as we have seen in the previous chapter, extended southwards to include southern France, north-eastern Spain and much of Italy. Though northern and western Europe were never fully incorporated, and showed considerable continuity from earlier traditions, some specific areas in these regions did have very marked connections with the Urnfield

complex. The concentration of wealth, particularly of bronze, in the agriculturally more productive areas in the north and west has already been mentioned, and it is precisely these which were the foci for Urnfield connections, especially in weapons, ornaments and other prestige items.

Later Bronze Age social organization was, therefore, markedly hierarchical and characterized by competition for prestige and status. Within a society, the elite controlled subsistence resources not so much by force or through direct ownership, but by the ability to manipulate surplus production in exchange perhaps for security and guarantees of subsistence offered by a successful leader, as well as the status given to the group as a whole by its elite. Both within and between groups status could be achieved by success in arms, by generosity in the exchange of gifts and by lavish entertaining. The nature of this competitive interaction could therefore vary from completely peaceful to openly aggressive. Individuals could form alliances, through the exchange of gifts or marriage partners, as a step towards increasing the basis for their competition. In such a system the distinction between social, economic and political activity is difficult to draw and may be inappropriate.

Such a system of social organization was inherently expansive. It encouraged intensification of production within the community, and through many forms of competitive interaction tended to draw more people into an ever widening social network. The degree of political centralization was generally small, but the potential existed for individuals to build a position of some considerable status, and possibly of considerable spatial extent. To judge from the distribution of rich burials and the evidence, such as it is, for the occupation of the defended sites, however, these positions were basically unstable, for no such focus seems to have lasted for long.

The same pattern of social organization lasted into the earlier part of the Iron Age. During the eighth century the level of wealth deposited in the richest graves once again began to increase, and this may have been due to the first contacts with the expanding Mediterranean economy, described in the previous chapter. From about 700 BC, however, as we have seen, there were significant changes in the burial record; the new rites, and the new vehicle and horse burials for expressing status, mark the end of the

Urnfield world, though there was considerable continuity in non-funerary items such as pottery and settlements.

One important factor in this change may have been the change from bronze to iron for many purposes at this time. Control of the supply and circulation of bronze had been one basis for social ranking in the Bronze Age, but with the switch to iron the significance of bronze was greatly reduced. Unlike copper and tin, iron ores were of very general occurrence, and though some sites seem to have grown wealthy by exploiting iron ores (Driehaus, 1965), the supply of metal could not be controlled in anything like the same way. The decline of the bronze industry also meant that those relationships which had been conducted primarily through the exchange of bronze, at least on one side, and those local social systems that depended mainly on prestige goods acquired through such exchanges could no longer be maintained in the same way (Kristiansen, 1978, 1982).

Another factor, which has already been mentioned, was the steady growth from the late ninth century of the economies of the Mediterranean world, which brought them into closer contact with temperate Europe (Wells, 1980; Fischer, 1973). The demand for raw materials and slaves produced new opportunities for the enhancement of status and a consequent redirection of surplus towards the south, which will be discussed more fully in the next section. Those people nearest to the consumers in the Mediterranean region stood to gain most, and a new set of burial rites may have been appropriate to symbolize a new basis for social organization.

The transition from bronze to iron and the reorientation of surplus production towards the Mediterranean had particularly marked effects on the connections established in the later Bronze Age between central Europe and areas to the north and west. Although some interaction continued, and the successive styles of weapons in particular were copied broadly throughout Europe, the intensity of these relationships was greatly reduced. The effect was particularly marked in northern Europe, which had depended almost entirely on the exchange of bronze for local products, especially amber, as a basis for its social ranking; from the seventh century, however, the supply of bronze was no longer forthcoming. For the rest of the first millennium there are few signs of any marked social differentiation in northern Europe.

The new opportunities offered by this exchange with the Mediterranean seem to have allowed at least some leaders to establish their position with a greater degree of stability. Some of the defended sites of the sixth century in central Europe, such as the Heuneburg and the Hohenasperg, appear to have maintained their status over several generations. These sites were the climax of the whole phase of hierarchical development that had characterized Bronze Age social organization. By the beginning of the Iron Age, the technology, subsistence economy, settlement pattern and to some extent the social organization of temperate Europe had been transformed, and the developments in the Mediterranean world had begun to have an effect, but the underlying principle of competition for status had not changed.

Central European society was not just influenced by the Mediterranean world, but it seems actually to have tried to imitate it, even if somewhat palely. The adoption of Mediterranean materials and architecture for defences, of Mediterranean technology and styles for pottery, perhaps even of Mediterranean fashions in furniture, clothing and tableware all point to something more profound than merely interaction through trade. That parts of central Europe were not incorporated into the Mediterranean world as completely and as permanently as, for instance, the south of France or eastern Spain may have been due to their greater distance from the Mediterranean and the less intense interaction. The collapse of these early Iron Age hierarchies will be discussed further below, but their demise marked the end of one phase of European prehistory. They were replaced by a different pattern of social organization, to be described in the next chapter, in which competition for status was still important, but was practised in different ways.

EXCHANGE

One of the most obvious archaeological traces of the far-flung social networks through which the elites of the later Bronze Age and early Iron Age operated are the prestige objects deposited at often considerable distances from their point of origin or manufacture. Exchange was a means of demonstrating and thus achieving status through the giving of generous gifts, and also a means of acquiring objects or materials, especially ones of exotic origin, whose possession would likewise confer status. Objects could thus pass through a succession of such transactions, until by stages they had reached somewhere far from their origin. Thus amber from the Baltic reached Ireland and Italy, bronze vessels made in central or eastern Europe reached Britain and Ireland, and northern Europe at different times attracted bronzes from Ireland, western and central Europe.

The value of the status conferred by such objects, however, depended on control over their supply and on limitation of the quantity available; the more bronze there was in a society, for instance, the harder it would be to restrict access to it, with the consequent risk of diminution in the status to be derived from its manipulation. One solution to this problem was to take prestige items out of circulation by depositing them where they would not be recovered; it would then be possible to continue to acquire them by exchange without the risk of lowering their value. The deposition of wealthy grave goods was, therefore, not just a means of demonstrating the status of the deceased, but also a way to keep up the value of the items still in circulation. In central Europe most of these deposits were indeed in burials, but other methods were adopted elsewhere. In eastern Europe hoards of metal were deposited, containing the same range of types as were used as grave-goods further west. In western Europe there is no regularly recoverable burial rite in many areas and many of the hoards seem to have a connection with industrial production. There are, on the other hand, large numbers of finds of exactly the same sorts of objects in rivers and bogs (Torbrügge, 1970/71). Some of the finds could be from eroded riverside settlements, but the large numbers and the exotic nature of these objects suggest a widespread practice of ritual deposition in watery places. In some areas of north-western Europe this practice had a long history from the second millennium BC until nearly AD 1000 or even later, but had a particular importance in the late Bronze Age (von Brunn, 1980; Levy, 1982).

At the highest level of the elite, these exchange networks, and the social networks of which they are the most visible part, extended over most of Europe. Deposition coincided with successful integration into the network, and the quantity and quality of the objects deposited can give a good indication of the changing patterns of status in the first millennium. As Kristiansen (1978) has pointed out, the less productive parts of Denmark experienced increasing difficulty in participating in these exchanges during the Bronze Age, and the bronzes deposited there had been kept in circulation longer and were therefore more worn than in other areas. These patterns of exchange, circulation and deposition are as yet little understood.

About 700 BC these patterns were disrupted, as has already been mentioned, by the impact of the expanding Mediterranean economies. The transformation of the Mediterranean world has been described in the previous chapter, and through its demand for slaves, foodstuffs and raw materials it had the most profound effect on temperate Europe (Wells, 1980; Frankenstein and Rowlands, 1978). Those areas nearest to the colonies of the central and western Mediterranean and the Black Sea were most able to capitalize on the appearance of a new demand; their very position made it easy for them to supply the kinds of material they themselves could produce and also to profit as middlemen from goods coming from further afield. Surplus production was channeled southwards and those communities on the fringe of the classical world stood to profit most.

The effects of this trade with the classical world can be seen from Russia to Spain (Boardman, 1980), in the imported goods and other wealth found in fortified sites and rich burials, such as Kul Oba in the Crimea, Trebenište in Yugoslavia or Vix in eastern France. As the intensity of these interactions increased, there was a tendency for the affected areas to be incorporated more fully into the economic and social sphere of the classical world. The first Greek colonies in the west had been in central Italy, which was then assimilated in this way, to be followed by southern France and north-eastern Spain, which all then became consumers rather than producers. Temperate Europe was not drawn into the classical world in this way, but the very proximity of some of the richest sites to the Mediterranean must have made it difficult to maintain restricted control over access to the imported classical goods. As the volume of trade increased it may have become easier for enterprising individuals to gain independent access to exchange connections, thus undermining the basis for much of the elite's position. This may have been an important factor in the decline of the wealthy early Iron Age sites of central Europe such as the Heuneburg in the period shortly after 500 BC; the competitive interaction between the sites may also have been important, since as well as sustaining them it may have led to their collapse at the same time. Mediterranean goods continued to be imported in the fifth century, but now passed through the area of the former elites and are found especially in the rich graves of Champagne and the Rhineland.

Imported classical goods are seldom found in central and western Europe after 400 BC. Their disappearance may have been due to the reorientation of Mediterranean demand to other directions, for such items continue to be found in some areas of eastern Europe, exchanged through the Greek colonies of the Black Sea. Before this date, however, first in parts of central Europe and then more generally elsewhere, a pattern of social organization had appeared in which control of prestige exchange played little part. This will form one of the themes of the next chapter.

SUGGESTIONS FOR FURTHER READING

The sheer quantity of material recovered from this period is enormous and has led to a vast literature, which is scattered through many journals and monographs, in many languages. Much of it is detailed presentation of material or sites, and the approach is predominantly regional, typological or chronological.

For the late Bronze Age, the earlier part of the period covered in this chapter, J. M. Coles and A. F. Harding, *The Bronze Age in Europe* is again an excellent introduction to this scattered literature. For Britain, J. Barrett and R. Bradley (eds), *Settlement and Society in the British Later Bronze Age* contains detailed reports of recent work and its interpretation.

There is no similar introductory book for the earlier Iron Age, though T. G. E. Powell, *The Celts* and J. Filip, *Celtic Civilization and its Heritage* are both useful. European reaction to Greek colonization is described in J. Boardman, *The Greeks Overseas*, and in more detail for Central Europe in P. S. Wells, *Culture Contact and Culture Change: Early Iron Age Central Europe and the Mediterranean World*. For the Scythian material see A. Artamanov, *Treasures from Scythian Tombs*.

Various papers in A. C. Renfrew and S. J. Shennan (eds), *Ranking, Resource and Exchange: Aspects of the Archaeology of Early European Society* deal with the emergence and development of social ranking in this period. A case study of the rise of one regional hierarchy is given in P. S. Wells, *The Emergence of an Iron Age Economy*.

The literature concerning the art of the earlier Iron Age is enormous. Useful introductions can be found in J. V. S. Megaw, *Art of the European Iron Age*, P. M. Duval, *Les Celtes*, and N. Sandars, *Prehistoric Art in Europe*.

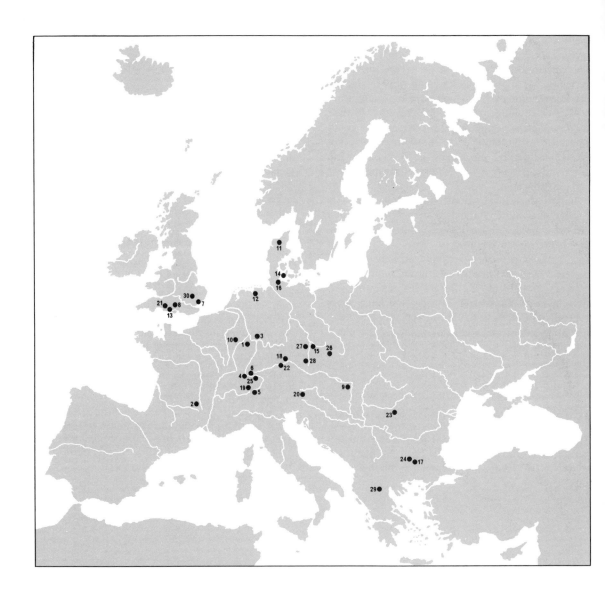

Fig. 10.1   Principal sites mentioned in Chapter 10. 1 Altburg bei Bundenbach. 2 Aulnat. 3 Bad Nauheim. 4 Basel. 5 Bern.
6 Breisach. 7 Colchester. 8 Danebury. 9 Gellerthegy-Taban, Budapest. 10 Goeblingen-Nospelt. 11 Grøntoft. 12 Hatzum.
13 Hengistbury Head. 14 Hjortspring. 15 Hrazany. 16 Husby. 17 Kazanluk. 18 Kelheim. 19 La Tène. 20 Magdalensberg.
21 Maiden Castle. 22 Manching. 23 Sarmizegethusa. 24 Seuthopolis. 25 Sissach. 26 Staré Hradisko. 27 Stradonice. 28
Třísov. 29 Vergina. 30 Welwyn Garden City.

10

Towns and the State in Temperate Europe

In the final phases of the Iron Age, before the expansion of the Roman empire northwards in the first century BC, major changes are apparent in the economy and society of temperate Europe from central France to the Black Sea. The settlement pattern was transformed by the growth of large sites which functioned as towns, and new centres of industrial production distributed standardized wares over larger distances. At the same time, political power was becoming increasingly centralized, and early forms of the state had emerged. Coinage was introduced, initially for political purposes, though later it facilitated commercial exchange. The use of writing was known, at least for keeping official records. Thus even before the Roman conquest, large parts of 'barbarian' Europe were occupied by literate societies with a high degree of social, economic and political development.

In the last centuries of the first millennium BC transformations of society and the economy similar to those that had occurred in the Mediterranean region 500 years earlier now took place in much of central and western Europe. Only northern and far north-western Europe remained outside the scope of these developments.

REGIONAL SEQUENCES – 400 BC–AD 50

After the decline of the rich burials described in the previous chapter, most of western and central Europe was dominated by the La Tène cultural group (Filip, 1977, pp.60–80) (Fig.10.2). This is best known from its burials, and indeed in many areas the archaeology of the accompanying settlements is almost unknown. The burials show considerable diversity from region to region (e.g. Bretz-Mahler, 1971; Haffner, 1976), both in the nature of the rites adopted and the selection of the grave goods. There is, nevertheless, a considerable degree of homogeneity (Lorenz, 1978), particularly in the deposition of weapons with men and jewellery with women, the general forms of both weapons and ornaments, and the art style developed from that initiated in the fifth

century. Some examples are shown in Fig.10.3, and the sub-divisions of the La Tène period and their chronology are shown in Fig.10.2.

During the fourth century BC this culture group expanded eastwards from its earlier location in France, Switzerland and Germany, to include most of Austria, Czechoslovakia and Hungary (Fig.10.4). This expansion is frequently attributed to migration from the former area (Filip, 1956), but this explanation is not without serious difficulties. It is true that there were migrations in the third century from central Europe south-eastwards into the Balkans, but they do not match the observed archaeological changes in either chronology or geography. Furthermore, there were no accompanying changes in other things such as settlements and pottery, and it seems more likely that it was the burial rite, together with the appropriate articles for inclusion in the grave, that was being adopted over a progressively wider area.

Some elements of this La Tène material culture were adopted over an even wider area. The art style was copied in Britain and Ireland (Megaw, 1970; Fox, 1958), and reached its full development there in the first century BC, at a time when it was hardly in use any more on the continent (Fig.10.5). The

BC	France/ Switzerland	Germany	Czechoslovakia/ Hungary	Eastern Europe	Britain/ Northern Europe
500	Hallstatt D	Hallstatt D	Late Hallstatt	Scythian/ Thracian	Pre-Roman Iron Age
	La Tène Ia	La Tène A			
400	La Tène Ib	La Tène B			
			La Tène B	La Tène B	
300	La Tène Ic				
	La Tène II	La Tène C	La Tène C	La Tène C	
200					
100	La Tène III	La Tène D	La Tène D	Dacian	
	Gallo-Roman				
0		Roman			

Fig. 10.2   Chronological chart for temperate Europe in the first millennium BC.

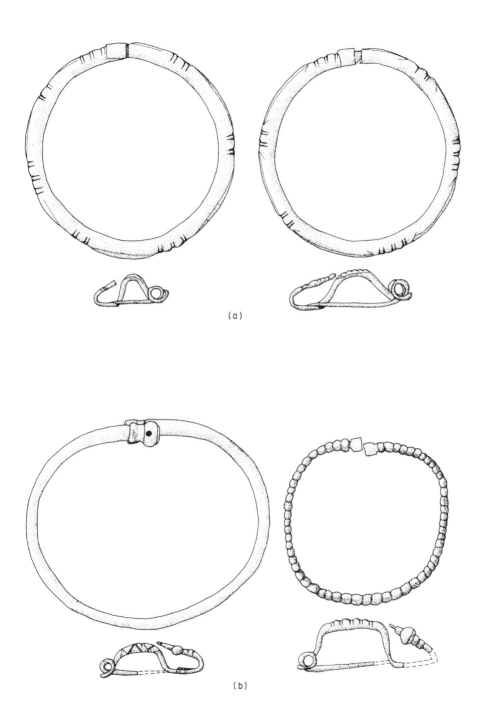

Fig. 10.3   Early La Tène burial groups from central Europe: (a) from Switzerland (after Hodson); (b) from Czechoslovakia (after Waldhauser).

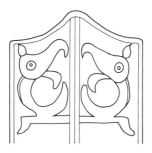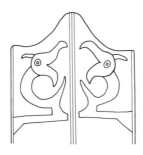

Fig. 10.4 La Tène decorated sword scabbards: (a) from Switzerland, (b) from Hungary (after Navarro).

fashionable styles of La Tène weapons and ornaments were also widely adopted and transformed into local variations, in particular the brooch. By the end of the millennium brooch styles derived from La Tène originals were found throughout northern Europe from Ireland through Scandinavia to Russia. These brooches, which are so widespread and show considerable changes in form through time, are also one of the main foundations for the chronology of the period: some of the variations are shown in Fig.10.6.

During the second century BC these burials disappear, and the La Tène III period of the first century BC is almost devoid of burial evidence. In an area of north-western Europe, however, including the Rhineland and northern France, cremation had been adopted during the second century (Collis, 1977), and that rite continued through the first century and into the Roman period, also spreading to south-eastern England in the late first century BC (Birchall, 1965).

Until these late cremations, most of Britain and northern France had been without burials throughout the first millennium, though inhumations in the La Tène mode do occur in cemeteries in Yorkshire in northern England (Stead, 1979). The main concern of archaeology in these areas has, therefore, been with settlements and domestic artifacts, in particular pottery.

In contrast to the earlier periods, the evidence for the first century BC on the continent, the La Tène III period, is derived mainly from settlements. A new settlement pattern with larger centres, frequently fortified, had appeared (Collis, 1975), with new styles of pottery, much of it now wheel-made (Fig.10.7).

In eastern Europe, the burial rites established in the sixth century (see Chapter 9), including the so-called 'Scythian' material continued, but were replaced around the fourth century by specifically La Tène customs, or by rites in which La Tène fashions were reflected (Szabo, 1971; Todorovic, 1968; Zirra, 1971). There too, in the first century BC a new material assemblage appeared, termed 'Dacian' (Collis, 1972), including wheel-made pottery with characteristic forms of jugs, bowls and pedestalled dishes (Fig.10.8).

From the end of the second century BC to the early first century AD, the political power of the Roman empire was gradually extended northwards, and in its wake came major changes. The settlement pattern was transformed by the establishment of towns as the key element in the new system of government, new architectural styles were adopted and new industries produced new forms of artifacts such as pottery; an unprecedented degree of cultural homogeneity ultimately prevailed in the Roman provinces.

In northern Europe and Scandinavia, however, the cultural sequence had been very different (Hachmann, 1960). The period before the development of relations with the newly consolidated Roman empire in the early first century AD is termed the Pre-Roman Iron Age, and was characterized by settlements and burials very different from those to the south, though directly derived from those of the local late Bronze Age (see previous chapter). The burials were almost exclusively by cremation, with the ashes placed in an urn accompanied by few, if any, grave goods, and with no superimposed mound. La Tène brooches were copied from the south, until by the first century they had almost totally replaced

Fig. 10.5   Decorated bronze mirror from Desborough, Northamptonshire, England.

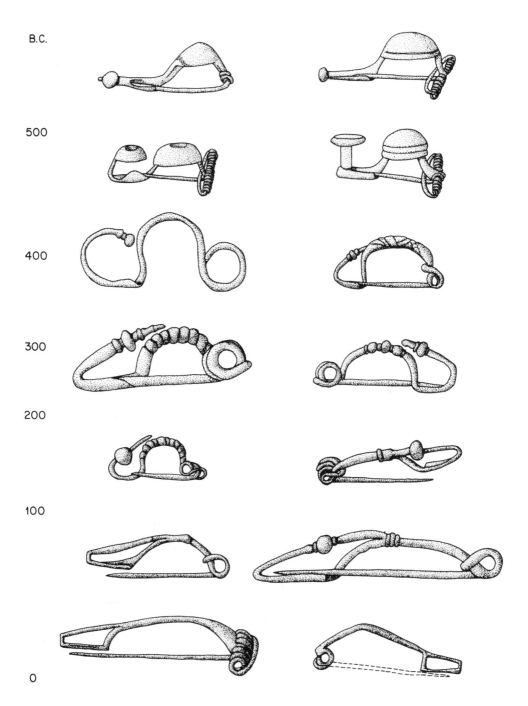

B.C.

500

400

300

200

100

0

Fig. 10.6 Development of the brooch in La Tène Europe: the constant change in brooch styles makes this type an important chronological marker throughout the Iron Age.

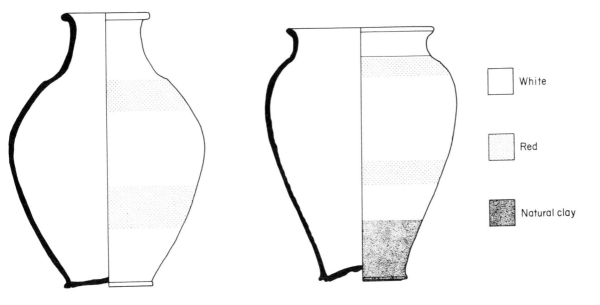

Fig. 10.7 Late La Tène painted pottery from Manching (after Maier, 1970).

White

Red

Natural clay

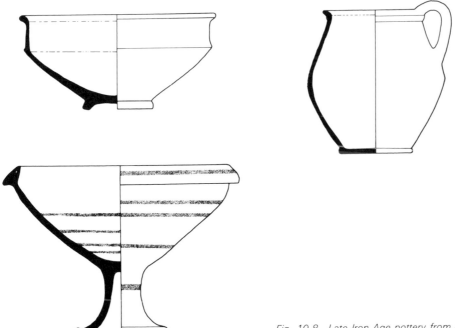

Fig. 10.8 Late Iron Age pottery from eastern Europe.

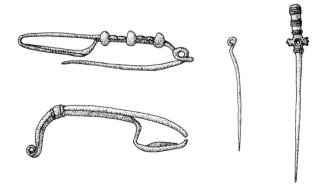

Fig. 10.9 Late Iron Age ornament types from northern Europe, showing survival of local pin types and the adoption of the brooch.

the local pin types; some examples are shown in Fig.10.9.

SUBSISTENCE

The evidence for subsistence activities is once again in most areas very slight, because few settlements have been excavated in a way designed to recover it. The rare studies of animal bone and seed data can, however, be supplemented by pollen analysis from several regions to build up at least a preliminary picture.

The largest sample of bone data is from Manching, where over 400 000 fragments were analysed (Boessneck *et al.*, 1971). Cattle were the most prominent of the domestic species represented, totalling over 40%, followed by pig and sheep. If, however, the ratios of the consumable meat from each of the species are estimated, then cattle must have supplied about 85% of the meat; sheep and pig were comparatively unimportant, both contributing less than horses. At a site further north in an upland location, at Altburg bei Bundenbach near Trier (Schindler, 1977), a similar heavy reliance on cattle is also seen, but there pig played a much more important role and sheep were of little significance; this can be most readily understood in terms of the very different terrain, since pollen analysis suggests that the surrounding hilly country was still somewhat wooded. The interpretation of these figures is difficult, since they cannot be compared with others from contemporary sites of the same or different type. Manching in particular is problematical, in representing a very

special type of large nucleated site with a mainly non-agricultural function (see below); the problem of provisioning such settlements may have demanded special arrangements, and the surviving bone remains cannot, therefore, be taken as typical of all late Iron Age sites.

Seed evidence, mainly from Germany and especially the Rhineland (Körber-Grohne and Piening, 1979, Fig.1; Knörzer, 1976), shows that there were no significant changes in the major species of crops grown. Barley and spelt continued to be the most important grain species, though more rye was being cultivated. Other crops of increasing importance were flax and hemp, grown for their fibres.

The evidence of pollen analysis shows that in several upland areas clearance was continuing and agriculture being pushed to higher altitudes than previously. In the Vosges mountains of eastern France, cereal agriculture is first documented c. 300 BC and expanded until the first century BC (Guillet *et al.*, 1976); much the same pattern is seen in the Jura (Borel, 1976), and high-level clearance is also known from the Austrian Alps. Traces of narrow terraced fields probably of late Iron Age date have been found in many upland areas, including the Vosges in France, the Vogelsberg and Westerwald in central Germany and the Swiss Alps, at heights where agriculture would not now be thought possible (Bradley, 1978a). Although the picture is a very patchy one, it is consistent in suggesting a considerable expansion of clearance, in particular for arable crop raising.

One of the reasons for this expansion may have

been an increasing population, although in the absence of firm data from settlements or cemeteries it is difficult to confirm such an argument. Nevertheless, on the evidence of the classical sources there was extreme population pressure in at least some parts of central and northern Europe from at least the fifth and possibly the sixth century BC. Large groups known historically as Celts or Gauls are recorded as migrating first into Italy and then later in the third century south-eastwards into the Balkans, Greece and ultimately into Asia Minor, where part of them survived as the Celtic-speaking Galatians. Though these migrations are hard to distinguish archaeologically in the pattern of more general diffusion of central European objects and styles, the historical sources are united in ascribing these movements to over-population and a desire for new land for settlement and agriculture (T. Champion, 1980).

There is also some further evidence to be derived from the classical literary sources, for there are references to the export of foodstuffs. Strabo records the export of surplus grain from southern England, and of salted pork from central Europe and cheese and other agricultural by-products from the southeast Alpine area into Italy. In view of the great growth in trade across the Alps in the second and first centuries BC, in which raw materials and foodstuffs must have been major exports, it seems likely that agricultural production would have undergone a change in aim, away from producing simply for local demand towards the production of surpluses for export; it would also have been necessary to supply the large non-agricultural sites that were developing at that time. Expansion, intensification and specialization of agriculture might all be expected, but unfortunately the evidence is as yet too sparse to be able to substantiate such a suggestion, except in the most general way. Expansion certainly occurred, and the number and quality of agricultural tools also rose, but little is known about the detailed organization of agriculture.

PRODUCTION AND EXCHANGE

Towards the end of the first millennium many areas of western, central and eastern Europe witnessed changes of far-reaching importance in the technology and organization of their craft industries, comparable to those that had taken place in the Mediterranean region several centuries before. Though no fundamentally new technologies were introduced, improvements were made in the quality of some products, new tools and equipment were developed, specialization increased, and new levels of industrial organization were reached. Production became more localized, but at the same time more specialized and at a higher technological level, so that new methods of distribution and exchange were also needed. These patterns of internal trade are often difficult to discern, since at the same time there was a trend towards widespread uniformity of style and design, especially in such archaeologically plentiful items as pottery and brooches; without more detailed evidence for the actual centres of production, it is therefore hard to analyse the patterns of distribution. It is clear, however, that major changes were taking place, which in their turn related to changes in the settlement pattern and in the broader economic and social structure.

The introduction of new techniques of production can be seen most clearly in the case of pottery. Though some pots had been made on a wheel from perhaps as early as the sixth century BC in central Europe, in the first century its use became much more common, and wheel-thrown pottery comprised the great majority of the finer wares and a considerable proportion of the entire pottery output (e.g. Pingel, 1971). The adoption of a new piece of production equipment, even a comparatively simple form of wheel, represented a major step in pottery manufacture and probably a new level of specialization. No potter's workshop has survived from the period with evidence of its wheel, but another important innovation of the first century BC is well documented archaeologically, the kiln. These are known from a number of sites such as Gellerthegy-Taban near Budapest, Hungary (Bonis, 1969), and Staré Hradisko, Czechoslovakia (Meduna, 1970); at Sissach, Switzerland, no less than twelve kilns were found (M. Frey, 1935). The site at Gellerthegy-Taban is of particular interest since it was part of a large pottery-working complex, with clay pits nearby.

In other industries the evidence for technical advance is mainly in the form of new tool types. Partly because of the greater number of settlement sites of first century BC date excavated, and partly because of an apparent increase in the ready availability of iron for tools, many more tools of this period are known than of any earlier one. But as well as an increase in their quantity, they also show a much wider range of types and a greater degree of specialization (G. Jacobi, 1974a). Hammers, for instance, were made in different shapes and sizes for different purposes. Carpenter's tools included hammers, files, saws and adzes of various types; wooden products, though only rarely surviving, included lathe-turned cups and bowls, as well as major constructions such as houses, ships and bridges, while the technical superiority of central European wheeled vehicles led to their adoption in the Roman world. A full range of tools was also developed for other industries such as leather and iron; the blacksmith's toolkit now included hammers, pincers, anvils, punches and files.

The growing elaboration and specialization of the toolkits suggests that the craftsmen themselves were also becoming specialists to a greater degree. Greater economic dependence on a developed craft speciality created a new basis for relationships within Iron Age society, and these new identities were sometimes indicated in the grave goods selected for burial with the dead; graves are known where the speciality of the dead was displayed by the inclusion of the tools of his trade, such as a doctor (Navarro, 1955) or a blacksmith (Taus, 1963). Increasing specialization may also have been accompanied by a new pattern of production. Study of small ornament types such as brooches suggests that whereas previously craftsmen were producing to actual demand and perhaps to the precise specification of the customer, and therefore individual objects show extreme diversity, increasingly the products became standardized, with the emphasis on the production of a stock of items to meet anticipated future demand. By the first century BC there was a marked pattern of standardization in certain products, so that, for example, brooches from France and Czechoslovakia might be indistinguishable. In the case of pottery, one individual tradition spread from France to Hungary (Maier, 1970; Kappel, 1969) and another from Hungary to the Black Sea (Collis, 1972), reflecting the increased output of a smaller number of more specialized production centres, and the greater dependence of the different areas on an integrated regional economic system.

Increasing individual specialization was accompanied by increasingly centralized production. The growing demand for iron led to more intensive exploitation of the larger and richer ore deposits, and easy access to these ores was an important factor in the location and development of some major late Iron Age settlements. In southern Germany sites such as Manching (see below) and Kelheim (F.-R. Hermann, 1975) were located near to extensive and easily worked iron ores, while many of the major centres of Czechoslovakia, such as Třisov (Břeň, 1966) and Staré Hradisko (Meduna, 1970) and Hengistbury Head (Cunliffe, 1978b) in southern England were similarly sited. The area known to the Romans as Noricum, in modern Austria, was famed for its iron products, as the evidence from its most important trading centre at the Magdalensberg bears out (Alföldy, 1974, pp. 62-75). Excavation has revealed extensive traces of iron working, including slag and furnaces, and the products were of a regularly high quality. Inscriptions tell of the complicated financial arrangements involved in the trade, including loans and credit, and of the origins of the traders who came to the site from the Roman world, especially from Italy but also from as far afield as north Africa. Another region with especially valuable iron deposits was the Holy Cross Mountain area of southern Poland, where many large smelting centres developed by the end of the first millennium (Bielenin, 1964). They did not introduce any particular technical improvement, but in the scale of their operation they represented a new level of economic complexity.

In the case of iron, smelting operations were concentrated on the ore deposits themselves in view of the difficulty of transporting the bulky ores any great distance. So too with another industry, salt, the location of the industrial development was determined by the occurrence of the deposits, and major production centres grew up on the coasts of western France and eastern England (de Brisay and Evans, 1975) and around Bad Nauheim (Jorns, 1960), to exploit marine and terrestrial salt respectively. With pottery, however, considerations were rather different. For many classes of pots suitable clay was widely available, and the fragile nature of the finished product demanded that production was sited near to the centres of demand. Hence, as the evidence of the kilns shows, pottery production tended to concentrate in or near to the largest settlements.

For some purposes, however, special clays were sought out. A graphite-rich clay was in particular demand for its heat resistant qualities (Kappel, 1969) and the two main sources of such clay, at Passau in Bavaria and Ceské Budĕjovice in Czechoslovakia, were both exploited. The products of the two sources can be distinguished, and there were probably two or three main production centres using clay from Passau. The raw clay was transported as far west as Manching in southern Germany, though pots made from it there reached even further afield (Fig.10.10).

The corollary of increased specialization and centralization of production was a more complex system of distribution. The archaeological evidence for this is very largely in the pattern of finished artifacts from known production centres, but there are also other signs of the increasing importance of exchange in the economy. In particular, systems of weights were in use, and two such systems based on units or 'pounds' of 309 and 638 grammes were common throughout western Europe in pre-Roman and Roman times (Schwarz, 1964). Balances, scale-pans and actual weights survive, though the known examples were mostly for weighing small amounts, possibly precious metals. Larger stone weights are known, however, from southern England for bulkier commodities, possibly grain. Other goods were also produced to standard sizes, especially iron ingots

(Allen, 1967; Mariën, 1970, pp.125–29); though different forms are known from different regions, such as double pyramidal ones in central Europe and sword-shaped ones in England (Fig.10.11), within each region, the ingots were remarkably uniform in size, shape and weight.

One special case of standardized units of weight was coinage (Allen, 1980). During the third century BC coins came into widespread use throughout Europe from France to Rumania, originally copying Mediterranean prototypes, especially those of Philip II and Alexander the Great of Macedonia. The earliest issues were entirely of large denomination coins, in the east of silver and in the west of gold. They represented a standard unit of wealth which was accepted as such without the need for weighing, but they were of too high a value to have been used like modern coins for everyday commercial transactions, and must have had some other function (Allen, 1976) (see below). From early in the first century BC, however, new coin types of much lower value were being minted, in silver as fractions of the larger values, or in bronze or potin, a tin–bronze alloy with a very high proportion of tin. In eastern Europe, copies of the Roman bronze denarius may have served the same purpose. These new small denomination coins are found especially in central France and to a lesser extent Germany and other areas of central Europe;

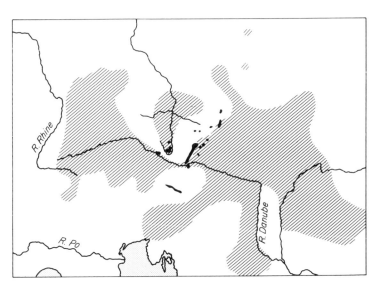

Fig. 10.10 Distribution of graphite pottery in central Europe in the late La Tène period (after Kappel, 1969).

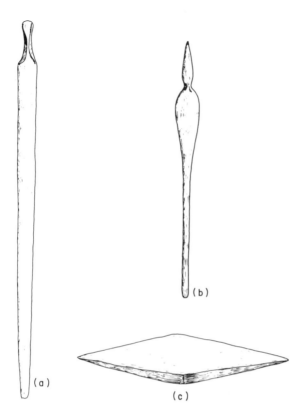

(b)

(c)

Fig. 10.11   Iron ingots (a) British sword-shaped type; (b) north-west European Wartburg type; (c) central European double pyramidal type (after Allen, 1967 and Marien, 1970).

by the end of the first century BC they were also in common use in southern England. They are found particularly on the large and developing urban sites of the period in these areas, and also on sites whose main function was as temples, but which may have also been the location for periodic markets or fairs. These sites were the centres for a new and more complex form of economy in which the surrounding areas took little part. Whether or not these coins can be taken to indicate the origin of a market economy in the sense of free exchange in which the relative values of commodities are fixed by laws of supply and demand divorced from any social control, they clearly represent an innovation which served to meet the need for a common medium of exchange to facilitate an unprecedented complexity of transactions. This was necessary not only because of the increasing specialization in food production and craft industries, but also because of renewed trade links with the expanding urban markets of the Mediterranean world.

Trade with Greece and Italy had reached an apparent peak in the sixth and fifth centuries BC, and thereafter declined, at least as far as western and central Europe were concerned; in eastern Europe, however, there seems to have been a steady flow of Greek material through the colonies of the Black Sea coast into the hinterland (Glodariu, 1976). Towards the end of the millennium this trade began once again to grow as the Roman world with its towns, markets and enormous demand for manpower and raw materials expanded. From the third century in eastern Europe and from the mid-second further to the west, Mediterranean goods again flowed into temperate Europe. Fine pottery, bronze and silver cups, jugs and strainers for serving wine (Werner, 1954) and the wine itself in amphorae (Peacock, 1971), the universal pottery storage vessels of the

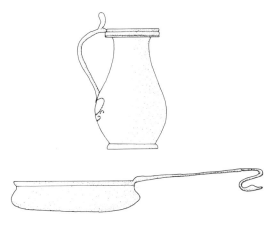

Fig. 10.12   Roman bronze jug and patera: such vessels connected with the serving of wine were frequently traded beyond the borders of the early Roman empire.

Mediterranean world, were traded northwards in increasing numbers (Fig.10.12).

The circumstances in which these luxury imports are found are totally different from those that prevailed in the earlier period. Instead of the rich graves and the aristocratic residences to which the imports had previously been confined, they are now found predominantly in the major settlements which formed the centres of the local economy and society. Especially in central France the imports are densely concentrated on the largest settlements (Peacock, 1971), but the same pattern can be seen from Rumania to southern England. Only in one area on the northern fringe of this zone is this pattern altered, for in northern France and south-eastern England in the period from *c.* 50 BC to AD 50 these imports also occur in rich graves, such as those from Goeblingen-Nospelt, Luxemburg (Thill, 1966, 1967), and Welwyn Garden City, England (Stead, 1967). These graves are remarkably similar in their wealth and imported goods to those of the sixth and fifth centuries in central Europe, and suggest that in this area at least trade to the south was still firmly in the control of an aristocratic elite (Fig.10.13).

SETTLEMENT

The new patterns of production and exchange were matched by new patterns of settlement (Collis, 1975).

From southern England to Rumania new types of site appear towards the end of the first millennium, and in the sites chosen for their development they frequently show a new location strategy. To the Romans, and especially to Julius Caesar who conquered France around 50 BC and saw these sites at first hand, it was natural to refer to them as *oppida* (Latin *oppidum* = town), and indeed they have many of the characteristics that we would expect of a town. They were comparatively large nucleated centres of a permanent population, and the archaeological evidence demonstrates that they were engaged in craft production far beyond their own immediate needs, producing goods to exchange for food from elsewhere. They were frequently defended with massive walls and gateways, and form the top level of a new settlement hierarchy; Caesar describes the settlement of the Helvetii of Switzerland as consisting of towns, villages and individual houses. They were centres of exchange, both long-distance and short-distance; they show the greatest concentration of imports from the Mediterranean world such as wine amphorae, and they were also the sites where the new low-denomination coinage introduced in the first century BC was particularly used to facilitate exchange.

The sites chosen show a distinct preference for locations on or near to trade routes and good lines of communication such as major river valleys and estuaries, and to important sources of raw materials. Good potting clay, gold and, perhaps most important of all, iron ore, all attracted settlements to exploit them (Kruta, 1975, pp. 100). The range of industries seen on these sites is very wide (Jacobi, 1974a; Wyss, 1974; Collis, 1976, pp.10–12). Smelting and forging of iron is particularly common, but other metals, especially bronze, were also worked; everyday domestic items and tools were produced in quantity, but so too was personal jewellery and on some sites also coins. Enamel, glass (Haevernick, 1960) and amber imported from northern Europe (Beck *et al.*, 1978) were turned into ornaments. Carpentry, leather-working and potting were also of great importance.

The precise form of these sites and their preferred locations vary considerably from region to region, but throughout central and western Europe their function as local centres of production and exchange

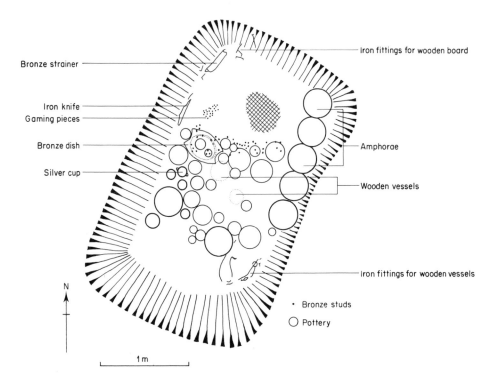

Bronze strainer

Iron fittings for wooden board

Iron knife

Gaming pieces

Bronze dish

Silver cup

Amphorae

Wooden vessels

Iron fittings for wooden vessels

N

• Bronze studs

○ Pottery

1 m

Fig. 10.13   Late La Tène burial from Welwyn Garden City, England (after Stead, 1967).

is broadly constant. Many of the sites are as yet unexcavated, and many others known in detail only from old excavations; extensive modern excavation is still a rarity, and hence those few sites where such work has taken place are of particular importance. Of these, the site of Manching in southern Germany is the key to the understanding of this phase of urban development (see box).

Manching clearly had many of the characteristics that would be associated with a town: the physical form of a large and permanently occupied concentration of population, with a planned and well-maintained internal layout, standardized types of buildings and zoning of activities; an economic function as a centre of non-agricultural production; and a role as a focus of local and distant exchange. Manching is, moreover, unique in the extent of its excavation and in the opportunity it offers to see the growth of such a site through time. At other sites, the limited excavation (if any) that has taken place

seldom allows the earlier phases of such a development to be seen.

Nevertheless, there is some evidence to suggest that the sequence at Manching can be matched at other sites elsewhere in a region from central France to Switzerland and southern Gemany. Large open sites of a similar nature are known at Breisach and Basel on the upper Rhine, at Bern in Switzerland and at Aulnat in France, during the course of the second century BC (Collis, 1976, pp.5–8, 1980). The development of fortified sites, the *oppida* of the first century BC, was only a secondary phenomenon; at some sites, such as Manching, defences were built around the open site, but elsewhere a shift in settlement took place and occupation moved to higher and more defensible locations. Aulnat, for instance, was abandoned and the neighbouring hilltops became the sites for occupation in the first century BC.

To the east of this region, a similar pattern of settlement was emerging in Czechoslovakia (Břeň,

1976), but there the new centres of urban occupation grew up on defended hilltops from the start. Excavation at Staré Hradisko has shown regular stone buildings aligned along the roughly rectangular grid of streets, and industrial production including the working of iron, glass and imported amber; coins were also minted. Occupation certainly began no later than the second century BC, as it also did at two other important sites further west at Stradonice and Hrazany (Jansová, 1965); the latter had cobbled streets flanked by courtyard houses, and produced evidence of iron and bronze working. Despite the difference in location, these sites all fulfilled identical functions as centres of non-agricultural population, production and exchange.

Though the best known examples of this new type of settlement are found in the belt from central France through Germany and Switzerland to Bohemia, similar sites are also known from a wider area to the north, in northern France, the Rhineland and central Germany. The same phenomenon is also found in England; though the chronology is not clear, sites performing similar functions, though taking a variety of actual forms, had certainly emerged, by the later part of the first century BC (Cunliffe, 1978a, pp.243–86). In eastern England large open sites developed, while in the south certain of the hilltop defended sites that had been founded in great numbers earlier in the millennium developed as centres of social and economic organization, while others faded. By the first century BC these sites, such as Maiden Castle (Fig.10.14) (Wheeler, 1943) and Danebury (Cunliffe, 1981), were massively defended and densely occupied. In addition to their role in production and exchange, some of these sites have also produced evidence of temples, a type of structure hitherto unknown. They suggest not only a further role for these sites as centres of religious organization, but also a new form of religion or ritual and a new importance for that religion in the social changes that were taking place.

In south-eastern England, however, a different pattern was emerging, of sites in river valleys or at river mouths. The locations were clearly chosen for

Fig. 10.14   Maiden Castle, Dorset, England: the defences of the hillfort were the result of several phases of enlargement.

MANCHING

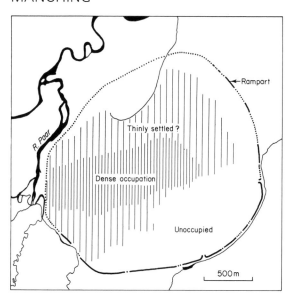

1. Extent of settlement in Manching in the first century BC (after Krämer and Schubert, 1970).

Manching lies at the junction of two rivers, the Danube and the Paar; the former is the major east–west route through central Europe and the latter gives easy access southwards to the Alpine passes. The surrounding land is not of high quality agriculturally, but provides reasonable pasture and has plentiful iron ore. The site was therefore chosen for its resources and communications, and occupation began certainly by about 200 BC and perhaps somewhat earlier (Krämer and Schubert, 1970). At first the area of occupation was small and undefended, but by the end of the second century it had grown considerably and was provided with walls. The defences were a massive operation, involving the diversion of a stream and the construction of seven kilometres of wall and four gates; excavation suggests that the entire system was rebuilt at least once throughout its entire length, and more frequently in places. The construction involved massive quantities of timber and nails, and stone was brought in from considerable distances to face part of the walls and to pave the gateways. The eastern entrance had a double carriageway for wheeled vehicles and a narrow passage for pedestrians on either side.

The internal occupation had already expanded to a considerable extent in the second century while the site was still undefended, and it grew even further during the first century. Some areas within the defences were apparently never built up, but may have been used for agricultural purposes, and the densest occupation was always at the centre of the site. In all, 200 hectares was occupied.

From the beginning, there were clear signs of a planned organization of the settlement. Streets up to ten metres wide were laid out and kept open with very little encroachment throughout the life of the site. In some areas, these streets were fronted by regular rows of rectangular timber buildings, behind which were zones given over entirely to pits. In some areas, large palisaded enclosures were found and it is suggested that these were agricultural in function; some contained large wooden structures interpreted as granaries. In one place there was evidence for the stalling of horses kept for transport.

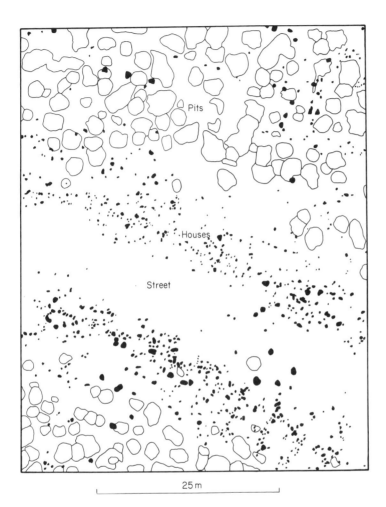

2. *Planned settlement within Manching: houses are aligned along roads, with pit and working areas behind (after Krämer and Schubert, 1970).*

Many different industries were practised at Manching, and from the limited evidence of the excavations there seems to have been some degree of zoning of craft specialities. One area was mainly inhabited by wood-workers and leather-workers, while another was the centre of iron-working. Glass rings and bracelets were manufactured, and pottery must also have been made somewhere on or near the site. Coins were certainly minted and widely used.

ease of communication, and many were succeeded without interruption by Roman, mediaeval and modern towns. Camulodunum, the first capital of Roman Britain and the predecessor of Colchester, is known historically to have been also the most important site in pre-conquest times and the centre of the local king (Hawkes and Hull, 1947; Rodwell, 1976, pp.339–59). The site was at the mouth of a river and heavily defended by earthworks, and contained an industrial area, a royal residence and a temple complex (Fig.10.15) (Crummy, 1980, pp.258–64). Such sites as this, like those on the continent, were centres of the long distance trade to the Mediterranean and of the local money-using exchange system.

In eastern Europe, from Hungary and eastern Czechoslovakia to the Black Sea, sites of similar status and function took a rather different form.

Hilltop locations, many of them used earlier, were chosen and heavily defended (Petres, 1975); in Rumania they have the appearance of small fortresses. Less is known about other features of these sites, but occupation was focused on terraces below these fortified citadels; the site of Gellerthegy-Taban, already mentioned for its pottery-making quarter, is one example. Sometimes the sites also have sanctuaries attached. The most important of the Rumanian sites is Gradistea Muncelului, the ancient Sarmizegethusa, which extended for about 3km over many terraces (Daicoviciu and Daicoviciu, 1963). The core of the site was the defended enclosure, joined by a paved road to the sanctuary complex; below this there was much evidence for large-scale industrial production, including iron, bronze and pottery.

All the sites described above were of local inspiration and derivation, but further south in the

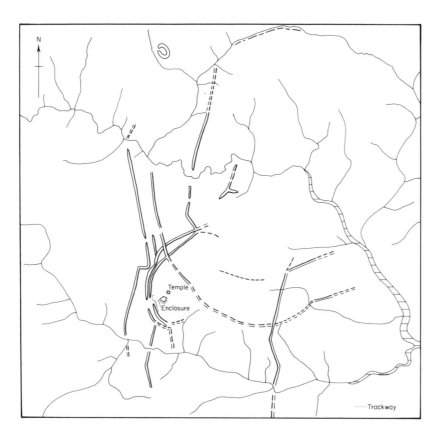

Fig. 10.15 Colchester, showing late Iron Age dyke system and some internal features (after Rodwell, 1976 and Crummy, 1980).

Balkans on the northern fringe of the Greek world other types of settlement were being founded. The first towns had, of course, been the northern Greek colonies at the head of the Aegean and in the Black Sea, and more foundations followed in the wake of the Macedonian expansion northwards in the fourth century, as a symbol of their conquest and as a means of governing the new territories. The towns survived after the collapse of the short-lived Macedonian empire, and inspired local imitation. The site of Seuthopolis in Bulgaria (Dimitrov and Čičikova, 1978), founded by the Thracian Seuthes at the end of the fourth century, copied Greek styles of planning and architecture for its defences and houses, but was not the equivalent of a Greek town in its function. It was, in fact, the seat of a powerful local ruler and his court, with a fortified residence for the chief, which included an important sanctuary, and grand houses for his immediate followers; unlike a town, it did not have a role as a producer of non-agricultural goods.

This discussion of settlements has concentrated on the sites at the top of the settlement hierarchy, partly because these are the most important in the new pattern of human settlement, but also because very little is yet known about the contemporary sites of lower status. It would be reasonable to suppose that the enormous changes in production and exchange taking place at this time would affect the function and location of rural settlements, and although there is some evidence to support this conclusion, it is very difficult to describe the nature of these developments in any detail.

SOCIAL ORGANIZATION: THE EMERGENCE OF THE STATE

The changes described above in agriculture, craft production, exchange and settlement were accompanied by far-reaching changes in social and political organization, and by the first century early forms of the state had emerged in many areas of Europe. The precise form taken by these emerging polities varied considerably from region to region, but our understanding of them is made easier by the availability of a written historical record from the classical world.

This record is best for those peoples of central and western Europe known to the Greek and Roman writers as the Celts (Fischer, 1972), and from it a picture can be built up of their social institutions and how they developed during the second half of the first millennium. Celtic society (Tierney, 1960; Nash, 1976b) was divided into three main classes, the nobles, the druids and the mass of common people. The nobles were the dominant political and military group, and the focus of all effective power within the society. Though groups of nobles might recognize a common tribal identity or acknowledge the superior status of a particular noble or dynasty of nobles, and though they might meet together in warrior assemblies, that did not amount to effective centralized control, and, in the period before the second century BC, there are few signs of the institutions of central coercive power in Celtic society. The individual nobles were greatly concerned to maintain their status by demonstrations of wealth and power, through eloquence, feats of physical strength and bravery, and by lavish generosity of gifts and hospitality. The druids (Piggott, 1975a), though later remembered mostly as mere magicians or mystics, were an important element in this social and political structure; they were the learned class, and included prophets and bards as well as priests. Of equal importance was their function as the guardians and interpreters of customary law. Through the ideology of Celtic society expressed in religious and bardic ceremonies, and through their interpretation of the laws and customs, they played an important part in the perpetuation of the position of the nobles; they enjoyed in return immunity from tribute and military service, and through their freedom to travel widely helped to establish a considerable homogeneity in western Europe.

The third and naturally most numerous class, the common people, attracted less attention from the classical writers, who generally portrayed them as reduced to near-servility. One of the most important institutions in Celtic society was the patron–client relationship which bound the nobles and the common people. The patron offered to his clients protection against violence and a guarantee of subsistence at times of economic hardship, while in return the client offered tribute, esteem, political support and service in a military retinue. Political power rested with the nobles and was exercised by the maintenance of such clients and retinues; a noble's status could be calculated by the size of the retinue that he could mobilize. Competition took place between nobles to increase the number of their clients and thus to improve their status through lavish generosity, better offers of protection or even violent aggression.

Celtic society was thus aristocratic, competitive and originally lacking in central institutions. Though other areas of Europe are less well documented, if at all, broadly similar forms of social organization may have prevailed. The particular institution of clientage is indeed well known elsewhere, among the Germans of northern Europe and the Thracians in particular, and may have been a general feature of European society.

By the beginning of the second century at the latest, however, more centralized political units had begun to appear, under monarchical rule. Some such kingdoms are known from earlier periods, especially in south-eastern Europe. Mention has already been made in a previous chapter of Macedonia, which achieved a centrally organized kingdom in the fifth century and expanded rapidly in the fourth, before declining into fragmentation. The short-lived state of the Thracian Seuthes at the end of the fourth century has also been mentioned. Kingship later seems to have become the prevailing political institution throughout much of central and western Europe. Among the Arverni of central France, for example, a strong centralized and hereditary monarchy had been established by the middle of the second century, and had ambitions to extend the area of its dominance (Nash, 1976a, 1978). In south-eastern England, local dynasties had emerged by the end of the first century BC, whose leaders exercised full political and military control from such elaborate centres as Colchester (see above), and minted coins on which they styled themselves 'king' (Cunliffe, 1978a, pp.67–114). Some of these kingdoms, such as the successive states of the Thracians in Bulgaria and the Dacians in Rumania, hardly survived as effective centralized authorities beyond the death of their respective founders, but others were more stable. Noricum, for instance, in modern Austria, which had been founded by the early second century, survived until its incorporation into the Roman empire around 15 BC (Alföldy, 1974).

These kingdoms were a form of state, with centralized authority, a hierarchical structure and a specialized ruling elite. This elite comprised the king himself and his immediate retinue of companions; supreme power rested with the king, and the companions were his political and military lieutenants, in a relationship not unlike clientage. The king's position could be reinforced by increasing the returns of spoils and power to his companions, and hence such kingdoms could be aggressively militaristic, as most spectacularly in the case of Macedonia. Much, however, depended on the ability of the individual king to keep the system together; there were few safeguards against challenge from within the companions, and kingdoms were particularly vulnerable at the death of a strong king. Thus, although they could expand rapidly, they could also collapse rapidly.

Kingdoms survived in some areas until the end of the first millennium and the Roman conquest, but by the end of the second century a different pattern was beginning to take its place in parts of western Europe, in particular central France and Switzerland (Nash, 1978). In this region a new structure of centralized institutions was developed. Political and military power still rested firmly with the nobles, but it was now exercised through a system of laws, a council and magistrates. Among the Aedui, for example, the chief magistrate, the *Vergobretos*, was the most powerful individual, but his power was qualified; he was elected according to known laws for one year only, there were strict limitations on what he could do in office, and detailed safeguards against the possibility of establishing a dominant position for himself or his family. Thus the king and his companions were replaced by a council and magistrates. The new institutions offered increased stability; in return for excluding the possibility of a single individual holding power personally, control was retained in the hands of the nobility as a whole, and each individual had the opportunity to exercise it, albeit in a qualified manner and for a limited period, through the rotation of office.

By the first century, a network of societies with elements of such a centralized and institutionalized system of government existed from western France to Switzerland (Fig.10.16). This system can be compared in general terms to that evolved some centuries earlier in the Mediterranean world, but it differed considerably from the classical Greek city-state or *polis*; there was not the same focus on a

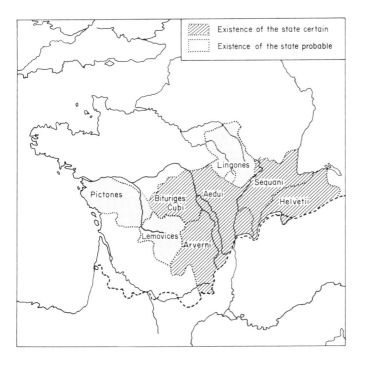

Existence of the state certain

Existence of the state probable

Fig. 10.16   Extent of the civitas form of early state organization in France (after Nash, 1978).

single city—indeed, many of these late Iron Age states in France seem to have had several towns of more or less equal status—and the concept of an exclusive citizenship was not developed at all. Nevertheless to Caesar, who saw and conquered this region of France, it was natural to describe such a system of government as a *civitas*, a term restricted to a society with a state organization.

A full account of the explanation of the emergence of these various forms of complex sociopolitical organization cannot yet be given, not least because of the limitations of the archaeological evidence and the poverty of information concerning such matters as economy and settlement system. It seems clear, however, that it was the result of a combination of internal and external processes. Internally, it is reasonable to assume, from the evidence currently available, that the population was growing, perhaps rapidly, and it is certain, as has been described above, that social and economic organization was becoming much more complex, with agricultural expansion, innovation and intensification, growth of craft specialization and the development of new production and exchange methods. As in the case of

the comparable development in the Mediterranean region described in Chapter 8, the role of population increase and the need for adequate managerial control of a more complex economy were no doubt important factors, but the aggressively competitive nature of Iron Age society was fundamental in stimulating this growth in pursuit of power.

External relations were also important, and may, indeed, have played a part in promoting these internal developments, for exchange with the Mediterranean world again had a profound effect on society to the north. In eastern Europe, constant contact through the Greek colonies in the north Aegean and the Black Sea (Glodariu, 1976) provided opportunities for the local nobility to demonstrate and enhance their position through control of the luxuries imported from Greece, but it also led to competition for the control of the local resources for export. Similarly in the west, after a period of little apparent contact, renewed Roman expansion in the late second century BC into the south of France provided new opportunities for exchange. The exports sent south included not only locally available raw materials, but also manpower, in the form of mercenaries for the armies of the Greek world, and later, after the subjugation of the Mediterranean world by Rome, slaves to support the Roman economy. Readjustment to provide these commodities, and competition to control their provision, were important factors in shaping society in the late Iron Age.

As well as providing for the basic economic needs of Mediterranean society, exchange was a symbol of wider political relationships, which could also take other forms. The expansionist aims of the Athenian empire in the fifth century, the Macedonian in the fourth, and the Roman in the second and first centuries played an important part in stimulating the centralization of power in temperate Europe, either to coordinate resistance or to enforce a policy of cooperation.

It was a combination of these various factors that led to the emergence of larger and more complex political groupings towards the end of the first millennium. The opportunities provided by exchange with the Mediterranean world, the necessity of developing political relations with it, the growing complexity of local social organization and the competitiveness of the noble elite produced a period of social change which culminated in two rather different results. In both cases power was firmly held by the nobles but in eastern Europe it was exercised supremely by a single individual, the king, with the support of his retinue of companions, while in western Europe it was exercised by the nobles as a group in a system designed to deny the chance of total domination by any single individual.

The centralization of power in this way into larger groupings was accompanied by more complex institutions of political organization. Coinage in particular played an important part, and its adoption and development clearly coincided with this phase of growth. Among the Thracians, for instance, the first coins appeared at the time of political centralization under Seuthes at the end of the fourth century BC, while further west coins became more standardized and more common with the growth of the early states from the late second century onwards (Nash, 1976a). As in the Mediterranean region, these early coin issues were all of large denominations and not for ordinary commercial use; they are rather a sign of the increasing role of the central political authority and were designed to facilitate such exchanges as payment by the state for military service and of tax

and tribute to the state (Allen, 1976). Literacy too was an important innovation, but only for limited bureaucratic and ceremonial purposes. Little now survives except for occasional inscriptions on coins and monuments, but the use of writing implements, wax tablets (G. Jacobi, 1974b) and papyrus (Wild, 1966) can all be documented. What they were used for is shown by Caesar's discovery in the baggage of the defeated Helvetii in 59 BC of written records of their population strength. Such details of population, production and tribute would have been essential to the new centralized political powers.

One of the characteristics of such early states is the construction of monumental buildings to symbolize the new political identity. In western Europe, however, no buildings of this sort are known, though this may be only the result of the very limited excavation that has taken place on sites of this period. The picture is very different in eastern Europe where new political groups were regularly marked by new programmes of building. The consolidation of the Macedonian state was symbolized by the construction of new cities in the current Greek style, as also was its rapid expansion northwards and eastwards; sites such as Philippopolis (Plovdiv in Bulgaria) symbolized not only Macedonian conquest, but in particular the power of their king, Philip. Similarly, the Thracian Seuthes celebrated the foundation of his short-lived state at the end of the fourth century by the building of Seuthopolis, aping Greek and Macedonian fashions in both architecture and nomenclature (Fig.10.17); as shown above, however, the site was not a town, but a fortified royal residence and sanctuary. In the first century BC, the Dacian state founded by Burebistas was also characterized by monumental building (Daicoviciu, 1972). Many of the major settlements were located at the foot of hills crowned by citadels with massive stone defences, and at the major ones religious sanctuaries were also built; the sanctuary area at Sarmizegethusa (Fig.10.18) was the largest and most important and contained several separate buildings and shrines.

This emphasis on sanctuaries and religion underlines another important feature of these early states, the use of ideology to project and promote the new political order, for their foundation is regularly accompanied by the appearance of new forms of ritual practice. The new sanctuaries associated with the Thracian and Dacian states have already been

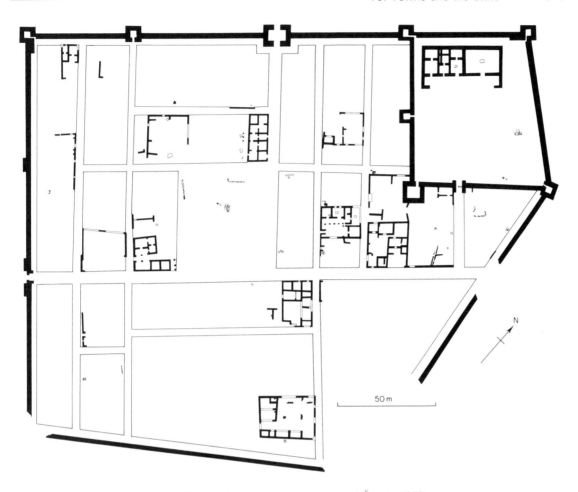

Fig. 10.17   Seuthopolis (after Dimitrov and Čičikova, 1978).

mentioned, and there is a similar phenomenon in western Europe. From central France eastwards to southern Germany and Bohemia, a new form of rural sanctuary, comprising a square ditched enclosure (*Viereckschanze*) with shafts containing votive deposits (Planck, 1982), appeared in the first century BC at the same time as the early states were developing (Fig.10.19). In southern England too the centres of political power, such as Colchester (Crummy, 1980), contained the first recognizable temples (Fig.10.20).

This ideological underpinning of society also found expression in the prevailing burial rites. In eastern Europe the position of the nobles was demonstrated by a continuing series of rich burials, distinguished not only by the wealth of the grave goods deposited in them, but also by new and exotic architectural styles. In Bulgaria *tholos* tombs which were sometimes in stone, sometimes in sun-dried brick, were built, and in a cemetery near Seuthopolis, at Kazanluk, the corbelled roof of such a tomb was painted with scenes of a funerary banquet (Jivkova, 1974). This series of rich aristocratic burials reaches its peak in the royal cemetery of the Macedonians at Vergina in northern Greece, where the most powerful dynasty of prehistoric Europe was fittingly commemorated with some of its richest burials (Andronikos, 1980).

The burial tradition of central and western Europe in this period is rather better known, and has formed one of the main themes of Iron Age studies for the

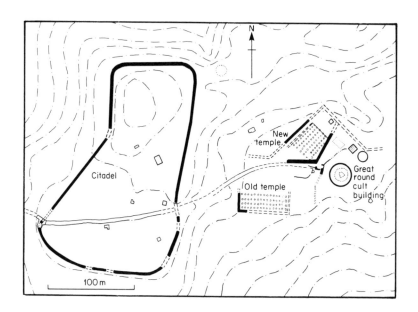

Fig. 10.18   The main sanctuary area at Sarmizegethusa.

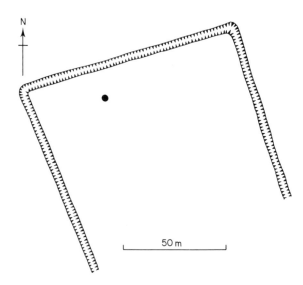

Fig. 10.19   Late Iron Age ritual enclosure, Viereckschanze,
at Fellbach-Schmieden, West Germany, showing shaft in
which votive deposits were made (after Planck, 1982).

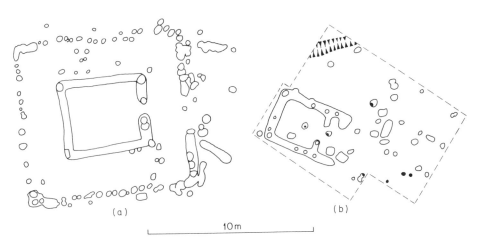

Fig. 10.20   Iron Age temple plans in Britain: (a) Heathrow (after Grimes); (b) South Cadbury (after Alcock).

last century. The rich burials described in the last chapter had disappeared by the early fourth century, but the cemeteries continued to reflect social distinctions. Differences of age and sex were important for the choice of grave goods, but so also were differences in status; men of higher status were accompanied by weapons, particularly sword and shield, and women by a variety of ornament types which varied considerably from region to region. Increasingly, though, new forms of social identity were symbolized in the graves, particularly that of craftsmen. In the first century BC, however, this burial tradition disappears and no new regular rite is found in its place. This does not, of course, imply that burial was no longer a matter of concern or that social distinctions were not expressed in funerary rituals, whatever form they took, but only that the established forms of displaying such distinctions were now abandoned. A new, and so far unknown, rite was adopted to accompany the new social order that was emerging in the early states.

In an area to the north, in north-eastern France and the Rhineland, burial rites changed in a different way, for from the second century BC onwards inhumation increasingly gave way to cremation, and by the end of the first century this new rite had also been adopted in south-eastern England (Collis, 1977). This was also the area in which sociopolitical developments took a different form from the institutionalized

structures of the early states of central France and Switzerland, with the survival of kingdoms. This difference was reflected in the different burial traditions, for the cremation practice also included those rich burials mentioned above, such as those from Goeblingen-Nospelt in Luxemburg and the Welwyn group in south-eastern England, in which the status of the noble was again asserted by the deposition of luxury imports from the Mediterranean and the equipment for feasting and drinking. In south-eastern England the new burial rite was clearly adopted at the same time as the emergence of centralized political powers and the pattern was probably similar on the continent. In this area, too, therefore, changes in ritual and ideology accompanied changes in social and political organization.

NORTHERN EUROPE IN THE IRON AGE

The changes described above, which in the course of the later part of the first millennium fundamentally changed the economy, settlement pattern and, above all, the social and political organization of much of Europe from France to the Black Sea, left untouched a broad zone to the north. Society and economy in this area were not totally static, but the changes that did take place were more akin to those described in

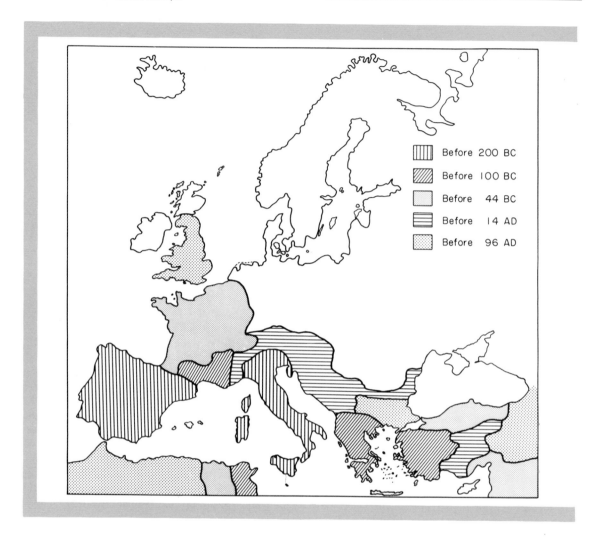

Before 200 BC
Before 100 BC
Before 44 BC
Before 14 AD
Before 96 AD

the previous chapter, that had occurred in the region to the south in the late second and early first millennia, and were largely similar responses to similar crises and opportunities.

By the middle of the first millennium BC the agricultural subsistence economy of northern Europe was under pressure from two different threats. In the first place, climatic deterioration was beginning to make agricultural production, at worst, impossible and, at best, more uncertain. Cooler, wetter summers and colder winters reduced the

growing seasons for crops and restricted the area in which they could be cultivated successfully; in the better climate of the earlier part of the millennium the agricultural frontier had been pushed far to the north in Scandinavia, but some of these northern areas now had to be abandoned for farming purposes. The second threat came from the falling yields of agricultural crops, due to the impoverishment of the soils through millennia of human exploitation. Already before 500 BC some of the poorer soils were being exhausted, and in Denmark, for instance, there

THE EXPANSION OF THE ROMAN EMPIRE IN EUROPE

By the beginning of the third century BC Rome had established control over much of peninsular Italy and was ready to embark on a period of wider territorial expansion. Defeat of the Carthaginian empire in the later third century led to the annexation of regions formerly under Carthaginian domination, and the beginnings of expansion into the western Mediterranean. Sicily was incorporated as a province in 241 BC, Sardinia and Corsica in 238 and Spain, except for the northwestern part, in 197 as two separate provinces. During the later third and early second centuries Rome conducted further military campaigns in northern Italy, the Po valley and the foothills of the Alps, and after final victory in 181 BC this area became the province of Cisalpine Gaul. From the mid-second century BC Rome was increasingly involved in the affairs of southern France, and with the foundation of a colony at Narbo (Narbonne) in 118, this area too became a province. Meanwhile, in the east, Greece and the coast of Yugoslavia became the provinces of Achaea, Macedonia and Illyria in 146 BC, and western Asia Minor was annexed in 133 BC.

Julius Caesar completed the conquest of France in the 50s BC, and under Augustus (33 BC–AD 14) more areas were added; north-western Spain was secured, and the northern frontier of the empire established along the Danube, thus taking in modern Switzerland, southern Germany, Austria, Hungary and Bulgaria. An attempt to advance from the Rhine further east across Germany ended in disastrous defeat in AD 9, and the conquest of England, Wales and southern Scotland took forty years form AD 43. Though there was some further expansion in Europe in the second century AD, in south-western Germany and Romania, the northern frontier had largely been established by the early first century.

The limits of the empire, therefore, corresponded approximately to the limits of the social development in prehistoric Europe towards early forms of the state and urban patterns of settlement and economy. Indeed, conquest was easiest where these developments were furthest advanced at the time of invasion, as in central France or south-eastern England, and hardest where they had scarcely begun, for example, in north-western Spain, Brittany or northern Britain.

are signs of settlement clustering on the better and more productive soils (Kristiansen, 1981).

Possible responses to these threats were limited. Expansion of agriculture was no longer possible, since the geographical and ecological limits of such an economy had been reached, and the frontier was indeed retreating in the face of deteriorating climate. Short of actual migration, intensification of agricultural effort to produce more from the same area was the only option, and this was attempted in a number of ways. Declining crop yields were countered by greater use of manuring, and more regular use of livestock for this purpose. About 500 BC field systems appear in a number of regions of northern Europe, including Holland (Brongers, 1976), Denmark (Müller-Wille, 1965) and Sweden; on Gotland, off the east coast of Sweden, extensive systems of this date have been traced, which were apparently laid out using a standard measure (Lindquist, 1974). Such fields would have served to concentrate the animals and hence control the manuring of specific areas. Animals were also increasingly stalled to provide a supply of manure, but this in turn necessitated the provision of fodder, especially for the winter, and hence the development of grass meadows for hay. The relationships became crops and animals became increasingly complex, and, especially in view of the greater intensity of land use, needed careful management.

Other innovations also occurred. New crops were introduced, especially rye, which is resistant to cold, wet winters, and became increasingly important. New installations are also found, such as wells to provide water for cattle. Soils which had hitherto been largely ignored were exploited, such as the clays and marshes of Holland (Waterbolk, 1965).

These new practices helped to restore the productivity of agriculture, but were clearly not a permanent solution. At the end of the second century BC a large horde of emigrants from north Germany and Denmark, known to the Romans as the Cimbri and the Teutones, wandered in western and central Europe for several years, and made repeated attempts to settle, before being defeated by the Romans, to whom they posed a considerable threat. The cause of their migration was the precarious balance of subsistence in the north, though possibly by this period marine transgression, the raising of sea level to innundate coastal areas, may have further compounded the problem. From the first century BC onwards, throughout the first millennium AD, there were constant attempts to maintain the balance between population and production by successive reorganizations of the agrarian landscape, and to ensure more intensive use of the land by increased efforts to farm the poorer soils and by other phases of emigration.

As in temperate Europe to the south, developments in subsistence were linked to those in technology. Iron working in particular grew rapidly in technical competence and scale of output from 500 BC onwards, using the wide-spread and easily available ores of the region. The greatly increased labour expended on agriculture, in constructing fields, new buildings and new installations, working new soils and transporting produce, fodder and manure, was aided by the use of new and improved tools of iron. This relationship is not yet well understood, but it seems clear that changes in subsistence were both the cause and the consequence of technological development, for agriculture both stimulated the production of new tools and benefited from their availability.

The new pattern of subsistence economy also formed the basis for a new mode of social organization. The cessation of the bronze supply to northern Europe around 600 BC had brought to an end the system of prestige goods on which the social hierarchy of the later Bronze Age had been founded (see Chapter 9). Exchange with the region to the south did continue, but on a much reduced scale; amber from the Baltic was still exported to central Europe (Beck *et al.*, 1978), and southern imports are occasionally found (Klindt-Jensen, 1950), most notably the cauldron from Gundestrup in Denmark probably made in south-eastern Europe in the second or first century BC (Powell, 1971). Other contacts with the south are also shown in the increasing adoption of the fashion for brooches, copying styles in central Europe to replace the native pins for clothes fastening. The scale of this exchange was very different, however, from earlier periods, and social organization now revolved around control of the land, which was the critical element in subsistence.

In contrast to the later Bronze Age, there is little evidence for differentiation in social status. The settlement pattern was characterized by individual farmsteads and small villages, with no sign of any centres of higher rank (e.g. Grøntoft, Becker, 1971; Hatzum, Haarnagel, 1969). By the end of the millennium, however, this pattern was beginning to change, for in some villages a single farm larger than its neighbours, with more stalling for cattle, was beginning to emerge, while in some areas of the north the first strongly defended sites were being constructed (Schmid, 1978). The burial evidence presents a similar picture, for from the sixth to the first century the cemeteries show a comparatively uniform cremation tradition with no marked differences of wealth. The first indications of such differentiation begin to appear in the first century BC, with the deposit of distinctive grave goods; in Denmark, following the established form of rich burial already seen in central Europe, waggons were included in the burials (e.g. Husby, Raddatz, 1967), and in other areas weapons or horse equipment such as sets of harness were beginning to be buried (Todd, 1975, p. 133).

Already by the first century BC, therefore, the first signs of marked social stratification since the end of the Bronze Age were appearing, and it was greatly enhanced in the following centuries. The northwards expansion of the Roman empire until the consolidation of a frontier along the Rhine in the early first century AD (see box) brought northern Europe for the first time into direct contact with Mediterranean civilization, and exchange relationships of the sort that had successively influenced the development of different areas of Europe from the seventh century onwards were again established (Hedeager, 1978). From early in the first century AD, rich graves appear which are characterized not only by physical separation from normal cemeteries, use of inhumation instead of cremation and possession of a large range of grave goods, but in particular by the inclusion of luxury imports from the Roman world (Gebühr, 1974); as elsewhere, many of these were associated with drinking, especially fine silver and bronze jugs and cups. Control over access to these imports was clearly an important factor in the increasing differentiation in society at this time.

These social changes were accompanied by innovations in ritual, though the ideology behind them and their connection with the growth of a social hierarchy cannot yet be clearly understood. From about 200 BC onwards, ritual deposits were made with increasing frequency in the peat bogs of northern Europe (Todd, 1975, pp.187-97). For the most part, these were of animals or animal products such as milk or butter, probably made as offerings to promote the fertility of the soil, but there were also more extravagant deposits. At Hjortspring in Denmark the collection included a boat, many weapons and much armour as well as domestic items such as bowls and dishes. The significance of such large deposits is difficult to estimate, but the practice as a whole may demonstrate a particular concern with fertility and productivity and may have emphasized the role of the emerging elite in controlling and ensuring these ends.

From the third century AD onwards there were significant changes in the archaeology of northern Europe; there were reorganizations of the agrarian landscape, emergence of centres of higher status in the settlement pattern, increased differences of wealth in the burials and a greater proportion of weapons in the bog deposits. These were all elements in a period of social and economic change that was to culminate later in barbarian pressure on the later Roman empire, the Anglo-Saxon migrations and the rise of northern Europe. Though these are more appropriately part of post-Roman and early mediaeval

archaeology, they had their roots in the changes set in motion in the middle of the first millennium BC.

SUGGESTIONS FOR FURTHER READING

There is again no general introduction to the period, though J. Filip, *Celtic Civilisation and Its Heritage* and S. Piggott, *Ancient Europe* are useful. For Britain, see B. W. Cunliffe, *Iron Age Communities in Britain.*

A series of regional studies of urban development is presented in B. W. Cunliffe and R. T. Rowley (eds), *Oppida: the Beginnings of Urbanisation in Barbarian Europe*, while J. Collis, *Defended Sites of the Late La Tène in Central and Western Europe* has a detailed catalogue of sites and much discussion.

The classical sources for Celtic society are briefly discussed in T. G. E. Powell, *The Celts* and S. Piggott, *The Druids.* For eastern Europe, R. Hoddinott, *The Thracians* gathers together much useful information.

D. F. Allen, *The Coinage of the Ancient Celts* is a detailed introduction to a vast topic; some possible interpretations of the coins are given in B. W. Cunliffe (ed.), *Coinage and Society in Britain and Gaul.*

For the non-urbanized communities of northern Europe, see M. Todd, *The Northern Barbarians 100 BC–AD 300.*

References

Abramova, Z. A. (1967). Palaeolithic art in the U.S.S.R., *Arctic Anthropology* **4** (2), 1–179.

Aguirre, E. and Lumley, M.-A. de. (1977). Fossil men from Atapuerca, Spain: their bearing on human evolution in the middle pleistocene, *Journal of Human Evolution* **6**, 681–88.

Albrecht, G. (1979). *Magdalénien-Inventare von Petersfels.* Archaeologica Venatoria 6. Institut für Urgeschichte, Tübingen.

Albrecht, G., Hahn, J. and Torke, W. G. (1972). *Merkmalanalyse von Geschossspitzen des mittleren Jungpleistozäns in Mittel- und Osteuropa.* Archaeologica Venatoria 2. Institut für Urgeschichte, Tübingen.

Albrethsen, S. E. and Petersen, E. B. (1976). Excavation of a mesolithic cemetery at Vedbaek, Denmark, *Acta Archaeologica* **47**, 1–28.

Alexander, J. and Hopkin, S. (1982). The origins and early development of European fibulae, *Proceedings of the Prehistoric Society* **48**, 401–16.

Alföldy, G. (1974). *Noricum.* Routledge and Kegan Paul, London.

Allen, D. F. (1967). Iron currency bars in Britain, *Proceedings of the Prehistoric Society* **33**, 307–35.

Allen, D. F. (1976). Wealth, money and coinage in a Celtic society, in *To Illustrate the Monuments: Essays on Archaeology presented to Stuart Piggott* (Ed. J. V. S. Megaw), 199–208. Thames and Hudson, London.

Allen, D. F. (1980). *The Coins of the Ancient Celts.* Edinburgh University Press, Edinburgh.

Almagro, M. (1966). *Las Estelas Decoradas del Suroeste Peninsular.* Biblioteca Praehistorica Hispana, Madrid.

Altuna, J. (1979). La faune des ongulés du Tardiglaciaire en Pays Basque et dans le reste de la région Cantabrique, in *La Fin des Temps glaciaires* (Ed. D. de Sonneville-Bordes), 85–95. C.N.R.S., Paris.

Ammerman, A. J. and Cavalli-Sforza, L. L. (1971). Measuring the rate of spread of early farming in Europe, *Man* **6**, 674–88.

Anati, E. (1961). *Camonica Valley.* Knopf, New York.

Anderson, P. C. (1980). A testimony of prehistoric tasks: diagnostic residues on stone tool working edges, *World Archaeology* **12**, 181–94.

Andersen, S. H. (1975). Ringkloster: en jysk inlandsboplads med Ertebøllekultur, *Kuml* 1973–4, 10–108.

Andersen, S. H. (1979). Aggersund. En Ertebølleboplads ved Limfjorden, *Kuml* 1978, 7–56.

Andresen, J. M., Byrd, B. F., Elson, M. D., McGuire, R. H., Mendoza, R. G., Staski, E. and White, J. P. (1981). The deer hunters: Star Carr reconsidered, *World Archaeology* **13**, 31–46.

Andronikos, M. (1980). The royal tombs at Aigai (Vergina), in *Philip of Macedon* (Ed. M. B. Hatzopoulos and L. D. Loukopoulos), 188–231. Ekdotike Athenon, Athens.

Angel, L. (1972). Ecology and population in the eastern Mediterranean, *World Archaeology* **4**, 88–105.

Annable, F. K. and Simpson, D. D. A. (1964). *Guide Catalogue of the Neolithic and Bronze Age Collections in the Devizes Museum.* Wiltshire Archaeological and Natural History Museum, Devizes.

ApSimon, A. M. (1976). Ballynagilly and the beginning and end of the Irish neolithic, in *Acculturation and Continuity in Atlantic Europe* (Ed. S. J. de Laet), 15–30. Dissertationes Archaeologicae Gandenses. De Tempel, Bruges.

ApSimon, A. M. (1980). The last Neanderthal in France? *Nature* **287**, 271–72.

Arnal, J. (1973). Le Lébous à Saint-Mathieu-de-Tréviers (Hérault). Ensemble du Chalcolithique au Gallo-Romain, *Gallia Préhistoire* **16**, 131–200.

Arora, S. K. (1973). Mittelsteinzeitliche Formengruppen zwischen Rhein und Weser, in *The Mesolithic in Europe* (Ed. S. K. Kozłowski), 9–21. University Press, Warsaw.

Arribas, A. (1963). *The Iberians.* Thames and Hudson, London.

Artamanov, A. (1969). *Treasures from Scythian Tombs.* Thames and Hudson, London.

Ashbee, P., Smith, I. F. and Evans, J. G. (1979). Excavations of three long barrows near Avebury, Wiltshire, *Proceedings of the Prehistoric Society* **45**, 207–300.

Atkinson, R. J. C. (1956). *Stonehenge.* Penguin, Harmondsworth.

Austin, M. and Vidal-Naquet, P. (1977). *Economic and Social History of Ancient Greece.* University of California Press, Los Angeles.

Bader, O. N. (1978). *Sunghir* (in Russian). Nauka, Moscow.

Bahn, P. G. (1977). Seasonal migration in south-west France during the late glacial period, *Journal of Archaeological Science* **4**, 245–57.

Bailey, G. N. (1978). Shell middens as indicators of postglacial economies: a territorial perspective, in *The Early Postglacial Settlement of Northern Europe* (Ed. P. Mellars), 37–64. Duckworth, London.

Bailey, G. N. (Ed.) (1983). *Hunter-gatherer Economy in Prehistoric Europe.* Cambridge University Press, Cambridge.

Bailey, G. N., Carter, P. L., Gamble, C. S. and Higgs, H. P. (1983). Epirus revisited: seasonality and inter-site variation in the upper palaeolithic of north-west Greece, in *Hunter-gatherer Economy in Prehistoric Europe* (Ed. G. N. Bailey), 64–78. Cambridge University Press, Cambridge.

Bailloud, G. (1976). Les civilisations néolithiques du Bassin Parisien et du Nord de la France, in *La Préhistoire Francaise*, Vol. 2 (Ed. J. Guilaine), 375–86. C.N.R.S., Paris.

Bakels, C. C. (1978). *Four Linearbandkeramik Settlements and their Environment: a palaeoecological study of Sittard, Stein, Elsloo and Hienheim.* Analecta Praehistorica Leidensia 11. University Press, Leiden.

Bakker, J. A. (1979). *The TRB West Group.* Institute of Pre- and Protohistory, Amsterdam.

Balaam, N. D., Smith, K. and Wainwright, G. J. (1982). The Shaugh Moor Project: fourth report—environment, context and conclusion, *Proceedings of the Prehistoric Society* **48**, 203–278.

Balkwill, C. (1976). The evidence of cemeteries for later prehistoric development in the Rhine valley, *Proceedings of the Prehistoric Society* **42**, 187–214.

Bandi, H. G. (1967). Die Auswertung von Ausgrabungen im neolithischen Uferdorf Seeberg, Burgäschisee-Süd, Kt. Bern, *Palaeohistoria* **12**, 17–32.

Bánesz, L. (1976). Prírodné prostredie hospodárska základňa a materiálna kultúra aurignacienu strednes Európy, *Slovenská Archaeológia* **24**, 5–82.

Banner, J. (1956). *Die Peceler Kultur.* Archaeologia Hungarica 35. Akadémiai Kiadó, Budapest.

Banti, L. (1973). *Etruscan Cities and their Culture.* Batsford, London.

Barfield, L. (1971). *Northern Italy before the Romans.* Thames and Hudson, London.

Barker, G. (1975). Prehistoric territories and economies in central Italy, in *Palaeoeconomy* (Ed. E. Higgs), 111–75. Cambridge University Press, Cambridge.

Barker, G. (1976). Morphological change and neolithic economies: an example from central Italy, *Journal of Archaeological Science* **3**, 71–82.

Barker, G. (1977). The archaeology of Samnite settlement in Molise, *Antiquity* **51**, 20–24.

Barker, G. (1981). *Landscape and Society: Prehistoric Central Italy.* Academic Press, London and New York.

Barrett, J. and Bradley, R. J. (Eds) (1980). *Settlement and Society in the British later Bronze Age.* British Archaeological Reports 83, Oxford.

Barta, J. (1967). Stratigraphische Übersicht der paläolithischen Funde in der Westslowakei, *Quartär* **18**, 57–80.

Bartolomei, G., Broglio, A. and Palma di Cesnola, A. (1979). Chronostratigraphie et écologie de l'Epigravettien en Italie, in *La Fin des Temps glaciaires* (Ed. D. de Sonneville-Bordes), 297–324. C.N.R.S., Paris.

Baudou, E. (1960). *Die regionale und chronologische Einteilung der jüngeren Bronzezeit im nordischen Kreis.* University of Stockholm, Stockholm.

Bay-Petersen, J. (1978). Animal exploitation in mesolithic Denmark, in *The Early Postglacial Settlement of Northern Europe* (Ed. P. Mellars), 115–45. Duckworth, London.

Beck, C. W., Greenlie, J., Diamond, M. P., Macchiarulo, A. M., Hannenberg, A. A. and Hauck, M. S. (1978). The chemical identification of Baltic amber at the Celtic oppidum Staré Hradisko in Moravia, *Journal of Archaeological Science* **5**, 343–54.

Becker, C. J. (1971). Früheisenzeitliche Dörfer bei Gröntoft, Westjütland. 3. Vorbericht: Die Ausgrabungen 1967–68, *Acta Archaeologica* **42**, 79–110.

Behm-Blanke, G. (1960). Altsteinzeitliche Rastplätze im Travertingebiet von Taubach, Weimar, Ehringsdorf. *Alt-Thüringen* **4**, 1–246.

Behrens, H. (1973). *Die Jungsteinzeit im Mittelelbe-Saale-Gebiet.* German Academy of Sciences, Berlin.

Behrens, H. (Ed.) (1981). Schnurkeramik-Symposium Halle 1979, *Jahresschrift für mitteldeutsche Vorgeschichte* **64**, 1–239.

Behrens, H. and Schlette, F. (Eds) (1969). *Die neolithischen Becherkulturen im Gebiet der DDR und ihre europäischen Beziehungen.* German Academy of Sciences, Berlin.

Behrens, H. and Schröter, E. (1980). *Siedlungen und Gräber der Trichterbecherkultur bei Halle (Saale).* German Academy of Sciences, Berlin.

Benac, A. and Čović, B. (1956). *Glasinac I: Bronzezeit.* Sarajevo.

Benac, A. and Čović, B. (1957). *Glasinac II: Eisenzeit.* Sarajevo.

Bender, B. (1975). *Farming in Prehistory. From Hunter-gatherer to Food Producer.* John Baker, London.

Bender, B. (1978). Gatherer-hunter to farmer: a social perspective, *World Archaeology* **10**, 204–22.

Bender, B. (1981). Gatherer-hunter intensification, in *Economic Archaeology* (Ed. A. Sheridan and G. N. Bailey), 149–57. British Archaeological Reports S96, Oxford.

Benoit, F. (1965). *Recherches sur l'hellénisation du Midi de la Gaule.* Annales de la Faculté des Lettres 43, Aix-en-Provence.

Benoit, F. (1968). Résultats historiques des fouilles d'Entremont, *Gallia* **26**, 1–31.

Bhattacharya, D. K. (1977). *Palaeolithic Europe.* Humanities Press, Atlantic Highlands, NJ.

Bicchieri, M. G. (Ed.) (1972). *Hunters and Gatherers Today.* Holt, Rinehart and Winston, New York.

Biddittu, I., Cassoli, P. F., Radicati di Brozolo, F., Segre, A. G., Segre Naldini, E. and Villa, I. (1979). Anagni, a K–Ar dated lower and middle pleistocene site, central Italy: preliminary report, *Quaternaria* **21**, 53–71.

Biel, J. (1982). Ein Fürstengrabhügel der späten Hallstattzeit bei Eberdingen-Hochdorf, Kr. Ludwigsburg (Baden-Württemberg). Vorbericht, *Germania* **60**, 61–104.

Bielenin, K. (1964). Das Hüttenwesen in Altertum im Gebiet

der Góry Świętorkrzyskie, *Prähistorische Zeitschrift* **42**, 77–96.

Bietti Sestieri, A. M. (1973). The metal industry of continental Italy, 13th–11th century, and its Aegean connections, *Proceedings of the Prehistoric Society* **39**, 383–424.

Bietti Sestieri, A. M. (1975). Elementi per lo studio dell' abitato protostorico di Frattesina di Fratta Polesine (Rovigo), *Padusa* **11**, 1–14.

Bietti Sestieri, A. M. (1981). Economy and society in Italy between the late Bronze Age and early Iron Age, in *Archaeology and Italian Society* (Ed. G. Barker and R. Hodges), 133–55. British Archaeological Reports S102, Oxford.

Bill, J. (1973). *Die Glockenbecherkultur und die frühe Bronzezeit im französischen Rhonebecken und ihre Beziehungen zur Südwestschweiz*. Schweizerische Gesellschaft für Ur- und Frühgeschichte, Basel.

Binford, L. R. (1968). Post-pleistocene adaptations, in *New Perspectives in Archaeology* (Ed. S. R. and L. R. Binford), 313–41. Aldine, Chicago.

Binford, L. R. (1972). *An Archaeological Perspective*. Seminar Press, New York.

Binford, L. R. (1973). Interassemblage variability: the mousterian and the 'functional' argument, in *The Explanation of Culture Change* (Ed. C. Renfrew), 227–54. Duckworth, London.

Binford, L. R. (1977). Forty-seven trips, in *Stone Tools as Cultural Markers* (Ed. R. V. S. Wright), 24–36. Australian Institute of Aboriginal Studies, Canberra.

Binford, L. R. (1978a). *Nunamiut Ethnoarchaeology*. Academic Press, London and New York.

Binford, L. R. (1978b). Dimensional analysis of behaviour and site structure: learning from an Eskimo hunting stand, *American Antiquity* **43**, 330–61.

Binford, L. R. (1980). Willow smoke and dogs' tails: hunter-gatherer settlement systems and archaeological site formation, *American Antiquity* **45**, 4–20.

Binford, L. R. (1981). *Bones: Ancient Men and Modern Myths*. Academic Press, London and New York.

Binford, L. R. (1982). The archaeology of place, *Journal of Anthropological Archaeology* **1**, 5–31.

Binford, L. R. and Bertram, J. B. (1977). Bone frequencies and attritional processes, in *For Theory Building in Archaeology* (Ed. L. R. Binford), 77–153. Academic Press, London and New York.

Binford, L. R. and Binford, S. R. (1966). A preliminary analysis of functional variability in the mousterian of levallois facies, *American Anthropologist* **68**(2), 238–95.

Binford, L. R. and Binford, S. R. (1969). Stone tools and human behavior, *Scientific American* **220**, 70–84.

Binford, S. R. (1968a). A structural comparison of disposal of the dead in the mousterian and the upper palaeolithic, *Southwestern Journal of Anthropology* **24**, 139–54.

Binford, S. R. (1968b). Early upper pleistocene adaptations in the Levant, *American Anthropologist* **70**, 707–17.

Birchall, A. (1965). The Aylesford-Swarling culture: the problem of the Belgae reconsidered, *Proceedings of the Prehistoric Society* **31**, 241–367.

Blance, B. (1971). *Die Anfänge der Metallurgie auf der iberischen Halbinsel*. Mann, Berlin.

Blegen, C. W. (1963). *Troy and the Trojans*. Thames and Hudson, London.

Boardman, J. (1980). *The Greeks Overseas: their Early Colonies and Trade* (3rd edition). Thames and Hudson, London.

Boessneck, J. (1971). *Die Tierknochenfunde aus dem Oppidum von Manching*. Franz Steiner, Wiesbaden.

Bohmers, A. (1951). Die Höhlen von Mauern, *Palaeohistoria* **1**, 1–107.

Boitani, F., Cataldi, M. and Pasquinucci, M. (1975). *Etruscan Cities*. Cassell, London.

Bökönyi, S. (1974). *The History of Domestic Mammals in Central and Eastern Europe*. Akadémiai Kiadó, Budapest.

Bona, I. (1975). *Die mittlere Bronzezeit Ungarns und ihre südöstlichen Beziehungen*. Akadémiai Kiadó, Budapest.

Bonís, E. B. (1969). *Die spätkeltische Siedlung Gellerthegy-Taban in Budapest*. Akadémiai Kiadó, Budapest.

Bordaz, J. (1970). *Tools of the Old and New Stone Age*. Natural History Press, New York.

Bordes, F. (1961a). *Typologie du Paléolithique ancien et moyen*. Delmas, Bordeaux.

Bordes, F. (1961b). Mousterian cultures in France, *Science* **134**, 803–10.

Bordes, F. (1968). *The Old Stone Age*. Weidenfeld and Nicholson, London.

Bordes, F. (1972a). *A Tale of Two Caves*. Harper and Row, New York.

Bordes, F. (1972b). Du paléolithique moyen au paléolithique supérieur: continuité ou discontinuité, in *The Origins of Homo Sapiens* (Ed. F. Bordes), 211–17. UNESCO, Paris.

Bordes, F. (1973). On the chronology and contemporaneity of different palaeolithic cultures in France, in *The Explanation of Culture Change* (Ed. C. Renfrew), 217–26. Duckworth, London.

Bordes, F. (1980). Le débitage levallois et ses variants, *Bulletin de la Société Préhistorique Française* **77**, 45–49.

Bordes, F. and Bourgon, M. (1951). Le complex moustérienne: moustérien, levalloisien et tayacien, *L'Anthropologie* **55**, 1–23.

Bordes, F. and Prat, F. (1965). Observations sur les faunes de Riss et du Würm I en Dordogne, *L'Anthropologie* **69**, 31–45.

Bordes, F. and Sonneville-Bordes, D. de. (1970). The significance of variability in palaeolithic assemblages, *World Archaeology* **2**, 61–73.

Borel, J.-L. (1976). La végétation pendant le Post-glaciaire dans le Jura et les Alpes du Nord, in *La Préhistoire Française*, Vol. 2 (Ed. J. Guilaine), 67–73. C.N.R.S., Paris.

Boserup, E. (1965). *The Conditions of Agricultural Growth*. Allen and Unwin, London.

Bosinski, G. (1967). *Die mittelpaläolithischen Funde im westlichen Mitteleuropa*. Fundamenta Reihe A, Band 4. Böhlau, Cologne.

Bosinski, G. (1979). *Die Ausgrabungen in Gönnersdorf 1968–76 und die Siedlungsbefunde der Grabung 1968*. Franz Steiner, Wiesbaden.

Bosinski, G. and Fischer, G. (1974). *Die Menschdarstellung von Gönnersdorf der Ausgrabung von 1968.* Franz Steiner, Wiesbaden.

Bottema, S. (1978). The late glacial in the eastern Mediterranean and the Near East, in *The Environmental History of the Near and Middle East since the last Ice Age* (Ed. W. C. Brice), 16–28. Academic Press, London and New York.

Bouchud, J. (1966). *Essai sur le Renne et la Climatologie du Paléolithique moyen et supérieur.* Magne, Périgueux.

Boule, M. (1908). L'homme fossile de La Chapelle aux Saints, *L'Anthropologie* 19, 519–25.

Bourdier, F. (1976). Les industries paléolithiques anté-würmiens dans le Nord-Ouest, in *La Préhistoire Française*, Vol. 1 (Ed. H. de Lumley), 956–63. C.N.R.S., Paris.

Bouvier, J.-M. (1977). *Un Gisement préhistorique: La Madeleine.* Pierre Fanlac, Périgueux.

Bouzek, J. (1978). Zu den Anfängen der Eisenzeit in Mitteleuropa, *Zeitschrift für Archäologie* 12, 9–14.

Bouzek, J., Koutecký, D. and Neustupný, E. (1966). *The Knovíz Settlement of North-west Bohemia.* Fontes Archaeologici Pragenses. National Museum, Prague.

Bowen, D. Q. (1978). *Quaternary Geology.* Pergamon Press, Oxford.

Brace, C. L. (1964). A consideration of hominid catastrophism, *Current Anthropology* 5, 3–43.

Brace, C. L. (1979). Krapina, 'classic' neanderthals and the evolution of the European face, *Journal of Human Evolution* 8, 527–50.

Bradley, R. J. (1978a). Prehistoric field systems in Britain and north-west Europe—a review of some recent work, *World Archaeology* 9, 265–80.

Bradley, R. J. (1978b). *The Prehistoric Settlement of Britain.* Routledge and Kegan Paul, London.

Bradley, R. J. (1981). Economic growth and social change: two examples from prehistoric Europe, in *Economic Archaeology* (Ed. A. Sheridan and G. N. Bailey), 231–37. British Archaeological Reports S96, Oxford.

Bradley, R. J. (1982). Position and possession: assemblage variations in the British neolithic, *Oxford Journal of Archaeology* 1, 27–38.

Bradley, R. J. and Richards, J. (1978). Prehistoric fields and boundaries on the Berkshire Downs, in *Early Land Allotment in the British Isles* (Ed. H. C. Bowen and P. J. Fowler), 53–60. British Archaeological Reports 48, Oxford.

Branigan, K. (1968). *Copper and Bronze Working in early Bronze Age Crete.* Studies in Mediterranean Archaeology 19. Paul Åström, Göteborg.

Brea, B. L. (1946/56). *Gli Scavi nella Caverna della Arene Candide, Parte 1: gli strati con ceramiche.* Instituto Internazionale di Studi Liguri, Bordighera.

Břeň, J. (1966). *Třisov: a Celtic Oppidum in South Bohemia.* Czechoslovak Academy of Sciences, Prague.

Břeň, J. (1976). Earliest settlements with urban character in central Europe, in *Oppida: the Beginnings of Urbanisation in Barbarian Europe* (Ed. B. W. Cunliffe and R. T. Rowley), 81–94. British Archaeological Reports S11, Oxford.

Bretz-Mahler, D. (1971). *La Civilisation de la Tène I en Champagne.* Gallia Supplement 23. C.N.R.S., Paris.

Breuil, H. (1939). The pleistocene succession in the Somme valley, *Proceedings of the Prehistoric Society* 5, 33–38.

Breuil, H. (1952). *Quatre Cents Siècles d'Art pariétal.* Centre d'études et de documentation préhistoriques, Montignac.

Breuil, H. and Kozłowski, L. (1932). Études de stratigraphie paléolithique dans le nord de la France, la Belgique et l'Angleterre, *L'Anthropologie* 42, 27–47, 291–314.

Brézillon, M. (1971). *La Dénomination des Objets de Pierre taillée.* Gallia Préhistoire Supplement 4. C.N.R.S., Paris.

Briard, J. (1965). *Les Depôts Bretons et l'Age du Bronze Atlantique.* Laboratoire d'Anthropologie préhistorique, Rennes.

Brisay, K. W. de and Evans, K. A. (Eds) (1975). *Salt: the Study of an Ancient Industry.* Colchester Archaeological Group, Colchester.

Broadbent, N. (1979). *Coastal Resources and Settlement Stability: a Critical Study of a Mesolithic Site Complex in Northern Sweden.* Uppsala University, Uppsala.

Broholm, H. C. (1931). Nouvelles trouvailles du plus ancien age de la pierre: les trouvailles de Holmegaard et de Svaerdborg, *Mémoires de la Société Royale des Antiquitaires du Nord* 1926–31, 1–128. Copenhagen.

Broholm, H. C. and Hald, M. (1935). *Danske Bronze-alders Dragter.* Nordiske Fortidsminder 2, Hefte 5–6, Copenhagen.

Brongers, J. (1976). *Air Photography and Celtic Field Research in the Netherlands.* ROB, Amersfoort.

Brongers, J. and Woltering, P. (1978). *Prehistorie van Nederland.* Fibula-van Dishoeck, Haarlem.

Brose, D. S. and Wolpoff, M. H. (1971). Early upper palaeolithic man and late middle palaeolithic tools, *American Anthropologist* 73, 1156–94.

Brunnacker, K. (1967). *Seeberg Burgäschisee-Süd. 4: Chronologie und Umwelt.* Acta Bernensia 2. Stampfli, Bern.

Bunn, H. T. (1981). Archaeological evidence for meat-eating by Plio-Pleistocene hominids from Koobi Fora and Olduvai Gorge, *Nature* 291, 574–77.

Burch, E. S. (1972). The caribou/wild reindeer as a human resource, *American Antiquity* 37, 339–67.

Burch, E. S. and Correll, T. C. (1972). Alliance and conflict: inter-regional relations in north Alaska, in *Alliance in Eskimo Society* (Ed. L. Guemple), 17–39. Proceedings of the American Ethnological Society, Supplement. University of Washington Press, Seattle.

Burenhult, G. (1973). *The Rock Carvings of Götaland.* Acta Archaeologica Lundensia Series in 4°, 8, Lund.

Burenhult, G. (1981). *The Carrowmore Excavations: Excavation Season 1980.* Institute of Archaeology, Stockholm.

Burgess, C. B. (1980). *The Age of Stonehenge.* Dent, London.

Burkitt, M. C. (1933). *The Old Stone Age: a Study of Palaeolithic Times.* Cambridge University Press, Cambridge.

Burow, G. M. (1973). Die mesolithischen Kulturen im äussersten europäischen Nordosten, in *The Mesolithic in*

Europe (Ed. S. K. Kozłowski), 129–49. University Press, Warsaw.

Butler, J. J. (1963). Bronze Age connections across the North Sea, *Palaeohistoria* **9**, 1–286.

Butler, J. J. (1978). Rings and ribs: the copper types of the 'ingot hoards' of the central European early bronze age, in *The Origins of Metallurgy in Atlantic Europe* (Ed. M. Ryan), 345–62. Irish Stationery Office, Dublin.

Butzer, K. W. (1971). *Environment and Archaeology* (2nd edition). Methuen, London.

Cadogan, G. (1976). *The Palaces of Minoan Crete*. Barrie and Jenkins, London.

Campbell, J. M. (1968). Territoriality among ancient hunters: interpretations from ethnography and nature, in *Anthropological Archaeology in the Americas* (Ed. B. J. Meggers), 1–21. Anthropological Society of Washington, Washington, D.C.

Campbell, J. B. (1977). *The Upper Palaeolithic of Britain*. Clarendon, Oxford.

Capitan, L. and Peyrony, D. (1928). *La Madeleine. Son Gisement, son Industrie, ses Oeuvres d'Art*. Publications de l'Institut International d'Anthropologie 2, Paris.

Carciumaru, M. (1973). Analyse pollinique des coprolithes livrés par quelques stations archéologiques des deux bords du Danube dans la zone des 'Portes de Fer', *Dacia* **17**, 53–60.

Cardini, L. (1946). Gli strati mesolitici e paleolitici della Caverna delle Arene Candide, *Rivista di Studi Liguri* **12**, 29–37.

Carriazo, J. de Mata. (1973). *Tartessos y el Carambolo*. Ministry of Education and Science, Madrid.

Caskey, J. L. (1954). Excavations at Lerna 1952–3, *Hesperia* **23**, 3–30.

Caskey, J. L. (1955). Excavations at Lerna 1954, *Hesperia* **24**, 25–49.

Caskey, J. L. (1972). Investigations in Keos. Part II: a conspectus of the pottery, *Hesperia* **41**, 357–401.

Caulfield, S. (1978). Neolithic fields: the Irish evidence, in *Early Land Allotment in the British Isles* (Ed. H. C. Bowen and P. J. Fowler), 137–43. British Archaeological Reports 48, Oxford.

Cave, A. J. E. and Straus, W. L. (1957). Pathology and posture of neanderthal man, *Quarterly Review of Biology* **32**, 348–63.

Chadwick, A. J. (1978). A computer simulation of Mycenean settlement, in *Simulation Studies in Archaeology* (Ed. I. Hodder), 47–57. Cambridge University Press, Cambridge.

Chadwick, J. (1958). *The Decipherment of Linear B*. Cambridge University Press, Cambridge.

Chadwick, J. (1976). *The Mycenean World*. Cambridge University Press, Cambridge.

Chadwick, J. (1977). The interpretation of Mycenean documents and Pylian geography, in *Mycenean Geography* (Ed. J. Bintliff), 36–40. British Association for Mycenean Studies, Cambridge.

Champion, S. (1976). Coral in Europe: commerce and Celtic ornament, in *Celtic Art in Ancient Europe* (Ed. P.-M. Duval and C. F. C. Hawkes), 29–37. Seminar Press, London.

Champion, S. (1982). Exchange and ranking: the case of coral, in *Ranking, Resource and Exchange* (Ed. C. Renfrew and S. J. Shennan), 67–72. Cambridge University Press, Cambridge.

Champion, T. (1980). Mass migration in later prehistoric Europe, in *Transport Technology and Social Change* (Ed. P. Sörbom), 31–42. Tekniska Museet, Stockholm.

Champion, T. (1982). Fortification, ranking and subsistence, in *Ranking, Resource and Exchange* (Ed. C. Renfrew and S. J. Shennan), 61–66. Cambridge University Press, Cambridge.

Chapman, J. (1981). *The Vinča Culture in South-east Europe*. British Archaeological Reports S117, Oxford.

Chapman, R. W. (1978). The evidence for prehistoric water control in south-east Spain, *Journal of Arid Environments* **1**, 261–74.

Chapman, R. W. (1981a). The megalithic tombs of Iberia, in *Antiquity and Man: Essays in Honour of Glyn Daniel* (Ed. B. W. Cunliffe, J. D. Evans and C. Renfrew), 93–106. Thames and Hudson, London.

Chapman, R. W. (1981b). Archaeological theory and communal burial in prehistoric Europe, in *Pattern of the Past* (Ed. I. Hodder, G. Isaac and N. Hammond), 387–411. Cambridge University Press, Cambridge.

Chapman, R. W. (1982). Autonomy, ranking and resources in Iberian prehistory, in *Ranking, Resource and Exchange* (Ed. C. Renfrew and S. J. Shennan), 46–51. Cambridge University Press, Cambridge.

Chapman, R. W. (in press). Los Millares and the relative chronology of the Copper Age in south-east Spain, *Cuadernas Prehistoricas Universita Granada* **6**.

Chernysh, A. P. (1961). *The Palaeolithic Station of Molodova V* (in Russian). Academy of Sciences, Kiev.

Cherry, J. F. (1977). Investigating the political geography of an early state by multidimensional scaling of Linear B tablet data, in *Mycenean Geography* (Ed. J. Bintliff), 76–83. British Association for Mycenean Studies, Cambridge.

Chertier, B. (1976a). *Les Nécropoles de la Civilisation des Champs d'urnes dans la région des marais de Saint-Gond (Marne)*. Gallia Préhistoire Supplement 8. C.N.R.S., Paris.

Chertier, B. (1976b). Les civilisations de l'age de bronze en Champagne, in *La Préhistoire Française*, Vol. 2 (Ed. J. Guilaine), 618–29. C.N.R.S., Paris.

Childe, V. G. (1925). *The Dawn of European Civilisation*. Routledge and Kegan Paul, London.

Childe, V. G. (1929). *The Danube in Prehistory*. Clarendon, Oxford.

Chmielewska, M. (1954). Grob kultury tardenavskiej pow. Skierncewice, *Wiadomisci Archeoloziczne* **20**, 23–48.

Christlein, R. (1964). Beiträge zur Stufengliederung der frühbronzezeitlichen Flachgräberfelder in Süddeutschland, *Bayerische Vorgeschichtsblätter* **29**, 25–63.

Clark, J. D. and Walton, J. (1962). A late stone age site in the Erongo Mountains, South-west Africa, *Proceedings of the Prehistoric Society* **28**, 1–16.

Clark, J. G. D. (1952). *Prehistoric Europe: the Economic Basis*. Methuen, London.

Clark, J. G. D. (1954). *Excavations at Star Carr*. Cambridge University Press, Cambridge.

Clark, J. G. D. (1972). *Star Carr: a Case Study in Bioarchaeology*. Addison Wesley, Reading, Mass.

Clark, J. G. D. (1975). *The Earlier Stone Age Settlement of Scandinavia*. Cambridge University Press, Cambridge.

Clark, J. G. D. and Rankine, W. F. (1939). Excavation at Farnham, Surrey, 1937–8, *Proceedings of the Prehistoric Society* 5, 61–118.

Clark, R. M. (1975). A calibration curve for radiocarbon dates, *Antiquity* 49, 251–66.

Clarke, D. L. (1968). *Analytical Archaeology*. Methuen, London.

Clarke, D. L. (1970). *Beaker Pottery of Great Britain and Ireland*. Cambridge University Press, Cambridge.

Clarke, D. L. (1976). Mesolithic Europe: the economic basis, in *Problems in Economic and Social Archaeology* (Ed. G. de G. Sieveking, I. H. Longworth and K. E. Wilson), 449–82. Duckworth, London.

CLIMAP (1976). The surface of ice age earth, *Science* 191, 1131–37.

Close, A. (1978). The identification of style in lithic artefacts, *World Archaeology* 10, 223–37.

Clottes, J. and Costantini, G. (1976). Les civilisations néolithiques dans les Causses, in *La Préhistoire Française*, Vol. 2 (Ed. J. Guilaine), 279–91. C.N.R.S., Paris.

Clough, T. H. McK. and Cummins, W. A. (Eds) (1979). *Stone Axe Studies: Archaeological, Petrological, Experimental and Ethnographic*. Council for British Archaeology Research Report 23, London.

Coldstream, J. N. (1977). *Geometric Greece*. Benn, London.

Coles, J. M. (1962). European Bronze Age shields, *Proceedings of the Prehistoric Society* 28, 156–90.

Coles, J. M. (1971). The early settlement of Scotland: excavations at Morton, Fife, *Proceedings of the Prehistoric Society* 37(2), 284–366.

Coles, J. M. (1976). Forest farmers: some archaeological, historical and experimental evidence relating to the prehistory of Europe, in *Acculturation and Continuity in Atlantic Europe* (Ed. S. J. de Laet), 59–66. Dissertationes Archaeologicae Gandenses. De Tempel, Bruges.

Coles, J. M. and Higgs, E. S. (1969). *The Archaeology of Early Man*. Faber and Faber, London.

Coles, J. M. and Harding, A. F. (1979). *The Bronze Age in Europe*. Methuen, London.

Coles, J. M., Hibbert, F. and Orme, B. (1973). Prehistoric roads and tracks in Somerset: 3. The Sweet Track, *Proceedings of the Prehistoric Society* 39, 256–93.

Coles, J. M., Orme, B. and Woolley, A. R. (1974). A jade axe from the Somerset Levels, *Antiquity* 48, 216–20.

Collins, D. (1969). Culture traditions and environment of early man, *Current Anthropology* 10, 276–316.

Collins, D. and Onians, J. (1978). The origins of art, *Art History* 1, 1–25.

Collis, J. R. (1972). The Dacian horizon — settlements and chronology, *Slovenská Archaeológia* 20, 313–16.

Collis, J. R. (1975). *Defended Sites of the Late La Tène in central and western Europe*. British Archaeological Reports S2, Oxford.

Collis, J. R. (1976). Town and market in Iron Age Europe, in *Oppida: the Beginnings of Urbanisation in Barbarian Europe* (Ed. B. W. Cunliffe and R. T. Rowley), 3–23. British Archaeological Reports S11, Oxford.

Collis, J. R. (1977). Pre-Roman burial rites in north-western Europe, in *Burial in the Roman World* (Ed. R. Reece), 1–13. Council for British Archaeology Research Report 22, London.

Collis, J. R. (1980). Aulnat and urbanisation in France: a second interim report, *Archaeological Journal* 137, 40–49.

Conkey, M. W. (1978). Style and information in cultural evolution: toward a predictive model for the palaeolithic, in *Social Archaeology* (Ed. C. Redman *et al.*), 61–85. Academic Press, London and New York.

Conkey, M. W. (1980). The identification of prehistoric hunter-gatherer aggregation sites: the case of Altamira, *Current Anthropology* 21, 609–30.

Coope, G. R. (1977). Fossil coleopteran assemblages as sensitive indicators of climatic changes during the Devensian (Last) cold stage, *Philosophical Transactions of the Royal Society of London* B280, 313–40.

Cordier, G. (1976). Les civilisations de l'age du bronze dans le centre-ouest et les pays de la Loire moyenne, in *La Préhistoire Française*, Vol. 2 (Ed. J. Guilaine), 543–60. C.N.R.S., Paris.

Courtin, J. (1976a). Les civilisations néolithiques en Provence, in *La Préhistoire Francaise*, Vol. 2 (Ed. J. Guilaine), 255–66. C.N.R.S., Paris.

Courtin, J. (1976b). Le camp de Laure, Le Rove (Bouches-du-Rhone), *Gallia Préhistoire* 19, 589–93.

Cristofani, M. (1975). Il 'dono' nell'Etruria archaica, *Parolo del Passato* 30, 132–52.

Cristofani, M. (1979). *The Etruscans: a New Investigation*. Orbis, London.

Cronin, J. E., Boaz, N. T., Stringer, C. B. and Rak, Y. (1981). Tempo and mode in hominid evolution, *Nature* 292, 113–21.

Crummy, P. (1980). The temples of Roman Colchester, in *Temples, Churches and Religion: recent research in Roman Britain* (Ed. W. Rodwell), 243–83. British Archaeological Reports 77, Oxford.

Čujanová-Jilková, E. (1970). *Mittelbronzezeitliche Hügelgräberfelder in Westböhmen*. Archaeological Institute, Czechoslovak Academy of Sciences, Prague.

Cunliffe, B. W. (1978a). *Iron Age Communities of the British Isles* (2nd edition). Routledge and Kegan Paul, London.

Cunliffe, B. W. (1978b). *Hengistbury Head*. Paul Elek, London.

Cunliffe, B. W. (1981a). Danebury, Hampshire: third interim report on the excavations 1976–80, *Antiquaries Journal* 61, 238–54.

Cunliffe, B. W. (Ed.) (1981b). *Coinage and Society in Britain and Gaul*. Council for British Archaeology Research Report 38, London.

Dabrowski, M. J. (1971). Pollen analysis of cultural layers from Sarnowo, district of Włocławek, *Prace I Materialy* 18, 163–64.

Daicoviciu, C. and Daicoviciu, H. (1963). *Sarmizegethusa*. Bucharest.

Daicoviciu, H. (1972). *Dacia de la Burebista la Cucerirea Romana*. Bucharest.

Dakaris, S. I., Higgs, E. S. and Hey, R. (1964). The climate, environment and industries of stone age Greece: part 1, *Proceedings of the Prehistoric Society* 30, 199–244.

Daniel, G. E. (1975). *150 Years of Archaeology*. Duckworth, London.

Dansgaard, W. S., Johnsen, S. J., Clausen, H. B. and Langway, C. C. (1971). Climatic record revealed by the Camp Century ice core, in *The Late Cenozoic Glacial Ages* (Ed. K. K. Turekian), 37–56. Yale University Press, New Haven, Conn.

Darwin, C. R. (1859). *On the origin of species*. Murray, London.

Davidson, I. (1974). Radiocarbon dates for the Spanish solutrean, *Antiquity* 48, 63–65.

Davis, J. L. (1979). Minos and Dexithea: Crete and the Cyclades in the later Bronze Age, in *Papers in Cycladic Prehistory* (Ed. J. L. Davis and J. F. Cherry), 143–57. Institute of Archaeology, University of California, Los Angeles.

Day, M. H. (1977). *Guide to Fossil Man* (3rd edition). Cassell, London.

Degerbol, M. and Fredskild, B. (1970). *The Ursus (Bos primigenius Bojanus) and neolithic domesticated cattle (Bos taurus domesticus Linne) in Denmark*. Det Kongelige Danske Videnskabernes Selskab, Biologiske Skrifter 17,1. Copenhagen.

Dehn, R. (1972). *Die Urnenfelderkultur in Nordwürttemberg*. Müller and Gräff, Stuttgart.

Delano Smith, C. (1972). Late neolithic settlement, land-use and *garrigue* in the Montpellier region, France, *Man* 7, 397–407.

Delano Smith, C. (1979). *Western Mediterranean Europe*. Academic Press, London and New York.

Delibrias, G. and Evin, J. (1980). Sommaire des datations 14C concernant la préhistoire en France, *Bulletin de la Société Préhistorique Française* 77, 216–24.

Delluc, B. and Delluc, G. (1978). Les manifestations graphiques aurignaciennes sur support rocheux des environs des Éyzies (Dordogne), *Gallia Préhistoire* 21, 213–438.

Delporte, H. (1968). L'abri Facteur à Tursac (Dordogne). Étude générale, *Gallia Préhistoire* 11, 1–112.

Delporte, H. (1979). *L'Image de la Femme dans l'Art Préhistorique*. Picard, Paris.

Dennell, R. W. (1974). The purity of prehistoric crops, *Proceedings of the Prehistoric Society* 40, 132–35.

Dennell, R. W. (1978). *Early Farming in Bulgaria from the VI to the III Millennia BC*. British Archaeological Reports S45, Oxford.

Dennell, R. W. (1979). Prehistoric diet and nutrition — some food for thought, *World Archaeology* 11, 121–35.

Dennell, R. W. and Webley, D. (1975). Prehistoric settlement and land-use in southern Bulgaria, in *Palaeoeconomy* (Ed. E. Higgs), 97–109. Cambridge University Press, Cambridge.

Desittere, M. (1968). *De Urnenvelden Kultuur in het gebied tussen Neder-Rijn en Nordzee (Periodes Ha A en B)*. Dissertationes Archaeologicae Gandenses. De Tempel, Bruges.

Dickinson, O. T. P. K. (1977). *The Origins of Mycenean Civilisation*. Studies in Mediterranean Archaeology 49. Paul Åström, Göteborg.

Dimbleby, G. W. and Evans, J. G. (1974). Pollen and land snail analysis of calcareous soils, *Journal of Archaeological Science* 1, 117–33.

Dimbleby, G. W. and Simmons, I. (1974). The possible role of ivy (*Hedera helix* L.) in the mesolithic economy of western Europe, *Journal of Archaeological Science* 1, 291–96.

Dimitrov, D. P. and Čičikova, M. (1978). *The Thracian City of Seuthopolis*. British Archaeological Reports S38, Oxford.

Doumas, C. and Puchelt, H. C. (Eds) (1980). *Thera and the Aegean World II*. Thera and the Aegean World, London.

Drack, W. (1958). Wagengräber und Wagenbestandteile aus Hallstatt-Grabhügeln der Schweiz, *Zeitschrift für schweizerische Archäologie und Kunstgeschichte* 18, 1–67.

Driehaus, J. (1965). 'Fürstengräber' und Eisenerze zwischen Mittelrhein, Mosel und Saar, *Germania* 43, 32–49.

Dunnell, R. C. (1980). Evolutionary theory and archaeology, in *Advances in Archaeological Method and Theory* (Ed. M. B. Schiffer), Vol. 3, 35–99. Academic Press, London and New York.

Dušek, M. (1966). *Thrakisches Gräberfeld der Hallstattzeit in Chotín*. Slovak Academy of Sciences, Bratislava.

Dušek, M. (1974a). Die Thraker in Karpatenbecken, *Slovenská Archaeológia* 22, 362–434.

Dušek, M. (1974b). Die junghallstattzeitliche Fürstensitz auf dem Molpir bei Smolenice, in *Symposium zur Problemen der jüngeren Hallstattzeit in Mitteleuropa* (Ed. B. Chropovský, M. Dušek and V. Podborský), 137–50. Slovak Academy of Sciences, Bratislava.

Duval, P.-M. (1977). *Les Celtes*. Gallimard, Paris.

Dvořák, F. (1938). *Wagengräber der älteren Eisenzeit in Böhmen*. Prague.

Ecsedy, I. (1979). *The People of the Pit-grave Kurgans in Eastern Hungary*. Akadémiai Kiadó, Budapest.

Efimenko, P. P. (1958). *Kostenki I* (in Russian). Akademiya nauk, Moscow and Leningrad.

Ehrenberg, V. (1969). *The Greek State* (2nd edition). Methuen, London.

Ehrich, R. W. and Pleslova, E. (1968). *Homolka: an Eneolithic Site in Bohemia*. Academia, Prague.

Ekholm, K. (1980). On the limitations of civilisations: the structure and dynamics of global systems, *Dialectical Anthropology* 5, 155–66.

Eogan, G. (1969). Excavations at Knowth, Co. Meath, 1968, *Antiquity* 43, 8–14.

Eogan, G. (1974). Report on the excavations of some passage graves, unprotected inhumation burials and a settlement site at Knowth, Co. Meath, *Proceedings of the Royal Irish Academy* 74C, 11–112.

Escalon de Fonton, M. (1966). Du paléolithique supérieur au mésolithique dans le Midi méditerranéen, *Bulletin de la Société Préhistorique Française* 63, 66–180.

Escalon de Fonton, M. (1967). Origine et développement des

civilisations néolithiques méditerranéennes en Europe occidentale, *Palaeohistoria* **12**, 209–48.

Evans, J. D. (1971). Neolithic Knossos: the growth of a settlement, *Proceedings of the Prehistoric Society* **37**, 95–117.

Evans, J. G. (1972). *Land Snails and Archaeology*. Academic Press, London.

Evans, J. G. (1975). *The Environment of Early Man in the British Isles*. Paul Elek, London.

Evans, J. G., Limbrey, S. and Cleere, H. (Eds) (1975). *The Effect of Man on the Landscape: the Highland Zone*. Council for British Archaeology Research Report 11, London.

Farrand, W. (1975). Analysis of the Abri Pataud sediments, in *Excavation of the Abri Pataud, Les Éyzies (Dordogne)* (Ed. H. L. Movius), 27–68. American School of Prehistoric Research Bulletin 30, Peabody Museum, Harvard University, Cambridge, Mass.

Farruggia, J. P., Kuper, R., Lüning, J. and Stehli, P. (1973). Untersuchungen zur neolithischen Besiedlung der Aldenhovener Platte III, *Bonner Jahrbücher* **173**, 226–56.

Felgenhauer, F. (1956/9). *Willendorf in der Wachau*. Mitteilungen der Prähistorisches Kommission 8/9, Vienna.

Filip, J. (1956). *Keltové ve Střední Evropě*. Czechoslovak Academy of Sciences, Prague.

Filip, J. (1977). *Celtic Civilisation and its Heritage* (2nd edition). Collett's, Wellingborough.

Fischer, F. (1972). Die Kelten bei Herodot, *Madrider Mitteilungen* **13**, 109–124.

Fischer, F. (1973). KEIMHΛIA. Bemerkungen zur kulturgeschichtlichen Interpretation des sogenannten Südimports in der späten Hallstatt- und frühen Latènezeit des westlichen Mitteleuropa, *Germania* **51**, 436–59.

Flannery, K. V. (1972a). The origins of the village as a settlement type in Mesoamerica and the Near East: a comparative study, in *Man, Settlement and Urbanism* (Ed. P. J. Ucko, R. Tringham and G. W. Dimbleby), 23–53. Duckworth, London.

Flannery, K. V. (1972b). The cultural evolution of civilisations, *Annual Review of Ecology and Systematics* **3**, 399–426.

Fleming, A. (1972). The genesis of pastoralism in European prehistory, *World Archaeology* **4**, 179–91.

Fleming, A. (1973). Tombs for the living, *Man* **8**, 177–93.

Flint, R. F. (1971). *Glacial and Quaternary Geology*. Wiley, New York.

Florescu, A. C. (1964). Contribuţii la cunuaştera culturii Noua, *Arheologia Moldovei* **2**/3, 143–216.

Fox, C. (1958). *Pattern and Purpose: Early Celtic Art in Britain*. National Museum of Wales, Cardiff.

Frankenstein, S. and Rowlands, M. J. (1978). The internal structure and regional context of early Iron Age society in south-west Germany, *Bulletin of the Institute of Archaeology, University of London* **15**, 73–112.

Freeman, L. G. (1973). The significance of mammalian faunas from palaeolithic occupations in Cantabrian Spain, *American Antiquity* **38**, 3–44.

Freeman, L. G. (1975). Acheulian sites and stratigraphy in

Iberia and the Maghreb, in *After the Australopithecines* (Ed. K. W. Butzer and G. Isaac), 661–743. Mouton, The Hague.

Frenzel, B. (1973). *Climatic Fluctuations of the Ice Age*. Case Western Reserve University, Cleveland.

Freund, G. (1952). *Die Blattspitzen des Paläolithikums in Europa*. Quartär-Bibliothek 1, Berlin.

Freund, G. (1963). Die ältere und die mittlere Steinzeit in Bayern, *Jahresberichte der Bayerischen Bodendenkmalpflege* **4**, 9–167.

Frey, M. (1935). Ein spätgallische Töpfersiedlung in Sissach, *Tätigkeitsbericht der Naturforschenden Gesellschaft Baselland* **10**, 70–82.

Fried, M. H. (1967). *The Evolution of Political Society*. Random House, New York.

Friis Johansen, K. (1919). Une station du plus ancien âge de la pierre dans la tombière de Svaerdborg, *Mémoires de la Société Royale des Antiquaires du Nord* 1914–19, 241–359.

Fugazzola Delpino, M. A. (1979). The Protovillanovan: a survey, in *Italy before the Romans: the Iron Age, Orientalizing and Etruscan Periods* (Eds D. Ridgway and F. R. Ridgway), 31–51. Academic Press, London and New York.

Furmanek, V. (1970). Hromadný nález bronzových předmětů v Liptovské Ondrašové, *Slovenská Archeológia* **18**, 451–68.

Gábori, M. (1976). *Les Civilisations du Paléolithique moyen entre les Alpes et l'Oural*. Akadémiai Kiadó, Budapest.

Gábori-Csánk, V. (1968). *La Station du Paléolithique moyen d'Érd, Hongrie*. Akadémiai Kiadó, Budapest.

Gabrovec, S. (1974). Die Ausgrabungen in Stična und ihre Bedeutung für die südostalpine Hallstattkultur, in *Symposium zu Problemen der jüngeren Hallstattzeit in Mitteleuropa* (Ed. B. Chropovský, M. Dušek and V. Podborský), 163–87. Slovak Academy of Sciences, Bratislava.

Gabrovec, S., Frey, O.-H. and Foltiny, S. (1970). Erster Vorbericht über die Ausgrabungen im Ringwall von Stična (Slowenien), *Germania* **48**, 12–33.

Galbenu, D. (1963). Neolitičeskaya masterkaya dlya obrabotki ukrašenii v Hîrşove, *Dacia* **7**, 501–9.

Gallay, A. (1976). The position of the Bell Beaker civilisation in the chronological sequence of Petit Chasseur (Sion, Valais, Switzerland), in *Glockenbechersymposium Oberried 1974* (Ed. J. N. Lanting and J. D. van der Waals), 279–306. Fibula-van Dishoeck, Bussum.

Gamble, C. S. (1978). Resource exploitation and the spatial patterning of hunter-gatherers: a case study, in *Social Organisation and Settlement* (Ed. D. Green, C. Haselgrove and M. Spriggs), 153–85. British Archaeological Reports S47, Oxford.

Gamble, C. S. (1979). Hunting strategies in the central European palaeolithic, *Proceedings of the Prehistoric Society* **45**, 35–52.

Gamble, C. S. (1982). Interaction and alliance in palaeolithic society, *Man* **17**, 92–107.

Gamble, C. S. (1983a). Alternative hunter-gatherer strategies in the upper pleistocene of Europe, in *Community*

Ecology and Human Adaptation in the Pleistocene (Ed. R. Foley). Academic Press, London and New York.

Gamble, C. S. (1983b). Culture and society in the upper palaeolithic of Europe, in *Hunter-gatherer Economy in Prehistoric Europe* (Ed. G. N. Bailey), 201–11. Cambridge University Press, Cambridge.

Garrod, D. A. E. and Bate, D. M. A. (1937). *The Stone Age of Mt. Carmel.* Oxford University Press, Oxford.

Gazdapuzstai, G. (1967). Caucasian relations of the Danubian basin in the early Iron Age, *Acta Archaeologica Academiae Scientiarum Hungaricae* **19**, 307–34.

Gebuhr, M. (1974). Zur Definition älterkaiserzeitlicher Fürstengräber von Lübsow-Typ, *Prähistorische Zeitschrift* **49**, 82–128.

Georgiev, G. (1959). Kulturgruppen der Jungstein- und Kupferzeit in der Ebene von Thrazien, in *L'Europe à la Fin de l'Age de la Pierre* (Ed. J. Böhm and S. J. de Laet), 45–100. Czechoslovak Academy of Sciences, Prague.

Georgiev, G. (1965). The Azmak mound in southern Bulgaria, *Antiquity* **39**, 6–8.

Gerloff, S. (1975). *The Early Bronze Age Daggers in Great Britain.* Prähistorische Bronzefunde VI.2. C. H. Beck, Munich.

Gilman, A. (1976). Bronze Age dynamics in south-east Spain, *Dialectical Anthropology* **1**, 307–19.

Gilman, A. (1981). The development of social stratification in Bronze Age Europe, *Current Anthropology* **22**, 1–23.

Gimbutas, M. (1965). *Bronze Age Cultures of Central and Eastern Europe.* Mouton, The Hague.

Gimbutas, M. (1974). *The Gods and Goddesses of Old Europe.* Thames and Hudson, London.

Giot, P. R., Monnier, J. L. and l'Helgouach, J. L. (1979a). *Préhistoire de la Bretagne.* Ouest France, Rennes.

Giot, P. R., Briard, J. and Pape, L. (1979b). *Protohistoire de la Bretagne.* Ouest France, Rennes.

Glodariu, I. (1976). *Dacian Trade with the Hellenistic and Roman World.* British Archaeological Reports S8, Oxford.

González-Echegaray, J. and Freeman, L. G. (1973). *Cueva Morín: Excavaciones 1969.* Publications del patronatò de las cuevas prehistóricas de la provincia de Santander 10, Santander.

Goretsky, G. I. and Ivanova, I. K. (1982). *Molodova I: unique mousterian settlement in the middle Dniestr region* (in Russian). Nauka, Moscow.

Gould, R. A. (1971). The archaeologist as ethnographer: a case from the Western Desert of Australia, *World Archaeology* **3**, 143–77.

Gould, R. A. (1980). *Living Archaeology.* Cambridge University Press, Cambridge.

Gould, S. J. and Eldredge, N. (1977). Punctuated equilibria: the tempo and mode of evolution reconsidered, *Paleobiology* **3**, 115–51.

Grahmann, R. (1955). The lower palaeolithic site of Markkleeberg and other comparable localities near Leipzig, *Transactions of the American Philosophical Society* **45**(6), 509–687.

Gramsch, B. (Ed.) (1981). *Mesolithikum in Europa.* Veröffentlichungen des Museums für Ur- und Früh-geschichte Potsdam, 14/15. German Academy of Sciences, Berlin.

Graziosi, P. (1960). *Palaeolithic Art.* Faber and Faber, London.

Green, H. S. (1981). The first Welshman: excavations at Pontnewydd, *Antiquity* **55**, 184–95.

Green, H. S., Stringer, C. B., Collcutt, S. N., Currant, A. P., Huxtable, J., Schwarcz, H. P., Debenham, N., Embleton, C., Bull, P., Molleson, T. I. and Bevins, R. E. (1981). Pontnewydd cave, Wales—a new middle pleistocene hominid site, *Nature* **294**, 707–13.

Grinsell, L. V. (1959). *Dorset Barrows.* Dorset Natural History and Archaeological Society, Dorchester.

Guilaine, J. (Ed.) (1976). *La Préhistoire Française*, Vol. 2. C.N.R.S., Paris.

Guilaine, J. (1981). *Premiers Bergers et Paysans de l'Occident Méditerranéen* (2nd edition). École des Hautes Etudes des Sciences Sociales, Paris.

Guillet, B., Janssen, C., Kalis, A. and Valk, E. de (1976). La végétation pendant le post-glaciaire dans l'est de la France, in *La Préhistoire Française*, Vol. 2 (Ed. J. Guilaine), 82–87. C.N.R.S., Paris.

Guth, C. (1974). Découverte dans la Villafranchien d'Auvergne de galets aménagés, *Comptes rendus de l'Académie des Sciences*, 23/9/1974, 1071–73.

Guyan, W. U. (Ed.) (1954). *Das Pfahlbauproblem.* Basel.

Guyan, W. U. (1967). Die jungsteinzeitlichen Moordörfer im Weier bei Thayngen, *Zeitschrift für schweizerische Archäologie und Kunstgeschichte* **25**, 1–39.

Haarnagel, W. (1969). Die Ergebnisse der Grabung auf der ältereisenzeitlichen Siedlung Boomburg/Hatzum, Kr. Leer, in der Jahren von 1965 bis 1967, *Neue Ausgrabungen und Forschungen in Niedersachsen* **4**, 57–97.

Hachmann, R. (1957). *Die frühe Bronzezeit im westlichen Ostseegebiet und ihre mittel- und südosteuropäischen Beziehungen.* Flemming, Hamburg.

Hachmann, R. (1960). Die Chronologie der jüngeren vorrömischen Eisenzeit. Studien zum Stand der Forschung im nördlichen Mitteleuropa und in Skandinavien, *Bericht der Römisch-Germanischen Kommission* **41**, 1–275.

Hadingham, E. (1979). *Secrets of the Ice Age.* Walker, New York.

Haevernick, T. (1960). *Die Glasarmringe und Ringperlen der Mittel- und Spätlatènezeit auf dem europäischen Festland.* Habelt, Bonn.

Haevernick, T. (1975). Hallstatt-Glasarmringe und Haguenauer Perlen, *Trierer Zeitschrift* **38**, 63–73.

Haevernick, T. (1978). Urnenfelderzeitliche Glasperlen, *Zeitschrift für schweizerische Archäologie und Kunstgeschichte* **35**, 145–57.

Haffner, A. (1976). *Die westliche Hunsrück-Eifel-Kultur.* Römisch-Germanische Forschungen 36. De Gruyter, Berlin.

Hahn, J. (1972a). Das Aurignacien in Mittel- und Osteuropa, *Acta Praehistorica et Archaeologica* **3**, 77–107.

Hahn, J. (1972b). Aurignacian signs, pendants and art objects in central and eastern Europe, *World Archaeology* **3**, 252–66.

Hahn, J. (1977). *Aurignacien: das ältere Jungpaläolithikum in Mittel- und Osteuropa*. Fundamenta Reihe A, Band 9. Böhlau, Cologne.

Hahn, J. (1979). Essai sur l'écologie du Magdalénien dans le Jura souabe, in *La Fin des Temps glaciaires en Europe* (Ed. D. de Sonneville-Bordes), 203–14. C.N.R.S., Paris.

Hahn, J. (1981). Abfolge und Umwelt der jüngeren Altsteinzeit in Südwestdeutschland, *Fundberichte aus Baden-Württemberg* **6**, 1–27.

Hahn, J., Müller-Beck, H.-J. and Taute, W. (1973). *Eiszeithöhlen im Lonetal*. Müller and Gräff, Stuttgart.

Hallam, B., Warren, S. and Renfrew, C. (1976). Obsidian in the western Mediterranean: characterisation by neutron activation analysis and optical emission spectroscopy, *Proceedings of the Prehistoric Society* **42**, 85–110.

Hallström, G. (1960). *Monumental Art of Northern Sweden from the Stone Age. Namforsen and other localities*. Almquist and Wiksell, Stockholm.

Halstead, P. (1981a). From determinism to uncertainty: social storage and the rise of the Minoan palace, in *Economic Archaeology* (Ed. A. Sheridan and G. N. Bailey), 187–213. British Archaeological Reports S96, Oxford.

Halstead, P. (1981b). Counting sheep in neolithic and bronze age Greece, in *Pattern of the Past* (Ed. I. Hodder, G. Isaac and N. Hammond), 307–339. Cambridge University Press, Cambridge.

Halstead, P. and O'Shea, J. (1982). A friend in need is a friend indeed: social storage and the origins of social ranking, in *Ranking, Resource and Exchange* (Ed. C. Renfrew and S. J. Shennan), 92–99. Cambridge University Press, Cambridge.

Hänsel, B. (1968). *Beiträge zue Chronologie der mittleren Bronzezeit im Karpatenbecken*. Habelt, Bonn.

Hansen, J. and Renfrew, J. (1978). Palaeolithic-neolithic seed remains at Franchthi Cave, Greece, *Nature* **271**, 349–52.

Harbison, P. (1969). The chariot of Celtic funerary tradition, in *Marburger Beiträge zur Archäologie der Kelten* (Ed. O.-H. Frey), 34–58. Fundberichte aus Hessen, Beiheft 1. Rudolf Habelt, Bonn.

Harcourt, R. A. (1971). The animal bones, in *Durrington Walls: Excavation 1966–68* (Ed. G. Wainwright and I. Longworth), 338–50. Society of Antiquaries Research Report 29, London.

Harding, A. F. (1976). Bronze agricultural implements in Bronze Age Europe, in *Problems in Economic and Social Archaeology* (Ed. G. de G. Sieveking, I. H. Longworth and K. E. Wilson), 513–22. Duckworth, London.

Harding, A. F. and Hughes-Brock, H. (1974). Amber in the Mycenean world, *Annual of the British School of Archaeology at Athens* **69**, 145–72.

Harding, D. W. (1978). *Prehistoric Europe*. Elsevier Phaidon, Oxford.

Härke, H. G. H. (1979). *Settlement Types and Settlement Patterns in the West Hallstatt Province*. British Archaeological Reports S57, Oxford.

Harlan, J. R. (1972). Crops that extend the range of agricultural settlement in *Man, Settlement and Urbanism* (Ed. P. J. Ucko, R. Tringham and G. W. Dimbleby), 239–43. Duckworth, London.

Harmon, R. S., Glazek, J. and Nowak, K. (1980). ^{230}Th/^{234}U dating of travertine from the Bilzingsleben archaeological site, *Nature* **284**, 132–35.

Harrison, R. J. (1977). *The Bell Beaker Cultures of Spain and Portugal*. American School of Prehistoric Research Bulletin 35, Peabody Museum, Harvard University, Cambridge, Mass.

Harrison, R. J. (1980). *The Beaker Folk*. Thames and Hudson, London.

Harrison, R. J. and Gilman, A. (1977). Trade in the second and third millennia BC between the Maghreb and Iberia, in *Ancient Europe and the Mediterranean* (Ed. V. Markotic), 90–104. Aris and Phillips, Warminster.

Harrold, F. B. (1980). A comparative analysis of Eurasian palaeolithic burials, *World Archaeology* **12**, 196–211.

Hásek, I. (1959). *The Early Únětician Cemetery at Dolní Počernice near Prague*. Fontes Archaeologici Pragenses 2. National Museum, Prague.

Häusler, A. (1976). *Die Gräber der älteren Ackergrabkultur zwischen Dnepr und Karpaten*. German Academy of Sciences, Berlin.

Häusler, A. (1981). Zur Frage der Beziehungen zwischen dem nordpontischen Raum und den neolithischen Kulturen Mitteleuropas, *Jahresschrift für mitteldeutsche Vorgeschichte* **64**, 229–36.

Hawkes, C. F. C. (1940). *The Prehistoric Foundations of Europe*. Methuen, London.

Hawkes, C. F. C. and Hull, M. R. (1947). *Camulodunum*. Society of Antiquaries Research Report 14, London.

Hawkes, C. F. C. and Smith, M. A. (1957). On some buckets and cauldrons of the Bronze and early Iron Ages, *Antiquaries Journal* **37**, 131–98.

Hayden, B. (Ed.) (1979a). *Lithic Use-wear Analysis*. Academic Press, London and New York.

Hayden, B. (1979b). *Palaeolithic Reflections*. Australian Institute of Aboriginal Studies, Canberra.

Heath, M. C. (1958). Early Helladic clay sealings from the House of Tiles at Lerna, *Hesperia* **27**, 81–121.

Hedaeger, L. (1978). A quantitative analysis of Roman imports north of the Limes (0–400 AD) and the question of Roman-Germanic exchange, in *New Directions in Scandinavian Archaeology* (Ed. K. Kristiansen and C. Paludan-Muller), 191–216. National Museum of Denmark, Copenhagen.

Hencken, H. (1968). *Tarquinia, Villanovans and Early Etruscans*. American School of Prehistoric Research Bulletin 23, Peabody Museum, Harvard University, Cambridge, Mass.

Hennig, G. J., Herr, W., Weber, E. and Xirotiris, N. I. (1981). ESR-dating of the fossil hominid cranium from Petralona Cave, Greece, *Nature* **292**, 533–36.

Herity, M. and Eogan, G. (1977). *Ireland in Prehistory*. Routledge and Kegan Paul, London.

Herrmann, F.-R. (1966). *Die Funde der Urnenfelderkultur in Mittel- und Südhessen*. Römisch-Germanische Forschungen 27. De Gruyter, Berlin.

Hermann, F.-R. (1975). Grabungen im Oppidum von Kelheim 1964–1972, in *Ausgrabungen in Deutschland*, Vol. 1, 298–311. Römisch-Germanisches Zentralmuseum, Mainz. Mainz.

Herrmann, J. (1969). Burgen und befestigte Siedlungen der jüngeren Bronze- und frühen Eisenzeit in Mitteleuropa, in *Siedlung, Burg und Stadt* (Ed. K.-H. Otto and J. Herrmann), 56–94. German Academy of Sciences, Berlin.

Higgs, E. S. (Ed.) (1972). *Papers in Economic Prehistory*. Cambridge University Press, Cambridge.

Higgs, E. S. (Ed.) (1975). *Palaeoeconomy*. Cambridge University Press, Cambridge.

Higgs, E. S. (1976). The history of European agriculture — the uplands, *Philosophical Transactions of the Royal Society of London* **B275**, 159–73.

Higgs, E. S. and Jarman, M. R. (1972). The origins of animal and plant husbandry, in *Papers in Economic Prehistory* (Ed. E. S. Higgs), 3–13. Cambridge University Press, Cambridge.

Higgs, E. S. and Vita-Finzi, C. (1966). The climate, environment and industries of stone age Greece: Part II, *Proceedings of the Prehistoric Society* **32**, 1–29.

Higham, C. W. (1967). Stock rearing as a cultural factor in prehistoric Europe, *Proceedings of the Prehistoric Society* **33**, 84–106.

Hillman, G. (1978). On the origins of domestic rye — secale cereale: the finds from aceramic Çan Hasan III in Turkey, *Anatolian Studies* **28**, 157–74.

Hodder, I. (1979). Economic and social stress and material culture patterning, *American Antiquity* **44**, 446–54.

Hodder, I. (1982). *Symbols in Action*. Cambridge University Press, Cambridge.

Hoddinott, R. F. (1981). *The Thracians*. Thames and Hudson, London.

Hoffman, G. W. (Ed.) (1977). *A Geography of Europe* (4th edition). Ronald Press Company, New York.

Holloway, R. R. (1975). Buccino: the early Bronze Age village of Tufariello, *Journal of Field Archaeology* **2**, 11–81.

Hooker, J. T. (1976). *Mycenean Greece*. Routledge and Kegan Paul, London.

Hortz, N. and Winge, H. (1906). Om Urozen fra Vig, *Aarboger for Nordisk Oldkyndighed og Historie* **21**, 225–36.

Howell, F. C. (1966). Observations on the earlier phases of the European lower palaeolithic, *American Anthropologist* **68**, 88–201.

Howell, F. C. (1971). *Early Man*. Time-Life International, Nederland, N.V.

Howells, W. W. (1974). Neanderthals: names, hypotheses and scientific method, *American Anthropologist* **76**, 24–38.

Howells, W. W. (1975). Neanderthal man: facts and figures, in *Palaeoanthropology* (Ed. R. Tuttle), 389–407. Mouton, The Hague.

Hulle, W. (1977). *Die Ilsenhöhle unter Burg Ranis*. Gustav Fischer, New York.

Humphreys, S. (1978). *Anthropology and the Greeks*. Routledge and Kegan Paul, London.

Ingold, T. (1980). *Hunters, Pastoralists and Ranchers*. Cambridge University Press, Cambridge.

Ingold, T. (1981). The hunter and his spear: notes on the cultural mediation of social and ecological systems, in *Economic Archaeology* (Ed. A. Sheridan and G. N. Bailey), 119–30. British Archaeological Reports S96, Oxford.

Isaac, G. (1978). The food-sharing behaviour of protohuman hominids, *Scientific American* **238**, 90–106.

Ivanov, I. S. (1978). Les fouilles archéologiques de la nécropole chalcolithique à Varna (1972–1975), *Studia Praehistorica* **1–2**, 13–26.

Jacobi, G. (1974a). *Werkzeug und Gerät aus dem Oppidum von Manching*. Franz Steiner, Wiesbaden.

Jacobi, G. (1974b). Zum Schriftgebrauch in keltischen Oppida nördlich der Alpen, *Hamburger Beiträge zur Archäologie* **4**, 171–81.

Jacobi, R. M. (1978). Northern England in the eighth millennium bc: an essay, in *The Early Post-glacial Settlement of Northern Europe* (Ed. P. Mellars), 295–332. Duckworth, London.

Jacobi, R. M., Tallis, J. H. and Mellars, P. (1976). The southern Pennine mesolithic and the ecological record, *Journal of Archaeological Science* **3**, 307–20.

Jacobsen, T. W. (1973). Excavations in the Franchthi Cave 1969–71, *Hesperia* **42**, 45–88, 253–83.

Jacobsthal, P. (1944). *Early Celtic Art*. Clarendon, Oxford.

Jannoray, J. (1955). *Ensérune. Contributions à l'étude des civilisations préromaines de la Gaule méridionale*. Paris.

Jansová, A. (1965). *Hrazany, keltské oppidum na Sedlčansku*. Czechoslovak Academy of Sciences, Prague.

Jarman, M. R. (1971). Culture and economy in the north Italian neolithic, *World Archaeology* **2**, 255–65.

Jarman, M. R. (1972). European deer economies and the advent of the neolithic, in *Papers in Economic Prehistory* (Ed. E. S. Higgs), 125–47. Cambridge University Press, Cambridge.

Jarman, M. R. and Webley, D. (1975). Settlement and land-use in Capitanata, in *Palaeoeconomy* (Ed. E. S. Higgs), 177–221. Cambridge University Press, Cambridge.

Jeffery, L. H. (1961). *The Local Scripts of Archaic Greece*. Clarendon, Oxford.

Jelinek, A. J. (1977). The lower palaeolithic: current evidence and interpretations, *Annual Review of Anthropology* **6**, 11–32.

Jivkova, L. (1974). *Le Tombeau de Kazanluk*. Sofia and Recklinghausen.

Joachim, H.-E. (1969). Unbekannte Wagengräber der Mittel- und Spätlatènezeit aus dem Rheinland, in *Marburger Beiträge zur Archäologie der Kelten* (Ed. O.-H. Frey), 84–111. Fundberichte aus Hessen, Beiheft 1. Rudolf Habelt, Bonn.

Jochim, M. A. (1976). *Hunter-gatherer Subsistence and Settlement: a Predictive Model*. Academic Press, London and New York.

Jochim, M. A. (1983). Palaeolithic cave art in ecological perspective, in *Hunter-gatherer Economy in Prehistoric Europe* (Ed. G. N. Bailey), 212–19. Cambridge University Press, Cambridge.

Jockenhövel, A. (1974). Zu befestigten Siedlungen der Urnenfelderzeit aus Süddeutschland, *Fundberichte aus Hessen* **14**, 19–62.

Joffroy, R. (1954). *Le Trésor de Vix (Côte d'Or)*. Monuments et Mémoires Piot 48.1. Presses Universitaires de France, Paris.

Joffroy, R. (1957). *Les Sépultures à Char du Premier Age du Fer en France*. Paris.

Joffroy, R. (1960). *L'Oppidum de Vix et la Civilisation hallstattienne finale dans l'est de la France*. Publications de l'Université de Dijon 20. Société Les Belles Lettres, Paris.

Jordan, T. G. (1973). *The European Culture Area*. Harper and Row, New York.

Jorns, W. (1960). Zur Salzgewinnung in Bad Nauheim während der Spätlatènezeit, *Germania* **38**, 178–84.

Jürgens, A. (1979). Die Rössener Siedlung von Aldenhoven, Kreis Düren, in *Beiträge zur Urgeschichte des Rheinlandes* (Ed. H.-E. Joachim), 385–505. Rheinische Ausgrabungen 18. Rheinland-Verlag, Cologne.

Kahlke, H. D. (1975). The macro-faunas of continental Europe during the middle pleistocene: stratigraphic sequence and problems of intercorrelation, in *After the Australopithecines* (Ed. K. W. Butzer and G. Isaac), 309–74. Mouton, the Hague.

Kaiser, K. (1960). Klimazeugen des periglazialen Dauerfrostbodens in Mittel- und Westeuropa, *Eiszeitalter und Gegenwart* **11**, 121–41.

Kalicz, N. (1963). *Die Peceler Kultur und Anatolien*. Akadémiai Kiadó, Budapest.

Kalicz, N. (1968). *Die Frühbronzezeit in Nordostungarn*. Akadémiai Kiadó, Budapest.

Kappel, I. (1969). *Die Graphittonkeramik von Manching*. Franz Steiner, Wiesbaden.

Keeley, L. H. (1974). Technique and methodology in microwear studies: a critical review, *World Archaeology* **5**, 323–36.

Keeley, L. H. (1980). *Experimental Determination of Stone Tool Uses: a Microwear Analysis*. University of Chicago Press, Chicago.

Keller, F. (1878). *The Lake Dwellings of Switzerland and Other Parts of Europe*. Longmans Green, London.

Kerney, M. P., Brown, E. H. and Chandler, T. J. (1964). The late-glacial and post-glacial history of the chalk escarpment near Brook, Kent, *Philosophical Transactions of the Royal Society of London* **B248**, 135–204.

Kibbert, K. (1980). *Die Äxte und Beile in Mittleren Westdeutschland*. Prähistorische Bronzefunde IX, 10. C. H. Beck, Munich.

Killen, J. (1964). The wool industry of Crete in the late Bronze Age, *Annual of the British School of Archaeology at Athens* **59**, 1–15.

Killen, J. (1977). The Knossos texts and the geography of Mycenean Greece, in *Mycenean Geography* (Ed. J. Bintliff), 40–54. British Association for Mycenean Studies, Cambridge.

Kimmig, W. (1964). Seevölkerbewegung und Urnenfelderkultur. Ein archäologisch-historischer Versuch, in *Studien aus Alt-Europa* (Ed. R. von Uslar and K. J. Narr), Vol. 1, 220–83. Bonner Jahrbücher Beiheft 10. Böhlau, Cologne.

Kimmig, W. (1975). Early Celts on the upper Danube: the excavations at the Heuneburg, in *Recent Archaeological Excavations in Europe* (Ed. R. L. S. Bruce-Mitford), 32–64. Routledge and Kegan Paul, London.

Klein, R. G. (1966). Chellean and Acheulean on the territory of the Soviet Union: a critical review of the evidence as presented in the literature, *American Anthropologist* **68**(2), 1–45.

Klein, R. G. (1969a). The mousterian of European Russia, *Proceedings of the Prehistoric Society* **35**, 77–111.

Klein, R. G. (1969b). *Man and Culture in the Late Pleistocene: a Case Study*. Chandler Publishing Company, San Francisco.

Klein, R. G. (1973). *Ice Age Hunters of the Ukraine*. University of Chicago Press, Chicago.

Klíma, B. (1954). Pavlov, nové paleolitické sídliště na jižní Moravě, *Archeologické Rozhledy* **6**, 721–28.

Klíma, B. (1957). Übersicht über die jüngsten paläolithischen Forschungen in Mähren, *Quartär* **9**, 85–130.

Klíma, B. (1963). *Dolní Věstonice*. Czechoslovak Academy of Sciences, Prague.

Klindt Jensen, O. (1950). Foreign influences in Denmark's early Iron Age, *Acta Archaeologica* **20**, 119–57.

Knörzer, K.-H. (1976). Späthallstattzeitliche Pflanzenfunde bei Bergheim, Erftkreis, *Rheinische Ausgrabungen* **17**, 151–85.

Körber-Grohne, U. and Piening, U. (1979). Verkohlte Nutz- und Wildpflanzenreste aus Bondorf, Kreis Böblingen, *Fundberichte aus Baden-Württemberg* **4**, 151–69.

Kossack, G. (1954). *Studien zur Symbolgut der Urnenfelder- und Hallstattzeit Mitteleuropas*. Römisch-Germanische Forschungen 20. De Gruyter, Berlin.

Kossack, G. (1959). *Südbayern während der Hallstattzeit*. Römisch-Germanische Forschungen 24. De Gruyter, Berlin.

Kovacs, T. (1977). *L'Age du Bronze en Hongrie*. Corvina, Budapest.

Kozłowski, J. (1974). Upper palaeolithic site with dwellings of mammoth bones—Cracow, Spadzista Street B, *Folia Quaternaria* **44**, 1–110.

Kozłowski, J. and Kozłowski, S. K. (1979). *Upper Palaeolithic and Mesolithic in Europe: Taxonomy and Palaeohistory*. Polish Academy, Warsaw.

Kozłowski, S. K. (1973a). Introduction to the history of Europe in early holocene, in *The Mesolithic in Europe* (Ed. S. K. Kozłowski), 331–66. University Press, Warsaw.

Kozłowski, S. K. (Ed.) (1973b). *The Mesolithic in Europe*. University Press, Warsaw.

Kraay, C. M. (1964). Hoards, small change and the origins of coinage, *Journal of Hellenic Studies* **84**, 76–91.

Krämer, W. and Schubert, F. (1970). *Die Ausgrabungen in Manching 1955–61. Einführung und Fundstellungübersicht*. Franz Steiner, Wiesbaden.

Kretzoi, M. and Vértes, L. (1965). Upper Biharian (intermindel) pebble-industry occupation site in western Hungary, *Current Anthropology* **6**, 74–87.

Kristiansen, K. (1978). The consumption of wealth in Bronze Age Denmark: a study of the dynamics of economic process in tribal societies, in *New Directions in Scandinavian Archaeology* (Ed. K. Kristiansen and

C. Paludan-Muller), 158–90. National Museum, Copenhagen.

Kristiansen, K. (1981). Economic models for Bronze Age Scandinavia—towards an integrated approach, in *Economic Archaeology* (Ed. A. Sheridan and G. N. Bailey), 239–303. British Archaeological Reports S96, Oxford.

Kristiansen, K. (1982). The formation of tribal systems in later European prehistory: northern Europe 4000–800 BC, in *Theory and Explanation in Archaeology* (Ed. C. Renfrew, M. Rowlands and B. Seagraves), 241–80. Academic Press, London and New York.

Kromer, K. (1959). *Das Gräberfeld von Hallstatt*. Sansoni, Florence.

Kruk, J. (1973). *Studia Osadnicze nad Neolitem Wyzyn Lessowych*. Polish Academy, Wroclaw.

Kruk, J. (1980). *The Neolithic Settlement of southern Poland*. British Archaeological Reports S93, Oxford.

Kruta, V. (1975). Les habitats et nécropoles laténiens en Bohême, in *L'Habitat et la Nécropole à l'Age de Fer en Europe occidentale et centrale* (Ed. P.-M. Duval and V. Kruta), 95–102. Librairie Honoré Champion, Paris.

Kukla, G. J. (1975). Loess stratigraphy of central Europe, in *After the Australopithecines* (Ed. K. W. Butzer and G. Isaac), 99–188. Mouton, The Hague.

Kukla, G. J. (1977). Pleistocene land-sea correlations. I: Europe, *Earth Science Review* 13, 307–74.

Kuper, R. and Piepers, W. (1966). Eine Siedlung der Rössener Kultur in Inden (Kreis Jülich) und Lamersdorf (Kreis Düren). Vorbericht, *Bonner Jahrbücher* 166, 270–76.

Kuper, R., Lohr, H., Lüning, J., Stehli, P. and Zimmerman, A. (1977). *Der Bandkeramische Siedlungplatz Langweiler 9, Gem. Aldenhoven, Kr. Düren*. Rheinische Ausgrabungen 18. Rheinland-Verlag, Bonn.

Kurtén, B. (1968). *Pleistocene Mammals of Europe*. Weidenfeld and Nicholson, London.

Lalanne, J. G. and Bouyssonie, J. (1941–6). Le gisement paléolithique de Laussel, *L'Anthropologie* 50, 1–163.

Lalanne, G. and Breuil, H. (1911). L'abri sculpté du Cap-Blanc à Laussel (Dordogne), *L'Anthropologie* 22, 385–402.

Lanting, J. N. and van der Waals, J. D. (Eds) (1975). *Glockenbechersymposium Oberried 1974*. Fibula-van Dishoeck, Bussum.

Laplace, G. (1966). *Recherches sur l'Origine et l'Évolution des Complexes leptolithiques*. École Française de Rome, Mélanges d'Archaeologie et d'Histoire 4 (XII), Rome.

László, A. (1977). Anfänge der Benutzung und der Bearbeitung des Eisens auf dem Gebiete Rumäniens, *Acta Archaeologica Academiae Scientiarum Hungaricae* 29, 53–75.

Laville, H., Rigaud, J.-P. and Sackett, J. (1980). *Rock Shelters of the Périgord*. Academic Press, London and New York.

Lee, R. B. (1968). What hunters do for a living, or how to make out on scarce resources, in *Man the Hunter* (Ed. R. B. Lee and I. DeVore), 30–48. Aldine, Chicago.

Lee, R. B. and DeVore, I. (Eds) (1968). *Man the Hunter*. Aldine, Chicago.

Lee, R. B. and DeVore, I. (Eds) (1976). *Kalahari Hunter-gatherers*. Harvard University Press, Cambridge, Mass.

Legge, A. J. (1972). Cave climates, in *Papers in Economic Prehistory* (Ed. E. S. Higgs), 97–103. Cambridge University Press, Cambridge.

Leonardi, P. and Broglio, A. (1962). *Le Paléolithique de la Vénétie*. Annali dell'Universita di Ferrara, Ferrara.

Leroi-Gourhan, A. (1968). *The Art of Prehistoric Man in Western Europe*. Thames and Hudson, London.

Leroi-Gourhan, A. (1982). *The Dawn of European Art*. Cambridge University Press, Cambridge.

Leroi-Gourhan, A. and Brézillon, M. (1966). L'habitation magdalénienne no. 1 de Pincevent (Seine-et-Marne), *Gallia Préhistoire* 9, 263–385.

Leroi-Gourhan, A. and Leroi-Gourhan, Arl. (1964). Chronologie des grottes d'Arcy-sur-Cure (Yonne), *Gallia Préhistoire* 7, 1–64.

Leroi-Gourhan, Arl. and Allain, J. (1979). *Lascaux Inconnu*. Gallia Préhistoire Supplement 12. C.N.R.S., Paris.

LeRoux, C. T. and Cordier, G. (1974). Étude pétrographique des haches polies de Touraine, *Bulletin de la Société Préhistorique Française* 71, 335–54.

Lévêque, F. and Vandermeersch, B. (1980). Les découvertes de restes humains dans un horizon castelperronien de Saint-Cesaire (Charente-Maritime), *Bulletin de la Société Préhistorique Française* 77, 35.

Levy, J. E. (1982). *Social and Religious Organization in Bronze Age Denmark: an Analysis of Ritual Hoard Finds*. British Archaeological Reports S142, Oxford.

Lewthwaite, J. (1981). Plains tails from the hills: transhumance in Mediterranean archaeology, in *Economic Archaeology* (Ed. A. Sheridan and G. N. Bailey), 57–66. British Archaeological Reports S96, Oxford.

Lichardus, J. (1980). Zur Funktion der Geweihspitzen des Typus Ostorf, *Germania* 58, 1–24.

Lieberman, P. (1976). Interactive models for evolution: neural mechanisms, anatomy and behaviour, in *Origins and Evolution of Language and Speech* (Ed. S.Harnad, H. D. Steklis and J. Lancaster), 660–72. Annals of the New York Academy of Sciences 280, New York.

Lieberman, P. and Crelin, E. S. (1971). On the speech of neanderthal man, *Linguistic Enquiry* 11, 203–22.

Lindquist, S.-O. (1974). The development of the agrarian landscape on Gotland during the early Iron Age, *Norwegian Archaeological Review* 7, 6–32.

Lomborg, E. (1973). *Die Flintdolche Dänemarks*. Nordiske Fortidsminder, B1,1. Copenhagen.

Lorenz, H. (1978). Totenbrachtum und Tracht: Untersuchungen in der frühen Latènezeit, *Bericht der Römisch-Germanischen Kommission* 59, 1–380.

Louis, M., Taffanel, O. and Taffanel, J. (1955/60). *Le premier Age de Fer languedocien*, Vols I–III. Instituo di Studi Liguri, Bordighera.

Louwe Kooijmans, L. P. (1974). *The Rhine/Meuse Delta*. Analecta Praehistorica Leidensia 7. University of Leiden Press, Leiden.

Lubbock, J. (1865). *Pre-historic Times*. Williams and Norgate, London.

Lumley, H. de (1969a). *Le Paléolithique Inférieur et Moyen*

du Midi Méditerranéen dans son Cadre Géologique.
I: Ligurie-Provence. Gallia Préhistoire Supplement 5.
C.N.R.S., Paris.

Lumley, H. de (1969b). *Une Cabane Acheuléenne dans la Grotte du Lazaret.* Mémoires de la Société Préhistorique Francaise 7, Paris.

Lumley, H. de (1976). Les premières industries humaines en Provence, in *La Préhistoire Francaise*, Vol. 1 (Ed. H. de Lumley), 765–76. C.N.R.S., Paris.

Lumley, H. de, Fontvielle, M. E. and Abelanet, J. (1976). Les gravures rupestres de l'age du bronze dans la region du Mont Bego (Tende, Alpes-Maritimes), in *La Préhistoire Francaise*, Vol. 2 (Ed. J. Guilaine), 222–36. C.N.R.S., Paris.

Lumley, M.-A. de (1973). *Anté-néandertaliens et Néandertaliens du Bassin Mediterranéen Occidental.* Études Quaternaires 2. C.N.R.S., Paris.

Lumley, M.-A. de (1975). Ante-neanderthals of western Europe, in *Palaeoanthropology* (Ed. R. Tuttle), 381–87. Mouton, The Hague.

Lumley, M.-A. de (1976). Les anténéandertaliens dans le sud, in *La Préhistoire Francaise*, Vol. 1 (ed. H. de Lumley), 547–60. C.N.R.S., Paris.

Lüning, J. (1969). Die Entwicklung der Keramik beim Übergang vom Mittel- zum Jungneolithikum in süddeutschen Raum, *Bericht der Römisch-Germanischen Kommission* 50, 1–98.

Luttropp, A. and Bosinski, G. (1971). *Der altsteinzeitliche Fundplatz Reutersruh bei Ziegenhain in Hessen.* Fundamenta Reihe A, Band 6. Böhlau, Cologne.

Lynch, A. (1981). *Man and Environment in south-west Ireland, 4000BC–AD800.* British Archaeological Reports 85, Oxford.

Maier, F. (1970). *Die bemalte Spätlatènekeramik von Manching.* Franz Steiner, Wiesbaden.

Maier, F. (1974). Gedanken zur Entstehung der industriellen Grosssiedlung der Hallatatt- und Latènezeit auf dem Dürrnberg bei Hallein, *Germania* 52, 326–47.

Malinowski, T. (1961). Obrazadek pogrzebowy ludności kultury łuzyckiej w Polsce (with summary in French), *Przegląd Archaeologiczny* 14, 5–135.

Malinowski, T. (1971). Über die Bernsteinhandel zwischen den südlichen baltischen Üfergebieten und dem Süden Europas in der frühen Eisenzeit, *Prähistorische Zeitzchrift* 46, 102–10.

Maluquer de Motes, J. M. (1954–58). *El Poblado hallstattico de Cortes de Navarra*, Vols I–II. Barcelona.

Maluquer de Motes, J. M. (1971). Late Bronze Age and early Iron Age in the valley of the Ebro, in *The European Community in Later Prehistory* (Ed. J. Boardman, M. A. Brown and T. G. E. Powell), 105–20. Routledge and Kegan Paul, London.

Mania, D. (1975). Bilzingsleben (Thüringen): eine neue altpaläolithische Fundstelle mit Knochenreste des *Homo erectus*, *Archäologisches Korrespondenzblatt* 5, 263–72.

Mania, D. and Dietzel, A. (1980). *Begegnung mit dem Urmensch.* Urania, Leipzig.

Mania, D. and Toepfer, V. (1973). *Königsaue.* Veröffentlichungen des Landesmuseums für Vorgeschichte in Halle, Band 26, Berlin.

Mania, D., Toepfer, V. and Vlček, E. (1980). *Bilzingsleben I.* Veröffentlichungen des Landesmuseums für Vorgeschichte in Halle, Band 32, Berlin.

Mansuelli, G. A. (1979). The Etruscan city, in *Italy before the Romans: the Iron Age, Orientalizing and Etruscan Periods* (Ed. D. Ridgway and F. R. Ridgway), 353–71. Academic Press, London and New York.

Marazzi, M. and Tusa, S. (1979). Die mykenische Penetration im westlichen Mittelmeerraum, *Klio* 61, 309–51.

Mariën, M. E. (1970). *Le Trou de l'Ambre au Bois de Wérimont, Éprave.* Monographies d'Archéologie Nationale, 4. Musées Royaux d'Art et d'Histoire, Brussels.

Marshack, A. (1972). *The Roots of Civilization.* McGraw Hill, New York.

Mateescu, C. N. (1975). Remarks on cattle breeding and agriculture in the middle and late neolithic on the Lower Danube, *Dacia* 19, 13–18.

Mathers, C. (n.d.). Beyond the grave: the wider context of burial in south-east Spain. Unpublished paper.

Mathiassen, T., Degerbol, M. and Troels-Smith, J. (1942). *Dyrholmen. En stenalderboplads pa Djursland.* Det Kongelike Danske Videnskabernes Selskab, Archaeologisk-Kunsthistorisk Skrifte 1,1. Copenhagen.

Matthias, W. (1974). *Kataloge zur mitteldeutschen Schnurkeramik Teil IV: Südharz-Unstrut Gebiet.* German Academy of Sciences, Berlin.

Matthias, W. (1976). Die Salzproduktion—ein bedeutender Faktor in der Wirtschaft der frühbronzezeitlichen Bevölkerung an der mittleren Saale, *Jahresschrift für mitteldeutsche Vorgeschichte* 60, 373–94.

McBurney, C. B. M. (1950). The geographical study of the older palaeolithic stages in Europe, *Proceedings of the Prehistoric Society* 16, 163–83.

McBurney, C. B. M. (1976). *Early Man in the Soviet Union.* British Academy, London.

McBurney, C. B. M. and Callow, P. (1971). The Cambridge excavations at La Cotte de Saint Brelade, Jersey—a preliminary report, *Proceedings of the Prehistoric Society* 37, 167–207.

McDonald, W. and Rapp, G. R. (1972). *The Minnesota Messenia Expedition.* University of Minnesota Press, Minneapolis.

Meduna, J. (1970). Die keltische Oppidum Staré Hradisko in Mähren, *Germania* 48, 34–59.

Megaw, J. V. S. (1970). *Art of the European Iron Age.* Adams and Dart, Bath.

Meier-Arendt, W. (1974). Zur Frage der Genese der Rössener Kultur, *Germania* 52, 1–15.

Meiklejohn, C. (1978). Ecological aspects of population size and growth in late-glacial and early post-glacial north-western Europe, in *The Early Post-glacial Settlement of Northern Europe* (Ed. P. Mellars), 65–79. Duckworth, London.

Meiklejohn, C. and Constandse-Westermann, T. S. (1979). The human skeletal material from Swifterbant, earlier neolithic of the northern Netherlands. 1: Inventory and demography, *Palaeohistoria* 20, 39–89.

Mellaart, J. (1967). *Catal Hüyük: a Neolithic Town in Anatolia.* Thames and Hudson, London.

Mellars, P. A. (1969). The chronology of mousterian industries in the Périgord region of south-western France, *Proceedings of the Prehistoric Society* **35**, 134–71.

Mellars, P. A. (1970). Some comments on the notion of 'functional variability' in stone tool assemblages, *World Archaeology* **2**, 74–89.

Mellars, P. A. (1973). The character of the middle-upper palaeolithic transition in south-west France, in *The Explanation of Culture Change* (Ed. C. Renfrew), 255–76. Duckworth, London.

Mellars, P. A. (1976a). Fire ecology, animal populations and man: a study of some ecological relationships in prehistory, *Proceedings of the Prehistoric Society* **42**, 15–46.

Mellars, P. A. (1976b). Settlement patterns and industrial variability in the British mesolithic, in *Problems in Economic and Social Archaeology* (Ed. G. de G. Sieveking, I. H. Longworth and K. E. Wilson), 374–99. Duckworth, London.

Mellars, P. A. (1978a). Excavation and economic analysis of mesolithic shell middens on the island of Oronsay (Inner Hebrides), in *The Early Post-glacial Settlement of Northern Europe* (Ed. P. Mellars), 371–96. Duckworth, London.

Mellars, P. A. (Ed.) (1978b). *The Early Post-glacial Settlement of Northern Europe*. Duckworth, London.

Mercer, R. J. (1980). *Hambledon Hill*. Edinburgh University Press, Edinburgh.

Mercer, R. J. (1981a). *Grimes Graves, Norfolk. Excavations 1971–2*. H.M.S.O., London.

Mercer, R. J. (Ed.) (1981b). *Farming Practice in British Prehistory*. Edinburgh University Press, Edinburgh.

Mesolella, K. J., Matthews, R. K., Broecker, W. S. and Thurber, D. L. (1969). The astronomical theory of climatic change, Barbados data, *Journal of Geology* **77**, 250–74.

Mezzena, F. and Palma di Cesnola, A. (1972). Scoperta di una sepoltura gravettiana nella Grotta Paglicci (Rignano Garganico), *Rivista di Scienze Preistoriche* **27**, 27–50.

Mikov, V. (1959). The prehistoric mound of Karanovo, *Archaeology* **12**, 88–97.

Milisauskas, S. (1978). *European Prehistory*. Academic Press, London and New York.

Mook, W. G., Munaut, A. V. and Waterbolk, H. T. (1972). Determination of age and duration of stratified prehistoric bog settlements, *Proceedings of the 8th International Radiocarbon Dating Conference*, Vol. 2, 27–40. Royal Society of New Zealand, Wellington.

Moore, A. M. T. (1975). The excavation of Tell Abu Hureyra in Syria: a preliminary report, *Proceedings of the Prehistoric Society* **41**, 50–77.

Moosleitner, F., Pauli, P. and Penninger, E. (1974). *Der Dürrnberg bei Hallein*. Vol. 2. Münchener Beiträge zur Vor- und Frühgeschichte 17. C. H. Beck, Munich.

Mörner, N. A. and Wallin, B. (1977). 10,000 year temperature record from Gotland, Sweden, *Palaeogeography, Palaeo-climatology, Palaeoecology* **21**, 113–38.

Moscati, S. (1973). *The World of the Phoenicians*. Cardinal, London.

Movius, H. L. (1966). The hearths of the upper perigordian and aurignacian horizons at the Abri Pataud, Les Éyzies (Dordogne) and their possible significance, *American Anthropologist* **68**(2), 296–325.

Movius, H. L. (1969). The châtelperronien in French archaeology: the evidence of Arcy-sur-Cure, *Antiquity* **43**, 111–23.

Movius, H. L. (1977). *Excavation of the Abri Pataud, Les Éyzies (Dordogne): Stratigraphy*. American School of Prehistoric Research Bulletin 31, Peabody Museum, Harvard University, Cambridge, Mass.

Mozsolics, A. (1967). *Bronzefunde des Karpatenbeckens. Depotfundhorizont von Apa und Hajdúsamson*. Akadémiai Kiadó, Budapest.

Mozsolics, A. (1973). *Bronze- und Goldfunde des Karpatenbeckens. Depotfundhorizont von Forró und Ópályi*. Akadémiai Kiadó, Budapest.

Muckelroy, K. (1981). Middle Bronze Age trade between Britain and Europe: a maritime perspective, *Proceedings of the Prehistoric Society* **47**, 279–97.

Müller, H.-H. (1964). *Die Haustiere der mitteldeutschen Bandkeramiker*. German Academy of Sciences, Berlin.

Müller-Beck, H.-J. (1965). *Seeberg Burgäschisee-Süd. 5: Holzgeräte und Holzbearbeitung*. Acta Bernensia 2. Stampfli, Bern.

Müller-Karpe, H. (1956). Das urnenfelderzeitliche Wagengrab von Hart a. d. Alz, Oberbayern, *Bayerische Vorgeschichtsblätter* **21**, 46–75.

Müller-Karpe, H. (1959). *Beiträge zur Chronologie der Urnenfelderzeit nördlich und südlich der Alpen*. Römisch-Germanische Forschungen 22. De Gruyter, Berlin.

Müller-Karpe, H. (1962). Zur spätbronzezeitlichen Bewaffnung in Mitteleuropa und Griechenland, *Germania* **40**, 255–87.

Müller-Karpe, H. (1966). *Handbuch der Vorgeschichte. I: Altsteinzeit*. C. H. Beck, Munich.

Müller-Karpe, H. (1974). *Handbuch der Vorgeschichte. III: Kupferzeit*. C. H. Beck, Munich.

Müller-Wille, M. (1965). *Eisenzeitliche Fluren in der festländischen Nordseegebieten*. Geographischen Kommission für Westfalen, Münster.

Musil, R. (1980–1). *Ursus spelaeus. Der Höhlenbär*. Museum für Ur- und Frühgeschichte Thüringens, Weimar.

Nash, D. (1976a). The growth of urban society in France, in *Oppida: the Beginnings of Urbanisation in Barbarian Europe* (Ed. B. W. Cunliffe and R. T. Rowley), 95–133. British Archaeological Reports S11, Oxford.

Nash, D. (1976b). Reconstructing Poseidonios' Celtic ethnography, *Britannia* **7**, 111–26.

Nash, D. (1978). Territory and state formation in central Gaul, in *Social Organisation and Settlement* (Ed. D. Green, C. Haselgrove and M. Spriggs), 455–75. British Archaeological Reports S47, Oxford.

Navarro, J. M. de (1955). A doctor's grave from the Middle La Tène period from Bavaria, *Proceedings of the Prehistoric Society* **21**, 231–48.

Navarro, J. M. de (1972). *The Finds from La Tène. I: Scabbards and Swords found in them*. Oxford University Press, Oxford.

Needham, S. (1979). Two recent British shield finds and their continental parallels, *Proceedings of the Prehistoric Society* **45**, 111–34.

Neustupný, E. (1973). Factors affecting the variability of the Corded Ware culture, in *The Explanation of Culture Change* (Ed. C. Renfrew), 725–30. Duckworth, London.

Newcomer, M. H. (1971). Some quantitative experiments in handaxe manufacture, *World Archaeology* 3, 85–94.

Newcomer, M. H. (1974). Study and replication of bone tools from Ksar Akil (Lebanon), *World Archaeology* 6, 138–53.

Newell, R. R. (1973). The post-glacial adaptations of the indigenous population of the north-west European plain, in *The Mesolithic in Europe* (Ed. S. K. Kozłowski), 399–440. University Press, Warsaw.

Nikolov, B. (1978). Développement du chalcolithique en Bulgarie de l'ouest et du nord-ouest, *Studia Praehistorica* 1–2, 121–29.

Nobis, G. (1971). *Vom Wildpferd zum Hauspferd*. Fundamenta Reihe B, Band 6. Böhlau, Cologne.

Noe-Nygaard, N. (1974). Mesolithic hunting in Denmark illustrated by bone injuries caused by human weapons, *Journal of Archaeological Science* 1, 217–48.

Northover, P. (1980). Bronze in the British Bronze Age, in *Aspects of Early Metallurgy* (Ed. W. A. Oddy), 63–70. British Museum Publications, London.

Northover, P. (1982). The metallurgy of the Wilburton hoards, *Oxford Journal of Archaeology* 1, 69–109.

Novotná, M. (1973). Einige Bemerkungen zur Datierung der Kupferindustrie in der Slowakei, *Musaica* 13, 5–21.

Oakley, K. P. (1949). *Man the Tool-maker* (1st edition; 6th edition, 1972). British Museum, London.

Oakley, K. P., Campbell, B. G. and Molleson, T. I. (1971). *Catalogue of Fossil Hominids. Vol. 2: Europe*. British Museum (Natural History), London.

Oakley, K. P., Andrews, P., Keeley, L. H. and Clark, J. D. (1977). A reappraisal of the Clacton spearpoint, *Proceedings of the Prehistoric Society* 43, 13–30.

O'Connor, B. (1980). *Cross-channel Relations in the Later Bronze Age*. British Archaeological Reports S91, Oxford.

O'Kelly, M. J. (1973). Current excavations at Newgrange, Ireland, in *Megalithic Graves and Ritual* (Ed. G. E. Daniel and P. Kjaerum), 137–46. Jutland Archaeological Society Publication 11, Copenhagen.

O'Kelly, M. J. (1979). The restoration of Newgrange, *Antiquity* 53, 205–10.

O'Kelly, M. J. (1981). The megalithic tombs of Ireland, in *Antiquity and Man: Essays in Honour of Glyn Daniel* (Ed. B. W. Cunliffe, J. D. Evans and C. Renfrew), 177–90. Duckworth, London.

O'Shea, J. (1981). Coping with scarcity: exchange and social storage, in *Economic Archaeology* (Ed. A. Sheridan and G. N. Bailey), 167–83. British Archaeological Reports S96, Oxford.

Östenberg, C. E. (1967). *Luni sul Mignone e Problemi della Preistoria italiana*. Gleerup, Lund.

Oswalt, W. H. (1976). *An Anthropological Analysis of Food-getting Technology*. John Wiley and Sons, New York.

Ottaway, B. (1973). The earliest copper ornaments in northern Europe, *Proceedings of the Prehistoric Society* 39, 294–331.

Ottaway, B. and Strahm, C. (1975). Swiss neolithic copper beads: currency, ornament or prestige items, *World Archaeology* 6, 307–21.

Otte, M. (1979). *Le Paléolithique Supérieur Ancien en Belgique*. Monographies d'archéologie nationale, 5. Musées Royaux d'Art et d'Histoire, Brussels.

Otte, M. (1981). *Le Gravettien en Europe centrale*. Dissertationes Archaeologicae Gandenses. De Tempel, Bruges.

Otto, K.-H. (1955). *Die sozialökonomischen Verhältnisse bei den Stämmen der Leubinger Kultur in Mitteldeutschland*. Ethnographische-archäologische Forschungen 3, Pt. 1. Berlin.

Ovey, C. D. (Ed.) (1964). *The Swanscombe Skull*. Occasional Paper 20. Royal Anthropological Institute, London.

Pales, L. (1976). *Les Gravures de la Marche. II: Les Humains*. Ophrys, Paris.

Pallottino, M. (1978). *The Etruscans* (2nd English edition). Penguin, Harmondsworth.

Pallottino, M. (1979). The origins of Rome: a survey of recent discoveries and discussions, in *Italy before the Romans: the Iron Age, Orientalizing and Etruscan Periods* (Ed. D. Ridgway and F. R. Ridgway), 197–222. Academic Press, London and New York.

Palmer, L. R. (1965). *Myceneans and Minoans*. Faber, London.

Pareti, L. (1947). *La Tomba Regolini-Galassi*. Tipographia Poliglotta Vaticana, Vatican City.

Passard, F. (1980). L'habitat du néolithique et début de l'âge de bronze en Franche-Comté, *Gallia Préhistoire* 23, 37–114.

Pauli, L. (1971). *Studien zur Golasecca-Kultur*. Kerle Verlag, Heidelberg.

Pauli, L. (1978). *Der Dürrnberg bei Hallein*. Vol. 3. Münchener Beiträge zur Vor- und Frühgeschichte 18. C. H. Beck, Munich.

Paulík, J. (1963). K. problematike čakanskej kultúry v karpatskej kotline (with German summary), *Slovenská Archaeológia* 11, 269–338.

Pavelčik, J. (1973). Befestigte Industriezentren der Träger der Badener Kultur und ihr Platz in der gesellschaftlich-ökonomischen Entwicklung des östlichen Teiles Mitteleuropas, *Musaica* 13, 41–50.

Payne, S. (1972). On the interpretation of bone samples from archaeological sites, in *Papers in Economic Prehistory* (Ed. E. S. Higgs), 65–81. Cambridge University Press, Cambridge.

Payne, S. (1975). Faunal change at Franchthi Cave from 20,000 BC to 3000 BC, in *Archaeozoological Studies* (Ed. A. T. Clason), 120–31. North-Holland Publishing Company, Amsterdam.

Peacock, D. P. S. (1969). Neolithic pottery production in Cornwall, *Antiquity* 43, 145–49.

Peacock, D. P. S. (1971). Roman amphorae in pre-Roman Britain, in *The Iron Age and its Hill-forts* (Ed. M. Jesson and D. Hill), 161–88. University of Southampton, Southampton.

Penninger, E. (1972). *Der Dürrnberg bei Hallein*. Vol. 1. Münchener Beiträge zur Vor- und Frühgeschichte 16. C. H. Beck, Munich.

Pericot, L. G. (1942). *La Cueva des Parpalló*. Consejo superior de Investigaciones Cientificas, Instituto Diego Velázquez, Madrid.

Peroni, R. (1971). *L'Età del Bronzo nella Penisola italiana. 1: L'antica Età del Bronze*. Olschki, Florence.

Peroni, R., Carancini, G. L., Coretti Irdi, P., Ponzi Bonomi, L., Rallo, A., Saronio Masolo, P. and Serra Ridgway, F. R. (1975). *Studi sulla Cronologia delle Civiltà di Este e Golasecca*. Florence.

Pescheck, C. (1972). Ein reicher Grabfund mit Kesselwagen aus Unterfranken, *Germania* **50**, 29–56.

Peters, E. (1930). *Die altsteinzeitliche Kulturstätte Petersfels*. Benno Filser Verlag, Augsburg.

Petersen, E. B. (1970). Ølby Lyng: en ostjaellandsk Kystboplads med Ertebøllekultur, *Aarbøger for Nordisk Oldkyndighed og Historie*, 5–42.

Petersen, E. B. (1973). A survey of the late palaeolithic and mesolithic in Denmark, in *The Mesolithic in Europe* (Ed. S. K. Kozłowski), 77–128. University Press, Warsaw.

Peterson, G. M., Webb, T., Kutzbach, J. E., van der Hammen, T., Wijmstra, T. A. and Street, F. A. (1979). The continental record of environmental conditions at 18,000 yr B.P.: an initial evaluation, *Quaternary Research* **12**, 47–82.

Petersson, M. (1951). Microlithen als Pfeilspitzen. Ein Fund aus dem Lilla Loshult Moor, Ksp. Loshult, Skåne, *Meddelanden fra Lunds Universitets Historiska Museum*, 123–37.

Petres, E. (1975). The late pre-Roman age in Hungary with special reference to oppida, in *Oppida: the Beginnings of Urbanisation in Barbarian Europe* (Ed. B. W. Cunliffe and R. T. Rowley), 51–80. British Archaeological Reports S11, Oxford.

Peyrony, D. (1930). Le Moustier: ses gisements, ses industries, ses couches géologiques, *Revue Anthropologique* **40**, 48–76, 155–76.

Peyrony, D. (1933). Les industries aurignaciennes dans le bassin de la Vézère: aurignacien et périgordien, *Bulletin de la Société Préhistorique Française* **30**, 543–59.

Peyrony, D. (1934). La Ferrassie — moustérien, périgordien, aurignacien, *Préhistoire* **3**, 1–92.

Peyrony, D. (1938). La Micoque: les fouilles récentes — leur significations, *Bulletin de la Société Préhistorique Française* **6**, 257–88.

Pfeiffer, J. E. (1978). *The Emergence of Man*. Harper and Row, New York.

Phillips, P. (1975). *Early Farmers of West Mediterranean Europe*. Hutchinson, London.

Phillips, P. (1980). *The Prehistory of Europe*. Allen Lane, London.

Pidoplichko, I. G. (1969). *Upper Palaeolithic Mammoth Bone Dwellings in the Ukraine* (in Russian). Mukova dumka, Ukraine.

Piggott, S. (1938). The early Bronze Age in Wessex, *Proceedings of the Prehistoric Society* **4**, 52–106.

Piggott, S. (1962). *The West Kennet Long Barrow: Excavations 1955–6*. H.M.S.O., London.

Piggott, S. (1965). *Ancient Europe*. Edinburgh University Press, Edinburgh.

Piggott, S. (1975a). *The Druids* (2nd edition). Thames and Hudson, London.

Piggott, S. (1975b). The beginnings of wheeled transport, in *Avenues to Antiquity* (Ed. B. Fagan), 212–20. W. H. Freeman, San Francisco.

Pilcher, J., Smith, A. G., Pearson, G. and Crowder, A. (1971). Land clearance in the Irish neolithic: new evidence and interpretation, *Science* **172**, 560–62.

Pingel, V. (1971). *Die glatte Drehscheiben-Keramik von Manching*. Franz Steiner, Wiesbaden.

Piperno, M. and Biddittu, I. (1978). Studio tipologico ed interpretazione dell'industria acheuleana e pre-musteriana dei livelli *m* ed *d* di Torre in Pietra (Roma), *Quaternaria* **20**, 441–536.

Pittioni, R. (1980). *Geschichte Österreichs. I: Urzeit*. Austrian Academy of Sciences, Vienna.

Pitts, M. (1979). Hides and antlers: a new look at the gather-hunter site at Star Carr, North Yorks., England, *World Archaeology* **11**, 32–42.

Piveteau, J. (1976). Les anté-néandertaliens du Sud-ouest, in *La Préhistoire Française*, Vol. 1 (Ed. H. de Lumley), 561–66. C.N.R.S., Paris.

Planck, D. (1982). Ein neuentdeckte keltische Viereckschanze in Fellbach-Schmiden, Rems-Murr-Kreis, *Germania* **60**, 105–72.

Pleiner, R. (1980). Early iron metallurgy in Europe, in *The Coming of the Age of Iron* (Ed. T. A. Wertime and J. D. Muhly), 375–415. Yale University Press, New Haven and London.

Popham, M., Sackett, L. H. and Themelis, P. G. (Eds) (1979). *Lefkandi I: the Iron Age*. Thames and Hudson, London.

Poser, H. (1948). Boden- und Klimaverhältnisse in Mittel- und Westeuropa während der Würmeiszeit, *Erdkunde* **2**, 53–68.

Potter, T. W. (1976). *A Faliscan Town in south Etruria: Excavations at Narce 1966–71*. British School of Archaeology at Rome, London.

Potter, T. W. (1979). *The Changing Landscape of South Etruria*. Paul Elek, London.

Potts, R. and Shipman, P. (1981). Cutmarks made by stone tools on bones from Olduvai Gorge, Tanzania, *Nature* **291**, 577–80.

Powell, T. G. E. (Ed.) (1969). *Megalithic Enquiries in the west of Britain*. Liverpool University Press, Liverpool.

Powell, T. G. E. (1971). From Urartu to Gundestrup: the agency of Thracian metal-work, in *The European Community in Later Prehistory* (Ed. J. Boardman, M. A. Brown and T. G. E. Powell), 181–210. Routledge and Kegan Paul, London.

Powell, T. G. E. (1980). *The Celts* (2nd edition). Thames and Hudson, London.

Preuss, J. (1966). *Die Baalberger Gruppe in Mitteldeutschland*. German Academy of Sciences, Berlin.

Price, T. D. (1978). Mesolithic settlement systems in the Netherlands, in *The Early Post-glacial Settlement of Northern Europe* (Ed. P. Mellars), 81–113. Duckworth, London.

Protsch, R. and Berger, R. (1973). Earliest radiocarbon dates for domesticated animals, *Science* **179**, 235–39.

Rackham, O. (1977). Neolithic woodland management in the Somerset Levels: Garvin's, Walton Heath and Rowland's tracks, *Somerset Levels Papers* **2**, 65–71. Department of Archaeology, University of Cambridge, Cambridge.

Raddatz, Z. (1967). *Das Wagengrab der jüngeren vorrömischen Eisenzeit von Husby, Kreis Flensburg.* Offa-Bücher 20. Karl Wachholtz, Neumünster.

Radley, J. and Mellars, P. A. (1964). A mesolithic structure at Deepcar, Yorkshire, England, and the affinities of its associated flint industry, *Proceedings of the Prehistoric Society* **30**, 1–24.

Radmilli, A. M. (1974). *Gli scavi nella grotta Polesini a Ponte Lucano di Tivoli e la più antiche arte nel Lazio.* Samsoni, Florence.

Randsborg, K. (1974). Social stratification in early Bronze Age Denmark: a study in the regulation of cultural systems, *Prähistorische Zeitschrift* **49**, 38–61.

Randsborg, K. (1975). Social dimensions of early neolithic Denmark, *Proceedings of the Prehistoric Society* **41**, 105–18.

Randsborg, K. (1980). Resource distribution and the function of copper in early neolithic Denmark, in *The Origins of Metallurgy in Atlantic Europe* (Ed. M. Ryan), 303–18. Irish Stationery Office, Dublin.

Rankine, W. F. (1949). Pebbles of non-local rock from mesolithic chipping floors, *Proceedings of the Prehistoric Society* **15**, 193–94.

Ranov, V. and Davis, R. (1979). Toward a new outline of the Soviet Central Asian palaeolithic, *Current Anthropology* **20**(2), 249–70.

Rathje, A. (1979). Oriental imports in Etruria in the eighth and seventh centuries BC: their origins and implications, in *Italy before the Romans: the Iron Age, Orientalizing and Etruscan periods* (Ed. D. Ridgway and F. R. Ridgway), 145–83. Academic Press, London and New York.

Reader, J. (1981). *Missing Links.* Collins, London.

Renfrew, A. C. (1967). Colonialism and megalithismus, *Antiquity* **41**, 276–88.

Renfrew, A. C. (1969). Trade and culture process, *Current Anthropology* **10**, 151–69.

Renfrew, A. C. (1971). Sitagroi, radiocarbon and the prehistory of south-east Europe, *Antiquity* **45**, 275–82.

Renfrew, A. C. (1972). *The Emergence of Civilisation. The Cyclades and the Aegean in the third millennium B.C.* Methuen, London.

Renfrew, A. C. (1973a). Monuments, mobilisation and social organization in neolithic Wessex, in *The Explanation of Culture Change* (Ed. C. Renfrew), 539–58. Duckworth, London.

Renfrew, A. C. (1973b). *Before Civilization.* Jonathan Cape, London.

Renfrew, A. C. (1974). Beyond a subsistence economy: the evolution of social organization in prehistoric Europe, in *Reconstructing Complex Societies* (Ed. C. B. Moore), 69–95. Bulletin of the American Schools of Oriental Research, Supplement 20.

Renfrew, A. C. (1977). Alternative models for exchange and spatial distribution, in *Exchange Systems in Prehistory* (Ed. T. K. Earle and J. E. Ericson), 71–90. Academic Press, London and New York.

Renfrew, A. C. and Shennan, S. J. (Eds) (1982). *Ranking, Resource and Exchange: Aspects of the Archaeology of Early European Society.* Cambridge University Press, Cambridge.

Renfrew, A. C. and Wagstaff, J. M. (Eds) (1982). *An Island Polity. The Archaeology of Exploitation in Melos.* Cambridge University Press, Cambridge.

Renfrew, J. M. (1973). *Palaeoethnobotany: the Prehistoric Food Plants of the Near East and Europe.* Methuen, London.

Ridgway, D. (1973). The first western Greeks, in *Greeks, Celts and Romans* (Ed. C. F. C. Hawkes and S. Hawkes), 5–36. Dent, London.

Ridgway, D. and Ridgway, F. R. (Eds) (1979). *Italy before the Romans: the Iron Age, Orientalizing and Etruscan Periods.* Academic Press, London and New York.

Ridgway, F. R. (1979). The Este and Golasecca cultures: a chronological guide, in *Italy before the Romans: the Iron Age, Orientalizing and Etruscan Periods* (Ed. D. Ridgway and F. R. Ridgway), 419–87. Academic Press, London and New York.

Riek, G. (1934). *Die Eiszeitjägerstation am Vogelherd. I: Die Kulturen.* Heine, Tübingen.

Riek, G. (1973). *Das Paläolithikum der Brillenhöhle bei Blaubeuren, Schwäbische Alb.* Müller and Gräff, Stuttgart.

Riek, G. and Hundt, H.-J. (1962). *Der Hohmichele.* Römisch-Germanische Forschungen 25. De Gruyter, Berlin.

Rittatore Vonwiller, F. (1975). La cultura protovillanoviana, in *Popoli e Civiltà dell'Italia antica*, Vol. 4, 11–60. Rome.

Roche, J. (1972). Les amas coquilliers (concheiros) mésolithiques de Muge (Portugal), in *Die Anfänge des Neolithikums vom Orient bis Nordeuropa* (Ed. H. Schwabedissen), Vol. VII: *Westliches Mittelmeergebiet und Britische Inseln* (Ed. J. Lüning), 72–107. Böhlau, Cologne.

Rochna, O. (1962). Hallstattzeitliches Lignit- und Gagatschmuck: zur Verbreitung, Zeitstellung und Herkunft, *Fundberichte aus Schwaben* **16**, 44–83.

Rodden, R. J. (1965). An early neolithic village in Greece, *Scientific American* **212**, 83–91.

Rodwell, W. (1976). Coinage, oppida and the rise of Belgic power in south-eastern Britain, in *Oppida: the Beginnings of Urbanisation in Barbarian Europe* (Ed. B. W. Cunliffe and R. T. Rowley), 181–366. British Archaeological Reports S11, Oxford.

Roe, D. A. (1964). The British lower and middle palaeolithic: some problems, methods of study and preliminary results, *Proceedings of the Prehistoric Society* **30**, 245–67.

Roe, D. A. (1968). British lower and middle palaeolithic handaxe groups, *Proceedings of the Prehistoric Society* **34**, 1–82.

Roe, D. A. (1981). *The Lower and Middle Palaeolithic Periods in Britain.* Routledge and Kegan Paul, London.

Rolland, N. (1981). The interpretation of middle palaeolithic variability, *Man* **16**, 15–42.

Rosenfeld, A. (1977). Profile figures: schematisation of the human figure in the magdalenian culture of Europe, in *Form in Indigenous Art* (Ed. P. J. Ucko), 90–109. Duckworth, London.

Roth, H. (1974). Ein Ledermesser der atlantischen Bronzezeit aus Mittelfranken, *Archäologisches Korrespondenzblatt* **4**, 37–47.

Roudil, J. L. and Soulier, M. (1976). La salle sépulchrale Ia (de la grotte du Hasard, Gard) et le commerce de l'ambre en Languedoc-oriental, *Gallia Préhistoire* **19**, 173–200.

Rowlands, M. J. (1976). *The Production and Distribution of Metalwork in the Middle Bronze Age in southern Britain*. British Archaeological Reports 31, Oxford.

Rowlands, M. J. (1980). Kinship, alliance and exchange in the European Bronze Age, in *Settlement and Society in the British Later Bronze Age* (Ed. J. Barrett and R. J. Bradley), 15–55. British Archaeological Reports 83, Oxford.

Rowlett, R. M. and Schneider, M. J. (1974). The material expression of neanderthal child care, in *The Human Mirror* (Ed. M. Richardson), 41–58. Louisiana State University Press, Bâton Rouge.

Royal Commission on Historical Monuments, England. (1979). *Stonehenge and its Environs*. Edinburgh University Press, Edinburgh.

Rozoy, J. G. (1978). *Les Derniers Chasseurs: l'Épipaleolithique en France et en Belgique. Essai de synthèse*. Bulletin spécial de la Société Archéologique Champenoise, Charleville.

Sackett, J. R. (1977). The meaning of style in archaeology: a general model, *American Antiquity* **42**, 369–80.

Sackett, J. R. (1982). Approaches to style in lithic archaeology, *Journal of Anthropological Archaeology* **1**, 59–112.

Sahlins, M. (1972). *Stone Age Economics*. Aldine, Chicago.

Sahlins, M. (1977). *Culture and Practical Reason*. University of Chicago Press, Chicago.

Saint-Périer, R. de (1930, 1936, 1950). *La Grotte Isturitz*. Archives de l'Institut de Paléontologie Humaine, Mémoires 7/17/25, Paris.

Sakellaridis, M. (1979). *The Economic Exploitation of the Swiss Area in the Mesolithic and Neolithic Periods*. British Archaeological Reports S67, Oxford.

Sandars, N. K. (1968). *Prehistoric Art in Europe*. Penguin, Harmondsworth.

Sangmeister, E. (1976). Das Verhältnis der Glockenbecherkultur zu den einheimischen Kulturen der ibersichen Halbinsel, in *Glockenbechersymposium Oberried 1974* (Ed. J. N. Lanting and J. D. van der Waals), 423–38. Fibula-van Dishoeck, Bussum.

Sangmeister, E. and Schubart, H. (1972). Zambujal, *Antiquity* **46**, 191–97.

Santonja, M., López-Martínez, N. and Pérez-González, A. (1980). Occupaciones achelenses en el valle del Jarama (Arganda, Madrid), *Arquelogia y Paleoecologia* **1**, 1–352.

Savory, H. N. (1968). *Spain and Portugal*. Thames and Hudson, London.

Schaaf, U. (1969). Versuch einer regionalen Gliederung frühlatènezeitlicher Fürstengräber, in *Marburger Beiträge zur Archäologie der Kelten* (Ed. O.-H. Frey), 187–202. Fundberichte aus Hessen, Beiheft 1. Habelt, Bonn.

Schaaf, U. and Taylor, A. (1975). Südimporte im Raum der Alpen (6.-4. Jahrhundert v. Chr.), in *Ausgrabungen in Deutschland*, Vol. 3, 312–16. Römisch-Germanisches Zentralmuseum, Mainz.

Schauer, P. (1975a). Die Bewaffnung der 'Adelskrieger' während der späten Bronze- und frühen Eisenzeit, in *Ausgrabungen in Deutschland*, Vol. 3, 305–11. Römisch-Germanisches Zentralmuseum, Mainz.

Schauer, P. (1975b). Beginn und Dauer der Urnenfelderkultur in Südfrankreich, *Germania* **53**, 47–63.

Schiek, S. (1953). Das Hallstattgrab von Vilsingen, in *Festschrift für Peter Goesller: Tübinger Beiträge zur Vor- und Frühgeschichte*, 150–67. Kohlhammer, Stuttgart.

Schild, R. (1971). Location of the so-called chocolate flint extraction sites on the north-eastern footslopes of the Holy Cross Mountains (in Polish), *Folia Quaternaria* **39**, 1–61.

Schild, R. (1975). Późny paleolit, in *Prahistoria ziem Polskich. I: Paleolit i Mezolit* (Ed. W. Chmielewski, R. Schild and H. Więckowska), 159–338. Polish Academy, Warsaw.

Schild, R. (1976). The final palaeolithic settlements of the European plain, *Scientific American* **234**, 88–99.

Schindler, R. (1968). *Stüdien zum vorgeschichtlichen Siedlungs- und Befestigungswesen der Saarlandes*. Paulinus-Verlag, Trier.

Schindler, R. (1977). *Die Altburg von Bundenbach*. von Zabern, Mainz.

Schlette, F. (1969). Das Siedlungswesen der Becherkulturen, in *Die neolitischen Becherkulturen im Gebiet der DDR und ihre europäischen Beziehungen* (Ed. H. Behrens and F. Schlette), 155–68. German Academy of Sciences, Berlin.

Schmid, E. (1969). Cave sediments and prehistory, in *Science in Archaeology* (Ed. D. Brothwell and E. S. Higgs), 151–66. Thames and Hudson, London.

Schmid, P. (1978). New archaeological results of settlement structures (Roman Iron Age) in the northwest German coastal area, in *Lowland Iron Age Communities in Europe* (Ed. B. W. Cunliffe and R. T. Rowley), 123–45. British Archaeological Reports S48, Oxford.

Schubart, H. (1975). *Die Kulturen der Bronzezeit im Südwesten der iberischen Halbinsel*. Madrider Forschungen 9. German Archaeological Institute, Madrid.

Schubart, H. (1976). Eine bronzezeitliche Kultur im Südwesten der iberischen Halbinsel, in *Acculturation and Continuity in Atlantic Europe* (Ed. S. J. de Laet), 221–34. Dissertationes Archaeologicae Gandenses 16. De Tempel, Bruges.

Schubert, E. (1973). Stüdien zur frühen Bronzezeit an der mittleren Donau, *Bericht der Römisch-Germanischen Kommission* **54**, 1–105.

Schuldt, E. (1961). *Hohen Viecheln: ein mittelsteinzeitlicher Wohnplatz in Mecklenburg*. German Academy of Sciences, Berlin.

Schüle, W. and Pellicer, M. (1966). *El Cerro de la Virgen*,

Orce (Granada). Ministry of Education and Science, Madrid.

Schwab, H. (1974). Neue Ergebnisse zur Topographie von La Tène, *Germania* **52**, 348–67.

Schwabedissen, H. (1954). *Die Feddermesser-Gruppen des nordwesteuropäischen Flachlandes*. Offa-Bücher 7. Karl Wachholtz, Neumünster.

Schwabedissen, H. (1970). Zur Verbreitung der Faustkeile in Mitteleuropa, in *Frühe Menschheit und Umwelt*, 61–98. Fundamenta Reihe A, Band 2. Böhlau, Cologne.

Schwappach, F. (1973). Frühkeltisches Ornament zwischen Marne, Rhein und Moldau, *Bonner Jahrbücher* **173**, 53–112.

Schwarz, G. T. (1964). Gallo-Römische Gewichte in Aventicum, *Schweizer Münzblätter* **13/14**, 150–57.

Scott, K. (1980). Two hunting episodes of middle palaeolithic age at La Cotte de Saint-Brelade, Jersey (Channel Islands), *World Archaeology* **12**, 137–52.

Scullard, H. H. (1967). *The Etruscan Cities and Rome*. Thames and Hudson, London.

Semenov, S. A. (1964). *Prehistoric Technology*. Cory, Adams and Mackay, London.

Service, E. R. (1962). *Primitive Social Organization: an evolutionary perspective*. Random House, New York.

Sevink, J., Hebeda, E. H., Priem, H. N. A. and Verschure, R. H. (1981). A note on the approximately 730,000-year-old mammal fauna and associated human activity sites near Isernia, central Italy, *Journal of Archaeological Science* **8**, 105–6.

Shackleton, N. J. (1969). The last interglacial in the marine and terrestrial record, *Proceedings of the Royal Society of London* **B174**, 135–54.

Shackleton, N. J. and Opdyke, N. D. (1973). Oxygen isotope and palaeomagnetic stratigraphy of Equatorial Pacific core V28-238, *Quaternary Research* **3**, 39–55.

Shackleton, N. J. and Renfrew, A. C. (1970). Neolithic trade routes realigned by oxygen isotope analysis, *Nature* **228**, 1062–64.

Shanks, M. and Tilley, C. (1982). Ideology, symbolic power and ritual communication: a re-interpretation of neolithic mortuary practices, in *Symbolic and Structural Archaeology* (Ed. I. Hodder), 129–54. Cambridge University Press, Cambridge.

Shennan, S. E. (1975). The social organization at Branč, *Antiquity* **49**, 279–88.

Shennan, S. E. (1982). From minimal to moderate ranking, in *Ranking, Resource and Exchange* (Ed. C. Renfrew and S. J. Shennan), 27–32. Cambridge University Press, Cambridge.

Shennan, S. J. (1976). Bell beakers and their context in central Europe, in *Glockenbechersymposium Oberried 1974* (Ed. J. N. Lanting and J. D. van der Waals), 231–39. Fibula-van Dishoeck, Bussum.

Shennan, S. J. (1977a). The appearance of the Bell Beaker assemblage in central Europe, in *Beakers in Britain and Europe: four studies* (Ed. R. J. Mercer), 51–70. British Archaeological Reports S26, Oxford.

Shennan, S. J. (1977b). *Bell Beakers and their Context in*

Central Europe: a New Approach. Unpublished Ph.D. dissertation, University of Cambridge.

Shennan, S. J. (1982a). Exchange and ranking: the role of amber in the earlier Bronze Age of Europe, in *Ranking, Resource and Exchange* (Ed. C. Renfrew and S. J. Shennan), 33–45. Cambridge University Press, Cambridge.

Shennan, S. J. (1982b). Ideology, change and the European early Bronze Age, in *Symbolic and Structural Archaeology* (Ed. I. Hodder), 155–61. Cambridge University Press, Cambridge.

Sheridan, A. and Bailey, G. N. (Eds) (1981). *Economic Archaeology: Towards an Integration of Ecological and Social Approaches*. British Archaeological Reports S96, Oxford.

Sherratt, A. (1976). Resources, technology and trade: an essay in early European metallurgy, in *Problems in Economic and Social Archaeology* (Ed. G. de G. Sieveking, I. H. Longworth and K. E. Wilson), 557–82. Duckworth, London.

Sherratt, A. (1980). Water, soil and seasonality in early cereal cultivation, *World Archaeology* **11**, 313–30.

Sherratt, A. (1981). Plough and pastoralism: aspects of the secondary products revolution, in *Pattern of the Past* (Ed. I. Hodder, G. Isaac and N. Hammond), 261–305. Cambridge University Press, Cambridge.

Silberbauer, G. B. (1972). The G/wi bushmen, in *Hunters and Gatherers Today* (Ed. M. Bicchieri), 271–326. Holt, Rinehart and Winston, New York.

Simmons, I. (1975). Towards an ecology of mesolithic man in the uplands of Britain, *Journal of Archaeological Science* **2**, 1–15.

Simmons, I. and Tooley, M. (Eds) (1981). *The Environment in British Prehistory*. Duckworth, London.

Sims, R. E. (1973). The anthropogenic factor in East Anglian vegetational history: an approach using A.P.F. techniques, in *Quaternary Plant Ecology* (Ed. H. J. B. Birks and R. G. West), 223–36. Blackwell, Oxford.

Singer, R., Wymer, J. J., Gladfelter, B. G. and Wolff, R. G. (1973). Excavation of the clactonian industry at the Golf course, Clacton-on-Sea, *Proceedings of the Prehistoric Society* **39**, 6–74.

Smiley, F. E., Sinopoli, C. M., Jackson, H. E., Wills, W. H. and Gregg, S. A. (1979–80). *The Archaeological Correlates of Hunter-gatherer Societies: Studies from the Ethnographic Record*. Michigan Discussions in Anthropology 5. University of Michigan, Ann Arbor.

Smith, I. F. (1965). *Windmill Hill and Avebury*. Clarendon, Oxford.

Smith, J. G. E. (1978). Economic uncertainty in an 'original affluent society': caribou and caribou-eater Chipewyan adaptive strategies, *Arctic Anthropology* **15**, 68–88.

Smith, K., Copen, J., Wainwright, G. J. and Beckett, S. (1981). The Shaugh Moor project: Third report—settlement and environmental investigations, *Proceedings of the Prehistoric Society* **47**, 205–73.

Smith, P. E. L. (1964). The solutrean culture, *Scientific American* **211**, 86–94.

Smith, P. E. L. (1966). *Le Solutréen en France*. Mémoire 5. Institut de Préhistoire de l'Université de Bordeaux, Bordeaux.

Snodgrass, A. M. (1971). *The Dark Age of Greece*. Edinburgh University Press, Edinburgh.

Snodgrass, A. M. (1980a). *Archaic Greece*. Dent, London.

Snodgrass, A. M. (1980b). Iron and early metallurgy in the Mediterranean, in *The Coming of the Age of Iron* (Ed. T. A. Wertime and J. D. Muhly), 335–74. Yale University Press, New Haven and London.

Soergel, W. (1943). *Der Klimacharakter der als nordisch geltenden Säugetiere des Eiszeitalters*. Heidelberg Academy of Sciences, Heidelberg.

Solier, Y. (1976/8). La culture ibéro-languedocienne aux VIe–Ve siècles, *Ampurias* **38–40**, 211–64.

Sonneville-Bordes, D. de (1960). *Le Paléolithique Supérieur en Périgord*. Delmas, Bordeaux.

Sonneville-Bordes, D. de (1973). The upper palaeolithic: c. 33,000–10,000 BC, in *France before the Romans* (Ed. S. Piggott, G. E. Daniel and C. McBurney), 30–60. Thames and Hudson, London.

Sonneville-Bordes, D. de (Ed.) (1979). *La Fin des Temps glaciaires en Europe*. C.N.R.S., Paris.

Sonneville-Bordes, D. de and Perrot, J. (1954–6). Lexique typologique du paléolithique supérieur: outillage lithique, *Bulletin de la Société Préhistorique Française* **51**, 327–35; **52**, 76–79; **53**, 408–12, 547–59.

Soudsky, B. (1969). Étude de la maison néolithique, *Slovenská Archaeológia* **17**, 5–96.

Spiess, A. E. (1979). *Reindeer and Caribou Hunters: an Archaeological Study*. Academic Press, London and New York.

Sprockhoff, E. (1930). *Zur Handelsgeschichte der germanischen Bronzezeit*. De Gruyter, Berlin.

Šramko, B. (1974). Zur Frage über die Technik und die Bearbeitungszentren von Buntmetallen in der Früheisenzeit, in *Symposium zur Problemen der jüngeren Hallstattzeit in Mitteleuropa* (Ed. B. Chropovský, M. Dušek and V. Podborský), 469–85. Slovak Academy of Sciences, Bratislava.

Srejovic, D. (1972). *Lepenski Vir*. Thames and Hudson, London.

Startin, W. and Bradley, R. J. (1981). Some notes on work organization and society in prehistoric Wessex, in *Astronomy and Society in Britain during the Period 4000–1500 BC* (Ed. C. L. N. Ruggles and A. W. R. Whittle), 289–96. British Archaeological Reports 88, Oxford.

Stead, I. M. (1967). A La Tène III burial at Welwyn Garden City, *Archaeologia* **101**, 1–62.

Stead, I. M. (1979). *The Arras Culture*. Yorkshire Philosophical Society, York.

Steiner, W. and Wagenbreth, O. (1971). Zur geologischen Situation der altsteinzeitlichen Rastplätze in unteren Travertin von Ehringsdorf bei Weimar, *Alt-Thüringen* **11**, 47–75.

Straus, L. G. (1977). Of deerslayers and mountain men: palaeolithic faunal exploitation in Cantabrian Spain, in *For Theory Building in Archaeology* (Ed. L. R. Binford), 41–76. Academic Press, London and New York.

Straus, L. G. (1982). Carnivores and cave sites in Cantabrian Spain, *Journal of Anthropological Research* **38**, 75–96.

Stringer, C. B. (1974). Population relationships of later pleistocene hominids: a multivariate study of available crania, *Journal of Archaeological Science* **1**, 317–42.

Stringer, C. B. (1982). Towards a solution of the neanderthal problem, *Journal of Human Evolution* **11**, 431–38.

Stringer, C. B., Clark Howell, F. and Melentis, J. K. (1979). The significance of the fossil hominid skull from Petralona, Greece, *Journal of Archaeological Science* **6**, 235–53.

Stubbings, F. H. (1972). *Prehistoric Greece*. Hart Davis MacGibbon, London.

Stuiver, M. (1970). Long-term C14 variations, in *Nobel Symposium 12: Radiocarbon Variations and Absolute Chronology* (Ed. I. V. Olsson), 197–213. Almqvist and Wiksell, Stockholm.

Sturdy, D. A. (1972). The exploitation patterns of a modern reindeer economy in West Greenland, in *Papers in Economic Prehistory* (Ed. E. S. Higgs), 161–68. Cambridge University Press, Cambridge.

Sturdy, D. A. (1975). Some reindeer economies in prehistoric Europe, in *Palaeoeconomy* (Ed. E. S. Higgs), 55–95. Cambridge University Press, Cambridge.

Sulimirski, T. (1970). *Prehistoric Russia*. John Baker, London.

Szabo, B. J. and Collins, D. M. (1975). Ages of fossil bone from British interglacial sites, *Nature* **254**, 680–82.

Szabo, M. (1971). *The Celtic Heritage in Hungary*. Corvina, Budapest.

Tabaczynski, S. (1972). Gesellschaft und Güteraustauch in Neolitkikum Europas, *Neolithische Studien* **1**, 31–95. Berlin.

Tauber, H. (1970). The Scandinavian varve chronology and C14 dating, in *Nobel Symposium 12: Radiocarbon Variations and Absolute Chronology* (Ed. I. V. Olsson), 173–96. Almqvist and Wiksell, Stockholm.

Taus, M. (1963). Ein spätlatènezeitliches Schmied-Grab aus St. Georgen a. pB. St. Pölten, NÖ, *Archaeologia Austriaca* **34**, 13–16.

Taute, W. (1967). Das Felsdach Lautereck, eine mesolithisch-neolitisch-bronzezeitliche Stratigraphie an der oberen Donau, *Palaeohistoria* **12**, 483–504.

Taute, W. (1968). *Die Stielspitzen-gruppen im nördlichen Mitteleuropa*. Fundamenta Reihe A, Band 5. Böhlau, Cologne.

Theocharis, D. (1973). *Neolithic Greece*. National Bank of Greece, Athens.

Thill, G. (1966). Goeblingen-Nospelt, *Hémecht* **18**, 482–91.

Thill, G. (1967). Goeblingen-Nospelt, *Hémecht* **19**, 87–98, 199–203.

Thomson, D. F. (1939). The seasonal factor in human culture, *Proceedings of the Prehistoric Society* **10**, 209–21.

Thrane, H. (1975). *Europæiske Forbindelser. Bidrag til studiet af fremmede forbindelser i Danmarks yngre bronzealder (periode IV–V)* (in Danish with English summary). National Museum, Copenhagen.

Tierney, J. J. (1960). The Celtic ethnography of Posidonius, *Proceedings of the Royal Irish Academy* **60C**, 189–275.

Točík, A. (1964). *Opevnená osada z doby bronzovej vo Veselom*. Slovak Academy of Sciences, Bratislava.

Točík, A. (1981a). *Malé Kosihy: osada zo staršej doby bronzovej*. Slovak Academy of Sciences, Nitra.

Točík, A. (1981b). *Nitriansky Hrádok-Zámaček: bronzezeitliche befestigte Ansiedlung der Madarovce Kultur*. Slovak Academy of Sciences, Nitra.

Točík, A. and Paulík, J. (1960). Výskum mohyly v Čake v rokoch 1950–51 (with German summary), *Slovenská Archaeológia* **8**, 59–124.

Točík, A. and Vladár, J. (1971). Prehl'ad bádania v problematike vývová Slovenska v dobe bronzovej (with German summary), *Slovenská Archaeológia* **19**, 365–422.

Todd, M. (1975). *The Northern Barbarians 100BC–AD300*. Hutchinson, London.

Tode, A. (Ed.) (1953). Die Untersuchung der paläolithischen Freilandstation von Salzgitter-Lebenstedt, *Eiszeitalter und Gegenwart* **3**, 144–220.

Todorova, H. (1974). Kultszene und Hausmodell aus Ovcarovo, Bez. Targovishte, *Thracia* **3**, 39–46.

Todorova, H. (1978). *The Eneolithic Period in Bulgaria in the Fifth Millennium BC*. British Archaeological Reports S49, Oxford.

Todorova, H. and Toncheva, E. (1975). Die äneolithische Pfahlbausiedlung bei Ezerovo im Varnasee, *Germania* **53**, 30–46.

Todorović, J. (1968). *Kelti u jugostoćnoj Evropi*. Belgrade.

Toepfer, V. (1957). *Die Mammutfunde von Pfännerhall in Geisetal*. Veröffentlichungen des Landesmuseum für Vorgeschichte, Halle.

Toepfer, V. (1963). *Tierwelt des Eiszeitalters*. Geest and Portig, Leipzig.

Toepfer, V. (1976). Alt-, Mittel- und Jungpaläolithikum, *Ausgrabungen und Funde* **21**, 17–24.

Torbrügge, W. (1970/71). Vor- und frühgeschichtliche Flussfunde, *Bericht der Römisch-Germanischen Kommission* **51/52**, 1–146.

Torelli, M. (1971). Gravisca (Tarquinia) — Scavi nella città etrusca e Romana. Campagna 1969 e 1970, *Notizie degli Scavi*, 195–299.

Torelli, M. (1977). Il santuario greco di Gravisca, *Parola del Passato* **32**, 398–458.

Torrence, R. (1983). Time budgeting and hunter-gatherer technology, in *Hunter-gatherer Economy in Prehistoric Europe* (Ed. G. N. Bailey), 11–22. Cambridge University Press, Cambridge.

Tringham, R. (1971). *Hunters, Fishers and Farmers of Eastern Europe 6000–3000 BC*. Hutchinson, London.

Tringham, R. (1973). The mesolithic of southeastern Europe, in *The Mesolithic in Europe* (Ed. S. K. Kozłowski), 551–72. University Press, Warsaw.

Trinkaus, E. and Howells, W. W. (1979). The neanderthals, *Scientific American* **241**, 94–105.

Troels-Smith, J. (1960). Ivy, mistletoe and elm: climate indicators — fodder plants, *Danmarks Geologiske Undersogelse* (4th series) **4**(4), 1–32.

Troels-Smith, J. (1967). The Ertebølle culture and its background, *Palaeohistoria* **12**, 505–529.

Trump, D. (1966a). *Southern Italy before Rome*. Thames and Hudson, London.

Trump, D. (1966b). *Skorba*. Society of Antiquaries Research Report 22, London.

Turner, C. (1970). The middle pleistocene deposits of Marks Tey, Essex, *Philosophical Transactions of the Royal Society of London* **B257**, 373–437.

Turner, J. (1965). A contribution to the history of forest clearance, *Proceedings of the Royal Society* **B161**, 343–54.

Turner, J. (1981). The Iron Age, in *The Environment in British Prehistory* (Ed. I. Simmons and M. Tooley), 250–81. Duckworth, London.

Tylecote, R. F. (1962). *Metallurgy in Archaeology*. Edward Arnold, London.

Ucko, P. J. and Rosenfeld, A. (1967). *Palaeolithic Cave Art*. Weidenfeld and Nicholson, London.

Valoch, K. (1968). Evolution of the palaeolithic in central and eastern Europe, *Current Anthropology* **9**, 351–68.

Valoch, K. (1980). Vorläufiger komplexer Bericht über die Erforschung der Kůlna Höhle bei Sloup (Bez. Blansko) in den Jahren 1961–76, *Přehled Výzkumů 1977 Brno*, 11–22.

van der Hammen, T., Wijmstra, T. A. and Zagwijn, W. H. (1971). The floral record of the late Cenozoic of Europe, in *The Late Cenozoic Glacial Ages* (Ed. K. K. Turekian), 391–424. Yale University Press, New Haven, Conn.

van der Waals, J. D. (1964). *Prehistoric Disc Wheels in the Netherlands*. Wolters, Groningen.

van der Waals, J. D. and Glasbergen, W. (1955). Beaker types and their distribution in the Netherlands, *Palaeohistoria* **5**, 39–51.

van der Waals, J. D. and Waterbolk, H. T. (1976). Excavations at Swifterbant — discovery, progress, aims and methods, *Helinium* **16**, 3–14.

van Wijngaarden-Bakker, L. H. (1974). The animal remains from the Beaker settlement at Newgrange, Co. Meath: first report, *Proceedings of the Royal Irish Academy* **74C**, 313–83.

van Zeist, W. (1957). De mesolithische Boot van Pesse, *Provinciaal Museum van Drenthe Museumbulletin 1956*, 4–11.

Vasić, M. M. (1932). *Preistoriska Vinča*. Isdanye Drshavne Stamparije, Belgrade.

Vereschagin, N. K. (1974). The mammoth 'cemeteries' of north-east Siberia, *Polar Record* **17**, 3–13.

Vértes, L. (1955). Neuere Ausgrabungen und paläolithische Funde in der Höhle von Istállóskö, *Acta Archaeologica Academiae Scientiarum Hungaricae* **5**, 111–31.

Vértes, L. (1964). *Tata — eine mittelpaläolithische Travertinsiedlung in Ungarn*. Akadémiai Kiadó, Budapest.

Vita-Finzi, C. (1978). *Archaeological Sites in their Setting*. Thames and Hudson, London.

Vita-Finzi, C. and Higgs, E. S. (1970). Prehistoric economy in the Mount Carmel area: site catchment analysis, *Proceedings of the Prehistoric Society* **36**, 1–37.

Vladár, J. (1973a). *Pohrebiska zo staršej doby bronzovej v Branči*. Slovak Academy of Sciences, Bratislava.

Vladár, J. (1973b). Osteuropäische und mediterrane Einflusse im Gebiet der Slowakei während der Bronzezeit, *Slovenská Archaeológia* **21**, 253–357.

Vlček, E. (1978). A new discovery of *Homo erectus* in Central Europe, *Journal of Human Evolution* **7**, 239–51.

Vogt, E. (1969). Siedlungswesen, in *Ur- und frühgeschicht-liche Archäologie der Schweiz II: Die jüngere Steinzeit* (Ed. W. Drack), 157–74. Schweizerische Gesellschaft für Ur- und Frühgeschichte, Basel.

von Brunn, W. A. (1968). *Mitteldeutsche Hortfunde der Jüngeren Bronzezeit*. Römisch-Germanische Forschungen 29. De Gruyter, Berlin.

von Brunn, W. A. (1980). Eine Deutung spätbronzezeitlicher Hortfunde zwischen Elbe und Weichsel, *Bericht der Römisch-Germanischen Kommission* **61**, 91–150.

von Koenigswald, W., Müller-Beck, H.-J. and Pressmar, E. (1974). *Die Archäologie und Paläontologie der Weinberg-höhlen bei Mauern (Bayern)*. Archaeologica Venatoria 3. Institut für Urgeschichte, Tübingen.

von Merhart, G. (1970). *Hallstatt und Italien*. Römisch-Germanisches Zentralmuseum, Mainz.

Vulpe, A. (1967). *Necropole Hallstattiana de la Ferigile*. Bucharest.

Wagner, E. (1981). Eine Löwenkopfplastik aus Elfenbein von der Vogelherdhöhle, *Fundberichte aus Baden-Württemberg* **6**, 29–57.

Wainwright, G. J. (1979). *Mount Pleasant, Dorset: Excavations 1970–71*. Society of Antiquaries Research Report 37, London.

Wainwright, G. J. and Longworth, I. H. (1971). *Durrington Walls: Excavations 1966–68*. Society of Antiquaries Research Report 29, London.

Warren, P. (1972). *Myrtos: an Early Bronze Age Settlement in Crete*. British School of Archaeology at Athens, London.

Waterbolk, H. T. (1956). Pollen spectra from neolithic grave monuments in the northern Netherlands, *Palaeohistoria* **5**, 39–51.

Waterbolk, H. T. (1958/59). Bandkeramische Siedlung von Geleen, *Palaeohistoria* **6/7**, 121–62.

Waterbolk, H. T. The occupation of Friesland in the prehistoric period, *Berichten van de Rijksdienst voor het Oudheidkundig Bodemonderzoek* **15**, 13–35.

Waterbolk, H. T. and van Zeist, W. (1978). *Niederwil. Eine Siedlung der Pfyner Kultur*. Academica Helvetica 1. Haupt, Bern.

Watts, W. A. (1980). Regional variation in the response of vegetation to late glacial climatic events in Europe, in *Studies in the Late Glacial of North-west Europe* (Ed. J. Lowe *et al.*), 1–21. Pergamon Press, Oxford.

Welinder, S. (1975). *Prehistoric Agriculture in Eastern Middle Sweden*. Acta Archaeologica Lundensia, Lund.

Welinder, S. (1978). The concept of ecology in mesolithic research, in *The Early Post-glacial Settlement of Northern Europe* (Ed. P. Mellars), 11–25. Duckworth, London.

Wells, P. (1980). *Culture Contact and Culture Change: Early Iron Age Central Europe and the Mediterranean World*. Cambridge University Press, Cambridge.

Wells, P. (1981). *The Emergence of an Iron Age Economy*. American School of Prehistoric Research Bulletin 33, Peabody Museum, Harvard University, Cambridge, Mass.

Werner, J. (1954). Die Bronzekanne von Kelheim, *Bayerische Vorgeschichtsblätter* **20**, 43–73.

West, R. G. (1977). *Pleistocene Geology and Biology with Especial Reference to the British Isles*. Longman, London.

West, R. G. and McBurney, C. B. M. (1955). The quaternary deposits at Hoxne, Suffolk, and their archaeology, *Proceedings of the Prehistoric Society* **20**, 131–54.

Wheeler, R. E. M. (1943). *Maiden Castle, Dorset*. Society of Antiquaries Research Report 12, London.

White, L. (1959). *The Evolution of Culture*. McGraw-Hill, New York.

White, R. (1982). Rethinking the middle/upper palaeolithic transition, *Current Anthropology* **23**, 169–92.

Whitelaw, T. M. (in press). Fournou Korifi, Myrtos and aspects of early Minoan social organization, in *Minoan Society* (Ed. L. Nixon and O. Kryskowska). Bristol Classical Press, Bristol.

Whittaker, C. R. (1974). The western Phoenicians: colonisation and assimilation, *Proceedings of the Cambridge Philological Society* **200**, 58–79.

Whittle, A. W. R. (1977). *The Earlier Neolithic of southern England and its Continental Background*. British Archaeological Reports S35, Oxford.

Whittle, A. W. R. (1978). Resources and population in the British neolithic, *Antiquity* **52**, 34–42.

Whittle, A. W. R. (1981). Later neolithic society in Britain: a re-alignment, in *Astronomy and Society in Britain during the period 4000BC–1500BC* (Ed. C. L. N. Ruggles and A. W. R. Whittle), 297–342. British Archaeological Reports 88, Oxford.

Wilkinson, P. (1976). 'Random' hunting and the composition of faunal samples from archaeological excavations: a modern example from New Zealand, *Journal of Archaeological Science* **3**, 321–28.

Winterhalder, B. and Smith, E. A. (Eds) (1981). *Hunter-gatherer Foraging Strategies*. University of Chicago Press, Chicago.

Wislanski, T. (Ed.) (1970). *The Neolithic in Poland*. Polish Academy of Sciences, Warsaw.

Wobst, H. M. (1974). Boundary conditions for palaeolithic social systems: a simulation approach, *American Antiquity* **39**, 147–78.

Wobst, H. M. (1977). Stylistic behaviour and information exchange, in *For the Director: Essays in Honor of James B. Griffin* (Ed. C. E. Cleland), 317–42. Anthropological Papers 61. University of Michigan Museum of Anthropology, Ann Arbor.

Woillard, G. M. (1978). Grand Pile peat bog: a continuous pollen record for the last 140,000 years, *Quaternary Research* **9**, 1–21.

Woodman, P. C. (1977). Recent excavations at Newferry, Co. Antrim, *Proceedings of the Prehistoric Society* **43**, 155–99.

Woodman, P. C. (1978). *The Mesolithic in Ireland: Hunter-gatherers in an insular Environment*. British Archaeological Reports 58, Oxford.

Woytowitsch, E. (1978). *Die Wagen der Bronze- und frühen Eisenzeit in Italien*. Prähistorische Bronzefunde XVII, 1. C. H. Beck, Munich.

Wright, H. (1977). Recent research on the origin of the state, *Annual Review of Anthropology* **6**, 379–97.

Wymer, J. J. (1968). *Lower Palaeolithic Archaeology in*

Britain, as represented by the Thames Valley. John Baker, London.

Wymer, J. J. (Ed.) (1977). *Gazetteer of Mesolithic Sites in England and Wales*. Council for British Archaeology Research Report 20, London.

Wymer, J. J. (1982). *The Palaeolithic Age*. Croom Helm, London.

Wyss, R. (1969). Die Gräber und weitere Belege zur geistigen Kultur, in *Ur- und frühgeschichtliche Archäologie der Schweiz II: Die jüngere Steinzeit* (Ed. W. Drack), 139–56. Schweizerische Gesellschaft für Ur- und Frühgeschichte, Basel.

Wyss, R. (1971). Siedlungswesen und Verkehrswege, in *Ur- und frühgeschichtliche Archäologie der Schweiz III: Bronzezeit* (Ed. W. Drack), 103–22. Schweizerische Gesellschaft für Ur- und Frühgeschichte, Basel.

Wyss, R. (1974). Technik, Wirtschaft, Handel und Kriegswesen der Eisenzeit, in *Ur- und frühgeschichtliche Archäologie der Schweiz IV: Eisenzeit* (Ed. W. Drack), 104–38. Schweizerische Gesellschaft für Ur- und Frühgeschichte, Basel.

Wyss, R. (1976). *Das jungsteinzeitliche Jäger-Bauerndorf von Egolzwil 5 im Wauwilermoos*. Schweizerisches Landesmuseum, Zurich.

Yellen, J. E. (1977). *Archaeological Approaches to the Present: Models for Reconstructing the Past*. Academic Press, London and New York.

Zagorskis, F. (1973). Das Spätmesolithikum in Lettland, in *The Mesolithic in Europe* (Ed. S. K. Kozłowski), 651–69. University Press, Warsaw.

Zeuner, F. E. (1959). *The Pleistocene Period*. Hutchinson, London.

Zirra, V. (1971). Stand der Forschung der keltischen Spätlatènezeit in Rumänien, *Archeologicke Rozhledy* 23, 529–47.

Zuffa, M. (1976). La civilta villanoviana, in *Popoli e Civiltà dell'Italia antica*, Vol. 5, 199–363. Rome.

Zürn, H. and Herrmann, H.-V. (1966). Der 'Grafenbühl' auf der Markung Asperg, Kr. Ludwigsburg: ein Fürstengrabhügel der späten Hallstattzeit. Vorbericht, *Germania* **44**, 74–102.

Index

Figures that appear in *italics* refer to figures

Abbeville, 41
Abri Cap Blanc, 78
Abri Facteur, 50
Abri Pataud, 50, 70–72, 81, *2.24*, *3.7*
Acheulean tradition, 41, 42, 43, 44
Acholshausen, 290
Adzes, 92, 124, 126, 145
Aedui, 316
Aggersund, 99
Agriculture, 100–101, 117–131, 156–160, 184–186,
    205–209, 225–226, 257–258, 277–280, 304–305,
    322–324
  expansion, 133–134, 160, 184, 185, 205, 208,
    277–278, 291, 304, 305, 317
  intensification, 139–140, 147, 194, 209, 226, 244,
    258, 264, 277–278, 305, 317, 322–324
  shifting, 126–127
Ahrensburgian industry, 56, *2.26*
Aibunar, 146, 165
Akrotiri, 231
Aldenhoven plateau, 132, 135, *5.10*, *5.13*
Alexander the Great, 261, 307
Allerød interstadial, 48, *2.5*
Al Mina, 251
Altamira, 18, 65, 80
Amber, 163, 213, 218–219, 221, 225, 226, 257, 283,
    287, 290, 293, 294, 309, 311, 324
Ambrona, 42
Amersfoort interstadial, 21, 43, *2.4*, *2.5*
Amiens (Rue de Cagny), 42
Amphoras, 258, 287, 308, 309
Ampurias, 251
Anagni, 28
Anglian glacial, *2.2*
Antler, 38, 39, 40, 50, 56, 94, 287, *2.16*

Antrea, 94
Apennine Bronze Age, 222
Arago, 26, 30, 75, *2.7*
Arcy-sur-Cure, 49, 76
Arene Candide, 91, 108, 116
Argaric culture, 223–225, 244
Argissa, 101, 131
Aricia, 264
Armour, 244, 257, 259, 266, 270, 271, 284, 290, 292,
    8.19, *9.15*
Arrows, 38, 56, 276
Arverni, 316
Asprochaliko, 67, *3.5*
Ass, 66
Atapuerca, 26
Athens, 241, 246, 248, 251, 254, 257, 258, 262, 263,
    318, *8.9*, *8.12*
Atlantic Bronze Age, 223
Aulnat, 310
Aurignacian industry, 48, 50–53, 77, *2.25*
Aurochs, 90, 94, 100, 129
Avebury, 173
Axes
  bronze, 198, 216, 217, 271, 279
  copper, 165, 168, 189, 192, 226, *6.13*
  flint, 92, 124, 145
  iron, 279
  stone, 92, 116, 124, 126, 145, 146, 163, 177
Ayia Triadha, 230
Azilian industry, 57, 92, *2.26*
Azmak, 126, 148

Baden culture, 159, 160, 165, 168, 178, *6.3*
Bad Nauheim, 306
Bakers Hole, 42

Ballynagilly, 136
Balve, 44
Band societies, 107
Barberini Tomb, 259
Barley, 100, 101, 118, 126, 278, 304
Barnenez, *5.20*
Basel, 310
Bâtons, 56
Bear, 23, 64, 73
Beaver, 21, 94
Beestonian glacial, *2.2*
Bell Beakers, 155–156, 163, 168, 171, 175, 177, 183,
    192, 193, 198, 199, 207, 211, 220, 221, 222–224,
    6.6
Belsk, 280
Bern, 310
Bernardini Tomb, 259, *8.20*
Big Elephant Cave, 70–72, *3.6*
Bilzingsleben, 26–27, 43, 69
Birds, 99
Biskupin, 280
Bison, 23, 64
Blades, 38, 48, 50
Bleibeskopf, 280
Boats, 94
Bockstein, 44, *2.20*
Bølling interstadial, 48, *2.5*
Bologna, 248, 251
Bone tools, 38, 39, 48, 49, 50, 56, 94
Borers, 34, 38, 43
Bow, 38, 94
Boyne valley, 149
Brancˇ, 212
Breisach, 310
Brillenhöhle, 76
Bronze, 181, 182, 198–204, 207, 211–213, 215–218,
    226, 244, 270–271, 279, 280, 284–289, 292, 293,
    294, 309, 311, 314, 322
  arsenical, 181, 192, 215
  sheet-working, 270–271, 284–285
Brørup interstadial, 21, 43, 44, *2.4*, *2.5*
Bruniquel, 77, *3.13*
Budakalasz, 159
Bug-Dniester culture, 101, 116, 131
Burebistas, 318
Burgäschisee, 126, 131, 136, 137
Burials
  Bell Beaker, 168, 171–175, 176, 193, *6.14*
  Corded Ware, 168, 171–175, 176
  early Bronze Age, 180, 186–188, 189, 209–213
  early neolithic, 142–143, 149
  La Tène, 298–300, 309, 319–321

  mesolithic, 108–109, *4.11*
  palaeolithic, 75–76, 86, *3.11*
  Urnfield, 290
  with vehicles, 273, 274, 283, 291, 324, *9.6*
Burins, 34, 38, 40, 44, 50, 56
Bush Barrow, *7.9*
Bygholm, 146
Bylany, 132

Caesar, C. Julius, 309
Cˇaka, 290
Camp Century, 21, *2.4*
Camp de Château, 290
Camp du Laure, 225
Cannibalism, 109
Canoes, 94
Cap Ragnon, 99
Carambolo, 251
Carrowkeel, 149
Carrowmore, 109, 149
Carthage, 251
Cˇascioarele, 142
Çatal Hüyük, 120
Cattle, 118, 120, 126, 128, 130, 132, 137, 304
Cauldrons, 271, 283, 285
Cave paintings, 18, 65, 80–83, 87
Cayla de Mailhac, 241, 251, 259
Celts, 305, 315–316
Cereals, 98–99, 100–101, 118, 126, 132, 136, 147, 160,
    182, 185, 228, 257, 258, 264, 277, 278–279, 304
Cernavoda, 134
Cerro de la Virgen, 185, 223
Cerveteri, 248, 254, 259
Cˇeské Budeˇjovice, 307
Chamois, 65
Chassey culture, 136, 140, 154, 185, *6.4*
Châteauneuf-les-Martigues, 98
Chatelperronian industry, 49–50, *2.25*
Chert, 32
Chevdar, 126, 127, 130
Chicken, 287
Chiefdom societies, 149, 170, 180, 182, 211, 230
Childe, V. G., 3, 19, 204, 221
Chillac, 28
Chopping tools, 32, 34, 41, 43, *2.17*
Chotin, 276
Cimbri, 324
City-state, *see* Polis
Clacton, 34, 38, 41, 43, 70, *2.13*, *2.14*
Clactonian industry, 41, 43
Cleavers, 32, 43
Clientship, 315–316

Climate, 11–14, 20–23, 48, 90, 114, 278–279, 322
Coinage, 244, 263, 307–308, 309, 311, 313, 314, 316, 318
Colchester, 314, 316, 319 *10.15*
Colonies, 248, 250–251, 262, 294, 315, 317
Combe Grenal, 46, 47, 62, 69, 76, *2.22, 3.3*
Commont's workshop, 42
Constanţa, 145
Copper, 137, 145–146, 147–148, 163–168, 180–181, 186, 188, 189, 190–191, 192, 211–213, 215–218, 225, 226, 289, 293
    suphide ores, 165, 215
Coppicing, 98, 124
Coral, 284, 287, 290
Corded Ware, 155, 159–160, 162, 163, 166, 168–169, 171, 175, 177, 220, *5.15, 6.5, 6.8*
Cortes de Navarra, 258
Coveta de l'Or, 133
Craft specialization, 147, 148, 180, 182, 186, 217, 244, 254, 255, 256, 264, 290, 305, 306, 309, 313, 317, 321
Crakow (Spadzista street), 50
Crô Magnon, 30, *2.7*
Cromerian interglacial, *2.2*
Cucuteni, 134
Cueva Morín, 50
Curation, 53

Dacian horizon, 300
Dacians, 316, 318
Daggers, 181, 200, 225, 276
    bronze, 200
    copper, 163, 168, 175, 177, 189, 192, 226
    flint, 163, 189, 192, 202, *7.4*
Danebury, 311
Dartmoor, 278
Darwin, C., 2
Deepcar, 106
Deer, 129, 131, 137
    fallow, 21, *3.2*
    red, 23, 62, 65, 66, 87, 90, 94, 96, 97
    roe, 65, 90, 94, 96
Delphi, 264
Denekamp interstadial, 21, 48, *2.4, 2.5*
Denticulates, 34, 43, 44, 46
Desborough, *10.5*
Devensian glacial, *2.2*
Dhimini, 134, 147
Diffusion, 3, 204, 264
Disc core, *see* Lithic technology
Dnieper glacial, *2.2*
Dog, 96

Dolní Věstonice, 50, 78, 81
Dover, 217
Druids, 315
Dufour bladelets, 50, *2.25*
Durrington Walls, 160, 173, 174
Dürrnberg bei Hallein, 290
Duvensee, 106
Dyrholm, 109

Early Celtic art, 276, 298–300
Eberdingen-Hochdorf, 283
Eemian interglacial, *2.2*
Egolzwil, 129, 136
Ehringsdorf, 41, 43
El Argar, 223
Elephant, 21, 69
Elk, 90, 94, 96, 129
Elm, 114
Elsloo, 132, *5.18*
Elster glacial, 21, *2.2*
Enamel, 290, 309
Ensérune, 241, 251
Entremont, 251, *8.15*
Epi-gravettian industries, 57, 92
Epi-palaeolithic industries, 57
Erd, 44
Ertebølle-Ellerbek culture, 101, 116
Este culture, 241
Ethnoarchaeology, 68, 70, 98
Ethnos, 259–261
Etruscans, 241, 244, 246, 248, 257, 258, 262, 263, 264, 266
Exchange, 143–147, 148, 162–169, 181–182, 189–194, 213–216, 217–221, 225–226, 231, 255, 257, 264, 287, 289, 292–295, 305–309, 310, 311, 317, 323
Exogamy, 163, 213
Ezero, 162

Federmesser assemblages, 56–57, *2.26*
Fellbach-Schmieden, *10.19*
Ferigile, 276
Fields, 127, 160, 205–206, 279, 323, *7.7*
Fig, 131
Figurines, 72, 76–77, 120, 142, 148
Fish, 68, 87, 96, 99, 101, 118, 132, 136
Fishing-nets, 94
Flax, 207, 304
Flint, 31–33, 83, 91, 192
    mines, 163, *6.9*
Flynderhage, 99
Fontbouisse culture, 189
Fontéchevade, 26, 43, *2.7*
Font Robert points, 50, *2.25*

Forest, 14, 90–91, 98–99, 114
    clearance, 21, 97, 98, 124, 126, 127, 129, 140, 160,
        162, 163, 277–278, 304, *5.12*
    regeneration, 140, 160
Fortification, 134, 137, 147, 148, 162, 171, 175, 180,
        186, 193, 208, 213–215, 225, 244, 251, 254,
        280–283, 300
Fossil hominids, 24–30
Franchthi Cave, 98, 99, 100–101, 132
Frattesina, 244, 290
Furs, 94, 96

Galatians, 305
Gaudo group, 189
Gauls, 305
Gazelle, *3.2*
Geleen, 132
Gellerthegy-Taban, 305, 314
Geometric period, 241
Glasinac, 273
Glass, 244, 284, 290, 309, 311, 313
Glauberg, 280
Goat, 91, 94, 98, 100, 101, 118, 128, 130, 132
Goeblingen-Nospelt, 309, 321
Golasecca culture, 241
Gold, 147–148, 191, 283, 290, 307, 309
Gönnersdorf, 57, 78, *3.13*, *3.15*
Gordion, 273
Gortyn, 263
Gotland, 322
Gradeshnitsa, 148
Gradistea Muncelului, *see* Sarmizegethusa
Grafenbühl, 283
Granaries, 279, 280
Grand Pressigny, 163, 168
Grapes, 131
Gravettian industry, 50–53, 56
Gravina, 250
Graviscae, 254
Greeks, 244
Grimaldi cave, 76
Grimes Graves, 163, *6.9*
Grøntoft, 324
Grotta del Santuario della Madonna, 116
Grotta Paglicci, 76, *3.11*
Grotte du Hasard, 225
Gundestrup, 324
Günz glacial, 21, *2.2*

Hajar Qim, 149
Halle-Dölauer Heide, 171
Hallstatt, 270, 273, 290

Hallstatt period, 270, 273
Hal Saflieni, 149
Hambledon Hill, 127, 130
Hamburgian industry, 56, *2.26*
Handaxes, 31, 32–33, 34, 41, 42, 43, 44, *2.9*
Harpoons, 56, *2.26*
Hart an der Alz, 290
Hatzum, 324
Heathrow, *10.20*
Helmsdorf, 211
Helvetii, 309, 318
Hemp, 304
Hengelo interstadial, 23, 45, 48, *2.4*, *2.5*
Henges, 171, 172–174
Hengistbury Head, 306
Heuneburg, 274, 283, 286–287, 293, 295
Hienheim, 116
Hieroglyphic script, 229, 231
High Lodge, 43
Hippopotamus, 21
Hjortspring, 325
Hoards, 203, 217, 218, 271, 273, 285–289, 294
Hoëdic, 108
Hohenasperg, 283, 293
Hohen Viecheln, 91, 94
Hohmichele, 287, 291
Holly, 114
Holmegaard, 94, 96, 98, 99, 103, 106
Holstein interglacial, 27, *2.2*
Holy Cross Mountains, 83, 306, *3.19*
Homo erectus, 26–27
Homolka, 160, 171, 177, 214, *6.15*
Homo sapiens, 26–30
    sapiens, 29–30
    neanderthalensis, 27–30
Horse, 23, 62, 65, 131, 207, 273, 276, 304
Horse harness, 207, 213, 273, 276, 283, 324
Horsham group, 109
Houses, 106, 140–142
Hoxne, 21, 34, 41, 69, 70, *2.13*
Hoxnian interglacial, 21, *2.2*
Hrazany, 311
Hülstener group, 109
Hunter-gatherer subsistence, 60–70, 73–75, 93–101
    facilities, 67, 94
    diversity, 94, 99
    mobility, 60–61, 66, 94–96, 99–100, 101–106
    plant resources, 91, 98–99
    sedentism, 100, 106, 120
    settlement organization, 70–75
    settlement systems, 65–73, 103–106
    storage, 66, 67–70

Husby, 324
Hyena, 23, 64, 73

Iberians, 244, 251, 257
Ibex, 64, 65, 90, 94
Icoana, 98
Ilsenhöhle, 44
Ilskaia, 44
Inden-Lamersdorf, 136
Ipswichian interglacial, *2.2*
Iron, 241, 255, 256, 258, 264, 273, 279, 280, 284,
    289–290, 293, 306, 309, 311, 313, 314, 324
    ingots, 307, *10.11*
Irrigation, 185
Isernia, 28
Istállóskö, 48, 50
Isturitz, 39
Ivory, 38, 76–77, 148, 186, 188, 190–191, 244, 257, 283
Ivy, 97, 114

Jadeite, 145
Janislawice, 109
Jericho, 121
Jerzmanovice, 48, *2.21*

Karanovo, 115, 122, 126, 131, 132, 134, 140, *5.2*, *5.3*,
    5.17
Karatau, 43
Karbuna hoard, 146
Kastritsa, 56, 66, *3.5*
Kazanluk, 127, 130
Kelheim, 306
Kents Cavern, 48
Klaussenische, 44
Knives, 34, 38, 44, 56
Knossos, 115, 130, 180, 183, 207, 228, 229, 230, 231,
    235
Knowth, 149, 170, *5.22*
Kokkinopilos, 44, *2.21*
Königsaue, 44
Körös culture, 101
Kostienki, 40, 50, 77, 78, 83, *2.21*
Kostienki knives, 38, 40, 50
Krapina, 27, 29, 30, 43
Krasny-Iar, 44
Krems-Hundssteig, 50
Krzemionki, 163, *6.10*
Kůlna, 44
Kul Oba, 294

La Adam, 98
La Chaise, 27

La Chapelle-aux-Saints, 29, 76, *2.7*
La Cotte de St. Brelade, 42, 73
La Ferrassie, 30, 50, 78, *2.7*
La Madeleine, 56, 78, *3.16*
La Marche, 78, *3.14*
La Micoque, 43, *2.20*
Langweiler, *5.13*
La Quercia, 132
La Quina, 30
Lascaux, 80
La Tène, 274
La Tène period, 274–276, 298–300
Laugerie-Basse, 77
Laugerie-Haute, 54
Lausitz group, 270, 276, 280
Laussel, 78, 81
Lautereck, 115
Lazaret, 72
Leather, 290, 306, 309, 313
Lébous, 189, 225, *6.24*
Lecce, 50
Lefkandi, 244
Legumes, 118, 127
Lehringen, 69
Łeki Małe, *7.10*
Le Moustier, 43
Lengyel culture, 140, *5.15*
Lepenski Vir, 99, 106, 109
Lerna, 180, *6.20*
Les Combarelles, 80
Le Tuc d'Audoubert, 80
Leubingen, 211
Levallois technique, *see* Lithic technology
Lichwin interglacial, *2.2*
Lignite, 287, 290
Linear A script, 231
Linear B script, 207, 231, 234–236
Linear Pottery Culture, 123, 132, 147, *5.10*, *5.13*, *5.15*,
    5.18
Linen, 130, 160
Linienbandkeramik, *see* Linear Pottery Culture
Lion, 23, 64
Lipari, 145
Lithic technology, 31–40
    anvil technique, 33, 41
    disc core, 33
    indirect percussion, 38
    levallois technique, 33, 34, 41, 42, 43, 48, *2.10*
    preheating, 38
    pressure flaking, 38, 54
    tortoise core, 33, 42
Loess, 23, 24, 43, 44, 97, 114, 116, 123

Loomweights, 209, 290
Loshult, 93
Los Millares, 137, 148, 186, *6.23*
Los Murcielagos, 132
Loughcrew, 149
Luni, 226, 244, 258
Lyell, C., 2

Macedonians, 260, 266, 315, 316, 318, 319
Magdalenenberg, *9.5*
Magdalenian industry, 38, 56–57, 65, 66, 73, *2.26*
Magdalensberg, 306
Maglemosian complex, 92
Magnetic polarity, 21, 27, 28, *2.3*
Maiden Castle, 311, *10.14*
Malé Kosihý, 209, 213
Mallia, 228, 230, *7.21*, *7.22*
Malta, 137, 149
Mammoth, 23, 44, 64, 69, 73–74, 76, 77
Manching, 304, 306, 307, 310, 312–313
Markleeberg, 42, 43
Marseilles, 250, 251
Marzabotto, 251, *8.18*
Mas d'Azil, 77
Mauer, 26, 30
Mauern *see* Weinberg caves
Megalithic tombs, 109, 143, 147, 149, 186, 193, 211
Meilen-Rohrenhaab, 131
Melos, 94, 178, 231
Mercenaries, 266, 317
Mezhirich, 73, 78
Michelsberg culture, 136, 140
Micoquian industry, 43–44, *2.20*
Microliths, 92
Microwear, *see* Use-wear analysis
Mikulino interglacial, *2.2*
Milk, 120, 130, 156, 159, 160, 178
Millaran culture, 137, 184, 186, 190, 223
Mindel glacial, 21, *2.2*
Minoan civilization, 221, 228–235
Mirrors, 277, 283, *10.5*
Mnajdra, 149
Mobilization, 230
Moel y Gaer, *9.11*
Molodova, 44, 50, 73, *2.8*
Molpir, 280
Monte Bego, 208
Montelius, O., 202, 270
Mont Lassois, 274, 283
Montmaurin, 26
Morfi, 44
Morgantina, 250

Morton, 99
Moscow glacial, *2.2*
Mt. Carmel, 30, 62, 69, 76, *3.2*
Mount Pleasant, 173, 215, *7.12*, *7.13*
Mount Sandel, 106, *4.10*
Mousterian tradition, 34, 43, 46–48, 49, 65, 73, *2.20*
Mureybit, 121
Mycenae, 218, 231, *7.23*
Mycenaean civilization, 221, 222, 226, 228, 231–237, 240–241, 244, 270
Myrtos, 180

Naples, 250, 251
Narce, 226, 244, 258
Naukratis, 251
Nea Nikomedeia, 132, 142
New Archaeology, 8
Newferry, 91, 98, 99
Newgrange, 149, 170, 207
Niaux, 80
Niederwil, 124, 136
Nitra, 143, *5.19*
Nitriansky Hrádok, 213
Noailles burins, 50, *2.25*
Nollheider group, 109
Noricum, 306, 316
Noua culture, 273

Oats, 101, 118
Obsidian, 83, 109, 145, 189–190, *6.27*
Ocean cores, 21, *2.3*
Odderade interstadial, 21, *2.4*, *2.5*
Odemira, *7.18*
Odintzovo interglacial, *2.2*
Offenbach-Rumpenheim, *9.6*
Ofnet, 45
Oka glacial, *2.2*
Ølby Lyng, 99
Old Smyrna, 247
Olive, 131, 179, 181–182, 185, 228, 257, 264
Olympia, 264
Oppida, 309–311
Orientalizing period, 244
Oronsay, 99
Ostia, 254
Ostrich eggshell, 148, 186, 188, 190–191, 244, 257
Ovcharovo, 148
Oxygen isotope analysis, 21, *2.3*

Pantelleria, 145
Papyrus, 318
Parpalló, 38, 56, *2.26*, *3.13*

Passau, 307
Passo di Corvo, 132
Pavlov, 50, 77, 78
Pear, 131
Pech Merle, 80, 82–83
Perigordian industry, 49, 50, 53, 72
Peristeria, 231
Pesse, 94
Petersfels, 56
Petralona, 26, 27, *2.7*
Pfyn, 136
Phaistos, 228, 230
Philip of Macedon, 261, 307, 318
Philippopolis, 318
Phoenicians, 244
Phylakopi, 178, 231
Piage, 50
Picks, 92
Pig, 90, 94, 98, 101, 118, 120, 131, 137, 304
Pincevent, 73
Piraeus, 254
Plough, 126–127, 129, 139, 156, 160, 162, 175, 208,
    220
Points, 34, 40, 41, 44, 50, 56
    leaf-shaped, 38, 44–45, 48, 54, *2.21*, *2.26*
Polada culture, 222, 226
Polesini, 56
Poliochni, *6.21*
Polis, 259, 262–264, 266, 316
Polyanitsa, 134, 148, *5.14*
Pontine islands, 145
Pontnewydd, 27
Population, 84, 100, 139–140, 228
    decline, 230, 231, 237, 244, 257
    density, 147, 175, 237
    growth, 84, 87, 100, 122, 139–140, 179, 194, 208,
        244–247, 254, 264–265, 280, 305, 317, *6.18*, *8.9*,
        8.10
Populonia, 248, 259
Postoloprty, 140
Potin, 307
Pottery, 101, 115, 116, 120, 147, 148, 163, 199, 203,
    240, 250, 254, 255–256, 257, 258, 270, 274, 287,
    306–307, 308, 309, 313, 314
    kilns, 137, 255–256, 305, 306
    wheel-thrown, 244, 255–256, 300, 305
Praeneste, 259
Předmost, 50
Prestige goods, 145–146, 148, 175, 177, 183, 193,
    207–208, 211, 217–221, 226, 228, 257, 259, 270,
    283, 290, 293, 294, 321
Přezletice, 41, 43

Protogeometric period, 241
Proto-Villanovan culture, 241, 244, 259
Pylos, 235–236
Pyrgi, 254
Pyrgos, 231

Quanterness, *5.20*
Quartzite, 32, 42, 44

Rabbit, 101
Radiocarbon dating, 3–5, 92, 116, 198, 204, 222, 240,
    270
Redistribution, 170, 181–183, 230
Regolini-Galassi Tomb, 259
Reindeer, 23, 44, 63, 65–66, 68, 87, 90
Reinecke, P., 270
Reutersruh, 42
Rhinoceros, 21, 23, 64, 69, 73
Rinaldone graves, 189, 192
Ringkloster, 94, 99
Riss glacial, 21, *2.2*
Roc de Combe, 50
Rock art, 207–209
Roessen phase, 136
Roman empire, 308, 316, 317, 318, 322–323, 325
Rome, 244, 248, 251, 254, 257, 258, 262, 263, 264, 266
Rouffignac, 80
Roundway, *6.14*
Rudna Glava, 146, 163
Rye, 118, 278, 304, 324

Saale glacial, 21, *2.2*
St Césaire, 30
Saguntum, 262
Salamis, 273
Salcombe, 217
Salpêtrière, 50
Salt, 220, 280, 284, 290, 306
Salzgitter-Lebenstedt, 44
Salzmünde group, *6.4*
Samnites, 260
Sanctuaries, 264, 314, 315, 318
Sardinia, 145
Sarmizegethusa, 314, 318, *10.18*
Sarnowo, 124, 136, *5.11*
Sauveterrian industry, 92, 93
Scalene triangle tools, 38
Scrapers, 34, 38, 41, 43, 44, 46, 48, 50, 56
Scythians, 277
Seal, 99, 101, 136
Sea level, 90, 99, 101, 114, 324
Segesta, 250, 251

Segmentary societies, 147
Seine-Oise-Marne culture, 160
Selinus, 251, *8.17*
Senftenberg, 280, *9.10*
Service, E. R., 6
Sesklo, 134, 147
Settlement location, 122–123, 131–137
Settlement patterns, 131–137, 160–162, 179–181,
    186–189, 228, 244–254, 280–283, 309–315, 323
  hierarchy, 147, 171, 180, 213–215, 225, 229, 244,
    309
  nucleation, 231, 247–254, 309
Seuthes, 315, 316, 318
Seuthopolis, 315, 318, 319, *10.17*
Shale, 290
Shanidar, 30
Sheep, 90, 94, 98, 100, 101, 118, 128, 130, 132, 160,
    178, 183, 185, 207, 234, 304
Shell-fish, 65, 101, 132
Shells, 76, 83, 163
    Spondylus gaederopus, 144–145, 146
Shell middens, 99, 101, 106
Shields, 271
Sickles, 127, 217, 279
Silbury Hill, 173
Silk, 287
Silver, 191, 307
Sion-Petit Chasseur, 194, *6.29*
Sissach, 305
Sitagroi, 115, 130, 131, 148
Site catchment analysis, 62–64, 67, 124, *3.2*
Sittard, 132
Skis, 94
Slate, 109
Slaves, 258, 293, 294, 318
Social organisation, 140–151, 169–177, 186–189,
    209–215, 220–221, 224–225, 258–266, 290–293,
    315–321, 324–325
Social storage, 182–183
Soils, 114, 118, 122–124, 127, 140, 162, 185, 205, 277,
    278, 322, 324
Solutrean industry, 38, 54–56, *2.26*
Somerset Levels, 115, 124
Soroki, 98
South Cadbury, *10.20*
South Street, 127, *5.11*
Sparta, 262
Spears, 38, 39
Spear throwers, 39, 56, *2.16*
Speech, 30
Spina, 251
Spindle whorls, 160, 209

Spišský Štvrtok, 214
Spy cave, 83
Stadel cave, 77, *3.12*
Star Carr, 91, 94, 96, 98, 99, 106, *4.4, 4.6*
Staré Hradisko, 305, 306, 311
State societies, 170, 230, 259–267, 315, 316–318
Statue-menhirs, 193
Stein, 132
Steinheim, 26, *2.7*
Stellmoor, 56
Stična, 273
Stonehenge, 172–174, 209
Storage, 279, 280
Stradonice, 311
Stranská Skála, 41, 43
Submycenaean period, 241
Sunghir, 76, 78
Svaerdborg, 94, 99
Swanscombe, 26, 41, 69, *2.8*
Sweet Track, 126, 145
Swifterbant, 101, 109
Swords, 198, 200, 217, 285, 290, 291, *7.5, 7.6*
Syracuse, *8.22*
Szeleta, 48, *2.21*
Szeletian industry, 48, 53

Tanged point assemblages, 56, 66, *2.26*
Tardenoisian industry, 92
Tarquinii, 248, 254, 259, *8.8, 8.13*
Tarxien, 149
Tata, 43
Tavoliere, 122, 132
Tell Abu Hureyra, 121
Tell settlements, 115, 122, 127, 131, 132, 133, 134,
    137–140, 148, 160, 203–204
Temples, 142, 148, 244, 251, 256, 263, 308, 311, 319,
    8.22, 10.20
Teutones, 324
Téviec, 108
Textiles, 163, 207–208, 220, 234, 283, 290
Thayngen-Weier, 129, 136
Thera, 231
Tholos tombs, 231, 319
Thomsen, C. J., 2
Thracians, 316, 318
Timber Grave culture, 273
Tin, 216, 289, 293
Tisza phase, 134
Tiszapolgar-Basatanya, *5.19*
Tiszapolgar phase, 134, 160
Torralba, 42, 69
Torre in Pietra, 42, 69

Tortoise core, *see* Lithic technology
Toszeg, 204
Toya, 259
Transhumance, 129, 185, 226
TRB culture, 136, 140, 154, 160, *5.15*
Trebeniŝte, 294
Trevener group, 109
Trichterrandbecherkultur, see TRB culture
Tripolye, 134
Tr̆isov, 306
Troy, 116, 178, 180, *6.20*
Tufariello, 222, *7.17*
Tumulus culture, 198, 202

Ulkestrup, 106
Ullastret, 251, *8.14*
Uluzzian industry, 50
Uluzzo, 50
Únĕtice, 211
Únĕtice culture, 198, 213
Urmitz, 136
Urnfield culture, 198, 224, 241, 259, 270–271, 273, 291–293
Urspring, 45
Use-wear analysis, 34–38, 40, 69, 127, *2.13*

Val Camonica, 208
Vallonet, 27, 41
Varna, 134, 148
Vedbaek, 108
Veii, 248, 251, *8.16*
Venus figurines, 72, 81, *3.18*
Vergina, 319
Vergobretos, 316
Vértesszöllös, 26, 27, 41, 43
Veselé, 213
Vetulonia, 259
Viereckschanzen, 318
Vig, 93, 94
Vila Nova de São Pedro, 137, 188, 193, *6.24*
Vila Nova de São Pedro culture, 188, 190
Villanovan culture, 241
Vinĉa, 115, 134

Vinĉa culture, 116, 148
Vines, 179, 181–182, 185, 228, 257, 264
Vix, 283, 291, 294
Vogelherd, 50, 77
Voltumna, 264
Vuĉedol, 175

Waldai glacial, *2.2*
Warthe glacial, *2.2*
Wauwilermoos, 131, 136, *5.16*
Weichselian glacial, 21, *2.2*
Weights, 307
Weinberg caves, Mauern, 45, 75, *2.21, 3.10*
Wells, 279, 322
Welwyn Garden City, 309, *10.13*
Welwyn type burials, 321
Wessex culture, 209–211, 221, *7.9*
West Kennet, 143, *5.20*
Whale, 99
Wheat, 118, 278
  bread wheat, 126
  emmer, 100, 126, 278
  spelt, 126, 278, 304
Wheeled vehicles, 156, 159, 208, 273, 274, 283, 287, 291, 306, 323, *6.7, 9.6*
Willendorf, 53
Windmill Hill, 116
Wine, 178, 257, 258, 274, 287, 308
Wis, 94
Wolf, 23, 64, 73, 96
Wolstonian glacial, 21, *2.2*
Wood-working, 306, 309, 313
Wool, 120, 130, 156, 159–160, 163, 179, 183, 185, 207
Worsaae, J. J. A., 2
Writing, 229, 231, 234–236, 244, 263, 318
Würm glacial, 21, 23, 43, 46, 48, *2.2*

Zagora, 247, *8.11*
Zakro, 230
Zambujal, 188, 193
Zaminets, 148
Zürich-Kleiner Hafner, 136
Zvejnieki, 109